DEVELOPING ORACLE
FORMS APPLICATIONS

Albert Lulushi

For book and bookstore information

http://www.prenhall.com

Prentice Hall PTR
Upper Saddle River, New Jersey 07458

Library of Congress Cataloging-in-Publication Data

Lulushi, Albert.
    Developing Oracle Forms applications / by Albert Lulushi.
        p.   cm.
    Includes index.
    ISBN 0–13–531229–9
        1. Oracle (Computer file)   2. Relational databases.
    3. Client/server computing.   I. Title.
    QA76.9.D3L855   1997
    005.75′65—dc20   96–16603
                                                                        CIP

Acquisitions editor: Mark L. Taub
Cover designer: Design Source
Cover design director: Jerry Votta
Manufacturing manager: Alexis R. Heydt
Compositor/Production services: Pine Tree Composition, Inc.

© 1996 by Prentice Hall PTR
Prentice-Hall, Inc.
A Simon & Schuster Company
Upper Saddle River, New Jersey 07458

The publisher offers discounts on this book when ordered in bulk quantities.

For more information contact:

Corporate Sales Department
Prentice Hall PTR
One Lake Street
Upper Saddle River, New Jersey 07458

Phone: 800-382-3419
Fax: 201-236-7141
email: corpsales@prenhall.com

Printed in the United States of America
10 9 8 7 6 5

ISBN: 0-13-531229-9

Prentice-Hall International (UK) Limited, *London*
Prentice-Hall of Australia Pty. Limited, *Sydney*
Prentice-Hall Canada Inc., *Toronto*
Prentice-Hall Hispanoamericana, S.A., *Mexico*
Prentice-Hall of India Private Limited, *New Delhi*
Prentice-Hall of Japan, Inc., *Tokyo*
Simon & Schuster Asia Pte. Ltd., *Singapore*
Editora Prentice-Hall do Brasil, Ltda., *Rio de Janeiro*

This book is for Steve, Romina, Silvia, Henry, Edina, Lauren, and Livia, and all the good things that the future holds for them.

CONTENTS

PREFACE

Oracle Forms is the most important tool used to create client/server applications that run against Oracle databases. *Developing Oracle Forms Applications* is a handbook for those who use Forms to build sophisticated database systems rapidly and productively. The book covers in detail all the aspects, features, and functionality of Oracle Forms. It also focuses on how modern application development concepts such as client/server computing and object-oriented programming are applied in the Oracle Forms environment.

ORGANIZATION OF THE BOOK

Developing Oracle Forms Applications is divided in four parts. Part I will introduce you to Oracle Forms programming. Following the detailed instructions provided in this part you will build your first form. In the process, important concepts of Oracle Forms Designer, Generate, and Runtime tools are presented. At the end of this part, you will have completed the first form and become familiar with terms and concepts that will be encountered throughout the rest of the book.

Part II equips you with the necessary tools to create, design, and enhance forms. It begins with an overview of Developer/2000, the larger family of Oracle development tools. Then it discusses the Oracle Forms Designer and its components: Object Navigator, Layout Editor, Properties Window, and Menu Editor. Separate chapters discuss the purpose, access methods, components, and usage of each tool. Elements of the Standard Query Language (SQL) used in Oracle Forms applications are discussed. The last chapter of this part introduces the Oracle's own PL/SQL language, the unified programming language used by the Oracle RDBMS and development tools.

Part III presents Oracle Forms as an object-oriented and event-driven programming environment. It explains the features, properties, and functionality of its objects, including blocks, items, windows, record structures, menus, etc. It also discusses events associated with each object, triggers they fire, and how they can be used to enhance Forms applications. Object-oriented programming principles, such as inheritance, reusability, encapsulation, and polymorphism, are other important topics of Part III. Following the chapters in this part you will develop a full-blown Oracle Forms application.

Part IV covers advanced programming with Oracle Forms. It begins with advanced PL/SQL topics, such as cursors and exception handling. Debugging concepts and tools are discussed as well. Then it discusses the integration of Forms with other Oracle tools such as Reports and Graphics. It then moves on to the broader issue of integration with other MS Windows applications through Dynamic Data Exchange (DDE), OLE Documents, and OLE Automation technologies, controls (such as VBX and OCX controls), user exits, and PL/SQL interfaces to foreign functions.

AUDIENCE

Developing Oracle Forms Applications is intended primarily for software engineers whose mission is to create database applications for the Oracle RDBMS. As such, the book primarily addresses the needs of this group of Information Technology (IT) professionals. Because of the way the material is organized, the book can be used by application developers at all levels of proficiency.

The first part is for the newcomers to the Oracle Forms environment. This part explains important Designer and Runtime concepts which benefits not just the beginner, but also end-users of Oracle applications.

The second part addresses the needs of intermediate programmers who do not have a vast experience with Oracle Forms. The chapters in this part are organized to serve as reference materials for the main components of Oracle Forms Designer, where most of the development activities occur.

The third part explains fundamental concepts that every serious Oracle Forms developer should know and master. The material covered in this part is for programmers dedicated to create applications conforming with object-oriented principles, Multiple-Document Interface (MDI) paradigm and well-established Graphical User Interface (GUI) principles.

The last part of the book provides information for advanced programmers who go the extra mile to deliver integrated and user-friendly applications. The focus in this part is not just the integration of Oracle Forms modules with other Developer/2000 tools, but, most importantly, the creation of unified multiple-component applications using DDE, OLE technologies, user exits, and PL/SQL interface to foreign functions.

The book provides concrete examples for each concept and technique discussed. All the sample code and software modules discussed here are provided in the companion disk, together with instructions on where to find them and how to use them.

SOFTWARE REQUIREMENTS AND PLATFORM CONSIDERATIONS

This book is first and foremost a hands-on guide to application development, and should be read as such. The only way to get a full understanding and appreciation of the concepts, properties, and sample code discussed in the book is to follow the discussion with the Oracle Forms Designer active in your machine.

Throughout the book, Oracle Forms will imply the version 4.5 of the software. The examples provided in the companion disk and the screen shots used throughout the book use Oracle Forms version 4.5.6.5.5 for MS Windows for Workgroups 3.11. However, they all use generic features that apply to the 4.5 release, therefore you should not experience any difficulties even if you are using a different version of the software. When a feature related to a particular release is discussed, the full version of that release will be mentioned.

Given the multitude of platforms on which Oracle Forms runs, it is impossible to discuss all the minute details of the software in every platform. The book discusses generic features as much as it is possible. In particular places, where the issues must be addressed for a particular environment, we chose to use MS Windows. This choice was made because this environment supports the MDI paradigm, OLE technology, VBX controls, and well-established GUI standards.

INSTALLING THE COMPANION DISK

As you read the book, you will be invited to explore the Oracle Forms environment, perform several activities, and carry out many different tasks. This will result in a number of applications that you will develop. These applications are all provided in the companion disk that accompanies this book. Files included in the companion disk are grouped in directories according to the chapters in which they are referenced. Throughout the book you will be provided with instructions on how to use these files. Here are instructions for installing them to your machine:

INSTALLING THE SOFTWARE MODULES

In order to install the modules provided in the companion disk to your environment, follow these steps:

1. Create a subdirectory off your C:\ directory and name it C:\ORAFORMS.
2. Copy the files from the companion disk onto C:\ORAFORMS.
3. Unzip the file OROFORMS.ZIP using the utility PKUNZIP. Since several directories are included in this file, you should use the switch -d in the PKUN-

ZIP command. Assuming that this utility is located in the DOS path, you should run the following command:

```
pkunzip -d oraforms.zip
```

4. Edit the file ORAWIN.INI to add the following environmental variables:
   - ❏ Add C:\ORAFORMS\ICONS to TK21_ICON
   - ❏ Add C:\ORAFORMS\PLL to FORMS45_PATH
   - ❏ Add C:\ORAFORMS\USEREXIT\UE_CH25.DLL to FORMS45_USER-EXITS

   All these variables are defined under the section [FORMS45] of ORAWIN.INI.

5. Copy the file ORAFORMS.GRP onto the \WINDOWS directory of your machine.

6. In the Program Manager, create a new program group based on the file ORACLEFO.GRP.

The program items created in this program group allow you to run the SQL*Plus scripts that create the necessary database objects for the examples, generate the Oracle Forms executables of these examples, and execute these executables. They assume that your ORACLE_HOME is set to C:\ORAWIN. If your environment is different, please make the necessary adjustments to the properties of the program items.

INSTALLING THE DATABASE OBJECTS

It is recommended that you create a separate account to store all the database objects required to run the applications provided in the companion disk. In order to do that, follow these instructions:

1. Execute the program *item Create New User* from the program group *Oracle Forms Applications* created previously.
2. Respond to the prompts according to your environment.

Alternatively, you may run the script C:\ORAFORMS\SQL\CR8USER.SQL from SQL*Plus. If you desire to remove this account at a later date, execute the program item *Drop User* or run the script C:\ORAFORMS\SQL\DROP-USER.SQL from SQL*Plus.

After creating the new user account, run the script that created the database objects and loads sample data in them.

1. Execute the program *item Create Database Objects* from the program group *Oracle Forms Applications* created previously.
2. Respond to the prompts according to your environment.

Alternatively, you may run the script C:\ORAFORMS\SQL\CR8OBJS.SQL from SQL*Plus. If you desire to remove these objects at a later date, execute the program item *Drop Database Objects* or run the script C:\ORAFORMS\SQL\DROPOBJS.SQL from SQL*Plus.

GENERATING THE EXECUTABLE VERSIONS OF THE SOFTWARE MODULES

You may easily accomplish this task by following the instructions provided in Chapter 1 on how to use the Oracle Forms Generator or by using the program item *Generate Applications* in the program group *Oracle Forms Applications*.

TYPOGRAPHIC CONVENTIONS

The following typographic conventions are followed throughout the book to make your reading and understanding of the material easier:

❑ All SQL, PL/SQL, and Oracle reserved words are shown in capital letters. This includes the different built-in program units that are provided by Developer/2000 in general and Oracle Forms in particular. Examples of such keywords are:

SELECT, COUNT, IF, THEN, EXECUTE_QUERY, and WHEN-BUTTON-PRESSED.

❑ All table, column names, and all Oracle Forms objects' names are shown in capital letters. Examples of these objects are:

HARDWARE table, FIRST_NAME column, CUSTOMER window, and SOFTWARE block.

❑ Selection from menu items is presented in the following format:

File I Open, Arrange I Size Objects..., or Edit I Copy.

❑ Properties that are set in the Oracle Forms Designer are shown in italics. The values they are set to are shown in italics, enclosed in single quotes. Example:

Set *Insert Allowed* to *'True'*.

❑ Everything that you should type is shown in Arial font. This will include names of variables, functions, and procedures that you will create. This will also include all the program statements that do not extend beyond one line of code. Example:

Enter HARDWARE in the property setting field.

or:

The body of the trigger contains this statement:

ENTER_QUERY;

❑   The contents of program units that you will create during development activities in the book are shown in the following format:

```
Procedure Check_Package_Failure IS
BEGIN
  IF NOT ( Form_Success ) THEN
    RAISE Form_Trigger_Failure;
  END IF;
END;
```

❑   Directory names and file names are shown in capital letters, as in this example:

C:\ETS\ETS.FMB.

❑   Window names, dialog box names, and options in a dialog box are shown in initial capitals, as in this example:

Layout Editor window, New Block Options dialog box, etc.

❑   Keyboard keys are shown in small capital letters, as in these examples:

ENTER, DELETE, and F10.

❑   KEY 1+KEY 2 will signify: Hold KEY 1 while you press KEY 2.
❑   KEY 1+CLICK, KEY 1+DOUBLE-CLICK, and KEY 1+DRAG will signify: Hold KEY 1 while performing the corresponding mouse action.
❑   Iconic buttons will be referred to by the balloon help name of the button, followed by the word *icon*, followed by the bitmap, as in this example:

Click the Save icon   in the toolbar.

❑ Label buttons will be referred to by the text label on the button, followed by the word *button*, as in this example:

Click Browse... button to display the Open dialog box.

❑ Steps that you must follow in order to accomplish a task are shown in the form of numbered lists as in this example:

1. Select Query | Enter from the menu.
2. Select Query | Execute from the menu.

❑ Actions that you may perform alternatively, instead of each other, are shown as lettered lists, as in this example:

a) Select File | Save from the menu, or
b) Press CTRL+S from the keyboard, or
c) Click the Save icon ▣ in the toolbar.

ACKNOWLEDGMENTS

George Pompidou, the famous French political leader and president of France in 1969–74 is attributed to saying, "Conception is much more fun than delivery." In these paragraphs I want to extend the warmest thanks to all those who helped me transform an idea conceived months ago into reality, in the form of this book.

In particular, many thanks to Enit Kaduku, who supported me from the very beginning and, by taking the load of many small things off my shoulders, allowed me to concentrate on the work. She also had the patience to read several drafts of this book and provide invaluable suggestions that helped improve its quality significantly.

Thanks to Lawrence James, for his technical editing and useful comments. His vast experience with Oracle databases and tools, and his willingness to share this experience with others, have helped me advance in my career and added quality to the book.

The clarity and preciseness of Chapters 15, 21, and 25 improved significantly thanks to the review and helpful comments of Steve Muench, longtime Product Manager of Oracle Forms, and currently, Senior Product Manager for the Project Sedona Development at the Oracle Corporation.

Special thanks go to the software engineers and management team at Sentient Systems, Inc., the Oracle solutions provider based in Kensington, Maryland, with whom I had the privilege to work in the initial phase of this project. Their commitment to excellence and, in particular, the support of Mr. Steve Casey, President, and Mr. William Schofield, Director of Enterprise, were of significant importance in the preliminary work and research activities that resulted in this book.

I would also like to express my acknowledgments to all the people at Prentice Hall who made this book possible, and in particular to Mr. Mark Taub, Senior Managing Editor at Prentice Hall, who offered his invaluable support and guidance throughout the life of this project and Beth Sturla, Total Concept Manager. The production team at Pine Tree Composition, Inc., played a significant importance in the timely completion of this book. My gratitude goes to all of them, and especially to Ms. Patty Sawyer and Mr. Dan Boilard.

Finally, I would like to thank you, dear reader, for the time you have spent, and will spend, with this book. I hope it will be a useful tool that will facilitate your work with Oracle Forms and will enhance your professional career. Enjoy!

Albert Lulushi

Part I

ORACLE FORMS 101

"He who has begun has half done. Dare to be wise; begin!"
—Horace

THE FIRST ORACLE
FORMS APPLICATION

"Look with favor upon a bold beginning."
—Virgil

- ◆ The Equipment Tracking System
- ◆ Creating the First Form
- ◆ The Object Navigator
- ◆ Creating a Base Table Block: *HARDWARE*
- ◆ Adding a Detail Block: *SOFTWARE*
- ◆ Saving and Generating
- ◆ Debugging and Debugger
- ◆ Summary

In this chapter you will develop the first Oracle Forms application to solve a real life problem. Before beginning the development activities, you will analyze the structure of entities, attributes, and database objects involved in this application.

You will then create a data entry form for the application. In the process, important elements of Oracle Forms Designer such as the Object Navigator, Designer toolbar, and message bar, will be discussed. The chapter also introduces basic Forms development techniques such as creating base table blocks, using master/detail relationships, and saving and generating modules.

1.1 THE EQUIPMENT TRACKING SYSTEM

Print and Press is a small desktop publishing company in Suburbia that prints everything from *The Suburban Sentinel*, to postcards, to wedding invitations. It has a dozen employees, including Mrs. White, the general manager, and Mr. Brown, the receptionist. They all use desktop computers that run different types of software applications. In addition, the print shop has three scanners, two photocopying machines, and several printers.

1.1.1 STATEMENT OF THE PROBLEM

Mrs. White has hired you to put her bills and receipts for hardware and software purchases in order. Mr. Brown currently stores them in a file folder each time a new item is purchased. The problem is that, periodically, someone has to go through all the receipts in order to figure out how much money was spent on hardware and on software. You assess the situation, interview some of the employees that need these data the most, and decide to create a small Oracle Forms application to solve their problem.

Before going any further, you should come up with a name for your application. Just like a sound bite, this name should convey as much information about the system as possible. The core functionality of the application should come across in no more than three or four words. Think of the name *MS Windows*, or *Oracle Forms*. In just two words they say what the application is about and who created it. The use of acronyms is acceptable, but you should be very careful to choose one that is easy to pronounce and remember. So, call the new application the Equipment Tracking System, or ETS for short.

1.1.2 DEFINING THE DATABASE OBJECTS FOR ETS

The main entities in the ETS application are *Hardware* and *Software*. *Hardware* is considered any electronic equipment purchased and located in the premises of Print and Press that is used in the daily activity of the employees. Examples of hardware items would by a personal computer (PC), a monitor, a scanner, or a printer. *Software* is any software package that is installed and runs on a particular hardware item. Examples of software items are MS DOS 6.0, Personal Oracle7, and other programs installed on Mr. Brown's PC. The entity relationship diagram for ETS is shown in Figure 1.1.

Each block in this diagram represents an entity. The line connecting the blocks represents the relationship between the entities. From left to right, it can be read as follows: "Each *Hardware* item runs zero or more *Software* items." It can also be read right to left: "Each *Software* item is installed on one and only one *Hardware* item."

Once the main entities of ETS and the relationship between them are defined, the attention shifts to identifying the attributes for each entity and the properties of each attribute. The most important property of an attribute is its datatype. Depending on the kind of data the attribute represents, its datatype can be alphanumeric, numeric, date, binary, and so on. Alphanumeric attributes represent character string data. The alphanumeric datatypes supported by the Oracle7 database server include CHAR (for fixed-length strings up to 255 bytes long), VARCHAR2 (for variable-length strings up to 2000 bytes long), and LONG (for variable-length strings up to 2 GB long). VARCHAR2 is the most flexible and frequently used alphanumeric datatype. Numeric attributes have NUMBER datatype and represent virtually any fixed and floating point numeric data, with up to 38 digits of precision. Attributes of DATE datatype represent dates in a flexible format that includes century, year, month, day, hours, minutes, and seconds. If the attribute will represent binary data up to 2000 bytes long, then RAW datatype is used. For larger binary objects (up to 2 Gb) such as graphics, bitmaps, and images, the LONG RAW datatype is used.

A primary key (PK) is the attribute that uniquely identifies an instance of the entity. For example, the attribute *Hardware Serial Number* uniquely identifies each *Hardware* record. A foreign key (FK) is the attribute of an entity that serves as primary key for another entity. Every foreign key represents a relation between two entities. More precisely, it describes the dependence or child/parent relationship between the entity that owns the foreign key on the entity pointed at by the key. In the ETS application, the attribute *Hardware Serial Number* is a foreign key for entity *Software*. It represents the relationship between a software item and the hardware unit on which the software is installed.

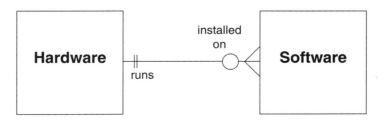

FIGURE 1.1   Entity Relationship diagram for ETS.

TABLE 1.1 Attributes for entity *Hardware*.

ENTITY	ATTRIBUTES	DATA TYPE	LENGTH	PK	FK	OTHER INTEGRITY CONSTRAINTS
Hardware	Hardware Serial Number	CHAR	6	Y		Internal tracking number, fixed length
	Name	VARCHAR2	30			Not NULL
	Manufacturer	VARCHAR2	30			
	Model	VARCHAR2	20			
	Purchase Cost	NUMBER	8, 2			Between $0.00 and $100,000.00
	Purchase Date	DATE				
	Customer Support Phone	VARCHAR2	10			
	Annual Customer Support Fee	NUMBER	8, 2			Between $0.00 and $100,000.00

Analyzing properties of attributes offers a good opportunity to identify the rules that data items will obey in the future application. For example, in the ETS application, it its reasonable to ask that data satisfy the following rules:

❑ Names of *Hardware* and *Software* items must be specified.
❑ *Purchase Cost* for *Hardware* and *Software* items and *Annual Customer Support Fee* for *Hardware* items should be positive values smaller than $100,000.
❑ All dollar values should be specified in dollars and cents.

Some of these requirements, such as the first one, will be enforced at the database level. The rest of them could be implemented there as well, but you will enforce them in the application you are about to develop. Properties that determine whether the attribute is a primary key, a foreign key, or whether the data it represents must not be NULL, must be unique, or obey other rules such as the ones described above, are also known as data integrity constraints. Table 1.1 lists the attributes of entity *Hardware* and their properties. Table 1.2 lists the attributes of entity *Software* and their properties.

1.1.3 CREATING THE DATABASE OBJECTS FOR ETS

In order to follow the development activities discussed in the rest of this chapter and in the following two chapters, you must create the ETS tables in your database and load sample data in them. The section *Installing the Companion Disk* in the preface provides the necessary instructions to complete this task. Please follow these instructions before continuing to the next section.

TABLE 1.2 Attributes for entity *Software*.

ENTITY	ATTRIBUTES	DATA TYPE	LENGTH	PK	FK	OTHER INTEGRITY CONSTRAINTS
Software	Software Serial Number	CHAR	6	Y		Internal tracking number, fixed length
	Hardware Serial Number	CHAR	6		Y	Equipment where software is installed
	Name	VARCHAR2	30			Not NULL
	Version	VARCHAR2	10			
	Purchase Cost	NUMBER	8, 2			Between $0.00 and $100,000.00
	Purchase Date	DATE				

1.2 CREATING THE FIRST FORM

Now you are ready to begin developing the form for the ETS application. First, create a separate directory in your hard disk to store it:

1. Open Windows Main group and double-click the File Manager program item.
2. Create a directory off the root directory and name it ETS.

Now, launch the Forms Designer.

3. Open the Developer/2000 group.
4. Double-click the Forms Designer program item.

After the Designer is loaded, you should see something similar to Figure 1.2 on the screen.

1.2.1 NAMING THE FORM

1. Click MODULE1 entry in the list, if it is not already selected.
2. Position the cursor over the text. When its shape changes to I-beam, click the mouse. The cursor is placed at the end of the module name.
3. Delete the existing name and type the new form's name: ETS.
4. Press ENTER when done.

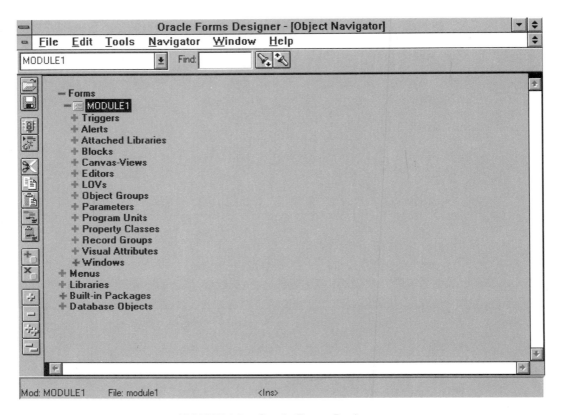

FIGURE 1.2 Oracle Forms Designer.

1.2.2 SAVING THE FORM

1. Select File | Save from the menu. Because this is a new module, the standard MS Windows Save As dialog box appears (see Figure 1.3).
2. Accept the proposed name: ets.fmb.
3. In the Directories list box, select the directory created in the previous steps to save the ETS form.
4. Click OK.

Oracle Forms saves the form according to your specifications.

1.2.3 CONNECTING TO THE DATABASE

1. Select File | Connect... from the menu. The Forms Designer Connect dialog box appears (see Figure 1.4).

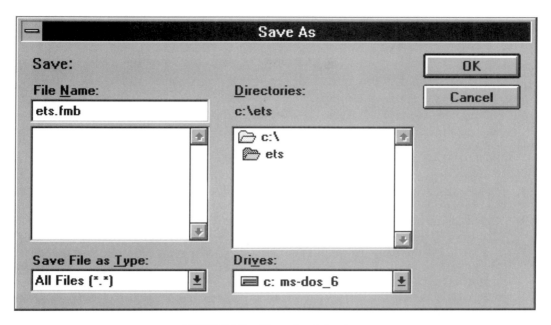

FIGURE 1.3 Save As dialog box.

2. Enter User Name and Password. The user name should be the Oracle account that owns the ETS tables, for example D2000.
3. Enter the Database connect string or alias, as it may apply to your environment. The connect string uniquely identifies the database where the ETS tables reside.
4. Click Connect button.

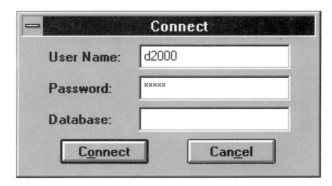

FIGURE 1.4 Connect dialog box.

Note

If the information you supplied is not correct, Oracle Forms will display an error message. Supply the appropriate user name, password, and database string; then, try connecting again.

When the connection is established, the little ✚ icon to the left of Database Objects changes color from light gray to deep blue. Now it looks like this: ✚. If you click it, you will see all the database users whose objects you can access. In the case of Figure 1.5, account D2000 has access to its own objects, and to some views owned by the SYS schema.

If you click the ✚ icon to the left of the account name, you can see that every database account may own stored program units, PL/SQL libraries, tables, and views. In the case of Figure 1.5, account D2000 owns only two tables: HARDWARE and SOFTWARE. The columns of each table are listed in alphabetical order and their data types are shown in parentheses. If there are database triggers associated with the table, they are listed as a separate heading, right under the table name.

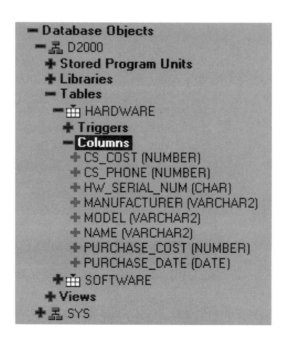

FIGURE 1.5 Viewing database objects in the Object Navigator.

1.3 THE OBJECT NAVIGATOR

The window you have been working on so far is the Oracle Forms Object Navigator. The Object Navigator is the heart of Developer/2000 tools in general and Forms 4.5 in particular. From here you can display, access, and edit just about every object in an application. Figure 1.6 represents the Object Navigator.

The most important part of the Object Navigator is the working area. The entries listed in the working area of Figure 1.6 are Oracle Forms object types. As you can see, a form can have triggers, alerts, blocks, and so on. Do not allow names such as LOVs or Canvas-Views discourage you. As cryptic as they may seem now, you will see that they are really easy to use and manipulate.

Entries in the list are also called nodes. The name of each node is preceded by small icons. These icons play a very important informational and navigational role. The light gray ✚ icon means that the object is not instantiated. In other words, there are no objects of that type in the application yet. To create one, double-click the ✚ icon. If the icon has a light azure color such as the ✚ icon, then there is at least one object of that type in the application. To see all the objects of a particular object type, click the ✚ icon or, as it is often said, *expand* the node. When the node is expanded, the previous icon is replaced by the ━ icon. All the instances of that object type are listed beneath, indented to the right. To hide them, click the ━ icon, or *collapse* the node.

On the left side of the Object Navigator window, there is a vertical toolbar. The buttons listed here allow fast access to often-used commands such as Open, Save, Cut, Paste, Expand, and Collapse. The bitmaps incorporated in these buttons clearly describe their purpose. However, you do not have to memorize the meaning of all these icons. Oracle Forms uses balloon help to assist you in identifying and selecting the right button. To display a brief description of an icon, place the mouse on the icon and do not move it for an instant. A little box will pop up on the side, displaying the icon's name on a yellow background. Later in the book, you will learn how to add balloon help functionality to your applications.

Another important component of the Object Navigator is the message bar. For clarity, it is shown separately in Figure 1.7.

For historical reasons, the message bar is often referred to as the message line, but the term is not fully correct. In reality, there are two lines in the message bar. The one on the top displays Oracle Forms informative messages such as the one captured in Figure 1.7. The bottom line displays the name of the module you are currently working with and the name of the file under which this module is saved. Further to the right, a group of status lamps is displayed. There can be up to three of these status lamps. In the case of Figure 1.7, only two are displayed. The first one, <Con>, indicates that Forms Designer is connected to the database. It will not appear if a connection is not established. The lamp on the right is a text editing mode indicator. It shows whether you are inserting (<Ins>) or replacing

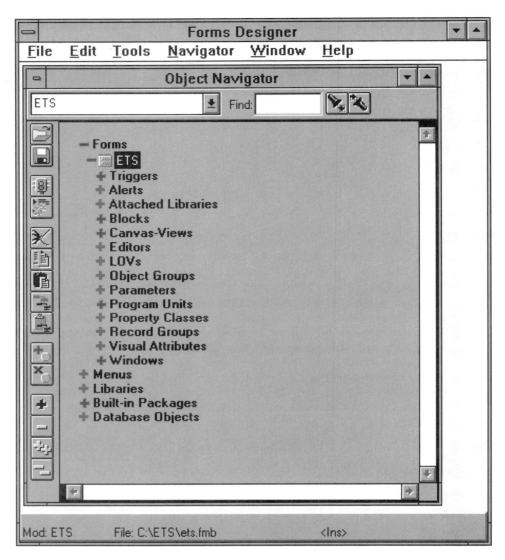

FIGURE 1.6   Oracle Forms Object Navigator.

FIGURE 1.7   Oracle Forms Designer message bar.

> # Note
>
> When developing a form, use the message bar the same way you would use the rear-view mirror in your car. Glance at it once in a while, but not for a long time. The information contained there can protect your application and provide helpful hints, but the fun stuff is right ahead in the Object Navigator and other editors that you will use.

(<Rep>) text as you type. There is a third status lamp, which is not shown in Figure 1.7. It indicates that the selected object is defined in another module and referenced in the current module.

1.4 CREATING A BASE TABLE BLOCK: *HARDWARE*

Ultimately, any Oracle Forms application is a collection of interface items and boilerplate objects that allow users to visually access and modify their data. The interface items may correspond to columns in database tables, or may represent derived data, formulas, and so on. All items in a form are grouped in abstract objects of a higher hierarchy, based on their meaning and functionality. These objects are called blocks. Blocks are often associated with a database table, in which case they are called base table blocks.

In the ETS application you will create two blocks that will interface with the tables HARDWARE and SOFTWARE. Begin by creating the first block in the ETS module.

1. In the Object Navigator, double-click the ✚ icon on the left of *Blocks*. New Block Options dialog box appears (see Figure 1.8). The window title is preceded by the name of your form.

The new block will organize data from the HARDWARE table. Let the Designer know about this.

2. Click the Select... button on the right of Base Table field. The Tables dialog box is displayed (see Figure 1.9).

The checked items in this dialog window mean that the Designer will display only those tables that are owned by the current user. Depending on the application, you may want to display other types of objects that you or other users own. Simply select the appropriate check boxes.

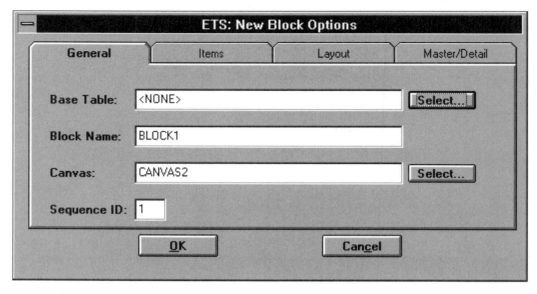

FIGURE 1.8   New Block Options dialog box. General tab is currently selected.

3. Click OK in the Tables dialog box. A list of available tables appears (see Figure 1.10).
4. Select the HARDWARE table, if not already selected.
5. Click OK, or double-click the HARDWARE entry in this list.

This and other similar pop-up windows are called List of Values, or often abbreviated as LOVs. They allow you to select an entry from the list onto a field in the

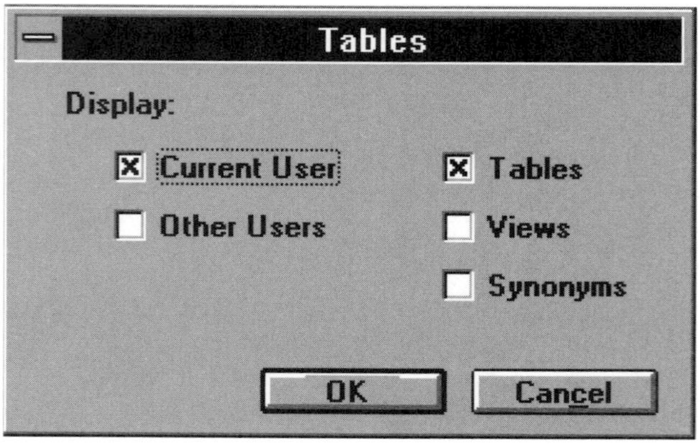

FIGURE 1.9   Tables dialog box.

FIGURE 1.10 Tables List of Values.

Designer. In addition, LOVs have two features that are especially useful when the number of listed entries is particularly large. By simply typing in the list area of the LOVs window, the list is automatically reduced to those items that match the characters you enter. The auto-reduction feature of LOVs allows you to select a particular entry by typing only a few initial characters of that entry. For more sophisticated search criteria, you can use the Find utility. Simply enter the text string in the Find text field of the LOVs window and click the Find button. Use standard SQL language wildcards such as %, to retrieve all those list items that contain the specific text you entered. The use of wildcards to specify search criteria is discussed in more detail later in Chapter 2 and 9.

After selecting from the LOVs, the control is returned to the New Block Options dialog box. Notice that Base Table and Block Name fields are automatically

Note

Oracle Forms allows you to incorporate similar LOVs in your applications. Their functionality is exactly the same and it all comes by default. In the chapters to come, you will learn how to attach LOVs to text items at design time or display them programmatically.

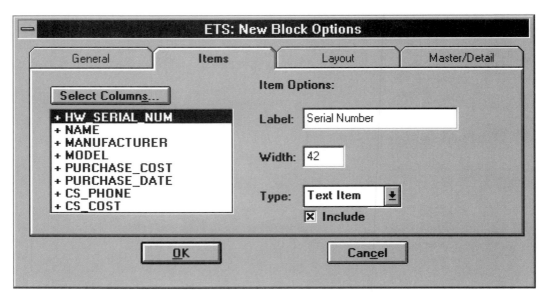

FIGURE 1.11   New Block Options dialog box. Items tab is currently selected.

filled by Forms. Now specify the columns from the HARDWARE table you want
to include in the new block.

6. Click the Items folder tab in the New Block Options dialog box. The content
    of the window will change to reflect item properties.
7. Click the Select Columns... button. All the columns of HARDWARE table
    will be displayed as in Figure 1.11.

The columns that are preceded by the + sign will be included in the block. Currently, all the columns from HARDWARE table are selected. If you want to deselect a column, double-click its name in the list, or uncheck the Include check box
under the item Type field. The – sign will replace the + sign to indicate that the
current column will not be included in the block. The Items folder tab allows you
to change some other properties such as width, type, or label. A label is the descriptive text associated with an item when Forms displays it in the block's boilerplate. As an example, change the label of HW_SERIAL_NUM column. Select
the column, click inside the Label text field, and type Serial Number. When Designer will draw its boilerplate, this label will be displayed on the side of
HW_SERIAL_NUM item.

Now specify layout settings for the new block.

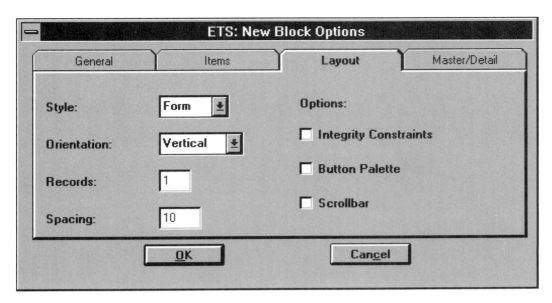

FIGURE 1.12   New Block Options dialog box. Layout tab is currently selected.

8. Click the Layout folder tab on the New Block Options dialog box. The content of the window will change to reflect layout properties (see Figure 1.12).
9. Click the Style list box, and select Form.

At this point, you are ready to complete the creation of your first block.

10. Click OK in the New Block Options dialog box.

Forms starts working, builds the block according to your specifications, and returns to the Object Navigator. The HARDWARE block is right there. If you expand it, you will see a list of items whose names correspond to the columns in the HARDWARE table. As you may have noticed, the Canvas-Views object type is populated now. The Designer has automatically created a canvas and drawn the new block on it.

1.5   ADDING A DETAIL BLOCK: *SOFTWARE*

In this section you will create a block that will interface with data in the SOFTWARE table. The ETS users are mainly interested to know which software products are installed and run on their hardware equipment. You want the Forms application to reflect this. In other words, if Mr. Brown's PC is displayed in the HARDWARE block, the SOFTWARE block should list all the programs installed there. If Mrs. White's PC is displayed, the software items should change accordingly.

In Oracle Forms, this type of coordination is implemented by defining a *master/detail* relationship between the HARDWARE and SOFTWARE blocks. The HARDWARE block will be the master block, because it will drive the information displayed in the other block. The SOFTWARE block will be the detail one, because it will supply additional information about the master record currently displayed in the HARDWARE block.

The process of creating any base table block is very similar to what you did in the previous section. Therefore, this section will not provide detailed instructions on how to create the SOFTWARE block, but only general guidelines that you can easily follow.

1. Select Blocks object type in the Object Navigator.
2. Click the Add icon ▣ in the toolbar.
3. Select SOFTWARE as the base table for the new block, and let all its columns be in the block.
4. Set the Layout properties as shown in Figure 1.13.

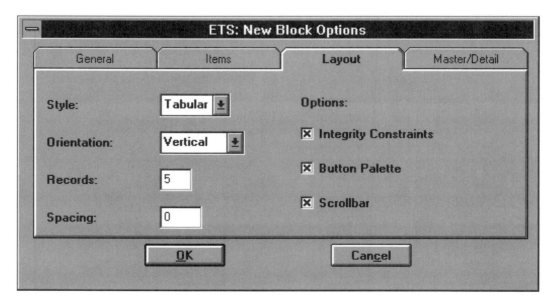

FIGURE 1.13   Layout settings for SOFTWARE block.

Setting Style to Tabular and Orientation to Vertical makes the SOFTWARE block display the records stacked vertically like a table. The settings for Records and Spacing mean that there will be five records displayed at a time, with no space between them. By checking the Button Palette check box, you are asking Oracle Forms to add a group of useful push buttons on the boilerplate. Finally, to facilitate the navigation between records, a vertical scrollbar will be added to the new block.

Now specify the master/detail relationship between HARDWARE and SOFTWARE blocks.

1. Click the Master/Detail folder tab on the New Block Options dialog box. The content of the window will change to reflect master/detail properties (see Figure 1.14).
2. Click the Select... button on the right of Master Block text field. The ETS:Blocks LOVs window appears.
3. Select HARDWARE from the list. Forms intelligently supplies the join condition, as shown in Figure 1.14, based on column, primary key, and foreign key definitions for both tables.
4. Click OK.

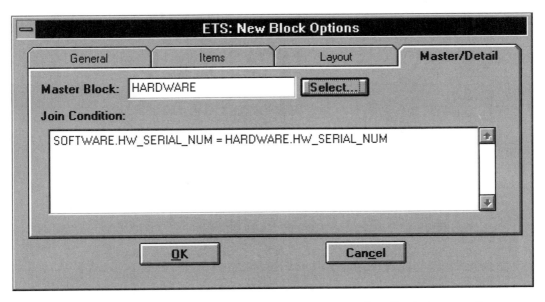

FIGURE 1.14 New Block Options dialog box. Master/Detail tab is currently selected.

Once again, Designer cranks its engine up, builds the specified block, and returns to the Object Navigator.

1.6 SAVING AND GENERATING

The significant improvements in the hardware and software products in use today have created a stable and robust environment for application development activities. However, unexpected events such as power failure, memory errors, file corruption, or viruses may result in loss of important work. Therefore, it is always a safe and good practice to save your application often. There are three ways to save an Oracle Forms module:

a) Select File | Save from the menu, or
b) Press CTRL+S from the keyboard, or
c) Click the Save icon ▣ in the toolbar.

1.6.1 GENERATING FROM DESIGNER

As in other programming environments, in order to run the newly created module, an executable file must be generated first. During the generating process, the Forms Designer checks and validates all the objects, their property settings, and the code attached to them. If conflicts are found, the appropriate error messages are generated and displayed to the user. The error messages are also written to a file that has the same name as the form module and the extension .ERR. For example, if errors are encountered during the generation of ETS.FMB module, they are written to the file ETS.ERR. The error file is created under the same directory as the binary file.

There are two ways to generate a Forms module that is open in the Designer:

a) Select File | Administration | Generate from the menu, or
b) Press CTRL+T from the keyboard.

If the generation is successful, an executable file with the extension .FMX is created under the same directory as the binary file. For example, the executable file of the ETS.FMB module will be ETS.FMX.

1.6.2 SETTING DESIGNER OPTIONS

Generating a module may seem more complicated than it should be. Indeed, you need to go through three levels of menus to access the command, and no button is provided in the toolbar. However, Oracle Forms, by default, provides a way to execute the application without explicitly generating it beforehand. The reason is that in Forms, like in other programming environments, the application development process is a repetition of the basic sequence:

1. Change the application by adding to or modifying its functionality.
2. Create the new executable version by compiling or generating.
3. Execute or run the application to assess the effects of additions and modifications.

Because it is so customary to generate the executable version of a module before running it, a setting in the Forms Designer Options allows you to bypass Step 2 in the sequence above. When developing a Forms application, you simply change the application and then run it to see the effect of the modifications. Designer implicitly generates the new executable, before running it. If you only need to generate the application, then follow the instructions provided above.

The setting for this and other options of Oracle Forms Designer and Runtime can be accessed and modified in the Options dialog box.

1. Select Tools | Options... from the menu. The Options dialog box appears (see Figure 1.15).
2. Set Designer Options or Runtime Options accordingly.

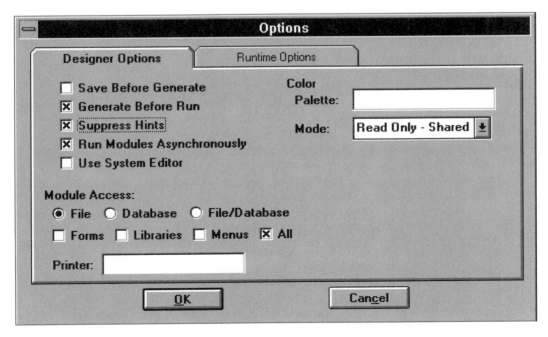

FIGURE 1.15 Options dialog box. Designer Options tab is selected.

As you can see from this figure, if you set the Save before Generate check box, you can skip the step of saving the form before generating and running it. Once an option is set, the setting will remain in effect until you change or reset it.

1.6.3 USING FORMS GENERATE

The methods described above generate a module from within the Designer, while you develop the application. There are instances when you may want only to generate a module without doing any other design activities. These situations are mostly encountered when you upgrade from older versions of Oracle Forms or when you port your application from one platform to another. In these cases, you may use the Oracle Forms Generate tool. Forms Generate takes as input the binary files created in the Designer. If the generation process is successful, the executable is created. To use the Forms Generate utility follow these steps:

1. Open the Developer/2000 program group.
2. Double-click Forms Generate program item. The Oracle Forms Generator Options window appears (see Figure 1.16).
3. Enter the name of the executable, as shown in Figure 1.16.
4. Fill in the Userid, Password, and Database fields according to your environment.
5. Click OK.

If you do not supply the full name of the module, Forms Generate will search only the directory %ORACLE_HOME%\BIN. For example, if ORACLE_HOME directory is C:\ORAWIN, then the directory searched by default is C:\ORAWIN\BIN. You can also click the Browse... button to display the standard MS Windows Open dialog box, and search for your module in the directory tree.

Note

If the information provided in the Forms Generator Options window is not sufficient or accurate enough for a database connection to be established, the generate process will terminate with the error message "ORA-01017: invalid userid/password; logon denied". You will have to start the program once again and hope that this time you will not make any mistakes. The window where the options are specified is too small and cannot be resized. You must use scrollbars to view almost every other option besides the ones specified in Figure 1.16.

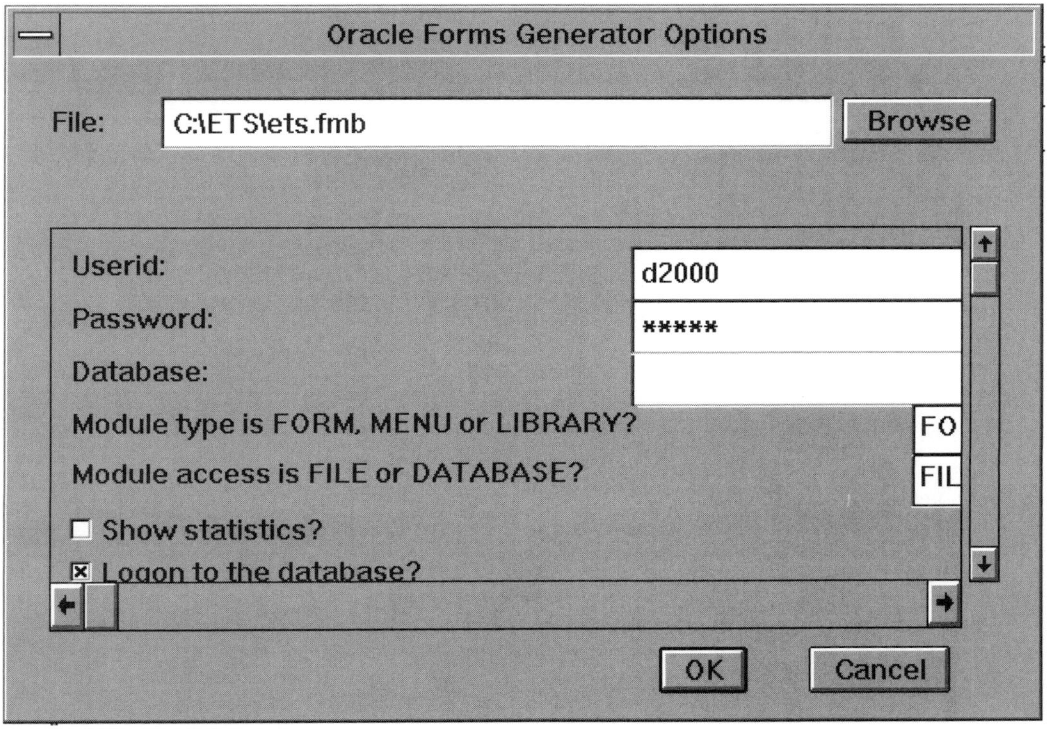

FIGURE 1.16   Oracle Forms Generator Options window.

1.7   DEBUGGING AND DEBUGGER

When you execute a module from within the Designer, depending on your Run-time Options settings, Forms may display the Debugger window (see Figure 1.17). If you do not plan to do any debugging, dismiss the window by clicking the Close button ⊠ in the Debugger toolbar.

As you develop a form in the Designer, you also debug it. During this process, you try to identify two categories of errors. The first category includes logical or design errors. Bugs of this category are identified in close interaction with the application users, during joint review sessions of the application. The second category includes the more traditional bugs, hidden in the PL/SQL code. The Debugger is a tool incorporated in Oracle Forms that facilitates the discovery of this type of bugs. The Fourth Generation Languages (4GL) tools, which include Oracle Forms and other Developer/2000 tools, revolutionized the process of application development. Compared with traditional 3GL tools, the code they pro-

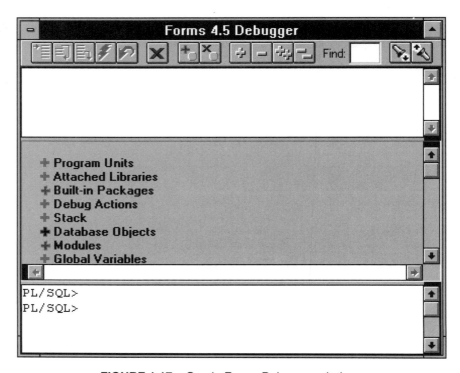

FIGURE 1.17   Oracle Forms Debugger window.

duce contains very few bugs of the second category. This allows developers to focus more on discovering inconsistencies of the first type, thus creating software systems that meet the real needs and requirements of their users.

In Oracle Forms, especially at the initial stage of development, there is very little coding done. Therefore, it is time-consuming to bring up the Debugger each time the form is executed, only to dismiss it right away, as you did previously. To avoid this, just turn off the Debug Mode property and use the Debugger only when you need it. There are several ways to toggle the Debug Mode on or off. The easiest one is to click the Debug button in the Object Navigator toolbar. This button is the fourth one from the top, with ... a bug in it. If the bug is bright and shiny, as in ▨, Forms is in Debug Mode. If the bug is hibernating, as in ▨, the Debug Mode is off.

You can set the Debug Mode from the Designer menu, as well. Choose Tools | Debug Mode menu item. If it is checked, debugging is on, otherwise it is off. Finally, you can set this mode in the Runtime Options folder tab of Options dialog box (see Figure 1.16). Check or uncheck the Debug Mode check box accordingly.

1.8 SUMMARY

This chapter introduced you to a simple application and guided you through the process of creating the first Oracle Forms module. Some of the most important concepts discussed in this chapter include the following:

- ❑ Application analysis and design
  - ❑ Rationale and core functionality of the Equipment Tracking System (ETS)
  - ❑ Entitites, entity relationship diagram, and attributes for ETS
  - ❑ Database objects for ETS
- ❑ Oracle Forms Object Navigator
  - ❑ Work area
  - ❑ Nodes
  - ❑ Expanding and collapsing nodes
  - ❑ Message bar
- ❑ Developing a new module
  - ❑ Connecting to the database
  - ❑ Creating base table blocks
  - ❑ Creating master/detail blocks
  - ❑ Oracle Forms List of Values (LOVs) functionality
  - ❑ Saving and generating
- ❑ Oracle Forms Generate utility
- ❑ Oracle Forms Debugger window

RUNNING THE FIRST FORM

"O young artist, you search for a subject—everything is a subject."
—Eugène Delacroix

- ◆ Oracle Forms Runtime
- ◆ Oracle Forms Runtime Window
- ◆ Querying the Database
- ◆ Normal Mode and Enter Query Mode
- ◆ Manipulating the Database
- ◆ Transactions in Oracle Forms
- ◆ Multi-User Applications and Record Locking
- ◆ What is Missing in ETS?
- ◆ Summary

In this chapter you will run the form created in the previous chapter and, in the process, discuss some important features of Oracle Forms Runtime. If you just completed reading Chapter 1, module ETS.FMB should be open in the Designer, and the generated executable ETS.FMX ready to run. To execute the current form follow one of the following instructions:

a) Select File | Run from the menu, or
b) Click the Run icon 🖾 in the Object Navigator toolbar.

If the debugger window appears, dismiss it and disable the Debug Mode option as discussed in the previous chapter.

2.1 ORACLE FORMS RUNTIME

You can also use Oracle Forms Runtime to execute the ETS.FMX module. During development efforts, when modules are executed mainly for debugging purposes, they are executed from within the Designer, as explained. Once they are finished and ready to be deployed in the users' workstations, the Runtime is used. To run the form using the Runtime utility follow these steps:

1. Open the Developer/2000 program group.
2. Double-click Forms Runtime program item. The Oracle Forms Runform Options window appears (see Figure 2.1).
3. Enter the name of the executable, as shown in Figure 2.1.
4. Fill in the Userid, Password, and Database fields according to your environment.
5. Click OK.

When specifying the name of the executable, provide the full path, otherwise Forms will search only the directory %ORACLE_HOME%\BIN, for example C:\ORAWIN\BIN. Click the Browse... button to display the standard MS Windows Open dialog box, and search for your executable.

If the information provided in the Userid, Password, or Database fields is not accurate and a database connection cannot be established, a Logon dialog window is displayed. Here you have the opportunity to specify the correct connect information.

These are the options you will use the most with Oracle Forms Runtime. Some of the other options are also accessible from the Runtime folder of the Designer's Options dialog box discussed in the previous chapter.

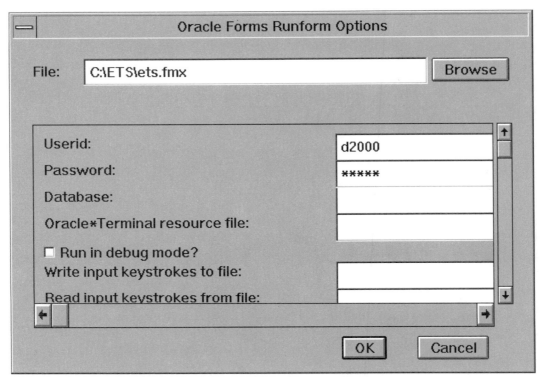

FIGURE 2.1   Oracle Forms Runtime Options window.

2.2   ORACLE FORMS RUNTIME WINDOW

Whether you decided to run the ETS module from within the Designer or using the Forms Runtime, when the module is loaded, the Oracle Forms Runtime window appears (see Figure 2.2). There are three important components of this window.

The *working area* is the normal MS Windows application workspace. All the interface objects of a form are located in this area. The chapters to come will discuss in detail how to make the application workspace as user-friendly and productive as possible.

The form has a *complete menu*, although you did not create one explicitly. This is the Oracle Forms default menu. It can be attached to any module you create. This menu provides useful commands to navigate between items and blocks, to specify and execute queries, to manipulate data, edit text, and so on.

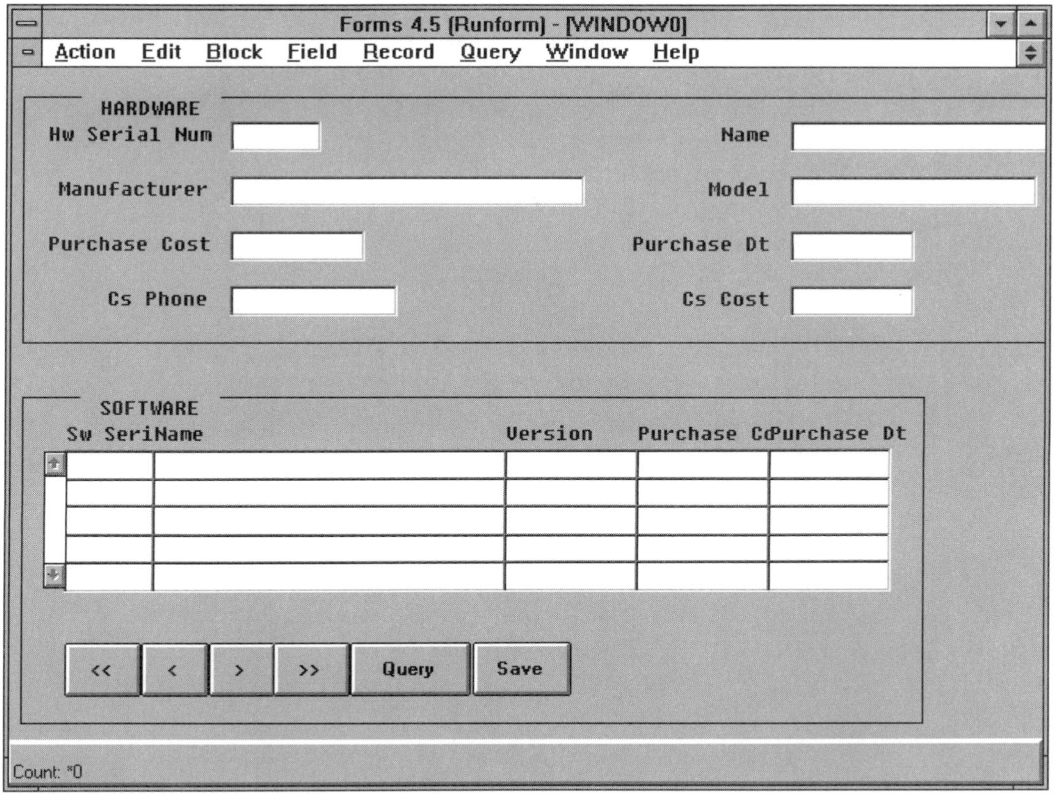

FIGURE 2.2   Oracle Forms Runtime window.

At the bottom of the Runtime window there is a *message bar* (see Figure 2.3). It is very similar in form and purpose to the Designer's message bar. This is also known as the application's *console*. The first line in the message bar displays useful processing information to the users. This information can be generated internally by Forms, or created programmatically at runtime. The second line contains several fields:

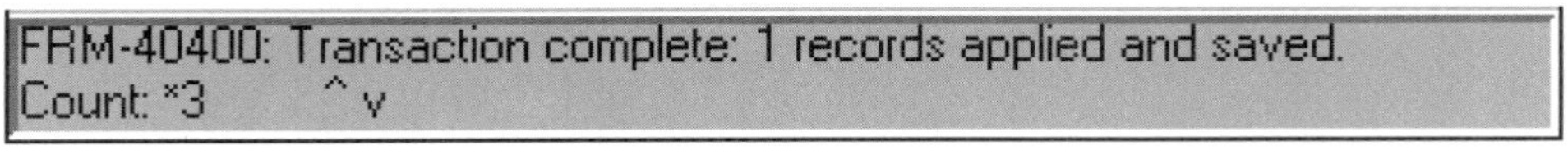

FIGURE 2.3   Oracle Forms Runtime message bar.

❏ Count indicates the number of records retrieved from the database by the most recent query. When an asterisk appears on the left of the number, as in the case of Figure 2.3, Forms has retrieved the last record.

❏ The symbols ∧ and ∨ appear if there is at least one record before or after the current record, respectively.

❏ If a List of Values is attached to a text item and Forms navigates to that item, the <LOV> lamp is displayed.

❏ When Oracle Forms is waiting for query criteria to be specified, the status indicator **ENTER QUERY** appears in the message bar. The following sections provide more details about the Enter Query mode.

2.3 QUERYING THE DATABASE

Retrieving data that already exist in the database, or querying, is the simplest way to use your application. In this section you will use the ETS form to perform several queries against the database. These data are inserted in the tables by the SQL*Plus script that creates them.

2.3.1 UNRESTRICTED QUERIES

First, click inside any text item in the HARDWARE block, if the cursor is not already there.

1. Select Query | Enter from the menu.
2. Select Query | Execute from the menu.

You could also click the Query button in the button bar twice. Each click corresponds to one of the steps listed above.

In both cases, Forms retrieves *all* the records from the HARDWARE table. The hardware records are displayed one at a time. There is a variety of ways to navigate between records in an application:

a) Scroll up and down by simply pressing the arrow keys, or
b) Select Record | Previous or Record | Next from the menu, or
c) Click the Previous (<) and Next (>) buttons in the button bar, or
d) Use the scrollbar on the left of the block.

As you can notice, each time the form displays a new hardware record, the records in the SOFTWARE block change to reflect the software items installed on that hardware equipment. This is the master/detail coordination at work. When the SOFTWARE block was created, you simply stated that it should be a detail block of the master block HARDWARE. Forms interpreted this and generated the code to automatically refresh the contents of the SOFTWARE block when the focus in the HARDWARE block moves to a different record.

In the previous example, you retrieved all the records from the HARD-WARE table. This type of query should be avoided as much as possible. The reason is very simple. Imagine the ETS application being used by a company with 1,000 employees. Its inventory contains 40,000–50,000 hardware items. It is not wise to query all those records, if probably only a few are needed. The issue is particularly important in client/server applications, which are very sensitive to network traffic and congestion. In the scenario presented above, each time this query is issued and users scroll through the records, a large quantity of data will be moved across the network, between the database server and the clients.

2.3.2 QUERY-BY-EXAMPLE INTERFACE

To avoid the situation described in the previous section, the number of records retrieved by queries should be restricted. Oracle Forms offers different methods to narrow the scope of queries. The most popular one is the query-by-example interface. The meaning of the term is that users can enter query criteria on the same screen in which they enter or manipulate data. They are not required to know any of the SQL language constructs to access the data. For example, suppose you want to know how many monitors there are in the database.

1. Select Query I Enter from the menu.
2. Click inside Name text item in the HARDWARE block.
3. Type **MONITOR**.
4. Select Query I Execute.

The query retrieves the records that match the criterion entered. This is called an exact match query because Forms retrieves only those hardware records whose name is exactly as you typed it.

2.3.3 RELAXING QUERIES USING WILDCARDS

Often, exact matches are too restrictive. They may not return all the necessary data. The inconsistency of data is one reason why this situation occurs. Sometimes, users of a database application will find compelling reasons to enter *MONITOR*, *Mntr.*, or *Monit.* when all they mean to enter is *Monitor*. Of course, if they want to see all the monitors in their system, the previous query will not work. A more flexible query is needed. Fortunately, Oracle Forms offers different ways to relax queries.

Using wildcards is one method. The wildcards used in the Oracle products, both database and tools, are the ones specified in the ANSI standard of SQL language: '%' and '_'. The wildcard '_' stands for any single character, whereas '%' stands for any number of characters, including no characters at all. For example, 'HO_SE' will represent 'HORSE' or 'HOUSE', but neither 'HORTICULTURE COURSE' nor 'HOSE'. 'HO%SE' on the other hand, will represent all of the above. Use your application to retrieve all the hardware items whose name begins with M.

1. Select Query | Enter from the menu.
2. Click inside Name text item in the HARDWARE block.
3. Type M%.
4. Select Query | Execute.

The query returns all the desired records.

2.3.4   RELAXING QUERIES USING SQL STATEMENTS

For users who are familiar with the syntax of SQL language, Forms provides ways to further restrict or customize a query. For example, suppose you want to retrieve all the hardware items that were purchased for $300 or more. At the same time, you want all the items manufactured by DELL or Compaq corporations without regard of the price. All the records should be ranked in descending order, based on the purchase price. The following steps show how to specify this rather complicated query in the HARDWARE block:

1. Select Query | Enter from the menu.
2. Click inside Manufacturer text item and type :manufacturer. The colon indicates that you will provide a variable rather than a static value for your query.
3. Click the Purchase Cost text item and type :cost.
4. Select Query | Execute from the menu. The Query/Where dialog box appears (see Figure 2.4).
5. At this point, you can enter your query criteria. Enter the text shown in Figure 2.4.
6. Click OK.

Forms executes the query according to your specifications.
   If you need to enter only ORDER BY criteria, the process becomes simpler:

1. Select Query | Enter from the menu.
2. Click any text item in the block and type &.
3. Select Query | Execute. The Query/Where dialog box appears.

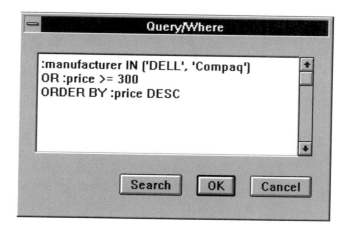

FIGURE 2.4 Query/Where dialog box.

4. Enter the ORDER BY statement. Do not prefix colons to the database column names. They are used only for variables or parameters. For example, you could enter ORDER BY purchase_cost.
5. Click OK.

The retrieved records will be ordered according to your statement. Notice that, in both cases, you do not have to specify a full-length SQL statement. Forms supplies most of it; you supply only the search or ordering criteria.

2.3.5 COUNTING QUERY HITS

A particularly useful feature in Oracle Forms is being able to count the query hits, or the number of records the query will return, without actually executing the query. This allows you as a users to carefully use computer resources. If a query will return thousands of records, there is no reason to load the database server and client machines with the burden of retrieving and sending these records to the requesting form. You can specify additional, more restrictive, query criteria that will retrieve the data faster and cheaper.

Use the Count Query feature in your form:

1. Select Query | Enter from the menu.
2. Select Query | Count Hits from the menu. A message similar to Figure 2.5 will be displayed in the message bar.

FRM-40355: Query will retrieve 3 records.
Count: *0   ENTER QUERY

FIGURE 2.5 Response of a Count Query Hits command.

Now, restrict the query criteria:

1. Click the Manufacturer text item and type D%.
2. Select Query | Count Hits again. The number of records the query will retrieve is now much smaller.
3. Either execute or cancel the query.

2.4 NORMAL MODE AND ENTER QUERY MODE

You may wonder why you must always select Query | Enter before specifying search criteria and executing queries. Oracle Forms has two modes of operations: Normal mode and Enter Query mode. The former is the default state. This is where records are created, deleted, or updated. Most of a form's life is spent in this mode. The Enter Query mode is used to specify criteria for retrieving records. These records are retrieved when the query is executed. After that, the form returns to Normal mode. If the query is canceled, Forms returns to Normal mode without further action. The transition diagram between these two states is presented in Figure 2.6.

As the diagram shows, Forms can navigate out of a block only if it is in Normal mode. If the block is in Enter Query mode, the query must be executed or canceled before users are allowed to leave the block.

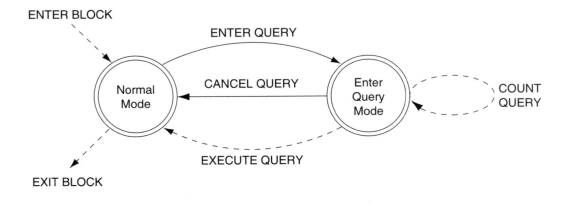

FIGURE 2.6   Transition diagram between Normal mode and Enter Query mode.

It is important to mention that all the functionality described in this section is available and can be used programmatically. This allows developers to design their own query interface, when the default interface is not sufficient to meet the application's requirements. As you read this book and become more confident with Oracle Forms, you may decide to do the same, thus providing your application with better, more flexible, and powerful queries. However, keep in mind the state transition diagram presented in Figure 2.6. If the custom-designed query interface follows the same model, your queries will be easier to understand, easier to use, and consistent with the Forms querying paradigm.

2.5 MANIPULATING THE DATABASE

So far, you have used your application rather passively; only to query data that already exist in the database. It is time to assume a more active role and start modifying the data by entering new records or updating and deleting existing ones. Before proceeding with the activities discussed in this section, keep in mind the following two points:

❑ Forms allows you to manipulate data only if it is in Normal mode. If you are in Enter Query mode, either execute or cancel the query to return to Normal mode.

❑ While you use an application to manipulate data, the changes are buffered by Oracle Forms in its internal memory structures. It is not until you save or commit, that these changes are sent to the database. Only at this point do the database transactions occur. If, for some reason, you clear or leave the block without saving to the database, your work since the last commit will be lost.

2.5.1 INSERTING

First, insert a new record. There is an easy way to do this is.

1. Select Record | Insert from the menu. Forms creates a blank record.
2. Enter data in the newly created record.
3. Select Action | Save from the menu to insert the record into the database.

You can also navigate to the last record and press the down-arrow key to move to a new record, but this is somewhat confusing to the users. It is preferable to create records with clearly defined actions such as selecting from a menu or clicking a button. Therefore, the navigation of Forms to a new record from the last one in the list is usually disabled. In the next chapter, you will implement this feature programmatically, together with other enhancements to the ETS form.

In order to facilitate the process of entering similar data in the database, Oracle Forms offers duplicating functionality, which can be used at the record level or at the item level. Suppose three identical PCs, have been received by Print and Press. You are assigned the task to enter these data into the database. Obviously, you can use the brute force approach and enter the same data three times. But you can also use the Forms Duplicate Record functionality, as described here.

1. Select Record | Insert from the menu.
2. Enter data for the first computer as shown in Figure 2.7.
3. Select Record | Insert again. A blank record is created for the next entry.
4. Select Record | Duplicate from the menu.

The newly created record is filled with information from the previous record. Enter a unique Serial Number for the second PC. Repeat the last two steps as many times as necessary. Commit the newly entered records to the database.

Suppose now that you are entering software data for one of the new PCs. This computer has DOS operating system and Windows installed in it. Obviously, the purchase date for both packages is the same. Enter data for the first two software records as shown in Figure 2.8. When you are ready to enter the Purchase Date item for Windows, do not retype **09-MAR-95**. Instead, select Field | Duplicate from the menu. Forms will automatically fill the item with text from the corresponding item in the previous record.

2.5.2 DELETING

If you want to delete a record, navigate to that record and select Record | Remove. Forms will remove the record from the block and flag it for delete processing during the next database commit. Let's delete a few records from the ETS database.

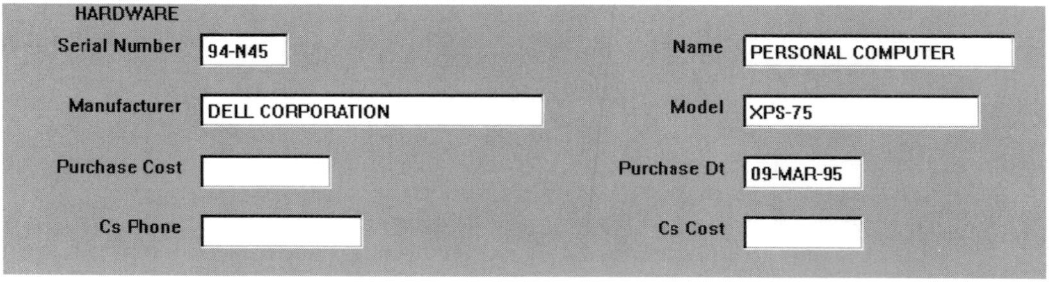

FIGURE 2.7   Sample data to illustrate the duplicate record functionality.

SOFTWARE				
Sw Seria	Name	Version	Purchase Cos	Purchase Dt
95-N33	DOS	6.2		09-MAR-95
95-N34	WINDOWS	3.11		

FIGURE 2.8   Sample data to illustrate the duplicate item functionality.

1. Go to HARDWARE block and query the monitor with serial number *95-N69*.
2. Select Record | Remove from the menu. The record is removed from the block.
3. Commit the delete action.

Now delete a PC.

1. Query the hardware item with serial number *95-N45*.
2. Select Record | Remove from the menu.

The action cannot be completed! The message bar displays, "**Cannot delete master record when matching detail records exit.**"

Once again, the master/detail relationship at work! Forms is protecting software records from becoming orphans, after their parent hardware record is deleted. To be able to delete this PC, you must first delete all the software items associated with it, and then commit the changes.

Of course, this is not a nice way to treat the users of your application. What you need here is a way to delete the master and all its detail records in one step. This process is also known as *cascade delete*. In the chapters that follow, you will learn how to implement cascade deletes in Oracle applications.

There is a menu item under the Record submenu, called Clear. Visually, Record | Clear and Record | Remove are similar. They both flush the current record from the block. But they are fundamentally different actions. Record | Remove requires interaction with the database. When a record is removed, it will be deleted from the database during the next commit and will no longer be available to this or any other application. When a record is cleared, it is flushed *only* from the working set of records buffered by Forms internally. It is not deleted from the database and can be retrieved again when needed.

2.5.3 UPDATING

Updating data in Oracle Forms is as easy as performing the changes, whether by typing or any other action, right in the screen. The Forms will flag the record for update. The actual update of the record in the database will occur during the next commit process.

2.6 TRANSACTIONS IN ORACLE FORMS

The previous sections emphasized the fact that changes made through inserts, deletes, or updates will not be permanently written to the database unless a COMMIT command is issued. In fact, the history of a database system is only a repetition of the basic cycle presented in Figure 2.9.

When users initially open a session and establish a connection with the database, the database is in a consistent state, shown in Figure 2.9 as *Database State T*. By selecting data from the database objects, they do not change the state of the database. However, it is by modifying data, that is, by inserting, deleting, and updating, that a database can become a really useful repository of information. When INSERT, DELETE, and UPDATE statements are issued, the changes users make are not applied to the database immediately. Instead, they are written to temporary structures such as the Oracle Forms internal memory buffers, or Oracle Server rollback segments.

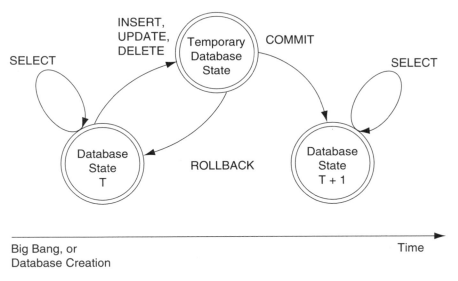

FIGURE 2.9   Basic cycle in the life of a database system.

In a situation like this, the user initiating the changes looks at a picture of data that is different from what other users may see. In fact, this user will see the changes while he or she is making them; the picture offered to him or her is the *Temporary Database State*. The other users will only see data as they were before the changes began; the picture offered to them is still the *Database State T*. This state of affairs gives users more flexibility and more control over their actions. It also protects them from unwanted accidental modifications of data. Users can rollback the changes, and go to the state they were in before any of the commands were issued. In that case, everybody will again look at the data in *Database State T*. They can also issue the COMMIT command that makes the changes permanent. In that case, all the users will move to a new database-consistent state, the *Database State T+1*.

All the commands issued in the scenario presented in Figure 2.9 form a transaction. If the COMMIT command is issued, it is said that the transaction is committed; if the ROLLBACK command is issued, it is said that the transaction is rolled back. In both cases, these commands end the current transaction. The first command issued after these statements initiates a new transaction.

2.7   MULTI-USER APPLICATIONS AND RECORD LOCKING

Applications being developed today are used by multiple users at the same time. This eventually leads to situations where more than one user may attempt to update or delete the same data, simultaneously. If the database application would allow that, then users would be overwriting each other's data inadvertently and chaotically. Data being modified by a user could be changed by another user before the first one had completed his or her transaction. In fact, imagine the following situation in the Print and Press print shop.

When the record for the PC with serial number *95-N60* was created in the ETS application, the Model name and Purchase Cost were not at hand, and therefore not entered in the database. At a later date, Tom finds the Model name in the back of the computer, pulls the record up on the screen, and begins entering the new information. At the same time, Linda finds the price in the shipping receipt. She also retrieves the record and supplies the Purchase Cost data. Next, Tom commits his changes and goes to lunch. Then, Linda commits her changes. Being the last one to commit, her record will overwrite Tom's record. Thus, the database will contain a record for PC *95-N60* that has a Purchase Cost, but not a Model name. Tom is up for a surprise when he comes back from lunch!

For the database, letting this situation occur is as disastrous as leaving a busy intersection without traffic lights during rush hours. In order to preserve and guarantee the consistency of data, some mechanism must be in place to manage the competing requests for the same data, also known as resource contention.

Every serious multi-user database package today uses *locking* to supervise the traffic of requests for updates and deletes of data. There are as many different implementations of locking as there are database vendors. The Oracle Server RDBMS follows this approach:

1. Place a lock on the resource when a user first modifies it.
2. From that moment, until the lock is released, do not allow other users to modify the resource.
3. Allow other users to query the locked resource. To maintain consistency, the view offered is that of the resource when the lock was placed.
4. Release the lock when the user commits or rolls back the transaction.

Although all the back-end database packages use some form of locking to protect the data, very few front-end development tools have a locking mechanism of their own. Oracle Forms not only provides this mechanism as part of its default processing, but also integrates it tightly with the locking mechanism implemented in the Oracle database server. The following sequence of figures shows how Oracle Forms and Oracle Server interact to handle the scenario presented at the beginning of this section.

In Figure 2.10, Tom has retrieved the PC with serial number *95-N60* and is entering the Model name. Automatically, Forms has sent an instruction to the database server to place an exclusive lock on the record in the HARDWARE table. This event occurred as soon as Tom started modifying the record.

The meaning of exclusive lock is that other users, such as Linda, can select the record, but cannot modify it. As Figure 2.10 shows, the record that Linda sees is the same as the one stored and locked in the database. Neither of them reflects any of the changes Tom is making. These changes are visible only to Tom and are maintained by the application instance running in his machine. In this case, if Linda attempts to enter the Purchase Cost on her screen, Forms will display the message FRM-40501: ORACLE error: unable to reserve the record for update or delete. She will have to wait until the lock on the record is released to proceed with her changes.

In Figure 2.11, Tom has finished entering the Model name. When he commits, Oracle Forms sends the changes over to the database server. This, in turn, applies the changes, and releases the lock from the record.

Now the view of data offered to Tom is consistent with what the database actually stores. Linda's view however is outdated, and her instance of Forms knows about this. If she attempts to do anything with the record displayed on her screen, she will get the message, FRM-40654: Record has been updated by another user. Re-query to see changes.

In the scenario presented in Figure 2.12, Linda has re-queried the database, retrieved the record with the Model name that Tom entered, and now is entering the purchase price.

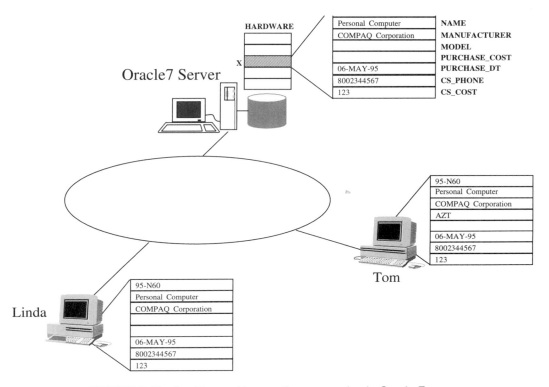

FIGURE 2.10   Locking and transaction processing in Oracle Forms.

Now she holds a lock on the record in the HARDWARE table, and it is Tom's turn to wait for her to commit and release the lock if he wants to modify that record.

It was said above that locks on records are held until the Oracle Forms operator commits or cancels his or her actions. It is not difficult to realize that if Tom goes to lunch before committing his changes, Linda will have to wait until he comes back in order to complete her job. This is not a good situation, especially in heavily used applications. From an application developer's perspective there are two things you can do to avoid it.

First, educate your users. Teach them not just what key strokes to press or actions to take when using your application, but also fundamental concepts behind the screens and windows they work with. Explain to them why they should commit their work regularly and often, and make them aware of the problems that may arise by not doing so.

Second, tailor your application to avoid unnecessary long transactions. It is not difficult to keep a count of records being modified and, when this count ex-

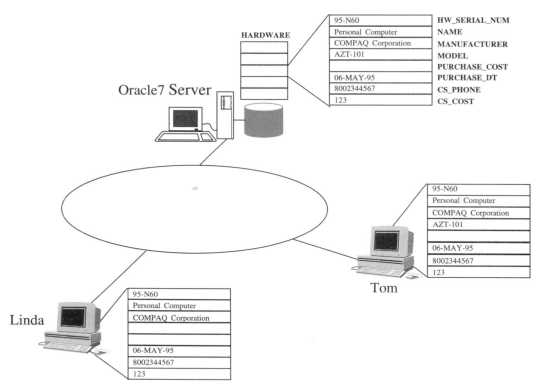

FIGURE 2.11 Locking and transaction processing in Oracle Forms (continued).

ceeds a certain threshold, you may remind the users to commit the changes. You can also create a timer that starts ticking when the first modification of data occurs. Then, if data are not committed within a certain interval of time, say five minutes, users are prompted to save their changes.

2.8 WHAT IS MISSING IN ETS?

The development of any Forms application, no matter how complicated or extensive it is, usually proceeds in two stages. Initially, you use the Object Navigator to lay out the framework for the application. You create the module, connect to the database under the appropriate account, and use the default functionality to quickly create the base table blocks and items the application will require. Then, you move on to fill the details and make the form a robust, user-friendly applica-

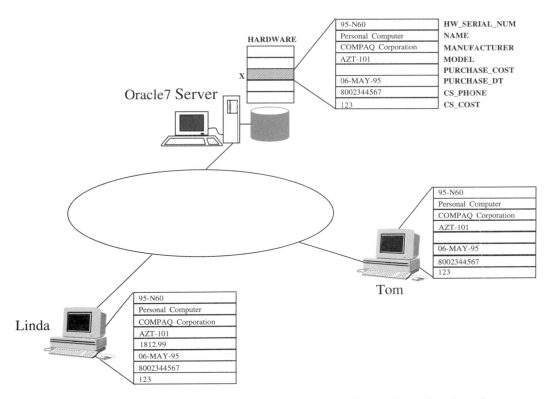

HARDWARE

95-N60	HW_SERIAL_NUM
Personal Computer	NAME
COMPAQ Corporation	MANUFACTURER
AZT-101	MODEL
	PURCHASE_COST
06-MAY-95	PURCHASE_DT
8002344567	CS_PHONE
123	CS_COST

Oracle7 Server

95-N60
Personal Computer
COMPAQ Corporation
AZT-101
06-MAY-95
8002344567
123

Tom

95-N60
Personal Computer
COMPAQ Corporation
AZT-101
1812.99
06-MAY-95
8002344567
123

Linda

FIGURE 2.12 Locking and transaction processing in Oracle Forms (continued).

tion. In this second stage, you use the Layout Editor to enhance and fine-tune the form's interface, set objects' properties in the Properties window, and modify or extend the form's functionality by using PL/SQL triggers and program units.

In Chapter 1 you took the ETS module through the first stage. This provided you with a usable application, and allowed you to explore some of the default features of two components of Oracle Forms: Designer and Runtime. However, what you have so far, is what many people call a "quick-and-dirty" application. As a matter of fact, the items on the screen can be arranged to look a little better, especially for the SOFTWARE block. Their functionality could be improved as well. For example, you may want to enforce some data standards with your form. One of them could be that users must enter all their data in uppercase. You may also want the dollar sign to precede the value in Purchase Cost items. These values must be positive, but should not exceed $100,000. In the next chapter you will implement these and other features that will make ETS not only fully functional, but also a user-friendly database application.

2.9 SUMMARY

In this chapter you became familiar with the Oracle Forms Runtime and how to operate a Forms application. Some of the basic concepts discussed here include the following:

❑ Oracle Forms Runtime
  ❑ Using Runtime to run modules
  ❑ Components of Runtime window
❑ Querying the database
  ❑ Unrestricted queries
  ❑ Query-by-example interface
  ❑ Relaxing queries using wildcards
  ❑ Relaxing queries using SQL statements
  ❑ Counting query hits
❑ Oracle Forms modes of operation
  ❑ Normal mode
  ❑ Enter Query mode
❑ Manipulating the database
  ❑ Inserting
  ❑ Duplicating
  ❑ Updating
  ❑ Deleting
❑ Transactions in Oracle Applications
  ❑ Commit
  ❑ Rollback
❑ Record locking in multi-user applications

Chapter 3

ENHANCING THE FIRST FORM

"Behold, I have refined thee . . ."
—Isaiah, *The Holy Bible* 48:10

- ♦ Arranging Items in the Layout Editor
- ♦ Modifying Visual Attributes
- ♦ Modifying Properties of Objects
- ♦ Enhancing the Functionality of Applications with PL/SQL Code
- ♦ Deploying Oracle Forms Applications
- ♦ What is the Rest of the Book About?
- ♦ Summary

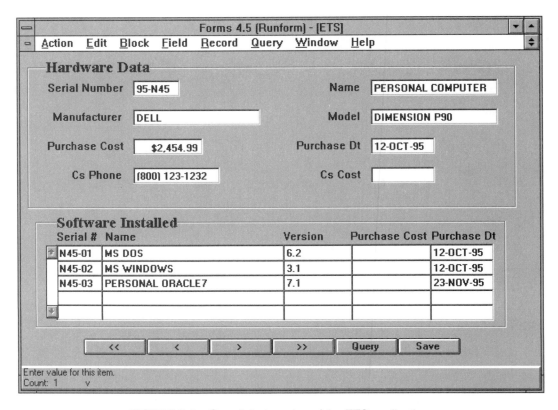

FIGURE 3.1   Completed version of the ETS application.

In this chapter, you will enhance the ETS form and add on to the default functionality that was created by the Designer when the form was created in Chapter 1. You will be introduced to important components of the Designer such as Layout Editor and Properties Window. You will arrange the items on the canvas, make them look nicer, and add some boilerplate objects to the existing form. You will also write your first triggers to improve the validation of data by your form. By the end of this chapter the ETS application will look like Figure 3.1.

The starting point for this chapter is the form you created in Chapter 1. Start Forms Designer and open the module ETS.FMB from your working directory. The companion disk also includes a copy of what the ETS form should look like at the end of this chapter. Consult with it any time during the discussion here, if you feel you need to do so.

3.1 ARRANGING ITEMS IN THE LAYOUT EDITOR

Begin now enhancing the display of the ETS form. As you may have noticed from the work done in Chapter 1, when objects are created, they are *painted* on a canvas. This canvas in turn is assigned to a *frame,* or window, and shown to the user at runtime. In order to modify the visual appearance of the application, you must paint on the canvas. The Layout Editor offers drawing tools, brushes, colors, and other utilities you may need in the process.

3.1.1 CLEANING UP AFTER THE DESIGNER

To edit a canvas, you must first open it in a Layout Editor window. The easiest way to do this is to double-click the Canvas-View icon ▦ on the left of the canvas name in the Object Navigator. Use this technique to open the canvas ETS in the Layout Editor.

The first impression you get by looking at this canvas is that too much screen space is wasted. Items are far from each other; text labels either extend the workspace even further, as in HARDWARE block, or are truncated as in SOFTWARE block; the push buttons are too big for a normal GUI application. Even by maximizing the window, you are not able to fit all the items in the screen. You have to use the scrollbars, thus making the use of the form more difficult than it should be. In this and coming sections, you fix all these problems.

First, you may have noticed that Designer has created rectangles around the blocks, when they were first created. Visually grouping together objects that are related logically is a good idea, but you can do a better job than that. So, delete the rectangles that surround the HARDWARE and SOFTWARE blocks.

1. Click any of the edges of the rectangle that belongs to HARDWARE block. The whole rectangle will be selected. Handles that appear in the corners and middle points of the edges indicate this.
2. Press DELETE.
3. Repeat Steps 1 and 2 to delete the SOFTWARE block rectangle.

Note

When the ETS form is created, the Designer assigns default names not only to the new module, but also to the new canvas where items were laid out and to the window that is displayed when the form is executed. Rename both these objects in the Object Navigator **ETS.** Refer to Chapter 1 if you need assistance with renaming objects in the Navigator.

3.1.2 RESIZING OBJECTS

It is a good practice to set the length of items that correspond to database columns to the length of the column itself. This saves your application from truncation errors that may occur if data from the database are fetched to items that are not long enough to hold them. But the length of an item is one thing, and the space it occupies on the canvas is another. The MANUFACTURER item, for example, is 30 characters long, but the average manufacturer name that ETS will handle will be 15–16 characters. There is no reason why this item should take more space than that on the window. To resize MANUFACTURER follow these steps:

1. Select the item by clicking it. The selection handles appear.
2. Drag the handle in the middle of the vertical right edge of the item to approximately two thirds of the original length.
3. Release the mouse button. The item is resized.

3.1.3 SETTING OBJECTS TO THE SAME SIZE

Your application will have a more uniform look and feel if other items in the HARDWARE block such as NAME and MODEL, have the same size as MANUFACTURER. However, you do not have to resize each item individually. Use the following steps instead:

1. Click MANUFACTURER to select it.
2. SHIFT-CLICK the NAME and MODEL items in HARDWARE block. Now all three items are selected.
3. Select Arrange I Size Objects... from the menu. The Size Object dialog box appears.
4. Click radio button Smallest in radio group Width.
5. Click OK.

The Layout Editor sets the width of the selected objects to the width of the smallest one, MANUFACTURER.

3.1.4 MOVING OBJECTS

Now bring the objects on the right half of the canvas closer to the ones on the left.

1. Click on the canvas higher up and further left than any of the labels on the right side of HARDWARE block.
2. Holding the mouse button down move the cursor diagonally, down, and to the right. You will see a rectangle being drawn as you drag the mouse.

Note

A quicker way to move selected objects is to click the mouse inside any of the objects, for example inside MODEL, keep the mouse button pressed, drag the whole group of objects to the new position, and, finally, release the mouse button.

---

3. When the rectangle includes all the items and their text labels, release the mouse button. Items NAME, MODE, PURCHASE_DT, CS_COST and their text labels are selected.
4. Press the left-arrow key a few times to move the selected items closer to the other items in the block.

3.1.5 CREATING BOILERPLATE OBJECTS

Now let us convey the idea that the items in HARDWARE block are logically related by enclosing them in a beveled rectangle.

1. Click the Rectangle icon ▢ in the toolbar. When the mouse navigates to the Layout workarea, the cursor changed shape from arrow to cross +.
2. Draw a rectangle that encloses all the items in the HARDWARE block and their text labels.

At this point, the text labels may go out of sight. Do not panic. The newly created object is hiding them from view. Select Arrange | Send to Back from the menu to redisplay the labels.

Now give this rectangle box the 3D look that is found in almost every other GUI application.

1. While the rectangle is still selected, click the Fill Color icon 🔳 at the bottom of the tool palette. The color palette is displayed.
2. Choose No Fill from the options at the bottom of the color palette. This way the rectangle will be transparent.
3. Select Format | Line from the menu and click the radio menu item 2 pt. to make the border thicker.
4. Select Format | Bevel from the menu and click the radio menu item Inset from the list of bevel options that appears.

3.1.6 CREATING TEXT LABELS

Finalize the redesign of HARDWARE block by placing a label with its name on top of it.

1. Click the Text icon ▣ in the toolbar. Again, the cursor changes shape to the crossed lines + when the mouse navigates inside the workarea.
2. Click somewhere on the upper edge of the rectangle drawn previously.
3. In the text box created type **Hardware Data** and click outside the box to exit the Text Edit mode.
4. Adjust the new label in a convenient position.

As you may notice, the text label inherits a beveled border line and transparent fill from the work you did previously to create the rectangle. To remove the border line and set the background color to that of the canvas follow these steps:

1. While the text label is still selected, click the Line Color icon ▣ at the bottom of the tool palette.
2. Choose 'No Line' from the options at the bottom of the color palette. The beveled border line around the label disappears.
3. Now, click the Fill Color icon ▣ at the bottom of the tool palette.
4. Click the cell at the intersection of the first column and the second row of tool palette. This cell corresponds to the gray background color of the canvas.

At this point, the HARDWARE block on the canvas should look similar to Figure 3.2.

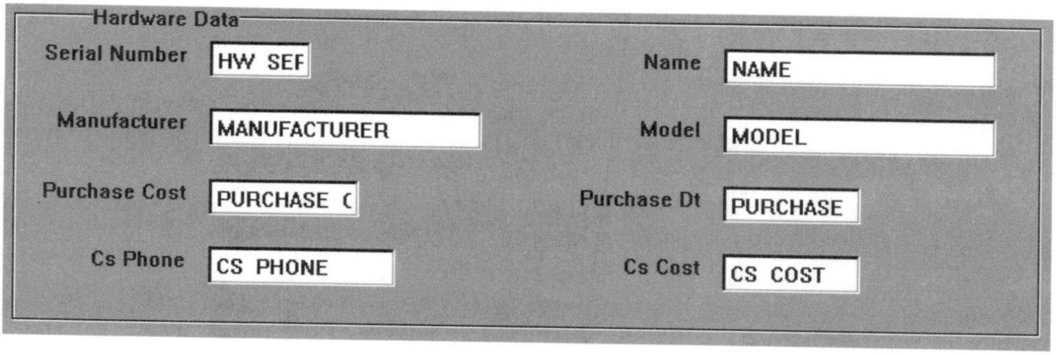

FIGURE 3.2   HARDWARE block rearranged.

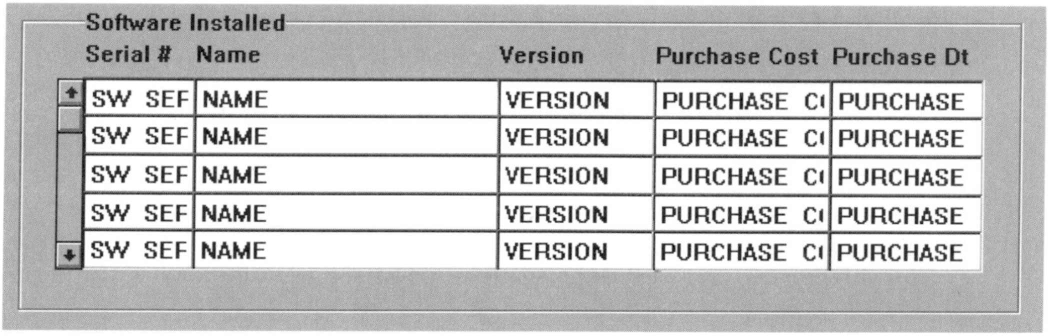

FIGURE 3.3   SOFTWARE block rearranged.

3.1.7   REARRANGING SOFTWARE BLOCK

Now you have the knowledge required to rearrange the SOFTWARE block as shown in Figure 3.3. Notice that you have to be a little creative in trying not to make text labels such as Serial Number, extend beyond the respective columns.

As you move and resize the items in of the SOFTWARE block, you may find the grid associated with the Layout Editor window to be helpful. In order to take advantage of it you must turn the Grid Snap property on. To do this, select View I Grid Snap check item from the Designer menu. To turn the property off, simply deselect the menu item. By turning the Grid Snap property on, you can accelerate the process of positioning and sizing objects on the canvas. Try moving and sizing objects with the property on and off to appreciate the differences.

3.1.8   REARRANGING BUTTON_PALETTE BLOCK

The buttons in the block BUTTON_PALETTE need to be resized to make them look like push buttons encountered in other GUI applications. First, you want to reduce their height. Then, you want to make them all have the same width. Both these goals can be achieved easily. First, set one button to the appropriate size.

1. Select the push button Save.
2. Drag one of the horizontal handles to bring the button to about half its original size.

Now that button Save has the appropriate size, you can set the others by using the Size Objects utility.

1. Select all the push buttons in the BUTTON_PALETTE block.
2. Select Arrange I Size Objects... from the Designer menu. The Size Objects dialog box appears.

> **Note**
>
> If you have set the Grid Snap property on, you may experience some difficulties resizing the button. In fact you will notice that the dimensions of the button cannot be made arbitrarily small. Grid Snap is good for coarse actions such as moving objects around, but it hinders you in finer actions such as the one described above. This is a typical situation when you want the Grid Snap property off.

3. Select radio button Largest in radio group Width.
4. Select radio button Smallest in radio group Height.
5. Click OK.

All the push buttons have the same size. Some of them now are overlapping, because they became wider in the process. You will fix this problem in the following section. Finally, move all the buttons closer to the other items in the form. Try to give your screen a balanced and symmetrical look. Objects should be distributed equally with respect to the vertical and the horizontal axis of the window. Crowded areas on one side of the screen and blank spaces on the other can be very tiring for the eyes of the users of your application.

3.1.9 ALIGNING OBJECTS

When arranging objects on the screen, it is not difficult to lose the alignment between them. For example, as you resize and move the push buttons, you may discover that they no longer form a nice, uniform horizontal bar. From the sizing actions in the previous section, they also overlap. To realign them follow these steps

1. Select all the push buttons.
2. Select Arrange | Align Objects.. from the Designer menu. The Alignment Settings dialog box appears.
3. Choose radio button Align Bottom from radio group Vertically.
4. Choose radio button Stack from radio group Horizontally. With this option, the sides of push buttons will barely touch, but will not overlap.
5. Click OK. All the buttons are aligned.

At this point, your form should look like Figure 3.4. Save the work you have done so far.

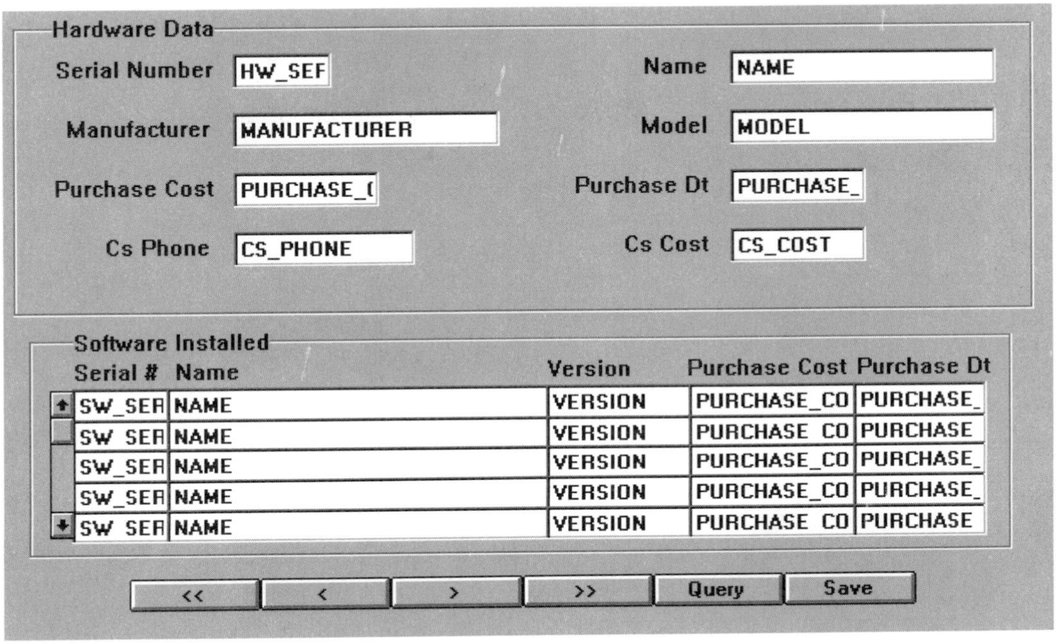

FIGURE 3.4 Final look of the ETS form after rearrangements.

3.2 MODIFYING VISUAL ATTRIBUTES

We will continue to modify the appearance of objects on the window by changing some of their properties. First, give the block labels some prominence and distinguish them from the other labels.

1. Select Hardware Data and Software Installed text labels.
2. Select Format | Font... from the Designer menu. The Font dialog box comes up.
3. Select Times New Roman in the Font list box; select Bold in the Font Style list box; select '14' in the Size list box.
4. Click OK.

Also change the color of these labels.

1. Select Hardware Data and Software Installed text labels.
2. Click the Text Color icon 🖳 from the Layout Editor toolbar.
3. From the color palette that is displayed, select a color that will make the block text labels more colorful than the rest of the text labels.

Save the changes in the ETS form and move on to some interesting features discussed in the next section.

3.3 MODIFYING PROPERTIES OF OBJECTS

In this section you will modify properties of several items in the form. For every object in the form, Designer displays its properties in a two-column sheet called Properties Window. Figure 3.5 represents the Properties Window for item MANUFACTURER.

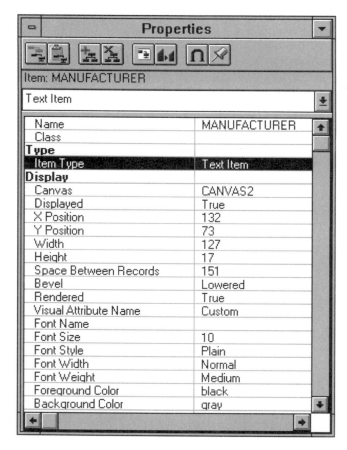

FIGURE 3.5 Properties Window for item MANUFACTURER.

3.3.1 PROPERTIES WINDOW

The left column in the window displays the properties of the object. Obviously, the contents of the list differ for different types of objects. For example, properties of blocks are different from properties of windows. To improve readability and understanding of an object's properties, Designer organizes them in logical groups. The header of each group is displayed in boldface characters. In Figure 3.5, you can see two groups of item properties: Type and Display. The right column in the window displays the actual settings of each property for the selected object. Of course, these settings may change from object to object. The setting for a property may be changed in the Set Property field, positioned between the toolbar and the properties sheet.

To display the Properties Window for an item from the Layout Editor, double-click the item. The window will remain open until you explicitly close it. If another item is selected, the content of the window is refreshed to represent the properties setting of the new item. If more than one item is selected, the properties that have the same setting for all the items will continue to display the value of that setting. If a property is set differently for at least one item, its setting field will display the string '*****'. To see an example of this follow these steps:

1. Double-click MANUFACTURER item in the Layout Editor. Its Properties Window will come up (see Figure 3.5).
2. CTRL+CLICK another item in the Layout Editor, for example NAME.

Looking at the Properties Window now you will notice that properties like *Data Type* or *Canvas* will continue to display their actual value, shared by both items. But properties related to each individual item such as *Name*, *X Position*, or *Y Position* will show '*****'.

3.3.2 SETTING PROPERTIES OF TEXT ITEMS

Now modify some of the item properties in your form. The following changes will apply to all the text items in HARDWARE and SOFTWARE blocks. As a preliminary step, select them all and switch to the Properties Window.

First, you want all the text items to accept and display data in upper-case characters. This will standardize data across the application. (Remember that SQL language, and, therefore, Oracle considers 'Personal Computer' and 'PERSONAL COMPUTER' as two different data values, although in real life they may mean the same thing.)

1. Select *Case Restriction* property. It is the first property under Functional group of properties. Its current setting is *'Mixed'*. The Set Property field is a drop-down list box.
2. Click the drop-down list button ▣ and choose *'Upper'* from the items of the list.

> ## Note
>
> A better way to standardize values of data elements such as NAME or MANU-FACTURER is to use lists of values. These lists can be static, with members that do not change during the life of the application. But they can also be dynamic lists maintained by users at runtime. Later in the book you will learn how to incorporate lists of values of both types in your applications.

You also want to display a hint message to the users, prompting them to enter the value for the current item whenever they navigate to that item.

1. Select *Auto Hint* property. It is the under the Miscellaneous group of properties. Its current setting is *'False'*. The Set Property field is again a drop-down list box.
2. Click the drop-down list button ▣ and choose *'True'* from the items of the list.
3. Select *Hint* property. It is immediately above *Auto Hint* property. Its Set Property field is a text field, in which the string '*****' is already selected and ready for your input.
4. Type Enter value for this item. in the Set Property field.

If you find this hint message too generic, or want to provide some additional information to the users, set it on an item-by-item basis.

3.3.3 SETTING FORMAT MASKS

Turn your attention now to items that display dollar values. According to established GUI standards, you want them to be indented to the right. You also want the dollar symbol to precede these values, but users should not be required to enter it. Finally, you want to enforce the business rule of Print and Press that dollar values must be non-negative and not to exceed $100,000.

First select PURCHASE_COST and CS_COST items from HARDWARE block, and PURCHASE_COST from SOFTWARE block. Switch to the Properties Window.

1. Select *Format Mask* property. It is part of the Data properties group. Its Set Property field is a text field.
2. Type $999,999.99 in the Set Property field. With this setting, users may enter only the numeric value of the item; for example 1199.99. Forms will automatically display it as $1,199.99.
3. Select *Range Low Value* property immediately below the *Format Mask* property, and enter 0 in its Set Property field.

4. Select *Range High Value* property immediately below *Range Low Value*, and enter **100000** in its Set Property field.

5. Select *Alignment* property. It is under the Functional group of properties. Its current setting is *'Left'*. The Set Property field is a drop-down list box.

6. Click the drop-down list button ▣ and choose *Right* from the items of the list.

With the previous setting of the *Format Mask* property, you save your users a few key strokes for each record they enter. This may seem like a minor issue, but it is very relevant for heavily used applications. You should set the *Format Mask* property so that it minimizes the key strokes necessary to enter data for an item. Good candidates for this are fixed length numeric items with embedded characters in them such as phone numbers or Social Security numbers.

Set the properties of CS_PHONE item with the goal of minimizing data entry time in mind. Select the item and switch to the Properties Window.

1. Set the *Format Mask* property to "("999") "999"-"9999. Note that the length of this item must be increased by 4 to make room for the embedded characters.

2. Select *Maximum Length* property three lines above *Format Mask*, and enter **14** in its Set Property field.

3. Select *Query Length* from the Database group and set its value to **14**. This property controls the length of data you can enter in the item when the form is in Enter Query mode. If this setting is not zero, it must be equal to or greater than the *Maximum Length*.

With these settings, users must enter only the ten digits that make up the phone number; for example **8001234567**. The application will format the entry to look like **(800) 123-4567**.

Finally, implement another business rule of the ETS application. It was mentioned in Chapter 1 that the serial numbers in Print and Press are all six characters long. This means that your application should not allow users to enter **NT-95** as a serial number either for hardware or software records. Since the serial numbers will be of fixed length, it would be nice if you make the application navigate to the next item as soon as the operators enter them. This way they do not have to explicitly navigate out of these items.

1. Select HW_SERIAL_NUM and SW_SERIAL_NUM items and switch to the Properties Window.

2. Set *Fixed Length* property in the Data group to *'True'*. This setting will require the users to enter the fill length of the serial numbers.

3. Set *Auto Skip* property in the Functional group to *'True'*. This setting will cause the application to navigate to the next item as soon as the user has entered the serial number.

By carefully setting properties of items, you guaranty that your application will enforce a great deal of data validation and business rules, without any explicit coding. If, however, more complicated rules must be implemented or additional actions will be performed, then PL/SQL code is written and organized in triggers, functions, procedures, and packages. The following section guides you through some activities performed in this stage. Make sure you save the changes made so far in the ETS application before moving on to the next section.

3.4 ENHANCING THE FUNCTIONALITY OF APPLICATIONS WITH PL/SQL CODE

In your application, HW_SERIAL_NUM is the primary key for the HARDWARE table. The Oracle database will not allow more than one hardware record to exist in the table with the same serial number. To see how this works, follow these steps:

1. Generate and run the ETS form.
2. Retrieve the hardware record with serial number *95-N45*. (If for some reason this record does not exist, create one and commit it to the database.)
3. Select Record I Insert from the menu to create a new record.
4. Select Record I Duplicate from the menu to make the new record an identical copy of the *95-N45* record.

If you try to commit the new record you will get the error message FRM-40408: ORACLE error: unable to INSERT record. Exit the ETS form you were running and return to the Forms Designer.

This type of behavior could be acceptable if users would commit each record when they insert or modify it. But, if they enter five more records before requesting the commit, the whole transaction will fail, even if only one record violates the uniqueness constraint. Because the message above does not identify the violator, users have to go through each individual record to identify the problem.

3.4.1 WRITING THE FIRST TRIGGER

You can improve the situation described above by checking for existing serial numbers when the record is validated. Later in the book, you will see in more detail when this event occurs. At this point it is sufficient to say that the record will be validated whenever users navigate out of it or commit. This event fires a trigger called WHEN-VALIDATE-RECORD for the particular block where the event occurred. You will place the code that does the check in this trigger, attached to the HARDWARE block.

1. In the Object Navigator, select the node Triggers immediately under the expanded node HARDWARE.
2. Click the Create icon 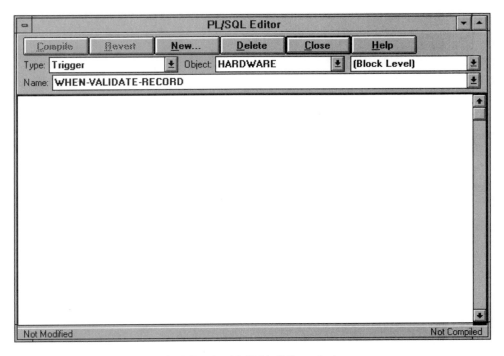 in the toolbar. A List of Values dialog box appears with all the trigger names in it.
3. Type **W**. The list will be restricted to only those entries that begin with WHEN-.
4. Type **V**. The list will be further restricted to only those trigger names that begin with WHEN-VALIDATE-. There are only two such triggers and WHEN-VALIDATE-RECORD is one of them.
5. Click the WHEN-VALIDATE-RECORD to select it.
6. Click OK. A PL/SQL Editor window will be displayed (see Figure 3.6).

The text pane of the window is blank, and the cursor is positioned in its upper left hand corner, waiting for your input. You also see that the Compile and Revert push buttons are disabled and the status bar at the bottom of the window

FIGURE 3.6 PL/SQL Editor window.

displays the status lamps **Not Modified** to the left and **Not Compiled** to the right. Enter the text shown in Figure 3.7.

Notice that as you enter the text, the Compile and Revert buttons are enabled and the status lamps of the trigger change to **Modified** and **Not Compiled**. When you are finished entering the text, click the Compile button. If you did not make any mistakes, the trigger compiles successfully and its status lamps become **Not Modified** and **Successfully Compiled**.

What you just entered in the PL/SQL Editor window is called a PL/SQL block. Let us briefly explain its components and the meaning of the PL/SQL statements that are part of it:

❑ Line 2 declares a variable of datatype NUMBER, called counter. This is a local variable whose value can be accessed only in this block. All the declarations of local variables are made in the declaration section of the PL/SQL block, which begins with the keyword DECLARE (Line 1) and end with the keyword BEGIN (Line 3).

❑ The statements enclosed between the keywords BEGIN and END (lines 3 through 15) are known as the executable part of the block. They are executed only if the record is a new record that will be inserted into the database. The status of the record is stored in the system variable SYSTEM.RECORD_ STATUS and is tested in line 4. The statements between lines 5 and 13 are re-

```
 1  DECLARE
 2    counter NUMBER;
 3  BEGIN
 4    IF :SYSTEM.RECORD_STATUS = 'INSERT' THEN
 5      SELECT COUNT(*)
 6      INTO counter
 7      FROM HARDWARE
 8      WHERE HW_SERIAL_NUM = :HARDWARE.HW_SERIAL_NUM;
 9      IF counter <> 0 THEN
10        BELL;
11        MESSAGE('Item with this serial number already exists.');
12        RAISE FORM_TRIGGER_FAILURE;
13      END IF;
14    END IF;
15  END;
```

FIGURE 3.7   Contents of WHEN-VALIDATE-RECORD trigger for HARDWARE block.

sponsible for the actions that will occur when the record is a newly-created one. There are basically two such actions.

❑ Lines 5 through 8 require the database to count all the records in HARD-WARE table in which the value of column HW_SERIAL_NUM equals the value stored in the Forms item HARDWARE.HW_SERIAL_NUM. The value retrieved is stored in the variable **counter**. If there are no such records, the value of **counter** will be 0; otherwise, **counter** will hold the number of these records. In the context of the ETS application, if **counter** is 0, the serial number entered in the form is valid; otherwise, it is duplicating the serial number of another record, and, therefore, is invalid.

❑ Line 9 decides what to do next, based on the value stored in variable **counter**. If the value is 0, everything is fine, and the trigger ends with no further action. But if **counter** is not 0, lines 10, 11, and 12 will be executed.

❑ Line 10 attracts the attention of the user by sounding the PC's bell. Oracle Forms built-in procedure BELL serves this purpose.

❑ Line 11 informs the user about what happened. The built-in procedure MESSAGE sends its argument string to the application's console.

❑ Line 12 prevents Forms from taking any further processing steps. A built-in named error, FORM_TRIGGER_FAILURE, is raised to stop the operations.

3.4.2 REUSING CODE IN THE SOFTWARE BLOCK

The process of implementing the same functionality for the SOFTWARE block is very similar. You can easily do it on your own, by adopting the approach described above. The following paragraph presents a technique that you may find useful when creating and working with your triggers. It takes advantage of the fact that you already have an open PL/SQL Editor window. It is easy to create a new trigger from here. In the process, you will also learn how to copy and paste text in these windows.

As a preliminary step, copy the contents of the trigger you created in the previous section:

1. In the PL/SQL Editor window, click before the keyword **DECLARE** in the first line.
2. Hold the left button down, drag the mouse down and to the right until the whole text of the trigger is selected.
3. Press CTRL-C or choose Edit I Copy from the menu to copy the text.

These steps place the contents of the trigger in the clipboard. When you create the new trigger, rather than entering its contents from scratch, you will paste this selection, and modify only a few lines that will be different between the two triggers. On one hand, you save yourself some typing. On the other, users will see

> **Note**
>
> There is a faster way to select the whole contents of the PL/SQL Editor window, useful especially when there are multiple lines in it.
>
> 1. In the PL/SQL Editor window, press CTRL+HOME. The cursor moves at the beginning of the first line in the window.
> 2. Holding the SHIFT key, press CTRL+END. The cursor moves at the end of the last line in the window and all the text is selected.

similar reactions for similar errors. Put in more academic terms, and you will reduce the application development time and create a consistent user interface. These are two basic paradigms for code sharing in software projects.

Now create the new trigger. Make sure your current window is the PL/SQL Editor.

1. Click the list button ▣ for the Object drop-down list box. This list is underneath the button Close.
2. Select SOFTWARE from the entries in the list. You will see the source pane clear. The Name list below the Object drop-down list box will display the value (None). This means that there are no triggers defined for the SOFTWARE block.
3. Click the New... button to create a new trigger. You will see the familiar List of Values window with the trigger names.
4. Choose WHEN-VALIDATE-RECORD from this list as explained in the previous section.
5. Press CTRL-V from the keyboard or select Edit | Paste to paste the text of the trigger.
6. Edit the text according to the context of SOFTWARE block.

When finished, the new trigger should look like Figure 3.8.

3.4.3   WRITING A PROCEDURE

It was mentioned in Chapter 2 that you may want to write some code that will not allow users to move to a new record from the last record in a block. This functionality would hold for any block, including HARDWARE and SOFTWARE. At the same time, it will be invoked by at least two events. One is when users try to navigate to the next record and the trigger fired in this case is KEY-NXTREC. The

```
DECLARE
  counter NUMBER;
BEGIN
  IF :SYSTEM.RECORD_STATUS = 'INSERT' THEN
    SELECT COUNT(*)
    INTO counter
    FROM SOFTWARE
    WHERE HW_SERIAL_NUM = :SOFTWARE.HW_SERIAL_NUM AND
          SW_SERIAL_NUM = :SOFTWARE.SW_SERIAL_NUM;
    IF counter <> 0 THEN
      BELL;
      MESSAGE('Item with this serial number already exists.');
      RAISE FORM_TRIGGER_FAILURE;
    END IF;
  END IF;
END;
```

FIGURE 3.8   Contents of WHEN-VALIDATE-RECORD trigger for SOFTWARE block.

other event is when users press the down-arrow key and the trigger fired in this case is KEY-DOWN.

In cases where the same code is invoked from several places in the application, it is advisable to place it in a procedure and issue calls to this procedure from the different triggers. In this section you will create the procedure **Move_Next_ Record** to implement the functionality mentioned here.

You can create the procedure from the Layout Editor window by following these steps:

1. Click the list button ▣ for the Type drop-down list box in the PL/SQL Editor window.
2. Select Program Unit from the list.
3. Click the New... button to create a new program unit. The New Program Unit dialog box appears. This allows you to specify the name and the type of the new program unit. The type Procedure is already selected.
4. Enter **Move_Next_Record** in the Name field.
5. Click OK.

At this point the control returns to the PL/SQL Editor window. A template for the procedure is already entered in the source code pane. Enter the contents of the procedure as shown in Figure 3.9.

In this procedure you are using the value stored in the Oracle Forms system variable SYSTEM.LAST_RECORD to decide whether the current record is the last

```
PROCEDURE Move_Next_Record IS
BEGIN
  IF :SYSTEM.LAST_RECORD <> 'TRUE' THEN
      NEXT_RECORD;
  ELSE
— No more records to move to.
    BELL;
    MESSAGE('At last record.');
    RAISE FORM_TRIGGER_FAILURE;
  END IF;
END;
```

FIGURE 3.9   Contents of procedure Move_Next_Record.

record in the block or not. If not, the built-in procedure NEXT_RECORD is used to navigate to the next record. Otherwise, the operation is halted in a way similar to the previous two triggers.

3.4.4   WRITING FORM-LEVEL TRIGGERS

Now that you have written the procedure **Move_Next_Record**, you should place calls to it from the form-level triggers KEY-NXTREC and KEY-DOWN. By creating these triggers at the form level rather than at each individual block level, you reduce the amount of code to create and maintain.

To create the trigger KEY-NXTREC from the PL/SQL Editor window follow these steps:

1. Click the list button ▣ for the Type drop-down list box in the PL/SQL Editor window.
2. Select Trigger from the list. The Object drop-down list box will display the entry (Form Level).
3. Click the New... button to create a new trigger.
4. From the List of Values dialog box with the names of the triggers, select KEY-NXTREC.
5. Enter the text of the trigger as follows:

                           Move_Next_Record;

To create the trigger KEY-DOWN from the PL/SQL Editor window follow these steps:

> # Note
>
> You may have noticed that there exists a form-level trigger called ON-CLEAR-DETAILS in the application. This trigger and the procedures CHECK_PACKAGE_FAILURE, QUERY_MASTER_DETAILS, and QUERY_ALL_MASTER_DETAILS are created by the Designer to implement the master/detail relationship between HARDWARE and SOFTWARE blocks.

1. Click the New... button to create a new trigger.
2. From the List of Values dialog box with the names of the triggers, select KEY-NXTREC.
3. Enter the text of the trigger as follows:

Move_Next_Record;

Now, you can say that you have a complete application that is full of functionality but also has a nice interface. Save and generate it, and feel free to use it to master the concepts discussed in Chapter 2.

3.5 DEPLOYING ORACLE FORMS APPLICATIONS

After completing the development process on your form, you should distribute it to the desktops of those Print and Press employees that will need to use the application. It is assumed here that you have installed at least the Oracle Forms Runtime software either on each individual client PC, or on a shared directory in a file server. It is also assumed that you have installed and configured the software required to connect to the database (SQL*Net 1.1 or SQL*Net 2.x).

To install the ETS application on a PC follow these steps:

1. Create a directory, for example C:\ETS, where the executable ETS.FMX will reside.
2. Copy in C:\ETS the file ETS.FMX from your development environment.
3. Create a new program group in the Program Manager and enter Equipment Tracking System in the Description field.
4. Create a new program item in the Equipment Tracking System group. In the Program Item Properties dialog box enter the following settings:
   ❑ Enter Equipment Tracking System in the Description field.

❑   The Command Line should contain the location and name of Oracle
    Forms Runtime executable followed by the location and name of
    ETS.FMX. If, for example, Oracle Forms Runtime is installed in
    C:\ORAWIN\BIN, then the Command Line for the new program item
    would be:

C:\ORAWIN\BIN\F45RUN.EXE C:\ETS\ETS.FMX

❑   The working directory of the new program unit should be C:\ETS.
❑   Click the Change Icon . . . button and either accept the Oracle Forms
    Runtime icon, or select an icon of your choice.

Now the ETS application is ready to be used.

3.6   WHAT IS THE REST OF THE BOOK ABOUT?

If you followed the material presented so far, you are up to a good start in your
Oracle Forms programming efforts. You know the basic components of Oracle
Forms Designer and Runtime. You have been exposed to concepts of database
applications development. You have an understanding of the principal stages in
which the development of a form evolves. What's more important, you just finished a useful application that rewards your work and places you among those
software engineers that can develop in Oracle Forms.

In order to learn more about Oracle Forms, you need to read the rest of
this book. Part Two equips you with the necessary tools to create, design, and
enhance forms. The purpose, access methods, components, and usage of important tools such as the Object Navigator, Layout Editor, Properties Window,
Menu Editor, and PL/SQL Editor, are discussed in detail. This part introduces
you to programming with the Standard Query Language (SQL). It concludes
with a coverage of programming techniques with the Oracle's own PL/SQL
language.

Part Three presents Oracle Forms as an object-oriented and event-driven
programming environment. It explains the features and functionality of its objects, including blocks, items, canvas-views, and windows. It also discusses
events, triggers, and how they can be used to enhance Forms applications.
Object-oriented programming principles such as inheritance, reusability, encapsulation, and polymorphism, are important topics discussed throughout this part.

Part Four covers advanced programming with Oracle Forms. It begins with
the discussion of integrating Forms with other Oracle tools such as Reports and
Graphics. Then, it moves on to the broader issue of integration with other MS
Windows applications through Dynamic Data Exchange (DDE), Object Linking
and Embedding (OLE), Visual Basic Custom (VBX) controls, user exits, and
PL/SQL call interfaces.

3.7 SUMMARY

In this chapter you turned the ETS form in a user-friendly GUI application. To achieve this, you worked to enhance the layout of the form in the Layout Editor and to customize the properties of its objects in the Properties Window. You also enhanced the application functionality by writing some PL/SQL code in the form of triggers and procedures. Important concepts discussed in this chapter include the following:

❑ Working with the Layout Editor
    ❑ Cleaning up after the Designer
    ❑ Selecting and moving objects
    ❑ Resizing objects
    ❑ Aligning objects
    ❑ Creating boilerplate objects
    ❑ Creating text labels
❑ Aligning objects and modifying visual attributes of objects
❑ Modifying properties of objects
    ❑ Properties window
    ❑ Setting properties of text items
    ❑ Format masks
❑ Enhancing the application functionality through PL/SQL objects
    ❑ PL/SQL Editor window
    ❑ Creating block-level triggers
    ❑ Creating procedures
    ❑ Creating form-level procedures
    ❑ Invoking built-in and user-named procedures
❑ Deploying Oracle Forms applications

Part II

ORACLE FORMS DEVELOPER TOOLBOX

"The tools we use have a profound . . . influence on our thinking habits, and, therefore, on our thinking abilities."

—*Edsger W. Dijkstra*

ORACLE FORMS DESIGNER

"Every tool carries with it the spirit by which it has been created."
—Werner Karl Heisenberg

- Oracle Developer/2000

- Components of Developer/2000

- Oracle Forms Designer

- Components of Designer

- Designer Menu

- Working with Modules

- Storing Modules in the Database

- Other Functionality of the Designer

- Summary

4.1   ORACLE DEVELOPER/2000

Developer/2000 is an application development suite of tools that was first introduced in January 1995 under the name of Cooperative Development Environment 2—CDE2. It was a major improvement of its predecessor, CDE. It is often called a second generation client/server development environment because it not only offers a sophisticated Graphical Users Interface (GUI), but also combines powerful forms, reports, and graphics into large, complex, and scaleable client/server applications. This section lists and briefly describes some of the main characteristics of Developer/2000 tools.

4.1.1   CLIENT/SERVER SUITE OF TOOLS FOR ORACLE DATABASES

Developer/2000 is considered the most powerful client/server application development environment for Oracle databases because it is tailored around and extensively supports its functionality. Many other programming tools can be used to create applications that run against Oracle databases. Developer/2000 tools offers a clear advantage over them because it shares the same programming language with the Oracle7 database server—PL/SQL. This means that if you are well-versed in writing stored functions or procedures for the Oracle database server, you can easily create functions and procedures in the client application, and vice-versa. One of the principal components of every tool in the Developer/2000 package, the Object Navigator, allows you to view and manipulate the code of your application in one window, no matter whether it resides on the client module or is stored in the database server. In the Navigator, you can move the routines from the client to the server, and vice-versa, with a simple drag-and-drop action. This process, also known as partitioning of application logic, enables you to optimize the distribution of your code based on the specific environment where the application will run.

4.1.2   POWERFUL SUPPORT FOR SQL

Structured Query Language (SQL) has become the standard language for interacting with relational database management systems. Its nonprocedural structure allows users to specify what they want done, without specifying how to do it. Its English-like syntax makes it easy to understand and learn. Oracle Corporation implemented the first commercial version of SQL in 1979. Since then, it has always played a leading role in defining and refining the language. Oracle database server and Developer/2000 tools utilize supersets of SQL compliant with the standards defined by the American National Standards Institute (ANSI), International Standards Organization (ISO), and the United States Federal Government.

PL/SQL is the programming language used by both Developer/2000 and Oracle server. It expands the SQL commands with procedural capabilities such as loops, conditional checks, and procedural calls.

4.1.3 RAPID APPLICATION DEVELOPMENT TOOLS

Rapid Application Development (RAD) is an approach to building high-quality and low-cost information systems in a significantly short amount of time. Under well-defined methodology principles, RAD combines Computer-Aided System Engineering (CASE) tools, highly skilled professionals, user-driven prototyping, and rigorous delivery time limits in a winning formula that has proved to guarantee success in the development of information systems. Developer/2000, combined with Designer/2000, provides a complete set of tools for the design, prototyping, development, and documentation of database systems according to RAD principles and methodology.

4.1.4 GRAPHICAL USERS INTERFACE TOOLS

Applications developed with Developer/2000 can utilize all the features of a GUI environment such as Multiple Documents Interface (MDI) paradigm, radio groups, check boxes, buttons, dynamic lists, and mouse support. They also offer powerful visual and graphical representation of data through interactive charts, boilerplate drawings, colors, patterns, and fonts. Each object developed with Developer/2000 can be used in any windows platform such as Microsoft Windows, Macintosh, and X Window System. It will automatically adapt to the native look of the underlying environment, thus enabling you to deploy your application in multiple platforms.

Developer/2000 also supports environment-specific features, for example, in MS Windows and Macintosh, you can implement Object Linking and Embedding (OLE) and Dynamic Data Exchange (DDE). You can also access functions developed in other languages such as C or C++, compiled in the form of Windows Dynamic Link Libraries (DLL).

4.1.5 OBJECT-ORIENTED PROGRAMMING ENVIRONMENT

Developer/2000 is an object-oriented application development environment. It is built around concepts such as object abstraction, event-driven control, inheritance structures, encapsulation, and reusability of data and processes. Operations such as object grouping, creation and use of property classes, compilation of reusable code in dynamic loadable libraries, combination of logically related data, and functions and procedures in packages, provide the power, capabilities, and flexibility of object-oriented programming in the Developer/2000 tools.

4.2   COMPONENTS OF DEVELOPER/2000

Developer/2000 is built around three main components: Oracle Forms, Oracle Reports, and Oracle Graphics. To further support you in the process of creating applications, other utilities such as Oracle Procedure Builder, Oracle Book, and Oracle Terminal, are included in Developer/2000. When you install the software, several program groups are created in your desktop:

❑   *Developer/2000* contains all the executables that are needed to design, generate, and execute the applications. This is the program group accessed the most during development activities with Oracle tools.

❑   *Developer/2000 Documentation* contains reference manuals, developer guides, user guides, and message and error manuals. All this information is provided in the form of Oracle Book documents. Part of the information contained in these documents is also accessible from within Developer/2000 tools as standard MS Windows Help files.

❑   *Developer/2000 Demos* contains applications developed by Oracle Corporation to demonstrate features and functionality of Forms, Reports, and Graphics. It also contains program items that create or drop the database objects required by these applications.

❑   *Developer/2000 Administration* contains program items that create or drop the database objects required to store Developer/2000 modules in the Oracle database.

❑   *Developer/2000 Components* contains Forms, Reports, and Graphics Reusable Component Libraries. These libraries contain software components such as Windows 95 style tabbed dialog boxes and PL/SQL libraries that you can use in your applications.

Developer/2000 bundles together the utilities that will be used most often in this book. Figure 4.1 shows the program items included in this group. They are not necessarily created in this order during the installation process, but are arranged for the sake of clarity.

From this picture, you can see that Forms, Reports, and Graphics have at least two components each: Designer and Runtime. Applications are created or modified from within the Designers. For example, to create, test, and debug a form you use Forms Designer. Runtime components are used to run the finished applications. They are primarily used by end-users and deployed with your application at the end of the development lifecycle.

Technically speaking, users could run executable modules from within Designers, as well. But this would compromise the integrity of the application and the database itself; therefore, separate runtime engines are considered as applica-

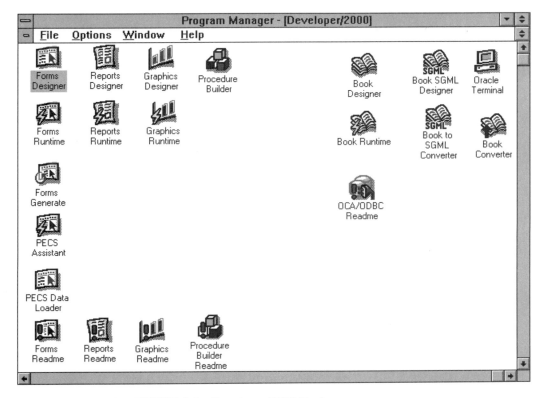

FIGURE 4.1 Developer/2000 Tools program group.

tion security features of Developer/2000. Licensing costs should also be considered since Oracle Corporation charges for Developer/2000 Designers but allows free distribution of Runtime engines. Finally, it is considered a good programming practice to offer users one single application entry point. They should be able to access all the features of the database systems from one program item icon. Forms, reports, and graphics created with Developer/2000 can be integrated in one unified application easily and seamlessly. This can be achieved only if the runtime interface is well-thought and carefully designed.

Oracle Forms is the environment where most of the Developer/2000 programming occurs. In order to help you create and optimize the application forms, some additional utilities are provided in the Developer/2000 Tools program group. Forms Generate takes binary files created in Forms Designer as input and creates executables that can be run from the Forms Runtime. PECS Assistant and PECS Data Loader collect useful data and statistics about internal and user-defined events. You can use this information to fine-tune and test Forms applications.

Other items included in the Developer/2000 program group are several Oracle Book tools and Oracle Terminal. Oracle Book can be used to design on-line documentation; Oracle Terminal allows remapping of keys and visual attributes for particular environments.

4.3   ORACLE FORMS DESIGNER

Oracle Forms Designer is the main development tool offered by Oracle Forms that allows you to create, access, modify, save, debug, and generate your application. Designer operates on objects, which it organizes according to certain rules of hierarchy and ownership. Modules are the objects at the highest level of the hierarchy. In Designer, you work with form, menu, or PL/SQL library modules. Each module contains objects, which, in turn, may contain other objects. PL/SQL objects are a special type of objects written by programmers to carry out the functionality of the applications. Some of these objects can be incorporated in form or menu modules. They can also be packaged and grouped together in the form of PL/SQL library modules.

4.4   COMPONENTS OF DESIGNER

When you launch the Oracle Forms Designer, you are presented with a window similar to Figure 4.2.

Oracle Forms Designer is a Multiple-Document Interface (MDI) application. As shown in Figure 4.2, it contains a master window, also known as the MDI

Note

Although forms, menus, and libraries share the highest level in the hierarchy of objects, from a runtime perspective, there is some ranking even among them. When users run a Forms application, they will first execute a form module. This form may have attached to it a menu from which the users can select available options. Depending on the situation and the functionality of the application, this menu can be replaced by another menu. The first form may call another form as well. A PL/SQL library may be attached to the menus, the forms, or even another library.

Oracle Forms Default Menu

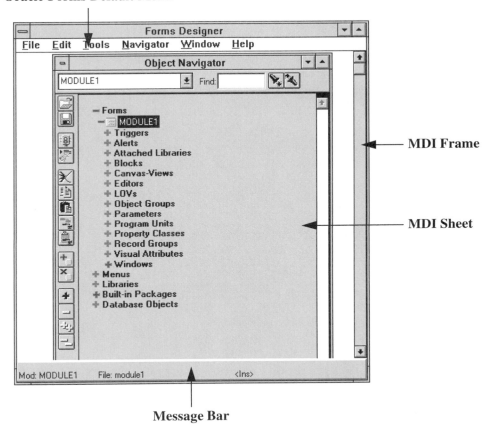

FIGURE 4.2 Components of Oracle Forms Designer.

frame, which serves as a repository for the application itself. This is referred to as the application window or, in this particular case, the Designer window. It has all the features of its siblings in the Windows environment in which Oracle Forms is running. It can be resized, moved, minimized, maximized, closed, and scrolled horizontally or vertically. Inside the Designer window there is always at least one window open: the Object Navigator. Other types of windows that can be open are Layout Editor, Properties Window, Menu Editor, and PL/SQL Editor windows. While the Forms Designer is running, there can be only one Object Navigator window, but multiple windows of the other types. In the MDI parlance, these windows are called MDI sheets. They can be resized, maximized, moved around,

Oracle Forms Default Menu

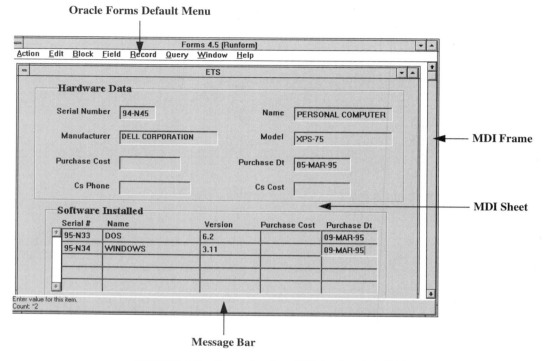

FIGURE 4.3   Example of an MDI Application: ETS.

scrolled horizontally and vertically, while always staying within the bounds of the Designer window. They can also be cascaded, tiled, and iconized (or minimized).

MDI applications have become widespread and a standard of measure for good quality, and serious programming efforts. Besides Oracle Forms, other MDI applications that you may encounter are Word, Excel, WordPerfect, Oracle Forms, Powerbuilder, and Visual Basic. Even the ETS application you developed in Part One is an MDI application (see Figure 4.3).

In the ETS application, and in all the Forms application you will develop, the Oracle Forms Runtime window will be the MDI frame. The forms and windows you create will be the MDI sheets.

4.5 DESIGNER MENU

Attached to the Designer window is also the Designer menu. In fact, there are four different menus that replace each other as you move from one MDI sheet to the other in the Designer. Figure 4.4 represents these menus.

Base Menu	Eile	Edit	Tools	Window	Help	

Base Menu Eile Edit Tools Window Help

Navigator Menu Eile Edit Tools Navigator Window Help

Layout Editor Menu Eile Edit Tools View Format Arrange Window Help

Menu Editor Menu Eile Edit Tools Menu Window Help

FIGURE 4.4 Oracle Forms Designer menus.

The base menu contains five submenus: File, Edit, Tools, Window, and Help. The functionality accessed through these submenus either applies to the entire module such as File menu, or is used throughout a Designer session such as Edit, Tools, Window, and Help menus. The contents of this menu are discussed in the following section.

The base menu is visible when the Designer context is a Properties Window or a PL/SQL Editor window. If the current context is the Object Navigator window, any Layout Editor, or any Menu Editor window, then this menu is replaced with the corresponding menus as shown in Figure 4.4. In these menus, additional submenus are added between Tools and Window submenus. These submenus handle functionality that is pertinent to the particular editor, but not to the rest of the application. The content and functionality of these menus will be explained in the context of the tools to which they belong. Namely, the Navigator submenu will be discussed in Chapter 5; the View, Format, and Arrange submenus in Chapter 6; and the Menu submenu in Chapter 8.

Each submenu is made up of several menu items. It is through selecting these items that you can access the functionality they represent. There are three different types of items in the Menu Designer:

❑ *Conventional menu items.* These items are the standard menu items that you find in any GUI application. Usually they execute a command such as File I Save, or Edit I Cut. If the command is complicated or requires additional specifications, a dialog box follows the selection of the item. In this dialog box, you can provide all the parameters necessary for the execution of the command. The labels of all those menu items that open a window or dialog box when selected, end with an ellipsis, as in File I Save As..., or Tools I Properties... .

❑ *Check menu items.* Tools I Debug Mode is a typical example of these kind of items. They are used to toggle the setting of a property. In unchecked mode, they look like any other menu item; in checked mode their name is preceded by a check mark (see Figure 4.5).

❑ *Radio button menu items.* You can see two such items in the Navigator menu (Navigator I Ownership View and Navigator I Visual View). They indicate

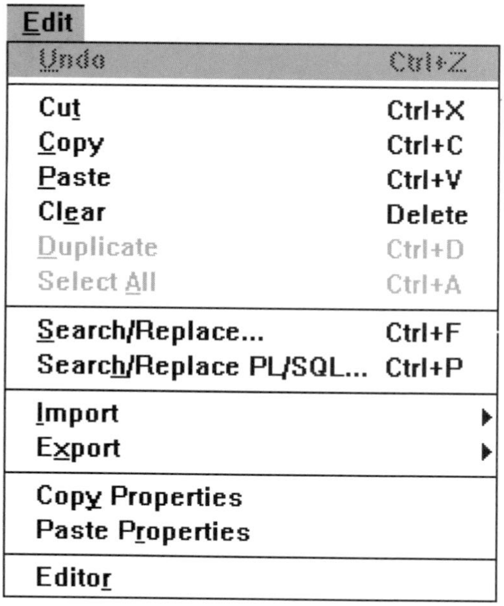

Edit	
Undo	Ctrl+Z
Cut	Ctrl+X
Copy	Ctrl+C
Paste	Ctrl+V
Clear	Delete
Duplicate	Ctrl+D
Select All	Ctrl+A
Search/Replace...	Ctrl+F
Search/Replace PL/SQL...	Ctrl+P
Import	▶
Export	▶
Copy Properties	
Paste Properties	
Editor	

FIGURE 4.5   Edit submenu.

or set an either ... or state in the application. Selecting one, deselects the other. Visually, their labels are preceded by radio buttons, which also indicate which of the items is selected from the radio group.

In the menus that you will develop for your applications, you can use the same types of menu items.

4.5.1   FILE SUBMENU

The File submenu controls the functionality that applies to the entire module. Section 4.6 later in the chapter discusses in detail the content of this menu.

4.5.2   EDIT SUBMENU

The Edit submenu is shown in Figure 4.5.
The first two groups of items in this menu provide all the usual Windows editing operations such as Undo, Cut, Copy, Paste, and Clear. These operations are accessible from different environments and are discussed throughout Part Two. The Search/Replace items allow you to search and replace text in PL/SQL objects of your application. Chapter 10 explains how to use the search/replace functionality in Oracle Forms. The Import | Export items allow you to transfer ob-

jects such as drawings, images, color palettes, and text between the application modules and the file system. Chapters 6 and 10 explain how to import and export color palettes and text, respectively. Finally, the Properties items are used to copy and paste properties of objects. These commands are also widely accessible from other environments and are explained throughout Part Two. The last item in this menu is used to display the Oracle Forms internal text editor for multiline text items.

4.5.3 TOOLS SUBMENU

The Tools submenu is used to access commonly used tools of the Designer (see Figure 4.6). The first five items in this menu open or navigate to windows of editors with the same name. The Designer enables and disables these items according to the context. In the example shown in Figure 4.6, the current context is a menu module, because the item Menu Editor..., unique to Menus, is enabled. If the current context is a form module, this item will be grayed out and the items Layout Editor... or New Block..., unique to Forms, will be enabled. In a PL/SQL module, none of the items above is available.

The item New Block... brings up the New Block Options dialog box, which can be used to create a new, default base table block. The item Tables | Columns... can be used to view the structure of database objects that you have privilege to access. The Debug Mode is a check menu item used to toggle the Debug Mode option of the Designer. Finally, Options menu item brings up the Options where Designer and Runtime options settings are set. Recall that all the functionality described in this paragraph was used during the development of the ETS application.

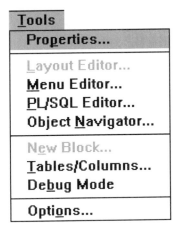

FIGURE 4.6   Tools submenu.

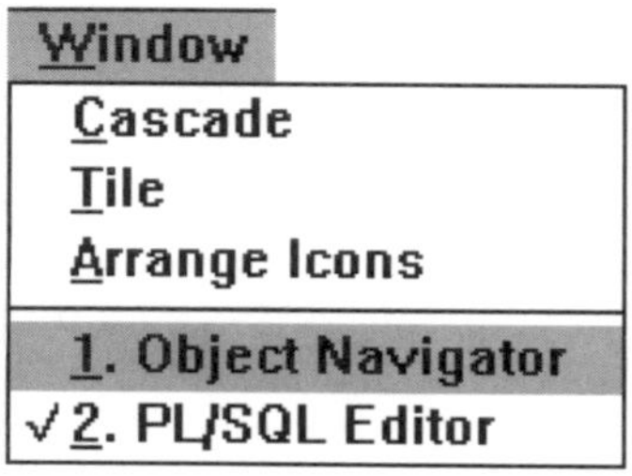

FIGURE 4.7   Window submenu.

4.5.4   WINDOW SUBMENU

Figure 4.7 shows an example of this submenu. The first two items of this menu manage the display of MDI sheets in the Designer. They can be tiled to fit the whole frame, or cascaded. If any or all the windows are minimized, use Window | Arrange Icons to arrange their icon in the lower part of the MDI frame. The second part of this submenu contains a list of the windows currently open in the Designer. By selecting any of the windows in this list, you can navigate to that window. The windows in the list are ordered by the time of access. The most recently accessed window is at the bottom of the list. In the case of Figure 4.7, there are two windows open; the PL/SQL Editor window is the current environment; it was accessed after the Object Navigator window, and the user is about to switch back to this window.

4.5.5   HELP SUBMENU

The Help submenu is shown in Figure 4.8. The most important item in this menu is Contents. It brings up the on-line help for the Designer. This is organized in the form of standard Windows Help files, and is an alternate way of browsing and searching the on-line documentation besides the Oracle Book files. If you want on-line help for a particular environment of the Designer, for example Object Navigator, Layout Editor, or Menu Editor, select the appropriate window and press F1 from the keyboard.

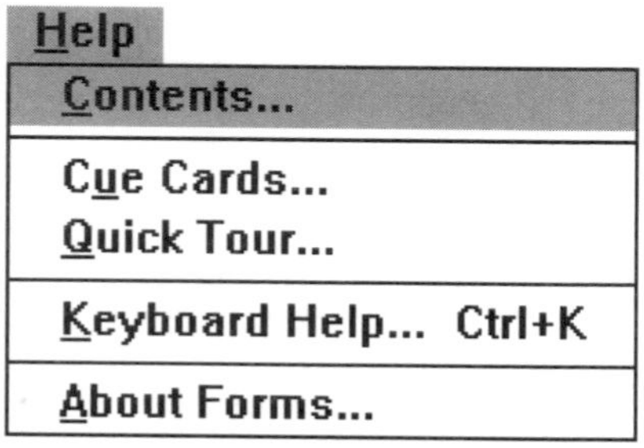

FIGURE 4.8   Help submenu.

Note

The menu items Help|Cue Cards... and Help|Quick Tour... were added with version 4.5.6.5.5 of Oracle Forms.

Two other important menu items that you may find very useful when you begin to program with Oracle Forms are Cue Cards... and Quick Tour... . The first option provides step-by-step instructions on how to perform basic tasks such as building a simple form, running a form, and adding interface items. The second option leads to a set of Computer-Based Training (CBT) courses on similar topics.

The item Keyboard Help displays a list of the Designer's functions available in the current context and the key sequence to access them from the keyboard. In graphical, mouse-driven environments this option is rarely needed or used.

The item About Oracle Forms... displays a scrollable list of all the software components used to build the version of Oracle Forms you are using. This information is not of any use, except in case you need to call the Oracle Corporation's Customer Support with a question or problem.

4.5.6 POPUP MENU

When you are working in the Object Navigator, Layout Editor, or Menu Editor windows, you can also click the right mouse button to display the popup menu shown Figure 4.9.

Use this menu to cut, copy, or paste objects; to navigate to or display any of the Properties, Layout Editor, or PL/SQL Editor windows; or to display context-sensitive help.

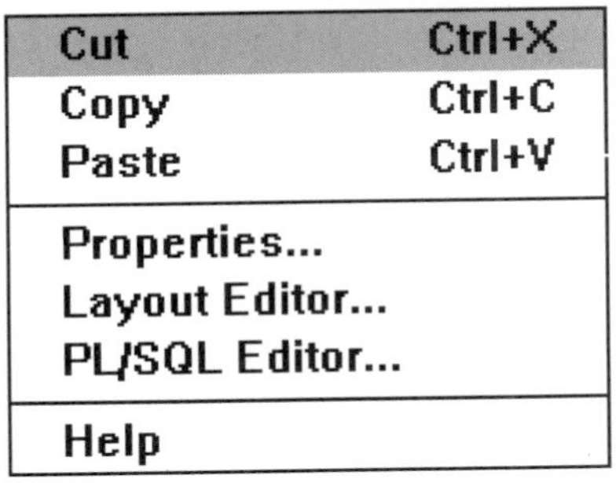

Cut	Ctrl+X
Copy	Ctrl+C
Paste	Ctrl+V
Properties...	
Layout Editor...	
PL/SQL Editor...	
Help	

FIGURE 4.9 Popup menu.

4.6 WORKING WITH MODULES

As mentioned previously, Oracle Forms follows a modular approach to building an application. Every object and piece of code is created, organized, and maintained in form, menu, or PL/SQL library modules. By default, modules are saved as files in the operating system directory structure.

4.6.1 TYPES OF MODULES

Each module can be in one of the following three forms:

❑ *Binary modules.* These are binary files that can be read only by the Designer. When you create and save a module, Designer saves it as a binary file. When you open the module for later modifications, the Designer will ask you to specify a binary file. The extension for binary forms is .FMB, for menus .MMB, and for PL/SQL libraries .PLL. The binary modules you create are portable from one platform to another. In other words, you can develop a form in MS Windows and then open that very same form in the Oracle Forms for Macintosh and continue working with it.

❑ *Executable modules.* These are files in machine-readable format that are created when the module is generated. The default extensions for forms is .FMX and for menus is .MMX. PL/SQL libraries are not generated; they are compiled and remain in the binary format. From within the Designer, you can generate the module by selecting File | Administration | Generate from the menu, or by pressing CTRL+T from the keyboard. You can also generate a module using the Forms Generate utility as explained in Chapter 1. Forms Runtime executes .FMX files and, implicitly, uses the .MMX and .PLL files, if menus or PL/SQL libraries are attached to the form. The format of the executable files depends on the operating system. In the example presented in the previous paragraph, you must generate your module both in MS Windows and Macintosh in order to run it in these environments. From within the Designer, you can run a form by selecting File | Run from the menu, or by pressing CTRL+R from the keyboard. Your users will execute the forms using the Forms Runtime tool.

❑ *Text modules.* These are text files that contain the information about the module in a human-readable format, that can be displayed in a text editor such as Notepad. The extension for forms is .FMT, for menus .MMT, and for PL/SQL libraries .PLD. The only reason to convert a module to a text format is to place it under the control of a version control utility.

To convert a module follow these steps:

1. Select File | Administration | Convert from the menu. The Convert dialog box appears (see Figure 4.10).
2. Select the module type. This can be *'Form'*, *'Menu'*, or *'Library'*.
3. Enter the name of the module. If you want to search the directory tree for the module name, click the Browse button.
4. Specify the direction of conversion. It can be either *'Binary-to-Text'* or *'Text-to-Binary'*.
5. Click Convert. The module is converted according to your specifications.

4.6.2 CREATING MODULES

To create a new module follow these steps:

1. Select File | New from the Designer menu. This displays the submenu of module types.
2. Select the type of module you want to create. It can be Form, Menu, or Library.

The Designer creates the new module and assigns it a default name. Note that when you launch the Designer, it creates a new form module by default, ready for you to use. If you want to work with an existing module, this default module is removed from the module list in the Navigator as soon as you open the other module.

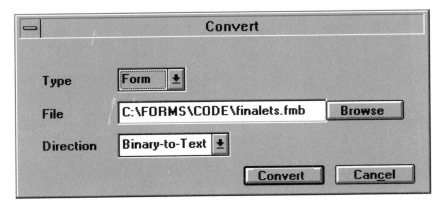

FIGURE 4.10 Convert dialog box.

4.6.3 OPENING MODULES

To open an existing module, select File | Open... from the Designer menu or press CTRL+O from the keyboard. A standard Open dialog box will be displayed (see Figure 4.11).

In this dialog box you can specify the drive, directory, and file name of the module you want to open. For the selected directory, you can list only the form modules (.FMB), menu modules (.MMB), or PL/SQL modules (.PLL). You can also choose to list all the files in the directory. This is the default way to access modules. You may change the settings to display only one type of module, or any combination of them. To do this, select Tools | Options... from the menu. In the Options dialog box that appears (see Figure 4.12 later in the chapter), set the check boxes according to your needs.

4.6.4 SAVING MODULES

To save an existing file, select File | Save from the menu or press CTRL+S from the keyboard.

To save a new file or to save an existing file under a new name, select File | Save As... from the menu. A dialog box very similar to the one shown in Figure 4.11 will appear. The only difference between these dialog boxes is the title bar. It is Open or Save As, depending on the command you are issuing.

Specify the location and the name of the file you want to save, and click OK.

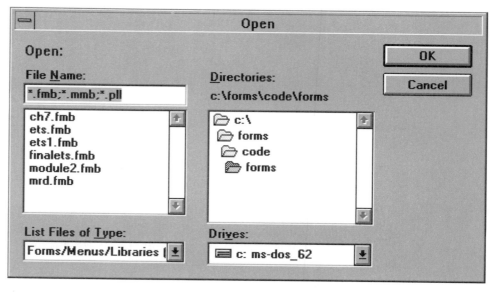

FIGURE 4.11 Open dialog box.

4.6.5 CLOSING MODULES

To close a module select File | Close from the menu or press CTRL+W from the keyboard. If there are unsaved changes in the module, you will be prompted to save them. If you chose to save a newly created module, the Save As dialog box appears, where you can specify the name of the module.

4.6.6 REVERTING MODULES

If you want to throw away all changes made on a module since the last save, choose File | Revert from the menu. This is a shortcut to closing the module without saving and then opening it again.

4.7 STORING MODULES IN THE DATABASE

By default, modules are stored as files in the directory structure of the operating system. However, Oracle Forms and all the other Developer/2000 tools have a rather unique feature that allows you to store the modules in the Oracle Server database. This section discusses how to store and access the modules in the database.

4.7.1 PREPARING THE DATABASE TO STORE MODULES

Together with the Developer/2000 software, Oracle Corporation provides the necessary SQL scripts to create the appropriate database objects that will store the information about modules. These scripts are located in the Developer/2000 Administration program group.

First, you create the Developer/2000 common database objects. To do this follow these steps:

1. Open Developer/2000 Administration program group.
2. Double-click the Common Build program item. The program invokes SQL*Plus.
3. Supply the password for SYSTEM as prompted by the program.
4. Supply the database connect string as it applies to your environment.

After this, the program executes the script and exits SQL*Plus.

Now, grant access to these objects to all users that will need to store the modules in the database:

1. Double-click the Common Grant program item. The program invokes SQL*Plus.
2. Supply the password for SYSTEM as prompted by the program.

> **Note**
>
> It is crucial that the database objects where the modules will be stored be created and owned by the account SYSTEM.

3. Supply the database connect string as it applies to your environment.
4. Enter the user name to whom you want to grant access. If you want to grant the privilege to several users, supply their names, separated by commas.

After this, the program executes the script and exits SQL*Plus.

Next, run the scripts that create Forms-specific objects and grant the users access to them. To do this, execute the Forms Build and Forms Grant program items in exactly the same fashion as described above.

4.7.2 SETTING MODULE ACCESS OPTIONS

To change the default way modules are accessed select Tools | Options from the Designer menu. The Options dialog box is displayed (see Figure 4.12). The three radio items in the Module Access section of the window are the options you want to set. By default, File is checked. If you check Database, modules can be opened from and saved to the database only. If you select File/Database, each time you open or save a module, you will see the Filter dialog box shown in Figure 4.13. Here you can specify whether you want to work with file or database modules.

4.7.3 OPENING AND SAVING

Everything that was said in Sections 4.6.3 and 4.6.4 about opening and saving modules in the file systems remains valid, with one exception. When working with database modules, the standard Windows dialog boxes are replaced with dialog boxes similar to the one shown in Figure 4.14.

This dialog box is displayed when you attempt to open a module. To retrieve a list of modules stored in the database that you can open, click Retrieve List button. Then, select the desired module from the list and click Open button.

The dialog box that is displayed when you try to save a module to the database is similar to the one shown in Figure 4.14. The only differences are the title of the dialog, which now is Save in Database. The name of the text field where you specify the module name and of the button you click to perform the action are now Save instead of Open.

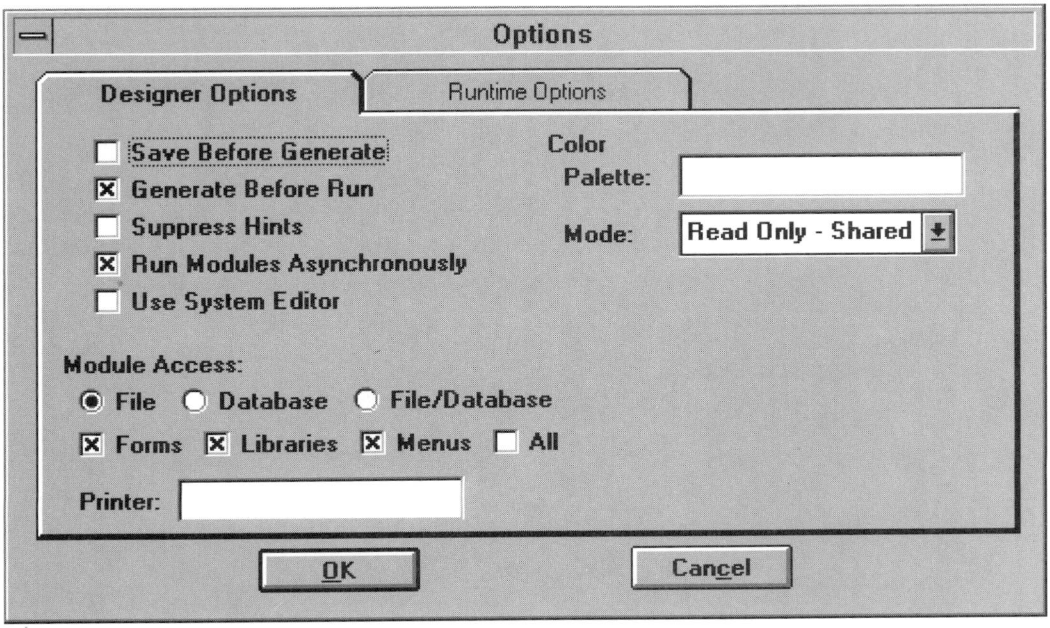

FIGURE 4.12 Changing module access settings in the Options dialog box.

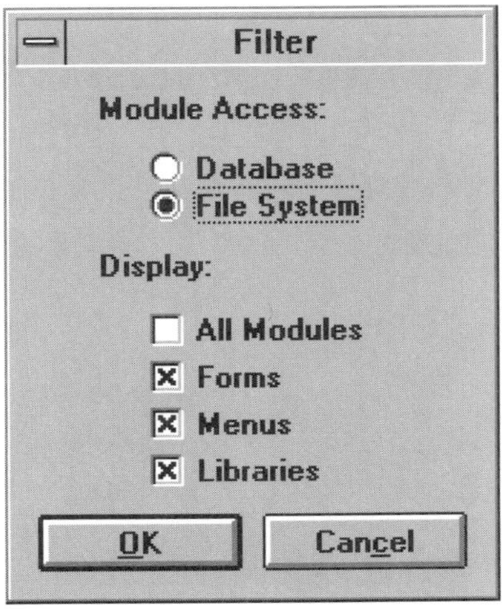

FIGURE 4.13 Filter dialog box.

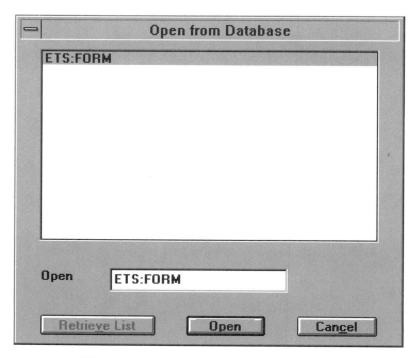

FIGURE 4.14 Open from Database dialog box.

4.7.4 DELETING AND RENAMING

You may delete a module from the database by performing these actions:

1. Choose File | Administration | Delete... from the menu. A dialog box similar to Figure 4.14 appears. In this case, the text labels Open are replaced by Delete.
2. Locate the module you want to delete using the Retrieve command if necessary.
3. Click the Delete button.

To rename a module follow these steps:

1. Select File | Administration | Rename... from the menu. The Rename in Database dialog box is displayed (see Figure 4.15).
2. Provide the name of the module to rename in the Old text field. Use the Retrieve functionality if necessary.
3. Enter the new name of the module in the New text field.
4. Click Rename button to proceed with the action.

> ## Note
>
> When working with file modules, deleting and renaming are carried out by operating system commands, outside the Designer. In MS Windows, for example, you can use File Manager to delete or rename modules.

4.7.5 GRANTING AND REVOKING ACCESS TO MODULES

If other users need to work with a module that you have stored in the database under your account, you must grant them access to it. When they are done with it, you may want to revoke them the privilege. To grant or revoke access to your module proceed as follows:

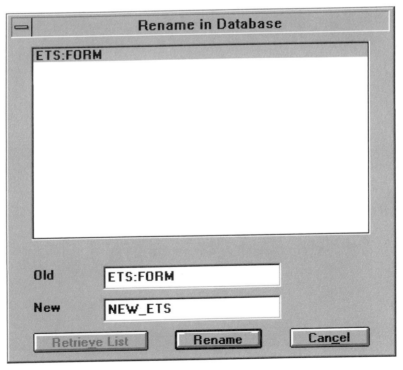

FIGURE 4.15 Rename in Database dialog box.

1. Select File|Administration|Module Access... from the menu. The Grant Module dialog box appears (see Figure 4.16).
2. Specify the name of the module in the Module text field. Use the retrieve functionality if necessary.
3. Enter the name of user in the User text field.
4. Check the radio button at the top of the window that describes the action you want to perform: Grant or Revoke.
5. Click OK to perform the action.

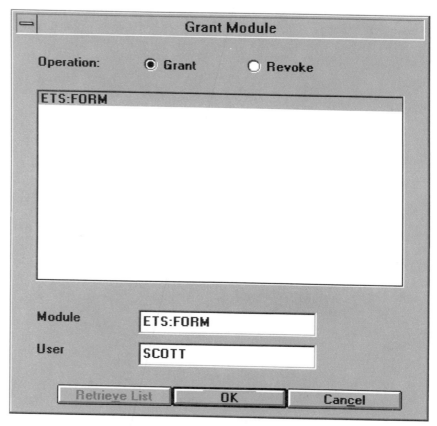

FIGURE 4.16   Grant Module dialog box.

> **Note**
>
> Unfortunately, there is not an easy way to grant access to multiple users with one single command, or to see which users have been granted access to the module. In order to effectively administer the privileges that other users have on your modules, you must rely on other forms of documentation for your application.

4.8 OTHER FUNCTIONALITY OF THE DESIGNER

There are some additional functions accessible from the Designer that will be discussed in the coming chapters. File | Compile... and File | Compile All... are used to compile the PL/SQL code in a module, and will be discussed in Chapter 10. File | Administration | Database Roles... is enabled only if you are connected to the database with DBA privileges. The functionality of this menu option will be discussed in Chapter 17. Finally, File | Administration | Check In, File | Administration | Check Out, and File | Administration | Source Control Options are enabled only if you have installed the source control software package Polytron Version Control System (PVCS) from Intersolv. They are used for source control and configuration management purposes in your software system.

4.9 SUMMARY

This chapter offered an overview of Developer/2000, Oracle Forms Designer, and issues related to working with modules in the Designer. Main topics discussed include the following:

- ❑ Features of Developer/2000
  - ❑ Client/Server suite of tools for Oracle databases
  - ❑ Powerful support for SQL
  - ❑ Rapid Application Development tools
  - ❑ Graphical Users Interface tools
  - ❑ Object-oriented programming environment
- ❑ Components of Developer/2000
  - ❑ Forms, reports, graphics
  - ❑ Designer versus Runtime
  - ❑ Other Developer/2000 components

- ❏ Components of Oracle Forms Designer
  - ❏ MDI frame
  - ❏ Object Navigator, Layout Editor, Properties Window, Menu Editor, and PL/SQL Editor
- ❏ Designer Menu
  - ❏ File, Edit, Tools, Window, Help, and Popup menus
- ❏ Working with Modules
  - ❏ Types of modules
  - ❏ Creating, opening, saving, closing, and reverting modules
- ❏ Storing Modules in the Database
  - ❏ Preparing the database to store modules
  - ❏ Setting module access options
  - ❏ Opening, saving, deleting, and renaming modules
  - ❏ Granting and revoking access to modules

Chapter 5

OBJECT NAVIGATOR

"Learn of the little nautilus to sail,
Spread the thin oar, and catch the driving gale."
—Alexander Pope

- ◆ Accessing Object Navigator
- ◆ Components of Object Navigator
- ◆ Object Types and Object Instances
- ◆ Getting Around Object Navigator
- ◆ Manipulating Objects in Object Navigator
- ◆ Different Views of Objects in Object Navigator
- ◆ Customizing Object Navigator
- ◆ Summary

The Object Navigator is used to represent the objects that make up an Oracle Forms application. These objects are organized hierarchically by object type. At the top level of the hierarchy are the five main groups of objects: Forms, Menus, Libraries, Built-in Packages, and Database Objects. Each of these groups can be expanded to several levels, thus allowing you to view all the details you need at a particular moment during your development activity. The Object Navigator provides ways to quickly search and locate the objects of an application. From the Object Navigator, you can create new objects or delete existing ones, and access and modify all their properties. You can also create or change PL/SQL code associated with an object.

5.1 ACCESSING OBJECT NAVIGATOR

The Object Navigator is always present when Forms Designer is running. It is the first window to come up and the last one to go. However, as you work with other editors, it may be temporarily hidden from view. In these cases, there are two ways to display the Object Navigator window:

a) Select Tools | Object Navigator... from the Designer menu, or
b) Select Window | Object Navigator from the Designer menu.

5.2 COMPONENTS OF OBJECT NAVIGATOR

Figure 5.1 represents a typical Object Navigator window. The main part of the Object Navigator window is occupied by an area where all the objects are displayed. This area will be called the Node Display area. Sometimes it is also referred to as the application object tree, because it offers a hierarchical view of all form, menu, and PL/SQL modules currently open. The horizontal toolbar of the Object Navigator contains the Context List and the Find Field. Along the left side of the window, there is a vertical toolbar. The following sections provide additional information about these four components.

The Object Navigator window is equipped with a horizontal and a vertical scroll bar. These allow you to display those areas of the window that contain objects but extend beyond the boundaries of the window at a particular moment. On top of the vertical scroll bar, there is the horizontal split pane bar. To the left of the horizontal scroll bar, you can see the vertical split pane bar. Split pane bars allow you to split the Object Navigator window in up to eight horizontal or vertical panes that can display the information independently. Section 5.7.1 discusses the functionality of split pane bars.

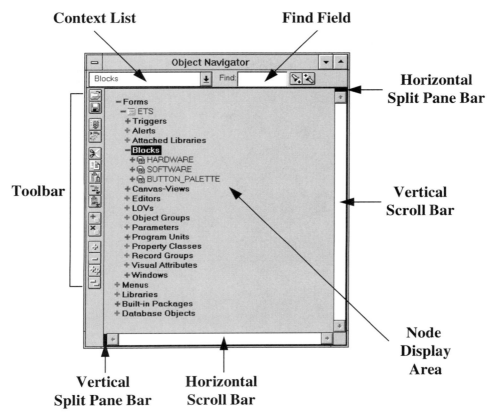

FIGURE 5.1   Components of Object Navigator window.

5.2.1 NODE DISPLAY AREA

The Node Display area, as the name suggests, is the part of the Object Navigator window where all the objects accessible in the current Forms development session are listed. As Figure 5.1 shows, these objects belong to forms, menus, and PL/SQL libraries. In addition, built-in program units and database objects can be displayed and accessed from here.

Each entry in the list is called a node. A node represents an object type such as a Form, Block, or Trigger; or it represents a user-created object such as ETS form, HARDWARE block, or MANUFACTURER item. Section 5.3 discusses in detail objects and their types in Oracle Forms.

5.2.2 FIND FIELD

The Find Field enhances the search capabilities of the Object Navigator. It is made up of a text field where search criteria are entered and has two iconic buttons that specify the direction of search. The Search Forward icon ⊠ searches from top down, whereas the Search Backward icon ⊠ searches from bottom up. By default, lists are searched forward. When the bottom of the list is reached, the search resumes from the top. To search backwards enter the search string and press Search Backwards icon ⊠. The search stops at the first entry in the list that satisfies the search criteria. This entry is highlighted by the Object Navigator.

The Find Field implements two powerful features that make it a very effective navigational tool. First, the objects are searched as you type. If, for example, T is entered in the text field, the search engine will locate the first object in the direction of search that begins with T. As more characters are typed in, the highlighted bar moves to entries of the list that match the additional criteria. If the current selection does not change as you type, then there are no objects whose names match the string being entered. Second, the Object Navigator performs a depth-first search on all the nodes in the direction of search. For each node, all its children and their children are searched recursively, even if they are not displayed in the Object Navigator in expanded state. When a match occurs, all parent nodes of the newly found entry are expanded as necessary.

5.2.3 CONTEXT LIST

The Context List displays all the modules currently open in the Object Navigator. If the name of a module is selected from the list, the Navigator jumps to the node in the Node Display area that represents that module. The Context List also displays the name of the object currently selected in the Navigator. This is the reason why it is often referred to as the Location Indicator. Together with the currently selected object, the Context List displays its parent and ancestors, indented based on their relationship to the object. Figure 5.2 shows typical information provided by the Context List.

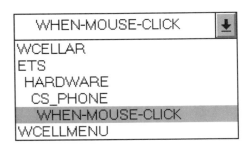

FIGURE 5.2 Context List.

In this example, the current object is WHEN-MOUSE-CLICK trigger, associated with CS_PHONE item. This item is a member of HARDWARE block, and they all are part of ETS form module. Currently there are two other modules open in the Navigator: WCELLAR and WCELLMENU.

The Context List becomes really advantageous if long lists of objects are displayed in the Navigator. For example, suppose you are working in a module and you want to use the built-in function USERENV. You want to look up its syntax, so you click inside the Find Field and start typing the function's name. After you have typed the fifth letter, the Find utility locates the function. At this point, between your original location in the node list and the current selection, there are several dozens of nodes. In fact, USERENV is among the very last entries in the list of functions included in the STANDARD package, under the node Built-in Packages. As explained in the previous section, on the way to locate the function, the Find utility has expanded all its parents.

Now, you want to navigate back to your module and continue work. If you decide to use the vertical scroll bar, it may take you some time to reach your destination. Use instead the Context List to navigate immediately to your module.

1. Click inside Context List field or on the list button ⊞ to its right. The drop-down list displays all the open modules and the function USERENV.
2. Click the module you want to navigate to from the list.

The Navigator will select the module automatically. From there, it is not difficult to navigate to your location prior to the function lookup.

Note

USERENV is a PL/SQL function that returns information about the current session such as a session identification number, or the language being used by the session. Its syntax is not complicated; it takes a VARCHAR2 argument and returns a VARCHAR2 value. For more complex functions, though, you may discover that by the time you return to the initial location, you have forgotten some small detail in their specification. The Object Navigator allows you to paste the name or the arguments of the PL/SQL object directly in your code by selecting Navigator|Paste Names or Navigator|Paste Arguments from the menu.

5.2.4 TOOLBAR

On the left-hand side of the Object Navigator window, there is a list of iconic buttons, also known as the Navigator toolbar. It is shown in Figure 5.3.

The toolbar allows developers to access often-used functionality with a click of the mouse. The buttons are grouped by functionality in five segments. The first one contains buttons that open and save form, menu, or PL/SQL library modules. The Run and Debug buttons in the second segment facilitate the process of developing and testing applications. The third segment of buttons offers editing functionality such as cut, paste, and copy for objects, and copy and paste for properties of objects. The buttons in the forth segment are used to add new or delete existing objects in the Navigator. Finally, the last four buttons that make up the fifth segment expand or collapse entries in the Node Display area.

The first three groups in the toolbar cover functionality that is available and accessible throughout the development process in Oracle Forms. These buttons are available in other editors such as Layout Editor or Menu Editor. The last two iconic segments of the toolbar cover functionality that is exclusive to the Object Navigator.

 Open

Save

 Run

Debug

 Create

Delete

 Cut

Copy

Paste

 Expand

Collapse

 Copy Properties

Paste Properties

 Expand All

Collapse All

FIGURE 5.3   Object Navigator's toolbar.

5.3 OBJECT TYPES AND OBJECT INSTANCES

As mentioned earlier, each entry listed in the Object Navigator's Node Display area is called a node. There are two kinds of nodes: object types and object instances. The following sections provide details for each of them.

5.3.1 OBJECT TYPES

The object types are names of categories of objects that can be used in Forms applications. Because each actual object falls under one of these categories, object type nodes are often called headings. Each object type node has the following format:

```
[Expand/Collapse Status Indicator] [Object Type Name]
```

The Expand/Collapse Status Indicator can have one of the following icons:

- Indicates that this category of objects is already populated. There is at least one object of that type in the application. Clicking the ✚ icon expands the object heading and displays the objects of that type. For clarity, the objects are indented below the corresponding object type node. For database objects, this icon has a dark blue color, like the ✚ icon.
- Indicates that there are no objects of this category in the application yet. Double-clicking the ✚ icon creates a new object of that type. This action is equivalent to clicking the Create icon 🖼 in the toolbar, or to selecting Navigator | Create from the menu.
- Indicates that the object category is already expanded. All the objects of that category are listed below the node, indented according to the hierarchy level. Clicking the ▬ icon collapses the object category and hides its instances from sight. For database objects, this icon has a dark blue color, like the ▬ icon.

The Object Type Name is preset in the Designer, and cannot be changed during development activities. Some examples of object types that can be encountered in a Forms application are Form, Block, Item, Menu, Menu Item, Attached Library, and Window. Feel free to explore the Object Navigator and see all the other types of objects not mentioned here.

5.3.2 OBJECT INSTANCES

The object instances represent actual objects created and used in the application. Figure 5.4 shows a typical listing of object types and object instances in the Object Navigator. The module used here is the module developed in Part One.

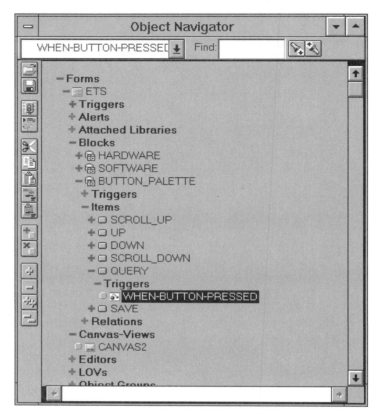

FIGURE 5.4 Object types and object instances.

In this figure, BUTTON_PALETTE is an instance of object type Blocks. A block, and therefore BUTTON_PALETTE, may own three other types of objects: triggers, items, and relations. Because the expand/collapse status indicators of nodes Triggers and Relations under BUTTON_PALETTE are grayed out, you can conclude that this block does not own any objects of these types. Currently, it owns only items.

Each object instance node has the following format:

```
[Expand/Collapse Status Indicator] [Object Type Icon]
                 [Object Name]
```

The Expand/Collapse Status Indicator can have one of the following states:

✦ Indicates that this object may own other objects. Clicking the ✦ icon expands the object and displays the types of objects it may own. These types may be populated or not, depending on the particular application. For database objects, this icon has a dark blue color, like the ✦ icon.

▬ Indicates that the object is already expanded. Clicking the ▬ icon collapses the object, and hides its children. For database objects, this icon has a dark blue color, like the ▬ icon.

▣ Indicates that the object cannot have any descendants in the object hierarchy tree. Such objects are also called atomic objects. For example, in Figure 5.4, the object CANVAS2 is an atomic object.

In the case of Figure 5.4, all the items under BUTTON_PALETTE block are collapsed, except for item QUERY, which contains a trigger named WHEN-MOUSE-CLICK. This trigger is an atomic object because it cannot own other objects.

The Object Type icon serves as a visual indicator of an object's type. Double-clicking this icon brings up the Properties window for all the objects, except for Canvases, Triggers, Program units, and Menus. Double-clicking the Canvases icon ▣ brings up a Layout Editor window for that canvas. Double-clicking the Triggers icon ▣ and the Program Units icon ▣ brings up the PL/SQL Editor. Double-clicking the Menu icon ▣ brings up the Menu Editor.

The Object Name uniquely identifies the instance of an object in the application. For each newly created object, Oracle Forms generates a name automatically. This is formed of the object type, or an abbreviation of it, followed by a sequence-generated number. Examples of such names are BLOCK1, ITEM10, WINDOW12, or LIB_029. Obviously, these names are not very helpful during development and maintenance activities. Mnemonic and more descriptive names should be used instead.

Note

The word atomic derives from the Greek *attomos*, which means undivided. It was used by philosophers in Ancient Greece to describe the smallest building block of the world. It is common knowledge today that atoms are made up of many other particles and subparticles. Nevertheless, the term atomic continues to be used in the discourse outside physics to indicate something indivisible.

5.4 GETTING AROUND OBJECT NAVIGATOR

Earlier in the chapter, you learned how to use the Context List and Find tools for locating and moving to target objects in the Navigator. The following sections provide additional information about navigating, selecting, expanding, collapsing, and marking objects.

5.4.1 NAVIGATING AND SELECTING OBJECTS

At first sight, navigating to and selecting an object may seem synonymous. Indeed, when you go to a node in the object hierarchical tree, Forms automatically highlights the name of the node, thus selecting it. Therefore, navigating to an object means selecting that object. But the reverse is not always true. As you will see later on, Forms allows you to select multiple objects. In this case, only the last object to be selected has the navigational focus.

The easiest way to navigate to an object is to click with the mouse in the area of the node list where the object is displayed. In order to do this, the target object must be visible in the Node Display area of the Object Navigator. If this is not the case, scrolling up and down the node list may be necessary. If the desired object is in a level of the hierarchy tree that is currently collapsed, expand the parent objects as necessary and then select the object. Expanding and collapsing are explained in the next section. The Find utility of the Object Navigator is very useful in locating target objects. This utility was discussed earlier in the chapter.

You can also use the arrow keys to navigate and select nodes in the Object Navigator. The up-arrow key navigates to the node immediately above the current node; the down-arrow key to the one immediately below.

5.4.2 SELECTING MULTIPLE OBJECTS

Using the mouse to select objects is not only easy but also powerful. This method allows selection of multiple objects, which cannot be done using the arrow keys. In order to better understand the process, perform the actions in the module ETS.FMB.

First, expand the blocks HARDWARE and SOFTWARE so that their items are visible (see Figure 5.5). Now select all the items that belong to HARDWARE block.

1. Click the HW_SERIAL_NUM item. It is selected.
2. SHIFT+CLICK CS_COST item. All the items between HW_SERIAL_NUM and CS_COST are selected.

This type of object selection is called range selection. In a range selection, all the entries between the initial and final selection points must be objects of the same

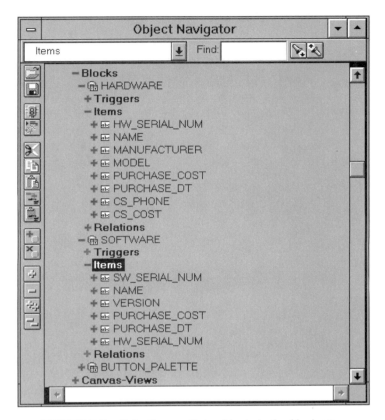

FIGURE 5.5 Selecting multiple objects in the Navigator.

type. When objects of a different type are included in the range, then only the objects of the same type that are in the same segment of the node list as the initial object are selected. As an example, try to select all the items of HARDWARE and SOFTWARE blocks.

1. Click the HW_SERIAL_NUM item in HARDWARE block. The item is selected.
2. SHIFT+CLICK the PURCHASE_DT item in SOFTWARE block.

All the items in the HARDWARE block are selected, but none from the SOFTWARE block is included in the range.

In order to select objects that are not adjacent in contiguous ranges, the CTRL key is used in conjunction with mouse clicks. For example, select NAME, MODEL, and PURCHASE_DT items of the HARDWARE block.

1. Click the NAME item in HARDWARE block. The item is selected.
2. CTRL+CLICK first MODEL then PURCHASE_DT. They are selected as you click.

If you want to deselect an already selected object, simply CTRL+CLICK that item.

For obvious reasons, range selecting and multiselecting are also known as shift-clicking and control-clicking. The two methods can be combined to provide more flexible and powerful selecting capabilities. For example, using shift- and control-clicking, you can now complete the task attempted earlier. Select all the items from HARDWARE and SOFTWARE blocks:

1. Click the HW_SERIAL_NUM item in HARDWARE block. The item is selected.
2. SHIFT+CLICK CS_COST in HARDWARE block. All the items in HARDWARE block are selected.
3. CTRL+CLICK SW_SERIAL_NUM in SOFTWARE block. The item is added to the already selected items from HARDWARE block.
4. SHIFT+CLICK PURCHASE_DT in SOFTWARE block. All the items in HARDWARE and SOFTWARE blocks are now selected.

Once the objects are selected, you can perform group operations on them such as moving them to another module, setting common properties, etc. As a matter of fact, performing these types of operations is the main purpose for selecting multiple objects.

5.4.3 EXPANDING AND COLLAPSING NODES

In order to better manage and organize the information about the many objects involved in an application, Oracle Forms provides expanding and collapsing services. These services include expand/collapse status indicators that show the state of a node and commands to actually expand or collapse nodes in the Navigator. The different status indicators were explained earlier in the chapter. The remainder of this section deals only with the commands to perform these operations.

There are four commands to expand or collapse nodes in the Object Navigator. The Expand command displays all the subnodes at the hierarchical level immediately below the currently selected object. It can be accessed in one of the following three equivalent methods:

a) Click the ✚ icon on the left of the node, or
b) Click the Expand icon 🔲 in the toolbar, or
c) Select Navigator | Expand from the Navigator menu.

The Collapse command hides the subnodes immediately below the currently selected object. To collapse a node in the Navigator do one of the following:

a) Click the ▬ icon on the left of the node, or
b) Click the Collapse icon ▣ in the toolbar, or
c) Select Navigator | Collapse from the menu.

The commands Expand and Collapse act upon nodes that are in the hierarchy
level immediately below that of the current node. For example, if the HARD-
WARE node is expanded, the nodes Triggers, Items, and Relations will be displayed. However, there are instances when there is a need to display or hide the
whole hierarchical tree of objects under a certain object. In the case above, you
may want to display also what is under Triggers, Items, and Relations. The commands Expand All and Collapse All are used in these situations.

The Expand All command displays all the subnodes at every hierarchical
level below the currently selected object. Each node expands recursively to the
atomic level under the current node. It can be accessed in one of the following
equivalent methods:

a) SHIFT+CLICK the ✚ icon on the left of the node, or
b) Click the Expand All icon ▣ in the toolbar, or
c) Select Navigator | Expand All from the menu.

The Collapse All command hides all the subnodes below the currently selected
object. It collapses all the hierarchies under the current node. To perform this action in the Navigator do one of the following:

a) SHIFT+CLICK ▬ icon on the left of the node, or
b) Click the Collapse All icon ▣ in the toolbar, or
c) Select Navigator | Collapse All from the menu.

Figure 5.6 shows the output of the Expand All action on the HARDWARE block
node.

It was mentioned earlier that up-arrow and down-arrow keys can be used
to navigate between nodes. Left- and right-arrow keys combine navigational and
expand/collapse functionality. The left-arrow key navigates to the parent node of
the currently selected object and collapses it. In the example of Figure 5.6, if the
current node is the relation HARDWARE_SOFTWARE, pressing the left-arrow
key will select the node Relations and collapse it. Repeating the action one more
time will select the HARDWARE block and collapse it.

The right-arrow key expands the current node and moves the focus to the
first node immediately below it. Still using the scenario presented above, pressing

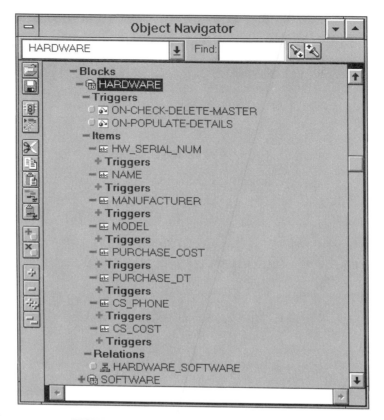

FIGURE 5.6   Effect of Expand All command.

the right-arrow key when the node HARDWARE is selected will expand this node and move the cursor one node down to Triggers.

In the conclusion of this section, let's mention that the Navigator memorizes the expand/collapse state of the object tree. An example provides the best explanation for this feature. Once again, you will use the module ETS.FMB and some of the commands discussed previously. If the HARDWARE block is expanded, perform a Collapse All on that node. Now follow these steps:

1. Expand the node HARDWARE.
2. Expand the node MANUFACTURER.
3. Collapse the node HARDWARE.
4. Expand the node HARDWARE for a second time.

As you see, the MANUFACTURER item remained expanded even after its parent, HARDWARE node was collapsed.

5.4.4 MARKING OBJECTS

Setting marks and navigating to them is another facility provided by Object Navigator to help you quickly access Forms objects. Every node in the Node Display Area can be marked. To mark an object, you simply select that object and choose Navigator | Mark from the menu.

Once a node is marked, Forms can navigate to that node from any position in the Navigator window, or in any other Editor. To navigate to a marked object, select Navigator | Goto Mark from the menu. If the target node is collapsed, the Object Navigator will expand the object tree as necessary.

Only one mark can be set in each Object Navigator pane. Later in the chapter you will see what the panes are and how to use multiple panes. A mark remains effective until one of the following events occur:

a) A new object is marked, thus overriding the current mark.
b) The marked object is deleted.
c) The module that contains the marked object is closed.
d) Forms Designer application terminates.

5.5 MANIPULATING OBJECTS IN OBJECT NAVIGATOR

The Object Navigator not only allows you to navigate to, search for, and select objects, but also gives you the possibility to act upon these objects. Actions such as create, delete, copy, and paste, can be accessed from other specialized editors, as well. For example, items can be created and modified in the Layout Editor, triggers, and program units in the PL/SQL Editor, and menu items in the Menu Editor. But, with its unified view of all the application objects, the Navigator gives uniformity and coherence to these actions. With its graphical view of the hierarchy tree, Navigator also greatly facilitates the process of placing an object in the appropriate position in the application.

5.5.1 CREATING OBJECTS

Before creating an object, the location of that object in the Navigator's hierarchy must be decided. This location depends on the type of the object. Form-dependent objects such as alerts, blocks, List of Values, and program units, go right under the respective object type nodes. If the object will depend from other objects within the module, than the parent object must be selected first. For example, before adding an item you must decide in which block that item will go; before creating a trigger you must decide to which object it will be attached.

If there are no objects of the same type as the object you want to create, the expand/collapse status indicator will be the greyed out ✚ icon. As it was explained earlier, double-clicking this icon creates a new object.

If there are already other objects for a given type, to create the new one, simply select the object type node or one of the existing objects to indicate the location in which the new object will be placed. The new object will be created immediately below the current selection.

To create an object follow these steps:

a) Click the Create icon ⊞ from the toolbar, or
b) Select Navigator | Create from the menu.

If multiple nodes are selected and the Create command is issued, Forms Designer will loop through all the selected nodes and, for each of them, will create a new object of the same type. You can convince yourself about this by opening the module ETS.FMB and expanding the HARDWARE block.

1. Select all items in the block.
2. Click the Create icon ⊞ in the toolbar.

New items are created under each existing item in the block. Even if selected objects are of different types, Designer will create new objects for each type. To see this perform these steps:

1. Select two object type nodes, for example Canvas-Views and Windows.
2. Click the Create icon ⊞ in the toolbar.

A new canvas-view and a new window are created. Forms Designer names the newly created objects as they are created.

5.5.2 DELETING OBJECTS

Objects in the Navigator can be deleted one at a time or in groups. The only difference in the process is during the selection of the candidates for deletion. There are different ways to delete an object, after it is selected.

a) Press DELETE key in the keyboard, or
b) Click the Delete icon ⊠ from the toolbar, or
c) Select Edit | Clear from the menu.

In all cases, the Navigator will remove the selected object from the tree. If the delete operation is performed on an object type node, then all the objects underneath the node will be deleted. The only exception to this is when the selected node is a module. In that case, the operation closes the module.

Note

Be careful when you delete objects in the Navigator! The delete command here is not reversible. You cannot get back what you delete, and even Edit I Undo will not work. If the deleted object existed before the last File I Save command, either issue a Revert command, or close the module without saving, and reopen it to get the object back. Of course, in the process you will lose all the work since the last time the module was saved. That's why saving your work periodically and frequently protects you from accidental losses of precious work efforts.

5.5.3 CUTTING AND COPYING OBJECTS

A milder form of deleting an object is to cut it. Cutting places the object in the clipboard—a memory buffer that temporarily stores the last copied or cut object. Once cut, the object will remain in the clipboard until the next cut operation. It can be pasted in the original position, or in as many other locations in the application as necessary. There are several ways to cut a selection:

   a) Press CTRL+X on the keyboard, or
   b) Click the Cut icon ▨ from the toolbar, or
   c) Select Edit I Cut from the menu.

In all cases, the selected objects will be removed from the Navigator tree and placed in the clipboard.
       If you want to place objects in the clipboard, but not remove them from the Navigator hierarchy tree, then select the desired objects and copy them. The ways to copy a selection are as follows:

   a) Press CTRL+C on the keyboard, or
   b) Click the Copy icon ▨ from the toolbar, or
   c) Select Edit I Copy from the menu.

5.5.4 PASTING AND DUPLICATING OBJECTS

Certain applications may contain objects which have identical or similar properties. To reduce development efforts, Forms Designer allows you to duplicate objects or copy and paste them to the desired location.

To duplicate an object first select it, then choose Edit | Duplicate from the menu. A duplicate copy is created immediately below the current selection. To paste an object to the desired location, first place it in the clipboard by either copying or cutting it. Then navigate to the position in the object tree where you want to insert the new object. Now, you can paste the contents from the clipboard in one of the following ways:

a) Press CTRL+V on the keyboard, or
b) Click the Paste icon ⬚ from the toolbar, or
c) Select Edit | Paste from the menu.

When pasting objects, the Navigator ensures that they are inserted in appropriate locations, according to their types. Items can be pasted under blocks, but not under windows or alerts.

Copying and duplicating conserves the hierarchy and ownership of objects as well. If the original object contains dependents, its copy will have exactly the same dependents. To see this property at work, open the form ETS.FMB:

1. Select the HARDWARE block.
2. Either copy and paste, or duplicate it.
3. Select the newly created block.
4. Click the Expand All icon ⬚ from the toolbar. You should see something similar to Figure 5.7.

Comparing this figure with Figure 5.6, it is not hard to see that the new block contains exactly the same objects as the original block.

5.5.5 MOVING OBJECTS

Often there is a need to move objects from one location to another in the Navigator. For example, you want to rearrange the TAB order of items in a certain block, or you want to move well-performing program units between modules and the database. One way to achieve this is to cut and paste. Another way is to use the drag-and-drop functionality that the Navigator provides:

1. Select the objects you want to move.
2. Holding the mouse button down, drag the selection to the target location.
3. Release the mouse button, or drop the object in the new location.

As with copying and pasting, Navigator will ensure that the drag-and-drop actions do not conflict with object types. It will not allow you, for example, to move triggers under alerts or windows under blocks. In addition, if you want to move multiple objects with one action, they must all be of the same type. In other

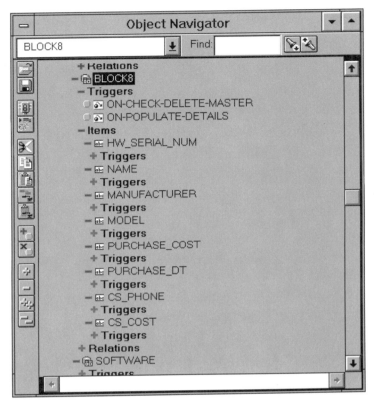

FIGURE 5.7 Copying or duplicating objects preserves their dependents.

words, you may move items or block-level triggers from one block to another separately, but you cannot mix and match the types.

5.5.6 RENAMING OBJECTS

When new objects are created, the Object Navigator automatically assigns them a name. These names indicate the type of the object (alert, block, item, etc.). They are padded with digits generated internally by the Designer to enforce their uniqueness. While assuring the consistency and robustness of the application, names such as BLOCK1 and ITEM13, do not add any value to its readability and maintainability. The need for informative and mnemonic names is explained and understood in every introductory programming course. However, it is important to emphasize that this need becomes crucial for applications developed by teams

> **Note**
>
> There is hope, though! Oracle Graphics V2.5 has an option that allows you to check the naming consistency of your application, and resolve the discrepancies that were mentioned above. Sooner or later Oracle will put this feature in Forms as well.

of programmers. In such cases, you should select names that describe the purpose and functionality of the application objects clearly and concisely. To rename an object follow these steps:

1. Select the object to be renamed.
2. Move the mouse pointer over the highlighted object's name. The cursor changes shape to I-beam.
3. Click. The cursor is placed at the end of the name field.
4. Edit the object's name as needed.

When renaming objects, additional checking must be done to ensure that there are no referencing conflicts in the application. Frequently, triggers, functions, and procedures reference objects by name. If the object's name changes, the new name should be propagated in all the statements that use it throughout the application. Unfortunately, this process may be very tedious at times. Therefore, it is important to establish naming conventions for the application early in the development stage, before any extensive coding is done. You may also try to write object-independent code. This is code in which the objects are not referenced directly by their name, but indirectly. In the chapters to come you will see several examples of such statements.

5.6 DIFFERENT VIEWS OF OBJECTS IN OBJECT NAVIGATOR

In all the examples presented thus far, you have used the Object Navigator in its default and most common state. Other ways to view the objects of an application exist as well. The following sections discuss each of them.

5.6.1 OWNERSHIP VIEW

This is the default and most comprehensive view offered by the Navigator. It allows you to look at all the objects in an application, organized by ownership hierarchy. The position and indentation of objects in the hierarchical tree clearly indicate their parent objects and objects that they own. This hierarchy represents the internal ordering of objects used by Oracle Forms and was discussed throughout this chapter.

5.6.2 VISUAL VIEW

Sometimes, it is helpful to organize objects in an application from a visual perspective. In other words, display only the tip of the iceberg that the users will see, but hide the remaining objects in the application that are visible to developers in the Ownership View. For this purpose, the Visual View of the Object Navigator is used. To switch to Visual View, select Navigator | Visual View radio item from the menu. To switch back to Ownership View, select Navigator | Ownership View radio item from the menu. Figure 5.8 represents the module ETS.FMB in Visual View.

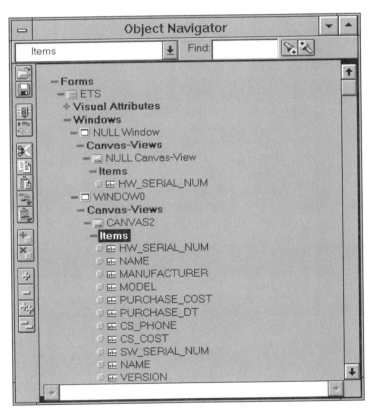

FIGURE 5.8 Visual View of Object Navigator.

As it can be seen from this figure, only visual attributes, windows, canvases, and items are displayed in Visual View. In this view, items are no longer owned by blocks, but by the canvases on which they are drawn. Items that are not assigned to a canvas are owned by the fictitious NULL Canvas-View. Each canvas in turn, is owned by the window to which it is attached. Canvases that are not assigned to any window are owned by the virtual NULL Window. Note here that if a canvas is assigned to multiple windows, the Visual View of the Object Navigator will display it under each of these windows. The information is repeated, but the canvases and their items are not replicated. Once again, this is what the windows will contain when users will see them.

5.6.3 DISPLAYING ONLY OBJECTS THAT CONTAIN PL/SQL CODE

Sometimes, it is useful to display only PL/SQL objects and the application objects to which they may be attached. This feature becomes especially important in the second stage of the development of an application. In this phase, the layout and interface design are more or less completed. The main activities now are coding and debugging triggers, procedures, and functions. It may be convenient to keep in the Navigator only those objects that are directly involved in these activities.

Objects that may contain PL/SQL code are triggers, attached libraries, blocks and their items, program units, and property classes. To view only these objects check the item Navigator | Only Objects with PL/SQL from the Designer menu. By default, this option is not set. This option can be set in both Ownership and Visual Views, but it has effect only in the Ownership View. As mentioned earlier, the Visual View displays visual attributes, canvases, items, and windows.

Figure 5.9 shows the Ownership view of ETS.FMB with the option Only Objects with PL/SQL set.

Notice in the figure that the block SOFTWARE is not present in the hierarchy tree because it does not contain any triggers.

5.7 CUSTOMIZING OBJECT NAVIGATOR

When working with the Object Navigator, you may want to further customize its behavior. The following two sections describe how to set up multiple panes of the Navigator and how to synchronize the contents of other open editors with that of the Navigator.

5.7.1 WORKING WITH MULTIPLE PANES

Forms applications can be made up of a large number of objects, resulting in long lists of entries in the Node Display area. During the development process, it may

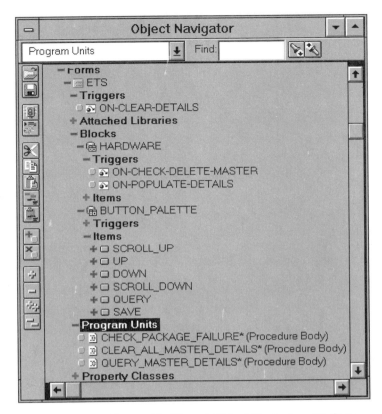

FIGURE 5.9 Ownership View of Object Navigator with Only Objects with PL/SQL option set.

be necessary to view objects in distant locations in the hierarchy tree. Rather than scrolling up and down each time these objects must be accessed, you can use multiple panes in the Object Navigator. Each pane is an identical view of the Navigator, which can be scrolled independently of views in other panes. There can be up to eight panes in the Navigator window. This window can be split either in horizontal or vertical panes. Figure 5.10 represents the form ETS.FMB displayed in two vertical panes.

Split bars are used to divide the Navigator window in different panes. They are thick black lines attached to the scroll bars of the Navigator window. The horizontal split bar is on top of the vertical scroll bar, and the vertical split bar is on the left of the horizontal scroll bar. If the Navigator window is not large enough, one split bar, or both of them, may be hidden. To display them, simply enlarge or maximize the window. When the mouse moves on top of split bars, it changes

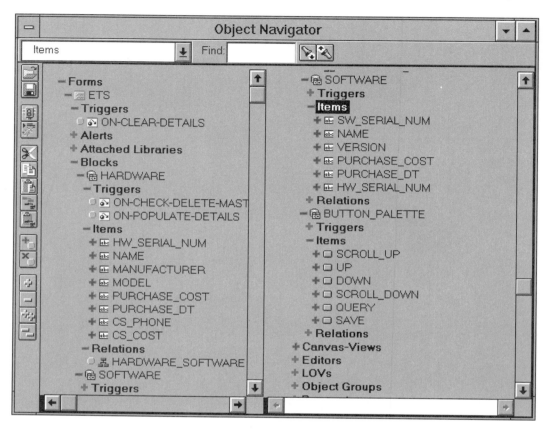

FIGURE 5.10   Vertical panes.

shape to the horizontal split indicator ÷ , or the vertical split indicator ⊪ , as the case may be.

Let us use the horizontal split bars to divide the Navigator window in two panes, similar to Figure 5.10. Open the module ETS.FMB in the Designer and follow these steps:

1. Move the cursor on the vertical split bar to the left of the horizontal scroll bar of the Navigator window. The mouse shape changes to the vertical split indicator ⊪ .
2. Hold down the mouse button. The thick black line of the split bar now extends all the way across the screen to the top of the Navigator window.
3. Holding the button down, drag the mouse to the right. The long vertical split line follows the mouse movement across the window.
4. Drop the split line in the middle of the Navigator window. A new pane is created.

> ## Note
>
> In this section, you worked with vertical panes. Splitting the Navigator in horizontal panes is a similar process that you can easily practice on your own.

Once a pane is created, you can grab the split bar with the mouse, and adjust the size of each pane to your preference. Expand objects as necessary and scroll up and down each pane to obtain a picture of the Navigator similar to Figure 5.10.

To remove an existing pane, grab the pane's split handle and move it outside the pane area. For example, to remove the vertical pane you just created, grab the vertical split bar and move it all the way either to the left or to the right of the Navigator window.

5.7.2 SYNCHRONIZING CONTENTS OF EDITORS

Objects in Oracle Forms can be accessed not only from the Navigator, but also from other editors such as the Layout Editor or the Menu Editor. All these editors may be open at the same time during the development process. It is understandable to require that if an object is selected, say, in Layout Editor, the correspondent entry in the Navigator must be selected, and vice-versa. The Object Navigator has an option which allows you to synchronize the contents of these editors with the selections in the Navigator. When the Synchronize option is on, selecting any item in the Navigator simultaneously selects that item in the other editors.

To set the Synchronize option, select Navigator | Synchronize from the menu. This is a check menu item. If it is checked, synchronizing is on, otherwise it is off. If the Synchronize option is off, then the selections in the Navigator are independent of those in the Layout and Menu Editors.

> ## Note
>
> Most of the time you want the synchronization on, but there are occasions when it becomes handy to turn it off. Suppose, for example, that you have selected several items in the Layout Editor for alignment and resizing purposes. Suddenly you realize that you need to look up the properties of another item which is displayed in the Navigator window. If the Synchronize option is on and you click the item in the Navigator, that item will also be selected in the Layout Editor, thus deselecting all your previous items. This problem does not occur if Synchronize is off.

5.8 SUMMARY

This chapter explained the components and properties of the Object Navigator. It also focused on the different actions that you can perform in this environment. Some key concepts covered include the following:

- ❑ How to access Object Navigator
- ❑ Components of Object Navigator
  - ❑ Node Display Area
  - ❑ Find Field
  - ❑ Context List
  - ❑ Toolbar
- ❑ Object types
- ❑ Object instances
- ❑ Navigating and selecting objects in the Navigator
  - ❑ Navigating and selecting objects
  - ❑ Selecting multiple objects
  - ❑ Expanding and collapsing nodes
  - ❑ Marking objects
- ❑ Working with objects in the Navigator
  - ❑ Creating and deleting objects
  - ❑ Copying, cutting, and pasting
  - ❑ Moving and renaming objects
- ❑ Different Views of the Object Navigator
  - ❑ Ownership View
  - ❑ Visual View
  - ❑ Displaying only objects that contain PL/SQL code
- ❑ Customizing the Object Navigator
  - ❑ Working with mulitple panes
  - ❑ Synchronizing contents of editors

LAYOUT EDITOR

"Right now a moment of time is fleeting by! Capture its reality in paint!"
—Paul Cézanne

- ◆ Accessing Layout Editor
- ◆ Components of Layout Editor
- ◆ Working with Objects in Layout Editor
- ◆ Setting Visual Attributes in Layout Editor
- ◆ Customizing the Layout Editor
- ◆ Customizing Drawing Options
- ◆ Customizing Color Palettes
- ◆ Summary

The Layout Editor allows Oracle Forms developers to graphically view, access, and modify the interface objects of their applications. These objects establish and maintain the communication of users with their data in database structures. When creating a landscape, artists paint on a canvas. When the work is completed, the canvas is framed and exhibited to viewers. Metaphorically, creating an Oracle Forms application is a similar process. The Layout Editor provides you with the tools to create and paint different objects on a canvas. The canvas then is "framed", or attached to a window. It is through a window that users can access the objects of the application at runtime.

Mastery of techniques and functionality of the Layout Editor is even more important because it conforms with the What-You-See-Is-What-You-Get (WYSIWYG) programming paradigm. This means that objects created and modified at design time in the editor will have the same look and feel that users will see at runtime.

6.1 ACCESSING LAYOUT EDITOR

As mentioned earlier, the Layout Editor allows for the creating and editing of visual objects on a canvas. Each instance, or window, of the Layout Editor displays exactly one canvas. Because Forms may utilize more than one canvas, it is possible to have multiple Layout Editor windows, each displaying a different canvas. If there are no canvases in the form, the Layout Editor will create one when invoked. If there is only one canvas, the Layout Editor automatically displays it. If there is more than one canvas, the Designer displays a list of canvases first, from which one can be chosen for editing.

There are several ways to access the Layout Editor in the Forms Designer:

a) Select Tools | Layout Editor... from the Designer menu, or
b) Select Layout Editor... from the popup menu displayed by a right-button mouse click, or
c) In Object Navigator, double-click the Canvas type icon ▣ to the left of the canvas you want to edit.

When a canvas is loaded in a Layout Editor window, the name of the canvas becomes part of the title of that window. This allows you to easily find it in the list of open windows under Window menu and return to this window at a later moment. Although several Layout Editor windows can be open at any one time, it is a good habit to close a window when you finish editing the canvas. You will free precious system resources and make them available for other activities in your environment.

6.2 COMPONENTS OF LAYOUT EDITOR

Figure 6.1 represents a Layout Editor window. This window is made up of several components. The most important one is the layout workarea where objects are created and edited. Above the layout workarea there is a toolbar, and along the left side of the window there is another group of iconic tools, called the tool palette. At the bottom of the window, the status bar displays important information such as mouse position and magnifying level. The following sections provide detailed information for each of these components.

6.2.1 LAYOUT WORKAREA

The layout workarea allows access to all the objects on a canvas. Its size does not depend on the size of the Layout Editor window. If this window is not large enough to display the whole layout workarea, vertical and horizontal scrollbars may be used to navigate to its hidden parts.

The canvas displayed in the layout workarea is an object in itself that is displayed by default. You can hide it by unchecking the View | Show Canvas from

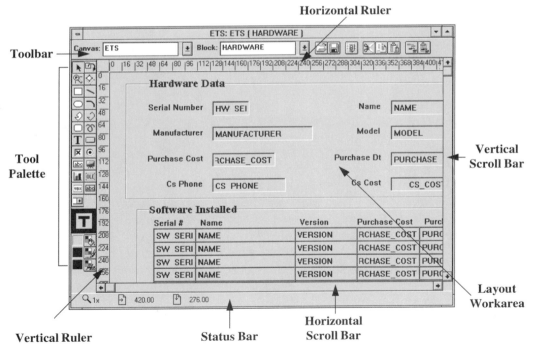

FIGURE 6.1   Components of the Layout Editor window.

the Layout Editor menu. Another basic object that is always present in the Layout Editor window is the view of the canvas. By default the view is hidden, but it can be displayed if needed. To display the view of a canvas check View | Show View menu item from the Layout Editor menu.

Canvases and views go hand in hand in Oracle Forms. Think of the metaphor of the painter creating a landscape. While working, she paints on the canvas. When she is finished, the canvas is framed and some cloth may be wrapped in the back of the frame, invisible to the viewers. The area of the painting smaller than the original canvas and surrounded by the frame is the view of the painting. In Oracle Forms, objects can be created or placed all over the canvas. But only those objects that are within the boundaries of the canvas-view will be seen by the users at runtime.

On top and along the left side of the workarea there are two rulers, also shown in Figure 6.1. These rulers form a system of coordinates for the layout workarea. Its origin is the top left corner of the canvas, and the unit of measurement can be expressed in inches, centimeters, points, or character cells. Points is the default unit. Section 6.5.1 explains how to change the measurement unit.

By expressing the distance of the current mouse position from the origin of coordinates, the rulers assist you in the process of sizing and moving objects. Rulers are displayed by default, but can be hidden by unchecking the View | Rulers menu item.

The current position of the cursor is projected on the rulers in the form of two markers. These are small lines that slide alongside both rulers as the mouse moves in the layout workarea. They are hidden or displayed together with the rulers.

Note

The question is a little more complicated than that. As a matter of fact, Oracle Forms operates with four types of canvases: content, horizontal toolbar, vertical toolbar, and stacked canvases. For content canvases the view size determines the original size of the window on which the canvas is attached. If the window has scrollbars, users can navigate to hidden parts of the canvas, even if they are not inside the view. For stacked views, which are not attached to a window frame, users can see only those objects that are enclosed within the view. Objects outside the view boundaries remain invisible.

So far, you have worked only with content canvases. Chapters 15 and 17 provide additional details on these and other concepts related to windows, canvas-views, and toolbars.

To further assist you in the process of creating, sizing, and moving objects, the Layout Editor provides horizontal and vertical ruler guides. These are dashed lines that can be very useful especially when aligning objects in the workarea. To create a ruler guide, click either the horizontal or the vertical ruler, and, holding the mouse button down, drag the ruler to the desired location. Multiple ruler guides can be created and used. When you don't want to use a guide any longer, simply drag it over the respective ruler to remove it. Ruler guides can also be hidden without being removed. To do this, uncheck the View | Ruler Guides menu item. All the guides will be hidden from sight. When you check the View | Ruler again, the guides appear in the previous positions.

To help position objects in the workarea, the Layout Editor provides a grid. The grid is a set of horizontal and vertical lines that cover the whole workarea. The distance between the lines, also known as the grid density, is specified in the units used by the ruler, and is set in the Ruler Settings dialog box. In Section 6.5.2 you will see how to use the Ruler Settings dialog box. The grid can be hidden from view by unchecking View | Grid menu item. If the canvas is visible, as in Figure 6.1, it will cover the grid.

6.2.2 TOOLBAR

On top of the layout workarea, there is the Layout Editor toolbar. It is shown separately in Figure 6.2.

The toolbar provides quick access to often-used functionality. The first drop-down list box displays all the canvases in the module and allows you to replace the canvas currently displayed in the Layout Editor with another canvas. The second list box maintains all the blocks in the application. It is used to set the context of the Designer when you create items in the Layout Editor window.

The first two buttons are used to open and save form, menu, and PL/SQL library modules. The third button executes the form from the Designer. The last five buttons offer editing functionality for objects and their properties such as cut, copy, and paste. These buttons can be found in other Designer windows such as Object Navigator and Menu Editor.

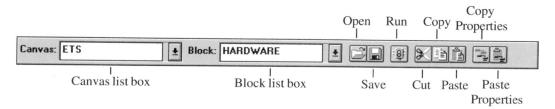

FIGURE 6.2   Layout Editor toolbar.

6.2.3 TOOL PALETTE

Along the left side of the Layout Editor window there is a group of iconic buttons, commonly known as the tool palette. These buttons allow application developers to create new objects on a canvas and modify the appearance of existing ones. Figure 6.3 shows the tool palette of the Layout Editor.

The Select icon ⬛ is used to select objects in the Layout Editor. It is maybe the most important tool because you must select an object first, before moving,

Handle

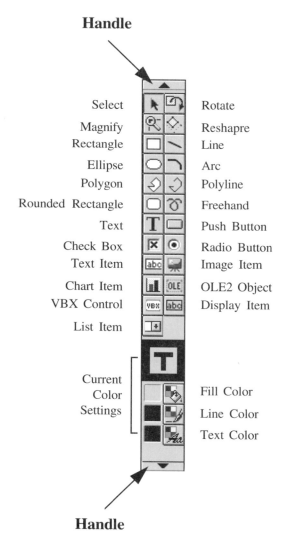

Select	Rotate
Magnify	Reshapre
Rectangle	Line
Ellipse	Arc
Polygon	Polyline
Rounded Rectangle	Freehand
Text	Push Button
Check Box	Radio Button
Text Item	Image Item
Chart Item	OLE2 Object
VBX Control	Display Item
List Item	

Current Color Settings	Fill Color
	Line Color
	Text Color

Handle

FIGURE 6.3   Layout Editor tool palette.

resizing, changing properties, or performing any other action on it. This is also the default tool of the Layout Editor.

The Magnify icon ⊞ is used to modify the view size of the objects. Its functionality is duplicated and complemented by the Zoom In, Zoom Out, Normal Size, and Fit to Window menu items of View menu.

Based on the functionality they provide, the remaining tools can be classified in the following groups:

❑ Tools that create new boilerplate objects on the canvas. This group includes the following tools: Rectangle ▢, Line ◣, Ellipse ▢, Arc ◥, Polygon ◪, Polyline ◪, Rounded Rectangle ▢, Freehand Object ▨, and Text Ⓣ.

❑ Tools that create new items on the canvas. There is one icon for each item type: Push Button ▣, Check Box ⊠, Radio Button ◉, Text Item ▣, Image Item ▣, Chart Item ◫, OLE2 Object ▣, VBX Control ▣, Display Item ▣, and List Item ▣.

❑ Tools that modify visual properties of existing objects. There are five tools that make up this group: Rotate ▣, Reshape ⊠, Fill Color ◪, Line Color ▣, and Text Color ▣.

To activate any of these tools, simply click on them. This allows the functionality associated with the activated tool to execute only once. If the tool must be used repeatedly, double-click on it and perform the operation as many times as necessary. Double-clicking a tool sets it in pinned state. Visually, a red pin appears across the tool button, as in the case of the Rectangle icon shown here: ▣. The tool remains pinned until another tool is selected.

If the Layout Editor window is not big enough to display the whole tool palette, handles appear on top and on the bottom of the palette, as shown in Figure 6.3. Use these handles to scroll the tool palette as necessary.

6.2.4 STATUS BAR

At the bottom of the Layout Editor window there is a status bar that displays information that may come in handy when creating, sizing, moving, and rotating objects in the Layout Editor. The information is presented in the form of small icons followed by digits. When coordinates or dimensions are measured, the digits are units as defined in the ruler settings. Angles are measured in degrees ranging from 0 to 360. The horizontal direction is an angle of 0 degrees. The leftmost icon, which is always present, expresses the current magnification level as a factor of the normal size. A factor of 2x means that the displayed size of objects is 200% of their actual size. A factor of 1/2x means that the currently displayed objects are 50% of their actual size.

The content of the status bar is different for different actions on different objects. Figure 6.4 shows some typical information displayed in the status bar. The

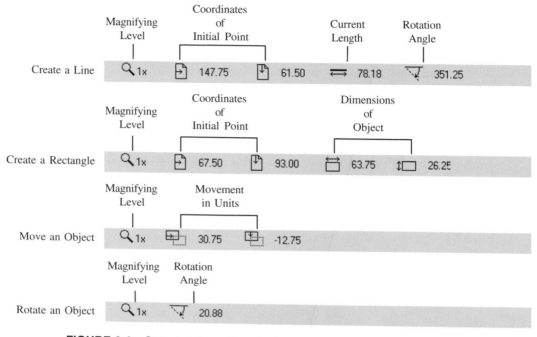

FIGURE 6.4 Sample information displayed by the Layout Editor status bar.

status bar also displays brief information about the iconic buttons in the tool palette. For this, the mouse should be positioned above any of the buttons and not moved for an instant. The Designer displays balloon help next to the button and a longer description of the tool in the status bar. For example, if the mouse is positioned on top of the Select button, the status bar will display the message, Selects objects on the layout.

6.3 WORKING WITH OBJECTS IN LAYOUT EDITOR

This section describes the main actions that can be performed in the Layout Editor. These include such actions as creating different types of objects, selecting, reshaping, and moving them around.

6.3.1 WHAT IS DONE CAN BE UNDONE

Before moving further in the discussion, let us introduce the Undo command. It reverses the last action performed in the Editor. It is a very helpful command that protects the application from accidental and unwanted actions. It is important to understand that Forms implements only a one-level Undo command. This means that if you want to undo something, you should do so immediately after the action or command is executed, without performing anything else in between.

There are two ways to invoke the Undo utility:

a) Select Edit | Undo from the Designer Menu, or

b) Press CTRL+Z from the keyboard. This is also the standard MS Windows Undo command.

In both cases your last action is reversed. When you issue the Undo command, the Undo menu item in the Edit menu changes to Redo.

Like any other command, you can undo the Undo command as well. In other words, the action you wanted to undo can be redone. You can perform the Redo command only if nothing else has happened since your last Undo.

To redo an undone command take any of the following steps:

a) Select Edit | Redo from the Designer Menu, or

b) Press CTRL+Z from the keyboard.

6.3.2 CREATING OBJECTS

Creating objects in the Layout Editor is simply a matter of drawing them where you want on the canvas. All Forms items and most of the boilerplate objects can be created with an easy two-step procedure:

1. Activate the tool icon in the tool palette that corresponds to the type of object you want to create. The cursor changes shape to $+$.

2. Click on the canvas where you want to create the object.

When you release the mouse button a new object is created.

Designer assigns default sizes to newly created objects. But it also allows you to specify their dimensions when you create them. To do this, follow the additional Step 3:

3. While holding the mouse button down, draw the object to the desired size.

A rectangle that will include the new object helps you estimate its size. The width and height of the object are displayed on the status bar.

The procedure to create lines, polygons, polylines, freehand, and text objects is slightly different. To create a line follow these steps:

1. Activate the Line icon in the tool palette.

2. Click on the canvas where you want the line to begin.

3. Hold the mouse button down and move the mouse towards the terminal point of the line. To guide you in the process, Designer draws a virtual line and displays its length and angle on the status bar.

4. Release the mouse button when the other extremity of line is reached. The line is created.

To create polygons or polylines follow this procedure:

1. Activate the Polygon icon or Polyline icon in the tool palette.

2. Click on the canvas where you want the first vertex of the object to be.

3. Click on the canvas where you want each subsequent vertex to be. Note that you do not need to keep the mouse button pressed. As each edge is drawn, Designer displays it on the canvas, and its angle is displayed on the status bar.

4. Double-click when the final vertex is reached.

At this point, the polyline is complete. For the polygon, Designer automatically draws the last edge between the last and first vertices. To draw a freehand object follow these steps:

1. Activate the Freehand Object icon in the tool palette.

2. Click on the canvas where you want the drawing to begin.

3. Hold the mouse button down and draw the object.

4. Release the mouse button when done.

To create a text object on the boilerplate follow these steps:

1. Activate the Text icon in the tool palette.

2. Click on the canvas where you want to create the text object. A box is created and the cursor is positioned inside the box waiting for input.

3. Type the text. The rectangle around the text objects is expanded as needed.

4. When done, click anywhere outside the text object.

To help you create objects of regular shapes, the tools in the Layout Editor can be used in Constraint mode. In this mode, rectangles become squares, ellipses become circles, and lines of any direction become horizontal, vertical, or 45-degree-angle lines. To use a tool in Constraint mode, activate the tool and hold down SHIFT while using it.

6.3.3 SETTING THE CONTEXT OF LAYOUT EDITOR

While boilerplate objects are simply owned by the canvas on which they reside, Oracle Forms items are owned by blocks. This is an important fact that must be kept in mind when creating items in the Layout Editor. It is very common for items from different blocks to share the same canvas. For example, the same canvas in the ETS application holds items that belong to three different blocks: HARDWARE, SOFTWARE, and BUTTON_PALETTE. If you want to add a new push button item to block BUTTON_PALETTE, you need to make sure that the current context of Layout Editor is set to this block.

The context is displayed in the title bar of the Layout Editor window. It can also be seen in the list of open windows under Window menu. Its format is as follows:

FORM_NAME:CANVAS_NAME(BLOCK_NAME)

In the case of Figure 6.1, the Layout Editor context in the ETS form is the ETS canvas and HARDWARE block. Therefore, the window title is ETS:ETS(HARDWARE). Change the block context of the Layout Editor as follows:

1. Click the list button of Block drop-down list box. The list of blocks in the module appears.
2. Select the desired block from the list.

To replace the canvas currently displayed in the Layout Editor window with a different canvas from the same form follow these steps:

1. Click the list button of Canvas drop-down list box. The list of canvases in the module appears.
2. Select the desired canvas from the list.

In the earlier versions of Oracle Forms 4.5, the Canvas and Block list boxes were not in the Layout Editor toolbar. If you have one of these earlier versions of the product, you can use two items from the Arrange menu to set the context in your application. To change the block context proceed as follows:

1. Select Arrange | Set Block... from the menu. A List of Values with the block names in the current form appears.
2. Select the block name from the list.
3. Click OK.

To change the canvas context follow these steps:

1. Select Arrange | Switch... from the menu. A List of Values with names of canvas-views in the current form appears.
2. Select the canvas-view you want to display.
3. Click OK.

> ## Note
>
> When you create items in the Layout Editor, the Object Navigator assigns them generic names and displays them under the appropriate block in the object tree. As explained in the previous chapter, these default names are not very useful, and should be replaced with more explanatory names. Use the Navigator to change names of newly created objects.
>
> Boilerplate objects on the other hand are not assigned any names and do not appear anywhere in the Object Navigator hierarchy tree. They are static objects, attached to the canvas on which they are created. Their properties can be set and modified by directly acting upon them in the Layout Editor but cannot be displayed in property sheets or accessed dynamically at runtime.

In both versions, you cannot replace the content of the Layout Editor with a canvas-view from a different Forms module. You must open a new window to display that canvas.

6.3.4 SELECTING OBJECTS

As mentioned earlier, selecting is probably the most important action in the Layout Editor. Before moving, resizing, cutting, pasting, aligning, or before doing anything with an object, you must first select it. Selecting is also the most frequent action in this Editor. This is the reason why Select is the default tool in the tool palette and why the action of selecting is so easy.

To select an object, just move the mouse on the object and click. When the object is selected, handles appear around it. Handles are dark gray boxes on the corners and middle points of the virtual rectangle that encircles the object. Each object, except for lines, has eight handles. Lines have only two. Figure 6.5 represents handles around an ellipse and a line.

Often, there is the need to select more than one object. Layout Editor provides two ways to select multiple objects. The first one selects one object at a time:

1. Select the first object.
2. Hold down either SHIFT or CTRL and select each additional object.

This method allows you to select only those objects you need, anywhere on the canvas. But, it can be tedious if the number of objects to be selected is large. The second method is used in this case:

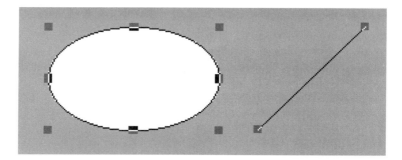

FIGURE 6.5 Selection handles around an ellipse and a line.

1. Place the mouse pointer further to the left and higher up than any object.
2. Holding the mouse button down, draw a virtual selection rectangle large enough to entirely encircle all the objects to be selected.

When you release the mouse button, all the objects completely inside the selecting rectangle are selected. Selecting objects this way is particularly helpful if the objects are adjacent or near each other. However, undesired objects may be selected together with the desired objects. If this is the case, deselect any unwanted objects. To deselect an object follow these steps:

1. Hold down SHIFT or CTRL key.
2. Click the object.

Sometimes, there may be a need to select all the objects on the current canvas. Any of the following two commands can be used to achieve this:

a) Select Edit | Select All from the menu, or
b) Press CTRL+A from the keyboard.

In either case, all the objects on the canvas are selected.

> ## Note
>
> Selecting multiple objects is similar in the Layout Editor and the Object Navigator. The only difference is that the concept of range selections does not exist in the Layout Editor. Therefore SHIFT+CLICK and CTRL+CLICK are synonymous actions here, but are different in the Navigator.

6.3.5 MOVING, RESIZING, AND RESHAPING OBJECTS

As discussed in Section 6.3.2, the Layout Editor allows you to place new objects you create where you want on the canvas. It also allows you to size the object as you create it. Nevertheless, after an object is created, or later, when the application's look is fine-tuned, you may need to move and resize it. You can perform these actions on individual objects or multiple objects simultaneously. The only difference is when you select them. Multiple objects will be moved as a group and, when resized, their dimensions will change proportionally.

To move an object after it is selected follow these steps:

1. Click anywhere inside the object and hold the mouse button down. Make sure not to click one of the handles.
2. While holding the button down, drag the object to the position you want on the canvas. The status bar displays the distance of the current position from the original one.
3. Release the button when you are satisfied with the new position.

You can also use the arrow keys to move an object. Each time the arrow key is pressed, the object moves one unit in the direction of the arrow. If the Grid Snap property is on, the unit is as specified in the Number of Snap Points Per Grid Spacing field of the Ruler Settings dialog box (see Section 6.5.2 for more details about this dialog box). If the Grid Snap property is not set, the unit of movement equals the ruler unit specified in the Ruler Settings dialog box.

To resize an object after it is selected, you must click and drag its handles. If only the width of the object needs to be changed, handles on the vertical edges of selecting rectangle are used. Handles on horizontal edges are used to adjust the object's height. The handles on all four vertices of the selecting rectangle are used to resize an object horizontally and vertically at the same time.

To resize an object proceed as follows:

1. Click the appropriate handle of the object.
2. While holding the button down, drag the handle until the object reaches the desired size. The status bar displays the dimensions of the original object and the dimensions of the current object.
3. Release the mouse button when you are satisfied with the new size of the object.

The Layout Editor allows you to change the shape of three boilerplate objects: polygons, polylines, and freehand drawings. This action is different from resizing because it allows you to change proportions and position of single vertices or parts of these objects, rather than change them proportionally, as a whole.

To reshape an already selected polygon, polyline, or freehand object follow these steps:

> ## Note
>
> As you can see from the actions above, the curves of a freehand object are nothing but polylines with vertices too close to each other. It is a well-known fact in mathematics that curves can be approximated by polylines if their vertices are drawn close enough.

1. Click the Reshape icon ▨ in the tool palette. The selecting rectangle around the object is replaced by selecting handles in each vertex of the object.
2. Click the desired handle and drag it to the new position.
3. Repeat these steps as necessary.

You can reshape only one object at a time. If you attempt to use the Reshape tool when multiple objects are selected, you will get the Oracle Forms message VGS-206: More than one object selected. If the Reshape tool is used with any of the other objects on the canvas, it simply resizes the object.

6.3.6 ALIGNING OBJECTS

When objects are moved around the canvas, it is difficult to keep them aligned and spaced properly. Although these may seem to be superfluous issues that are not directly related to the main functionality of the application, they are also known to affect the users reaction to the interface of the application. The Layout Editor provides several alignment settings for objects on a canvas. The process itself is simple:

1. Select the objects to align.
2. Select Arrange | Align Objects... from the menu. The Alignment Settings dialog box appears (see Figure 6.6).
3. Specify the alignment settings according to your application needs.
4. Click OK.

The selected objects are aligned according to the settings you specified.

If you want to align other objects using the same settings proceed as follows:

1. Select the objects to align.
2. Select Arrange | Repeat Alignment from the menu, or press CTRL+L from the keyboard.

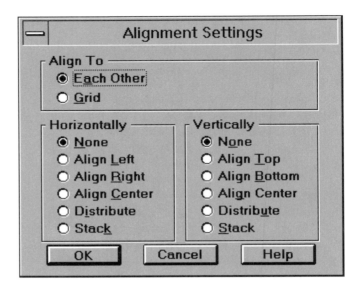

FIGURE 6.6   Alignment Settings dialog box.

Once set, the alignment settings will remain in effect for the canvas until they are reset, or the module is closed. The settings will remain in effect even if the Layout Editor window holding that canvas is closed.

The Alignment Settings dialog box has two mutually exclusive modes of aligning objects: Align to Each Other and Align to Grid. Align to Each Other mode aligns objects with respect to each other. Two or more objects must be selected for this mode to be active. Objects can be aligned vertically or horizontally. For each direction, there is a set of six exclusive options that can be specified.

❑ **None** is chosen by default for both horizontal and vertical alignments, meaning that by default no alignment occurs. If you want to align objects, some settings must be specified beforehand.

❑ **Align Left** means that the left side of each selected object will be aligned with the left side of the left-most object. Align Right, Align Top, and Align Bottom have similar meaning for the respective directions.

❑ **Align Center** aligns the middle-point handles of selected objects on a common center line between them.

❑ **Distribute** spreads selected objects in the horizontal or vertical direction so that there is an equal distance between them. The left-most and right-most objects are not moved for Horizontally Distribute option. The top-most and bottom-most objects are not moved for Vertically Distribute option.

❑ **Stack** aligns objects so that there is no space between them in the respective direction. Combined with other options, Stack can be used to create adjacent rows or columns of objects.

Figure 6.7 displays the outcome of Align command for three push button objects, for a few alignment settings.

As mentioned earlier, each of the six horizontal alignment settings can be combined with any of the six vertical ones. Therefore, there are thirty-six different ways to align a group of selected objects with respect to each other. You may want to practice your aligning skills by experimenting with each of them.

Align to Grid mode allows you to align one or more objects with respect to the grid lines. For example, Align Left will move the selected object so that its left side falls in the closest vertical grid line. Align Top will snap the top side of an object to the closest horizontal line. Similar actions result from Align Right and Align Bottom settings. Align Center will place the center handles of the object on the closest horizontal or vertical grid line.

Align to Grid affects each object individually. Even if multiple objects are selected, each of them will be moved to the closest grid line, according to specified settings. If View | Grid Snap option is set, the Align to Grid settings do not

Horizontally	Vertically	Outcome
None	None	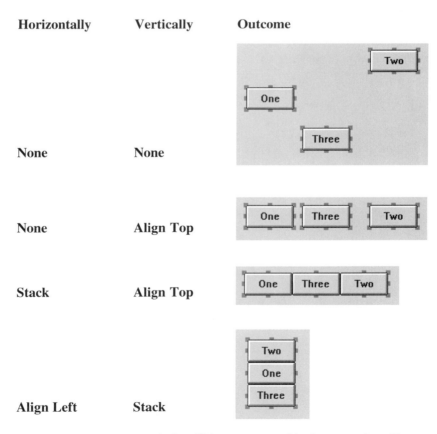
None	Align Top	
Stack	Align Top	
Align Left	Stack	

FIGURE 6.7 Outcome of Align Objects command for four sample settings.

result in any position changes, because the sides of objects are already along grid lines. However, this mode of alignment is independent from Grid Snap settings.

6.3.7 SETTING OBJECTS TO SAME SIZE

As said, alignment of canvas objects plays an important role in the overall look and feel of an application. Setting objects to the same size is equally important. Modern GUI development practices emphasize the use of standards across applications. One of these important standards is that the size of identical or similar objects should be the same. Forms Designer provides extended functionality to help developers size objects uniformly. Set objects to the same size as follows:

1. Select the desired objects.
2. Select Arrange | Size Objects... from the menu. The Size Objects dialog box appears (see Figure 6.8).
3. Specify the sizing settings according to your needs.
4. Click OK.

The selected objects are sized according to the settings you specified.

If you want to size other objects using the same settings follow these steps:

1. Select the objects to size.
2. Select Arrange | Repeat Sizing from the menu.

Once set, the sizing settings will remain in effect for the canvas until they are reset or the module is closed. The settings will remain in effect even if the Layout Editor window with that canvas is closed.

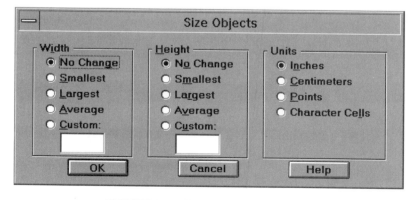

FIGURE 6.8 Size Objects dialog box.

The Size Objects dialog box allows you to set the width and height of selected objects. For each of the dimensions, one setting can be chosen out of five available options. By default, No Change is selected. If Smallest is set, the width or height of all selected objects will be set to that of the object with the smallest dimension. Largest option sets the dimension to the highest value of dimensions for all selected objects. If Average is selected, then Designer computes an arithmetic average of the appropriate dimension for all selected objects and sets this dimension to the computed average.

You can also specify exactly how many units of measurements the dimensions for each object will be. To do this, click the Custom radio button and enter the size or width or height in the field below. The units of measurement are those of the Layout Editor grid. You can specify them in the Units column to the right. Inches is the default unit. The Size Objects dialog box allows you to set these units in any case, but they are meaningful only if custom width or height dimension settings are specified.

Figure 6.9 presents effects of Size Objects command on three push button objects, for sample settings.

6.3.8 DELETING OBJECTS

To delete objects in the Layout Editor, you must first select them. Then

a) Press DELETE key in the keyboard, or
b) Select Edit | Clear from the menu.

In both cases, the objects will be removed from the canvas and, simultaneously, from the Navigator's hierarchy tree.

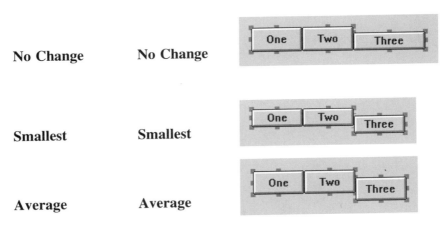

FIGURE 6.9   Outcome of Size Objects command for three sample settings.

The effects of accidentally issuing the Delete command in the Layout Editor are not as severe as in the Object Navigator. Fortunately, there is the Undo that saves the day. As long as you do not perform any other actions since the accidental delete, the Undo command will restore the objects unintentionally deleted on the canvas. Remember that you cannot do this if the objects are deleted from the Navigator.

6.3.9 CUTTING AND COPYING OBJECTS

Cutting and copying in the Layout Editor is very similar to the same actions in the Navigator. A copy of the object will be placed in the clipboard and will remain there until the next cut or copy operation. To cut an object or group of objects from the canvas do one of two things:

    a) Press CTRL+X, or
    b) Select Edit | Cut from the menu.

Selected objects will be removed from the canvas and the Navigator object tree and placed in the clipboard. If you want to place just a copy of the objects in the clipboard, without removing them from the existing position in the form, then use the Copy command. You can copy an already selected object or group of objects

    a) Press CTRL+C, or
    b) Select Edit | Copy from the menu.

6.3.10 PASTING AND DUPLICATING OBJECTS

To duplicate an object in the Layout Editor, first select it, then choose Edit | Duplicate from the menu. A duplicate copy is created beside the current selection. Duplicate will replicate the selected object on the same canvas as the original one. For a more flexible replication scheme, a combination of Cut or Copy and Paste is used.

To Paste an object to a target location, first place it in the clipboard by either copying or cutting it. If you want to Copy the object to a different canvas, switch to the Layout Editor window that contains that canvas if it is already loaded, or open a new window to display it. Paste the objects from the clipboard in one of the following ways:

    a) Press CTRL+V, or
    b) Select Edit | Paste from the menu.

Pasted object will be placed in exactly the same location on the canvas as their original versions. If pasting within the same canvas, the objects will overlap, with the new one immediately on top of the existing object. You will have to move the newly pasted object to the desired location.

If when pasting to a different canvas, the position of the new object falls outside the canvas' boundaries, the Designer will display the message, One or more Object will extend off the canvas.

Finally, to close this section, note that when items are created, whether new from scratch or copied from existing objects, the Layout Editor will assign them generic names. To change these names to more meaningful ones, either rename the items in the Object Navigator, or double-click the object to display its property sheet and change its name there. The following chapter provides detailed information about Properties Window.

6.3.11 GROUPING AND UNGROUPING OBJECTS

Often, during the process of laying out a form, it may be convenient to treat several separate objects as one single object. For example, after certain items are aligned and sized, you would want to move them together, with one single operation, rather than moving each one separately, and then having to repeat the realignment process. Grouping is the process that combines two or more selected objects into one larger entity that includes these objects. To perform this operation, select the objects that will be grouped. Proceed as follows:

a) Select Arrange | Group from the menu, or
b) Press CTRL+G.

Visually, you will notice that all the selecting handles around individual objects will disappear and will be replaced by handles of a selecting rectangle that includes all the grouped objects. This rectangle will represent the newly grouped objects. It can be considered as a single object, and you can perform on it all moving, sizing, cutting, pasting, and other actions that you want to perform on each individual member of the group.

To select a group, click any of its members once. Selecting handles will appear around the virtual rectangle that includes all objects in the group. If you need to select a particular member of the group, click that object a second time.

If an object is already selected and you want to know its parent group, choose Arrange | Group Operations | Select Parent from the Designer menu. If the object is not a member of any group, Designer will display the message VGS-213: Object has no parent. But, if the object is already grouped, its parent group will be selected.

If a group is already selected and you need to select all its children as individual objects, choose Arrange | Group Operations | Select Children from the Designer menu. Selecting handles will appear around each group member.

To add new objects to an existing group follow these steps:

1. Select the group.
2. SHIFT+CLICK or CTRL+CLICK each object to be added to the group.
3. Choose Arrange | Group Operations | Add to Group from the menu.

Step 3 above can be replaced by either of the following steps:

a) Choose Arrange | Group from the menu, or
b) Press CTRL+G from the keyboard.

In all cases, the resulting group will be expanded to include the new members.

A group may contain individual objects, but also other groups. The grouping operation Add to Group described above acts only upon individual objects that have not been previously included in other groups. If you need to include existing groups in groups of a higher hierarchy, select Arrange | Group from the menu or press CTRL+G from the keyboard. Figure 6.10 presents a situation when both commands would result in the same group.

In the situation presented in this figure, objects A and B have been previously grouped under Group One. Objects C and D can be merged with Group One to a larger Group Two following either of the methods presented above.

Figure 6.11 presents a situation where only CTRL+G or Arrange | Group command can be used.

This situation differs from the previous one in that there are two additional objects, E and F, already grouped under Group Three that must be grouped with the other objects. Attempting to use Arrange | Group Operations | Add to Group in this case would result in the message, **VGS-207: Must select exactly one group.**

Objects bundled together in a group can be ungrouped as well. To remove one or more objects from an existing group follow these steps:

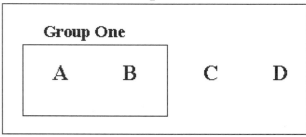

FIGURE 6.10   Situation where Add to Group command is the same as Group.

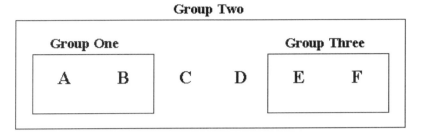

FIGURE 6.11 Situation where Add to Group command is different from Group.

1. Select the group.
2. Select the objects to be removed from the group.
3. Choose Arrange|Group Operations|Remove from Group from the Designer menu.

Ungrouping is another way to break up the structure of an existing group. To ungroup, first select the desired group then follow these steps:

a) Select Arrange|Ungroup from the menu, or
b) Press CTRL+U from the keyboard.

Here, again, there is a difference between Ungroup and Remove from Group operations. Look again at Figure 6.11. If in this situation Group Three is removed from Group Two, then the resulting structure of Group Two will be similar to Figure 6.10. However, if Group Two is ungrouped, the outcome would be two separate groups, Group One and Group Three, and two separate atomic objects C and D. Group Two will no longer exist. Clearly, these operations produce different results.

The group names in Figure 6.10 and Figure 6.11 are provided only for clarity purposes. Forms maintains the identity of groups internally; no names are assigned to them, and you cannot access them in the Designer. Finally, note that a different type of groups encountered in Forms are radio groups. They group together radio group items to ensure that only one value is chosen from a number of choices. Radio groups are discussed in Chapter 14.

6.3.12 ROTATING OBJECTS

It was mentioned earlier that boilerplate objects are used to enhance the look of Forms applications. To increase the variety of shapes and objects that can be built on a canvas, the Layout Editor allows rotating these objects to any angle from the original position. To rotate a boilerplate object or group of objects, first select them. Then proceed as follows:

1. Select the Rotate icon ▨ from the tool palette.
2. Click any of the handles and hold the mouse button down.
3. While holding the mouse down, drag the handle to the new position.
4. When the object is rotated as desired, release the mouse button.

During rotating operations, Designer displays a virtual rectangle that encircles the selected object or group of objects, and follows your mouse movements. Designer also displays a line connecting the current clicked handle and the center of this rectangle. The status bar displays the current rotation angle in degrees.

If, during rotation, part of the selected objects falls outside the layout workarea, the Designer will display the message, **One or more objects will extend off the canvas. Operation disallowed.**, and will cancel the action.

6.3.13 WORKING WITH OVERLAPPING OBJECTS

The Layout Editor allows developers to create several basic drawing objects. But creative use of these objects allows for a variety of designs to be created on the canvas. For example, the *Clair de Lune* by a certain yet-to-be-discovered painter shown in Figure 6.12 is created by using the rectangle, circle, and freehand object of Figure 6.13. These basic objects are copied, resized, moved around, and colored appropriately, but the fact remains that only three simple objects were used.

Overlapping objects is a technique often used to create additional boilerplate drawings. The moon in Figure 6.12 is nothing more than a copy of the initial circle, colored blue, and positioned on top of the white-colored circle, shifted a little bit.

Overlapping objects form a stack. You see only the view from the top of this stack. Objects can be moved up and down the stack to create different images or visual illusions. There are four helpful operations to help developers in the process:

FIGURE 6.12   Clair de Lune...

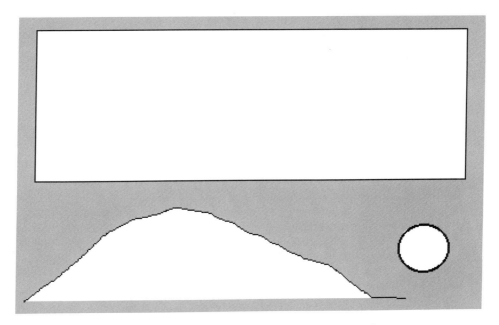

FIGURE 6.13 ...and the objects used to create it.

❑ Bring to Front moves the selected object to the top of the stack, above every other overlapping object. To bring to front an already selected object or group of objects do one of two things:
 a) Select Arrange | Bring to Front from the menu, or
 b) Press CTRL+SHIFT+B from the keyboard.

❑ Send to Back moves the selected object at the bottom of the stack, immediately above the canvas. To send to back an already selected object or group of objects do one of two things:
 a) Select Arrange | Send to Back from the menu, or
 b) Press CTRL+SHIFT+S from the keyboard.

❑ Move Forward moves the selected object one level up the stack, that is above the object that was immediately overlapping it. To move forward an already selected object or group of objects do one of two things:
 a) Select Arrange | Move Forward from the menu, or
 b) Press CTRL+SHIFT+F from the keyboard.

❑ Move Backward moves the selected object one level down the stack, under the object it was overlapping. To move backward an already selected object or group of objects do one of two things:
 a) Select Arrange | Move Backward from the menu, or
 b) Press CTRL+SHIFT+C from the keyboard.

6.4 SETTING VISUAL ATTRIBUTES IN THE LAYOUT EDITOR

Each object in the Layout Editor has a variety of properties. Some of these properties define its functionality and behavior, others define the appearance of the object. Properties of the first type are called functional properties. Only Forms items can have functional properties. Properties of the second type are known as visual attributes of an object. All objects on a canvas, items, and boilerplate objects, have visual attributes. Visual attributes are the text, color, and pattern properties of an object. This section discusses how to set and modify them in the Layout Editor.

6.4.1 FONT ATTRIBUTES

Font attributes include the font name, size, and style. By default all text items and labels on the canvas are created using the System font, but you can change the font settings for any item or boilerplate object:

1. Select the object or group of objects that you want to modify.
2. Choose Format | Font... from the menu. Font dialog box appears (see Figure 6.14).
3. Specify font settings such as name, type, style, size, and special effects.
4. Click OK.

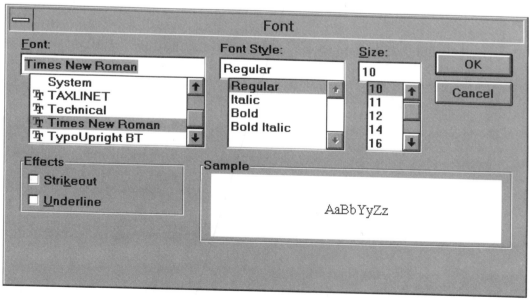

FIGURE 6.14 Font dialog box.

> ## Note
>
> Some fonts may be specific to the installation of Windows in your machine, which may be different from what the users have. Furthermore, the appearance and size of non-TrueType fonts depends on the resolution of the Windows desktop (640x480, 800x600, 1024x768, etc.). Therefore, it is important that you develop your applications in those fonts and resolutions that are available and used by the users' community.

Font attributes of the selected objects will change according to your specifications.

The main components of the Font dialog box are the lists of options from which attributes settings can be selected. The list on the left displays all the fonts available to your application. Windows TrueType fonts are preceded by the indicator **T**. TrueType fonts have enough variety and scalability to meet virtually all the needs of your applications. They allow you to set different sizes and styles for text items on the canvas, thus making the applications look better and feel more user-friendly. Some fonts used frequently are Arial, Courier New, and Times New Roman. You can add additional TrueType fonts to further enhance your Windows applications.

The list in the middle allows you to select the Font Style. It can be regular, **bold**, *italic*, or ***bold italic***. The list to the right allows you to specify the size of the chosen font. Usually, only TrueType fonts support different sizes of their characters. For example, Times New Roman font shown in Figure 6.14, supports a whole range of font sizes, but System font, which is not TrueType, supports only characters of size 10.

On the lower left corner of the Font dialog box you can specify two additional font attributes: Underline and Strikeout. If the check boxes are marked, then the text will have <u>underline</u> and ~~strikeout~~ effects respectively.

The Font dialog box offers you a chance to see the outcome of your selections in the Sample field. In this field, you can see what the text objects you are modifying will look like, before actually making the changes.

6.4.2 SPACING AND ALIGNMENT SETTINGS

Besides setting font attributes, you can also specify spacing and alignment settings for text labels on the canvas. Spacing applies only to boilerplate text objects, and it does not have any effect on text items. It affects the distance between lines of text, therefore, it will have a visual effect only on multiline text labels. To set the text spacing follow these steps:

FIGURE 6.15   Items of Format|Spacing menu.

1. Select the object or group of objects that you want to modify.
2. Choose Format | Spacing from the menu. A list of radio button menu items appears (see Figure 6.15).
3. Select the setting that meets your needs.

By default, text is single-spaced. Designer allows you to quickly space text at 1.5 lines and double lines. If you are not satisfied with these settings, you can specify custom spacing parameters. To do so, follow Steps 1 and 2 above, and select Custom... from the menu items of Format | Spacing. Custom Spacing dialog box will appear (see Figure 6.16).

You can set the distance between lines of text to 6, 12, or 18 points. You can also check Other radio button and specify any number of points in the field to the right. Specifying 0 points is equivalent to Format | Spacing | Single; 6 points to Format | Spacing 1½; and 12 points to Format | Spacing | Double.

Alignment settings control whether the boilerplate text objects or text items display text aligned to the left, center, or right. Other forms of text on the canvas such as labels for radio button or check box items are not affected visually by the alignment settings. By default, Oracle Forms aligns text to the left. Follow these steps to set the alignment:

1. Select the object or group of objects whose text you want to align.
2. Choose Format | Alignment from the menu. A list of radio button menu items appears (see Figure 6.17).
3. Select either Left, Center, or Right.

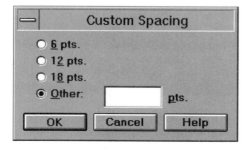

FIGURE 6.16   Custom Spacing dialog box.

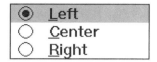

FIGURE 6.17 Items of Format|Alignment menu.

Note that settings for fonts, spacing, and alignment not only apply to the currently selected objects, but become the default setting for objects that you create thereafter.

6.4.3 COLOR ATTRIBUTES

The Layout Editor allows you to change the color of border lines, background, and text of objects. The tools that perform these operations are located in the bottom part of the tool palette.

Before modifying the color settings of an object, you must first select it. To change the background color and pattern, click the Fill Color icon ▣; to change the borderline color, click Line Color icon ▣; finally, to change the text color, click Text Color icon ▣. In all cases, a color palette will appear, similar to the Fill Color palette shown in Figure 6.18.

Move the mouse pointer around the palette to search for the color you want. As you do so, the colored box to the left of the button you clicked will display the color. The sample square on top will also update its color with the color currently pointed at by the mouse. Once you find a good color that you like, click on it. The fill, line, or text color will change according to your specifications.

From the Fill Color palette, you can also change the background pattern of the selected object. To do so, click the Patterns... menu item. The Fill Pattern Palette dialog box will appear (Figure 6.19).

Selecting a pattern here is similar to selecting a color from the color palette. By default, the pattern is black on white. If you want to change, it click the drop-down list buttons. This action displays the color palette from which you can select a replacement for these colors. When satisfied with your changes, close the dialog box.

FIGURE 6.18 Fill Color palette.

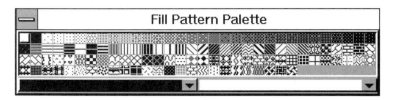

FIGURE 6.19   Fill Pattern Palette.

For Fill Color you can also specify the No Fill option. In this case, the background will not have a fill color. Similarly, for Line Color you can specify the No Line option, which removes the border line from the object. This option is meaningless for the Text Color tool, therefore it is not available.

By default, the color palettes for all three tools pop up when the tool icon is clicked and are closed by the next mouse click, no matter whether a color selection was made or not. To keep the color palette displayed until you decide to dismiss it, select Tear Off Palette menu item, which is present in all the palettes. This places the palette in a dialog box like the Fill Pattern Palette dialog box shown in Figure 6.19.

As with fonts, spacing, and alignment settings, color settings discussed in this paragraph will apply to all the objects that will be created subsequently, after the changes take effect.

6.4.4 LINE AND BORDER ATTRIBUTES

The Layout Editor provides additional functionality that developers can use to enhance the image of boilerplate objects. The features presented in this section apply only to borders of boilerplate objects and objects created with the line, polyline, and freehand tools. They do not apply to items.

First, border lines of these objects can have different thickness. Follow these steps to change the width of the lines:

Note

Like fonts, colors may vary from workstation to workstation. The first 4x4 grid on the color palette represents the basic sixteen colors that are found in every Windows configuration. The purity of other colors will depend on the Windows setup. It is important that you know the configuration of your users' environment.

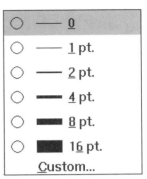

FIGURE 6.20   Items of Format|Line menu.

1. Select the object or group of objects whose border lines you want to change.
2. Choose Format | Line from the menu. A list of radio button menu items appears (see Figure 6.20).
3. Select the appropriate setting for the width of selected lines.

Designer lists six commonly used width settings, from which you can choose one that suits your needs. You can also directly set the line width by choosing Custom... option from the above menu. The Custom Line Width dialog box appears (see Figure 6.21). Here you can specify the line width in inches, centimeters, or points.

The process of changing the width of lines, polylines, and freehand objects is identical. Rectangles you create on the canvas can have a 3D look if their *Bevel* properties are set. To do this follow these steps:

1. Select the rectangle on the canvas.
2. Choose Format | Bevel from the menu. A list of radio button menu items appears.
3. Select the appropriate bevel for the rectangle.

Note that if thickness of line is set to the default, 0 points, the rectangle cannot have any bevel. Figure 6.22 shows how a boilerplate rectangle looks when each of the bevel options is set.

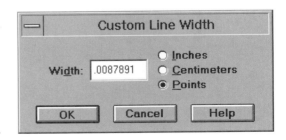

FIGURE 6.21   Custom Line Width dialog box.

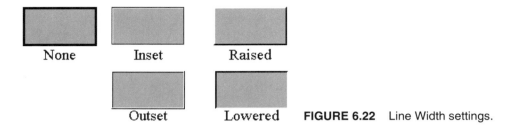

None   Inset   Raised

Outset   Lowered   **FIGURE 6.22** Line Width settings.

As mentioned, bevel settings can be specified for rectangles only. Nevertheless, using overlapping techniques discussed in Section 6.3.13, 3D rectangles can be used as background for other boilerplate objects and items that do not have a 3D look inherently. Items such as text items, radio buttons, and check boxes, come beveled by default. Their bevel settings can be changed by accessing their properties, as explained in Chapters 13 and 14.

By default, borders of boilerplate objects, as well as lines, polylines, and freehand drawings, are solid lines. The Layout Editor allows you to use a variety of dashed lines as well:

1. Select the object you want to modify
2. Choose Format | Dash from the menu. A list of radio button menu items appears (see Figure 6.23).
3. Select the appropriate dashed line.

Note that dashed lines must have default width. Also, note that objects with dashed border lines cannot have bevel settings specified.

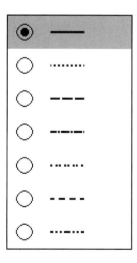

FIGURE 6.23 Items of Format|Dash menu.

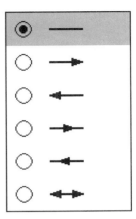

FIGURE 6.24 Items of Format|Arrow menu.

The Layout Editor also allows drawing arrows of different types. Only line objects can be transformed in arrows. To do this, follow these steps:

1. Select the line to be transformed into an arrow.
2. Choose Format | Arrow from the menu. A list of radio button menu items appears (see Figure 6.24).
3. Select the appropriate arrow type.

As with other settings explained in the previous two paragraphs, border and line settings discussed here not only apply to the selected objects, but will be default setting for all the objects that will be created in the future.

6.5 CUSTOMIZING THE LAYOUT EDITOR

Once you become familiar with the Layout Editor, you may want to customize some of its settings. The following sections explain the main activities you can do to make this Editor better suit the needs of your application.

6.5.1 CUSTOMIZING LAYOUT WORKAREA

There are two parameters of the Layout workarea that can be customized: size and page direction. The size is the height and width of the workarea, expressed in inches or centimeters. The page direction instructs the File | Print command to print pages left to right or top to bottom. If you want to see the page borders on the screen, check View | Page Breaks from the Layout Editor menu.

To change the Layout workarea settings select View | Settings | Layout... from the menu. The Layout Settings dialog box appears (see Figure 6.25).

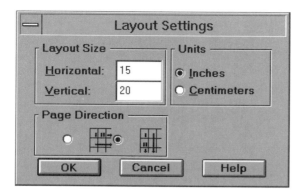

FIGURE 6.25   Layout Settings dialog box.

This dialog box displays the current size and page direction settings. The default size of the layout workarea is 15 inches wide by 20 inches long. The default page direction is top to bottom. When changing the dimensions of the workarea, make sure that all the existing objects will fit in the newly sized canvas. The Layout Editor will not move them automatically if they fall outside boundaries, and their behavior and properties may be unpredictable. Obviously, you will not be able to create new objects outside the layout workarea.

6.5.2 CUSTOMIZING RULER SETTINGS

The settings you can customize for rulers are the unit of measurement, the grid spacing, and the number of snap points per grid. To view or change these settings, choose the View | Settings | Rulers... item from the Layout Editor menu. The Ruler Settings dialog box appears (see Figure 6.26). It shows the current settings of the parameters for the canvas displayed in the Layout Editor.

The upper part of the Ruler Settings dialog box is where the rulers' units are specified. They can be inches, centimeters, points, or character cells. If the last unit is used, then the fields on the right are used to specify the size of each character cell in points. The default settings for units and character cell size are form properties. They can be accessed and set in the dialog box associated with the property *Coordinate Information* of the current form.

The middle part of the Ruler Settings dialog box is where you specify the grid spacing, or the distance between grid lines. You can choose any of the five predetermined settings on the left. You can also enter any value you desire by clicking Other radio button and entering the value in the field to its right. In the case of Figure 6.26, the grid lines will be 12 points apart.

The lower part of the Ruler Settings dialog box allows you to set the number of snap points allowed between the grid lines. If the Grid Snap property of the canvas is set, then the ratio between the Grid Spacing and Number of Grid Points per Grid spacing becomes the basic unit of measurement. If for example,

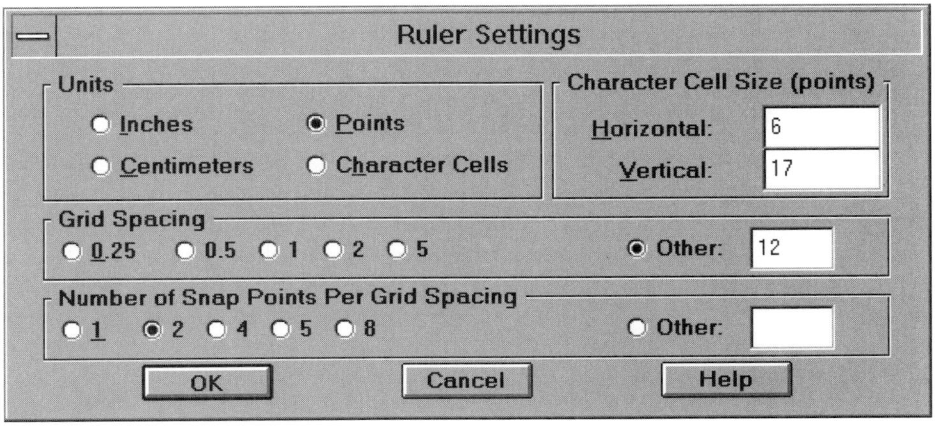

FIGURE 6.26 Ruler Settings dialog box.

the ruler unit is inches, the grid spacing is 1 inch, and the number of snap points is 4, then the smallest distance an object can be moved in any direction is ¼ of an inch (grid spacing divided by number of snap points per grid spacing). Similarly, the smallest dimension of any newly created object will be ¼ of an inch. Distances and dimensions will now be multiples of ¼ of an inch. In other words, a line can be ½ inch or 2.75 inches long, but not 2⅓ inches long. Thus, when Grid Snap is on, the ratio between grid spacing and number of grid points per grid spacing defines a new virtual coordinate system, or grid, that is coarser than the base system. When the Grid Snap property is not set, then the previous settings do not affect the dimensions of, or distances between, objects in the Layout Editor.

6.5.3 CUSTOMIZING THE APPEARANCE OF THE LAYOUT EDITOR

The Layout Editor can be used in different magnification levels: the higher the magnification level, the larger the objects will look on the screen. To increase the magnification level of the Editor proceed as follows:

Note

Turning the Grid Snap property on does not affect the position or dimensions of existing objects.

1. Select the Magnify icon ▧ in the tool palette.
2. Click anywhere on the canvas.
3. The current size of the layout is doubled.

A synonymous way to magnify the current layout is to select View I Zoom In from the Editor's menu. To reduce the magnification level of the Layout Editor choose View I Zoom Out from the menu. Each zoom out reduces the layout size in half.

If you get too carried away zooming in and out and lose track of the original size of the objects, then select View I Normal Size from the menu. If you select View I Fit to Window from the menu, the whole layout workarea is reduced to fit in the current Layout Editor window. Remember that the size of this area is defined in Layout Settings dialog box (see Figure 6.25).

You also have the option to hide and display certain components of the Layout Editor window such as the tool palette, status bar, page breaks, canvas, and view. Their display status is controlled by checking menu items under the View menu. For example to hide the tool palette, uncheck View I Tool Palette. By default, the tool palette, status bar, and canvas are displayed, while page breaks and the view are not.

6.6 CUSTOMIZING DRAWING OPTIONS

You can change the way objects are drawn in general, and the way arcs, rounded rectangles, and text objects are created, in particular. You can also change the way images are treated by the Designer.

6.6.1 GENERAL DRAWING OPTIONS

To view or modify general drawing options, select Format I Drawing Options I General... from the Layout Editor menu. The General Drawing Options dialog box appears (see Figure 6.27). It shows the current settings of these options.

The Cap Style area of this dialog box specifies how endpoints of lines should be rendered. The Join Style applies to rectangles and specifies how their corners should be rendered. The Object Creation is where you specify how new objects are drawn on the canvas. Recall from the discussion earlier in the chapter that one way to create an object in the Layout Editor is to select the appropriate tool from the palette, click on the canvas, and draw the object to the desired size. If Draw from Corner option is selected, as in Figure 6.27, the point where you click the mouse initially is the corner of the new object. If Draw from Center is set instead, the clicking point becomes the center of the object.

Draw from Corner is the default option. When the Draw from Center option is initially set, the boilerplate object icons in the tool palette, that are affected by the change, display a little plus sign in their center. Now, the Rectangle tool looks

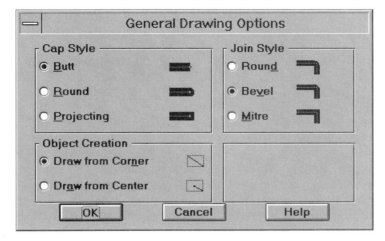

FIGURE 6.27 General Drawing Options dialog box.

like 🔳, the ellipse tool looks like 🔳, and the rounded rectangle tool looks like 🔳. After they are used for the first time, they assume the usual look. The objects that are not affected by setting Draw from Center option are lines, polylines, polygons, arcs, and freehand drawings.

6.6.2 ARC DRAWING OPTIONS

To view or modify arc drawing options, choose Format | Drawing Options | Arc... from the menu. The Arc Drawing Option dialog box appears (see Figure 6.28). The current settings for these options are displayed. The upper half of this dialog

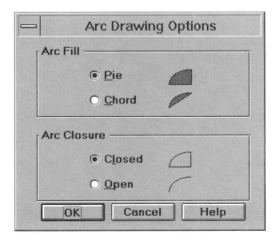

FIGURE 6.28 Arc Drawing Options dialog box.

box, Arc Fill, specifies which part of the canvas region defined by the arc will be the fill region for the arc. Pie option sets the fill region for the arc to the quarter of the ellipse or circle described by the arc. Chord option sets it to the area bound by the arc itself and the chord that connects its two endpoints.

The lower half of the dialog box, Arc Closure, allows you to specify the border lines for the fill region defined by the arc. The arc itself will always be a border line for the region. If Open option is set, the arc is the only border line. If Closed is set instead, borders will also include the segment lines that define the cord or pie fill region of the arc.

The fill region for an arc should be considered like the interior of any other object on the canvas. You can change its color and pattern by using the Fill Color icon ▓ from the palette. In particular, if all you want to display is the arc line, set the Arc Closure option to Open and set the fill color to No Fill, as explained previously in this chapter.

6.6.3 TEXT DRAWING OPTIONS

To view or modify text drawing options, choose Format | Drawing Options | Text... from the menu. The Text Drawing Option dialog box appears (see Figure 6.29). The current settings for these options are displayed.

Horizontal Origin and Vertical Origin areas in the upper half of this dialog box control the alignment of the text. The horizontal alignment of text can be overridden for each text object on the canvas by using the Format | Spacing menu items as shown earlier in this chapter.

The lower part of the dialog box contains general options that can be applied to boilerplate text objects. By default, the font of text objects is fixed, and

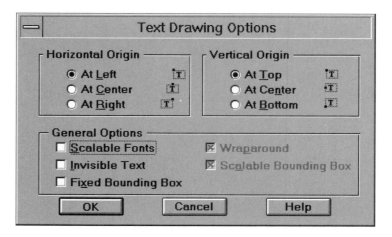

FIGURE 6.29 Text Drawing Options dialog box.

the objects themselves cannot be resized like other boilerplate objects. If you want to be able to resize text objects and keep the font proportional to their dimensions, then set the Scaleable Fonts check box. Once this option is set, you can resize the text object by dragging its corner handles. If, for some reason, you need to have text on the canvas that is invisible to the users, then set the Invisible Text option.

When text objects are created on the canvas, by default their dimensions are adjusted dynamically, as you type, to enclose the text being entered. Even when you edit them, the box around the text is modified according to the amount of text it encloses. If you want to use a fixed-size text object whose dimensions will not depend on the text, set the Fixed Bounding Box option. With this option on, you can resize the text object without being restricted to display all and only the text it contains. As you type text in an object with this property on, Designer will expand it if necessary, to show you what is being typed. But, as soon as you leave the text edit mode, the object will be reset to its original size.

When the Fixed Bounding Box option is set, two additional options are enabled. Wraparound, when set, allows text being typed to wrap to the next line to fit within the text object. Scaleable Bounding Box, when set, allows you to resize the text object independently of the text it contains.

6.6.4 ROUND RECTANGLE DRAWING OPTIONS

To view or modify round rectangle drawing options, choose Format I Drawing Options I Rounded Rectangle... from the menu. The Rounded Rectangle Drawing Option dialog box appears (see Figure 6.30). The current settings for these options are displayed.

The Corner Radius area specifies how much the Layout Editor will round the corners of the rectangle. Larger values entered in Horizontal and Vertical field, cause more rounded corners to be drawn. If any of these two fields is set to zero, no rounding occurs; the rounded rectangle becomes just a regular rectangle. The corner radius units are specified on the right side of the dialog box.

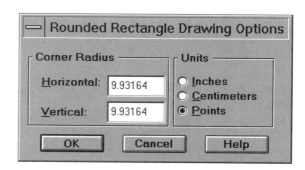

FIGURE 6.30 Rounded Rectangle Drawing Options dialog box.

6.6.5 IMAGE DRAWING OPTIONS

To view or modify image drawing options, choose Format | Drawing Options | Image... from the menu. The Image Drawing Options dialog box appears (see Figure 6.31). The current settings for these options are displayed.

Images are imported on the canvas using the Edit | Import | Image... command. Once set on the canvas, their quality can be set to an appropriate level in the dialog box shown in Figure 6.31. Higher image quality causes better appearance on the screen. However, the screen drawing process will be more resource intensive, and, therefore, slower.

The colors accessible from Oracle Forms are defined in the current color palette (see Figure 6.18). The color palette contains more than two hundred different colors, nuances, and shades. However, it is possible that imported images may contain colors not specified in the current palette. When this happens, Designer either replaces the missing colors with colors from the palette that most resemble them, or simulates their appearance. The process of simulating an image's color when it is not available in the current palette is called *dithering*. When dithering is on, the image colors will more closely resemble the original colors, thus resulting in a better quality of the image itself. But the dithering algorithm will consume more resources and time, thus resulting in slower screen drawings. When dithering is off, the quality of the images may slightly deteriorate, but screens are drawn and displayed faster. Usually resource gains and time savings offset the image quality loss. Therefore, by default, dithering in Forms is not set.

Another way to save some precious computing resources when working with boilerplate images is to reduce their resolution. Resolution is the amount of detail provided for each image. The resolution of an image is proportional to its quality, but also to the resources it consumes and the time it takes to be displayed on the screen. Often, an acceptable compromise is reached and low resolution images that are easier to manipulate by Forms are used. To reduce the resolution of an image follow these steps:

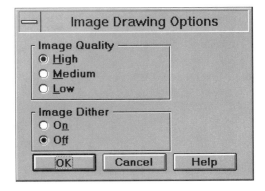

FIGURE 6.31 Image Drawing Options dialog box.

> ## Note
>
> The reverse action is not available; the resolution of an image cannot be increased. This may result in loss of the image's details. For example, consider an image that is imported on the canvas, and its size is reduced. If the image resolution is reduced, the quality of the image will deteriorate. Due to the small size of the image, this deterioration may not be noticeable. But, if the image is restored to its original size, degradation of its quality will be noticeable.

1. Select the image to modify.
2. Select Format | Reduce Resolution from the menu.

You can reduce the resolution only for one image at a time.

6.7 CUSTOMIZING COLOR PALETTES

Earlier in the chapter, it was explained how you can change fill, line, and text colors of objects in the Layout Editor. In all cases, a color palette like the one in Figure 6.18 is used. This color palette contains 228 cells. Each of the cells represents a different combination of red, green, and blue (RGB) levels, which make up a distinct color or nuance on the palette. Each form can use one color palette, which most often is the Oracle Forms Designer default palette. However, if the application requires special colors that do not exist in the palette, the Layout Editor gives you the ability to create these colors and save them in the file system or to the database for later use in the form of color palettes. A session of the Forms Designer can use only one color palette. If the default palette is not used, its name is specified in the Designer Options tab of the Options dialog box, as shown in Figure 6.32. If the Color Palette field of this dialog box is blank, the default palette is in use. To access Options dialog box, select Tools | Options... from the Designer menu.

In the Options dialog box, the Mode field specifies one of the ways to use this color palette: Read Only - Shared, Read Only - Private, or Editable. When custom palettes are used, it is important, especially in team development efforts, that all developers use the same baseline palette in read only and shared mode. This ensures that the color scheme used by all the forms in the application is independent from individual programmers and protected from accidental changes. If the settings of the color palette options are changed, Forms Designer must be restarted for the changes to take effect.

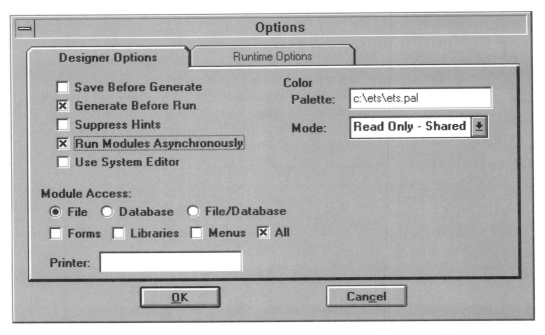

FIGURE 6.32   Options dialog box where a custom color palette is defined.

6.7.1 EXPORTING AND IMPORTING COLOR PALETTES

If an application needs a customized color palette, you must ensure that all the forms are being developed using the same palette. It would be unwise to ask each developer to change the color palette and to expect these palettes to be the same. Instead, only one color palette must be modified. Then, it can be exported either as a file or as an object in the database. This exported palette is and should be treated like part of the application source code. It must be protected from acci-

---

Note

Make sure to NEVER edit the default color palette. This should be used as a reference points for the colors in your application. Follow the discussion presented next with a copy of your default palette. To do this, you can export the default color palette to a named file in your hard disk, for example C:\ETS\ETS.PAL, or to the database.

dental damages, backed up regularly, and made available, in Read Only Shared mode, to all those programmers that need it. To use the master color palette, the programmers, in turn, import it in their environment. Follow these steps to export a color palette:

1. Open the Layout Editor if it is not already opened.
2. Select Edit|Export|Color Palette... from the menu. The Export dialog box appears (see Figure 6.33). Color Palette... item of Edit|Export menu is enabled only if the Layout Editor window is opened and currently selected.
3. Specify where to export the color palette and under which name.
4. Click OK. The color palette is exported according to your specifications.

To help you specify the destination of the exported color palette, the Export dialog box offers a browse utility. If you choose to export to the file system, clicking Browse... button will display a standard Save As dialog box. Designer will prompt you to save the file in the same directory and with the same name as the current module. The extension of an exported color palette is PAL. If you choose to export to the database, clicking Browse... will display the Export to Database dialog box (see Figure 6.34)

The list in this dialog box displays palettes currently exported to the database. Enter the palette name in the Name field and click OK. The control will return to the Export dialog box. The name of the palette is prefixed by the user identification you are logged on.

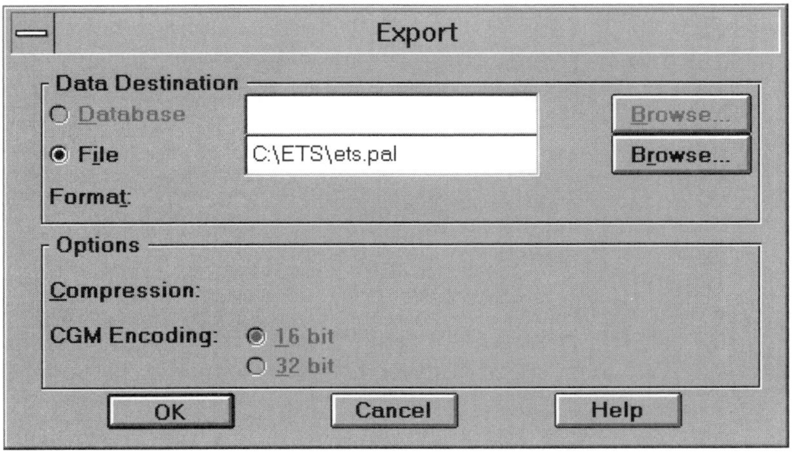

FIGURE 6.33   Export dialog box.

FIGURE 6.34 Export to Database dialog box.

To import a color palette follow these steps:

1. Open the Layout Editor if it is not already opened.
2. Select Edit | Import | Color Palette... from the menu. The Import dialog box appears (see Figure 6.35). Color Palette... item of Edit | Import menu is enabled only if the Layout Editor dialog box is selected and the Designer's color palette mode is set to Editable.
3. Specify the location and file name of the palette file to be imported.
4. Click OK. The color palette is imported from the file or database object you specified.

To help you locate the color palette, the Import dialog box offers a Browse utility. If you chose to import a file, clicking Browse... button will display a standard

FIGURE 6.35 Import dialog box.

Open dialog box. If you are importing the palette from the database, clicking Browse... button displays a dialog box almost identical to the one shown in Figure 6.34. The only difference is that the title is, Import from Database. Select the palette from the list, and click OK to return to the Import dialog box.

6.7.2 EDITING COLOR PALETTES

If you want to edit the color palette, you must load it in Edit mode:

1. Select Tool I Options... from the menu. Options dialog box appears (see Figure 6.32).
2. Enter the name of the color palette in the Color Palette field. For example, enter C:\ETS\ETS.PAL.
3. Choose Editable from the Color Mode drop-down list.
4. Click OK.
5. Exit and restart the Designer for the new option settings to take effect.

When the Designer is restarted you may modify the color palette to meet your needs. As a first step, open a Layout Editor window and select Format I Color Palette... from the Layout Editor menu. The Color Palette dialog box appears (see Figure 6.36). Note that the Format I Color Palette... menu item is enabled only if the current color palette is editable.

The central part of the Color Palette dialog box displays the colors defined in the current palette. The Palette Name field under it displays the name of the palette. Each color in the palette can be selected for editing by clicking its cell. The currently selected color cell has a raised bevel status, and its name is displayed in the Current Color field. In the default palette, sixteen colors in the 4 × 4 cells square in the upper left corner of the palette use descriptive English names such as *black, green, magenta*, or *darkgrey*. Eight cells underneath them are named *cus-*

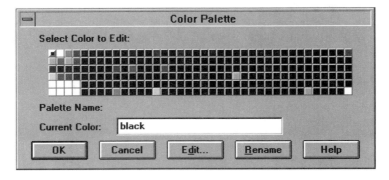

FIGURE 6.36 Color Palette dialog box.

tom1 through *custom8*. In the default palette, they are blank. These are additional colors that you can create, besides editing the existing ones. The rest of the colors have names that describe their saturation level of red, green and blue such as *r100g25b100*.

If you want to rename a selected color follow these steps:

1. Click inside the Current Color name field.
2. Type the new name.
3. Click Rename button on the Color Palette dialog box.

The color now assumes the new name. To edit an already selected color, or to add a custom color to the palette, click Edit... button on the Color Palette dialog box. The Select Color dialog box appears (see Figure 6.37). You could select any of the forty-eight Basic Colors on the upper left quarter of the window as your new color. However, since they are already defined in the color palette, you will end up with duplicate cells.

What you want to do instead, is use the Basic Colors to define a Custom Color:

1. Click one of the sixteen Custom Color rectangles. You will fill this rectangle with the color that you will define in the following steps.
2. Click the Basic Color rectangle that most resembles the color you want to create.

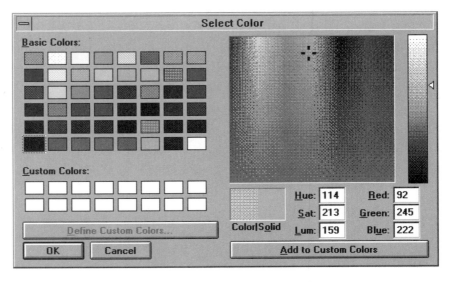

FIGURE 6.37 Select Color dialog box.

3. Refine the color by dragging the cross hair icon around the big color spectrum box on the right half of the window. You may also drag the white triangle up and down the vertical bar further right, or directly enter numeric values from 0 to 255 in the fields under the box.

4. Click the Add to Custom Colors button, when you have defined the color you want. The newly defined color is placed in the Custom Color rectangle selected in Step 1.

You can specify up to sixteen different Custom Colors. To use one of them in the color palette, select it and click OK in the Select Color dialog box. The control is returned to the Color Palette dialog box shown in Figure 6.36. The cell that was selected before the Edit... button was pressed, now displays the new color.

If you are finished editing colors or creating new ones, click OK to dismiss the Color Palette dialog box. Export the new palette to the file system or the database if it must be distributed to other developers.

It is very important not to proceed with Forms development with the tool palette in Editable mode. Set its mode to Read Only - Shared:

1. Select Tool | Options... from the menu. Options dialog box appears (see Figure 6.32).
2. Choose Read Only - Shared from the Color Mode drop-down list.
3. Click OK.
4. Restart the Designer for the changes to take effect.

6.8 SUMMARY

This chapter provided information about one of the most important components of Oracle Forms Designer: the Layout Editor. The main concepts disussed are listed here:

❑ Accessing Layout Editor
❑ Components of Layout Editor
    ❑ Layout workarea
    ❑ Toolbar
    ❑ Tool palette
    ❑ Status bar
❑ Working with Objects in Layout Editor
    ❑ Undo command
    ❑ Creating objects
    ❑ Setting the context of Layout Editor

- ❏ Selecting
- ❏ Moving, resizing, and reshaping objects
- ❏ Aligning and setting objects to same size
- ❏ Deleting objects
- ❏ Copying, cutting, pasting, and duplicating objects
- ❏ Grouping and ungrouping
- ❏ Rotating
- ❏ Working with overlapping objects
- ❏ Setting visual attributes in Layout Editor
    - ❏ Font attributes
    - ❏ Spacing and alignment
    - ❏ Color attributes
    - ❏ Line and border attributes
- ❏ Customizing Layout Editor
    - ❏ Customizing layout workarea
    - ❏ Customizing ruler settings
    - ❏ Customizing the appearance of Layout Editor
- ❏ Customizing Drawing Options
    - ❏ General drawing options
    - ❏ Arc drawing options
    - ❏ Text drawing options
    - ❏ Round rectangle drawing options
    - ❏ Image drawing options
- ❏ Customizing Color Palettes
    - ❏ Exporting and importing color palettes
    - ❏ Editing color palettes

PROPERTIES WINDOW

"It is quality rather than quantity that matters."
—Seneca

- ◆ Accessing Properties Windows
- ◆ Components of Properties Windows
- ◆ Using Properties Windows
- ◆ Properties Classes
- ◆ Visual Attributes
- ◆ Practical Examples
- ◆ Other Ways to Access Properties of Objects
- ◆ Summary

The behavior and functionality of objects in an Oracle Forms application is determined by their properties. Upon creation, each object is assigned a set of default properties, which can be changed and reset based on the needs of the application. The Properties Windows are the interface that Designer provides to access and modify properties of objects. In these windows you can display and edit the properties of one or more objects. They also allow you to copy properties of one object to an other, to organize them in properties classes, and inherit properties of objects from these properties classes.

7.1 ACCESSING PROPERTIES WINDOWS

There is a variety of ways to access Properties Windows in the Oracle Forms Designer. From anywhere in the application, you can select Tools | Properties... from the menu. This will always display a Properties Window. If there are no objects selected when the command is issued, the window is blank; if one or more objects are previously selected, a list of their properties will be displayed in the window.

From Object Navigator, Layout Editor, or Menu Editor you can also right-click to display the popup menu described in Chapter 4, and select Properties... from this menu. This command has a slight advantage over the previous one. If you want to view or edit the properties of only one object, right-clicking the object will select it and display the popup menu at the same time, thus saving you a Select command that the first option requires.

Another way to access the properties of most objects displayed in the Object Navigator is to double-click the object type icon to the left of the object's name. The only exception to this are canvases, menus, and PL/SQL objects. Double-clicking their icons brings up the Layout Editor, Menu Editor, and PL/SQL Editor, respectively.

If you are in the Layout Editor window, double-clicking items on the canvas displays their properties. Also, in the Menu Editor, double-clicking menu objects and menu items brings up their Properties Window.

All the actions discussed above will open a Properties Window if none has been opened up to that point. If there is a Properties Window already open, these actions will simply activate it, thus making that window the current window in the Designer. Often, there is a need to compare properties of objects while developing applications. To do this, you can display each of them in its own Properties Window. To open additional Properties Windows you can still use the commands above, but double-clicking is replaced with SHIFT+DOUBLE-CLICKING. In other words, to open a second Properties Window, hold down the SHIFT key from the keyboard while double-clicking the object in the Navigator, Layout Editor, or Menu Editor.

If a Properties Window is already open and you want to navigate to it, you can select it from the list of currently open windows accessible from the Window menu of the Designer. Unfortunately, the title of the window is simply Properties, without any reference to the name of the object. This may not be very helpful if more than one Properties Window is open.

7.2 COMPONENTS OF PROPERTIES WINDOWS

Figure 7.1 displays the Properties Window for a trigger in the ETS application. It can be seen from the figure that this window cannot be maximized, which is different from other windows in the Designer, but that will not impact the development of your applications, since it can be resized and scrolled to display all the information it contains.

There are four major components of each Properties Window. The toolbar allows access to common commands related to properties; the context bar provides information about the type and name of the currently selected object; the property setting bar displays the setting for the currently selected property in the properties list; the properties list contains all the properties that apply to the current selection of objects and their settings. The rest of this section discusses each of these components in detail.

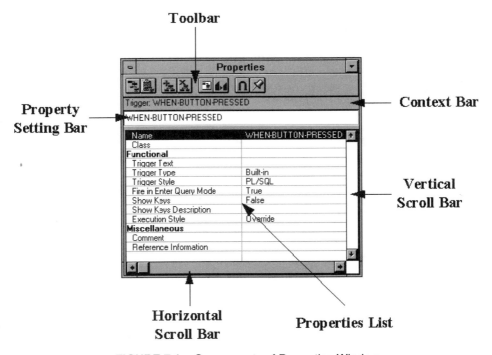

FIGURE 7.1 Components of Properties Window.

7.2.1 TOOLBAR

Like the Object Navigator, the Layout Editor, and the Menu Editor, Properties Windows come with a toolbar that allows developers to quickly access commands closely associated with them. The toolbar is displayed horizontally, right under the window's title bar. Table 7.1 lists all the icons of the toolbar, their names, and a brief description for each of them.

You will notice that the first two icons used to copy and paste properties of objects are also found in the Navigator, Layout Editor, and Menu Editor. This is done so that you can access these functions directly from within these environments, without having to display any Properties Window. Their functionality can also be accessed by selecting Edit | Copy Properties and Edit | Paste Properties items from the Designer menu.

7.2.2 CONTEXT BAR

The context bar is located immediately below the toolbar, and displays information that identifies the object whose properties are currently displayed in the window. The context of the window is defined by the type and name of the object. In

TABLE 7.1   Iconic Tools in Properties Window toolbar.

ICON	NAME	FUNCTIONALITY
	Copy Properties	Copy the properties settings displayed in the window.
	Paste Properties	Paste properties settings in the current window.
	Add Property	Add a property to the property class displayed in the window.
	Delete Property	Remove the selected property from the property class displayed in the window.
	Property Class	Create a property class based on the properties displayed in the window.
	Inherit	Set the currently selected property to its default value.
	Intersect/Union	Properties Window is in Intersect mode; it displays only the common properties of the selected objects. Clicking the icon toggles the window's mode to Union.
	Intersect/Union	Properties Window is in Union mode; it displays all the properties of selected objects. Clicking the icon toggles the window's mode to Intersect.
	Freeze/Unfreeze	Properties Window is in Unfreeze mode; its content is updated each time a new object is selected to reflect properties of the current selection. Clicking the icon toggles the window's mode to Freeze.
	Freeze/Unfreeze	Properties Window is in Freeze mode; it displays the properties of only one object and is not synchronized with objects selected in the Navigator and other editors. Clicking the icon toggles the window's mode to Unfreeze.

Figure 7.1 for example, the Properties Window shows information about the trigger WHEN-BUTTON-PRESSED.

When more than one object is selected, the context bar displays the message Multiple selection. When no objects are selected, the message displayed becomes No selection.

7.2.3 PROPERTIES SETTING BAR

The properties setting bar is positioned under the context bar. It is here that settings for the currently selected property are specified. The content of the properties setting bar depends on the type of property selected.

If the property setting can be specified by a text string or a digit, the bar displays a text field, where you can enter the desired value. If the property is already set, the text in the text field is highlighted, so that it can be typed over more easily. For properties whose setting is long text, the Text Editor iconic button 🖻 appears to the right of the text field. Clicking this button brings up the Designer's text editor, where you can type and edit the text more easily.

If the property setting must be chosen from a list of predefined values, the properties setting bar displays a drop-down list box. This list contains the valid settings for the property, from which one must be chosen. When appropriate, this list allows you to set the property to NULL.

If the list is one of the Designer's Lists of Values, the drop-down list box is replaced by a text field with the List of Values iconic push button 🔳 to its right. Clicking this button displays the LOVs, from which you can select the desired value for the property.

If setting a property requires more complicated actions, then the property setting bar displays the More... push button. Clicking on the button displays a dialog box in which you can specify the settings accordingly. In the case of *Trigger Text* property for triggers, clicking More... button launches the PL/SQL Editor for that trigger. Figure 7.2 shows all the different views that the properties setting bar can take.

Note

For List of Values Properties you can directly type text in the text field. For some properties, Designer will validate your entry against the List of Values. If the test fails, you will not be allowed to continue without entering a valid value. However, for a few properties such as *Font Name* for items, the validation test is not done until the form is generated. Until this feature becomes more consistent, use only the List of Values to choose a valid setting for your property.

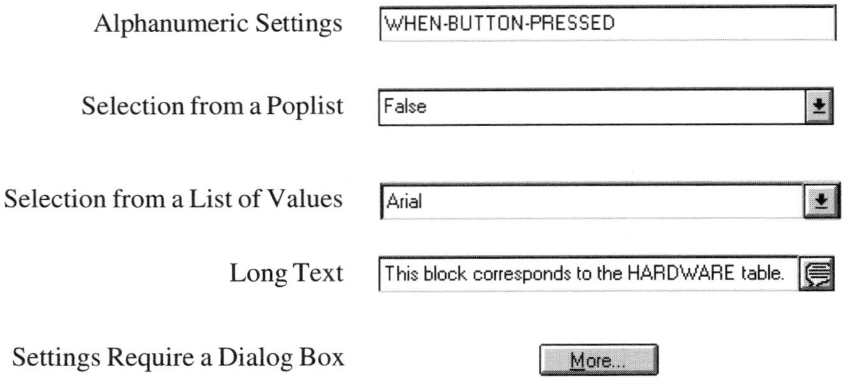

Alphanumeric Settings | WHEN-BUTTON-PRESSED

Selection from a Poplist | False

Selection from a List of Values | Arial

Long Text | This block corresponds to the HARDWARE table.

Settings Require a Dialog Box | More...

FIGURE 7.2   Different views of properties setting bar.

There are instances, especially when multiple objects are selected, when you cannot set a property. For example, you cannot set the name of multiple objects with one command. In these cases, the Designer disables the property setting bar. In disabled state, the first four types of fields are not displayed at all, whereas the More... button takes the default grayed-out appearance of a disabled push button in MS Windows.

7.2.4 PROPERTIES LIST

The properties list takes up most of the Properties Window. It has the form of a two-column sheet. The left column contains the names of properties, and the right one the setting for each property displayed in the window. The length of this list depends on the object or group of objects selected. All objects in Oracle Forms share the first two entries in the properties list: *Name* and *Class*. The reason is simple: Each object must have a name and settings for its properties may be derived from a properties class.

The properties in the list are grouped by functionality. Each functional group begins with a header entry in bold typeface. For example, trigger properties are grouped in two categories: Functional and Miscellaneous (see Figure 7.1). The Miscellaneous group is shared by all the objects. One property member of this group shared by all objects is *Comment*. This is where you can enter text to document your application.

When more than one object is selected, the properties displayed in the properties list depend on the mode of the Properties Window. If it is in Intersect mode, which is also the default mode, only common properties are listed. If the Properties Window is in Union mode, all the properties of selected objects are listed. If the selected objects share a common property, the actual value of its setting is displayed only if it is the same for all objects. If at least one object contains a different setting, the right column of the properties list will display the string, "*****".

7.3 USING PROPERTIES WINDOWS

This section explains how to use the Properties Window to set object properties, copy and paste them, to create property classes, and use them to inherit properties.

7.3.1 SETTING PROPERTIES OF OBJECTS

You can set only one property at a time for one or more objects in the Properties Window. Section 7.2.3 described different forms that this bar can take. It also introduced ways to set the values of the property displayed in the bar. This section mentions one additional method that can be used for the same purpose: the almighty double-click.

Double-clicking an entry in the property list can result in different outcomes depending on the value of that property and what is displayed in the properties setting bar. Table 7.2 lists the different results of double-clicking a property. For clarity and consistency purposes, this table uses the same types of property setting bars used in Figure 7.2.

If more than one object is selected, setting a property will propagate the setting in all the objects that contain that property. The action will overwrite any existing settings of that property. This can be especially helpful to create applications with objects that share a consistent look and interface such as text font, color schemes, and style.

TABLE 7.2 Double-Clicking Properties in a Properties Window.

PROPERTY SETTING BAR	OUTCOME OF DOUBLE-CLICKING THE PROPERTY
WHEN-BUTTON-PRESSED	The text contained in the field is selected.
False	The next entry in the list is selected. For True/False properties, it toggles the value.
Arial	The appropriate List of Values is displayed.
This block corresponds to the HARDWARE table.	Designer's editor is displayed with the text in it.
More...	The dialog window where the property can be set is displayed. For properties whose setting is PL/SQL code, the PL/SQL Editor is launched.

> # Note
>
> There is a caveat here, though. The Designer does not warn you about over-written properties. Nor does it allow you to undo a property setting action. Therefore you should be careful not to lose precious work when setting properties this way.

7.3.2 COMPARING PROPERTIES OF OBJECTS

A quick way to compare the properties of two or more objects is to select them and navigate to a Properties Window in Intersect (default) mode. The properties displayed in the properties list are the ones the objects share. If the settings have a value displayed, all the objects share that value; if the setting displays, "*****", at least one object has a different setting for that property.

For a more detailed comparison, you need to display each object in its separate Properties Window. Earlier in the chapter you learned how to open more than one of these windows. By default, each Properties Window is synchronized with the Object Navigator, Layout Editor, and Menu Editor. This means that it will display the properties of the current selection in one of these windows. If they are left in this default state, all the Properties Windows in the Designer will contain exactly the same information.

In order to display the properties of two or more objects simultaneously in separate windows, you must brake this synchronization. To do this, click the Unfreeze button ▨ from the toolbar. This action toggles the state of the window to Freeze and replaces the icon on the Freeze/Unfreeze button with the Freeze icon ▣ . Now, the properties of the object are "pinned" to the window and will remain displayed there even after you select another object in the Navigator or the other editors. You can navigate to a second Properties Window and display, side-by-side, the properties of different objects.

7.3.3 COPYING AND PASTING PROPERTIES OF OBJECTS

Oracle Forms extends the concept of copying and pasting objects to that of copying and pasting their properties. The commands Copy Properties and Paste Properties can be accessed from the Object Navigator, Layout Editor, Menu Editor, and Properties Window. To copy properties follow these steps:

1. Select the object or group of objects whose properties you want to copy.
2. Click Copy Properties icon ▣ from the window's toolbar or choose Edit I Copy Properties from the menu.

The Designer places the properties settings in the clipboard, ready to be pasted onto another object. If you are copying properties of multiple objects, only the common properties of these objects are copied. This means that property settings that look like, "*****", in the Properties Window will not be copied to the clipboard.

To paste properties follow these steps:

1. Select the object or group of objects on which you want to paste the properties.
2. Click Paste Properties icon 🖳 from the window's toolbar or choose Edit | Paste Properties from the menu.

The objects where you paste the properties need not be of the same type as the objects from which these properties were copied. When issuing a Paste Properties command, Designer will paste only those properties that have a meaning for the target object. This feature allows you, for example, to copy the properties of an item in a form module and paste them on a menu item. Only shared attributes such as Font Name, Size, and Style will be applied to the menu item.

You should be cautious when copying and pasting properties, because these commands act upon all the properties of the selected objects. If, for example, you copy the properties of an item and paste them onto another item, all their properties, except name, will become identical. Thus, you will end up with two overlapping items that have the same functionality. This may be a little more than what you were trying to achieve!

To remedy this brute force approach to sharing common properties of similar objects in an application, Oracle Forms allows you to create and use property classes and visual attributes.

7.4 PROPERTIES CLASSES

Properties classes is one way to implement inheritance in Oracle Forms applications. Inheritance is one of the pillars of object-oriented programming. Inheritance techniques give programmers the capability to create new objects in an application based on a set of previously defined objects. It not only significantly cuts the development time, but also creates applications which share a common and consistent look and behavior.

For example, in a financial application, you may want to align fields that contains dollar values right, rather than left, which is the default alignment setting for text items. You may also want to display them in the currency format, preceded by the dollar sign and expressed as dollars and cents. Furthermore, negative values may be presented differently from non-negative ones to attract the attention of the user. A method, or trigger, must be attached to the text item field which checks the current value stored there, and based on it, changes the font, color, or any other visual attribute considered appropriate.

In traditional programming environments, each time a text field that displays dollar values is added to the application, the programmer must specify its size, format, alignment settings, and replicate the code that sets its attributes based on the value of the item. Programming applications this way is a lengthy, costly, and very tedious process. Maintaining them is not easy either. If there is a slight change in the requirements, programmers need to go and apply the change to all the dollar value items in their modules.

In object-oriented environments, an object class is created instead. General attributes and methods are specified for this class. Then, for example, each time the application needs a dollar value item, that item is inherited from the base class. No additional programming is needed to set its format or create the check method. If, in the future, the requirements change, attributes or methods need to be modified in only one place, the base class. All the objects derived from this class will automatically inherit the new settings with no further effort from the developers.

If you are implementing the financial application in Oracle Forms, you need to create and embellish only one currency item. Then, based on the properties settings of this item, you create a property class. From that moment on, each time a new currency item needs to be created, its properties are inherited from this class. Of course, any of the inherited properties can be overwritten if necessary.

7.4.1 CREATING PROPERTY CLASSES

Property classes are objects in a module; therefore, they can be created from the Navigator like any other object. When you do so, an entry is created in the object tree and a default name is given to it. After you create the new class, you need to populate it with the necessary attributes.

If an object that will serve as model for the properties settings in the class already exists, the class can be created directly from the content of the Properties Window for this object:

1. Display the Properties Window for the object.
2. Click Property Class ⊞ from the window toolbar. Designer displays a message of the form, Creating property class PROPERTY_CLASS2.
3. Click OK.
4. Rename the newly created property class in the Navigator.

This is the most common way to create a property class because it allows you to quickly specify the properties included in the class. Most, if not all of them, are already present in the Properties Window. All you have to do to bring the class to the state you want is to add, delete, or reset just a few properties.

7.4.2 ADDING AND DELETING PROPERTIES IN A PROPERTIES CLASS

Once a properties class is created, it may need some adjustments in its content. To change the content of a property class, display it in a Properties Window. Here you can change settings as explained in Section 7.3.1. You can also add or delete other properties in the existing list.

You can add a property to the class:

1. Click Add Property icon 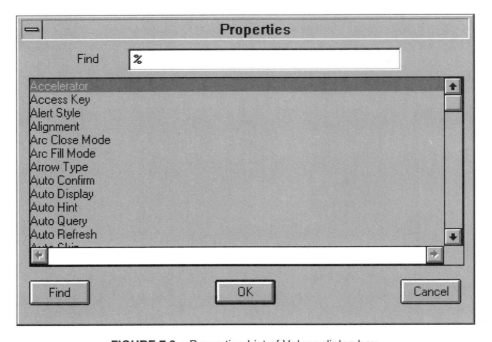 from the toolbar. The Properties List of Values dialog box appears (see Figure 7.3).
2. Select the property you want to add. Remember that the List of Values supports autoreduction and search features.
3. Click OK.

The property is added and set to its default value. Designer places the new property in its own place under the appropriate functional category. If the category is not present in the list, it is automatically created when one of its properties is added to the class.

Another way to quickly add multiple properties to an existing class is to use the Copy Properties and Paste Properties commands presented in the previous

FIGURE 7.3 Properties List of Values dialog box.

sections. You copy the properties of the source object and then paste them in the target property class window. If the class already contains any of the properties of the source, their settings will be overwritten; all the other properties will be added to the class.

To delete a property from the class follow these steps:

1. Select the property you want to delete from the list.
2. Click Delete Property icon ▧ from the toolbar.

The selected property is deleted. Note that you can add or delete only one property at a time.

7.4.3 INHERITING PROPERTIES FROM PROPERTIES CLASSES

Once a properties class is created, it can be used to define the properties of other objects in the application. To inherit properties of an object from an existing class follow these steps:

1. Display the Properties Window for that object.
2. Click the list icon ▤ for the *Class* property of the object. A list of all property classes currently defined in the module is displayed.
3. Select the property class from which the properties will be inherited.

An object can inherit properties from only one class at any one time. To inherit properties from another properties class, simply change the setting of the *Class* property for the object. Inheriting from a class affects only those properties that are included in the class. Visually, they are distinguished from the rest in the properties sheet by the sign '=' that precedes their name. Properties of the object that are not included in the class remain unchanged.

Settings of inherited properties can be changed in two different ways. If the change applies to only one object, set the property of that object in the Properties Window. The '=' in front of its name will disappear to indicate that the property is no longer inherited. If you want to apply the change to all the objects that inherit their properties from the same class, modify the setting at the class level. Designer will automatically apply the change to all objects inherited from that class.

If you change the setting of an inherited property, you also break the link between this property and its setting in the property class. If settings for that property are modified in the properties class, the changes will not be applied to the object. To reestablish this link and reset a modified property to the value specified in the properties class use the Inherit command in the Properties Window:

1. Select the property to reset.
2. Click the Inherit icon ▧ from the toolbar.

The inheritance indicator '=' reappears to the left of the property. You can use the Inherit command even if the property is not inherited. In this case, clicking the Inherit icon sets the property to its default value maintained by the Oracle Forms Designer.

Properties classes, like any other object in Forms, can inherit their properties from other classes, thus leading to multiple levels of inheritance. In the scenario introduced above, if your financial application will display currencies other than dollars, you can create a new class that inherits all the properties and triggers from the class used in dollar values text items. Then, necessary adjustments, such as format and currency symbol, are made to this class. Text items inherited from it will share common characteristics with other currency items, while preserving their differences.

7.5 VISUAL ATTRIBUTES

Visual attributes, in a sense, are an explicit type of properties classes, managed as separate objects by Oracle Forms. The basic functionality that can be achieved using visual attributes can also be implemented with properties classes. However, your application will benefit and gain in clarity if properties that regulate only the visual appearance of objects are grouped separately in the form of visual attributes.

The properties that make up a visual attribute are *Font Name, Size, Style, Width,* and *Weight; Foreground Color* and *Background Color; Fill Pattern, Charmode Logical Attribute,* and *White on Black.* You can create and name a visual attribute like any other object in the Navigator. You can specify the properties settings of a visual attribute as you would do for any object in the Properties Window.

Each interface object contains among other properties the font, color, and pattern properties specified above. The settings of these properties are controlled by the object's *Visual Attribute Name* property. If this property is set to *'Default',* then the visual attributes will be the Oracle Forms default attributes. If any of these attributes are modified, either in the Properties Window or the Layout Editor, the *Visual Attribute Name* changes to *'Custom',* which instructs the Oracle Forms Runtime engine to use the specified settings rather than the default ones.

To base the attributes on an existing visual attributes object, you simply select its name from the drop-down list box of *Visual Attributes Name* property. Designer places the sign '=' in front of all the visual attributes, from *Font Name* to *White on Black.* Only properties that are meaningful for the object being modified are applied to the selected object. Thus, setting attributes based on a visual attributes objects is similar to inheriting properties from a properties class. However, if you change the setting of even one of these attributes, the inheritance sign '=' will be removed from all of them, and the name of the visual attribute will be set to *'Custom'.* Thus, as a rule of thumb, to set all the visual attributes as a group, either

'Default' or a predefined visual attribute object must be used; to change the setting of attributes individually, the name of the visual attribute name is set to *'Custom'*.

The one and only purpose of visual attributes objects is to control the visual appearance of other objects in an application. Therefore, it is reasonable that they have precedence over properties classes, which may specify these and other properties. If an object inherits some visual properties from a class, and, at the same time, its *Visual Attributes Name* property is set to a visual attributes object, the settings specified in the visual attributes object override the settings of the property class.

Another difference between visual attributes objects and properties classes is that the assignment of a named visual attribute for an object can be changed programmatically at runtime, whereas the properties class is specified at design time and cannot be changed programmatically. On the other hand, properties classes can contain all the properties contained in visual attribute objects and other additional ones. What is more important, they allow PL/SQL triggers to be associated with the class, and then inherited to all the objects derived from the class.

It is difficult to say when it is more advantageous to use visual attributes objects or properties classes. Clearly, a combination of the functionality from both types would provide more benefits, power, and flexibility than each of them separately. In the following section, you create visual attributes and properties classes that can be used in the financial application described earlier in this chapter.

7.6 PRACTICAL EXAMPLES

In this section you will work with the ETS application that you developed in Part One. Open the form in the Designer. In Chapter 3 you modified the visual attributes, alignment settings, and format mask for the currency value items. Here you will take advantage of that effort.

Start by creating two visual attributes objects that will be used in this section. Initially, their properties will be set exactly like those of item PURCHASE_COST in block HARDWARE:

1. Select item HARDWARE.PURCHASE_COST in the Navigator or Layout Editor.
2. Click Copy Properties icon ▣ from the toolbar.
3. Create a new visual attribute object in the Navigator, and name it NON_NEGATIVE.
4. Click Paste Properties icon ▣ while visual attribute NON_NEGATIVE is still selected.

5. Create another visual attribute object in the Navigator, and name it NEGA-TIVE.

6. Click Paste Properties icon ▣ while visual attribute NEGATIVE is still selected.

The components of the visual attribute NON_NEGATIVE will have the same settings as their counterparts in the item PURCHASE_COST. The properties of the visual attributes NEGATIVE will be similar to NON_NEGATIVE, except for the *Foreground Color*, which will be set to *'red'*:

1. Double-click the visual attribute NEGATIVE to display its Properties Window.

2. Double-click the *Foreground Color* property. Colors List of Values dialog box appears.

3. Select *'red'* from the list.

Now, create a property class that will contain properties characteristic for currency value items. Once again you will use the settings of HARDWARE.PURCHASE_COST item. As you create and populate the new properties class, you will need to reference the properties of this item. Therefore, *pin* its properties in a window and create the properties class in a second window:

1. Double-click the PURCHASE_COST item to display its Properties Window.

2. Click the Freeze/Unfreeze icon ▣ to freeze the contents of the window. The icon now is replaced by the icon ▣.

3. Create a new Property Class object in the Navigator, and name it US_CURRENCY.

4 SHIFT-DOUBLE-CLICK the property class US_CURRENCY to display its settings in a second Properties Window.

The new property class has only three members in it: *Name, Class,* and *Reference Information*. Begin adding more properties to it. The Properties Window for PURCHASE_COST will help you figure out what properties to add, therefore arrange it by the side of the Properties Window for US_CURRENCY.

Add *Item Type* property to the US_CURRENCY class:

1. Click the Add Property icon ▣ in the toolbar.

2. Select *Item Type* from the Properties LOVs window that comes up.

Perform these two steps to add the following properties: *Data Type, Format Mask, Range Low Value, Range High Value, Alignment, Hint, Auto-Hint,* and *Comment* properties. Set the properties as shown in Figure 7.4.

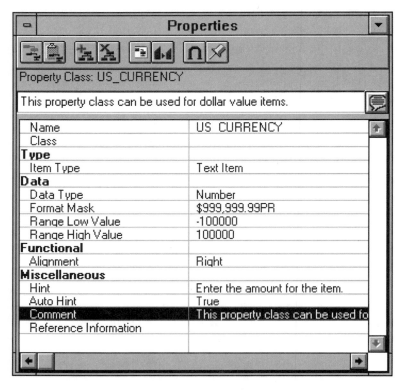

FIGURE 7.4   Settings of a properties class.

Finally, add a trigger to this property class. The trigger will fire during the validation of any item that inherits its from the US_CURRENCY class. Based on the value stored in the item, the trigger will set the *Visual Attribute Name* of the item to *'NON_NEGATIVE'* or *'NEGATIVE'*:

1. Expand the US_CURRENCY node in the Object Navigator, and select the node Triggers underneath it.
2. Click the Create icon ▦ from the toolbar. The LOVs dialog box with trigger names appears.
3. Select WHEN-VALIDATE-ITEM from the list of trigger names. The new trigger is created and a PL/SQL Editor window is displayed.
4. Enter the text of the trigger as shown in Figure 7.5, compile it, and close the PL/SQL Editor window.

In this trigger, if a negative value is entered in the item, that item is assigned the visual attribute NEGATIVE. One the other hand, if a non-negative

```
IF :SYSTEM.CURSOR_VALUE < 0 THEN        -- Negative value entered
-- Attach NEGATIVE visual attribute to item
  SET_ITEM_PROPERTY (:SYSTEM.CURSOR_ITEM, VISUAL_ATTRIBUTE,
  'NEGATIVE');
ELSE                                   --Non-negative value entered
-- Attach NON_NEGATIVE visual attribute to item
  SET_ITEM_PROPERTY (:SYSTEM.CURSOR_ITEM, VISUAL_ATTRIBUTE,
  'NON_NEGATIVE');
END IF;
```

FIGURE 7.5 Adding a trigger to a properties class.

value is entered, the visual attribute for the item becomes NON-NEGATIVE. The value of the item is stored in the system variable SYSTEM.CURSOR_VALUE, the name of the item is retrieved from the system variable SYSTEM.CURSOR_ITEM, and the visual attribute is replaced using the built-in procedure SET_ITEM_ PROPERTY.

Now, whenever you will need money items in your forms, you can inherit their characteristic properties from the US_CURRENCY class created here. As an example, inherit the properties of item PURCHASE_COST in blocks HARD-WARE and SOFTWARE from US_CURRENCY and execute the application to see how the visual attributes are replaced when non-negative dollar amounts are replaced by negative ones and vice-versa.

7.7 OTHER WAYS TO ACCESS PROPERTIES OF OBJECTS

At the conclusion of this chapter let us mention that Properties Windows are not the only way to set properties of objects in Oracle Forms applications. Often, upon creation, Designer offers you the possibility to specify the properties for the

Note

The code you have written in this trigger should not depend on the particular item that will inherit it. The use of system variables such as SYSTEM.CUR-SOR_ITEM (that returns the name of the item at runtime) and SYSTEM.CUR-SOR_VALUE (that returns the value stored in that item) enables you to write the trigger in an object-independent fashion.

new object. A typical example for this is the New Block Window dialog box, which you have used to create the blocks for the ETS application.

Other properties, primarily visual attributes and Display properties, can be accessed and modified from the Layout Editor, as shown in Chapter 6. Finally, there are objects whose properties cannot be displayed in a Properties Window. These are boilerplate objects such as arcs, lines, and rectangles. Chapter 6 explained how to access and modify their drawing options.

7.8 SUMMARY

This chapter focused on Properties Windows and how they are used to inspect and modify the properties of objects in Oracle Forms applications. Important concepts discussed are listed here:

❑ Accessing Properties Windows
❑ Components of Properties Windows
    ❑ Toolbar
    ❑ Context bar
    ❑ Properties setting bar
    ❑ Properties list
❑ Using Properties Windows
    ❑ Setting properties
    ❑ Comparing properties of objects
    ❑ Copying and pasting properties
❑ Property classes
    ❑ Creating property classes
    ❑ Adding and deleting properties to a class
    ❑ Inheriting properties from a class
❑ Visual attributes
    ❑ Advantages of visual attributes
    ❑ Differences between visual attributes and property classes

MENU EDITOR

"We must learn to explore all the options and possibilities that confront us in a complex and rapidly changing world."

—James William Fulbright

The Menu Editor is a tool that facilitates the visual development of menus for Oracle Forms applications. It is tightly integrated with the functionality of the Object Navigator. In many aspects, it is the counterpart of the Layout Editor in menu's development. By graphically displaying the menu while it is being designed, the Menu Editor allows application developers to get a real picture of its behavior at runtime.

8.1 ACCESSING THE MENU EDITOR

In order to access the Menu Editor, at least one menu module must be open in the Object Navigator. Chapter 4 provides instructions on how to open or create new modules in the Forms Designer.

There are three ways to access the Menu Editor. The most generic one launches a Menu Editor window from the Node Display area of the Object Navigator. Follow these steps to do this:

1. Click anywhere in the hierarchy tree of the menu module you want to display in the editor.
2. Select Tools|Menu Editor... from the Navigator menu. The Menu Editor window appears.

The Menu Editor window displays only one menu object at a time. With this method, the menu that is on top of the menu hierarchy for the current module will be displayed in the editor's window. If you want to work with a different menu object in that module, either follow the steps above and then display the menu you want in the Menu Editor window, or simply double-click the Menu Type icon 🗒 to the left of the menu you want to display. This action opens a Menu Editor window and displays the selected menu in it. If there is an editor window already open for that module, double-clicking the Menu icon 🗒 sets the focus to that window, but does not replace the menu displayed there with the new selection.

The Menu Editor window displays only one menu module at a time. The name of the module is displayed on the title bar of the editor window. If you need to access several menu modules simultaneously, follow any of the techniques described above to load each additional module in its own window.

If there is a Menu Editor window already open for a module, but is hidden, you can navigate to the window by double-clicking the Menu type icon 🗒 of any menu in the module or by selecting the window from the Window menu.

8.2 COMPONENTS OF THE MENU EDITOR

Figure 8.1 presents a typical Menu Editor window, with a sample menu in it. The main component of this window is the workarea in which menus and menu items are displayed, created, modified, or deleted. Above the workarea, there is a toolbar that allows you to quickly display a different menu in the workarea, or perform frequently used commands.

8.2.1 MENU EDITOR WORKAREA

This is the heart of the Menu Editor, where all the menu design activities occur. It allows you to visualize the structure of the menu being created and to access the properties of all the objects that are part of it. There are no size limits for the workarea. It will accommodate as many objects as necessary. If they extend beyond the limits of the Menu Editor window, vertical and horizontal scrollbars can be used to navigate to them. The orientation of the objects in the workarea can be switched from horizontal, as shown in Figure 8.1, to vertical. Later in the chapter you will see how to do this.

There are two types of objects displayed in the Menu Editor workarea: menus and menu items. Although they look similar, they are fundamentally different. Menu items are owned by menus. They carry out the actual actions in the application such as connecting, disconnecting, saving, cutting, and pasting. On

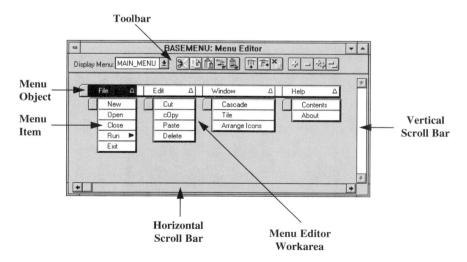

FIGURE 8.1   Components of Menu Editor window.

> **Note**
>
> There must always be one menu with at least one menu item displayed in the Menu Editor workarea. If, for example, you delete all the menus in the current module while the Menu Editor window is open, the Designer will create one menu with a generic name like MENU2, and with a <New Item> menu item underneath.

the other hand, menus organize the menu items, and the functionality they make available, in a logical, user-friendly fashion. Visually, menus are represented by menu handles ▯ , whereas menu items by rectangles. For example, in Figure 8.1, the rectangles displayed horizontally, containing the labels File, Edit, Window, and Help are the menu items of the MAIN_MENU menu object. This menu itself is represented by the gray-colored box at the left of menu item File. Similarly, FILE menu is represented by the handle on the left of the New menu item, and all its items are listed vertically underneath.

8.2.2 TOOLBAR

The toolbar for the Menu Editor is a group of iconic tools that make often-used actions and commands as easy as one mouse click. For clarity, it is shown separately in Figure 8.2.

On the left of the toolbar there is a drop-down list box called Display Menu. It displays the name of the menu object currently loaded in the workarea. The Display Menu drop-down list box makes the process of switching from one menu to another in the editor very simple:

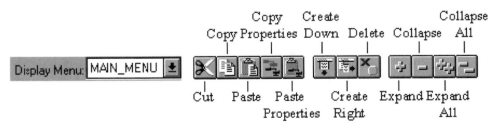

FIGURE 8.2 Menu Editor toolbar.

1. Click the List icon 🔳 to its right. A list of all the menu objects in the current menu module appears.

2. Select the menu you want to work with from this list. The Menu Editor replaces the menu currently displayed in the workarea with the one you selected.

The first group of icons in the toolbar is also present in the Object Navigator and Layout Editor windows. The icons here provide quick access to commands for cutting, copying, and pasting objects, or for copying and pasting their properties. The next three buttons are used to create or delete menu objects in the editor. The Create Down icon 🔳 is used to create menus under the current object; the Create Right icon 🔳 places the new menu to the right of the current selection; the Delete icon 🔳 deletes the selected objects. The functionality of the last four iconic buttons is similar to the functionality of these very same tools in the Object Navigator. The Expand icon 🔳 expands the selected menus to display its items. The Collapse icon 🔳 hides the menu items of the selected menu. The Expand All icon 🔳 expands all the levels of the selected menu. If, for example, one of its menu items is a menu itself, the Expand All command will expand it and display its items. The Collapse All icon 🔳 collapses all the hierarchy levels of the selected menu. The same actions can be performed by selecting Menu I Expand, Menu I Collapse, Menu I Expand All, and Menu I Collapse All from the Designer menu.

8.3 USING THE MENU EDITOR

This section explains how to use the Menu Editor to create and design menus for Oracle Forms applications. Unlike the Layout Editor, where the Undo command protects the application from accidents and errors, in the Menu Editor you cannot undo commands. However, before accomplishing potentially destructive tasks such as deleting or replacing objects, the Menu Editor will warn you and prompt you to confirm the action.

To better understand the features and techniques explained in this section, use the menu module CH8.MMB provided in the companion disk. Start Forms Designer and open the module from the directory where you installed the utilities included in the diskette. Launch the Menu Editor and display MAIN_MENU menu in the workarea, as explained earlier in this chapter.

8.3.1 NAVIGATING AND SELECTING

In the Menu Editor you work with either menu objects or menu items. A variety of techniques is used to navigate to and select each of them. If the object you want to navigate to is visible, clicking it moves the Designer's focus on the object and selects it. To select a menu item simply click inside the rectangle that represents it. To select a menu, click the menu handle to its left. In both cases, the video status of the object is reversed, thus, clearly marking it.

If the object is not visible, you may use the Display Menu drop-down list box to display the object, if it is a menu, or the menu that owns it, if it is a menu item. If the object is not visible, but the parent menu is displayed on the workarea, you can expand the submenus of the parent until you see the desired object. Menu items are atomic objects in the menu hierarchy, they cannot be further expanded. Each submenu has an expand/collapse status indicator to the right of its label. The icon ▼ indicates that the menu is collapsed; the icon ⌂ indicates that the menu is expanded.

There are three ways to expand a menu. The simplest one is to click its ▼ icon. You can also select the menu to expand and then click the Expand icon ▣ in the toolbar, or choose Menu I Expand from the Designer menu.

The Expand command acts upon objects that are only one level below the current menu in the hierarchy. To expand all the menu levels below the current menu, use the Expand All command:

1. Select the menu to expand.
2. Click the Expand All icon ▣ from the toolbar, or choose Menu I Expand All from the Designer menu.

In the Menu Editor, as in the Object Navigator, the opposite of expanding the menu hierarchy is collapsing it. The quickest way to collapse a menu is to click its ⌂ icon. You can also select the menu you want to collapse and click the Collapse icon ▣ from the toolbar, or choose Menu I Collapse from the Designer menu.

The Menu Editor "remembers" the status of the hierarchical tree under the menu even after you collapse it. This means that when a menu with several levels underneath is collapsed and then expanded again, the hierarchy view will be exactly as it was before it was collapsed. To collapse all the submenus before collapsing the current menu, the Collapse All command is used. Follow these steps to do this:

1. Select the menu to collapse.
2. Click the Collapse All icon ▣ in the toolbar, or choose Menu I Collapse All from the Designer menu.

If you need to select more than one object, use either SHIFT-CLICK or CTRL-CLICK techniques similar to the ones used for the same purpose in the Object Navigator. The SHIFT-CLICK method is used to select a range of menu items that belong to one menu. For example, you can select all the menu items of MAIN_MENU menu displayed in the Menu Editor:

1. Click the File menu item.
2. SHIFT+CLICK the Help menu item.

All the items of this menu are selected. If CTRL+CLICK is used instead of the SHIFT+CLICK, the actions above would have resulted in the selection of only File and Help menu items.

The SHIFT and CTRL selecting techniques can be combined to provide for a variety of ways to select objects in the Menu Editor. Suppose, for example, that you want to select all the items that belong to menus File, Window, and also the menu Help. Before you start, execute an Expand All command on MAIN_MENU menu. You should see something similar to Figure 8.1.

1. Click New menu item.
2. SHIFT+CLICK the Exit menu item. All items of File menu are selected.
3. CTRL+CLICK the Cascade menu item under Window menu.
4. SHIFT+CLICK the Arrange Icons menu item. All items of Window menu are selected.
5. CTRL+CLICK the menu handle to the left of the Contents menu item. This action selects the Help menu.

After these steps, you should see something similar to Figure 8.3.

Note that clicking the Help menu handle is different from clicking the Help menu item in the MAIN_MENU. The first action selects the menu Help; the second one selects the item Help in MAIN_MENU menu. This action is also different from selecting Contents and About menu items, which are items of the Help menu.

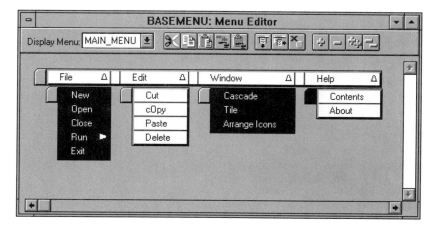

FIGURE 8.3   SHIFT and CTRL selecting objects in Menu Editor.

When the Synchronize property of the Object Navigator is on, each object you select in the Menu Editor will be automatically selected in the Navigator, and vice-versa. This means that, besides the Menu Editor, you can use the Navigator to select the menu objects you want to work with.

8.3.2 CREATING MENUS AND MENU ITEMS

In the Menu Editor you can create menus and menu items quickly and easily. To experience this, in this section you will build a menu similar to the menu provided in CH8.FMB that you have used so far.

First create and save a new menu module that will be used during this section:

1. Start Forms Designer.
2. Create a new menu module in the Object Navigator.
3. Replace the module's default name assigned by the Navigator with a more meaningful one, for example BASEMENU.
4. Save the newly created module to an appropriate directory in your file system.

Now you are ready to create the new menu.

Double-click the Menu type icon 📃, or select Tools | Menu Editor... to launch the Menu Editor. The Designer creates and displays a menu called MAIN_MENU and a menu item labeled <New_Item>, which is selected and waiting for you to type over.

1. Type **File** over the <New_Item> label.
2. Click the Create Right tool 📄 in the toolbar or select Menu | Create Right from the menu. The editor creates a new item to the right of File.
3. Type **Edit** in the label of the new item.
4. Follow the steps above to create the items Window and Help for the MAIN_MENU.

If your Navigator has the Synchronize property on, you will see that the new menu items fall in the appropriate location in the Navigator's object tree as you create them.

At this point, you have created the top level of the menu. Its items could be terminal nodes that execute a command or open a window; however, in a full-fledged application, they usually call other menus to offer more options to the user.

To create the submenu of the File item follow these steps:

1. Select the File menu item.
2. Click the Create Down tool ▣ in the toolbar, or select Menu | Create Down from the menu. The editor creates a new menu and a <New_Menu> item for this menu. The File item in the MAIN_MENU is now linked to the newly created menu, and the △ icon suggests that it is in an expanded state.
3. Type **New** over <New_Item> label.
4. Click the Create Down tool ▣ from the toolbar or select Menu | Create Down from the menu. This time, the editor creates a new menu item under **New**.
5. Label the new item **Open**.
6. Repeat the step above to create Close, Run, Print, and Exit menu items for the File submenu.

If you look at the Object Navigator window, you will notice that Designer has created a new menu and named it FILE_MENU. Its items are listed underneath as you created them. Furthermore, in the MAIN_MENU, Designer automatically has set the type of item File to menu (its icon is 団), and linked it to the FILE_MENU that you created. When users will run the application and select File from the menu, FILE_MENU will appear. As you see, the Menu Editor allows you to simply draw this relationship in the workarea. To practice your skills, create submenus for Edit, Window, and Help items, following the instructions above. They should contain the same items as the menu in Figure 8.1.

You can use the Layout Editor to create as many submenus as your application needs, all in one screen. For example, you may create a submenu under the Run menu item of FILE_MENU:

1. Select Run menu item.
2. Click the Create Right icon ▣ in the toolbar or select Menu | Create Right from the menu. The editor creates a new submenu to the right of Run. The Edit, Window, and Help submenus are shifted right to make room for the new submenu. The Object Navigator inserts this new submenu in the object tree and names it RUN_MENU. The type of RUN_ITEM in FILE_MENU changes to menu (its icon now is 団).
3. Label the first item of this submenu **Forms**.
4. Click the Create Down tool ▣ in the toolbar or select Menu | Create Down from the menu. Each time this action is executed the editor creates a new item for the RUN_MENU.
5. Type **Reports** over <New_Item> label.
6. Repeat Steps 4 and 5 to create the menu item Graphics.

When finished, your menu should look like the one shown in Figure 8.4. Save the module, because you will use it later in the chapter.

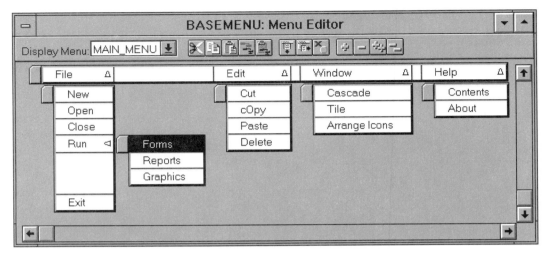

FIGURE 8.4   Base menu.

It took you only a few minutes to create the frame for the application menu. Its functionality must be embellished and useful actions attached to each menu item. Issues related to this process will be discussed in Chapter 17. By making the process of creating the menu simple and easy, Oracle Forms allows you to focus the attention on this functionality. Technicalities such as linking or naming menu objects become transparent and are handled automatically by the Designer.

8.3.3 DELETING MENUS AND MENU ITEMS

You can delete one menu item at a time or a selection of them:

1. Select the item or items you want to delete.
2. Press DELETE from the keyboard or choose Edit | Clear from the menu. An Oracle Forms alert box is displayed (see Figure 8.5). It wants you to confirm that you want to delete.
3. Click Yes if you want to proceed with the delete, or Cancel.

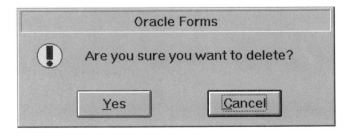

FIGURE 8.5   Delete confirmation alert.

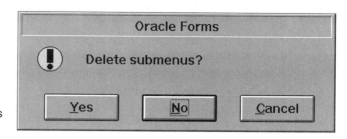

FIGURE 8.6 Delete submenus confirmation alert.

While Designer allows you to delete multiple menu items at a time, menus can be deleted only one at a time. To delete a menu object follow these steps:

1. Click the menu handle of the object you want to delete.
2. Press DELETE from the keyboard or choose Edit | Clear from the menu.

Depending on the selected object several things may happen here.

If you selected to delete the top-level menu, you will be prompted to confirm the action with the same alert as in Figure 8.5. If the menu does not have any submenus attached to it, clicking Yes removes it from the current module. But, if the menu has submenus attached, clicking Yes will bring up the alert shown in Figure 8.6.

Clicking Yes in this alert box will delete the selected menu and all its submenus. Clicking No will delete only the current menu, but leave the submenus attached to it intact. Clicking Cancel rolls back the whole delete action.

If, on the other hand, you selected to delete a submenu of the top-level menu, you will see the alert shown in Figure 8.7.

Clicking Detach will simply break the link between the selected menu and the menu item that owns it in the parent menu. The menu itself will not be removed from the current module. Clicking Delete will proceed with the deletion. Here, if the selected menu has submenus attached to it, you will be prompted to delete the submenus or not, as discussed previously.

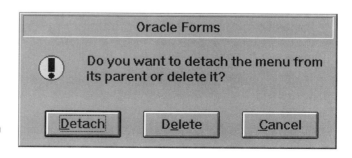

FIGURE 8.7 Detach confirmation alert.

8.3.4 CUTTING, COPYING, PASTING, AND MOVING

As in other Oracle Forms editors, cutting in the Menu Editor is a safer alternative to deleting because you can always paste the object from the clipboard. Cutting removes the object from the current menu module hierarchy tree and places it in the Windows clipboard, where it will remain until another object is placed there. To cut, follow these steps:

1. Select the object or objects you want to cut.
2. Press CTRL+X from the keyboard or choose Edit | Cut from the menu.

As with deleting, you can cut several menu items together, but only one menu object at a time.

To place the object in the clipboard without removing it from the Menu Editor, use the copy command. To copy, proceed as follows:

1. Select the object or objects you want to cut.
2. Press CTRL+C from the keyboard, or choose Edit | Cut from the menu.

Here again, copying works for more than one menu item, but only for one menu object at a time.

Once an object is placed in the clipboard, you can paste it to another location in the menu. To paste, follow these steps:

1. Click in the menu location where you want to paste the object.
2. Press CTRL+V from the keyboard, or choose Edit | Paste from the menu.

The Menu Editor will execute the paste command only if you clicked a menu item. If the object in the clipboard is another menu item, then it is added to the right or below the current selection, as yet another item in the parent menu. But, if the object in the clipboard is a menu, then this is not only copied to the new location, but also attached to the selected item.

Cut and paste can be used to move objects from one window of the Menu Editor to another. If you want to move objects to a location within the window, you can simply drag and drop them to the new location. To move menu items follow this procedure:

1. Select the item or items you want to move.
2. Click the selection and hold the mouse button down.
3. Holding the mouse button down, drag the selection to the new location. When the cursor moves outside the selected item, it changes shape into the cross hair cursor $+$.
4. Release the mouse button when the focus is on the new location.

Designer will guide you to move an item to the appropriate location. As soon as the cross hair cursor + moves on menu items, a light blue bar appears along the border lines of these items. If you release the mouse button at that moment, this is where the dragged items will be inserted. The light blue bar appears along vertical edges of menu items for horizontally displayed menus and along horizontal edges for vertically displayed ones.

Using drag-and-drop techniques with menus is slightly different than with menu items. First of all, as with other commands in this section, you cannot move multiple menus with one action. If you attempt to move more than one menu, Designer will display the error message, FRM-15205: Cannot drag more than one menu item at once.

Dragging the menu handle and dropping it to a new location detaches the menu from the original menu item and attaches it to the new item, but does not affect the menu itself. If during the move, the cross hair cursor + navigates inside an item to which this menu can be attached, that item is highlighted. If the menu item is not highlighted, then attaching the menu to that item is not allowed. For example, you cannot attach the menu to an item of its own.

When a menu is moved around and attached to another menu item, the *Command Type* property of that item is set to '*Menu*'. If the previous setting for this property was PL/SQL, and there is PL/SQL code attached to the menu item, the Designer will prevent accidental loss of code when *Command Type* changes to '*Menu*'. You will be prompted with the alert shown in Figure 8.8. If you do not want to save the code currently attached to the item, click Change Type button. Otherwise click Cancel and take the necessary steps to save the code. If another submenu is already attached to the item, an alert will appear and you can choose to either replace it with the selected menu or cancel the operation.

As you can see, drag-and-drop in its simple form does not create any new menus in the module; it simply detaches and attaches existing ones to different items. But, with a slight modification, you can make drag-and-drop replicate and expand the functionality of copy and paste. The modification is to keep the CTRL pressed while performing the actions described on the following page.

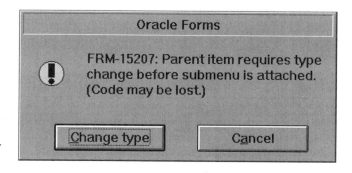

FIGURE 8.8   Replace confirmation alert.

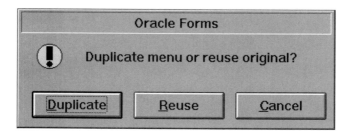

FIGURE 8.9 Duplicate confirmation alert.

1. Press CTRL from the keyboard.
2. Click the menu handle of the menu you want to drag and hold the mouse button down.
3. Holding down the mouse button, drag the menu to the new location.
4. Release the mouse button to drop the menu to the new location. At this point, the alert box shown in Figure 8.9 appears.

Clicking Duplicate will create a new menu with the same items as the original one, attached to the target item. The original menu is still in its place. Thus, this action is identical to a copy-and-paste action. Clicking Reuse button, will not create a new object. A pointer to the original menu is created, instead. The menu handle for both instances changes to the icon 🔲 that indicates that there are multiple instances of that menu. Not all the instances of a multiple-instance menu may be visible at any given moment in the Menu Editor. If one instance is displayed, and you want to locate the other instances, select Menu | Next Instance from the menu. This command moves in circular fashion among all the instances of a menu object.

8.3.5 HORIZONTAL AND VERTICAL ORIENTATION

By default, the Menu Editor will display the top-level menu horizontally. However, you may need to switch the orientation and display the menu vertically. To experiment with this feature, continue working with the File menu from the BASEMENU module you created earlier in the chapter:

1. Select FILE_MENU from the Display Menu drop-down list box in the toolbar. The menu is displayed horizontally in the editor's workarea.
2. Select Menu | Switch Orientation from the Designer menu.

Expand the FILE_MENU. You should see something similar to Figure 8.10.
Select Menu | Switch Orientation again to return to the original view of the editor.

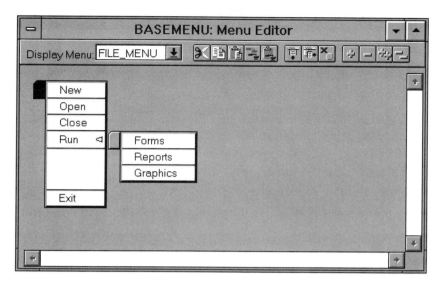

FIGURE 8.10   Vertical View of Menu Editor.

8.4 SUMMARY

The Menu Editor is the Designer's tool to create the menu modules for your applications. This chapter explained the components of the Menu Editor and how to
use it effectively. Basic concepts covered in this chapter include the following:

- ❏ Accessing the Menu Editor
- ❏ Components of the Menu Editor
    - ❏ Menu Editor workarea
    - ❏ Toolbar
- ❏ Using the Menu Editor
    - ❏ Navigating and selecting
    - ❏ Creating menus and menu items
    - ❏ Deleting menus and menu items
    - ❏ Cutting, copying, pasting, and moving
    - ❏ Horizontal and Vertical Orientation of the Menu Editor

Chapter 9

INTRODUCTION TO SQL

"God never sent a messenger save with the language of his folk, that he might make the message clear for them."

—The Koran

9.1 BRIEF HISTORY OF SQL LANGUAGE

SQL, an abbreviation for Structured Query Language, forms the foundations of all relational database systems. It is an English-like computer language that makes the process of interacting with databases very simple. For traditional and historical reasons, its name is pronounced "sequel," although a more recent way to say it is "es-que-el" (claimed by some to be the standard one). SQL and relational database management systems originate in an article titled "A Relational Model of Data for Large Shared Data Banks", published in June 1970 in *Communications of the Association for Computing Machinery* (CACM) Journal. Its author, Dr. Edgar F. Codd was a researcher at the IBM Research Laboratory in San Jose, California. Using concepts and results of branches of mathematics such as set theory and Boolean algebra, Codd laid the foundations of what would become the most widespread type of databases in the computer industry today.

Other researchers at the IBM San Jose Research Laboratory concentrated their efforts on implementing the ideas of Codd. In the mid-1970s, a number of languages were designed, based on his abstract relational model. One of these languages, known as Structured English QUEry Language (SEQUEL), was used in an IBM prototype called SEQUEL-XRM. In 1976, IBM launched the efforts for a second prototype of its relational database system under the code name System R. System R used a subset of the original SEQUEL language, called SQL.

The warm reception of System R in those IBM sites where it was deployed clearly showed that relational databases using SQL had a bright future. Other vendors began to move even faster than IBM to develop their own products. At least one of them, Relational Software, Inc., from Belmont, California, created in 1979 the first commercially available relational database called ORACLE. Based on the popularity of its product, the company later changed its name to Oracle Corporation. Today, it is the leading relational database vendor and one of the largest software companies worldwide. IBM and other vendors followed with their own SQL products. DB2 was introduced in 1983 and SYBASE in 1986.

Because of the large number of SQL-based products and the wide-spread use of SQL with relational database technologies, there has been a persisting need to standardize the language. The first SQL standard was approved by the American National Standards Institute (ANSI) in 1986. This standard was adopted by the International Standards Organization (ISO) in 1987. In late 1992, both ANSI and ISO approved a revised and greatly expanded standard of SQL under the name International Standard ISO.IEC 9075:1992, *Database Language SQL*.

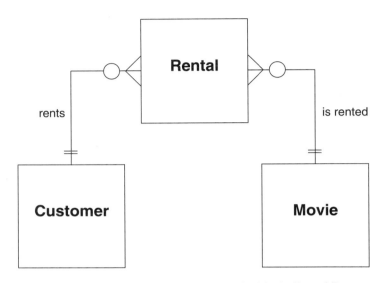

FIGURE 9.1   Entity relationship diagram for Movie Rental Database.

9.2 MOVIE RENTAL DATABASE

This chapter will discuss a number of SQL commands and functions. A small application provided in the companion diskette will help you follow the examples presented here. This application consists of only three tables: Customer, Movie, and Rental. They contain information that a movie rental store can find useful in keeping track of its business activities. The Customer table stores data about individual customers such as name, telephone number, date of birth, and membership date. The Movie table stores information about the movies that the video

TABLE 9.1   Attributes for entity CUSTOMER.

ENTITY	ATTRIBUTES	DATA TYPE	LENGTH	PK	FK	ATTRIBUTE CONSTRAINTS
Customer	Customer ID	NUMBER	6	Y		Internal tracking number
	Last Name	VARCHAR2	30			Not NULL
	First Name	VARCHAR2	30			
	Phone Number	VARCHAR2	14			
	Date of Birth	DATE				
	Membership Date	DATE				

TABLE 9.2 Attributes for entity MOVIE.

ENTITY	ATTRIBUTES	DATA TYPE	LENGTH	PK	FK	ATTRIBUTE CONSTRAINTS
Movie	Movie ID	NUMBER	6	Y		Internal tracking number
	Title	VARCHAR2	50			Not NULL
	Director Name	VARCHAR2	30			
	Main Actor	VARCHAR2	30			
	Main Actress	VARCHAR2	30			
	Rating	VARCHAR2	8			

store rents out to its customers. Such information includes the movie title, rating, names of director, lead actor, and lead actress. A Customer may rent several movies, and a Movie may be rented by more than one customer at any one time. The Rental table records every such transaction. The data stored in this table include the customer and movie identification numbers, rental date, return date, and rental rate.

Figure 9.1 represents the entity relationship diagram of the Movie Rental Database, which will be called MRD.

The relationship between Customer and Rental entities on the left side of the picture can be interpreted as follows: "A Customer may initiate zero or more Rental transactions, during which he or she rents a movie. A Rental transaction must be initiated by one and only one Customer." The relationship between Movie and Rental entities to the right states: "A Movie may be rented zero or more times during a Rental transaction by a Customer. A Rental transaction must involve one and only one Movie." Tables 9.1, 9.2, and 9.3 list the attributes of each entity.

TABLE 9.3 Attributes for entity RENTAL.

ENTITY	ATTRIBUTES	DATA TYPE	LENGTH	PK	FK	ATTRIBUTE CONSTRAINTS
Rental	Customer ID	NUMBER	6	Y	Y	ID of customer renting a movie
	Movie ID	NUMBER	6	Y	Y	ID of movie rented by the customer
	Rent Date	DATE		Y		
	Return Date	DATE				
	Daily Rate	NUMBER	4, 2			Up two digits after decimal point

> # Note
>
> The MRD database with which you will work in this chapter and the next is simplified in order to allow you to focus on the elements of the SQL and PL/SQL languages rather than on the complexity of a data modeling problem. Part Three expands on the problem of the neighborhood video rental store. The chapters in this part analyze, design, and build an Oracle Forms application to solve this problem.

The companion disk provided with this book installs a SQL*Plus script that creates these tables and loads sample data in them. Instructions to execute this script against your Oracle Server database are provided in the section *Installing the Companion Disk* in the preface.

At this point you are ready to follow the topics discussed in the rest of this chapter. It will be assumed that you are using the Oracle Corporation's SQL*Plus program to execute the commands discussed here. Start SQL*Plus and log on to the database with the user account used to run the script mentioned in the previous paragraph.

9.3 CATEGORIES OF SQL COMMANDS

The SQL language in itself does not have complicated syntactic structures or a large number of commands. The intentions of its designers were to allow a large number of users to access and to manipulate data stored in database structures easily. The idea was to provide users of SQL with a way to ask for the data they needed, without specifying how these data were to be retrieved. It is customary to classify the commands in the SQL language in four categories:

❑ Data Retrieval Command is a category that contains only one command: SELECT. This command is a cornerstone of SQL and allows users to query necessary data from the database. Because of its importance and widespread usage, it is often considered in a category of its own.

❑ Data Manipulation Language (DML) commands allow the user to INSERT, UPDATE, and DELETE data. Often it is necessary to use the SELECT command to specify the set of data that should be updated or deleted. This is the reason why SELECT sometimes is included with the other three commands in the DML category.

❑ Data Definition Language (DDL) commands modify the structure of the database by creating, replacing, altering, or dropping objects such as tables, indexes, and views.

❑ Data Control Language (DCL) commands protect the integrity of the database and the consistency of data by controlling and managing the access to the database structures.

A full discussion of SQL and all the categories of commands introduced above would be beyond the scope of this book. They are discussed thoroughly in other books and manuals. An excellent book on this subject is *The SQL Guide to ORACLE* by Rick F. van der Lans (1992, Addison-Wesley). This chapter will discuss only those SQL commands that are used in Oracle Forms applications. They belong to the first two categories and are SELECT, INSERT, UPDATE, and DELETE.

9.4 DATA RETRIEVAL WITH SELECT

A SELECT command is a query expression optionally followed by an ORDER BY clause. The first part of the command retrieves the data from the database according to the query specifications. If the ORDER BY clause is specified, the set of records is sorted or ordered, according to the clause. Figure 9.2 shows two SELECT commands, and the data they return. The first command contains only the query expression; the second command, in addition, contains ordering instructions, which affect the order in which the records retrieved by the query are displayed.

Let us mention at this point some conventions that will be used throughout this chapter:

❑ First, SQL language keywords like SELECT, FROM, WHERE, and ORDER BY will always be shown capitalized. Nothing would change in the outcome of these statements if lower-case letters were used, because SQL is not a case-sensitive language in itself. The purpose of this convention is to clearly distinguish the language constructs from database objects.

❑ Second, the outcome of a statement will be shown only when it helps in understanding the statement. Even in those cases, the outcome may have been formatted for clarity purposes. For example, the query in Figure 9.2 returns several records, but only a few of them are shown in the picture.

```
SQL> SELECT last_name, first_name
  2  FROM customer
  3  WHERE member_dt > '01-JAN-95';

LAST_NAME                         FIRST_NAME
----------------------------      --------------------------------
Smith                             Robert
Richard                           Joanne
Moore                             Suzanne
Moore                             Karla
Campbell                          Michael

SQL> SELECT last_name, first_name
  2  FROM customer
  3  WHERE member_dt > '01-JAN-95'
  4  ORDER BY last_name;

LAST_NAME                         FIRST_NAME
----------------------------      --------------------------------
Campbell                          Michael
Moore                             Suzanne
Moore                             Karla
Richard                           Joanne
Smith                             Robert
```

FIGURE 9.2 Examples of SELECT commands.

❑ Finally, breaking SQL statements in multiple lines is done primarily for clarity and ease of understanding. It is not a requirement of the language syntax. The statements shown in Figure 9.3 are equivalent, but more obscure and difficult to follow than the ones in Figure 9.2.

```
SELECT last_name, first_name FROM
customer WHERE member_dt > '01-JAN-95';

SELECT last_name, first_name FROM customer WHERE member_dt >
'01-JAN-95' ORDER BY last_name;
```

FIGURE 9.3 Examples of obscure SELECT statements.

9.4.1 SELECTING ALL ROWS FROM A TABLE

As a minimum, every query expression must contain a SELECT clause and a FROM clause. The SELECT clause defines the columns that must be retrieved from the query. The FROM clause specifies the table (or tables) from which the data will be retrieved. A query that contains only the SELECT and FROM clauses retrieves all the rows in the specified tables. A third clause, the WHERE clause, must be added to supply restrictive criteria that reduce the number of rows returned by the query.

Depending on the content of the SELECT clause, the query may retrieve one, more than one, or all the columns of data in a table. To retrieve just one column from a table, simply provide the name of the column after the SELECT command, as shown in Figure 9.4.

To retrieve more than one column, provide their name after the SELECT keyword. The name of each column, except for the last must be followed by a comma to separate it from the others. The query shown in Figure 9.5 selects the First Name, Last Name, and Membership Date from the Customer table.

When the query returns the data from the database, the columns will be listed in the order specified in the SELECT statement. In the previous example, FIRST_NAME is followed by the LAST_NAME for each customer, despite the fact that the data in the database are stored in the reverse order.

There are two ways to retrieve all the columns from a table. The first one uses the same format as the SELECT statement shown in Figure 9.5. You specify the names of all the columns, instead of just three. Obviously, this method requires you to know the names of all the columns beforehand, and may involve extensive typing, especially for tables with many columns. The advantages

```
SQL> SELECT title
  2   FROM movie;

TITLE
------------------------
Pulp Fiction
Jefferson in Paris
Howards End
The Remains of the Day
A Walk in the Clouds
Something to Talk About
Scent of a Woman
When a Man Loves a Woman
Amadeus
The Silence of the Lambs
```

FIGURE 9.4 One column SELECT command.

```
SQL> SELECT first_name, last_name, member_dt
  2  FROM customer;

FIRST_NAME                            LAST_NAME           MEMBER_DT
------------------------------        ----------------    ---------
John                                  Moore               27-MAR-94
Karen                                 Campbell            14-NOV-94
Robert                                Smith               01-SEP-95
Joanne                                Richard             25-JUL-95
Suzanne                               Moore               24-MAR-95
Karla                                 Moore               30-JUL-95
Michael                               Campbell            19-AUG-95
```

FIGURE 9.5   Multiple column SELECT command.

though are that you get exactly those data elements you ask for, in the order you supply. This type of statement is mostly used in applications that use SQL and embedded SQL statements.

A shortcut to this method is to use the asterisk symbol * after the SELECT keyword. An example of this follows:

SELECT * FROM customer;

When the query returns data from the database, the columns are listed in the same order as they are stored in the physical structure of the table. This type of query is usually used in interactive sessions such as a SQL*Plus session.

9.4.2 FILTERING ROWS—THE WHERE CLAUSE

Queries discussed in the previous section retrieve all the rows from the tables specified in the FROM clause. In systems with scarce computing resources, a high number of users, or in client/server environments, queries like these negatively affect the performance of the applications, and of the database system as a whole. On the other hand, there are very few applications that require all the records of a table to be queried and retrieved. In most database systems users need only a small subset of the large number of records that may be stored in tables.

In order to select only certain rows from a table, the WHERE clause is added to the previous query statements immediately after the FROM clause. This clause filters out rows that do not meet the needs of users and that would be otherwise returned by the query. Rows are included or excluded based upon the value of the condition specified by the WHERE clause. For every row in the table, if the condition is evaluated to TRUE, the row is returned by the query. If it is evaluated to FALSE or UNKNOWN the row is not returned.

A query statement now has the following form:

```
SELECT clause
FROM clause
WHERE condition;
```

In its most simple form, a condition uses an operator to compare data in a column with a character literal, numerical expression, or data in another column. If the column being compared has an alphanumeric datatype, the character literal it is being compared with must be enclosed in quotes.

Table 9.4 lists some of the logical operators used the most in SQL statements. The first column contains the form of the condition if the operator is used. The second column states in which case the condition evaluates TRUE.

9.4.3 SQL OPERATORS

Let us present some examples that use the operators presented above in the tables of the Movie Rental Database.

❑ **Equality Operator.** This operator is used to retrieve rows with a certain column value. The following statement retrieves all the movies in the database directed by Spielberg:

```
SELECT title
FROM movies
WHERE director = 'Spielberg';
```

TABLE 9.4   Frequently used SQL operators.

CONDITION...	... EVALUATES TRUE IF ...
A = B	A is equal to B
A != B, A <> B	A is not equal to B
A > B; A >= B	A is greater than B; A is greater than or equal to B
A < B; A <= B	A is smaller than B; A is smaller than or equal to B
A IN (List_Item_1, ... , List_Item_N)	A is equal to any member of the list
A BETWEEN x AND y	Value of A is between values x and y, inclusive
A LIKE y	A matches the pattern specified by y
A IS NULL	Value of A is missing
NOT	Reverses the truth value of any of the preceding four operators

❑ **Inequality Operators.** These operators are used to retrieve all those rows that do not contain a certain column value. For example, find all the movies that are not rated R:

```
SELECT title
FROM movies
WHERE rating <> 'R';
```

❑ **Greater Than/Less Than Operators.** These operators retrieve rows for which the value of the specified column is greater than or less than a particular value, respectively. The conditions can be relaxed in both cases by adding the equality operator '='. For example, retrieve all the records of Rental transactions for which the customers have paid $1.99 or more every day:

```
SELECT *
FROM rental
WHERE daily_rate >= 1.99;
```

Oracle adjusts the behavior of these operators to the datatype of the column being compared. Indeed, if the column's datatype is alphanumeric, the condition column_name > value retrieves all the rows for which the value of the column ranks behind the given value in alphabetic order. For example, list all the customers whose last names begin with 'L' and beyond:

```
SELECT first_name, last_name
FROM customer
WHERE last_name > 'L';
```

If the datatype of the column is date, then the equality or inequality operators compare the dates. For example, retrieve all the customers that have joined the club on or after January 1, 1995:

```
SELECT first_name, last_name
FROM customer
WHERE member_dt >= '01-JAN-95';
```

The ability of the same operator (or function) to perform differently depending, among others, on the datatype of parameters passed into it, is called overloading. Chapter 19 will discuss overloading in Oracle Forms applications in more detail.

❏ **IN Operator.** The general syntax of this operator is WHERE *column* IN (*list_item_1, ... list_item_N*). It selects only those rows whose column value is one of the list items included in parentheses. For example, select all the movies rated as PG-13 and R:

```
SELECT title
FROM movie
WHERE rating IN ('PG-13', 'R');
```

When the operator IN is preceded by the operator NOT, the query selects all those rows whose column value is not one of the list items. The following statement retrieves all the movies that are not rated PG-13 or R.

```
SELECT title
FROM movie
WHERE rating NOT IN ('PG-13', 'R');
```

❏ **BETWEEN Operator.** The syntax for this operator is WHERE *column* BETWEEN *value_1* AND *value_2*. This operator selects all rows whose column value is greater or equal to *value_1* and smaller than or equal to *value_2*. Again, Oracle uses polymorphism to implement the operator with different datatypes. The following query retrieves all the rental transactions for which the customers paid between $1.25 and $1.99 per day:

```
SELECT *
FROM rental
WHERE daily_rate BETWEEN 1.25 AND 1.99;
```

The following query retrieves all the customers that joined the video rental club on the Labor Day Weekend 1995:

```
SELECT first_name, last_name
FROM customer
WHERE member_dt BETWEEN '02-SEP-95' AND '04-SEP-95';
```

When the operator BETWEEN is preceded by the operator NOT, the query retrieves rows whose column value is less than *value_1* or greater than *value_2*. The following query retrieves all the customer records that were not retrieved by the previous one:

```
SELECT first_name, last_name
FROM customer
WHERE member_dt NOT BETWEEN '02-SEP-95' AND '04-SEP-95';
```

❑ **LIKE Operator.** The general syntax of this operator is WHERE *column* LIKE *pattern*. It selects all those rows whose column value matches the character pattern specified by *pattern*. The column datatype in this case must be either CHAR or VARCHAR2. When the equality operator is used, Oracle does an exact match of the values in the table column. But, when the LIKE operator is used, the query can be less restrictive thanks to the use of the two wildcard symbols '%' and '_' in the character pattern specification. The wildcard '%' is used to represent zero or more characters in the pattern string. The following query searches for the names of the directors of *ROCKY* and all its sequels in the database:

```
SELECT director
FROM movie
WHERE title LIKE 'ROCKY%';
```

The wildcard '_' represents one and only one character in the exact position in the string where the wildcard is used. The following query selects the directors of *ROCKY II* and *ROCKY IV*, but not the director of the initial movie itself, or of *ROCKY III:*

```
SELECT director
FROM movie
WHERE title LIKE 'ROCKY __';
```

Once again, the operator NOT can be used to logically negate the outcome of the LIKE operator. For example, the following query selects all the customers, except for those that live in Washington, D.C., where the area code of telephone numbers is 202:

```
SELECT first_name, last_name
FROM customer
WHERE phone NOT LIKE '(202)%';
```

❑ **IS NULL Operator.** The syntax of this operator is WHERE *column* IS NULL. It selects all those rows whose specified column does not contain any value at all. To select the columns that do contain any value the IS NOT NULL operator is used. The following query retrieves all the movies that are not rated:

```
SELECT title
FROM movie
WHERE rating IS NULL;
```

The statement below retrieves the movies that are rated:

```
SELECT title
FROM movie
WHERE rating IS NOT NULL;
```

9.4.4 BOOLEAN OPERATORS

Multiple conditions can be specified in the WHERE clause. These conditions can be combined with the Boolean operators AND and OR.

❑ The logical operator AND returns TRUE if both its operands evaluate to TRUE. It returns FALSE if at least one of the operands evaluates to FALSE. A query whose WHERE clause looks like

WHERE Condition_A AND Condition_B

will return only those rows that satisfy both Condition_A and Condition_B. For example, the following query retrieves all the customers whose last name begins with 'S' and who have been club members since January 1, 1995:

```
SELECT first_name, last_name
FROM customer
WHERE last_name LIKE 'S%'
AND member_dt >= '01-JAN-95';
```

❑ The logical operator OR returns TRUE if at least one of the operands evaluates to TRUE. It returns FALSE only if both of them evaluate to FALSE. A query whose WHERE clause looks like

WHERE Condition_A OR Condition_B

will return those rows that satisfy Condition_A or Condition_B. The following query selects all the movies in which Tom Hanks or Sharon Stone play the leading role:

```
SELECT title
FROM movie
WHERE actor = 'Tom Hanks'
OR actress = 'Sharon Stone';
```

Table 9.5 displays the results of these operations when the operands take different truth values. In Boolean algebra, this is known as a truth table.

Obviously, the operators NOT, AND, and OR can be combined to form complicated search criteria. In such cases, the truth value of the conditions is evaluated according to precedence rules. The NOT operator is highest in the hierarchy, then comes AND, and finally, the OR operator. For example, the following query retrieves all the customers whose last name begins with 'S' and have their phone number in the database. It also selects all the customers born after January 1, 1975 whether they meet the previous criteria or not.

```
SELECT first_name, last_name, phone, dob
FROM customer
WHERE last_name LIKE 'S%'
AND phone IS NOT NULL
OR dob >= '01-JAN-75';
```

9.4.5 USING PARENTHESES IN LOGICAL EXPRESSIONS

When several conditions are combined in a WHERE clause, the expression may become complicated and difficult to read. It is easy to introduce errors in such expressions and it is difficult to debug them. It is advisable to use parentheses in

TABLE 9.5 Truth table for Boolean operators AND and OR.

A	B	A AND B	A OR B
TRUE	TRUE	TRUE	TRUE
TRUE	FALSE	FALSE	TRUE
FALSE	TRUE	FALSE	TRUE
FALSE	FALSE	FALSE	FALSE

```
SQL> SELECT *
  2  FROM rental
  3  WHERE (movie_id = 203
  4    OR movie_id = 208)
  5    AND rent_dt BETWEEN '02-SEP-95' and '04-SEP-95';


CUSTOMER_ID  MOVIE_ID RENT_DT   RETURN_DT DAILY_RATE
-----------  -------- --------- --------- ----------
         70       203 02-SEP-95 03-SEP-95        .99
         70       208 02-SEP-95 04-SEP-95       1.99
         60       208 03-SEP-95 04-SEP-95       1.99
         40       203 03-SEP-95 04-SEP-95        .99
```

FIGURE 9.6   Importance of parentheses in logical expressions.

order to simplify the appearance of complicated logical expressions. Parentheses can also be used to override the default precedence rules of logical operators. Every expression enclosed in parentheses is evaluated before other expressions to its right or left. After this, the evaluation of the expression proceeds according to the precedence rules mentioned before. The query in Figure 9.6 selects all the rental transactions for movies *The Remains of the Day* (movie ID is 203) or *Amadeus* (movie ID is 208) that occurred during Labor Day Weekend 1995.

If the parentheses are omitted, the outcome of the query is different, as Figure 9.7 shows. In the statement presented here, the operator AND takes prece-

```
SQL> SELECT *
  2  FROM rental
  3  WHERE movie_id = 203
  4    OR movie_id = 208
  5    AND rent_dt BETWEEN '02-SEP-95' and '04-SEP-95';


CUSTOMER_ID  MOVIE_ID RENT_DT   RETURN_DT DAILY_RATE
-----------  -------- --------- --------- ----------
         70       203 02-SEP-95 03-SEP-95        .99
         70       208 02-SEP-95 04-SEP-95       1.99
         60       208 03-SEP-95 04-SEP-95       1.99
         40       203 03-SEP-95 04-SEP-95        .99
         30       203 12-JUN-95 13-JUN-95        .99
         60       203 21-NOV-95 23-NOV-95        .99
```

FIGURE 9.7   Importance of parentheses in logical expressions (continued).

dence over OR. Therefore, the query will retrieve all the transactions for the movie *The Remains of the Day* regardless of the rent date and the transactions for the movie *Amadeus* during Labor Day Weekend 1995.

9.4.6 GROUP BY CLAUSE

Often, there exists a need to group data returned from a query and display summary information for that group of data. The GROUP BY clause allows the SELECT statement to meet this requirement. The general syntax of this clause is GROUP BY *column.* The SELECT statement with a GROUP BY clause will return only one row displayed for each unique value of the column whose name is specified in the clause. The query presented in Figure 9.8 calculates how many rental transactions have occurred between August 20 and August 24, 1995 for movies *The Remains of the Day* (movie ID is 203) or *Amadeus* (movie ID is 208). The GROUP BY clause ensures that one record is displayed for each day, with the total number of the specified movies rented in that time period.

The GROUP BY clause can be used with more than one column. In the example above, you do not have a way to tell exactly how many copies of these two movies were rented each day. To retrieve the total of movies rented for each movie, for each day, you expand the GROUP BY clause as shown in Figure 9.9.

Now you can tell that on August 21 and August 22 both movies rented equally well. On August 23 *The Remains of the Day* rented one copy more than *Amadeus*. The situation was the reverse on August 24.

9.4.7 HAVING CLAUSE

When selecting rows from a table, you filter the unwanted ones by specifying restricting criteria in the WHERE clause. Similarly, when using the GROUP BY

```
SQL> SELECT rent_dt, count(*)
  2    FROM rental
  3    WHERE movie_id IN (203, 208)
  4    AND rent_dt BETWEEN '21-AUG-95' and '24-AUG-95'
  5    GROUP BY rent_dt;

RENT_DT          COUNT(*)
--------------------
21-AUG-95               2
22-AUG-95               2
23-AUG-95               3
24-AUG-95               3
```

FIGURE 9.8   GROUP BY clause.

```
SQL> SELECT rent_dt, movie_id, count(*)
  2  FROM rental
  3  WHERE movie_id IN (203, 208)
  4  AND rent_dt BETWEEN '21-AUG-95' and '24-AUG-95'
  5  GROUP BY rent_dt, movie_id;

RENT_DT       MOVIE_ID    COUNT(*)
---------   -----------   ----------
21-AUG-95        203          1
21-AUG-95        208          1
22-AUG-95        203          1
22-AUG-95        208          1
23-AUG-95        203          2
23-AUG-95        208          1
24-AUG-95        203          1
24-AUG-95        208          2
```

FIGURE 9.9   GROUP BY clause with multiple columns.

clause, you may need to filter out some of the grouped rows. In this case, the HAVING clause is used. The general format of this clause is HAVING *condition*, where *condition* is a logical expression that evaluates to TRUE or FALSE like the conditions in the WHERE clause. The query in Figure 9.10 is a slight modification of the statement shown in Figure 9.9.

This query lists on a day-by-day basis all the movies that have rented more than five copies per day during the specified period of time.

In a SELECT statement that contains WHERE, GROUP BY, and HAVING clauses, the records that do not fulfill the WHERE conditions are discarded first. Then, the remaining records are bundled together as specified in the GROUP BY clause. Finally, the HAVING clause removes those groups that do not meet its conditions. Obviously, you want to remove as many records in the first filtering performed by the WHERE clause. Therefore, the HAVING clause conditions should be designed to operate only on data that depend on the grouping of rows, but not on each individual record in the table.

```
SELECT rent_dt, movie_id, count(*)
FROM rental
WHERE rent_dt BETWEEN '21-AUG-95' AND '24-AUG-95'
GROUP BY rent_dt, movie_id
HAVING count(*) >=5;
```

FIGURE 9.10   HAVING clause.

9.4.8 JOINS

In the examples presented so far, you have queried data from single tables. One of the strongest features of SQL is the ease and flexibility it provides in selecting data from multiple tables. When data from more than one table are selected and displayed by the query as one logical record, it is said that the tables are joined. The easiest way to join two tables is to specify their column names in the SELECT clause and their names in the FROM clause of the query. However, this is not a type of query that should occur often, if at all. The reason is that it generates a Cartesian product of the rows in each table, or in other words, it matches each row in one table with all the rows in the second table, thus resulting in a large, often too large, number of records returned by the query.

Suppose, for example, that the Customer table has 100 records and the Movie table 1000 records, and you issue the following query:

```
SELECT last_name, first_name, title
FROM customer, movie;
```

In response to this statement, Oracle would return 100 x 1000 = 100,000 records from the database. This is certainly not needed or necessary.

The join that is used most frequently is the simple join, or equi-join. In this type of join, records from tables are joined based on the equality of data in columns from the respective tables. Obviously, similar data are compared together. The comparing occurs in the WHERE clause, or the HAVING clause if the GROUP BY clause is present. For example, the following query retrieves the names of customers and the dates they rented movies from the video store:

```
SELECT first_name, last_name, rent_dt
FROM customer, rental
WHERE customer.customer_id = rental.customer_id;
```

The condition for joining records from tables CUSTOMER and RENTAL is that the values in the respective CUSTOMER_ID columns must be the same. In order to avoid the ambiguity that arises when columns with the same name but from different tables are used in a SQL statement, the names of these columns must be prefixed by the table name, as shown in the example above.

You can join records from more than two tables. Be careful though to avoid a Cartesian product of rows, which has the undesired results explained earlier. As a rule of thumb, the number of conditions in the WHERE clause that compare columns from tables usually is one less than the number of tables. The following example selects the movies rented by each customer, together with rental dates and prices paid:

```
SELECT first_name, last_name, title, daily_rate
FROM customer, rental, movie
WHERE customer.customer_id = rental.customer_id
AND movie.movie_id = rental.movie_id;
```

In the last two queries the condition in the WHERE clause is responsible for joining data from different tables in a logical manner, but does little to further restrict the number of records returned by the queries. Additional conditions should be added to the statements as discussed in the previous sections.

Finally, let us mention that when multiple table names are involved in the query, the typing of their names can become cumbersome. To avoid the inevitable mistakes that can be made, pseudonyms or aliases can be used instead of the full names of tables. The following example is another version of the previous query, where aliases are used:

```
SELECT first_name, last_name, title, daily_rate
FROM customer C, rental R, movie M
WHERE C.customer_id = R.customer_id
AND M.movie_id = R.movie_id;
```

9.4.9 ORDER BY CLAUSE

What has been silently accepted in all the examples so far is the fact that the records returned by the queries do not appear in a particular order. In fact, records in relational databases are not stored in any particular order. However, the ORDER BY clause allows you to sort the outcome of a query based on the values of columns or expressions that will be returned by the query. For example, the query in Figure 9.11 lists the customers that have joined the video club during the month of September 1995, ordered alphabetically by LAST_NAME.

By default, SQL sorts the records in the ascending order, as shown in Figure 9.11. If you want to sort them in the descending order, add the keyword DESC at the end of the ORDER BY clause. Figure 9.12 shows a query that retrieves the same data as the query in Figure 9.11, but sorts them by LAST_NAME in descending order.

The output of a query can be ordered based on the data from more than one column. To do this, the additional columns are specified in the ORDER BY statement, separated by a comma. In a situation like this, the records are first sorted based on the value of the first column in the ORDER BY clause. Then, each set of records with the same value for the first column is sorted based on the second column, and so on. For example, the following query displays all the movies in the video rental database. The movies are sorted first based on the name of the leading actress, then actor, and finally, title.

```
SQL> SELECT last_name, first_name
  2  FROM customer
  3  WHERE member_dt >= '01-JAN-95'
  4    AND member_dt < '01-JAN-96'
  5  ORDER BY last_name;

LAST_NAME                          FIRST_NAME
--------------------------------   -------------------------
Campbell                           Michael
Moore                              Suzanne
Moore                              Karla
Richard                            Joanne
Smith                              Robert
```

FIGURE 9.11   ORDER BY clause.

```
SELECT actress, actor, title
FROM movie
ORDER by actress, actor, movie;
```

The columns to order by can be specified by supplying their name, as in all the examples presented here. They can also be specified by giving their position in the list of columns that appear in the SELECT clause. This is particularly useful when, instead of table columns, long expressions are evaluated. The following

```
SQL> SELECT last_name, first_name
  2 FROM customer
  3 WHERE member_dt >= '01-JAN-95'
  4   AND member_dt < '01-JAN-96'
  5 ORDER BY last_name DESC;

LAST_NAME                          FIRST_NAME
--------------------------------   -------------------------
Smith                              Robert
Richard                            Joanne
Moore                              Suzanne
Moore                              Karla
Campbell                           Michael
```

FIGURE 9.12   ORDER BY clause in descending order.

query is similar to another query encountered before. For each date between the specified dates, it calculates the number of the movies rented. It displays only those movies that have rented more than five copies each day, starting from the best rentals.

```
SELECT rent_dt, movie_id, count(*)
FROM rental
WHERE rent_dt BETWEEN '21-AUG-95' AND '24-AUG-95'
GROUP BY rent_dt, movie_id
HAVING count(*) > 5
ORDER BY 3 DESC;
```

This query sorts by the value calculated by the function COUNT, which is the third one in the SELECT clause.

9.5 EXPANDING QUERIES WITH SET OPERATIONS

It was mentioned earlier that the relational database model and SQL language are founded upon the mathematical theory of sets. For the purposes of this chapter, a *set* is a collection of items that share some common characteristics. These items are called elements of a set. Conventionally, sets are denoted with upper-case letters, whereas elements of a set are denoted with lower-case characters, sometimes followed by subscripts. Curled brackets are used to present a set and its elements or a part thereof. For example the following represents the set of days of the week:

WEEK = { Sunday, Monday, Tuesday, Wednesday, Thursday, Friday, Saturday }

Two constraints placed on the elements of a set are that a set cannot contain duplicate elements and the set cannot be considered as an element of itself. The need for the first one is fairly obvious. Weeks that contain two Mondays are not particularly helpful. The second constraint is less evident, but it should be sufficient to note that mathematics entered a deep crisis at the turn of the century, simply because mathematicians were not aware of the importance of this constraint.

There are three basic operations defined in set theory that allow for creation of new sets by combining elements of existing sets. These operations are UNION, INTERSECT, and MINUS. The UNION operation results in a set that contains elements that are in either set. It is denoted usually as $A \cup B$ or $A + B$. The INTERSECT operation results in a set that contains elements that are in both sets. It is denoted usually as $A \cap B$, $A \bullet B$, or simply AB. The MINUS operation results in sets with elements that are part of the first set, but are not part of the second one. It is denoted usually as A / B or $A - B$. Figure 9.13 visually displays the results of these operations.

> ## Note
>
> The blind alley the mathematicians of the early years of this century found themselves in is known as the Russell's paradox, after the great English mathematician and philosopher Lord Bertrand Russell (1872–1970). This paradox is often described in the popular literature as the barber's paradox.
>
> *Question: How would you define the barber of a village?*
>
> Answer: He shaves those that do not shave themselves.
>
> *Question: Who shaves the barber, then?*
>
> Answer: (Scratching the head) Well, there is no other barber to go to, since he's the only one in the village. But, he cannot shave himself either, because, being a barber, he must shave only those who do not shave themselves!

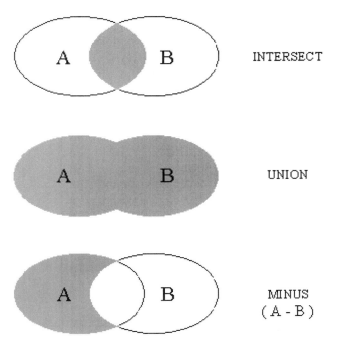

INTERSECT

UNION

MINUS
(A - B)

FIGURE 9.13   Visual example of set operations.

In relational databases, records returned by a query, or SELECT statement, form a set. Each individual record is an element of this set. The SQL language implements the three set operations described above, thus allowing you to further extend your ability to retrieve data from the database. The general syntax of statements that use set operators is

QUERY_1 Set Operator QUERY_2.

As an example, let QUERY_1 be the statement that selects all the movies where Anthony Hopkins plays the leading role:

```
SELECT title
FROM movie
WHERE actor = 'Anthony Hopkins';
```

Let QUERY_2 be the statement that selects all the movies where Emma Thompson plays the leading role:

```
SELECT title
FROM movie
WHERE actress = 'Emma Thompson';
```

Then, the statement in Figure 9.14 selects the movies in which Anthony Hopkins or Emma Thompson play leading roles.

```
SQL> SELECT title
  2    FROM movie
  3    WHERE actor = 'Anthony Hopkins'
  4    UNION
  5    SELECT title
  6    FROM movie
  7    WHERE actress = 'Emma Thompson';

TITLE
------------------------------
Howards End
Much Ado About Nothing
The Remains of the Day
The Silence of the Lambs
```

FIGURE 9.14   Using UNION in queries.

```
SQL> SELECT title
  2  FROM movie
  3  WHERE actor = 'Anthony Hopkins'
  4  INTERSECT
  5  SELECT title
  6  FROM movie
  7  WHERE actress = 'Emma Thompson';

TITLE
------------------------------
Howards End
The Remains of the Day
```

FIGURE 9.15 Using INTERSECT in queries.

Note that movies *Howard's End* and *The Remains of the Day* appear only once in the list, despite the fact that they are returned by both QUERY_1 and QUERY_2. This is how SQL implements the set theory constraint that elements in a set must be unique. However, in practice there may be instances when returning only the distinct rows of two queries is not desirable. To address this problem, SQL uses the operator UNION ALL, an extension of UNION, that simply merges the output of the two queries, without worrying about returning only the distinct rows.

Figure 9.15 shows the same two queries joined by the operator INTERSECT. The query returns all the movies in which the two actors play together.

Figure 9.16 shows QUERY_1 and QUERY_2 joined by the operator MINUS. The query returns the movies where Anthony Hopkins plays but not Emma Thompson.

```
SQL> SELECT title
  2  FROM movie
  3  WHERE actor = 'Anthony Hopkins'
  4  MINUS
  5  SELECT title
  6  FROM movie
  7  WHERE actress = 'Emma Thompson';

TITLE
------------------------------
The Silence of the Lambs
```

FIGURE 9.16 Using MINUS in queries.

The outcome of operators UNION, UNION ALL, and INTERSECT does not depend on the order in which the individual queries are listed. It is said that these operators are commutative. You can convince yourself by reversing the order of the queries in the first three statements. The operator MINUS however does not enjoy this property. Its outcome depends on the order in which the queries are executed. The query shown in Figure 9.17 uses the same individual queries as the one in Figure 9.16, but in reverse order. The different results are to be expected. The second query returns the movies where Emma Thompson plays without Anthony Hopkins.

This section concludes with a note on multiple uses of set operators. The examples shown previously use only two individual queries, but statements can be written where several queries can be combined using one or more set operators. In the set theory, the operator INTERSECT has the highest precedence of all. This means that $A \cup B \cap C$ is evaluated according to the following two steps:

1. $D = B \cap C$
2. $E = A \cup D$

Obviously, parentheses override this order by taking the highest precedence.

However, in the Oracle implementation of SQL language, all the set operators have the same precedence. Here, the same statement $A \cup B \cap C$ is evaluated as

1. $D = A \cup B$
2. $E = D \cap C$

Oracle will enforce the precedence rules of set operators in its upcoming versions. In the meantime, to ensure that SQL statements written today will return the same data in the future, resolve any potential ambiguity by using parentheses. For example, implement the previous statements as $(A \cup (B \cap C))$.

```
SQL> SELECT title
  2    FROM movie
  3    WHERE actress = 'Emma Thompson'
  4    MINUS
  5    SELECT title
  6    FROM movie
  7    WHERE actor = 'Anthony Hopkins';


TITLE
----------------------------
Much Ado About Nothing
```

FIGURE 9.17   MINUS is not commutative.

9.6 DATA MANIPULATION LANGUAGE COMMANDS

The next four sections will explain how to add, modify, or delete data from the database. The SQL commands that perform these tasks, INSERT, UPDATE, and DELETE are simple and straightforward. They form a category of SQL statements called Data Manipulation Language (DML). DML statements are slightly different from the SELECT command. SELECT is a passive command in the sense that it only displays data that already exist in the database. The content of the database does not change when a SELECT statement is issued. But, when a DML statement is issued, the content of the database changes.

9.6.1 COMMIT AND ROLLBACK

However, these changes do not occur instantaneously. As DML statements are issued, Oracle stores the data they modify in internal structures, known as rollback segments. At the same time, Oracle places locks on modified data, so that other users may not change them. Only when a COMMIT command is issued are these statements applied to the database, thus making the changes effective and available to all other users. At COMMIT time, the locks on data are released as well. In order to ensure the integrity of the database, Oracle issues an implicit COMMIT command each time Data Definition Language statements such as CREATE, MODIFY, or DROP commands are issued.

If you decide you want to undo the actions of DML commands issued during the current transaction, issue the ROLLBACK command. ROLLBACK throws away all changes made to data since the last COMMIT. Sometime, you may want to rollback just part of the transaction, but not the entire changes, since the last COMMIT. In such a case, *savepoints* are created in the transaction. Think of a savepoint as a picture of the database taken at the moment the savepoint is created. If at any time after that moment you are not happy with the outcome of some statement, you can undo the changes and move to the database state captured by the picture, or the savepoint. To achieve this, you issue a ROLLBACK TO SAVEPOINT statement. By doing so, you do not lose the modifications made since your last COMMIT up to the savepoint. Obviously, the next time you commit, everything will be written to the database. The savepoints are not needed any more and are automatically discarded. Figure 9.18 illustrates the COMMIT, ROLLBACK, and SAVEPOINT concepts in a typical database session.

9.6.2 INSERT

The SELECT command is important because it allows you to view what is stored in the database. However, at some point, somebody needs to enter those records in the database. SQL provides a simple command to insert data in a database. The INSERT command can be used to enter records one at a time. When combined

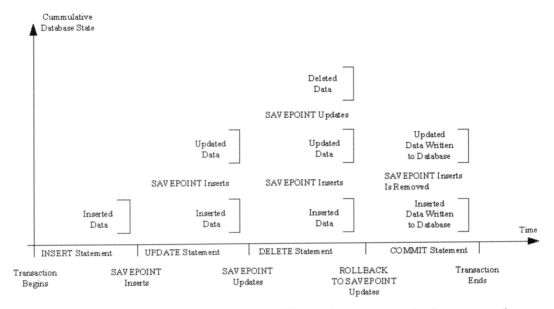

FIGURE 9.18 COMMIT, ROLLBACK, and SAVEPOINT concepts in a database transaction.

with the SELECT command, it can insert multiple records from data structures that already exist in the database. The general syntax of the command is as follows:

```
INSERT INTO table_name (column_1, column_2, ... column_N)
VALUES (value_1, value_2, ... value_N);
```

There must be a one-to-one relationship between the columns in the INSERT clause and the values provided in the VALUES clause; the datatypes must also match. Here is a typical INSERT statement:

```
INSERT INTO movie (movie_id, title, director, actor, actress,
rating)
VALUES (211, 'The Piano', 'Jane Campion', 'Harvey Keitel',
'Holly Hunter', 'R');
```

Alphanumeric and DATE values are always enclosed in single quotes, but the quotes are not needed if the values are of NUMBER datatype. If data is missing for a particular column, specify the keyword NULL. However, the INSERT statement will fail with an error if you do not provide a value for a column with the NOT NULL database constraint enabled. The order of the columns in the INSERT statement is not important as long as specified values follow the same order.

The INSERT statement can be used without column specification. In this case, the relational database assumes that all the columns in the table will be entered in the order in which they are stored in the physical table structure. The following example inserts a new customer in the database with this type of statement:

```
INSERT INTO customer
VALUES (122, 'Collins', 'David', NULL, '31-MAR-63', '05-SEP-95');
```

This statement relies too much on your knowledge of the database at a given point in time. For applications that access tables whose structure changes, commands like this are not flexible and may lead to errors and inability of users to insert data. The first type of INSERT statement is more flexible because the columns to be inserted are fixed.

The INSERT command followed by the VALUES clause allows you to insert data one record at a time. When data are retrieved from other existing tables, the INSERT statement can be combined with the SELECT clause to insert multiple records in a table. To see an example for this type of statement you will use an additional table called LATE_RETURN. This table records the customers that do not return their movies within one month from the rental date. Figure 9.19 shows the SQL statement used to create this table.

The table was created together with the other three tables of the Movie Rental Database, but it does not contain any records. You will populate it with the names and phone numbers of customers that have a gap of one month or more between the rental and return dates. You also want to store the title of the

```
CREATE TABLE late_return (
  customer_id    NUMBER,
  last_name      VARCHAR2 (30),
  first_name     VARCHAR2 (30),
  phone          VARCHAR2 (14),
  title          VARCHAR2 (30),
  rent_dt        DATE,
  return_dt      DATE
);
```

FIGURE 9.19   SQL statement to create the table LATE_RETURN.

movie they have rented. The following query retrieves all the records that meet these requirements:

```
SELECT customer.customer_id, first_name, last_name,
phone, title, rent_dt, return_dt
FROM customer, movie, rental
WHERE customer.customer_id = rental.customer_id
  AND movie.movie_id = rental.movie_id
  AND MONTHS_BETWEEN (return_dt, rent_dt) >= 1;
```

To insert these records into the table LATE_RETURN, simply add the INSERT clause before the SELECT clause as shown in the following statement:

```
INSERT INTO late_return
SELECT customer.customer_id, first_name, last_name,
phone, title, rent_dt, return_dt
FROM customer, movie, rental
WHERE customer.customer_id = rental.customer_id
  AND movie.movie_id = rental.movie_id
  AND MONTHS_BETWEEN (return_dt, rent_dt) >= 1;
```

This statement uses the fully qualified name for columns that are encountered in more than one table. The SQL function MONTHS_BETWEEN will be discussed in Section 9.7.2 later in the chapter.

9.6.3   UPDATE

To reflect the ever changing needs of users, the contents of the database are in constant change. Therefore, it is necessary to update data constantly. The UP-DATE command provided by the SQL language allows for updates on one or more columns and one or more rows in a table. The general syntax for this statement is shown here:

```
UPDATE table
SET column = value
WHERE condition;
```

It instructs the database to set the data of each column in the SET clause to the specified value for all rows in the table mentioned in the UPDATE clause that satisfy the WHERE clause. The following example updates the telephone number of customer Karen Campbell.

```
UPDATE customer
SET phone = '(800)   234-4323'
WHERE last_name = 'Campbell'
  AND first_name = 'Karen';
```

If the statement updates more than one column, they are separated by commas in the SET clause, as the following example shows:

```
UPDATE customer
SET phone = '(800)   456-7890', dob = '13-FEB-64'
WHERE last_name = 'Collins'
  AND first_name = 'David';
```

The WHERE clause in the UPDATE statement is very important because it decides which rows will be updated. If no WHERE clause is defined, all the rows in the table will be updated. The following statement can be issued when customer David Collins (CUSTOMER_ID = 112) returns the movie *Amadeus* (MOVIE_ID = 203):

```
UPDATE rental
SET return_dt = SYSDATE
WHERE customer_id = 112
  AND movie_id = 203
  AND return_dt IS NULL;
```

SYSDATE is another SQL function that returns the current date (and time) as maintained by the database.

In this query, you know the CUSTOMER_ID and the MOVIE_ID beforehand. If only the customer name or the movie title are known, the tables CUSTOMER and MOVIE must be queried to retrieve the ID numbers. A SELECT clause may be used in the WHERE clause to enable you to specify the records to be updated. The following query registers the return of the movie *Pulp Fiction* by Karen Campbell without explicitly using, or requiring you to know, ID numbers of the movie or the customer.

```
UPDATE rental
SET return_dt = SYSDATE
WHERE customer_id IN (
    SELECT customer_id FROM customer
    WHERE last_name = 'Campbell' AND first_name = 'Karen' )
  AND movie_id IN (
    SELECT movie_id FROM movie
    WHERE title = 'Pulp Fiction' )
  AND return_dt IS NULL;
```

The indentation of the subqueries is for readability purpose only and it does not affect the syntax of the query itself.

9.6.4 DELETE

The DELETE statement allows you to delete data from a table. Its general syntax is shown here:

```
DELETE FROM table
WHERE condition;
```

The following example purges the Rental table by deleting records for movies that were returned before January 1, 1987:

```
DELETE FROM rental
WHERE return_dt < '01-JAN-87';
```

The WHERE clause is very important because it specifies which records should be deleted from the table. If the clause is not present, *all* the records from the table will be deleted. As with the UPDATE statement, a SELECT command can be combined with the WHERE clause of a DELETE statement to better identify the records that should be removed. The following statement deletes from the table LATE_RETURN the records for those customers that returned their movies:

```
DELETE FROM customer
WHERE customer_id NOT IN (
   SELECT DISTINCT customer_id FROM rental
   WHERE return_dt IS NULL);
```

The subquery in this statement, retrieves the ID of those customers that have not returned their movies. Note here the significance of the keyword DISTINCT in the subquery. It ensures that the SELECT statement return only one customer ID, despite the fact that the customer may have several movies to return. The condition in the WHERE clause singles out for delete those customers that are not in the group identified by the subquery, that is, the customers that have returned their movies.

9.7 SQL FUNCTIONS

As some of the examples discussed previously show, data can be actively manipulated in SQL statements through arithmetic operators. But SQL language itself and its implementation by Oracle also provide a large number of functions that help perform computations that are beyond the scope of simple arithmetic expressions. Depending on the way they act upon records, the functions can be classified as single-row, or scalar, functions and group, or aggregate, functions.

Scalar functions act upon each row returned by the query. They can be placed in the SELECT clause, thus performing calculations of data returned by the query; or in the WHERE clause, thus enabling the query to specify more precise and sophisticated retrieval criteria. Depending on the parameters they take, and values they return, these functions are classified as character functions, date functions, and mathematical functions. A fourth category of miscellaneous functions such as those responsible for data conversion from one type to the other, or NULL value substitution, can also be considered separately.

The standard ANSI SQL language defines only the following functions: AVG, COUNT, MAX, MIN, and SUM—they are all group functions. This means that all the other functions discussed in this section are specific to the Oracle implementation of SQL. This is not to say that implementations of SQL by other database vendors do not have these or similar functions. Functions ROUND and TRUNC, for example, are implemented identically by INFORMIX SQL and Oracle SQL. The following sections discuss types of SQL functions and provide examples of such functions for each type.

9.7.1 SCALAR CHARACTER FUNCTIONS

Scalar character functions take alphanumeric data as arguments. Some of them return alphanumeric values, but a few return numeric values. Among the most important functions in this category are the case conversion functions (INITCAP, LOWER, UPPER), concatenation function (CONCAT), and substring function (SUBSTR):

❑ The case conversion functions transform the case of the input character string. INITCAP returns the input string with the first character of each word in upper-case; LOWER returns all the characters in the input string in lower-case; UPPER returns all the characters in the input string in upper-case. Figure 9.20 shows a statement that uses all three functions to display the last name of a customer in different formats.

```
SQL> SELECT INITCAP (last_name), UPPER (last_name), LOWER
(last_name)
  2 FROM customer
  3 WHERE customer_id = 20;

INITCAP (LAST_NAME)        UPPER (LAST_NAME)      LOWER (LAST_NAME)
-------------------        -------------------    -----------------
Campbell                   CAMPBELL               campbell
```

FIGURE 9.20 Case conversion SQL functions.

❏ The concatenation function has the syntax CONCAT (*string_1, string_2*). As the name suggests, it returns the input strings concatenated together:

```
SELECT CONCAT(first_name, last_name)
FROM customer
WHERE customer_id = 20;
```

Note that you can achieve the same result with the concatenation operator | |:

```
SELECT first_name||last_name
FROM customer
WHERE customer_id = 20;
```

Sometimes, especially when concatenating multiple strings, the concatenation operator | | is easier to write and read than multiple calls to the CONCAT function. Compare the following two statements:

```
SELECT CONCAT (CONCAT(title, ' was directed by '), director)
FROM movie
WHERE movie_id = 208;
```

```
SELECT title || ' was directed by ' || director
FROM movie
WHERE movie_id = 208;
```

They both result in the same string concatenated, but the second one is much more natural and easier to understand.

❏ The syntax of the substring function is SUBSTR(*input_string, n, l*), where *input_string* is the string from which you want to strip out a substring, *n* is the position in *input_string* from which you want to begin stripping the substring, and *l* is the number of characters to be included in the substring. Both *n* and *l* are integers. Value of *l* cannot be smaller than one. If *n* is positive, the substring will begin *n* positions starting from the beginning of *input_string*. If *n* is negative, the substring will begin *n* positions starting from the end of *input_string*.

```
SELECT SUBSTR (title, 5, 7) First, SUBSTR(title, -3, 3) Second
FROM movie
WHERE movie_id = 203;
```

In this statement, the first call to SUBSTR function returns string 'Remains'—seven characters starting from position 5 in string 'The Remains of the Day.' The second call returns substring 'Day'—three characters, starting three positions from the end of title.

❑ Among the most important character functions that return numeric values are INSTR and LENGTH. The syntax of the first function in INSTR(*string_1*, *string_2*, *n*, *m*). It searches *string_1*, starting from character *n* for the *m*th occurrence of *string_2*. The function returns the initial position of *string_2* with respect to the beginning of *string_1*. The function returns 0 if the *m*th occurrence of *string_2* does not occur starting from the *n*th position of *string_1*. If the value of *n* is positive, *string_1* is searched from the beginning; if the value of *n* is negative, the search of *string_1* begins from the end.

```
SELECT INSTR (title, 'he', 2, 2)
FROM movie
WHERE movie_id = 203;
```

The statement above returns 17, which is the position in which the second occurrence of substring 'he' begins in string 'The Remains of the Day.'

❑ The syntax of function LENGTH is LENGTH(*input_string*). It returns the length of the *input_string* in characters.

```
SELECT LENGTH (title)
FROM movie
WHERE movie_id = 203;
```

This statement returns 22, which is the length in bytes of string 'The Remains of the Day.'

9.7.2 SCALAR DATE FUNCTIONS

Scalar date functions take date values as input. They all return date values, except for the MONTHS_BETWEEN function, which returns the number of months between two dates. Other important functions in this category are ADD_MONTHS, LAST_DAY, NEXT_DAY, and SYSDATE:

❑ Function SYSDATE requires no arguments and returns the current system date and time.

❑ The syntax of ADD_MONTHS is ADD_MONTHS(*input_date*, *number_of_ months*). It adds the specified number of months to the input date and returns the new date. For example, in order to rent movies rated R, customers

```
SQL> SELECT ADD_MONTHS (dob, 17*12)
  2  FROM customer
  3  WHERE first_name = 'Karen'
  4    AND last_name = 'Campbell';


ADD_MONTH
---------
09-APR-97
```

FIGURE 9.21 ADD_MONTHS SQL function.

must be seventeen years or older. The query shown in Figure 9.21 displays the seventeenth birthday of the customer Karen Campbell. She cannot rent movies until that date.

❏ The general syntax of MONTHS_BETWEEN is MONTHS_BETWEEN (*date_1*, *date_2*). The function returns the months between the two input dates. The following query makes it easier for the clerk to decide whether to rent R rated movies to Karen Campbell. It calculates her age in months, then divides it by twelve to display it in years.

```
SELECT MONTHS_BETWEEN(SYSDATE, dob)/12 Age
FROM customer
WHERE first_name = 'Karen' AND last_name = 'Campbell';
```

The age of Karen, as returned by this statement is a decimal number.

❏ The syntax of function NEXT_DAY is NEXT_DAY(*input_date*, *day*). It returns the date of the first occurrence of the specified day of the week since the input date. The variable *day* can take any of the following values: 'MONDAY', 'TUESDAY', 'WEDNESDAY', 'THURSDAY', 'FRIDAY', 'SATURDAY', 'SUNDAY'.

Suppose that during the week a clerk wants to post a notice about the video rental store being closed the coming Monday. The following query supplies the needed date and can be executed any of the week days the store is open without requiring any changes.

```
SELECT NEXT_DAY (SYSDATE, 'MONDAY');
FROM DUAL;
```

DUAL is a dummy table that will be discussed in Section 9.8 of this chapter.

9.7.3　SCALAR MATHEMATICAL FUNCTIONS

Scalar mathematical functions take numeric values as input and return numeric values. Oracle provides functions for basic mathematical functions such as exponential, logarithmic, trigonometric, hyperbolic, and other functions. This section provides an example for the function TRUNC. Its general syntax is TRUNC(*input_number*, *m*). It truncates the *input_number* to *m* decimal places. The parameter *m* is optional. If it is omitted, the function will display only the whole part of the *input_number*. If *m* is positive, the function truncates the *input_number* to *m* digits after the decimal point. If *m* is negative, the function makes zero *m* digits before the decimal point. The following query displays the age of Karen Campbell, but this time only as a whole number.

```
SELECT TRUNC (MONTHS_BETWEEN (SYSDATE, dob)/12) Age
FROM customer
WHERE first_name = 'Karen' AND last_name = 'Campbell';
```

The age of Karen as shown by this statement is an integer and not a decimal number as in a similar query in Section 9.7.2.

9.7.4　MISCELLANEOUS FUNCTIONS

An important group of miscellaneous functions are those that convert data from one type to another. The most important functions in this group are TO_CHAR, TO_DATE, and TO_NUMBER. The general format of these functions is *conversion_function(data_to_be_converted, fmt)*. Each function takes the input data, converts them to the appropriate type and displays them in the specified format *fmt*. In all these functions, the format parameter *fmt* is optional. If not specified, Oracle supplies the default format for the data type in question.

```
SQL> SELECT dob,
  2  TO_CHAR (dob, 'DD MONTH YYYY') format_one,
  3  TO_CHAR (dob, 'Month DD, YYYY') format_two
  4  FROM CUSTOMER
  5  WHERE first_name = 'Karen' AND last_name = 'Campbell';

DOB       FORMAT_ONE                FORMAT_TWO
--------- ------------------------- ----------------------------
09-APR-80 09 APRIL      1980        April     09, 1980
```

FIGURE 9.22　Using TO_CHAR SQL function to convert dates.

```
SQL> SELECT daily_rate def, TO_CHAR (daily_rate, '0.99') frmt
  2  FROM rental;

      DEF FRMT
--------- ------
      .99 $0.99
     1.99 $1.99
     1.99 $1.99
      .99 $0.99
      .99 $0.99
      .99 $0.99
```

FIGURE 9.23   Using TO_CHAR SQL function to format numbers.

❑ TO_CHAR function is used in the query displayed in Figure 9.22. It converts DATE datatype to VARCHAR2. First, the default Oracle format is used, then two custom formats are invoked with the function.

❑ The function TO_CHAR can be used to convert NUMBER to VARCHAR2 datatype, as well. The query in Figure 9.23 displays dollar values stored as numbers in the database. The first column displays the data using Oracle's default format; the second column displays the same data according to the format '$0.99'.

❑ The function TO_DATE converts alphanumeric datatypes CHAR and VARCHAR2 to DATE datatype. It is usually used in INSERT and UPDATE operations to populate DATE columns of a table. It is also used to convert the datatype of input values to date functions. If no format is specified, the input string must be a valid date in the default Oracle format DD-MON-YY.

❑ TO_NUMBER is used to convert alphanumeric datatypes CHAR and VARCHAR2 to NUMBER datatype. Similar to TO_DATE, the function TO_NUMBER is used to specify numeric values in INSERT and UPDATE statements, or to convert the datatype of input values for mathematical functions.

❑ Another important function in the miscellaneous category is the NVL functions. NVL stands for NULL Value Substitution. The general syntax of this function is NVL(*parameter_1, parameter_2*). This function returns *parameter_1* if it is not NULL. When this parameter is NULL, rather than not displaying anything at all, the function NVL returns *parameter_2*. The following statement selects the return date of the movies. If the return date is NULL, the movie is not returned yet, therefore the query displays the string, *'Not Returned'*.

```
SELECT customer_id, NVL (TO_CHAR (return_dt), 'Not Returned')
FROM rental;
```

Note that the function NVL can be overloaded. Its parameters can be of NUMBER, CHAR, VARCHAR2, DATE, or BOOLEAN. However, they must both be of the same datatype. This is the reason why in the previous example you must convert the DATE column RETURN_DT using the function TO_CHAR.

❑ Let's close the section about scalar functions with the function DECODE. Its general syntax is DECODE(*input_value, S1, R1, S2, R2, ... Sn, Rn, default_value*). When this function is invoked, it compares the *input_value* with *S1*. If a match occurs, *R1* is returned. Otherwise, *input_value* is compared with *S2*. If a match occurs, *R2* is returned. Otherwise, the matching process continues. If the last search parameter *Sn* does not produce a match, the value *default_value* is returned. If *default_value* is not specified, DECODE returns NULL. The number of parameters in this function may vary, but cannot go beyond 255. The following statement selects the movie titles and a description for their rating from the database.

```
SELECT title, DECODE (rating, 'R', 'Restricted', 'G',
'General', 'Other')
FROM movie;
```

If the movie is rated R the string *'Restricted'* is displayed; if the movie is rated G the string *'General'* is displayed; for all other cases the string *'Other'* is displayed.

If you are familiar with procedural languages such as Pascal, C, or PL/SQL, you can easily conclude that DECODE is a way of implementing IF ... THEN ... ELSE statements, or CASE statements in SQL. Indeed, the following IF ... ELSE statement in a pseudo-language would result in the same outcome as the previous DECODE statement:

```
IF rating = 'R' THEN
  display 'Restricted'
ELSE IF rating = 'G' THEN
  display 'General'
ELSE
  display 'Other'
END IF
```

The following CASE statement produces the same result, see box on top of next page.

9.7.5 GROUP FUNCTIONS

While scalar functions operate on a record-per-record basis, the group functions operate on groups of records. The group functions include AVG, COUNT, MAX,

```
SWITCH (rating)
  CASE 'R'
    display 'Restricted'
  CASE 'G'
    display 'General'
  DEFAULT
    display 'Other'
```

MIN, STDDEV, SUM, and VARIANCE. All of these functions take numeric values as input, except for COUNT, MAX, and MIN that can take input of any datatype. Figure 9.24 provides examples of the use of each of these functions.

This example analyzes the data for DAILY_RATE fees. First, the function COUNT returns the number of different daily rates stored in the database. Then, the maximum, minimum, and average rates are computed using functions MAX, MIN, AVG. Finally, two important statistical parameters, the standard deviation and variance of daily rentals are computed using the functions STDDEV and VARIANCE.

All the previous functions, except for COUNT, operate on *all* the records as a group. Sometimes, it is necessary to perform actions based only on distinct values in the set of records. In this case, the DISTINCT keyword is specified inside parentheses, before any other parameters are specified. In the example from Figure 9.24, the keyword DISTINCT guarantees that the function COUNT retrieves the number of distinct daily rates. If it were omitted it would return the number of rental transactions recorded in the table.

Any NULL value in the set of records on which the functions act upon will be ignored. The only exception to this rule is the function COUNT when the syntax COUNT(*) is used. Under this condition, the function returns the number of all records that are returned by the query, including records that contain NULL values.

```
SQL> SELECT COUNT (DISTINCT daily_rate) count, MAX (daily_rate)
max,
  2    MIN (daily_rate) min, AVG (daily_rate) avg,
  3    STDDEV (daily_rate) stddev, VARIANCE (daily_rate) var
  4  FROM rental;

COUNT           MAX           MIN         AVG       STDDEV         VAR
_____ _____ _____ _____ _____ _____
    2          1.99           .99 1.4017647  .50729966 .25735294
```

FIGURE 9.24 Using group functions.

9.8 DUAL TABLE

Sometimes it is necessary to use a certain function or perform a certain calculation without having to query a table from the database. For example, you may want to display the system date, or select the next value from a sequence, or simply display a text string. For these instances, Oracle provides a construct called DUAL table. It is a table with only one column, DUMMY, and only one row, X, in it. It is owned by the user SYS, but every user of the database can select from it. Obviously, every table can be used to compute an expression by selecting from it, but the expression will be returned as many times as there are rows in the table. DUAL, by having only one row, guarantees that the calculated expression or constant will be returned only once.

The following query selects the current system date:

SELECT SYSDATE FROM DUAL;

The following query selects the next value from a sequence:

SELECT internal_id_seq.NEXTVAL from DUAL;

Finally, the next query simply selects a text string:

SELECT 'This is the last statement for this chapter.' FROM DUAL;

9.9 SUMMARY

This chapter introduces elements of the Structured Query Language that you will need as you develop your Oracle Forms applications. These are some of the highlights of this chapter:

- ❏ Historic view of SQL
- ❏ Categories of SQL commands
  - ❏ Data Retrieval Command
  - ❏ Data Manipulation Language
  - ❏ Data Definition Language
  - ❏ Data Control Language
- ❏ Data retrieval with SELECT
  - ❏ Selecting all rows from a table
  - ❏ WHERE clause
  - ❏ SQL operators
  - ❏ Boolean operators

- ❑ Using parentheses in logical expressions
- ❑ GROUP BY clause
- ❑ HAVING clause
- ❑ Joins
- ❑ ORDER BY clause
- ❑ Combining queries with set operations
- ❑ Data manipulation language commands
  - ❑ COMMIT and ROLLBACK
  - ❑ INSERT data
  - ❑ UPDATE data
  - ❑ DELETE data
- ❑ SQL Functions
  - ❑ Scalar character functions
  - ❑ Scalar date functions
  - ❑ Scalar mathematical functions
  - ❑ Scalar miscellaneous functions
  - ❑ Group functions
- ❑ DUAL table

INTRODUCTION TO PL/SQL

"High thoughts must have high language."
—Aristophanes

- ◆ Brief History of PL/SQL Language
- ◆ Approach and Advantages of PL/SQL
- ◆ Structural Elements of PL/SQL Blocks
- ◆ Variables in PL/SQL
- ◆ Manipulating Data in PL/SQL Blocks
- ◆ Procedural Constructs of PL/SQL
- ◆ Exception Handling
- ◆ Program Units in Oracle Forms
- ◆ PL/SQL Editor
- ◆ Summary

10.1 BRIEF HISTORY OF PL/SQL LANGUAGE

The previous chapter introduced elements of SQL language used in database applications development. You saw that with its simple syntax, SQL allows users to really focus on the data they need without worrying about how to access the data. In the infancy stage of relational databases, the functionality of SQL was sufficient to handle system programming needs. However, as the complexity of the applications began to increase, it became clear that the advantages of SQL as a result-oriented language would be increased by features of other programming languages such as parameters, language control structures, and subroutines. In one way or the other, by the mid-1980s all the relational database vendors were addressing the issue of a programming language for their products.

A solution offered initially was to open up the existing procedural languages, such as C, COBOL, and FORTRAN, to syntactic structures of SQL. This marked the birth of embedded SQL and precompilers. As input, precompilers take source files in which SQL statements are mixed with statements of the target procedural language, for example C, according to predefined rules of syntax. They interpret these source files and produce files that contain only target-language code. The files are then compiled, linked, and executed, according to the language specifications. Precompilers continue to be used today. In some environments they are very effective and successful.

Early front-end development tools were also developed to allow applications to better display and manipulate the data. Tools such as SQL*Forms V2 used a rudimentary script language. This "language" however was tedious to program and did not support much functionality. The increasing needs of data processing systems could be met only with a full-fledged programming language that would combine all the benefits of procedural languages with the nonprocedural characteristics of SQL language.

The response of Oracle Corporation to this need was PL/SQL (Procedural Language/Structured Query Language). Its first version was introduced in 1990 with the new generation of Oracle products: SQL*Forms Version 3.0 and RDBMS Version 6.0. Today, all the Developer/2000 tools have PL/SQL Version 1.1 implemented in them. The Oracle7 database server implements PL/SQL Version 2.

10.2 APPROACH AND ADVANTAGES OF PL/SQL

As mentioned, the PL/SQL engine is implemented on both sides of the Oracle database application. PL/SQL Version 2 being used by the database server has a few more features than PL/SQL Version 1.1 of Oracle Forms and other Developer/2000 tools. However, this chapter will focus on common features of both versions.

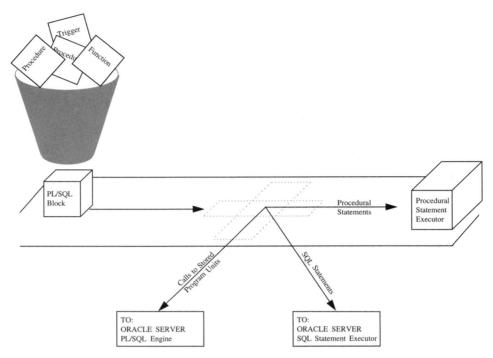

FIGURE 10.1   Graphical representation of the PL/SQL engine in Oracle Forms.

Figure 10.1 graphically presents the functionality of the PL/SQL engine in Oracle Forms. The objects that contain PL/SQL code such as triggers, functions, and procedures, are broken up in smaller units called PL/SQL blocks. Each of these PL/SQL blocks is processed separately. Its statements are divided in three major categories. Procedural statements such as IF ... ELSE, or LOOP statements, are handled internally by the Procedural Statement Executor. SQL statements such as SELECT, INSERT, UPDATE, and DELETE statements are stripped out and sent to the Oracle Server's SQL Statements Executor. Any calls to functions and procedures stored in database structures, also known as stored program units, are sent to the PL/SQL engine of the Oracle Server. The PL/SQL engine in the Oracle Server proceeds in a similar fashion. Its functionality is presented in Figure 10.2.

If the database server receives a call for one of its stored program units, the called object is retrieved and handed out for processing to the PL/SQL engine. Like its counterpart in Oracle Forms, this engine breaks up the stored unit in PL/SQL blocks, which then are processed individually. For each block, procedural statements are separated from SQL statements. The former are sent to the Procedural Statement Executor, the latter to the SQL Statement Executor. SQL statements from Oracle Forms pass through this engine as well.

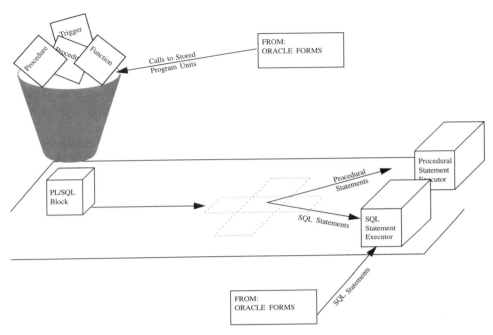

FIGURE 10.2   Graphical representation of the PL/SQL engine in Oracle Server.

From what has been said so far, a major advantage of PL/SQL can be immediately drawn. PL/SQL is a language shared by the Oracle database server and
all the tools in the Developer/2000 suite, including Oracle Forms, Reports, and
Graphics. This means that mastering programming in PL/SQL in any of these environments enables you to become proficient in all the other areas of systems development where PL/SQL is used. The return on the investment is pretty high.

The fact that the database server and the front-end tools have the same programming language makes code sharing a trivial task. The same PL/SQL procedure can be called from a form, report, or graphic. It can also be stored in the
database and be used by other front-end development tools such as Powerbuilder
or Visual Basic.

Another advantage provided by the use of PL/SQL on both sides of the application is that its code can be tuned and distributed easily between client and
server to maximize performance. It can be seen from the previous figures that nu-
merous SQL statements sent to the database and a large amount of data returned
to the client application can take a heavy toll on the performance of the application. The bottleneck can become significant, especially in a network where many
users access the data simultaneously. If, on the other hand, the PL/SQL code is
moved from the client application to the database, then all the application must
send to the server is a call to a stored procedure. The PL/SQL engine in the data-

base server executes the procedure and obtains the same results but without moving data back and forth across the network.

However, stored procedures are not the panacea to the application performance. If, for example, the procedure performs complicated calculations of data, it is not wise to take precious server resources to do this. In this situation, better performance may be achieved by keeping the code on the client side. There is a fine line here that application developers try not to cross during development and testing activities.

10.3 STRUCTURAL ELEMENTS OF PL/SQL BLOCKS

As the discussion in the previous paragraph showed, no matter how complicated a PL/SQL program unit is, it is ultimately broken up in units of code called PL/SQL blocks. Figure 10.3 represents a typical PL/SQL block.

```
DECLARE
   f_name VARCHAR2(30);
   l_name VARCHAR2(30);
BEGIN
   SELECT first_name, last_name
   INTO f_name, l_name
   FROM customer
   WHERE customer_id = :RENTAL.CUSTOMER_ID;

   IF (f_name IS NULL) AND (l_name IS NULL) THEN
     :RENTAL.CUSTOMER_NAME := 'Missing Name';
   ELSE
     f_name := UPPER(f_name);
     l_name := UPPER(l_name);
     :RENTAL.CUSTOMER_NAME := f_name ||' '||l_name;
   END IF;
EXCEPTION
   WHEN TOO_MANY_ROWS THEN
     BELL;
     MESSAGE('Duplicate customer records.');
     RAISE FORM_TRIGGER_FAILURE;
   WHEN OTHERS THEN
     BELL;
     MESSAGE('Error retrieving Customer Name.');
     RAISE FORM_TRIGGER_FAILURE;
END;
```

Declaration — marks the DECLARE section

Execution — marks the BEGIN section

Exception — marks the EXCEPTION section

FIGURE 10.3   Typical PL/SQL block.

Following the SQL language conventions, each statement in a PL/SQL block must be terminated by a semicolon (;). The statement may be in one line or span across multiple lines. The PL/SQL parser will process all lines until it reaches the semicolon as one statement. Multiple statements can reside in one line as well.

A PL/SQL block may have up to three distinct sections: declaration, execution, and exception. The declaration section begins with the keyword DECLARE. Variables that will be used in the block are declared and initialized here. Constants, and other PL/SQL constructs such as cursors and user-defined exceptions are defined in this section as well. If the block will not need any such variables or constructs, the declaration section is omitted. Figure 10.4 shows a PL/SQL block without a declaration section. If the declaration section is present, the keyword BEGIN must separate it from the rest of the code as shown in Figure 10.3. Note that the keywords BEGIN and END must always be in matching pairs.

The execution section contains statements that perform the core functionality of the PL/SQL blocks. Here is where all the data are selected and manipulated. The execution section must always be present in the block. Sometimes it can be the only section in it. Figure 10.4 shows a PL/SQL block that contains only the execution section. In the general case though, the execution section is preceded by the declaration section and followed by the exception section.

The exception section is used to protect the application from unexpected events or failures. In the example presented in Figure 10.3, the SELECT statement retrieves the first name and last name of the customers based on the CUSTOMER_ID stored in the RENTAL table. Many things can go wrong during the execution of this statement. In the example of Figure 10.3, you handle one abnormal situation explicitly. If any other error occurs, a generic message is displayed.

Like the declaration section, the exception section is also optional, but it is strongly suggested. Catching and handling all the exceptions that can be raised at

```
PROCEDURE Move_Next_Record IS
BEGIN
  IF :SYSTEM.LAST_RECORD <> 'TRUE' THEN
     NEXT_RECORD;
  ELSE
  -- No more records to move to.
    BELL;
    MESSAGE('At last record.');
    RAISE FORM_TRIGGER_FAILURE;
  END IF;
END;
```

FIGURE 10.4   Example of a PL/SQL block that contains only the execution section.

runtime protects the application from unexpected failures and is becoming a standard feature of serious application development efforts.

In every application development environment it is important to document the code. Oracle Forms provides a *Comments* property for every object, where developers can enter useful information about their behavior. When writing PL/SQL code, additional comments are strongly suggested. A program unit that is well-documented is much easier to maintain or modify without adversely affecting the rest of the application. PL/SQL allows you to write comments in one line or across multiple lines. The symbol '--' comments out everything until the end of line. The symbols '/* ... */' comment out everything enclosed between them, even if it spans across several lines.

```
DECLARE
  f_name VARCHAR2(30);
  l_name VARCHAR2(30);
BEGIN
  SELECT first_name, last_name
  INTO f_name, l_name
  FROM customer
  WHERE customer_id = :RENTAL.CUSTOMER_ID;

  IF (f_name IS NULL) AND (l_name IS NULL) THEN
    GOTO missing_name;
  END IF;

  f_name := UPPER(f_name);
  l_name := UPPER(l_name);
  :RENTAL.CUSTOMER_NAME := f_name ||' '||l_name;

  <<missing_name>>
  :RENTAL.CUSTOMER_NAME := 'Missing Name';
EXCEPTION
  WHEN TOO_MANY_ROWS THEN
    BELL;
    MESSAGE('Duplicate customer records.');
    RAISE FORM_TRIGGER_FAILURE;
  WHEN OTHERS THEN
    BELL;
    MESSAGE('Error retrieving Customer Name.');
    RAISE FORM_TRIGGER_FAILURE;
END;
```

FIGURE 10.5 PL/SQL block with labels.

PL/SQL blocks written in Oracle Forms triggers or from a SQL*Plus command line are often called anonymous blocks. In the early days of PL/SQL programming, labels were used to name separate parts of an anonymous PL/SQL block. The aim was to create a naming structure within the code so as to modularize the code itself and to allow unconditional jumps to sections of code according to the application's needs. Figure 10.5 presents an example of a PL/SQL block with labels. Note that the code presented in this figure has the same functionality as the code shown in Figure 10.3.

It is unusual today to find code that contains labels, due mainly to two factors. First, Oracle supports named PL/SQL constructs such as functions and procedures, not just in the front-end development tools, but also in the database side, in the form of stored program units. Second, improved program control constructs of PL/SQL make unconditional jumps in the application code unnecessary and unwarranted.

10.4 VARIABLES IN PL/SQL

As any other programming language, PL/SQL uses variables as placeholders of information or data. In the PL/SQL blocks presented so far, you have seen the use of different kinds of variables such as local variables, Forms objects and database columns. This section will provide more details for each of them.

10.4.1 LOCAL AND GLOBAL VARIABLES

Oracle Forms uses local and global variables. Local variables are accessible only within the PL/SQL block in which they are declared. Global variables are accessible from every object, trigger, function, and procedure in the running module. While local variables can be declared only in the declaration section of a PL/SQL block, global variables can be declared anywhere in the application. However, it is an established practice to declare globals when a form is first accessed, usually in a PRE-FORM trigger. The reason for this is that in Forms, a variable must be declared before being used. Normally, a global variable is used in more than one piece of code. Given the unpredictability and randomness with which pieces of code are executed—a characteristic for all GUI applications—it may happen that Forms runs into a global variable before executing the code in which it is declared. In this case a runtime error will occur. On the other hand, the code of the PRE-FORM trigger is executed in the initial moments of the form's existence, before any thing else happens. By declaring globals in this trigger, you protect the application from these runtime errors.

Another difference between local and global variables in Oracle Forms is the way the memory allocated to them is handled. For a local variable, the memory is allocated when the focus moves inside the PL/SQL block. As soon as the execution of that block of code ends, the memory for the variable is released. For a global variable, the memory is allocated when the variable is declared and it remains allocated until the form is closed or the global is explicitly erased, whichever comes first. It is important to understand this fact. In the case of large applications that keep multiple forms open, using a large number of global variables may consume memory resources and affect the performance. It is common to release the memory taken by globals when a form is exited. This is usually done in a POST-FORM trigger, which is the last one to be executed in a Forms module.

The names of all global variables must be preceeded by the keyword *GLOBAL,* as in GLOBAL.first_name, or GLOBAL.cost. Note that PL/SQL, like SQL, is not case-sensitive. However, as in the previous chapter, keywords and other language constructs will be used in upper-case letters to distinguish them from the rest of the code.

10.4.2 DATA TYPES OF VARIABLES IN ORACLE FORMS

An important characteristic of variables is their data type. For the sake of simplicity, the data types of Oracle Forms variables will be divided in two groups. The first group includes generic PL/SQL data types. Although PL/SQL supports a large number of data types and their subtypes, in Oracle Forms you would encounter only variables of NUMBER, VARCHAR2, DATE, and BOOLEAN data types. Table 10.1 provides a brief explanation for each data type.

The generic data types, being associated only with the PL/SQL language, can be used in all the Oracle tools that support the PL/SQL syntax. PL/SQL code that utilizes only these data types has the greatest potential for portability. Such code can be written in Forms and, with no modifications required, can run on the database as a stored procedure, can be included in an Oracle Reports or Oracle Graphics trigger, or can be executed from SQL*Plus.

In order to increase the efficiency of the code in a particular environment, PL/SQL allows data types specific to that environment. These data types normally correspond to the types of objects used by the tools. So, in Oracle Forms you have variables of type WINDOW, ITEM, BLOCK, and so on, that store internal identifiers for these objects. In Oracle Graphics you have variables of type

TABLE 10.1 PL/SQL generic data types.

DATA TYPE	DESCRIPTION
NUMBER	Data type for fixed and floating point numbers.
VARCHAR2	Data type for alphanumeric data of variable length. In Oracle Forms VARCHAR2 variables can store up to 2000 bytes of data.
DATE	Data type for date and time variables.
BOOLEAN	Data type for variables that take values TRUE, FALSE, or NULL in Boolean logic operations.

OG_LAYER or OG_RECTANGLE that store information about layers or rectangles. The data types used in Oracle Forms will be referred to as Forms-specific data types.

Declaring a Forms-specific data type variable is similar to declaring a generic data type variable. Indeed, both the following statements are equally valid:

```
score    NUMBER;
help_win WINDOW;
```

However, assigning values to them is a slightly different process. Generic data type variables can be assigned a value directly, as in the following statement:

score := 25;

To assign a value to a Forms-specific data type variable, the built-in FIND function that corresponds to the object of that data type must be used. There are fourteen such functions that correspond to as many objects in Oracle Forms. The general syntax of these functions is FIND_*object('object_name')*, where *object* can be FORM, BLOCK, ITEM, ALERT, CANVAS, or WINDOW. They return a unique identifier for the object with the specified *object_name*, if it exists. Otherwise they return NULL. This unique identifier is called the object ID and its value is assigned and maintained internally by the Forms. The object ID has the Forms-specific data type that correspond to the particular object. In the example above, the variable help_win can be assigned a value with this statement:

help_win := FIND_WINDOW('MAIN_HELP');

If there is a window named MAIN_HELP in the module, its object ID will be stored in the variable help_win. You can use help_win to access and modify all the properties of the MAIN_HELP window. If the module does not contain a window called MAIN_HELP, help_win will be NULL. To protect the application from unexpected failures, you must check that FIND_WINDOW returned a non-NULL value to variable help_win, before proceeding with the actions mentioned above. Figure 10.6 presents a way to handle the situation described here.

Another way to specify the data type of a variable is by referencing the %TYPE attribute of another variable that is already defined. In the following example, the first line defines a variable named price. The second line then defines a second variable, discount_price of the same type as price.

```
price             NUMBER;
discount_price    price%TYPE;
```

```
DECLARE
  help_win WINDOW;
  -- Other declarations go here
BEGIN
  help_win := FIND_WINDOW('MAIN_HELP');
  IF ID_NULL(help_win) THEN
     -- MAIN_HELP does not exist.
     -- Remedy for the situation
  ELSE
     -- Manipulate the window
  END IF;
  -- Other statements go here
END;
```

FIGURE 10.6   Using Forms-specific data type variables.

This type definition has a clear advantage. If the definition of price changes in the future, the change will automatically propagate to variable discount_price, or any other variable defined based on the type of price. You do not have to change the type definition of the derived variables. The technique is especially useful when variables are declared based on the data type of a table column in the database. In the following example, both price and discount_price are declared using the definition of the column DAILY_RATE in table RENTAL of the Movie Rental Database:

```
price                rental.daily_rate%TYPE;
discount_price       rental.daily_rate%TYPE;
```

This assures that the database structure will always be synchronized with the application code. If the requirements change in the future, the only place where you need to change the type definition is the database. The application will automatically reflect the change.

10.4.3   FORMS ITEMS AND DATABASE COLUMNS

Oracle Forms items can be used just like any variable in an application. They can be assigned values which then can be further manipulated. To access the values stored in Oracle Forms items, their names must be preceded by a colon. When items are created in the module, Oracle Forms ensures that there are no naming conflicts among them. You should be equally careful in your code in avoiding these conflicts. The best provision for this is to use the fully qualified names of the items. You should make it a habit to always reference items as :BLOCK_NAME.ITEM_NAME.

Suppose for example that you are working with a data entry form for the MRD application. The form contains three database blocks to interact with the Customer, Movie, and Rental tables. If you try to add a statement like

```
:CUSTOMER_ID := 155;
```

to a trigger, you will get a compilation error when you generate. Oracle Forms cannot decide whether you are trying to set the CUSTOMER_ID in CUSTOMER block or RENTAL block, and will inform you about the ambiguity of your statement. The situation gets worse if you have a statement like

```
GO_ITEM('CUSTOMER_ID');
```

Here, you are instructing Forms to jump from the current location to the item CUSTOMER_ID. The problem is that the Designer does not look inside the single quotes during the generation; it compiles the statement with the understanding that the address of the item will be resolved and will be available at runtime. Thus, you have an application that generates successfully but will certainly fail when the statement is executed. The address of CUSTOMER_ID, as specified above cannot be resolved.

Eliminate these problems by referring to the CUSTOMER_ID item using the name of the block. If you are working with RENTAL block, the statements will be

```
:RENTAL.CUSTOMER_ID = 155;
```

and

```
GO_ITEM('RENTAL.CUSTOMER_ID');
```

Thus, now you solve all ambiguities by instructing Forms to set the value of CUSTOMER_ID in RENTAL block to 155, or to navigate to this unique item.

Looking at the statements above, you may question the different usage of the quotation marks and colon. The two notations don't just happen to be different. In fact, they denote different objects. A notation like RENTAL. CUSTOMER_ID references the object; the place where some data resides. The value of the data per se is referenced by the notation :RENTAL.CUSTOMER_ID. Therefore, the statement

```
:RENTAL.CUSTOMER_ID = 155;
```

in reality means that the value stored in the object RENTAL.CUSTOMER_ID should become 155. Of course, this is often abbreviated as RENTAL.

:TABLE.WINE_GLASS := 'Charmes-Chambertin';

GO_ITEM('TABLE.WINE_GLASS') ⟶

FIGURE 10.7   Referencing names and values of Forms items.

CUSTOMER_ID is 155. Figure 10.7 contains a rather informal explanation of the concept.

In this figure the string enclosed in quotes points to the glass, but the same string, preceded with a colon denotes the precious wine inside the glass.

Database columns in PL/SQL can be used only in SQL statements. To avoid any conflicting names, it is good to fully qualify column names by preceding them with the table name. If ambiguities still exist, the name of the table owner can be added.

10.5 MANIPULATING DATA IN PL/SQL BLOCKS

Data in PL/SQL blocks can be selected and manipulated using SQL language statements. Statements discussed in the previous chapter, namely SELECT, INSERT, UPDATE, DELETE, COMMIT, and ROLLBACK are the only SQL commands that can be used in a PL/SQL block. DDL statements such as CREATE and DROP, or DCL statements such as GRANT and REVOKE, cannot be used.

The only major modification to what was discussed in Chapter 9 comes in the SELECT statement. A new clause, the INTO clause, is required immediately after the SELECT clause. Thus, the general form of the SELECT statement now reads as follows:

```
SELECT clause
INTO clause
FROM clause
WHERE clause;
```

The reason for the new INTO clause is simple and reflects one of the main reasons for the existence of PL/SQL as a supplement of SQL. SQL is an interactive language. You type a statement at the command prompt and wait to see the results on the screen. There is no need to redirect the data, except, probably, to a spooled file. PL/SQL though, being a procedural language aims at not just displaying the data, but also processing the information and making decisions based on its content. This task is greatly facilitated if data retrieved from the database is stored in memory locations that can be easily accessed and manipulated. These are PL/SQL variables and Oracle Forms items. The redirection is done by the INTO clause.

The following is an example of a SELECT statement in a PL/SQL program. It is taken from the PL/SQL block that is shown in Figure 10.3:

```
SELECT first_name, last_name
INTO f_name, l_name
FROM customer
WHERE customer_id = :RENTAL.CUSTOMER_ID;
```

It is evident that for each column or expression in the SELECT clause, there must be a variable or item in the INTO clause to store the value returned from the SELECT statement.

In general, the outcome of a SELECT statement is zero, one, or more rows returned from the database. In SQL this does not cause any problems. However, in PL/SQL, queries must be tailored so that they return one record, at most. The normal outcome of a SELECT statement in PL/SQL is to return only one row. If the query retrieves no rows, the exception NO_DATA_FOUND is raised; if more than one row is returned, the exception TOO_MANY_ROWS is raised.

The fact that the SELECT ... INTO statement should raise an exception if more than one row is found is an ANSI standard. To conform with this standard, whenever the first row of a query is returned, Oracle Forms must make another trip to the database to see whether the query returned more rows. If not, everything is fine; otherwise the TOO_MANY_ROWS exception is raised. In any event, from the front-end application perspective, the second trip is superfluous. In the best case, it returns little needed information (additional records are returned by the query but not retrieved by the PL/SQL engine); in the worst case, it is a waste of computing time and resources (extra trip to the database just to find out that the row you have already is the only one retrieved by the query). To remedy this restrictive and noneffecient behavior of the SELECT statement, PL/SQL cursors are used. Chapter 19 discusses the structure and functionality of PL/SQL cursors, together with other advanced PL/SQL programming techniques.

There is little to say about the use of INSERT, UPDATE, and DELETE statements in PL/SQL blocks that was not said in Chapter 9. The only novelty is that variables and values stored in Oracle Forms items can be used now. An example will be provided for each statement.

The following PL/SQL statement inserts a record in the LATE_RETURN table:

```
INSERT INTO late_return (customer_id, last_name,
title, rent_dt)
VALUES (:customer.customer_id, :customer.last_name,
:movie.title, :movie.rent_dt);
```

The following statement updates the record to add the FIRST_NAME and PHONE information:

```
UPDATE late_return
SET first_name = :customer.first_name, phone = :customer.phone
WHERE customer_id = :customer.customer_id;
```

The following statement deletes the record from LATE_RENTAL table:

```
DELETE FROM late_return
WHERE customer_id = :customer.customer_id;
```

What was said in Chapter 9 about the COMMIT and ROLLBACK commands in SQL applies to PL/SQL programming as well. Be aware though that Oracle Forms also keeps track of its base table blocks. If after a statement like the ones presented above, you add the statement COMMIT, Oracle Forms will commit not just the statement you issued, but also the changes that exist in these base table blocks.

Finally, let us mention that all the SQL functions discussed in the previous chapter can be used in SQL statements of PL/SQL blocks as well. It is easy to locate the names and the parameters of these functions in Oracle Forms. They are all listed under the STANDARD built-in package, the last one in the list of Built-in Packages in the Object Navigator. Do not confuse this with the STANDARD Extensions built-in package that contains all the Oracle Forms built-in functions and procedures, and is the first one in the list of Built-in Packages. As explained in Chapter 5, you can use the commands Navigator/Paste Name and Navigator/Paste Arguments from the Designer menu to add the specifications of these built-ins in your PL/SQL statements.

10.6 PROCEDURAL CONSTRUCTS OF PL/SQL

Procedural statements allow PL/SQL to control the flow of program execution. They include conditional branching statements such as the IF ... ELSE clause, loop statements such as LOOP, WHILE, or FOR clause, and the unconditional branching statement GOTO.

10.6.1 IF STATEMENT

The simplest form of this statement is shown here:

```
IF condition THEN
   PL/SQL statements;
ELSE
   PL/SQL statements;
END IF;
```

When this statement is executed, the logical condition between the keywords IF and THEN is first evaluated. If its value is TRUE, then the statements in the IF clause are executed. If it is FALSE or UNKNOWN, then statements in the ELSE clause are executed. The following example is an extract of the PL/SQL block shown in Figure 10.3:

```
IF (f_name IS NULL) AND (l_name IS NULL) THEN
   :RENTAL.CUSTOMER_NAME := 'Missing Name';
ELSE
   f_name := UPPER(f_name);
   l_name := UPPER(l_name);
   :RENTAL.CUSTOMER_NAME := f_name ||' '|| l_name;
END IF;
```

The ELSE clause is not required, and it can be omitted if no action should be taken when the condition is not fulfilled. Multiple IF statements can be nested inside each clause. This would be the structure of nested IF statements:

```
IF condition THEN
   PL/SQL statements;
   IF condition THEN
     PL/SQL statements;
   END IF;
ELSE
   PL/SQL statements;
END IF;
```

When the condition may have more than just a TRUE/FALSE outcome, the IF ... ELSE statements can be nested. The following diagram can be used to check for a three-values condition:

```
IF condition THEN
  PL/SQL statements;
ELSE
  IF condition THEN
    PL/SQL statements;
 ELSE
    PL/SQL statements;
  END IF;
END IF;
```

This representation can be tedious and difficult to understand, especially when multiple conditions are evaluated. To simplify this situation, PL/SQL allows the use of the ELSIF keyword. Now the previous construct is simplified to the following:

```
IF condition THEN
  PL/SQL statements;
ELSIF condition THEN
  PL/SQL statements;
ELSE
  PL/SQL statements;
END IF;
```

Note that only one ELSE clause and only one END IF statement are needed. Multiple ELSIF clauses can be specified if necessary, as shown in the next statement:

```
IF :rental.rating = 'R' THEN
  MESSAGE('Movie is rated R.');
ELSIF :rental.rating = 'PG-13' THEN
  MESSAGE('Movie is rated PG-13.');
ELSIF :rental.rating = 'G' THEN
  MESSAGE('Movie is rated G.');
ELSE
  MESSAGE('Movie has another rating or is not rated.');
END IF;
```

10.6.2 LOOPING STATEMENTS

Loops are used to perform actions repetitively. The iteration they control continues until a certain condition evaluates to TRUE, or while a certain condition holds

TRUE, for a specific number of times. Based on these three different situations, you can distinguish three types of loops.

The first type repeats the loop statements until the exit condition evaluates to TRUE. Its general syntax is shown here:

```
LOOP
   PL/SQL statements;
   EXIT WHEN condition;
END LOOP;
```

The PL/SQL statements within the loop are executed at least once. If the exit condition evaluates to FALSE or NULL, the loop will repeat its iteration. Only when the exit condition evaluates to TRUE will the loop stop, and control is passed to the rest of the statements outside the loop. The following PL/SQL block contains an example of this kind of loop:

```
DECLARE
   k NUMBER := 1;
LOOP
   MESSAGE('Iteration '||TO_CHAR(k));
   k := k + 1;
   EXIT WHEN k > 4;
END LOOP;
```

The second type executes the loop statements only if and while the entry loop condition is TRUE. Its general syntax is as follows:

```
WHILE condition LOOP
   PL/SQL statements;
END LOOP;
```

In this loop, the PL/SQL statements may be executed zero or more times. The execution will stop as soon as the condition evaluates to FALSE or NULL. Here is an example of the WHILE loop:

```
DECLARE
   k NUMBER := 1;
WHILE k < 5 LOOP
   MESSAGE('Iteration '||TO_CHAR(k));
   k := k + 1;
END LOOP;
```

The previous two loops are not equivalent, but with little coding added, one can be used to simulate the other.

The third type of loop is used when the iterations will be performed a certain number of times. Its general syntax is shown here:

```
FOR counter IN lower_bound..higher_bound LOOP
  PL/SQL statements;
END LOOP;
```

The following is an example of a FOR loop:

```
FOR k IN 1..4 LOOP
  MESSAGE('Iteration '||TO_CHAR(k));
END LOOP;
```

The implementation of the FOR loop in PL/SQL is slightly different from that of other programming languages such as C. First, the loop counter is declared internally as an integer, which means that you do not need to declare it explicitly. On the other hand, this counter can be referenced only inside the loop. The value of the counter can be assigned to other variables inside the loop. However, because the counter is maintained internally, you cannot assign a value to it, or change its existing value. This means that the counter will faithfully increment by one unit, starting from the lower bound of its range values all the way up to the upper bound.

The implicit handling of the loop counter by the PL/SQL engine, while being more rigid than in other languages, protects the loop from accidentally be-

Note

Another important note could be made about the first two types of loops. If proper care is not taken to update the loop exit condition, they both can degenerate in infinite loops. In a distributed, multi-user database environment, these events can be costly. Imagine an out-of-control loop that inserts a 10 Kb worth of data in each iteration. With a modest 10 iterations per second, the loop will pump every minute 6 Mb of useless data into the database. If 10 users issue the statement and it goes undetected or unstopped for 10 minutes, 600 Mb of data will have flooded, if not crashed, the database.

coming an infinite loop. You do not have to worry about incrementing the loop counter in each iteration. PL/SQL will make sure that the loop executes exactly the number of times allowed by its range.

10.6.3 UNCONDITIONAL BRANCHING

For backward compatibility and traditional reasons, more than for its usefulness, PL/SQL continues to support unconditional jumps to labels in the code using the command GOTO. This command does not provide any functionality that is not already implemented better and more elegantly by other constructs. Figure 10.5 contains an example of GOTO statements and labels.

10.7 EXCEPTION HANDLING

When discussing the components of a PL/SQL block, the purpose and usage of exceptions in PL/SQL code was also mentioned. They are abnormal conditions in the PL/SQL environment, associated with a warning or error of which the user of the application must be aware. When any of these abnormal conditions occur, an exception is raised. The execution flow of the program is interrupted. The control jumps to the EXCEPTION part of the block that the programmer should be careful to include. Otherwise, the error propagates outside the block in which it occurred. If the calling environment does not handle it, not-very-user-friendly situations may occur, at the very best. The exception section of the PL/SQL block is where you write the code that gracefully handles the error condition, or takes measures to correct it.

There are two types of exceptions that can occur in an Oracle application. The first category includes all the exceptions that the PL/SQL engine of the Oracle Server or Oracle Forms raises automatically when the abnormal condition occurs. These are called internal exceptions. The second category includes user-specified exception. They are not Oracle processing errors, but rather situations in the application about which the user's attention must be drawn.

10.7.1 INTERNAL EXCEPTIONS

Each internal exception is associated with an Oracle Server error number. The group of internal exceptions is further divided into named and unnamed exceptions. The named internal exceptions are a small number of exceptions, that occur most frequently, and are defined in the STANDARD package that is included in the PL/SQL engine of Oracle Forms. Table 10.2 lists some of these exceptions that you are likely to encounter the most in your development practice. Examples provided in this chapter (such as the PL/SQL block in Figure 10.3) show how to handle these exceptions.

TABLE 10.2 Examples of named internal exceptions.

EXCEPTION NAME	ORACLE ERROR	DESCRIPTION
NO_DATA_FOUND	ORA-01403	SELECT ... INTO statement returns no rows
TOO_MANY_ROWS	ORA-01427	SELECT ... INTO statement returns more than one row
ZERO_DIVIDE	ORA-01476	Numeric value is divided by zero
VALUE_ERROR	ORA-01403	Error occurred during a computation or data conversion
STORAGE_ERROR	ORA-06500	No sufficient memory available, or memory is corrupted
PROGRAM_ERROR	ORA-06501	Internal error of PL/SQL

The majority of internal errors are not named explicitly, although they automatically raise an exception when they occur. However, in order to trap and handle them appropriately, the code of these errors must be associated with an exception name. Figure 10.8 shows how to handle an unnamed internal exception.

In this case, it is assumed that there is a check constraint on table RENTAL, which does not allow the daily rate for rentals to be higher then $3.00. If the

```
DECLARE
-- Declare a name for the constraint
  check_constraint_violated  EXCEPTION;
-- Bind the constraint to an Oracle error code
  PRAGMA EXCEPTION_INIT (check_constraint_violated, -2290);
BEGIN
  INSERT INTO rental (customer_id, movie_id, rent_dt,
daily_rate)
  VALUES (:main.customer_id, :main.movie_id,
          :main.rent_dt, :main.daily_rate);
  -- INSERT fails if daily_rate > $3.00
  -- Violation of check constraint raises ORA-02290
  -- In such case control jumps to EXCEPTION section
  COMMIT;
EXCEPTION
  WHEN check_constraint_violated THEN
    MESSAGE('You are ripping this guy off!')
  WHEN OTHERS THEN
    MESSAGE('Internal error occurred.');
END;
```

FIGURE 10.8 Using unnamed internal exceptions.

record sent for INSERT to the database contains a higher value for DAILY_RATE, the statement will violate the check constraint defined in RENTAL. The error raised by the database server will be ORA-02290. The internal value of this error has a negative sign. In the PL/SQL block shown in Figure 10.8, this error is associated with the user-declared exception check_constraint_violated using the pragma EXCEPTION_INIT. A pragma is a directive that instructs the PL/SQL compiler to bind the internal error number to the specified exception name. Whenever the error occurs, the name can be used to handle the exception.

10.7.2 USER-DEFINED EXCEPTIONS

There are abnormal situations in an application that are not due to a failure or error of the database engine, but to a violation of the requirements or logic of the application. In that case, a user-specified exception may be used to trap and handle the situation. Figure 10.9 is an improvement of the previous code because it does check the DAILY_RATE before the record is sent to the database.

The difference between unnamed internal exceptions and user-named exceptions is that the second type must be raised explicitly when the abnormal condition occurs. The RAISE statement in a sense serves as a GOTO statement because the program execution is interrupted and the flow jumps to the exception.

```
DECLARE
-- Declare a name for the constraint
  check_constraint_violated  EXCEPTION;
BEGIN
  IF :main.daily_rate > 3 THEN
    RAISE check_constraint_violated;
  END IF;

-- If control comes here, daily_rate <= $3.00
  INSERT INTO rental (customer_id, movie_id, rent_dt, daily_rate)
  VALUES (:main.customer_id, :main.movie_id,
          :main.rent_dt, :main.daily_rate);
  COMMIT;
EXCEPTION
  WHEN check_constraint_violated THEN
    MESSAGE('You are ripping this guy off!')
  WHEN OTHERS THEN
    MESSAGE('Internal error occurred.');
END;
```

FIGURE 10.9   Example of a user-named exception.

> ## Note
>
> A user-defined exception that is declared in the built-in package STANDARD is FORM_TRIGGER_FAILURE. You can raise this exception any time you want to halt the processing of any Oracle Forms trigger.

However, using the RAISE command makes the code more uniform and consistent with other situations.

10.7.3 ERROR REPORTING FUNCTIONS

It is a known fact in the information technology environment that the number of things that could potentially go wrong with an application is proportional to its functionality. However, it is a recognized trend that the systems developed today are more robust and protected than systems developed in the past. This is due to great improvements in hardware and software development tools, and to a better preparation of programmers to handle different situations that a system can face. But, it is unrealistic to expect an application to handle every error that can occur. The developer must decide which errors can and must be corrected when they occur and which ones may simply be reported and taken care of later.

In PL/SQL programs, a good place to put error reporting code is in the OTHER clause of the EXCEPTION section. Whenever an error occurs, Oracle provides the number of that error and a brief descriptive message. They can both be retrieved and further manipulated by the functions SQLCODE and SQLERRM. These are PL/SQL specific functions that cannot be used in a SQL statement. SQLCODE returns the error number, and the SQLERRM returns the error message. Figure 10.10 expands the functionality of the PL/SQL block in Figure 10.9 by adding error reporting functionality. Chapter 19 provides additional details on exceptions, how they propagate and how you can trap and handle them.

10.8 PROGRAM UNITS IN ORACLE FORMS

The material presented so far has introduced some Forms-specific uses of PL/SQL such as global variables or Forms objects data types. This section introduces some additional information about Oracle Forms objects that contain only PL/SQL code.

PL/SQL code in Oracle Forms applications can be written in triggers and menu items. Triggers are attached to either a form, a block, or an item. Their code is executed upon the occurrence of the specific event for which they are written.

```
DECLARE
   err_code NUMBER;
   err_text VARCHAR2(255);
-- Declare a name for the constraint
  check_constraint_violated  EXCEPTION;
BEGIN
  IF :main.daily_rate > 3 THEN
    RAISE check_constraint_violated;
  END IF;

-- If control comes here, daily_rate <= $3.00
  INSERT INTO rental (customer_id, movie_id, rent_dt, daily_rate)
  VALUES (:main.customer_id, :main.movie_id,
          :main.rent_dt, :main.daily_rate);
  COMMIT;
EXCEPTION
  WHEN check_constraint_violated THEN
    MESSAGE('You are ripping this guy off!')
  WHEN OTHERS THEN
    err_code := SQLCODE; err_text := SQLERRM;
    MESSAGE('Error '||TO_CHAR(err_code)||' - '|| err_text);
END;
```

FIGURE 10.10   Using functions SQLCODE and SQLERRM.

The code written in triggers or menu items is in the form of anonymous PL/SQL blocks. All the features discussed in previous sections can be used to access and manipulate data. Oracle Forms also provides a large number of built-in program units that can be used in triggers. These built-ins implement actions and functionality that occur so often that they have become standards in Forms applications. User-defined functions and procedures can be called or used in these anonymous blocks.

The user-defined functions and procedures are separate Oracle Forms objects that belong to the form or menu module. They are listed under the Program Units node of the Object Navigator. Logically related functions and procedures can be grouped together in larger PL/SQL objects called packages. Packages will be discussed in Chapter 19, together with other advanced PL/SQL programming features.

As in other programming languages, PL/SQL procedures perform certain actions, whereas functions return a value. The syntax rules of PL/SQL do not forbid procedures to return values to the calling environment, or functions to perform tasks. However, the code is more clear if these two criteria are not violated. Figure 10.11 shows examples of how procedures or functions are called in a PL/SQL block.

```
DECLARE
  days NUMBER;
BEGIN
  days := Days_Between(:rental.rent_dt, :rental.return_dt);
  Set_Cust_Phone(:customer.customer_id, '(800) 345-5424');
END;
```

FIGURE 10.11 Calling user-defined program units.

10.8.1 PARTS OF PROGRAM UNITS

Figure 10.12 contains the definition of the function Days_Between.
Figure 10.13 contains the definition of the function Set_Cust_Phone.

Each program unit has a specification part and a body. The specification for a procedure is made up of the keyword PROCEDURE, the name of the procedure, and the argument list enclosed in parentheses. The specification for a function is made up of the keyword FUNCTION, the name of the function, the argument list enclosed in parentheses, and the RETURN clause, which defines the data type of the value returned by the function. The argument definition list contains the name, mode, and data type of each argument.

The arguments defined in the specification part of a program unit and used in its body are called formal arguments. For example, the arguments cust_id in Figure 10.12, or first_dt in Figure 10.13 are formal arguments. The values passed to the program unit when it is called are called actual arguments. Values :customer.customer_id or :rental.rent_dt in Figure 10.11 are actual arguments.

```
FUNCTION Days_Between(first_dt IN DATE, second_dt IN DATE)
RETURN NUMBER
IS
  dt_one NUMBER;
  dt_two NUMBER;
BEGIN
  dt_one := TO_NUMBER(TO_CHAR(first_dt, 'DDD'));
  dt_two := TO_NUMBER(TO_CHAR(second_dt, 'DDD'));

  RETURN(dt_two - dt_one);
END;
```

FIGURE 10.12 Example of a function.

```
PROCEDURE Set_Cust_Phone (cust_id IN OUT NUMBER,
                          cust_phone IN OUT VARCHAR2)
IS
BEGIN
  UPDATE customer
  SET phone = cust_phone
  WHERE customer_id = cust_id;
EXCEPTION
  WHEN OTHERS THEN
    MESSAGE('Internal error occurred.');
END;
```

FIGURE 10.13   Example of a procedure.

The mode of arguments can be IN, OUT, or IN OUT. It defines the way they handle the data passed in the program unit call. IN arguments are used to pass a value that should not be changed by the program unit. In the program unit's body, an IN argument behaves like a constant whose value cannot be modified by assignment statements. If not specified otherwise, an argument is by default an IN mode argument. OUT arguments are used to modify the value of the actual argument in the calling environment. The value of an OUT argument before the call is no longer available when the control returns from the function or procedure to the calling environment. For this reason, the program unit must assign a value to all its OUT arguments, otherwise their value after the unit's execution is complete, is undetermined. Assignments are the only operations in which OUT arguments can be used inside the program unit.

IN OUT arguments allow the calling environment to pass values to a program unit. In its body, they are treated like normal variables. The program unit may modify the value of the argument, and this modification is visible to the outside environment. Although nothing restricts functions from using OUT and IN OUT arguments, they are usually limited to using IN arguments only. Usually, a function takes a series of arguments as input, and computes and returns only one value as its output. The logic of a function is not very clear and is prone to errors if, on the side, the function modifies a few other variables passed as OUT or IN OUT.

The body of the program unit begins with the keyword IS. If local variables will be used, they must be declared between this keyword and the keyword BEGIN, as in the case of function Days_Between. Named program units do not use the keyword DECLARE to indicate the beginning of the declaration section. The executable statements followed by the EXCEPTION section are placed between the keywords BEGIN and END, which are mandatory for named functions and procedures.

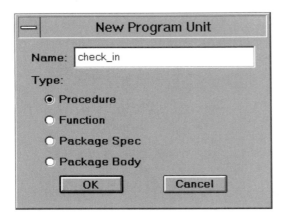

FIGURE 10.14   New Program Unit dialog box.

10.8.2 CREATING PROGRAM UNITS

A program unit can be easily created from the Object Navigator:

1. Select the Program Units node.
2. Click the Add button in the Navigator's toolbar. The New Program Unit dialog box appears (See Figure 10.14)
3. Specify the name of the program unit and its type.
4. Click OK.

Forms opens a PL/SQL editor window and provides a template that you can use to create the new program unit. Use the editor as described in the following section to define and compile the newly created function or procedure.

10.9 PL/SQL EDITOR

The PL/SQL Editor is a tool that facilitates the process of creating, modifying, compiling, and saving PL/SQL objects in an Oracle Forms database application. These objects include triggers, functions, procedures, and packages. In the Oracle Forms object, hierarchy triggers can be attached to forms, blocks, or items. Functions, procedures, and packages are all listed under the Program Units heading in the Object Navigator.

If you create a trigger or a program unit from the Navigator, a PL/SQL editor window will automatically open. If you want to edit the contents of an existing PL/SQL object, select it in the Navigator and use any of the following commands:

a) Double-click the trigger icon 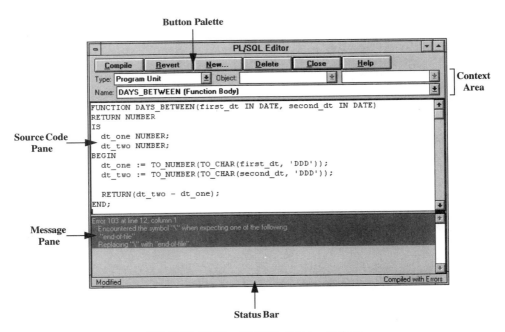 or program unit icon to the left of the object, or

b) Select Tools | PL/SQL Editor... from the Designer menu, or

c) Right-click and select PL/SQL Editor... from the popup menu.

Figure 10.15 shows a typical PL/SQL Editor window.

The components of the PL/SQL Editor window are the source code pane, the messages pane, the context definition area, and button palette. At the bottom of the window, you can see a status bar. The window also has horizontal and vertical scrollbars that allow navigating to hidden parts of it.

10.9.1   EDITING TEXT

In the source code pane you can use all the standard text editing functions. Namely, you can cut, copy, paste, and delete by either choosing the corresponding menu items from the Edit menu, or by pressing the hot keys from the keyboard. In the editing area, you can also search for a specific string or replace it with a new string.

FIGURE 10.15   PL/SQL Editor window.

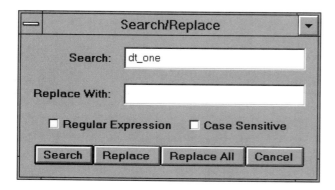

FIGURE 10.16   Search/Replace dialog box.

To search for or replace a string in the PL/SQL object currently displayed in the window follow these steps:

1. Select Edit | Search/Replace... from the menu. The Search/Replace dialog box appears (see Figure 10.16).
2. Enter the string to search for in the Search text field. If you want to replace it with another string, enter the new string in the Replace text field.
3. Check the respective boxes if you want to perform a case-sensitive search, or to search regular expressions.
4. Click Search to find the first occurrence of the string, or Replace to substitute the first occurrence of the string, or Replace All to substitute all the occurrences of the string.
5. Click Cancel when done.

When you click the Search, Replace, or Replace All buttons, the editor will search forward, starting from the current position of the cursor. If it reaches the end of the code, and no occurrences of the string are found, you will be asked if you want to continue searching from the beginning.

Note

The names of the Search/Replace menu items may lead to some confusion. They both search and replace PL/SQL code. Search/Replace... works with one object at a time; Search/Replace PL/SQL... acts upon all the triggers, functions, and procedures in the current module.

The PL/SQL editor allows you to perform global search-and-replaces on all the PL/SQL objects in the module. To do this follow the previous steps, but select Edit | Search/Replace PL/SQL... menu item, instead of Edit | Search/Replace. The rest is the same. When the editor reaches the end of a program unit, it asks you whether you want to continue to search to the next program unit.

10.9.2 EXPORTING AND IMPORTING TEXT

The PL/SQL editor also allows you to move the text in the source code area from the Designer to a file in the directory tree and vice-versa. Follow these steps to export the contents of a PL/SQL object:

1. Select Edit | Export | Text... . A standard Save As dialog box appears.
2. Specify the name and the location of the file.
3. Click OK.

To import the content of a text file into the source code area of a PL/SQL editor proceed as follows:

1. Select Edit | Import | Text... . A standard Open dialog box appears.
2. Specify the name and the location of the file you want to import.
3. Click OK.

The content of the file will be loaded starting from the current cursor position.

10.9.3 COMPILING CODE

After you enter code in the source pane you need to compile it. To do so, click the Compile button in the button palette. If the compilation is successful, the status bar of the window will display the Compiled Successfully status indicator to the right. If the PL/SQL engine encounters any syntax errors, the status indicator will be Compiled with Errors, and the errors will be displayed in the message pane as shown in Figure 10.15. If you click at the line number of the error, the editor places the cursor in the source code pane at the line where the error occurred. You can drag the bar that divides the panes to rearrange the sizes of the two panes. If you move it all the way to the bottom of the window, the message pane will be hidden.

You can compile PL/SQL objects from the Object Navigator as well. If you select the File | Compile... from the menu, only those objects that were not successfully compiled will be processed. If you want to compile the whole module, including those items that were compiled successfully earlier, select File | Compile All... from the menu. In both cases, a dialog box similar to Figure 10.17 will be displayed.

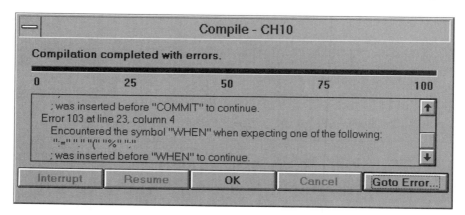

FIGURE 10.17   Compile dialog box.

The line across the window shows the percentage of the code compiled. It is filled dynamically during the compilation. At this time, you also can stop the process by clicking the Interrupt button. Click Resume when you are ready to continue compiling the rest of the code. The button Goto Error... opens a PL/SQL editor window and places the cursor at the line where the error occurred.

Finally, when the module is generated, all the PL/SQL objects are compiled as well. If errors occur, they are displayed in a scrollable window and, at the same time, written to a file with the extension .ERR.

10.9.4   CONTEXT AREA

The context area of the PL/SQL editor window is where the name and type of the PL/SQL object are defined. In the case of triggers, the type of trigger and the object they are attached to are displayed here as well. The context area is a combination of four drop-down list boxes. The first one, up and to the left, shows the type of the object currently loaded in the editor. Its value can be either Program Unit or Trigger. The two other drop-down lists to its right are enabled only if the type of objects is Trigger. They define the object (form, block, or item) that owns the trigger. The list box in the second row displays the name of the PL/SQL object. Figure 10.18 shows samples of the four possible context definitions that can be used in an application.

If the object type is Program Unit, the Object drop-down list boxes are disabled. If the PL/SQL object is a form-level or block-level trigger, the first one of them displays either (Form Level) or the name of the block that owns the trigger; the last list box is disabled.

By selecting different entries from the list boxes described above, you can quickly navigate to the PL/SQL objects you want to work with. Suppose, for example, that you just finished work with the function ADD_MONTHS (see Figure 10.18a); you want to call this function from the trigger WHEN-LIST-ACTIVATED attached to item DAILY_RATE of block RENTAL (see Figure 10.18d):

Program Unit	Type: Program Unit ± Object: ± ± **(a)** Name: DAYS_BETWEEN (Function Body) ±
Form-Level Trigger	Type: Trigger ± Object: (Form Level) ± ± **(b)** Name: PRE-FORM ±
Block-Level Trigger	Type: Trigger ± Object: RENTAL ± (Block Level) ± **(c)** Name: POST-QUERY ±
Item-Level Trigger	Type: Trigger ± Object: RENTAL ± DAILY_RATE ± **(d)** Name: WHEN-LIST-ACTIVATED ±

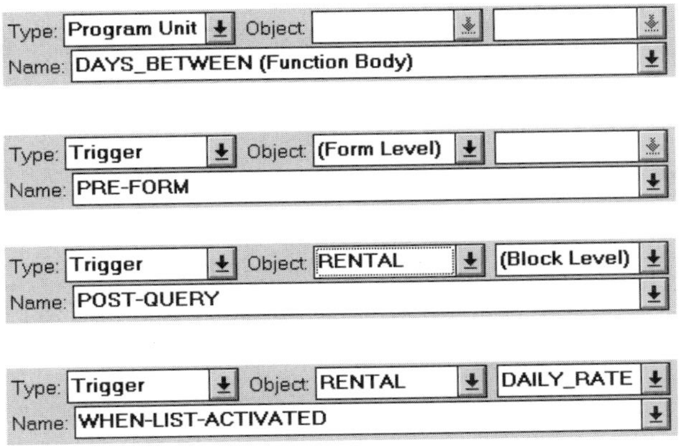

FIGURE 10.18   Four context settings of the PL/SQL Editor window.

1. Click the arrow button ± of the Type drop-down list box and change type to Trigger. The context switches to the first trigger in the module hierarchy. In the case of Figure 10.18b, it happens to be the form-level trigger PRE-FORM.
2. Click the arrow button ± of the first Object drop-down list box and select RENTAL from the list of blocks that appears (see Figure 10.18c). At this point, the arrow button of the second list is enabled.
3. Click the arrow button ± of the second Object drop-down list box and select DAILY_RATE from the list of columns that appears.
4. Click the arrow button ± of the Name drop-down list box and select WHEN-LIST-ACTIVATED from the list of trigger that appears (see Figure 10.18d).

10.9.5   USING TABLES/COLUMNS UTILITY

Oracle Forms gives you a hand in writing statements that select columns from a table. You can use the Tables/Columns utility to click at the columns you want to include in the SELECT statement and have the Designer paste the statement for you. To see an example of this, start the Designer, connect to the database, and create a new program unit. Suppose you want to select data from the table MOVIES in this program unit:

1. Choose Tools I Tables/Columns... from the menu. The Tables dialog box is displayed (see Figure 10.19). This is the same dialog box that is displayed during the process of creating a default base table block.
2. Click OK in the Tables dialog box. A list of tables that you own appears (see Figure 10.20).

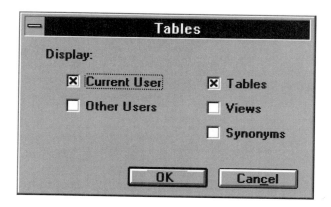

FIGURE 10.19 Tables dialog box.

3. Select MOVIE from the left pane. All the columns of the table are displayed in the left pane, as shown in Figure 10. 20.
4. Click column MOVIE_ID, then SHIFT+CLICK column RATING. All the columns are selected.
5. Click Select-from push button to paste a SELECT statement in the PL/SQL editor.
6. Complete the SELECT statement with the INTO clause, WHERE clause, and other clauses as the case may be.

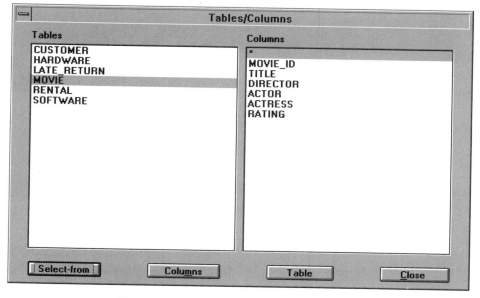

FIGURE 10.20 Tables/Columns dialog box.

If you need to write another SELECT statement, use the tool again. Click Close push button to dismiss it.

10.10 SUMMARY

This chapter introduces elements of PL/SQL programming language and how they are used in Oracle Forms applications. Major concepts discussed in this chapter are listed here:

- ❏ Brief history of PL/SQL language
- ❏ Approach and advantages of PL/SQL
- ❏ Structural elements of PL/SQL blocks
- ❏ Variables in PL/SQL
    - ❏ Local and global variables
    - ❏ Data types of variables in Oracle Forms
    - ❏ Forms items and database columns
- ❏ Manipulating data in PL/SQL blocks
- ❏ Procedural constructs of PL/SQL
    - ❏ IF statement
    - ❏ Looping statements
    - ❏ Unconditional branching
- ❏ Exception handling
    - ❏ Internal exceptions
    - ❏ User-defined exceptions
    - ❏ Error reporting functions
- ❏ Program units in Oracle Forms
    - ❏ Parts of program units
    - ❏ Creating program units
- ❏ PL/SQL Editor
    - ❏ Editing text
    - ❏ Exporting and importing text
    - ❏ Compiling code
    - ❏ Context area
- ❏ Using Tables/Columns Utility

Part III

ORACLE FORMS OBJECTS

When you strip away all the politics, rhetoric and other baggage . . . you find that an object is an instance of some class in which that object is anything that supports three fundamental notions:

- ❑ *Encapsulation*
- ❑ *Polymorphism*
- ❑ *Inheritance*

—Kraig Brockschmidt

OBJECT-ORIENTED ANALYSIS AND DESIGN

"Once the whole is divided, the parts need names."
—Lao Tsu

- Movie Rental Database Problem Restated
- Object-Oriented Terminology
- Structured Design versus Object-Oriented Design
- Designing the MRD Application
- User Interface Design and Conventions
- Summary

This chapter returns and expands on the problem of the neighborhood video rental store, which was used in the previous two chapters for the purpose of learning the syntax of SQL and PL/SQL languages. The statements issued and executed in those chapters help you create an idea about the problems that the employees in the store face in their everyday activity. This chapter will analyze in more detail these problems and create a design for the application that will be developed in the coming chapters. The approach taken here is not the one taken traditionally in the analysis and design of database systems with Oracle Forms. Because of the many object-oriented features incorporated in the software with the recent and upcoming releases, the more modern and increasingly more popular methodology of object-oriented analysis (OOA) and design (OOD) is used.

11.1 MOVIE RENTAL DATABASE PROBLEM RESTATED

Movie Rental Database (MRD) is an application that will serve the needs of a neighborhood video store. The jobs that employees perform there can be grouped in two broad groups. The first group is the one you are most familiar with, because you interact with it each time you rent or return a movie. The employees fulfilling duties included in this category stay behind counters and serve the customers. The range of services they provide is very broad. Not all of them require the use of the MRD application. Informing a customer about the business hours of the store is such a service. However, most of the functions in this job category will be greatly facilitated by your system. Such duties would be opening a new account for a customer, checking out videos, and responding to customers' inquiries about certain movies, actors, or other information in the system.

The second group includes functions that occur behind the counters; not necessarily in interaction with the customers. Some of these actions are simple, such as making sure that videos are in good working condition and rewound when they are returned. Others are more complex, such as analyzing the revenue generated by different movies and making decisions on what to buy next based on this analysis. Your application will accommodate functionality from both groups.

11.2 OBJECT-ORIENTED TERMINOLOGY

The purpose of this section is to explain some of the terms frequently used in object-oriented analysis, design, and programming. It also attempts to shed some light on the concepts they represent and how they apply to Oracle Forms programming. You should not consider this section conclusive in nature. As you will see, you will return to concepts mentioned here later in the chapter when you will use them to design the MRD application. You will put to practice these concepts in the chapters to come where the application will be developed.

11.2.1 OBJECTS, CLASSES, AND INSTANCES

The word object in the everyday life means something that we can touch, feel, or conceive intellectually. In software engineering, an object is something that the user can see and feel on the screen, click it with the mouse, drag from one point, and drop into another. The object in software engineering is an abstract representation of the real world. For example, in the real world, we consider videos as objects. But in the MRD application, videos are represented by a set of data items on the screen. Through the power of intellectual abstraction, we establish one or more conventional rules similar to this. In other words, we define the objects involved in the application. The purpose of this analysis is to establish some order and to group the amount of information that the system will process.

The colloquial language that we use at home, workplace, or school contains a considerable amount of fuzziness. When we refer to a table in our conversation, in some circumstances we may be thinking of a particular coffee table, and in other circumstances we think of a table as a category of objects. The marvelous information processing machine that is in our heads, the brain, is able to use a whole range of other inputs from the context or the situation to establish the appropriate meaning of the word. In software systems, where we tend to discard information deemed to be irrelevant to the problem, some additional conventions must be established in order to avoid this fuzziness. Thus, the concepts of *class* and *instance* are introduced.

A *class* is the generalization of the characteristics that a group of objects have in common. The class Table would represent all the tables in the world, and the class Customer would represent all the customers that do business with our video rental store. The *instance,* on the other hand, is specific information about a particular object in the class. The coffee table in my living room is an instance of class Table; Mary Jones is an instance of class Customer.

Note

The concepts described above are encountered, under different names, in more traditional approaches to software engineering. In relational databases for example, the concept of entity could substitute the concept of class to a great extent. When the database is physically implemented, tables represent these entities, or classes. Each table is populated with records, or instances of the entity. On the front-end, if the application is implemented in Oracle Forms, the entities are represented by blocks. Each record displayed in the block is an instance of the entity.

11.2.2 ATTRIBUTES

From what has been said above, you can conclude that common characteristics of similar objects can be grouped together in an abstract class. These characteristics are called attributes of the class. Each object instance derived from that class will, by definition, have the same attributes as the parent class. Imagine for a moment an Oracle Forms block that represents the class Customer on the screen. Attributes of this class such as datatype of FIRST_NAME, or maximum length of LAST_NAME, will be the same for all the instances or records of that class.

The concept of variables is introduced with the attributes. Settings that do not change from instance to instance are called class variables. They are given a value when the class is created and this value remains the same during the life of the class. There is a second type of variable called an instance variable, whose value changes from instance to instance. In the example above, the contents of data items such as FIRST_NAME and LAST_NAME, are instance variables. Their values will generally change from record to record.

11.2.3 METHODS

In the real life, objects are not a static picture of data, frozen in time. They interact with and constantly act upon each other. We buy and drive cars, rent and watch videos, take exams, or pass tests. This dynamic scenario of our life is reflected in the software systems we create. These systems perform actions upon data, from the simplest to the most complicated ones. Every computer system, whether it is programmed according to structured methodology principles or using object-oriented tools and approach must fulfill this requirement. The innovative approach that object-oriented programmers introduced in software engineering is not in what can be done, as much as in how intuitively things can be done. The object-oriented methodology premise is that the computer models you create will be closer to reality and easier to manipulate if they reflect this reality faithfully. Since objects and actions go hand-in-hand in the real life, that's how they must be implemented in a software system.

An object-oriented application bundles in one class not only the attributes and data that the class represents, but also actions to be performed upon these data. These actions are known as methods associated with the object class. These methods, when executed, manipulate the data encapsulated in the class structure. They may also initiate actions on other objects. True object-oriented programming languages allow access to the methods of a class only through that class. The methods cannot be called directly like functions or procedures in structured programming. In Oracle applications, methods associated with objects are called triggers.

11.2.4 MESSAGES

In the structured methodology, programmers are in the driver's seat. They establish a flow in the internal logic of the program which users must follow in order to perform the actions they need. Users are offered a very limited choice of options and typically are reduced to answering Yes/No type of questions. The object-oriented approach is different. Programmers no longer control the flow of the application. In fact, there is no deterministic way in which an application is executed. At any point in time, users have a variety of places to click on, windows to browse, and lists to select from. It is very unusual here to find long subroutines with several levels of calls to other routines. Instead, you have objects and small pieces of code attached to them. These objects patiently wait for the user to interact with them. The interaction can take several aspects. It can be a mouse-click, a change in the value of the data item, request for validation of the data entered, or creation of a new record. Whenever this happens, it is said that the object received a message. Another way to express this is that an event occurred for the object. Each object has a certain number of events, or messages, that can serve as a wake-up call. These events, commonly known as the protocol of the object, are mostly predefined, based on the type of object, but can also be defined by the programmer.

When the object receives a message that is part of its protocol, it checks to see if there is a method or trigger associated with it. In case there is one, the method is executed; otherwise, the object does not react to the message. In Oracle Forms, the number of messages an object can receive can be quite large, but most of them are ignored or handled by the default functionality. For example, it is typical for push buttons to respond to the mouse click, but not to dozens of other actions the user may try to do. Chapter 19 will discuss in greater detail the events and triggers in Oracle Forms applications.

11.2.5 INHERITANCE

Inheritance is the object-oriented programming principle that allows you to reuse object classes developed and tested previously. It reflects the gradual changes between reality objects that share similar characteristics, but have differences in a limited number of attributes or methods. Imagine for example a class of objects called Clothes. Some of its attributes may be Size, Price, Date of Purchase. Some methods associated with it could be Wash and Iron. Pants is a new class that inherits all the attributes and methods of class Clothes. This class may have additional attributes added to it such as Length and Seam. If there is a need to add more specific instructions for washing and ironing pants, the methods inherited from the parent class can be modified or overridden.

In the current version of Oracle Forms you can create classes based on properties of objects. Triggers may be attached to these classes as well. These classes are used to assign the set of properties and associated methods to an object using the inheritance mechanism.

11.2.6 ENCAPSULATION

As mentioned earlier, encapsulation is a method to group logically related data together with the methods that access and modify them. It is also a method to protect the data in the class from unwanted and potentially destructive access. A class is truly encapsulated in an object-oriented sense if its attributes are modifiable only through the methods of the class. The interface offered by this class to the outside application must be limited to the specifications of these methods. It is not necessary for the rest of the application to know how the methods are implemented internally, and to rely on or utilize this implementation. If that were allowed, a minor change in the body of the method could result in modifications throughout the application. If, on the other hand, the implementation of the method is hidden, the changes will be transparent to the rest of the application. PL/SQL offers a solid implementation of encapsulation through packages. These objects will be discussed in Chapter 19 as well.

11.2.7 POLYMORPHISM

Polymorphism is the object-oriented technique that allows the same message to generate different responses in different objects. The concept of polymorphism is encountered frequently in the everyday life. Suppose, for example, that there is a conference of Oracle Forms developers scheduled in three months. The organizing committee issues a call for papers to all the professionals in its mailing list. At this point, the committee does not care how each individual will react to the message. Some may prepare a demo, some may prepare a presentation, some may ignore the message altogether. The fact remains that the same message will generate different responses in different persons. Or take another example. Each year, the Federal Government announces the date in April when taxes are due. Different people will react differently to the message. Some will prepare their taxes themselves, some will hire an accountant, and some will buy a tax preparation software package. Again, the same message makes different people react differently.

In Oracle Forms, the polymorphism can be seen and used in several instances. For example, the built-in routine CREATE_RECORD will always create an empty record in any base-table block, despite the number of items in the block or the structure of the block itself. Furthermore, PL/SQL allows you to create program units with the same name, but that take variables of different datatypes. Based on these variables, different actions can be taken, but these differences remain transparent to the application that issues the call to the function.

11.3 STRUCTURED DESIGN VERSUS OBJECT-ORIENTED DESIGN

The process of analyzing the requirements for a soon-to-be-constructed software system follows a certain sequence of steps, recommended by the particular methodology you are following. The design of a system according to structured programming methodology will proceed following the steps listed below:

1. Define the data used by the application. In this step, software engineers define the entities used in the application, their attributes, and the type of relations they form with each other. Based on this analysis, a logical design for the database is prepared and stored in the system's knowledge repository. The logical database design includes, among others, entity-relationship diagrams, data dictionaries, and business rules that affect data items.

2. Create the physical database design model. Based on the logical database design, database specialists define the physical database structures that will store the information contained in the system. This step more or less concludes the design of the back-end, or the database side, of the application.

3. Identify and describe each process that the future system will perform. Complex processes are divided in simpler subprocesses until a satisfactory level of simplicity is reached. For each process, systems analysts define its input and output data, and outline its functionality. The outcome of this step is the process decomposition diagram of the system.

4. Define and describe the dependency among processes identified in the previous step. In other words, define how, and under what conditions, processes will pass the control to other processes. The outcome of this step is the process-flow diagrams, also known as data-flow diagrams. The last two steps often are merged together during system design sessions.

5. Design modules, procedures, and functions of the system to reflect the diagrams defined in the previous two steps. This step also includes designing screens, windows, menus, and other user-interface elements of the front-end application.

As you can see, the attention of the structured methodology shifts from the data objects (Steps 1 and 2) to the actions or processes that occur in the system (Steps 3, 4, and 5). The process decomposition diagrams and data-flow diagrams, when implemented by the software engineers, will inherently define the logical flow of the application. Users are often restricted to follow the system in order to perform the business transactions implemented there.

Object-oriented programming on the other hand, keeps the designers' attention focused on the objects. The first two steps of the traditional approach are still preserved, although different terminology may be used in each of them. Steps three, four, and five are quite different and look as follows:

3. Visualize the conduct of each object when it interacts with the users and specify the methods associated with it. As explained in the previous section, these methods maintain a low profile in the application. They are services that the object offers to the users only when they request them. Users request these services by sending messages to the objects. The number of methods that can be associated with an object is practically unlimited. However, a well-designed object has only a few pertinent methods explicitly de-

> ## Note
>
> Some debate exists in the IT community about the effectiveness of object-oriented techniques in applications that use relational databases. Object-oriented purists require that object class structures and their instances be stored in object-oriented databases. We take a more pragmatic approach to this problem by using the best that both sides have to offer. We utilize the extensive functionality, robustness, and maturity that relational database systems have achieved for the back-end implementation of the system. At the same time, we design and implement the front-end application following object-oriented principles. This is a *modus vivendi* reached in many modern data processing centers today.

fined. The rest of them are handled by the implicit default processing of the application. For example, to create a new record in a block, you may simply invoke the method CREATE_RECORD, without having to implement it.

4. Define the protocol of the object or the messages that will activate each method. Messages can be generated by user actions, by methods of other objects, or by internal processes such as navigation, data validation, or database interaction. However, as in the previous step, you do not identify every message that the object can intercept, but only the few ones that need special attention. These two steps are often performed together. The results are presented in a unified table known as the control-by-message matrix of the application. The first row of the matrix contains the objects involved in the system; the first column lists the messages that they can intercept. The matrix cell at the intersection of an object column with a message row contains the method of that object that is activated by the message. For an example of a control-by-message matrix see Table 11.5 later in the chapter.

5. Design screens, windows, menus, and other user-interface elements of the application to reflect the object-oriented design. The layout of the application should make the process of activating the methods associated with objects clear, easy, and intuitive. In this step you also identify objects that will benefit from inheritance or that will respond differently to the same message.

11.4 DESIGNING THE MRD APPLICATION

In this section you will apply the steps described in the previous section to design the Movie Rental Database Application.

11.4.1 OBJECTS DEFINITION AND ENTITY-RELATIONSHIP DIAGRAMS

By carefully analyzing the business process of the video store, it is not difficult to conclude that the main entities of this application are Customer, Movie, Tape, and Rental.

Customer represents the typical clients of the store that open an account and rent tapes for a limited amount of time. Movie is a play, story, or event in the form of a motion picture. A movie can be seen in movie theaters or on television, but for the purpose of this application, it is copied on one or more tapes and rented to customers. Tape is a magnetic tape used to record pictures of a movie. Customers in your application rent one or more tapes to watch the movies they contain. Finally, Rental is the object that represents the transaction between a customer and the video store in which a tape is rented for one or more days.

The definitions provided above, inherently contain the relationships between the objects in the MRD application. Nevertheless, they need some further clarification. Relationships, or relations, are significant associations or forms of interactions between objects. On both sides of a relation reside entities. Depending on the number of objects from one entity that can be associated with objects from the other entity, several types of entity relationships are distinguished. These types are shown and explained in Figure 11.1.

Figure 11.2 represents the entity-relationship diagram for the MRD application. There are three relationships between the entities of this application. They can be worded as follows:

1. Each Customer may initiate zero or more Rental transactions. Each Rental transaction must be initiated by one and only one Customer.

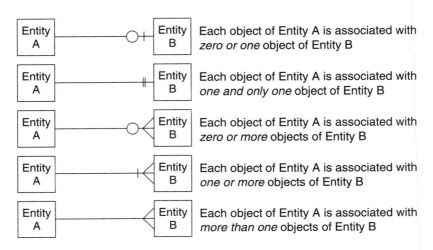

FIGURE 11.1   Types of entity relationships.

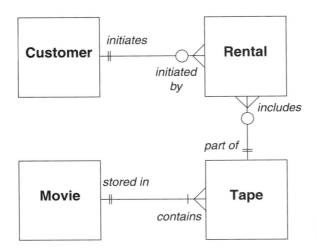

FIGURE 11.2 Entity relationship diagram for Movie Rental Database.

2. Each Tape may be part of zero or more Rental transactions. Each Rental transaction must include one and only one Tape.
3. Each Movie may be stored in one or many Tapes. Each Tape must contain one and only one Movie.

After the main entities of the application are defined, each entity is analyzed in detail to identify their attributes. As in other examples in this book, the characteristics of attributes that you try to capture in this stage are name, datatype, length, and referential integrity constraints such as primary key, foreign key, and uniqueness.

Table 11.1 shows the attribute definitions for entity Customer. Table 11.2 shows the attribute definitions for entity Tape. Table 11.3 shows the attribute definitions for entity Movie. Finally, Table 11.4 shows the attribute definitions for entity Rental. The next step after the logical design of the database is the physical design. In this phase, the database package is selected, and its particular features utilized. Each entity identified in the logical design is mapped to a table in the physical design. The tables for the MRD application will be CUSTOMERS, TAPES, MOVIES, RENTALS. Note that it is customary to use the plural of an entity's name as the name of its corresponding table. The storage parameters for each table are defined based on the analysis of data volume for each entity.

Other structures designed in this phase are sequence number generators, indexes, stored program units, and database triggers. The MRD application will use a sequence to generate the internal identification numbers for instances of the entities defined above. Oracle Server automatically creates indexes for all the columns of a table that are part of the primary key. These indexes will be sufficient for the needs of your application, given the modest size of the MRD database. The program units and database triggers are part of the application logic

TABLE 11.1 Attributes for entity Customer.

ENTITY	ATTRIBUTES	DATA TYPE	LENGTH	PK	FK	OTHER INTEGRITY CONSTRAINTS
Customer	Customer Id	NUMBER	6	Y		Membership Number
	First Name	VARCHAR2	30			Not NULL
	Last Name	VARCHAR2	30			Not NULL
	Gender	CHAR	1			(M)ale, (F)emale
	Date of Birth	DATE				
	Membership Date	DATE				
	Status	VARCHAR2	1			(A)ctive; (G)ood Credit; (B)ad Credit
	Address Line	VARCHAR2	50			
	City	VARCHAR2	30			
	State	CHAR	2			
	Zip Code	VARCHAR2	10			
	Daytime Telephone Number	VARCHAR2	10			
	Evening Telephone Number	VARCHAR2	10			
	Comedy	CHAR	1			Y if preferred, NULL otherwise
	Drama	CHAR	1			Y if preferred, NULL otherwise
	Mystery	CHAR	1			Y if preferred, NULL otherwise
	Foreign	CHAR	1			Y if preferred, NULL otherwise

placed on the back-end rather than the front-end application. They are considered methods associated with the database objects. The following section defines the methods of the MRD application in general and the stored program units in particular.

The companion disk provided with this book installs a SQL*Plus script that creates these tables and loads sample data in them. Instructions to execute this script against your Oracle Server database are provided in the section *Installing the Companion Disk* in the preface.

11.4.2 METHODS AND MESSAGES

This section defines the methods that will be encapsulated together with the data attributes of the entities. At the same time, you will specify the messages or

TABLE 11.2 Attributes for entity Tape

ENTITY	ATTRIBUTES	DATA TYPE	LENGTH	PK	FK	OTHER INTEGRITY CONSTRAINTS
Tape	Tape Id	NUMBER	6	Y		Internal tracking number
	Movie Id	NUMBER	6	Y	Y	Movie Id contained in tape
	Status	CHAR	1			(A)vailable; (R)ented; Re(T)urned

events that activate these methods. It is important to point out that at this stage you identify only the most important methods and messages in the highest level of the application. As you progress further in the development process, you will identify and document additional methods attached to objects in lower levels of the hierarchy of objects. Figure 11.3 graphically presents the MRD objects and the specifications of their methods.

TABLE 11.3 Attributes for entity Movie.

ENTITY	ATTRIBUTES	DATA TYPE	LENGTH	PK	FK	OTHER INTEGRITY CONSTRAINTS
Movie	Movie Id	Number	6	Y		Internal tracking number
	Title	VARCHAR2	30			Not NULL
	Status	CHAR	1			(A)vailable; (N)ot Available
	Director Name	VARCHAR2	30			
	Main Actor	VARCHAR2	30			
	Main Actress	VARCHAR2	30			
	Producer	VARCHAR2	30			
	Producing Company	VARCHAR2	30			
	Start Date	DATE				Date when rentals began
	End Date	DATE				Date when movie is discontinued
	Rating	CHAR	1			1 = NR, 2 = PG-13, 3 = R, 4 = NC-17

TABLE 11.4 Attributes for entity Rental

ENTITY	ATTRIBUTES	DATA TYPE	LENGTH	PK	FK	OTHER INTEGRITY CONSTRAINTS
Rental	Customer Id	NUMBER	6	Y	Y	Customer renting the tape
	Tape Id	NUMBER	6	Y	Y	Tape rented by the customer
	Rent Date	DATE		Y		
	Return Date	DATE				
	Daily Rate	NUMBER	4			

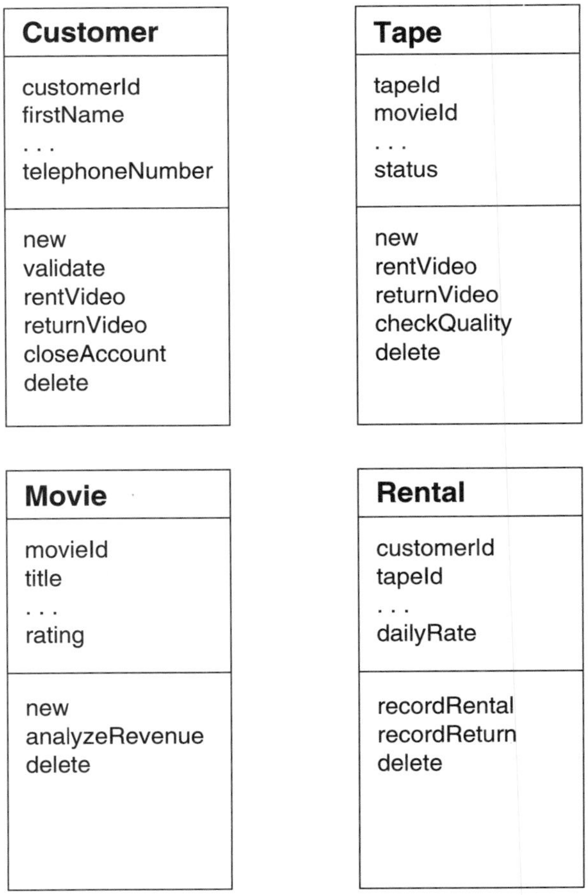

Customer

customerId
firstName
. . .
telephoneNumber

new
validate
rentVideo
returnVideo
closeAccount
delete

Tape

tapeId
movieId
. . .
status

new
rentVideo
returnVideo
checkQuality
delete

Movie

movieId
title
. . .
rating

new
analyzeRevenue
delete

Rental

customerId
tapeId
. . .
dailyRate

recordRental
recordReturn
delete

FIGURE 11.3 Data and methods encapsulated in Movie Rental Database objects.

Here is a brief description of the methods associated with object Customer:

- ❏ *New.* Invoked by the internal event CreateRecord. Creates a new record and assigns a unique identification number to the customer. Customer status is set to Active.
- ❏ *Validate.* Invoked by the internal event ValidateRecord. If the record is newly entered, check the database to see if the new customer was a member before.
- ❏ *RentVideo.* Invoked by the user-defined event RentVideo. Check the credit status of the customer.
- ❏ *ReturnVideo.* Invoked by the user-defined event ReturnVideo. Update the credit status if necessary.
- ❏ *CloseAccount.* Invoked by the user-defined event CloseAccount. If the customer has no tapes to return, set the status to Good Credit; otherwise, set the status to Bad Credit.
- ❏ *Delete.* Invoked by the internal event DeleteRecord. Sends DeleteRecord (Customer.CustomerId) message to object Rental to delete all the rental transactions initiated by this customer and deletes current record from Customer.

The following is a list of methods encapsulated with object Movie:

- ❏ *New.* Invoked by the internal event CreateRecord. Enter a new movie record and sent the message CreateRecord to Tape to create one or more tape records for the new movie.
- ❏ *AnalyzeRevenue.* Invoked by the user-defined event AnalyzeRevenue. Displays the revenue generated for the specified period.
- ❏ *Delete.* Invoked by the internal event DeleteRecord. Sends DeleteRecord (Movie.MovieId) message to object Tape to delete all the tapes for the movie and deletes the current record from Movie.

The methods of object Tape are listed below:

- ❏ *New.* Invoked by the internal event CreateRecord. Enter a new tape for a movie.
- ❏ *RentVideo.* Invoked by the user-defined event RentVideo. Set status of Tape to Rented.
- ❏ *ReturnVideo.* Invoked by the user-defined event ReturnVideo. Set status of Tape to Returned. Broadcast the CheckQuality message.
- ❏ *CheckQuality.* Invoked by the user-defined message CheckQuality. Manually check the tape for problems and rewind it, if necessary. If the tape is in good working condition, display it in the shelves and set the status to Available. Otherwise, issue DeleteRecord message and discard the tape.

TABLE 11.5 Object-oriented matrix for MRD application.

	CUSTOMER	MOVIE	VIDEO	RENTAL
CreateRecord	new	new	new	
ValidateRecord	validate			
DeleteRecord	delete	delete	delete	delete
CloseAccount	closeAccount			
RentVideo	rentVideo		rentVideo	recordRental
ReturnVideo	returnVideo		returnVideo	recordReturn
CheckQuality			checkQuality	
AnalyzeRevenue		analyzeRevenue		

❑ *Delete.* Invoked by the internal event DeleteRecord. Sends DeleteRecord (Tape.TapeId) message to object Rental to delete all the rental transactions for this tape, and deletes current record from Tape.

Finally, here is a description of the methods of object Rental:

❑ *RecordRental.* Invoked by the user-defined event RentVideo. Creates a new rental record for the particular Customer and Tape.

❑ *RecordReturn.* Invoked by the user-defined event ReturnVideo. Sets the return date to the current date. The appropriate fee is collected from the customer.

❑ *Delete.* Invoked by the internal event DeleteRecord. Deletes current record from Rental.

Table 11.5 summarizes the information presented so far in the form of a matrix. The first row of this matrix contains the objects in the MRD application: Customer, Movie, Video, and Rental. The first column of the matrix contains the events or messages generated in the application. The intersection cell of an object with an event contains the name of the method activated in that object by the corresponding event.

11.5 USER INTERFACE DESIGN AND CONVENTIONS

At this point you have an idea about what data entities and business rules the MRD application will cover. The next step before moving to the actual development activities is to create a high-level design of the user interface. Without worrying too much about the implementation details, you will identify the menu structure, types of windows, and any other relevant components that will be part of the application.

11.5.1 THE MDI FRAME

When the users will execute the application, they will first land in a window that does not contain any data items, except for the main menu of the application attached to it. The window will serve as the MDI frame for the MRD application. Its title will be Movie Rental Database, and the message bar will display information to help users in their data processing activities. The MDI frame window will also contain the application menu. In addition, a vertical and horizontal toolbar will be displayed and available to provide access to the main commands with a click of the mouse. At different points during the use of the application, some menu items may not be available. Upon such conditions, the logic of the application will disable these items by graying them out, as in other Windows applications. Figure 11.4 shows a prototype of the MDI frame for the MRD application.

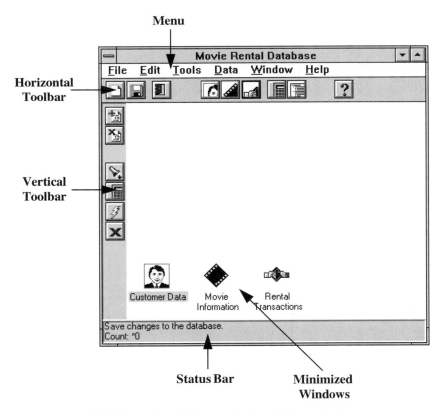

FIGURE 11.4   MDI frame for the MRD application.

11.5.2 THE APPLICATION MENU

The menu of the application will contain File, Edit, Tools, Data, Window, and Help submenus.

File
Clear
Save
Exit

The File menu contains only three items. File | Clear sets the whole application in a clean state, as it is when it is first loaded. File | Save commits changes to the database. File | Exit closes all the open windows and exits the application. These menu items correspond to the first three items of the horizontal toolbar of the MDI frame.

Edit	
Cut	Ctrl+X
Copy	Ctrl+C
Paste	Ctrl+V
Clear	Delete

The Edit menu contains the standard text editing menu items.

Tools
Customer...
Movie...
Rental...
Analyze...
Mailing Labels...

Tools menu contains menu items that invoke all the other windows in the application. The ellipses ... after the label indicates that a window will appear when the menu item will be selected. The iconic buttons located at the center of the horizontal toolbar will duplicate the functionality of these items.

Data	
Insert	
Duplicate	▶
Delete	
Enter Query	
Count Query Hits	
Execute Query	
Cancel Query	

The Data menu contains menu items used for database interaction. The first group of these items allows users to Insert, Duplicate, and Delete data in the current block. The second group controls the querying of the database. Items in this menu, except for Duplicate, correspond to the vertical toolbar icons under the editing buttons.

Window menu is the standard MDI menu that allows cascading and tiling of all open windows, or arranges the icons of minimized ones. The second part of it lists the windows currently open.

Finally, Help menu displays on-line help available for the application. The last item, About..., will display a copyright notice and a brief description of the application.

11.5.3 GUI STANDARDS FOR APPLICATION WINDOWS

As in every MDI application, the windows and dialog boxes in the MRD application will be displayed and manipulated within the boundaries of the MDI frame window. These windows, also known as MDI sheets, will all share the following characteristics:

1. Each window will contain data to support only one business function.
2. Windows will have Resize, Minimize, and Maximize capabilities.
3. The background color for the windows will be gray.
4. All the controls (items, buttons, etc.) will have a 3D look.
5. The title bar of the window will be a two or three word description of the business function accomplished by the window.
6. An appropriate icon must be displayed if the window is in Minimized state (see Figure 11.4). The icon title must be the same as the window title.
7. Each window will have at least two standard push buttons: Save and Close. Save will commit changes to the database and leave the window open. Close will prompt the user to save any uncommitted changes and close the window.
8. Text items will have white background color and black text color. Text will be in MS sans-serif font, size 8.
9. Text labels will have gray background color (to match windows background) and black text color. Text will be in MS sans-serif font, size 8.
10. Each navigable item, including any push buttons on the window must have micro-help displayed in the message bar.
11. The window must be sized and populated so that horizontal or vertical scrollbars will not be needed to view or access its objects.

Note that these are only suggested standards. You may modify or add to them if you find it necessary during the development process. The main point here is that, whatever the standards are, they must exist, be discussed, and be agreed upon in close interaction with the owners and users of the application. The issue is especially important when developing enterprise-wide applications using several software engineers to create the windows and screens.

11.5.4 WINDOWS AND DIALOG BOXES

This section describes in general terms the layout of each window in the MRD application.

- ❏ *Customer window.* This window will display data about customers in one record at a time. This format will allow users to view all information about a particular customer in the window. This window will be used to enter, update, delete, and query customer records.

- ❏ *Movie window.* The layout of this window is similar to that of Customer window. The upper part will display the movies in the MRD database one record at a time. The lower part will display the tapes for the current movie. The tapes that are currently available will be displayed first and those that are already rented will follow.

- ❏ *Rental window.* Front-desk clerks will use this window to record or update a rental transaction. The upper left quarter of the window will serve as a retrieval block for the customer; the upper right one for the movie. Remember that both these entities must be present when a tape is rented or returned. The lower half of the window will display by default the videos that the customer has not returned. Based on the number of the unreturned videos, additional requests for rentals may be turned down. Here the application users may also issue additional queries to review the customer's renting history.

- ❏ *Mailing Labels window.* This window will be used to generate mailing labels for specified groups of customers.

- ❏ *Analyze windows.* There will be two such windows that will be used to analyze the revenue generated by the store. One of them will display the amount of money customers spend on movie rentals in a given period of time, summed by zip code. The second window will display the amount in revenue generated by movies that the stores rent, based on their rating category.

Each of these windows can be invoked from the MDI frame by either clicking an iconic button in the toolbar, or by selecting the appropriate menu item. Users will be free to navigate from window to window while they are open. In addition, from the Customer and Movie window, users will be able to open or activate the Rental window to record a particular renting transaction that may occur. From the Rental window, they will be able to navigate to the Customer and Movie windows, in order to retrieve additional information that may be required. In such a case, the contents of the three windows will be synchronized accordingly. Push button items will be created in the respective windows to implement this functionality.

In addition to the windows above, the MRD application will also contain application modal dialog boxes that will supply additional information or will perform specific tasks related to a business function. While these dialog boxes are open, users cannot perform any other activity in the application. However, their ability to run other applications will not be affected. A special type of dialog boxes, Oracle Forms' Lists of Values, will be used to enter the appropriate state code in the address of a customer.

The layout of dialog boxes will follow the same guidelines as the ones presented earlier in the chapter. The only difference is that the push button Save will be replaced with OK, or another label that better describes the task accomplished in the dialog box. Activating this button will save the users' settings and close the dialog box.

The MRD application will communicate with the users in four ways. Hint messages and micro-help text will be displayed in the message bar. Informative messages will be displayed in dialog boxes with the icon ❶. Warnings and errors of low or medium severity will be displayed in dialog boxes with the icon ⓘ. If severe errors occur, dialog boxes with the icon ⬤ will attract the attention of users.

11.5.5 APPLICATION SECURITY

The users of the applications will be divided in two security groups, according to the job description and their need to view, access, and edit data. The members of the first group will be primarily the employees of the movie rental store that interact with the customers during the business hours of the store. They will have access to Customers, Movie, and Rental windows. They will also be able to print mailing labels for the customers, but will be restricted from accessing the Analyze window. The second group will have unrestricted access on all the windows of the application, including the Analyze window. Members of this group will be the managers and the financial analysts of the movie rental store. The logic of the application will decide in which group a user belongs upon logging to the database. Menu items and iconic buttons in the toolbar will be enabled and disabled accordingly.

11.6 SUMMARY

This chapter presented an overview of object-oriented analysis and design techniques, and how they apply to the Movie Rental Database problem. Some important concepts discussed in this chapter are listed here:

- ❑ Movie Rental Database problem restated
- ❑ Object-Oriented terminology
  - ❑ Objects, classes, and instances
  - ❑ Attributes
  - ❑ Methods
  - ❑ Messages
  - ❑ Inheritance
  - ❑ Encapsulation
  - ❑ Polymorphism
- ❑ Structured design versus object-oriented design
- ❑ Designing the MRD Application
  - ❑ Objects definition and entity-relationship diagrams
  - ❑ Methods and messages
- ❑ User interface design and conventions
  - ❑ The MDI frame
  - ❑ The application menu
  - ❑ GUI standards for application windows
  - ❑ Windows and dialog boxes
  - ❑ Application security

BLOCKS AND RELATIONS

"Go play with the towns you have built of blocks."
—Stephen Vincent Benét

- ♦ Base Table Blocks and Control Blocks
- ♦ Creating Blocks
- ♦ Properties of Blocks
- ♦ Relations
- ♦ Blocks and Relations for the MRD Application
- ♦ Summary

Blocks group together data elements based on the logical relationships that exist among them. In the front-end application, they represent an object type or class as defined in Chapter 11. This means that blocks are not only meant to bundle data, but also to define and contain the methods that access and manipulate these data. For example, the block CUSTOMER in the MRD application will be used as a container of data attributes related to the class of customers, and, at the same time, will allow you to enter, modify, and maintain these attribute for each customer.

An instance of the data object represented by the block is called a record. In Oracle Forms the term has a broader meaning that the same term used in the context of a relational database. In general, a record may not represent data from just one table. As a matter of fact it is common to have calculated data items in a block, which are not stored in the database. While a block is an object represented by a node in the Navigator hierarchy tree, records are objects maintained internally by Forms. Their properties and methods can be accessed at runtime by built-in program units. This chapter will discuss in detail the properties and features of blocks.

12.1 BASE TABLE BLOCKS AND CONTROL BLOCKS

As mentioned above, blocks are logical containers of data items in a form. Based on the source of data for these items, blocks are divided in base table blocks and control blocks. If at least one item in the block is directly linked with a column from a database table, the block is a base table block. Understandably, the items that correspond to table columns are called base table items. If none of the items included in a block is a base table item, then the block is called a control block. Items that do not represent data from database columns are referred to as control items. There are a few interesting facts that should be noted for base table and control blocks.

First, a base table block does not need to share the same name with the database table upon which the block is based. However, base table items in the block must have the same name as the table column. For example, later in this chapter you will create a multirecord block that will display data from the CUSTOMER table in the RENTAL window. You will name it CUST_RENT, a different name from the database table. But you will still keep the column names for the items of the block.

Second, a block may be based on one database table at most. If a block needs to display and manipulate data from more than one table, you must decide which one will be the base table for the block. Then, items that correspond to columns in other tables are created as control items within the same block. The logic of the application must ensure that these control items communicate correctly with their counterparts in the database. As an example, in the MRD application, the

RENTAL block will need to display data from three tables: CUSTOMER, TAPE, and RENTAL. Because the main functionality of this block is to describe a rental transaction, most of the database interaction will be handled by items that are derived from RENTAL table. For this reason, you will base the block upon this table. Then, programmatically, through triggers, functions, and procedures, you will complete the picture with detailed data about the customer and the video. Thus, the block will represent the data in the association in which they occur in real life, although this may not necessarily be the way they are stored in the database.

Third, base table blocks allow you to automatically inherit many of the attributes assigned to the database columns when the tables are created. Data type and length are the most trivial ones. In addition, data integrity constraints such as primary keys, foreign keys, NOT NULL, and unique values are inherited, if you choose to enforce these constraints when the block is created.

Finally, base table blocks greatly reduce the amount of SQL statements you must write in order to retrieve and manipulate the data. Consider, for example, the following scenario:

> The database contains a table THE_TABLE with only one column, THE_COLUMN. Two blocks are defined in a Forms module. The first one is based on THE_TABLE, and the second one is not. They are called BASE_TABLE and CONTROL respectively. Your task is to insert a new row in the table, then query the database to redisplay it. Figure 12.1 shows the steps to carry out the tasks with a base table block. Figure 12.2 shows the steps to carry the same task with a control block.

As you can see from this picture, the amount of code required in control blocks can be significantly larger than that in base table blocks. The task becomes even more complicated if the block displays and manipulates multiple records simultaneously. Keeping track of the status for each record—whether it is newly inserted, updated, or deleted—is overwhelming for control blocks, but is part of

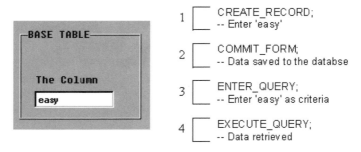

FIGURE 12.1   Base table blocks effectively use the default functionality of Oracle Forms.

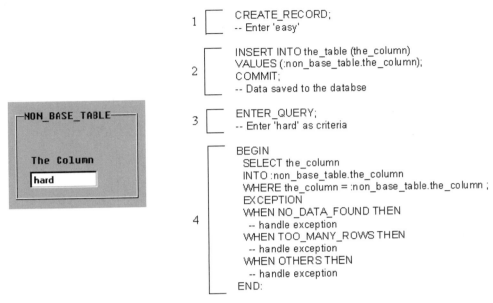

FIGURE 12.2 Control blocks usually require additional programming.

the default functionality of the base table block. Naturally, in the applications you will develop, data will be manipulated through base table blocks. Control blocks, as the name suggests will be used to further coordinate and enhance the default functionality of Oracle Forms.

12.2 CREATING BLOCKS

Blocks in a Forms module can be created in the Object Navigator in one of the following ways:

a) Select Tool | New Block... from the Designer menu, or

b) Select the node Blocks in the Navigator and click the Create button from the toolbar.

Any of these actions displays the New Block Options dialog box, where you can set many important properties of the block.

The New Block Options dialog box is a Windows-95 style dialog box with four tabs labeled General, Items, Layout, and Master/Detail. The following sections explain the block properties that can be set in each of these tabs.

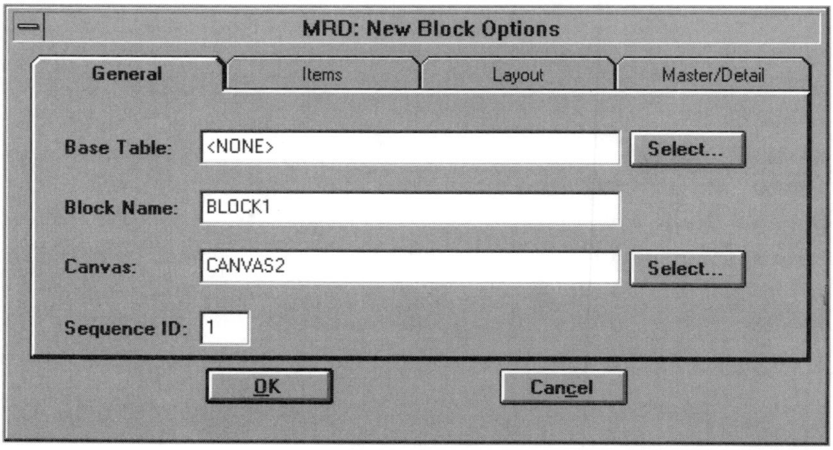

FIGURE 12.3   New Block Options—General tab.

12.2.1 NEW BLOCK OPTIONS—GENERAL TAB

The General tab is the first tab in the New Block Options dialog box. Each time a new block is created, its setting will be similar to the ones shown in Figure 12.3. Depending on the number of other objects you have created previously, the actual digits appended to the block and canvas names may be different from those shown in Figure 12.3. They are generated internally by a sequence number generator whose start value is set when the form module is initially created. If you want to create a control block follow these steps:

1. Enter the name of the block in the Block Name text item.
2. Click OK.

The New Block Options is closed and Designer creates the new block, with no items in it.

The New Block Options dialog box displays all its power and usefulness when base table blocks are created. In this case, the General tab allows you to

---

Note

The relationship between blocks and canvases is established through the items contained in the block. The entry in the Canvas field has no effect when a control block is created because such a block does not have any items yet.

specify the table name upon which the new block will be based. If you know the name of the table, enter it directly in the Base Table field. If not, click the Select... button to its right. You will be presented first with a filter dialog box, called Tables. Here you inform the Designer about the objects you want to look up—either tables, views, or synonyms—and whether these objects are owned by you or by other users. After entering the filtering criteria, you will see a List of Values dialog box. This dialog box will allow you to select the desired table. Remember to use the auto-reduction functionality of LOVs, your number of entries in the list is large.

When the LOVs dialog box is closed, the control is returned to the General tab. Both the Base Table and Block fields are filled with the name of the selected table. By default, a base table block has the same name as the database table from which it is derived, although this is an optional setting that you may change at your discretion.

However, if multiple blocks are based on the same table, their names must be different, in order to maintain the referential integrity of the application module. In order to facilitate the readability and maintenance of your application, choose mnemonic names that characterize the block. Suppose, for example, that you will need two blocks based on CUSTOMER table. One of them displays multiple records in tabular format, and the other one provides all the details for a customer one record at a time in a form format. You could name the first one CUSTOMER_MULTI and the second one CUSTOMER_DETAIL.

In the General tab you may also specify the canvas on which the items of the new block will be created. If the canvas already exists, click Select... to display the Canvas-Views LOVs dialog box, and choose the appropriate canvas name. If the canvas does not exist, enter the name in the Canvas field for a new canvas. Together with the new block, Designer will create the new canvas and place the items on it. Try to choose a name that clearly describes the data that will reside on the canvas.

The Sequence ID field allows you to place the new block in the position you want among other existing blocks. Remember that you can change the order of block, and therefore their Sequence ID, by dragging and dropping them in the Object Navigator.

Note

Be cautious when setting filtering criteria in the Tables dialog box to values other than Tables for Current User. Designer will retrieve the object names for all the schemas, including SYS and SYSTEM. This could result in a long list of entries in the LOVs dialog box.

The setting of Sequence ID is important in character-based environments, where users navigate from one part of the application to the other by pressing the keyboard keys. It is not as important in GUI platforms where the mouse is the primary means of navigation. In these environments, users should not be limited to following a certain sequence defined by the application developers when moving among blocks.

12.2.2 NEW BLOCK OPTIONS—ITEMS TAB

The next step in the process of creating a new base table block is to select the database columns that will become its items. This is accomplished in the Items tab of the New Block Options dialog box.

When the Items tab is initially displayed, it does not show any settings. If you want to select all the columns from the table, and will not modify the text label, the length, or the item type of any of them, you do not need to take any action in this tab. Designer will complete the task automatically. Otherwise, click Select Columns... push button to retrieve all the columns from the table (see Figure 12.4).

The + sign that precedes each column in the list box indicates that the column will be part of the new block. Double-clicking a column name excludes it from the block and replaces the + sign with the − sign. This is equivalent to unchecking the Include check box under the Type drop-down list.

Some properties of the items are displayed and can be modified on the right half of the dialog box, under the heading Item Options. You may change the text label that will appear by the item, the display size of the item, and you may set the type of the item in one of the nine Oracle Forms item types: Check Box, Display Item, Image, List Radio Group, Text Item, VBX Control, OLE Control, or User Area.

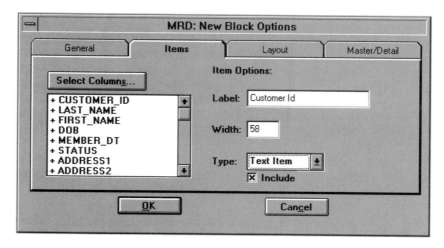

FIGURE 12.4 New Block Options—Items tab.

But why bother! You can easily set these properties in the Layout Editor, as you will see in the next two chapters. There you will get an immediate feedback about your changes by seeing their results on the screen.

12.2.3   NEW BLOCK OPTIONS—LAYOUT TAB

After choosing the items that will be included in the block, you are ready to specify how the Designer will arrange the items of the block in the canvas. This is done in the Layout tab of the New Block Options dialog box (see Figure 12.5).

The Style drop-down list box allows you to organize the items of the block either in a form or a tabular way. The form style will display the items of the block in a rectangular area, and is generally used to display more details about an entity one record at a time. The tabular style is used to display multiple records of an entity at the same time. In order to keep the records from stretching beyond the window, multiple record blocks usually contain only those data elements that are sufficient to identify an instance of the entity. For example, in a tabular CUSTOMER block, you would display the first name, last name, and telephone number for each individual, but not the address. All the data items about the address would be more suitable in a form style block.

The Orientation drop-down list box has two options: Horizontal and Vertical. The vertically oriented block keeps the records in the order you are used to seeing them. The next record is under the current record and the previous record is above it. In a horizontally oriented block the next record is to the right of the current record and the previous record is to the left. This orientation setting is very uncommon and far from what users would ordinarily expect to see. Practically speaking, you will never have to use it.

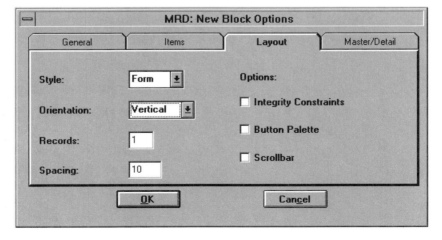

FIGURE 12.5   New Block Options—Layout tab.

The Records field controls the number of records that the block will display on the screen. Form-style records usually display one record at a time. If multiple records are displayed, their number is kept to a minimum, usually not more than three records per screen. This is done to conserve and better utilize the working area of the window that a form-style block displaying multiple records would otherwise occupy. On the other hand, it is very unusual to see tabular-style records that display less than five records at a time. In fact, the purpose of these blocks is to present as much information as possible in the least amount of screen area. The number of records displayed in tabular blocks should not be greater than eight, and users should be provided with ways to quickly navigate through and search the records displayed.

The Spacing field specifies the distance in character cells between the objects in the initial layout of the block. The default setting is 10, but you should consider setting it to a lower value to keep the items from spreading too much on the canvas. This setting has effect only when the Designer initially creates the block. You can move the items on the canvas as you wish after that.

The right half of the Layout tab is taken by the Options group of check boxes. If Integrity Constraints is checked, Designer will query the database dictionary for the constraints defined on the table and the columns that will be part of the block. Constraints such as primary key, foreign key, unique or NULL values, are transferred directly from the table definition to the item properties. If there are check constraints defined for a particular column or table, Designer will convert them to triggers that fire when the item or the record is validated in the form. Suppose, for example, that the check constraint (CUSTOMER_ID > 10) is defined on column CUSTOMER_ID of table CUSTOMER. Oracle7 RDBMS stores this constraint in the data dictionary. If you create a block based on this table with the Constraints option checked, Designer will create a WHEN-VALIDATE-ITEM for item CUSTOMER_ID of that block. The contents of this trigger are shown in Figure 12.6.

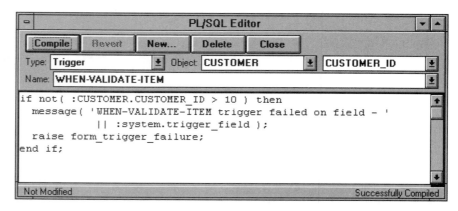

```
if not( :CUSTOMER.CUSTOMER_ID > 10 ) then
  message( 'WHEN-VALIDATE-ITEM trigger failed on field - '
           || :system.trigger_field );
  raise form_trigger_failure;
end if;
```

FIGURE 12.6   Trigger created when Oracle Forms enforces integrity constraints upon creation of block.

The trigger may need some customization such as a more informative message for the user. However, the business rule defined at the database level was implemented automatically for you by the Designer.

If the check constraint is defined for the table, rather than for a particular column, Designer will place the validation rule in a WHEN-VALIDATE-RECORD trigger.

The Button Palette option allows you to create a control block that contains six push button items. Two of them allow users to scroll the records in a block one at a time; two others, a screen at a time. The remaining two are used to enter and execute a query and save the changes made to the block. A nice feature of the BUTTON_PALETTE block is that the functionality of its items is not block dependent. Users can perform the operations on any block in the form by clicking the respective buttons. The support for iconic toolbars that Oracle Forms 4.5 provides has made the appearance of the default button palette obsolete. In fact, in the MRD application, you will implement this functionality through horizontal and vertical toolbars rather than with the default button palette.

Finally, the Scrollbar option attaches a scrollbar to the newly created block. Depending on the orientation of the block, this may be a horizontal or vertical scrollbar. In both cases, it allows fast scrolling through the records that currently populate the block. You may also add the scrollbar at a later time, by setting the properties of the block as explained in Section 12.3.1.

12.2.4 NEW BLOCK OPTIONS—MASTER/DETAIL TAB

The Master/Detail tab (see Figure 12.7) allows you to take advantage of the definition of foreign keys in the Oracle Server database. You can define a master/detail relationship between two base table blocks quickly, while creating the detail block. There are two conditions that must be met in order to use the Master/Detail tab from the New Block Options dialog box:

1. The master block must be a base table block already created in the module.
2. A foreign key constraint must be defined in the base table of the detail block. This key must reference the primary key of the master block base table.

To create a block as detail of an existing master block click the Master/Detail tab in the New Block Options dialog box. Then, click the Select... push button to the right of Master Block text item. This action displays a LOVs dialog box with the names of blocks that could be candidates for the master block position. When you click the Select... button, Designer performs internally a series of steps to populate the LOVs dialog box:

1. Get the base table name of the detail block from the General tab.
2. Query the database data dictionary for all the foreign key constraints of this

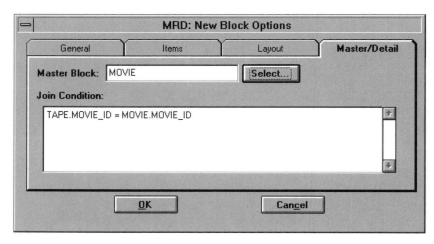

FIGURE 12.7   New Block Options—Master/Detail tab.

table. If no foreign key is defined or enabled, the operation stops. The block cannot become part of a master/detail relation at this time.

3. Compile a list of tables referenced by the foreign keys of the detail table.
4. Query the module for those blocks that are based on the tables defined in the previous step. The operation stops if no such blocks exist.
5. Populate the LOVs dialog box with block names from the previous step.

Once you select the name of a block, Designer closes the LOVs dialog box and fills in the join condition that will govern the master/detail relationship between the two blocks (see Figure 12.7).

When the detail block is created, Designer creates a series of additional objects that are responsible for the coordination of the two blocks. The most important of them is the relation object that describes the relationship between the blocks. The default name of this relation is *MasterBlockName_DetailBlockName*, for example MOVIE_TAPE. Then, there is a number of triggers and procedures that coordinate the querying and deleting of data between blocks. The last sections of this chapter will provide more details about relations. At this point, it is sufficient to mention that you do not need to worry about the content of these PL/SQL objects. Designer allows you to visually modify the properties of the relation object in its Properties Window. The code of the triggers is updated automatically by the Designer, in order to reflect the new settings of these properties. If you decide you want to break the master/detail relationship between blocks, simply delete the relation object. Designer will also delete the PL/SQL objects associated with it.

12.3 PROPERTIES OF BLOCKS

The New Block Options dialog box is a helpful tool that allows you to set some block properties upon creation. If the block is a base table block, the Designer sets its properties based on the definition of the table. However, in the development process you may need to change some of the block properties. If your application is to be really flexible, you may want to change some block properties dynamically as well. This section will discuss these issues.

12.3.1 ACCESSING AND MODIFYING BLOCK PROPERTIES IN THE DESIGNER

In the Designer, you can access and modify the properties of a block in its Properties Window. These properties are divided in the following groups: **Display**, **Records**, **Navigation**, **Database**, **Functional**, and **Miscellaneous**. The properties *Name* and *Property Class* lead the list of properties and are not part of any of these groups.

An important property in the **Display** group is *Scroll Bar*. Its value is *'False'* if the block does not have a scrollbar attached to it. When the *Scroll Bar* property is set to *'True'*, Designer will add a scrollbar to the block and insert a list of other properties related to it in the Properties Window. These properties control the location, position, size, orientation, and functionality of the scrollbar. *Scroll Bar Canvas* property allows you to specify the canvas on which the scrollbar will reside. If this setting is *'<Null>'*, you will not be able to see the scrollbar even if *Scroll Bar* property to *'True'*. This means that when you set *Scroll Bar* property to *'True'*, you should also set the *Scroll Bar Canvas* property. By default, scrollbars are vertical ones, but you can set the *Orientation* property to *'Horizontal'* to obtain a horizontal scrollbar. The scrollbar is initially positioned on the upper left-hand corner of the canvas, but you can drag and resize it in the Layout Editor to the desired location and dimension. This is much easier than setting *Scroll Bar X Position*, *Scroll Bar Y Position*, *Scroll Bar Width*, and *Scroll Bar Height* in the Properties Window. The default functionality of the scrollbar is to fetch additional records, or move to the next record if it is scrolled down, and move to the previous record if it is scrolled up. You may set the *Reverse Direction* property to *'True'* to make the scrollbar behave the opposite way, but this will make your application very nonintuitive. Finally, from all the visual attributes attached to the scrollbar, only *Background Color* and *Fill Pattern* have a visual effect. If, for example, you set the *Background Property* to *'red'*, then the bar in the scrollbar will appear red.

The only other property in the **Display** group besides the scroll bar properties is *Current Record Attribute*. This property is used to automatically assign a named visual attribute object to the current record. This attribute could be used to highlight the current selection in a multirecord block.

The properties *Records Displayed* and *Record Orientation* in the **Record** group control the number of records the block displays simultaneously, and whether the records flow vertically or horizontally. They have the same meaning as their correspondents in the Layout tab of New Block Options dialog box.

The properties under the **Navigation** group are used primarily in character mode applications, where users must move from item to item sequentially. GUI applications offer the flexibility to navigate to the desired destination by simply clicking there. However, even for these applications, good keyboard navigation features are signs of serious programming efforts, and may save the day if the mouse driver or hardware fail. The *Navigation Style* property defines the behavior of Forms when users are in the block's last item and try to navigate to the next item. If the property is set to *'Same Record'*, the focus will move to the first item within the same record; if the setting is *'Change Record'*, Forms will jump to the first item of the next record; if the setting is *'Change Block'*, the cursor will land in the first navigable item in the next block. Properties *Next Navigation Block* and *Previous Navigation Block* define which block is considered the next block and which one is considered the previous block relative to the given block. If these properties are not set, the sequence ID, or the ordering of the blocks in the Navigator, defines the navigation order. This default sequence can be overridden by setting these properties to the names of other blocks in the current module. If you do not want the users to navigate outside the block using the keyboard or the built-in procedures NEXT_BLOCK or PREVIOUS_BLOCK, set these properties to the name of the block itself.

The **Database** group contains the properties you will change the most for your blocks. *Base Table* property is not set if the block is a control block; for base table blocks, it contains the name of the table on which the block is based. Double-clicking this property has the same effect as selecting a table in the General tab of the New Block Options dialog box. A LOVs dialog box appears, from which you can choose the table name. All the other properties in this group have effect only if the block is a base table block. Worth mentioning here are *Delete Allowed, Insert Allowed, Query Allowed,* and *Update Allowed* properties. By default, they are all set to *'True'*, which means that users can perform all these four operations in the block. To disable any of these operations, set the corresponding property to *'False'*. Two other properties that can help you customize the queries issued from a base table block are *WHERE Clause* and *ORDER BY Clause*. They allow you to enter query and ordering criteria in addition to those entered by the users in the query-by-example interface of your block. For example, if you want to create a block that will display only the active customers, you may set the *WHERE Clause* to

STATUS = 'A'

Whenever users execute a query in this block, Oracle Forms will prepare the SELECT statement based on the criteria they specify, and, in addition, will append the condition **AND STATUS = 'A'** to the WHERE clause of the statement. Setting the *ORDER BY Clause* works in an entirely similar fashion.

> **Note**
>
> You do not need to add the keywords WHERE or ORDER BY when setting these properties.

The properties *Records Buffered* and *Records Fetched* play an important role in the process of fine-tuning the application in general and the queries issued in the base table block, in particular. *Records Buffered* is the number of records that Forms keeps in its internal memory structures at any one time. By default, this number is three units larger than the number specified in *Records Displayed* property. In other words, if the block displays seven records, Forms will buffer ten records in memory.

When a query is executed, Oracle Forms does not retrieve all the records in one trip to the database. Instead, the number of trips, or fetches, depends on the setting of *Records Fetched* property. The default value of this setting is the number in which the *Records Displayed* property is set. In the example above, it would be seven. In this case, if a query returns twenty records, the first fetch will bring over only the first seven records. When users are at the seventh record and try to navigate to the next record, Forms will fetch the next seven records, and so on. Forms does not display the records in the block until the whole set is fetched from the database. Therefore, a large setting of the *Records Fetched* may slow down the process of populating the block with the query results. On the other hand, a low setting may result in frequent calls to the database. The overhead cost of sending these bursts of information may degrade the performance in Local Area Network (LAN) and especially in Wide Area Network (WAN) environments.

Another block property that may have an impact on the performance in particular situations is *Update Changed Columns*. By default, this property is set to *'False'*. With this setting, during the commit of a changed record, Forms will construct an UPDATE statement that will include all the columns in the block, even

> **Note**
>
> The setting of *Records Displayed* serves as a minimum boundary for the setting of *Records Buffered*. In the scenario above, if you set *Records Buffered* to anything less than seven, at generate time, Designer will display the message **FRM-30033: Records buffered must be greater than records displayed.**

> ## Note
>
> The way the default settings of *Records Buffered* and *Records Fetched* are displayed in the Properties Window may be misleading. If not set manually, these settings are NULL (default values). However, they appear as zero, which is not consistent with the way other NULL settings are presented. You will notice this discrepancy with other properties that can be set to numeric values.

those whose value did not change. This saves some processing time and improves the performance of the server. The improvements result from the way the Oracle Server executes SQL statements. The first time the statement is encountered, for example an UPDATE statement, the SQL Statement Executor will parse it to identify the table and columns being updated. Then, the variables will be bound to the actual values passed in the statement and, finally, the statement will be executed. After that, each time the same statement is issued, the database server will bypass the parsing step because the table and column names do not change. The statements are considered the same if they are exactly the same, byte per byte. An extra white space or a character in the opposite case are enough to make the statements different.

However, there are situations when it is desirable to set the *Update Changed Columns* property to 'True'. Imagine, for example, that for each movie in the database you store twenty seconds of video clips in a column of LONG RAW data type. This video clip will be played at the customer's request, but almost never edited. Other data for the movie though, will be updated frequently. If the property in question is set to 'False', each time a column value is updated, the whole movie record, together with several megabytes of the video clip, will be sent across the network to the database for update. If, on the other hand, *Update Changed Columns* property is 'True' only the modified data will be sent for update.

Finally, let's conclude this section with two properties from the **Miscellaneous** group: *In Menu*, and *Block Description*. These are two other properties that are more useful in applications developed for character-based environments. Oracle Forms maintains internally a list of block names that can be displayed to the users and allows them to navigate to the desired block (see Figure 12.8).

You can display this menu programmatically by invoking the BLOCK_MENU built-in procedure, or by pressing [BLOCK MENU] key on the keyboard.

If the property *In Menu* is set to 'False', the block will not appear in the menu. If it is set to 'True' and the property *Block Description* is NULL, the block

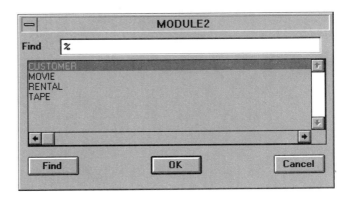

FIGURE 12.8 Oracle Forms block menu.

will not appear in the menu. The only time the block is displayed is when the property *In Menu* is set to 'True' and the *Block Description* contains a string value. The contents of *Block Description* will appear in the block menu.

12.3.2 ACCESSING AND MODIFYING BLOCK PROPERTIES AT RUNTIME

In order to make the application flexible and responsive to the user's actions, it may be necessary to retrieve or modify the setting of some block properties at runtime. The location and situation for which you place the code to perform these actions varies widely. However, certain steps must be followed in the trigger, function, or procedure where you plan to access or change the block properties.

In order to retrieve the setting for a particular property, you must first know the data type of this setting. For example, the setting of *Base Table* property is a character string that stores the base table name for the block. But the setting for *Records Displayed* is a number that corresponds to the number of records displayed in the block.

After you define the data type of the property setting, you must declare a variable of the same data type that will store the value of that setting. The function GET_BLOCK_PROPERTY is used to place the value of the property in the variable you declared.

The process of setting the value of a property is similar. Here you first declare a variable with the appropriate data type and store the new setting in it. Then, the procedure SET_BLOCK_PROPERTY is used to complete the action. Let us see some examples that follow the steps described above.

Figure 12.9 shows a function that returns the status of a block whose name is passed as an input argument. The property *STATUS* is a property that exists only at runtime. You cannot access or set it in the Properties Windows of the Designer. The status of a block is QUERY if the block contains only queried records. It is NEW if the block contains only one record that has just been created. It is

```
FUNCTION Get_Block_Status (block_name VARCHAR2)
RETURN VARCHAR2 IS
  block_status VARCHAR2(20) :=NULL;
BEGIN
  block_status := GET_BLOCK_PROPERTY(block_name, STATUS);
  RETURN block_status;
END Get_Block_Status;
```

FIGURE 12.9   Retrieving the status of a block at runtime.

CHANGED if at least one record in the block has been modified. If records are initially queried, and then new records are created, the status of the record is also CHANGED.

The next example implements some security features for the MRD application. You can think of the users of this application as divided in three categories, according to their job functions. Each category is represented by a database account, and their names are CLERK, STAFF, or MANAGER. Employees that interact with customers at the counter log on the system as CLERK; those that maintain the inventory in the back of the store use the STAFF account; supervisors and managers log on as MANAGER. The account MANAGER does not have any restrictions. This account can query, insert, update, and delete records in all the blocks. Front-desk clerks cannot delete records in any blocks. They can insert, update, and delete in blocks CUSTOMER and RENTAL, but only query in MOVIE and TAPE. Maintenance staff cannot delete any records as well. They are limited to just viewing data in CUSTOMER and TAPE blocks, but can insert, update, and delete from CUSTOMER and RENTAL.

Figure 12.10 shows the procedure that could be used to implement the business rules described above.

The program units in Figure 12.9 and Figure 12.10 are fairly easy to write and understand. However, they are vulnerable to errors. In both these routines you assume that there are no mistakes in specifying the block name. But, if one such error occurs, the code is not protected from the failure of the built-in routines GET_BLOCK_PROPERTY or SET_BLOCK_PROPERTY. To remedy for this problem, you must guarantee that the block is present before using any of the above built-ins.

The procedure **Set_Block_Security** has also a performance problem. As mentioned earlier, Forms assigns unique identifiers to objects in a module. These identifiers are used to access the object internally. If, in your code you refer to an object by its name, Forms has to perform a look up in its internal structures to find the ID of the object with that name. In this procedure, Forms must query the IDs of blocks MOVIE and TAPE three times. You could certainly improve the performance by retrieving the block ID and then issuing the call to SET_BLOCK_PROPERTY as many times as it is necessary.

```
PROCEDURE Set_Block_Security (username VARCHAR2) IS
BEGIN
  IF username = 'CLERK' THEN
    SET_BLOCK_PROPERTY('CUSTOMER',DELETE_ALLOWED,PROPERTY_FALSE);
    SET_BLOCK_PROPERTY('RENTAL',DELETE_ALLOWED,PROPERTY_FALSE);
    SET_BLOCK_PROPERTY('MOVIE',DELETE_ALLOWED,PROPERTY_FALSE);
    SET_BLOCK_PROPERTY('MOVIE',INSERT_ALLOWED,PROPERTY_FALSE);
    SET_BLOCK_PROPERTY('MOVIE',UPDATE_ALLOWED,PROPERTY_FALSE);
    SET_BLOCK_PROPERTY('TAPE',DELETE_ALLOWED,PROPERTY_FALSE);
    SET_BLOCK_PROPERTY('TAPE',INSERT_ALLOWED,PROPERTY_FALSE);
    SET_BLOCK_PROPERTY('TAPE',UPDATE_ALLOWED,PROPERTY_FALSE);
  ELSIF username = 'STAFF' THEN
    SET_BLOCK_PROPERTY('CUSTOMER',DELETE_ALLOWED,PROPERTY_FALSE);
    SET_BLOCK_PROPERTY('CUSTOMER',INSERT_ALLOWED,PROPERTY_FALSE);
    SET_BLOCK_PROPERTY('CUSTOMER',UPDATE_ALLOWED,PROPERTY_FALSE);
    SET_BLOCK_PROPERTY('RENTAL',DELETE_ALLOWED,PROPERTY_FALSE);
    SET_BLOCK_PROPERTY('RENTAL',INSERT_ALLOWED,PROPERTY_FALSE);
    SET_BLOCK_PROPERTY('RENTAL',UPDATE_ALLOWED,PROPERTY_FALSE);
    SET_BLOCK_PROPERTY('MOVIE',DELETE_ALLOWED,PROPERTY_FALSE);
    SET_BLOCK_PROPERTY('TAPE',DELETE_ALLOWED,PROPERTY_FALSE);
  END IF;
END Set_Block_Security;
```

FIGURE 12.10 Controlling users' access to blocks programmatically.

Figure 12.11 shows the modified and improved version of function Get_Block_Status. A new version of the Set_Block_Security procedure that incorporates the same feature would be similar. You would declare four variables of data type Block, and store the internal ID for each block in them using the FIND_BLOCK function. Then the SET_BLOCK_PROPERTY procedures are invoked as in Figure 12.10, but this time you use the ID rather than the name of the block.

It is worth noting here that you will use the same layout of code when accessing or modifying properties of other object in Forms. These are the general steps you will follow:

1. Use the object-specific FIND function to get the internal ID for the object, based on its name. This function could be FIND_BLOCK, FIND_ITEM, FIND_WINDOW, and so on.
2. Use the IS_NULL function to ensure that the ID is valid.
3. Use the object-specific GET function to retrieve the setting for a property. The function could be GET_BLOCK_PROPERTY, GET_ITEM_PROPERTY, GET_WINDOW_PROPERTY, and so on.

```
FUNCTION Get_Block_Status (block_name VARCHAR2)
RETURN VARCHAR2 IS
  block_status VARCHAR2(20) :=NULL;
  block_id    BLOCK;
BEGIN
  block_id := FIND_BLOCK(block_name);
  IF NOT ID_NULL(block_id) THEN
    block_status := GET_BLOCK_PROPERTY(block_name, STATUS);
  ELSE
    MESSAGE('Block '||block_name||' does not exist.');
    RAISE FORM_TRIGGER_FAILURE;
  END IF;

  /* If control comes here, no errors occurred.*/
  RETURN block_status;
END Get_Block_Status;
```

FIGURE 12.11   Internal identifiers improve the application's robustness and performance.

4. Use the object-specific SET function to set a property. The function could be SET_BLOCK_PROPERTY, SET_ITEM_PROPERTY, SET_WINDOW_PROPERTY, and so on.

12.4 RELATIONS

As mentioned previously, blocks in an Oracle Forms module correspond to logical groups of data in the world that the application is describing. When the system is designed, the relationships between these groups of data are discovered. It is natural to expect the application to reflect such relationships in its interface.

Oracle Forms has a separate class of objects, called Relations, to administer the coordination of blocks that represent related data. On one side of the relation object resides the master block. On the other side, there is the detail block. There may be zero or more records in the detail block that correspond to each record in the master block. The condition that records from each block must meet in order for them to be considered related, is called a join condition. The join condition is typically an equality condition. The value stored in the foreign key of the relation block must be equal to the value of the primary key in the master block.

12.4.1 CREATING RELATIONS AND SETTING THEIR PROPERTIES IN THE DESIGNER

Up to now you have created default master/detail relations from the New Block Options dialog box. A restriction in the functionality of this dialog box is that the relationship must already be defined at the database level, in the form of a foreign key constraint. When creating relations from the Object Navigator, this restriction fades away. Using relations, you can create links among any blocks to reflect the requirements of your application.

Relations are objects that hierarchically belong to blocks, or, more precisely, to the master blocks in the relation. In order to create a relation follow these steps:

1. Identify the master block and the detail block that will be joined by the relation.
2. Expand the master block node in the Navigator, and create a new Relation object. The New Relation dialog box appears (see Figure 12.12).
3. Enter the properties settings for the new relation according to your needs. The meaning of these settings is discussed in the rest of this section.
4. Click OK.

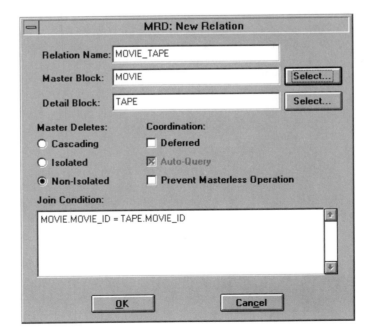

FIGURE 12.12 New Relation dialog box.

Note

When the New Relation dialog box is displayed, the Master Block text field contains the name of the block from where the operation originated. Nevertheless, you can supply any other block name in the field. When the relation will be created, the object will be placed under the hierarchy of the block you specify as master.

The New Relation dialog box allows you to set the properties of a relation at creation time. The name of the relation is specified in the Name text field. It corresponds to the *Name* property of the relation and it can be any valid Oracle Forms name. However, it is customary to concatenate the name of the master block followed by the name of the detail block, as shown in Figure 12.12. If you know which blocks you want to connect, supply their names directly in the Master Block and Detail Block text fields. You can also click the Select push buttons to their right to display a LOVs dialog box from which you can choose the block name.

Under the name fields, there is a group of three radio buttons called Master Deletes. Its settings correspond to the property *Master Deletes* in the Properties Window of the relation. The options you can choose here control if, when, and how detail records will be deleted if the master record is deleted. The *'Non-Isolated'* option is the default setting of the *Master Deletes* property. When this option is set, records in the master block cannot be deleted if the detail block contains records. This behavior may be too restrictive sometimes. If, for example, the database contains twenty copies of a movie that is being taken off the shelves, you would want to delete the movie record, and have the application ensure that the tape records that depend on it are deleted as well. At the application level, you can implement this functionality by selecting the Cascading radio button from the Master Deletes group.

The *'Isolated'* option is the least restrictive from all the possible settings of the *Master Deletes* property. This allows users to delete records in the master block independently from the records displayed in the detail block.

To the right of the Master Deletes radio group, there is a check box group called Coordination. Each member of this group corresponds to a property of relations with the same name. The settings of the check boxes under this group control the display of records in the detail block when a coordination event occurs in the master block. A coordination event would be any action that will cause moving of the focus from one record in the block to another record in that block. Examples of coordination events are moving to the next or previous record, creating a new record, or deleting an existing one. Moving to another item within a record, changing an item, or committing changes to the database do not constitute coordination events.

> ## Note
>
> Depending on the particular environment for each application, you may choose to place the cascade delete logic in the database server or in the client application. At the database level you may define foreign key constraints with the ON DELETE CASCADE option. For example, the table RENTALS that will be used in the MRD application has the following two constraints defined:
>
> ```
> CONSTRAINT rentals_cust_id_fk FOREIGN KEY (customer_id)
>          REFERENCES customers
>          ON DELETE CASCADE
> CONSTRAINT rentals_tape_id_fk FOREIGN KEY (tape_id)
>          REFERENCES tapes
>          ON DELETE CASCADE
> ```
>
> With these constraints enabled, each time a record is deleted in the table CUSTOMERS or TAPES, Oracle will automatically delete records in RENTALS associated with it.
>
> If for some reason the foreign key constraints are found to be too restrictive, the same functionality can be implemented by defining database triggers in tables MOVIES and CUSTOMERS, which fires each time a record is deleted, and remove all the related records from table RENTALS. Chapter 18 will discuss in more detail the process of creating database triggers.
>
> Whichever approach you take, you must not duplicate the effort by implementing the same feature at both levels.

The effects of selecting the check boxes in this group, the wording of the text labels, and the micro-help messages associated with them can be quite confusing and, at times, obscure. Therefore, you will go through them carefully and explain each combination separately.

The first two options are closely related to each other. If *Deferred* option is not checked, Forms will populate the detail block as soon as a coordination event occurs in the master block. But, if the *Deferred* option is checked, then the retrieval of records in the detail block is postponed, or deferred, in two ways. If *Auto-Query* is checked, the detail records are queried as soon as the focus navigates in the detail block. If the *Auto-Query* is not checked, the detail records are retrieved only if the users explicitly query the detail block. No automatic population of the block happens in this instance. Figure 12.13 graphically presents the meaning of these options.

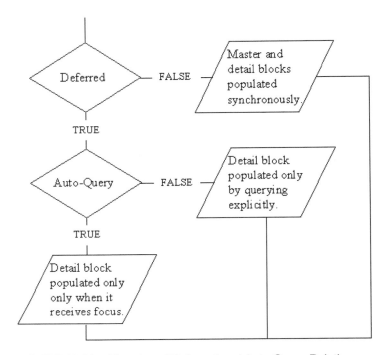

FIGURE 12.13   Meaning of Deferred and Auto-Query Relation properties.

By default, the *Deferred* property is turned off, thus resulting in an automatic and synchronized coordination of the blocks.

The third check box, *Prevent Masterless Operations*, is not dependent on the setting of the previous two properties. If the option is set, the records in the detail block could be queried even when there are no records present in the master block. If the option is not set, which is also the default behavior, Forms cannot navigate to the detail block if the master contains no records.

The multiline text field Join Condition is where you specify the condition that establishes the coordination of the block. In general terms, this condition specifies the data items in the detail and master blocks whose values must match. Usually, the join condition is fully qualified, as in Figure 12.12. However, if the items in both blocks share the same name, simply providing that common name will work equally well. In the example of Figure 12.12, the join condition could have simply been MOVIE_ID.

Once a relation is created, its properties can be modified at design time in the Properties Window for the relation. The properties for a relation object are divided in two main groups. The **Functional** group includes the properties *Detail Block*, *Join Condition*, *Master Deletes*, and *Prevent Masterless Operations*. The **Coordi-**

nation group includes the properties *Deferred* and *Auto-Query*. The settings of these windows in the Properties Window have the same meaning as in the New Relation dialog box.

12.4.2 SETTING THE PROPERTIES OF RELATIONS AT RUNTIME

The Oracle Forms built-ins routines FIND_RELATION, ID_NULL, GET_RELA-TION_PROPERTY, and SET_RELATION_PROPERTY allow you to manipulate the properties of a relation programmatically.

The function shown in Figure 12.14 takes as input the variable name of a relation and returns the coordination state between the related blocks. The logic of the function follows the meaning of *Deferred* and *Auto-Query* properties explained earlier, and the flow chart diagram presented in Figure 12.13.

The function Get_Coordination_Status returns SYNCHRONOUS if *Deferred* property is *'False'*, DEFERRED_AUTOMATIC if *Deferred* property is *'True'* and *Auto-Query* is *'True'*; and DEFERRED_MANUAL if *Deferred* property is *'True'* and *Auto-Query* is *'False'*.

The procedure shown in Figure 12.15, takes as input variable the name of a relation and a character string that represents the coordination state between the related blocks. If this string is SYNCHRONOUS, the procedure Set_Coordina-tion_Status will set the property *Deferred* to *'False'*; if it is DEFERRED_AUTO-MATIC, the properties *Deferred* and *Auto-Query* are set to *'True'*; and if it is DEFERRED_MANUAL, the *Deferred* property is set to *'True'* and *Auto-Query* to *'False'*.

You can use both these program units to give users the flexibility and ability to decide at runtime how the detail blocks in the application will be populated, rather than making a decision for them at design time.

Note

It is worth mentioning that the properties for relations and all the other objects in Oracle Forms have two names. The first one is what you see in the Properties Window at design time. For example, the names for two properties of records are *Deferred* and *Auto-Query*. The second name is what you should use with the object-specific built-in routines GET and SET to manipulate the settings of these properties at runtime. The names for the properties mentioned above are *DEFERRED_COORDINATION* and *AUTOQUERY*. In this book you will see used both names according to the context of the discourse.

```
FUNCTION Get_Coordination_Status (rel_name VARCHAR2)
RETURN VARCHAR2   IS
  deferred_status       VARCHAR2(20)  :=NULL;
  autoquery_status      VARCHAR2(20)  :=NULL;
  coordination_status VARCHAR2(20)  :=NULL;
  rel_id                RELATION;
BEGIN
  rel_id := FIND_RELATION(rel_name);
  IF NOT ID_NULL(rel_id) THEN
    deferred_status := GET_RELATION_PROPERTY(rel_id,
                                  DEFERRED_COORDINATION);
    autoquery_status := GET_RELATION_PROPERTY(rel_id,
                                  AUTOQUERY);
  ELSE
    MESSAGE('Relation '||relation_name||' does not exist.');
    RAISE FORM_TRIGGER_FAILURE;
  END IF;

  /* If control comes here, the relation exists in the module. */
  IF deferred_status = 'TRUE' THEN
    IF autoquery_status = 'TRUE' THEN
      coordination_status := 'DEFERRED_AUTOMATIC';
    ELSE
      coordination_status := 'DEFERRED_MANUAL';
    END IF;
  ELSE
    coordination_status := 'SYNCHRONOUS';
  END IF;

  RETURN coordination_status;
END Get_Coordination_Status;
```

FIGURE 12.14 Defining the coordination state of a relation at runtime.

The *Join Condition* of a relation specifies that two or more data items in the master and detail blocks will have the same values. If an item that is part of the relation's foreign key in the detail block is accessible, users may override its value, thus breaking the link with the master record. Usually this situation must not occur, therefore, Oracle Forms, by default, hides the item by setting its *Canvas* property to *'NULL'*. The item is still part of the detail block, but it is simply hidden from the users. If you need to override the default functionality in your application, set the item's *Canvas* property to the name of canvas where you want the item to be displayed.

```
PROCEDURE Set_Coordination_Status (relation_name VARCHAR2,
                                   status VARCHAR2) IS
  relation_id      RELATION;
BEGIN
  relation_id := FIND_RELATION(relation_name);
  IF NOT ID_NULL(relation_id) THEN
    IF status = 'SYNCHRONOUS' THEN
      SET_RELATION_PROPERTY(relation_id, DEFERRED_COORDINATION,
                                         PROPERTY_FALSE);
    ELSIF status = 'DEFERRED_AUTOMATIC' THEN
      SET_RELATION_PROPERTY(relation_id, DEFERRED_COORDINATION,
                                         PROPERTY_FALSE);
      SET_RELATION_PROPERTY(relation_id, AUTOQUERY,
                                         PROPERTY_TRUE);
    ELSIF status = 'DEFERRED_MANUAL' THEN
      SET_RELATION_PROPERTY(relation_id, DEFERRED_COORDINATION,
                                         PROPERTY_FALSE);
      SET_RELATION_PROPERTY(relation_id, AUTOQUERY,
                                         PROPERTY_TRUE);
  ELSE
    MESSAGE(UPPER(status)||' is not a valid coordination
status.');
    RAISE FORM_TRIGGER_FAILURE;
   END IF;
  ELSE
    MESSAGE('Relation '||relation_name||' does not exist.');
    RAISE FORM_TRIGGER_FAILURE;
  END IF;
END Set_Coordination_Status;
```

FIGURE 12.15 Setting the coordination state of a relation at runtime.

12.4.3 PL/SQL OBJECTS ASSOCIATED WITH RELATIONS

When you create a new relation, Designer automatically creates a series of triggers and program units that control the coordination between the master and detail blocks. The type of triggers will depend on the setting of the properties for the relation.

If at least one relation exists in the form, Designer creates the form-level trigger ON-CLEAR-DETAIL. This trigger fires when the focus moves from one record to another in the master block. It simply issues a call to the CLEAR_ALL_MASTER_DETAIL procedure, which is created and updated as relations are created. The purpose of this procedure is to go through the list of all the blocks that serve as detail blocks for the block being cleared, and to clear them from existing records.

The trigger ON-POPULATE-DETAIL is created for each relation. It is attached to the master block of a relation and is responsible for the way the records in the detail block are queried. This trigger fires when the focus of the form lands inside the record in the master block.

If the record is not committed to the database, or the item that is part of the *Join Condition* is NULL, the trigger does not act in any manner. This behavior is to be expected, since both conditions mean that the master record cannot have any detail records associated with it in the database.

If the master record already exists in the database and the *Join Condition* item is not NULL, the trigger invokes the procedure QUERY_MASTER_ DETAIL, which is created and maintained automatically by Designer when relations are created. The settings of the Coordination properties define the actions this procedure can perform. If *Deferred* is 'False', QUERY_MASTER_DETAIL issues a query in the detail block that synchronizes its contents with the record that has the focus in the master block. If *Deferred* is 'True', the only action of QUERY_MASTER_DETAIL is to set the *Coordination_Status* property of the detail block to NON_COORDINATED. If, during the execution of the application, users navigate to the detail block, this setting prompts Forms Runtime engine to act according to the *Auto-Query* property setting of the relation. If it is 'True', a query is issued to refresh the contents of the block; otherwise, no action occurs.

If the *Master Deletes* property of the relation is set to 'Isolated', these are the only triggers created by Designer. If this property is set to 'Non Isolated', Designer creates the trigger ON-CHECK-DELETE-MASTER, in addition to the other two. This trigger is attached to the master block, and fires when users attempt to delete a record in it. The trigger allows the delete process to continue only if there are no detail records in the database. Otherwise, it displays the message, **Cannot delete master record when matching detail records exist.** You have already seen this message in the ETS application that you created in Part One.

If the *Master Deletes* property is set to 'Cascading,' a PRE-DELETE trigger is created in addition to ON-CLEAR-DETAILS and ON-POPULATE-DETAILS triggers. This trigger is also attached to the master block and fires just before the DELETE statement for the master record is sent to the database. Its functionality is to delete the detail records. In addition to the triggers and procedures mentioned here, Designer also creates a procedure called CHECK_PACKAGE_FAILURE that halts any further processing if the last action in the form is not successful.

If you are a little confused by all the functionality that these program units perform, be assured that, with all likelihood, you will never have to edit them. Your task in the process of defining a relation is as simple as setting the properties of the relation in the New Relation dialog box or in the Properties Window. Designer will read these settings and create or edit the PL/SQL objects accordingly. Here are a few actions that Designer will perform in order to maintain the code of these objects for you:

1. If a block enters in several complicated relations with other blocks, Designer will expand the triggers and procedures mentioned above to reflect the position of the block as master or detail in all the relations in which it takes part.

2. If a relation is deleted, the PL/SQL objects will be edited according to the new relationship structure. If no longer needed, they will be removed altogether.

3. If the *Master Deletes* property of a relation changes, Designer will ask if you want to modify the generated triggers in addition to changing the relation. If you confirm the action, Designer will create or delete triggers according to the setting of the property. For example, if you change the setting from *'Non-Isolated'* to *'Cascading'*, Designer will delete the ON-CHECK-DELETE-MASTER trigger and create a PRE-DELETE trigger.

4. If you place code in the triggers mentioned here (ON-CLEAR-DETAILS, ON-POPULATE-DETAILS, ON-CHECK-DELETE-MASTER, and PRE-DELETE), Designer will preserve your code. The code necessary for the master/detail coordination will be appended to or removed from existing triggers, depending on the situation.

The elegant handling of all the code creation and maintenance activities, and the fact that relations in Oracle Forms represent purely logical connections between data elements, free from constraints specified in the database, makes them a powerful tool in Forms development activities.

12.5 BLOCKS AND RELATIONS FOR THE MRD APPLICATION

Before creating the blocks that will be part of the MRD application, perform these preliminary steps:

1. Create a subdirectory that will hold all the code for the MRD application; for example, C:\MRD.

2. Launch the Oracle Forms Designer and connect to the database with the account used to create the MRD database objects.

3. Replace the default name of the Forms module with MRD.

4. Save the module to the C:\MRD directory.

Now you can use the New Block Options dialog box to specify the initial properties of the base table blocks. The following steps contain the recommended settings for the properties that you will change. The rest of the properties may retain their default values.

1. Create block CUSTOMER based on table CUSTOMERS. Set the Canvas field to CUSTOMER to create a new canvas for the block. In the Layout tab, set Style to Forms.

2. Create block MOVIE based on table MOVIES. Enter MOVIE in the Canvas field. In the Layout tab, set Style to Forms.

3. Create block TAPE based on table TAPES. Make sure that Canvas property is set to MOVIE. In the Layout tab, set Records to 5 and check Scrollbar check box. In the Master/Detail tab, select MOVIE as the master block.

4. Create block RENTAL based on table RENTALS. Set the Canvas property to RENTAL to have Designer create it for you. In the Layout tab, set Records to 5 and check Scrollbar check box.

5. Create block CUST_RENT based on table CUSTOMERS. The Canvas property must be set to RENTAL. In the Items tab, select only CUSTOMER_ID, LAST_NAME, FIRST_NAME, DOB, MEMBER_DT, and STATUS as items to include in the block. In the Layout tab, set Records to 8 and check Scrollbar check box.

6. Create block MOVIE_RENT based on table MOVIES. The Canvas property must be set to RENTAL. In the Items tab, select only MOVIE_ID, TITLE, STATUS, and RATING as items to include in the block. In the Layout tab, set Records to 8 and check Scrollbar check box.

7. Create block TAPE_RENT based on table TAPES. The Canvas property must be set to RENTAL. In the Layout tab, set Records to 5 and check Scrollbar check box. In the Master/Detail tab, select MOVIE_RENT as the master block for TAPE_RENT.

Now change the properties of the newly created blocks and relations as follows:

1. Set the properties *Delete Allowed*, *Insert Allowed*, and *Update Allowed* for blocks CUST_RENT, MOVIE_RENT, and TAPE_RENT to *'False'*.

2. Set the properties *Deferred* and *Auto Query* to *'True'* for relation MOVIE_RENT_TAPE_RENT number block MOVIE_RENT.

Wrap up the work by saving and generating the module.

12.6 SUMMARY

This chapter discussed the properties of blocks and relations in Oracle Forms. Important concepts of this chapter are listed here:

❑   Base table blocks and control blocks
❑   Creating blocks

- ❑ New Block Options—General tab
- ❑ New Block Options—Items tab
- ❑ New Block Options—Layout tab
- ❑ New Block Options—Master/Detail tab
- ❑ Properties of blocks
  - ❑ Accessing and modifying block properties in the Designer
  - ❑ Accessing and modifying block properties at runtime
- ❑ Relations
  - ❑ Creating relations and setting their properties in the Designer
  - ❑ Setting the properties of relations at runtime
  - ❑ PL/SQL objects associated with relations
- ❑ Blocks and relations for the MRD Application

ITEMS

"We're making the users do more and more programming, but they don't know it."

—Dan Bricklin

Items are the most basic and, at the same time, the most important elements of an application's interface. It is by entering data in or selecting from items, that users establish links to the repository of data. In the Oracle Forms hierarchy, items must exist within blocks. Inside a block, items are associated with other items based on the logical representation of data. Items must also lay on a canvas. If users will interact directly with the items, the canvas is a named one. If items will be used to facilitate the internal processing, and will not need to be displayed to the users, they are "placed" on a virtual canvas, called the NULL canvas. This chapter discusses in detail the types of items that can be used in Oracle Forms and their properties.

13.1 TYPES OF ITEMS

Items are used to present data from the database to the users. They are a bridge between the back-end and the front-end parts of an application. This dichotomy displays itself in the classification of items. Based on the origin of data, items are divided in base table and control items. Based on the way the data are presented to users in a GUI environment, items are classified as data entry items and GUI controls. Data entry items include text and display items. GUI controls include push buttons, radio buttons, check boxes, and list boxes. In addition, applications developed with Oracle Forms can use image items, charts from Oracle Graphics, VBX controls, and OLE2 items.

13.1.1 BASE TABLE AND CONTROL ITEMS

Base table items can only be part of base table blocks. They are directly mapped to a column in the table that serves as the block's base table. When a query is executed, data from this column appear directly in the item. When a record is created or updated, data supplied in the item will be sent to the database and stored appropriately in the corresponding column.

Control items, on the other hand, do not directly map to a column in the database. They can be part of both base table and control blocks. When used in base table blocks, control items usually display data derived from other items in the block. For example, a control item may calculate the total revenue generated by a customer, based on the amounts paid over a period of time to rent videos, which are stored in the database. Another popular use of control items in base table blocks is to retrieve and display data based on values of base table items in the block. For example, in a block based on table RENTALS, you would like to display the full name of the customer renting a movie, rather than just the CUSTOMER_ID stored in this table. The name item in the block will be a control item, and it will be populated from the CUSTOMERS table, based on the value of CUSTOMER_ID for each particular rental transaction.

> ## Note
>
> During the analysis and design phase of the application, the most important activity is normalizing data entities and relations, or making sure that all the data elements of an entity depend on the entity's primary key, the whole key, and nothing but the key. The purpose of this activity is to create a clear understanding of the data involved and the rules that govern their relations and interaction. During the development phase, in order to represent the data in a way that is familiar and understandable to the users, some of the data entities are merged visually, in a process known as denormalization of the data model. Using control items to represent related data that are not stored in the base table of a block is an aspect of denormalizing the data model.

13.1.2 GUI INTERFACE ITEMS

As mentioned before, the interface between users and the database is maintained by data entry items, push buttons, radio buttons, check boxes, and list boxes. Figure 13.1 shows the example of a form that contains items from each of these categories.

The term *data entry item* is used for traditional and historical reasons. Usually, in GUI standards and reference guides, this term is used for single-line or multi-line text fields, as those shown in Figure 13.1. Push buttons are usually control items that initiate an action such as saving to the database or opening a dialog box where additional information is processed. Radio buttons are used to select only one choice from a short list of options. Check boxes are used to select more than one choice from a short list of options. If the number of options to choose from is large, list boxes are used to improve the readability of the application. Single-selection list boxes expand the functionality of radio groups; multiselection list boxes expand the functionality of check boxes.

The rest of this chapter will discuss issues related to the creation and use of items, and their generic properties. The second part of the chapter will focus on text and display items. The next chapter will discuss the GUI control items: push buttons, radio buttons, check boxes, and lists. Part Four will provide the necessary information for manipulating Oracle Graphics charts, OLE2, and VBX items.

13.2 CREATING ITEMS

For base table blocks, the fastest way to create items is to include the corresponding column names in the Items tab of the New Block Options dialog box, when the block is created. By default, items created with this method will be text items.

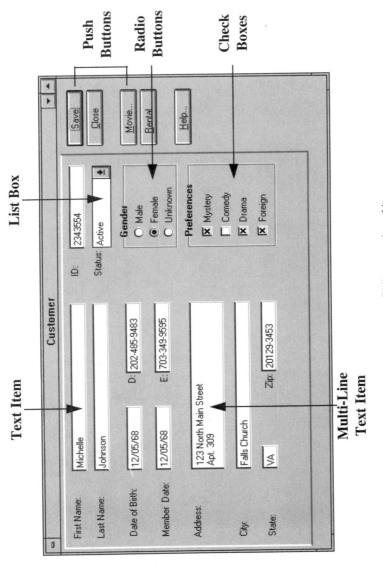

FIGURE 13.1 Major GUI categories of items.

You can create the item as a radio group, check box, or any other type, by selecting from the Type drop-down list in the Items tab. However, since additional editing is still required, it is easier to create the block with text items, and then change the *Type* property in the Properties Window of the item.

If the block already exists, you can add new items to it by creating them either in the Object Navigator, or in the Layout Editor. It is preferable to create items in the Layout Editor, since it is much easier to place and size them on the canvas. The context of the Editor, when the item is created, defines the block and the canvas that will own the item. You must ensure that the context is set appropriately before the item is created.

When base table items are created using the New Block Options dialog box, Oracle Forms sets at least the name, datatype, and size of the item according to the column specifications. If the Integrity Constraints option is checked in the Layout tab, additional formatting and validation information is transferred from the database to the item. When items are created in the Navigator or Layout Editor, Forms does not query the database for any of the data dictionary definitions mentioned above. You must manually set all the properties of the new item according to the needs of the application. If the item is a base table item, make sure that its name matches the column name in the table. You can use the Tables/Column dialog box, accessible from Tools | Tables/Columns... menu item of the Designer, to quickly look up these names. You must also make sure that the datatype and length of the new item do not conflict with the database settings. By default, an item created in the Navigator or the Layout Editor is a 30-characters-long CHAR item. If its database counterpart has settings different from the above, the application will be prone to several kinds of error. Some of the errors that may occur are listed here:

a) If the column datatype is different from the item datatype, you cannot perform any database actions. If, for example, you try to query the database, you will get the error message, FRM-40505: ORACLE error: unable to perform query, followed by, ORA-00932: Inconsistent datatypes.

b) If the column is longer than the item, truncation may occur when records are queries from the database. Forms will display the message, FRM-40831: Truncation occurs: value too long for field FIELD_NAME.

c) If the column is shorter than the item, you may not be able to insert or update records in the database. If, for example, the UPDATE command fails, Forms will display the error message, FRM-40509: ORACLE error: unable to UPDATE record, followed by ORA-01401: INSERTED value too large for column.

Given the many strings that you must pull together when adding a base table column to an already created block, it is natural to conclude that some up-front thinking before the block is created is always a good idea. True, you will spend some time defining all the database columns that will be included in the block.

> ## Note
>
> You may retrieve some of the information required to create a new base table item in the Object Navigator. Expanding the Database Objects node to an appropriate level, you can display the name and data type for each column in any table. For more detailed information, you must rely either on the database design and data dictionary documentation, or use other tools such as SQL*Plus or Object Manager.

However, the time invested pays itself off, by avoiding the extra effort required to add a column at a later date.

To conclude this section, let us mention that the type of block also defines the type that will be assigned to an item created in the Object Navigator or the Layout Editor. When creating an item for a base table block, the *Base Table Item* property for that item will be set to '*True*'. If you are creating a control item for the block, you must remember to set this property to '*False*'.

13.3 GENERIC PROPERTIES OF ITEMS

Two fundamental properties of an item are its name (*Name*), and the name of a property class (*Class*) from which other properties may be derived. The other properties are grouped in categories to facilitate the process of viewing and modifying their settings. The names of these categories are **Type**, **Display**, **Data**, **Records**, **Navigation**, **Database**, **Functional**, and **Miscellaneous**. All the items that can interact with the database have properties in each of these categories. This includes text, display, check box, radio group, image, VBX Controls, and OLE2 Object items. Push button items do not contain any properties in the **Data** or **Database** groups because their purpose is to initiate some action, and not to display or modify data. Similarly, chart items, used to store Oracle Graphics displays in the form, do not have properties in these two groups. In addition, because the functionality of these types of items is provided by Oracle Graphics, they do not have properties in the **Functional** group either. The following sections describe each property group and some of the properties shared among the majority of items.

13.3.1 TYPE PROPERTIES

The **Type** property group contains only one property: *Item Type*. By changing the setting of this property you change the type of the item. The contents of the Properties Window for the item will change according to the item type.

13.3.2 DISPLAY PROPERTIES

The **Display** group contains the *Canvas* and visual attributes properties for each item. The *Canvas* property contains the name of the canvas on which the item resides. If the item is hidden from users, this property is set to *'NULL'*.

Another way to hide an item from the users is to set the property *Displayed* to *'False'*. By default, this property is *'True'*, except for items that are part of the foreign key definition in a master/detail relationship between blocks. When you set this property to *'False'*, the item will not be visible at runtime, but it will continue to be displayed on the canvas at design time. If you want to hide the item altogether, set its *Canvas* property to *'NULL'*.

The **Display** group also includes properties that control the position of the item on the canvas (*X Position*, *Y Position*), and the size of the item (*Width*, *Height*).

If the item is part of a multi-record block, the property *Space Between Records* controls the distance between items that belong to different records. Normally it is set to zero, which means that the items will be adjacent.

The property *Visual Attribute Name* is set to *'Default'* if no changes are made to the default settings of Oracle Forms. If one attribute is changed, for example *Font Name* is set to *'Arial'*, *Visual Attribute Name* changes to *'Custom'*. If the item is inheriting the settings of visual attributes from a visual attribute object in the module, the name of this object is specified in the *Visual Attribute Name* property. Chapter 7 discussed more extensively the meaning and functionality of Visual Attribute objects and visual attribute properties.

The property *Current Record Attribute* is used to assign a named Visual Attribute object to the item for the current record. This can be used to visually distinguish an item from the other items in the record. This setting overrides the block-level setting of the same property, if it exists.

13.3.3 DATA PROPERTIES

The **Data** group contains properties that control data related properties of items such as length, datatype, and default value. As mentioned earlier, chart and push button items do not have any properties in this group. Depending on the type of item, some of the properties may not be meaningful and therefore, absent. For example, OLE Object and image items do not have properties such as datatype or length.

The *Data Type* property specifies what kind of data are represented by the item. The property is meaningful only for text, display, radio group, check box, and list items. The fundamental datatypes are CHAR, DATE, NUMBER, and LONG. CHAR datatype is used for items that manipulate up to 2 Kb of character data. DATE is used for items that contain date and time information. NUMBER is used to represent numeric data. LONG datatype is used for text items that manipulate character data up to 64 Kb long. For backward compatibility reasons, text items support a variety of other data types. Because they may be phased out in the future releases of Oracle Forms, you should stick with the fundamental datatypes in your applications.

The *Maximum Length* property specifies the size in bytes of data that can be manipulated by the item. It is important to set this property so that situations when information is truncated or cannot be applied to the database do not occur. Note that the *Maximum Length* property does not interfere with the size of the item on the canvas, defined by the *Width* and *Height* properties.

The *Default Value* property is used to fill the item with data when the record is first created. If carefully thought out, and properly set, this property can significantly reduce the data entry time and effort. If there is a value that is common for the majority of records in the database, you may want to specify it as the default value for the item. The rule of thumb is that if users pick a value more than fifty percent of the time, that should become the default value for the item. There are several things you may achieve by setting the *Default Value* property of an item:

1. Provide a hard-coded value such as 5, or **Active**, that users will enter frequently. To do this, set the property to that value in the Properties Window.

2. Populate the item with numbers generated by a sequence. You could use this approach in the MRD application to supply ID numbers for customers and movies stored in the database. In this case, the setting of *Default Value* property should be

:SEQUENCE.MRD_SEQ.NXTVAL.

3. Supply dates in the application, rather than having users type them in. In the MRD application, many records will bear a creation date stamp on them. For customer records this will be the MEMBER_DT; for rental records it will be RENT_DT. When the application is first loaded, you may store the system date in a global variable, called GLOBAL.Sysdate. Then, the *Default Value* for the items mentioned above will be set to :GLOBAL.Sysdate.

The *Mirror Item* property can be set for all items except OLE containers. It allows you to create within a block mirrored instances of the same item. All these instances will synchronously display the same data. Modifying one instance propagates the change in all the other instances. You can use this property if you need to display the same data item in different contexts within the block.

The *Copy Value from Item* property is a variation on the same theme. This property indicates that the value of the current item must be initially copied from another item in the form, as indicated by its setting. When a master/detail relation is created, Oracle Forms sets the *Copy Value from Item* property of the foreign key in the detail block to the primary key of the master block. Let me explain this with an example. Consider the relation MOVIE_TAPE, in which MOVIE is the master and TAPE is the detail block. The property *Copy Value from Item* of item MOVIE_ID in TAPE block is set to MOVIE.MOVIE_ID.

The *Copy Value from Item* property is different from *Mirror Item* property in two meanings:

1. The setting for *Copy Value from Item* can be any item in the current module. The setting for *Mirror Item* can be only an item within the same block.

2. *Copy Value from Item* property populates the item with data, but after that does not maintain the source and the destination of data synchronized. *Mirror Item*, on the other hand, ensures that both the source and destination items will contain the same data at any one moment.

13.3.4 RECORDS PROPERTIES

The **Records** group contains only one property: *Items Displayed*. For multi-record blocks, this property allows you to override the setting of the block's *Records Displayed* property for the individual item. Suppose, for example, that you want to include the scanned picture of each customer in a multi-record block that displays other biographical data about them. You can conserve screen space and computing resources by displaying only one image at a time. To do this set the *Items Displayed* property to '1'. Note that the default value for this property is zero. It means that the item will be displayed as many times as the setting of *Records Displayed* for the block.

13.3.5 NAVIGATION PROPERTIES

The **Navigation** group includes properties such as *Enabled, Navigable, Next Navigation Item,* and *Previous Navigation Item.* The *Enabled* property by default is set to '*True*', thus allowing users to access the item's data. If you set the property to '*False*', users have no way to access the item. Methods associated with events in a disabled item will not be executed, since none of these events occurs. Data displayed in the field will appear grayed out to indicate the unavailability.

The *Navigable* property controls the access to enabled items using the keyboard navigation keys. If the property is set to '*True*', users can use the keyboard's keys to navigate to the item. If the property is set to '*False*', the keyboard keys will not be able to place the form's focus inside the item.

Users may click the item to access it if the *Mouse Navigate* property is set to '*True*'. Clicking the mouse on items such as check boxes, radio groups, list items, push buttons, charts, VBX Controls, and OLE2 Objects, is done primarily to perform an action rather than to navigate to the item. To avoid placing the Forms focus on these items, set their *Mouse Navigate* property to '*False*'. This will still cause all the appropriate events to occur when the mouse is clicked, but will not move the focus from where it currently is to the clicked item.

Finally, the *Next Navigation Item* and *Previous Navigation Item* properties, if set, indicate the item where Forms should navigate when users press the TAB or

SHIFT+TAB keys from the keyboard, or the NEXT_ITEM or PREVIOUS_ITEM built-ins are issued programmatically. If not set, the default tab order for the item is specified by the order of items in the Object Navigator.

13.3.6 DATABASE PROPERTIES

The main properties included in this group are *Base Table Item*, *Query Only*, *Primary Key*, *Insert Allowed*, *Query Allowed*, and *Update Allowed*. The meaning of *Base Table Item* property was discussed earlier in the chapter. Without repeating the same information again, it suffices to mention that the rest of the properties in this group do not apply to control items, whose *Base Table Item* property is set to '*False*'.

Query Only property is set to '*False*' by default, thus allowing users not only to query, but also to insert or update the data managed by the item. Although this property appears in the Designer, and its value can be set in the Properties Window of an item, the setting specified at design time does not have any effects on its functionality at runtime. The default setting for this property can be overridden only programmatically.

The properties *Insert Allowed*, *Query Allowed*, and *Update Allowed* control the ability of users to include the item in the respective database transactions. By default, they are all set to '*True*'. Setting *Insert Allowed* to '*False*' does not allow users to enter data in the item when a new record is created. This feature can be used to populate items from sequence generators and prevent users from overriding the generated numbers. Setting *Query Allowed* to '*False*' prevents users from navigating to the item when the block is in Enter Query mode. Finally, if *Update Allowed* is '*False*' users can retrieve data for the item from the database, but cannot modify it. This feature can be used to protect sensitive data from unauthorized modifications.

13.3.7 FUNCTIONAL PROPERTIES

This group contains properties that are specific to each item type. Functional properties of text and display items will be discussed later in the chapter. Functional properties of push buttons, radio groups, check boxes, and lists will be explained in Chapter 14. Functional properties of charts, VBX controls, and OLE2 items will be discussed in Part Four.

13.3.8 MISCELLANEOUS PROPERTIES

All the items contain at least the properties *Comments* and *Reference Information*. *Comments* is used by programmers to provide any additional information about the item as part of the overall effort to document the software development project. *Reference Information* property contains values only for referenced objects. If the item is referenced, the setting of this property will be similar to Figure 13.2.

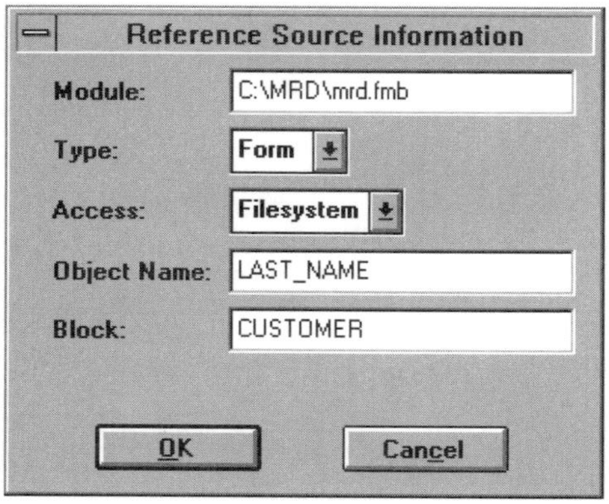

Reference Source Information	
Module:	C:\MRD\mrd.fmb
Type:	Form
Access:	Filesystem
Object Name:	LAST_NAME
Block:	CUSTOMER

OK   Cancel

FIGURE 13.2   Reference Source Information dialog box.

In addition to these properties, all items, except for display and chart items contain the *Hint* and *Auto Hint* properties. The setting for *Hint* is a message that can be displayed in the micro-help line of the MDI frame when the focus is on the current item. The message is displayed only if the property *Auto Hint* is 'True'. It is a good programming practice to always provide micro-help to the users of your application. The combination of *Auto Hint* and *Hint* properties offers a satisfactory solution for character-based applications. In these applications, users can only be at one item at any given time. In GUI-based applications, while the input focus of the form is still in only one item, users can move the mouse around to point at different items on the screen. It would be useful to display an item's micro-help message when the mouse is over the item, without requiring users to place the focus of the form in the item itself. The following section offers an example of how to do this in an application.

13.4 SETTING PROPERTIES OF ITEMS AT RUNTIME

By carefully setting the properties of items in the Designer, you can enhance the look and the functionality of your application. In addition, Oracle Forms allows you to set them at Runtime, thus making the form more dynamic and responsive to the changes that occur in the data. Programmatically, you can retrieve and store in PL/SQL variables the settings of any property and specify new settings for almost any property, except for a few. The general steps followed in the process are presented in Figure 13.3.

Note that the two parts of this pseudo-routine may be located in different PL/SQL objects. In one place you may just get the property of an item. In another place you may only set that property or a different one.

Figure 13.4 shows the procedure that retrieves the Hint message of the item whose name is passed as an input variable and displays it in the form of a micro-help message. To implement the functionality promised at the end of Section

```
PROCEDURE Generic_Item_Routine (item_name VARCHAR2) IS
   item_id                Item;
   property_setting       VARCHAR2;

BEGIN
   /* FIND_ITEM returns the appropriate item ID.       */
   item_id := FIND_ITEM(item_name);

   IF NOT ID_NULL(item_id) THEN
      /* PROPERTY_NAME will depend on the particular item type. */
      property_setting := GET_ITEM_PROPERTY(item_id,
                          PROPERTY_NAME);

   /* Additional processing may occur here              */

      /* PROPERTY_NAME will depend on the particular item type. */
      SET_ITEM_PROPERTY(item_id, PROPERTY_NAME, property_setting);
   ELSE
      MESSAGE('Item '||item_name||' does not exist.');
      RAISE FORM_TRIGGER_FAILURE;
   END IF;
END Generic_Item_Routine;
```

FIGURE 13.3 Guidelines for retrieving and setting properties of items at Runtime.

13.3.8, all you need to do is add the following line in a form-level WHEN-MOUSE-ENTER trigger:

Display_Hint(:SYSTEM.MOUSE_ITEM);

This trigger will fire whenever the mouse moves inside an item. The system variable **SYSTEM.MOUSE_ITEM**, stores the name of the item, which is passed to Display_Hint for processing.

If you want to see another example of getting and setting properties of items, open and run the module CLICKME.FMB provided in the companion disk. This is a form with only one push button item. Your task is to click the button with the mouse.

You will see that the button will jump sideways to a new position each time you click the mouse on it. Once you get tired or bored with the game, choose File I Exit from the menu to close the application.

Now open and run the module CLICKME1.FMB. This module is very similar to the first one except that the upper part of its window contains some informative data to help you understand how the application works (see Figure 13.5).

```
PROCEDURE Display_Hint (item_name VARCHAR2) IS
   item_id          Item;
   item_hint        VARCHAR2(80);

BEGIN
   IF item_name IS NOT NULL then
   /* FIND_ITEM returns the appropriate item ID.*/
     item_id := FIND_ITEM(item_name);

     IF NOT ID_NULL(item_id) THEN
       item_hint := GET_ITEM_PROPERTY(item_id, HINT_TEXT);
       MESSAGE(item_hint, NO_ACKNOWLEDGE);
     ELSE
       MESSAGE('Item'||item_name||' does not exist.');
       RAISE FORM_TRIGGER_FAILURE;
     END IF;
   END IF;
END Display_Hint;
```

FIGURE 13.4   Procedure to display the micro-help message for an item.

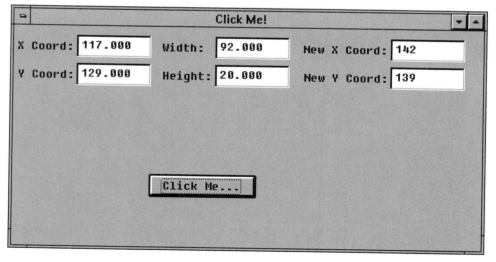

FIGURE 13.5   Manipulating the position of an item on the canvas at Runtime.

As soon as the mouse enters the push button area, the trigger WHEN-MOUSE-ENTER calls the functions that populate the items in the upper part of the window with the current coordinates and dimensions of the item. This trigger also computes the new position where the item will jump to, if the mouse is clicked.

Figure 13.6 shows the code for the function that retrieves the X coordinate of the item.

The functions that return the Y coordinate, width, and height of the button are entirely similar. Instead of returning the value of property *X_POS*, they return the setting for properties *Y_POS*, *WIDTH*, and *HEIGHT*, respectively. (Note that here the Runtime names of properties are used.)

Based on the current coordinates and dimensions of the item, the dimensions of the canvas, and on the current position of the mouse, the functions Compute_New_X and Compute_New_Y compute the new position of the item in a way that when the mouse is clicked, the item escapes out of the reach of the mouse. For a detailed explanation of the algorithm used to compute the new coordinates, refer to the comments in the body specification of the program units in modules CLICKME.FMB or CLICKME1.FMB.

```
FUNCTION Get_X_Coord (item_name VARCHAR2)
RETURN VARCHAR2 IS
  item_id    Item;
  x_coord    VARCHAR2(10);

BEGIN
  IF item_name IS NOT NULL then
  /* FIND_ITEM returns the appropriate item ID.*/
    item_id := FIND_ITEM(item_name);

    IF NOT ID_NULL(item_id) THEN
      x_coord := GET_ITEM_PROPERTY(item_id, X_POS);
    ELSE
      MESSAGE('Item'||item_name||' does not exist.');
      RAISE FORM_TRIGGER_FAILURE;
    END IF;
    RETURN x_coord;
  END IF;
END Get_X_Coord;
```

FIGURE 13.6   Retrieving the coordinates of items at Runtime.

```
PROCEDURE Set_X_Coord (item_name VARCHAR2,  .
                       x_coord        NUMBER)  IS
   item_id     Item;

BEGIN
   IF item_name IS NOT NULL then
   /* FIND_ITEM returns the appropriate item ID.*/
     item_id := FIND_ITEM(item_name);

     IF NOT ID_NULL(item_id) THEN
       SET_ITEM_PROPERTY(item_id, X_POS, x_coord);
     ELSE
       MESSAGE('Item'||item_name||' does not exist.');
       RAISE FORM_TRIGGER_FAILURE;
     END IF;
   END IF;
END Set_X_Coord;
```

FIGURE 13.7   Setting the coordinates of items at Runtime.

The procedures that place the item in the new position are Set_X_Coord and Set_Y_Coord. Figure 13.7 shows the implementation of the procedure Set_X_Coord.

The code for Set_Y_Coord resembles that of Set_X_Coord, except that here the y_coord input variable is used to set the Y_POS property.

Both these procedures are called from the WHEN-MOUSE-DOWN trigger, which fires when the event MouseDown occurs. The choice of this event is not casual. In the Oracle Forms mouse events protocol, a MouseClick event is a combination of a MouseDown and a MouseUp that occur sequentially. If you do not want the users to click the button, then you better move it to a new location before the event occurs. Placing the movement code in the WHEN-MOUSE-DOWN trigger moves the item when the users begin to click (with a MouseDown), but before completing the action (with a MouseUp).

Note

If you look closely at the implementation of function **Get_X_Coord** and procedure **Set_X_Coord** shown in Figures 13.6 and Figure 13.7, you will notice that the built-in function GET_ITEM_PROPERTY returns the setting of *X_POS* as a character value. However, the built-in procedure SET_ITEM_PROPERTY requires the setting for the same property to be a number.

13.5 VALIDATION OF ITEMS IN ORACLE FORMS

The validation of items is the event that checks the conformity of the data they contain with the requirements set forth for these items. If the validation process is successful, items are cleared to be sent to the database for storage. The time when the validation occurs depends on the setting of the *Validation Unit* property for the current module. For GUI environments, *Validation Unit* is set to '*Item*', which means that the validation event will occur as soon as the users try to navigate out of the item.

At any given point during the execution of an application, its items can be in one of the following states: NEW, CHANGED, or VALID. When a new record is created, all its items are NEW. As soon as users begin entering data in one of the items, the state of this and all other items in the block becomes CHANGED. When users request to commit the record, each item and the record itself are validated. If the validation process is successful, the state of each item is set to VALID. A record is sent to the database only if all its items are VALID. When records are brought in to the application from the database, the status of all their items is VALID. If one of the items in the record is modified, the status for all the items in that record is set to CHANGED. They must all be validated during the next database commit.

The requirements specified for an item can be as simple as the datatype or the length of data they represent. They are usually handled by appropriately setting different properties of the items. However, they can also be complicated business rules that the application must enforce upon data. In this case, these rules are implemented using PL/SQL and are placed in a method or trigger that fires when the ValidateItem event occurs. The name of the trigger is WHEN-VALIDATE-ITEM.

13.6 TEXT ITEMS AND DISPLAY ITEMS

Text items are, by far, the most widely used items in an Oracle Forms application, because of their ease of use, flexibility, and extended functionality. They can be used to retrieve, display, and manipulate data of several types, sizes, and formats. Display items can be used only for the purpose of displaying data. Users cannot navigate to or modify the information presented by display items. Because of the reduced functionality, display items also use less system resources.

13.6.1 BEVEL AND RENDERED PROPERTIES

In addition to generic properties discussed above, text and display items have other properties that are specific to them. Two properties that are worth mentioning in the **Display** group are *Bevel* and *Rendered*. *Bevel* controls the display of the item's border. By default, its setting is *'Raised'*. If you set it to *'None'*, the border will not be visible. This setting is useful if you use display items for dynamic text labels in the form.

In order to understand the meaning of property *Rendered*, you must understand how Oracle Forms manages the display of items at runtime. Visually, you get the impression that there are as many containers of data on the screen as there are items. In reality, this is not exactly true. By default, there is only up to one such container at any one moment. The real container is the text or display item where the current focus of Forms is. All the other items and widgets on the screen are just drawings on the boilerplate. To clarify the discussion, Figure 13.8 presents the state of a form at Runtime.

Here, the focus is initially on Item A. Oracle Forms uses Display properties of items such as *X Position*, *Y Position*, *Width*, and *Height*, to divide the boilerplate in context-sensitive areas. If the focus of Forms is placed on an item, say Item B, either by clicking it, or by tabbing into it, or by internal navigation, Forms initially retrieves the boilerplate position of this item. Then, it queries its internal structures to retrieve the context-sensitive information for that screen location. If this information indicates that the target is another text or display item, the data contained in the item are transferred from the internal structures of Forms into the container that is created for the item, and made available to the user for processing. Meanwhile, if the property *Rendered* of Item A is set to *'True'*, the boilerplate drawing that represents the item is updated, and the container of data for that item is erased from memory, thus releasing the system resources it occupies. If this property is set to *'False'*, as in the case of Item C, Forms maintains the container attached to the item. There are a few points to make here:

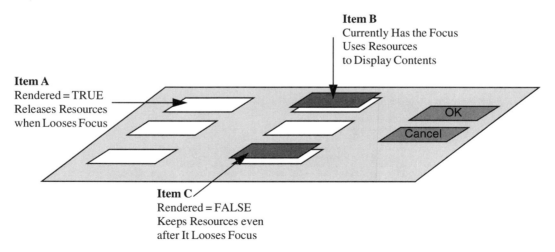

FIGURE 13.8 Oracle Forms renders its items by default.

1. There is no visual difference between an item that has the current focus, and other items with similar properties. The fact that Forms renders these items, or treats them as boilerplate drawings, does not affect their appearance.

2. Only text or display items need a container around them to manage the information they contain. Other items such as push buttons, check boxes, or radio buttons change their contents due to actions performed on them.

3. If the *Rendered* property of a text or display item is set to *'False'*, the item will continue to occupy resources even when it no longer has the focus of Forms.

4. If the *Rendered* property of a text or display item is set to *'True'*, there will be some processing overhead each time the item receives the focus. This additional processing is needed to create and populate the container that will display the item's data.

5. The benefits of setting *Rendered* property *'True'*, measured in saved system resources, clearly surpass the cost of overhead processing that will occur each time the item receives focus.

13.6.2 DATA PROPERTIES OF TEXT ITEMS

In addition to generic properties discussed in Section 13.3.3, text items have other useful properties in the **Data** group. Proper settings of these properties allow you to better display the data and to facilitate the task of entering the information in the database.

If the *Required* property is set to *'True'*, users cannot leave the item without entering a value in it. Items based on NOT NULL database columns that are created with the New Block utility automatically have the *Required* property set to *'True'*. For other items that are manually created, the default setting of the property is *'False'*. If they need this restriction, you must change the default setting in the Properties Window.

The *Format Mask* property is used to display data according to a certain predefined pattern. The variety of format masks that can be specified here is overwhelming. Being unable to cover all of them here, this section provides some examples that create a good idea about format masks.

1. If you want your users to enter only the digits of a dollar amount, but display it in the ordinary business format, set *Format Mask* to $999,999.99PR. Now, when users enter 1223.89, Forms will display the item as $1,223.89. When they enter −1223.83, the amount will be displayed as <$1,223.89>. (It is a common accounting practice to represent negative values in parentheses rather than preceeded by the minus sign.)

2. If you want to embed characters inside numeric strings, enclose them in double-quotes in the *Format Mask* setting. The format mask "("999") "999"-

"9999 can be used for telephone numbers; the format mask 999"-"99"-"9999 could be used for Social Security Numbers.

3. If you want to display the date in the format 12/05/95, set *Format Mask* to DD"/"MM"/"YY.

To spare users the effort of typing the extra characters included in the format mask, put the FM indicator in front of it. If, for example the *Format Mask* is specified as FM"("999") "999"-"9999, users need to type only 2220001111, and the input will be formatted as (222) 000-1111. For date formats the FM indicator does not have the same effect. You must enter the item as required by the format.

If the data of a particular item will be within a range of values, you can set the *Range Low Value* or *Range High Value* properties to the lower and upper bounds of the range. Forms will automatically ensure that the data entered do not extend beyond the allowed range.

13.6.3 DATABASE PROPERTIES OF TEXT ITEMS

Besides the generic properties from this group discussed in Section 13.3.6, text items have two additional properties that are used in the query-by-example interface of Oracle Forms. The *Query Length* property controls the length of query criteria that can be entered in the item when the block is in Enter Query mode. By default, the setting of *Query Length* equals that of *Maximum Length* property. It can be higher than *Maximum Length*, but never smaller. In Oracle Forms messages or documentation you will often see stated that this setting can be zero. Like other numeric settings of properties, a zero setting for the *Query Length* indicates that the property has its default value, which is *Maximum Length*. Misleading as this is, it can come in handy if you plan to change the *Maximum Length* property for an item frequently. With the *Query Length* set to zero, you do not need to worry about synchronizing its value each time you change the *Maximum Length*.

The advantage of setting *Query Length* to a higher value than *Maximum Length*, is that it allows users to enter more flexible criteria in Enter Query mode. For example, the usual setting for these two properties for date items is 9. Suppose that you keep these settings for the item MEMBER_DT in the block CUSTOMER of the application. Your users will be able to retrieve customers that became members of the video store on a certain date. However, by setting the *Query Length* to '11', you can offer them a more flexible way to query the table. Now they will be able to query the database for all the customers that opened an account on or after a certain date, simply by entering >=DD-MON-YY in the MEMBER_DT item. A variety of other queries can be issued using the operators <>, <, and <=.

The property *Case Insensitive Query* is set to '*False*' by default. This means that Oracle Forms will construct the query using criteria exactly as you enter them. If, for example, you enter John in the item FIRST_NAME of block CUSTOMER and issue a query, the WHERE clause of the SELECT statement sent to the database will contain the following criteria:

FIRST_NAME = 'John'

The query will return only the customers whose first name is John.

If your data is not consistent, and you have customers called John, JoHn, or JOHN, you can set the *Case Insensitive Query* property to *'True'* to retrieve these records. Be aware that Oracle Forms constructs the SELECT statements in a way that it may take longer to complete, unless the column in the table is indexed.

As mentioned, *Update Allowed* property controls the users' ability to update the data. If the property is set to *'False'*, the information presented in the item cannot be updated. This restriction can be relaxed a little by setting *Update Only if NULL* property to *'True'*. In this case, users can supply data if the item does not contain any information.

Chapter 2 explained how Oracle Forms locks a record in the database as soon as an item in that record is changed by the user. This item must be a base table item for the locking to be done automatically. All too often, control items are used in conjunction with base table items in a block. To have the locking process kick off automatically when a control item is modified, set its *Lock Record* property to *'True'*. By default, the property is set to *'False'*. This is the only property in the **Database** group of properties that is meaningful for control items.

13.6.4 FUNCTIONAL PROPERTIES OF TEXT ITEMS

The *Case Restriction* property can be used to enforce a particular case for the data entered in the item. For example, to enter data in upper-case letters, set this property to *'Upper'*. Note that this property converts the case only if information is entered through the item. If a value is stored in lower-case characters in the database, it will be displayed that way when retrieved by a query.

The *Align* property defines the alignment of data in the item. By default, items are aligned to the left. If your application displays monetary data, you may want to align these items to the right by setting this property.

If you want to protect the data at the item level, you may set the *Secure* property of the item to *'True'*. With this setting, the item will display the data as a sequence of asterisk characters. Because the property can be set dynamically, you can use it to hide certain data elements from unauthorized users.

If the data displayed in the item is too long to fit in a single-line item, you may display the item as a multi-line item. For this, set the *Multi-line* property to *'True'* and adjust the size of the item on the canvas to span across multiple lines. If the amount of data in the item will make scrolling necessary, you can add a vertical scroll bar to the item by setting the *Vertical Scroll Bar* property to *'True'*.

By default, when Oracle Forms navigates inside an item, it places the cursor at the beginning of the item. Especially for multi-line text items, it may be helpful to place the cursor where it was when users navigated out of the item. Forms will automatically do this for you, if the property *Keep Position* is set to *'True'*.

13.7 EVENTS OF TEXT ITEMS

There are three basic events that occur in an item: EnterItem, ValidateItem, and LeaveItem. The final outcome of the EnterItem event is to place the focus of the form inside the target item. In the process, Oracle Forms executes the PRE-TEXT-ITEM trigger, if it is specified. When the EnterItem event is completed and the cursor lands inside the item, the WHEN-NEW-ITEM-INSTANCE trigger is fired. When a new record is just created, the status of all its items is NEW.

Once inside the item, users can enter and edit data for that item. As soon as they do this the status of the item is set to CHANGED. If no changes are made to the contents of the item, its status remains the same as prior to entering the item.

When the users initiate the LeaveItem event, Forms decides whether to validate the item or not. If the item's status is NEW or CHANGED the validation event occurs. If the ValidateItem event is successful, the event LeaveItem proceeds to completion. The trigger POST-TEXT-ITEM is fired during this event.

For text items, the validation event is more extended than for other types of items. Depending on the settings of different properties for the item, each of the following checks may occur:

1. Check the value's format mask if *Format Mask* property is set.
2. Check that value is not NULL if *Required* property is *'True'* and *Input Allowed* is *'True'*.
3. Check that the length of entered value equals the item's *Maximum Length* if *Fixed Length* is set to *'True'*.

Note

Any action that modifies the data sets the item status to CHANGED, even if the final outcome of the item is the same as at the beginning. In other words, even if you cut and paste the contents of a text item, without any other action, its status will be CHANGED.

4. Check that the value's datatype does not conflict with the setting of *Data Type* property.

5. Check that the value is within *Range Low Value* and *Range High Value* settings, if defined.

6. Fire the WHEN-VALIDATE-ITEM trigger if it is defined in the item, block, or form level.

Failure to satisfy any of the checks, stops the validation process. If any of the first five checks fails, the focus of the form cannot leave the item. If the WHEN-VALIDATE-ITEM trigger fails, users will not be able to leave the item if the exception FORM-TRIGGER-FAILURE is raised. The status of the item is set to VALID only if all the checks that are applicable to that particular item are successful.

The ValidateItem event may be initiated programmatically from within the item, without necessarily having to wait for the LeaveItem event to occur. The built-in procedure ENTER is used for this purpose.

If the status of an item is NEW, that is, the record is just created, the only validation check will be Rule 2 in the list above. This is often very restrictive, as the following scenario demonstrates. Imagine that you just created a new record in the block CUSTOMER and the focus of the form is in a required item such as CUSTOMER_ID. However, you want to enter the new customer's name first. You will discover that you cannot navigate to any other item in that record, before entering some value for CUSTOMER_ID.

To avoid this situation, you may shift the checking for NULL values from Rule 2 to Rule 6. In other words, set the *Required* property to *'False'*, and place an IF statement that does not allow users to leave the item if it is NULL. The drawback to this approach is that it will add an extra level of complexity to the WHEN-VALIDATE-ITEM trigger for the item and must be done for each item with the *Required* property set to *'True'*.

A more elegant solution is to set the form property *DEFER_REQUIRED_ENFORCEMENT* to *'True'*. This is a property that can be set *only* programmatically. For example, to set it for the MRD module, you would use the following statement in a trigger that fires when the form module is initially launched such as PRE-FORM or WHEN-NEW-FORM-INSTANCE:

```
SET_FORM_PROPERTY('MRD', DEFERED_REQUIRED_ENFORCEMENT,
                  PROPERTY_TRUE);
```

With this setting, Oracle Forms will not apply the Rule 2 until the Validate Record event occurs. In other words, users are allowed to move freely among items of the same block, even if they do not enter values for required items. They will be asked to provide these values only when they will try to move outside the record.

> **Note**
>
> In older versions of Oracle Forms, the POST-CHANGE trigger fires right before the WHEN-VALIDATE-ITEM trigger fires. This trigger is still available for backward compatibility reasons, but its use is not recommended.

Figure 13.9 graphically summarizes the item-related events and triggers in Oracle Forms.

13.8 GUI GUIDELINES FOR DATA ITEMS

There are two goals that you must have in mind when creating applications for GUI environments such as MS Windows or Macintosh:

1. Be consistent. Every screen you design must have a look and feel that is standard across the entire application and, possibly in a wider range, across all the applications used by your organization.
2. Don't show off. The screens you create must not be used to display your talent as painters or designers, nor your latest ideas on color combinations.

The application must not attract the users attention or distract them from the main purpose they have when using it: to access and manipulate their data in the most productive and efficient manner. With all the new and fancy programming tools that proliferate in the market, the temptation to put all kinds of bells, whistles, and flashing lights in the application can be satisfied easily. But you must learn to overcome that temptation. Whenever the subject comes up, I like to quote

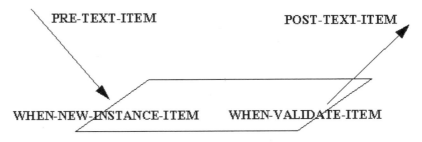

FIGURE 13.9   Triggers of text items in Oracle Forms.

one of the Microsoft Word Tips of the Day, "Plaid shirts and striped pants rarely make a positive fashion."

This section will discuss some guidelines to follow in the development of forms in GUI platforms. The topic will come up in the discussion about control items, windows, dialog boxes, and menus, in their respective chapters. The ideas presented in this and other chapters do not exhaust the question of how to create good GUI applications. This is not the goal of this book. If you want more information on the topic, two excellent books are *Secrets of Effective GUI Design*, by Mark Minasi (SYBEX, 1994), and *Guidelines for Enterprise-Wide GUI Design*, by Susan Weinschenk and Sarah C. Yeo (John Wiley & Sons, 1995).

13.8.1 COLORS

By default, a screen in Oracle Forms uses three basic colors. Light gray is used as background color for the canvas. White is used as background color for text items. Black is used as text color for text and display items, and for text labels on the canvas. Use additional colors sparingly, if you think you will need them.

If you decide to use other colors, do so for very specific situations, and choose colors that are associated with a cultural meaning. For example, use red to express urgency, or danger; use yellow to caution the users; or blue to simply inform them about an event. Sticking with the basic colors has another advantage. It will save system resources and reduce the time it takes your video driver and Oracle Forms to draw the screen.

Use colors to get the attention of users about very specific situations. Do not use them to simply draw fancy-looking boxes on the screen. They will wear out your users' patience very quickly. However, do not rely too much on your users reacting to the colors. There is a considerable number of people, that are color-blind. The phenomenon is particularly encountered in males 50 years or older.

13.8.2 TEXT

By default, text in Oracle Forms is displayed in System font. Although there are many other fonts you can choose, use a font that is an established standard in your environment. Applications designed for MS Windows use System font, or a sans-serif font such as MS sans-serif, or Arial. The regular size of the System font is ten; for the other two it is eight. MS sans-serif and Arial are widely used, because the items and labels take less space on the canvas. However, there may be people among your users that may have problems with any font smaller than ten points.

Do not use colors or other visual effects such as italics, strikeout, or underline. If you want to emphasize certain text items or labels, use bold typeface.

Avoid multi-line items that cannot display all the data they may contain. It was explained earlier in the chapter how to add scrollbars to help users view the text in these items. However, it is desirable to display all the data in one large dialog box. Oracle Forms comes to your aid in these types of situations, because it provides an editor window, sizable to your specifications, that can be displayed anywhere on the screen. This editor provides standard text editing utility and will be discussed in greater extent in Chapter 16.

13.8.3 TEXT ITEMS AND TEXT LABELS

Text items should have a white background, visible border, and should present the text in black color. Display items should have a light gray background that matches the background color of the canvas if they will serve as dynamic text labels. They may or may not have a border.

Text items must provide users with visual clues about the size of data they contain. If the average length of data in an item is fifty characters long, it is not a good idea to present it on the screen as ten characters long. If items are of similar size, set them to the same size. Use creatively the Size and Align utilities of Forms Designer to reduce to a minimum the different margins on the screen. See Figure 13.1 at the beginning of this chapter for an example of a form that contains very few margins.

In the process of rearranging the layout, it may be necessary to move some data items around the screen. Make sure that data elements that are logically related are visually grouped together. Do not overlook the tab order of the items on the screen, even if the mouse and not the keyboard will be the primary means of interface between users and the application. Remember that this order is defined by the sequence of items in the Object Navigator.

Each item must have a brief but descriptive text label associated with it. In form-type screens, the text labels are to the left of the data item they describe. They must all be aligned to the left. In tabular blocks, text labels stay on top of the data items and their bottoms are aligned horizontally.

Text labels must terminate with a colon (see Figure 13.1). However, if they represent a group of items such as Gender and Preferences in Figure 13.1, they should not end with a colon.

13.9 DATA ITEMS IN THE MRD APPLICATION

At this point, you are ready to go back to the MRD application you started developing in the previous chapter. In this section you will organize and set the properties of text items in the form.

13.9.1 CREATING VISUAL ATTRIBUTES AND PROPERTY CLASSES

As explained in Chapter 7, there are many reasons why you should always consider using visual attributes and property classes in your applications. The benefits of this aproach are even more clear in the MRD form, which contains a considerable number of items with common properties. In this chapter you will create a visual attribute object and four property classes.

1. Start by creating a visual attribute object and name it MS_SANS_SERIF. This object will control the settings for visual attributes of displayed objects in the MRD application. Set the *Font* property to '*MS Sans Serif*' and *Font Size* to '8'.

2. Create a property class and name it TEXT_ITEM. Items in the MRD form will by default inherit properties from this class. Include in this class the properties and settings shown in Figure 13.10.

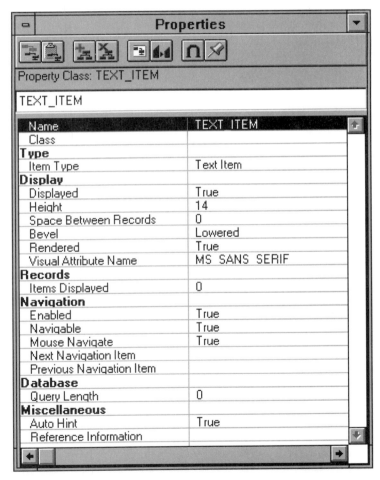

FIGURE 13.10 Contents of property class TEXT_ITEM.

3. Create a duplicate copy of the property class TEXT_ITEM and name it NUMBER_ITEM. This class will define generic properties of numeric items. For the property class NUMBER_ITEM add the property *Data Type* and set it to *'Number'*; add the property *Alignment* and set it to *'Right.'*

4. Create a duplicate copy of the property class NUMBER_ITEM and name it MONEY_ITEM. All items that will display dollar values in the MRD form will inherit their properties from this class. For the property class MONEY_ITEM add the property *Format Mask* and set it to *'$99.99'*; add the property *Range Low Value* and set it to *'0'*.

5. Create a duplicate copy of the property class TEXT_ITEM and name it DATE_ITEM. This class will define generic properties of date items. For the property class DATE_ITEM add the property *Width* and set it to *'60'*; add the property *Data Type* and set it to *'Date'*; add the property *Maximum Length* and set it to *'11'*; add the property *Case Restriction* and set it to *'Upper'*.

6. Create a duplicate copy of the property class TEXT_ITEM and name it PHONE_ITEM. This class will control properties of phone numbers. For the property class PHONE_ITEM add the property *Width* and set it to *'60'*; add the property *Maximum Length* and set it to *'12'*; add the property *Format Mask* and set it to *'FM999"-"999"-"9999'*.

13.9.2   ARRANGING CANVAS CUSTOMER

First, display the canvas in a Layout Editor window and set all the text labels to font MS Sans Serif and size eight. To quickly accomplish this task, follow these steps:

1. Select the text labels on the canvas.
2. Choose Format/Font... from the Designer menu. The Font dialog box appears.
3. Set Font to MS Sans Serif, Font Style to Regular, and Size to 8.
4. Click OK.

Now set the properties of items in the block CUSTOMER as follows:

1. For CUSTOMER_ID set *Class* to *'NUMBER_ITEM'*. In addition, set *Item Type* to *'Display Item'*. This will prevent users from manually entering or updating this item.
2. For items FIRST_NAME, LAST_NAME, ADDRESS, STATE, and ZIP, set *Class* to *'TEXT_ITEM'*.
3. For the date items DOB and MEMBER_DT set *Class* to *'DATE_ITEM'*.
4. For the telephone items, DAY_PHONE and EVE_PHONE set *Class* to *'PHONE_ITEM'*.

5. For the item ADDRESS, set *Multi-line* to *'True'*.

6. For STATE, set *Case Restriction* to *'Upper'*, *Auto Skip* to *'True'*, and *Fixed Length* to *'True'*.

Now arrange the items of the block CUSTOMER. Follow the GUI guidelines discussed earlier for the alignment and sizing of text items and labels. Do not worry too much at this point about the following items: STATUS, GENDER, MYSTERY, COMEDY, DRAMA, and FOREIGN. In the next chapter you will convert them to other types of items. Simply set them aside, out of the way. When finished, the CUSTOMER canvas should look similar to Figure 13.11. Notice that the item ADDRESS is expanded across multiple lines.

13.9.3 ARRANGING CANVAS MOVIE

Display the canvas MOVIE in the Layout Editor and for all of the text labels set the font to MS Sans Serif and size to eight. Now, set the properties of items displayed in this canvas as follows:

1. Hide item MOVIE_ID in block MOVIE by setting the *Canvas* property to *'<Null>'*, and *Displayed* property to *'False'*.

2. Set *Class* to *'TEXT_ITEM'* for items TITLE, ACTOR, ACTRESS, DIRECTOR, PRODUCER, and COMPANY.

3. Set *Class* to *'DATE_ITEM'* for items START_DT and END_DT.

4. Set *Class* to *'NUMBER_ITEM'* for item TAPE_ID in block TAPE.

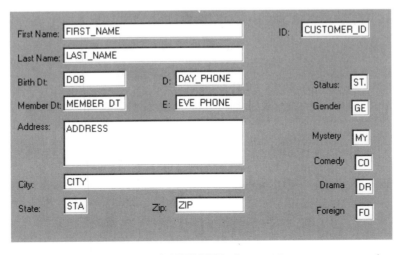

FIGURE 13.11 Canvas CUSTOMER after text items are arranged.

In the next chapter you will convert RATING, STATUS for block MOVIE and STATUS for block TAPE to different types of items; therefore, leave them as they are for the moment being.

Finally, arrange the items on the canvas to look like Figure 13.12. For the rectangle that groups items in block TAPE set Fill Color to No Fill, Line Color to black, and Bevel to Inset. For the text label "Tapes for Movie" set Fill Color to light gray, Line Color to No Line, and font to MS Sans Serif, bold, size eight.

13.9.4   ARRANGING CANVAS RENTAL

Display the canvas RENTAL in the Layout Editor and set the font to MS Sans Serif and size to eight for all the text labels on the canvas. Then, set the properties of items as follows:

1. Set *Displayed* to *'False'* and *Canvas* to *'<Null>'* for these items: CUSTOMER_ID in RENTAL block; CUSTOMER_ID, DOB, and MEMBER_DT in block CUST_RENT; and MOVIE_ID in block MOVIE_RENT.

2. Set *Class* to *'TEXT_ITEM'* for these items: LAST_NAME, FIRST_NAME, and STATUS in block CUST_RENT; TITLE, STATUS, and RATING in block MOVIE_RENT; STATUS in block TAPE_RENT.

3. Set *Class* to *'NUMBER_ITEM'* for TAPE_ID in blocks RENTAL and TAPE_RENT.

4. Set *Class* to *'DATE_ITEM'* for RENT_DT and RETURN_DT in block RENTAL.

5. Set *Class* to *'MONEY_ITEM'* for DAILY_RATE in block RENTAL.

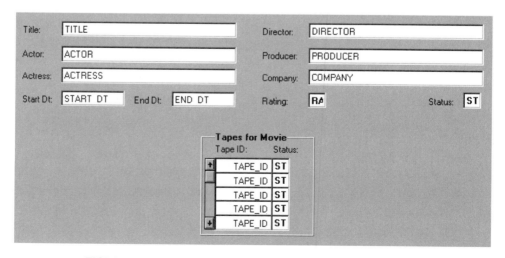

FIGURE 13.12   Canvas MOVIE after text items are arranged.

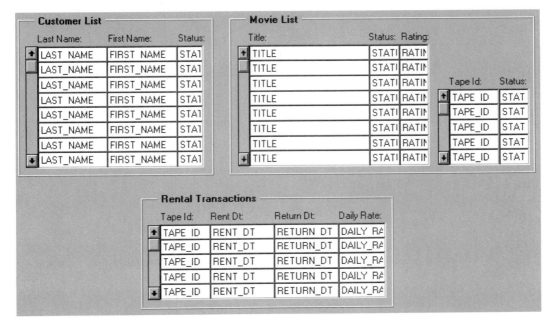

FIGURE 13.13   Canvas RENTAL after text items are arranged.

Finally, arrange, resize and align the items on the canvas until it looks similar to Figure 13.13. For the rectangles that group logically related data set Fill Color to No Fill, Line Color to black, and Bevel to Inset. For the text labels set Fill Color to light gray, Line Color to No Line, and font to MS Sans Serif, bold, size eight.

When you are finished save and generate the form.

13.10 SUMMARY

This chapter discusses the Oracle Forms items, their properties, and events. The first part of the chapter deals with generic properties of items of all types and the second part sets its focus on text items in particular. Major concepts of this chapter are listed here:

❑ Types of items
   ❑ Base table and control items
   ❑ GUI interface items
❑ Creating items
❑ Generic properties of items
   ❑ Type properties

❑   Display properties
❑   Data properties
❑   Records properties
❑   Navigation properties
❑   Database properties
❑   Functional properties
❑   Miscellaneous properties
❑   Setting properties of items at Runtime
❑   Validation of items in Oracle Forms
❑   Text items and display items
    ❑   Bevel and rendered properties
    ❑   Data properties of text items
    ❑   Database properties of text items
    ❑   Functional properties of text items
❑   Events of text items
❑   GUI guidelines for data items
    ❑   Colors
    ❑   Text
    ❑   Text items and text labels

CONTROLS

"I think the real challenge is to design software that is simple on the outside but complex on the inside."

—John Page

- ♦ Push Buttons
- ♦ Radio Buttons
- ♦ Check Boxes
- ♦ List Boxes
- ♦ GUI Guidelines for Controls
- ♦ Controls in the MRD Application
- ♦ Summary

In character-based applications, text items are the only way that users have to interact with the data. At any moment in the life of such applications, the focus of the form is in an item, and the users inspect, modify, or validate the data contained in it. The implementation of Oracle Forms for GUI environments increased dramatically not only their functionality and capabilities, but also the ability of users to decide the way the application is executed. Control items are the principal tools that users have to express their intentions, to initiate actions, or to influence the flow of the application. Oracle Forms supports four types of controls: push buttons, list boxes, radio buttons, and check boxes. This chapter discusses the properties and implementation of these controls.

14.1 PUSH BUTTONS

Push buttons are always used to initiate an action or navigate to a different context area in the application. Typical actions triggered by clicking these buttons are to commit changes to a database, cancel an operation, or close a dialog box.

Based on their appearance, push buttons are divided in label and iconic push buttons. Label push buttons contain a text label that clearly states their functionality such as Save, Cancel, or Print. If these buttons open other windows or dialog boxes, the label's text must end with an ellipsis, as in this button [Help...]. This is a well-established industry standard that you must observe in your applications. Label buttons are used primarily in windows and dialog boxes to indicate and perform the main functions associated with them. They should be placed prominently in such a way that users can immediately tell by looking at the window what functions they can perform there, or what to do next.

Iconic buttons contain an icon on their face instead of a label. The icon graphically presents the functionality of the button. This type of button is used mainly in toolbars, but it is not unusual to find them in windows and dialog boxes, as well.

Because of their nature, push buttons can only be control items in a Forms module. They cannot display any data, and, therefore, do not contain any properties in the Data or Database groups usually associated with other types of items. For the same reason, they can be created only from the Object Navigator of the Layout Editor, but not from the New Block Options dialog box, like other types of items in Oracle Forms.

14.1.1 FUNCTIONAL PROPERTIES OF PUSH BUTTONS

Most of the generic properties of Oracle Forms items discussed in the first part of Chapter 13 apply to push buttons as well. This section will discuss only their Functional properties.

The *Label* property contains the string of characters that will appear in the face of the label button. To allow users to access the button from the keyboard, without using the mouse, you can set the *Access Key* property. You can specify only one character in the setting of this property. At runtime, Forms will underline the first character of the label string that matches the access key. Users can select the button by pressing ALT and the access key simultaneously. For example, if the button's label is Close and the access key is C, the button will appear to the users as [Close] . They can navigate to it by pressing ALT+C, and then pressing the space bar to push the button. One button per block can be activated by the users from anywhere on the screen by pressing ENTER. This is known as the default button and can become such by setting the *Default Button* property to *'True'*. At runtime, as long as no other push button is selected, the default button will maintain the selection border around it as in this example: [Save] . This means that the button is always ready to fire, whenever ENTER is pressed. Because there is no need to navigate to the button in order to push it, default buttons do not need access keys.

The *Iconic* property of push buttons controls whether they are iconic or label buttons. When it is set to *'True'*, the button is an iconic button; when it is set to *'False'*, the button is a label button. For an iconic button, you must also specify the name of the icon that will be displayed on top of the button. This is done by setting the *Icon Name* property to the name of the file that contains the icon.

There are two things you should be careful about when specifying the name of an icon:

1. Oracle Forms expects the file to be with the extension .ICO in the file system and wants you to specify only the file name in the *Icon Name* property. If you add the extension of the file, Forms will not be able to attach it to the button. For example, if the icon file name is CUSTOMER.ICO, set the *Icon Name* property only to *'CUSTOMER'*.

2. The location of the icon file must be in one of the directories specified in the TK21_ICON environment variable. In MS Windows, this variable is specified in the [FORMS45] section of ORACLE.INI. The ORACLE.INI file, which contains the settings for all the environment variables used by Oracle database and tools, is located in the Windows directory of your machine. If you specify a fully qualified path for the icon file, Oracle Forms will not be able to attach it to the button, even if the path is included in the TK21_ICON environment variable.

Note

The possibility of pressing default buttons inadvertently is high. Therefore, do not use them to perform destructive actions such as deleting records from the database.

> **Note**
>
> By setting the property *Mouse Navigate* to '*False*', it is possible to fire the PressButton event without the ActivateButton event, because the focus cannot be placed on the button.

14.1.2 EVENTS OF PUSH BUTTONS

There are two major events that happen in the life of a push button: ActivateButton and PressButton. They can originate from the keyboard or from mouse clicks. The only way to activate a button without pressing it is to use the TAB or SHIFT+TAB keys, also known in the Oracle Forms terminology as [Next Item] and [Previous Item] until the focus navigates to the button. This requires that the *Navigable* property of the button be set to '*True*'. Once the button is activated, there are several ways to press it:

  a) Press the SPACE bar from the keyboard, or
  b) Press ENTER from the keyboard, or
  c) Click the button with the mouse.

When the mouse or the keyboard access keys are used, activating and pressing the button occur in rapid succession and are often considered as one event: PressButton.

You can associate the method WHEN-NEW-ITEM-INSTANCE with the ActivateButton event, and the method WHEN-BUTTON-PRESSED with the PressButton event. Usually, the second one is used to perform the functionality that the button is designed to do.

14.2 RADIO GROUPS AND RADIO BUTTONS

Radio buttons offer users a way to choose only one option from a list of mutually exclusive options. Each of the options is presented by a label and a radio button on the side of the label that indicates whether the option is currently selected or not. The radio buttons that represent all the choices available for a particular situation form a radio group. In Oracle Forms, items can be represented by radio groups. Those few data options that can be manipulated by a radio group item are the radio buttons that make up the group.

The easiest way to implement an item as a radio group is to change the *Item Type* in the Properties Window from, say, '*Text Item*' to '*Radio Group*'. When you do this, you will notice that properties such as *Displayed*, *X Position*, *Y Position*, *Width*, and *Height*, disappear from the list of item's properties. Because the radio group itself is not displayed on the screen, these properties do not have any meaning for this type of item. However, the *Canvas* property remains in effect, and its setting will determine where the members of that radio group will be displayed. In the Object Navigator, the item type icon to the left of the item's name changes to a radio group icon.

If you expand the radio group item, you will see that besides triggers, this type of item also owns radio buttons. You must create radio button objects under the radio group item to represent the different choices that users have on the screen. You can create these objects in the Object Navigator or from the Layout Editor. If you create radio buttons from the Layout Editor, you will be presented with a list of radio groups in the current block. From this list, you choose the group that will become the parent of the newly created button.

14.2.1 PROPERTIES OF RADIO GROUPS AND RADIO BUTTONS

Radio buttons inherit the *Canvas* property from their parent group. Their most important properties are *Value*, *Label*, and *Access Key*.

The *Value* property is the value that the radio button will pass to the parent group if it is selected from the user. It is also the value that must be fetched by a query or stored programmatically in the radio group item in order to select the radio button. For example, suppose that the item GENDER in the CUSTOMER block of the MRD application is implemented as a radio group. Two radio buttons, MALE and FEMALE, are members of this group. Their *Value* property is set to 'M' and 'F', respectively. Each time the users will click the button FEMALE on the screen, 'F' will be the value assigned to the item GENDER. If the record of a customer is queried from the database, and the value of GENDER item is 'F', the button FEMALE will be selected.

The *Label* property is the text that users will see on the side of the radio button. It should explain the meaning of the option clearly and concisely. The *Access Key* property has the same meaning here as in push button items. It is a character that users can type from the keyboard, in conjunction with the ALT key, that allows them to select the radio button without clicking it with the mouse. Radio buttons also have properties such as *Displayed*, *X Position*, *Y Position*, *Width*, and *Height*. These properties control their appearance, position, and dimensions on the canvas.

You can use the property *Other Values* to make the handling of the data by the radio group more robust. The default setting of the property is NULL. With such a setting, the block will reject all the queried records that do not contain any of the values assigned to the radio buttons in their radio group item. In the case presented above, if the query returns a customer whose GENDER is not set to 'M' or 'F', the record will not be allowed to appear in the block. Sometimes, this way of handling inconsistent data may be too restrictive. If you build an application on top of these data for the purpose of standardizing them, the default setting of *Other Values* will not allow you to view the erratic data items that you are trying to fix. In such situations, you may set this property (either its name, or its value) to one of the radio buttons in the group. After that, whenever a nonconforming record is queried, the radio button specified in the *Other Values* property will be selected.

The fact that radio buttons make one choice out of a number of mutually exclusive options, implies that a choice is always made. In other words, if an item is implemented as radio group, it will always contain a value as specified by the radio buttons. The value can be NULL if the property of one of the buttons is set as such.

Finally, although radio groups are not represented visually on the canvas, you must give the idea that their radio buttons are grouped together. Usually a box is drawn around the buttons and a text label placed on top of the box describes their functionality.

14.2.2 EVENTS OF RADIO GROUPS

The events that are associated with radio group items are ActivateRadioGroup and ChangeRadioGroupSelection. The first event occurs when users navigate to the group using the keyboard, or when they click on the radio button that is currently selected. At the successful completion of this event, the trigger WHEN-NEW-ITEM-INSTANCE will fire. The *Navigable* property of the radio group item must be set to '*True*', if the keyboard will be used to activate the item; the *Mouse Navigate* property must be set to '*True*', if the mouse will be used for the same purpose.

The selection of the radio group can be changed in one of two ways:

a) Click the appropriate radio button, or
b) Press simultaneously the ALT key and the character specified in the *Access Key* property, if it exists.

Any of these actions causes the event ChangeRadioGroupSelection, which, in turn, fires the trigger WHEN-RADIO-CHANGED. You can use this trigger to perform any actions that should be taken if the selection of the radio button changes.

It is interesting to note that when the selection of the radio group changes, the first event to occur is ChangeRadioGroupSelection, followed by Activate RadioGroup. The navigation to the item itself is completed after this event. Thus, the trigger WHEN-RADIO-CHANGED will fire before the trigger WHEN-NEW-ITEM-INSTANCE. Keep in mind this sequence if you are placing code in both triggers.

As with other controls, if the *Mouse Navigate* property of the radio group item is set to '*False*', you can click a radio button without moving the focus of the form to the radio group itself. In this case, only the trigger WHEN-RADIO-CHANGED will fire if the selection of the radio button is changed.

14.3 CHECK BOXES

Like radio buttons, check boxes are used to choose among some options, but unlike radio buttons, the choices that check boxes represent are not mutually exclusive. In other words, if your users need to make multiple selections out of a number of options, check boxes must be used to represent these options. But if they must choose only one of these options, you must use radio buttons.

You can create check box items either by converting the *Item Type* property of an existing item to '*Check Box*', or by creating the item from scratch in the Layout Editor. When you do so, the item type icon in the Object Navigator will change to a check box.

14.3.1 PROPERTIES OF CHECK BOXES

When you convert an existing text item to a check box, most properties are carried over to the new type, except for properties in the **Functional** group and a few properties specific to text items such as *Bevel* and *Status*. The check box *Label* property will be set to the name of the item and its dimensions to those of the original text item. This may require you to adjust the dimension of the check box, if its label is not fully visible, and to delete the text label previously associated with the text item. From the **Functional** properties of check boxes, *Label* and *Access Key* properties have the same meaning as the respective properties for radio buttons.

The *Checked Value* property contains the value that the item should contain if users check the box on the screen. If the item is populated with this value either by a query or programmatically, the status of the check box on the canvas will be checked.

The *Unchecked Value* property is set to the value that must be placed in the item if the check box is not checked. If this value is assigned to the item internally, the status of the box becomes unchecked.

The properties *Checked Value* and *Unchecked Value* must have different settings for the check box to be considered valid. If the properties are not set to different values, you will get the following error when generating the module: FRM-30174: Checked and unchecked values must be distinct.

As an example, consider the preferences a customer may have for movies. If the customer has an interest in Mystery movies, the MYSTERY column in the database will store the value Y; otherwise, no values will be stored. If you implement the item MYSTERY in block CUSTOMER as a check box, you would assign '*Y*' to its *Checked Value*, and leave blank the *Unchecked Value* property. Now users can check the box to express the fact that the customer is interested in Mystery movies, instead of entering Y in a text item. When the record is retrieved from the database, the Mystery item will be checked if the column contains Y, or unchecked if it contains no values at all.

The *Check Box Other Values* property has the same meaning as *Other Values* property for radio groups. It handles the case when the value stored in the database does not match the setting of *Checked Value* or *Unchecked Value* properties. By default, it is set to *'Checked'*, and sets the status of the box to checked if such values are returned from a query or assigned to the item programmatically. You can set it to *'Unchecked'* to reverse the effect, or to *'Not Allowed'* to reject records that contain inconsistent values.

14.3.2 EVENTS OF CHECK BOXES

Two events associated with a check box are activating and changing the check status of the item. You can activate the check box by using TAB or SHIFT+TAB keys to navigate to it. When this event is complete, the trigger WHEN-NEW-ITEM-INSTANCE fires. The ActivateCheckbox event occurs only when the *Navigable* property of the item is *'True'*.

Once the item is activated, you can change its state by pressing the SPACE bar on the keyboard. This causes the event ChangeCheckBox which, in turn, activates the trigger WHEN-CHECKBOX-CHANGED.

If you click the check box, or its label, both events will occur in rapid succession. The event that takes precedence in this case is changing the status of the check box. Therefore, WHEN-CHECKBOX-CHANGED trigger will fire before WHEN-NEW-ITEM-INSTANCE trigger. The effect of clicking the check box with the mouse can be replicated from the keyboard by pressing at the same time the ALT key and the access key, if one is defined.

As it is the case with push buttons and radio buttons, if the *Mouse Navigate* property is set to *'False'*, you can change the setting of the check box without placing the focus on the item itself. In such a case, only the event CheckboxChanged will occur, and therefore, only the trigger WHEN-CHECKBOX-CHANGED will fire.

At the conclusion of this section, recall that it is important that logically related check boxes be grouped visually on the canvas. In this case, as with radio buttons, you may want to draw a box around the items and place a text label on top of it that summarizes the purpose or the functionality of these items.

14.4 LIST BOXES

Given the amount of space they occupy on the screen, it is recommended that you limit the number of radio items or check boxes to five or less per group. If your application requires choosing from a larger number of options, then selection lists are used. Single-selection lists extend the functionality of radio buttons in the sense that they allow users to pick only one entry from a list of options presented to them. Multi-selection lists allow users to choose several options at the same time, and, therefore extend the functionality of check boxes. Oracle Forms, by default, supports only single-selection lists. Multi-selection lists can be implemented programmatically. In the rest of this section, referring to lists will mean single-selection lists.

To convert an existing item to a list, simply set its *Item Type* property to '*List Item*'. If you are converting a text item to a list, you will notice that the new items will inherit all the other properties of the original item, with the exception of properties in the **Functional** group and the properties *Bevel* and *Rendered*. You can also create a list item directly on the Layout Editor.

14.4.1 TYPES OF LISTS

There are three types of lists used in GUI environments and in Oracle Forms applications: drop-down list boxes, text lists, and combo boxes. The type of list is controlled by the property *List Style* under the **Functional** group.

❑ **Drop-down list boxes** take the appearance of text items when they are not in use. To their right, they have an arrow button, which, when activated, displays the elements of the list. If the number of options is larger than ten, a scrollbar will appear to help users navigate to the other items not displayed in the list. When users pick one option, the list folds back to its normal state and the selection appears in the text area of the list. By default, when a list is created, it is a drop-down list box. If you want to change another type of list to a drop-down list, set the *List Style* property to '*Poplist*'.

❑ **Text lists** in their normal state, are rectangular boxes where the list items are displayed. The size of the box is defined in the Layout Editor, when you create the list. If the list contains more items than can fit in the box, a scrollbar to the right of the box can be used to scroll the list. To make a list a text list set its *List Style* property to '*Tlist*'.

❑ With the two previous types of lists, users can only select one value that already exists and is displayed by the list. There are occasions when they

---

Note

Drop-down list boxes are also referred to as poplists. The first term is more descriptive for the behavior of the object. It also conforms with the terminology ordinarily used for this type of lists in other GUI development tools.

must be allowed to enter a value that is not in the list. **Combo boxes** combine the benefits of using a list of predefined data elements to populate an item with the flexibility to enter additional data that are not in the list. Visually, combo boxes are similar to drop-down list boxes, except that here, the text field is separated form the drop-down arrow button. Functionally, users can click this button to display the list of available options, and pick an option from the list to fill the text item. They can also type directly in the text item as they would with any other text items in the Form. The combo box will not automatically record the data they enter as elements of the list. If the application must update the list of options with the new data, the feature must be implemented programmatically. Later in the chapter you will see how to do this. To implement a list as a combo box, set its *List Style* property to '*Combo Box*'.

Figure 14.1 shows examples of the same item implemented using the styles of lists described above.

14.4.2 SETTING LIST PROPERTIES AT DESIGN TIME

The principal property of a list used in the Designer is the *List Elements* property. This property defines the options that users will see when they activate the list at runtime. This property is set in the List Items Elements dialog box that is displayed if you double-click it or if you click the More... button displayed in the properties settings bar (see Figure 14.2).

There are two parts in this dialog box. The List Elements text list is where you define the items that users will see when accessing your list. The List Item Value field is where you specify the value that will correspond to the list element in the Oracle Forms item. In the example shown in Figure 14.2, the current ele-

Drop-Down List Box   Text Box   Combo Box

FIGURE 14.1   Three types of lists in Oracle Forms.

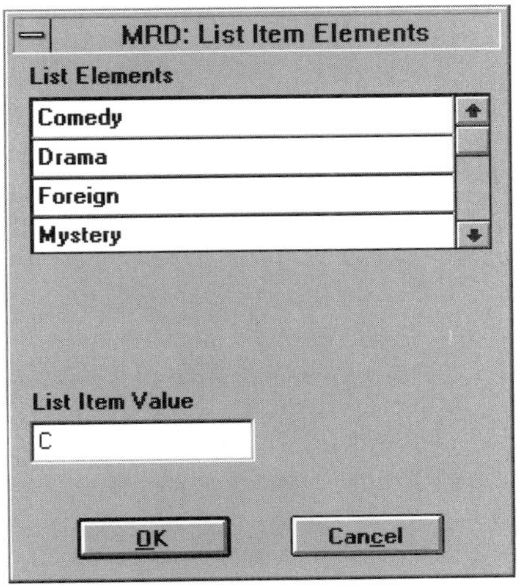

FIGURE 14.2 List Item Elements dialog box.

ment is Comedy and the item value that corresponds to it is C. This means that, if users select Comedy from the list, the CATEGORY item in the form will be assigned the value C. If a query or programmatic assignment places the value C in the CATEGORY item, Comedy will become the selected element in the list.

Unfortunately, the List Item Elements dialog box does not provide a way to sort the elements of the list in any order. If you want to sort them, you must populate the list dynamically via a SELECT statement that contains an ORDER BY clause. Once you enter all the elements of the list, you can click the OK button to accept the changes.

Two properties of list items, *Default Value* and *Other Values* have exactly the same meaning as the corresponding properties in radio group items. They are both set to either a list element such as Comedy, or to the list item value that corresponds to that element, for example C.

Note

Inserting or deleting entries in the text list is not a very intuitive process. In order to figure out the right key combination for these actions, press CTRL+K from the keyboard to display the list of keys that can be used in this dialog box. There, you can see that to insert an element you must press CTRL+> and to delete it CTRL+<.

14.4.3 EVENTS OF LISTS

As with other controls discussed in this chapter, the two most important events in the life of a list are activating it and changing its selection. Both events can be initiated by keyboard key strokes, or by mouse clicks. The *Navigable* property must be set to *'True'* to be able to access the list using the keyboard.

The ActivateList event occurs if the TAB or SHIFT+TAB keys are used to navigate to the list. At the completion of this event, the focus of the form is placed on the list, its current value is highlighted, and the WHEN-NEW-ITEM-INSTANCE trigger fires.

When drop-down list boxes or the combo boxes are activated, you must press the down-arrow key to display the list members. Once these types of lists are unfolded, you can scroll their elements to search for the choice you want. To pick one of the list items, highlight it and press ENTER. At this point, the Change-List event occurs and the trigger WHEN-LIST-CHANGED fires. At the conclusion of this event, the lists are folded back to their initial state.

When text lists are activated, the current list value will be selected. Scrolling the elements of the list will cause the event ChangeList and the trigger WHEN-LIST-CHANGED will fire.

The easiest way to activate or change the value of a list is to use the mouse clicks. If you click drop-down list boxes, the list elements will appear. The ActivateList event occurs, and the WHEN-NEW-ITEM-INSTANCE trigger fires only if *Mouse Navigate* property is set to *'True'*. From the list of options available, you can click one to change the value of the list. If the option you pick is different from the current value of the list, the ChangeList occurs; otherwise, nothing happens.

For text lists, their elements are displayed in the list box. If the focus is not on the list, and you click one of its elements, the ChangeList and ActivateList events will occur one after the other, in this order. Again here, if the *Mouse Navigate* property is *'False'*, the ActivateList event does not occur.

Text lists have two aspects in their behavior that are different from the other types of lists:

1. If the currently selected list element is clicked, the element will be deselected. Visually, the selection box around the element disappears. Internally, the value stored in the list item is set to NULL.
2. Forms recognizes double-clicking an element of the list as a separate event. This event triggers the WHEN-LIST-ACTIVATED method to fire.

The method is meaningful only for text list items. Because the ChangeList event occurs before DoubleClickListElement, the new value of the list item is available in the WHEN-LIST-ACTIVATED trigger and can be used to initiate actions such as display a dialog box, or perform a computation. You will utilize this feature of text lists to programmatically implement a multiple selection list in Chapter 16.

> ## Note
>
> If the combo list is changed via a mouse click, the ChangeList event will fire only once. However, if a new entry is typed in the text field, the ChangeList event will occur each time a character is typed. As a consequence, the WHEN-LIST-CHANGED trigger will fire as many times as you hit the keyboard. Be very careful with the code you place in this trigger for combo boxes.

The *Mouse Navigate* property of combo boxes is always '*True*'. If you set it to '*False*', Designer will display a warning when the module is generated, and the setting will be ignored at runtime. If you click inside the text field of the combo box, the current selection will be highlighted and the cursor will be placed inside the field. The same thing happens when the list button of the combo box is clicked, but, in addition, the list elements will be displayed as in a drop-down list box. At this point, you can either pick another element from the list, or type a new entry over the current selection. In both cases, the ChangeList event will occur. The new selection will be available to the trigger WHEN-LIST-CHANGED that fires in response to this event.

14.4.4 MANIPULATING LISTS PROGRAMMATICALLY

Besides creating list items at design time, you can also use a series of built-in functions and procedures to maintain them at runtime. In this section you will implement the COMPANY item in block MOVIE of the MRD application as a combo box list that will be populated by the users as the application is being used. In the process of implementing this functionality, you will understand the meaning of the built-in program units that you will use. You can follow the discussion in this section with the MRD module you are creating as you are reading this book.

Open the module, navigate to the MOVIE block, select the item COMPANY, and display its properties in a Property Window. Now follow these steps:

1. Set *Item Type* property to '*List Item*'.
2. Set *List Style* property in the **Functional** group to '*Combo Box*'.

In order for Forms Runtime to be able to initialize the list item, you must specify at least one element in the list:

1. Double-click *List Elements* property to display the List Item Elements dialog box.
2. Create a list element that will represent a movie-making company, for example MIRAMAX.

3. Set the list item value for that element to the same value as the label, for example MIRAMAX.

4. Enter additional companies if you wish.

5. Click OK when done.

Save and generate the form module before moving to the programmatic implementation of the functionality of COMPANY combo box.

As mentioned earlier in the chapter, combo boxes are "memoryless." They allow users to enter data that are not elements of the list, but do not incorporate the new entries in the list automatically. In order to make combo boxes record the new data elements, you will capture the value of the list item when the event ActivateList occurs (in the WHEN-NEW-ITEM-INSTANCE trigger). Then, during the event ValidateItem (in the WHEN-VALIDATE-ITEM trigger), you will compare the final value of the list item with the original value. If there is a change, the new value is a candidate to become an element of the list. You will decide whether to add this new value or not to the list by comparing it with the existing elements in the list.

You will store the initial value of the list in a global variable, which will be declared when the form module is first created. The safest place to declare global variables is a PRE-FORM form-level trigger. However, 255 bytes will be allocated for the entire life of the form to a global that is needed only when users access the COMPANY item in MOVIE block. A more efficient solution is to declare the global at the beginning of ActivateList event, use it during the ValidateItem event, and erase it at the end of this event.

1. In the Object Navigator, select the Triggers node under the item COMPANY in the MOVIE block.

2. Create a new trigger, and choose WHEN-NEW-ITEM-INSTANCE from the Triggers LOVs dialog box.

Note

The initial impulse would be to place this functionality in the WHEN-LIST-CHANGED trigger, but there is a possibility that this event occurs more than one time, that is, if the users pick several choices before making up their mind, or if they enter a new value from the keyboard. In your implementation, you will let the users pick and choose as much as they like. When they decide to leave the item, the value stored there will be validated, and here you will decide whether a new element must be added to the list or not.

```
IF (:GLOBAL.original_item <> :MOVIE.COMPANY) AND
   (Element_Label_Exists('MOVIE.COMPANY', :MOVIE.COMPANY)
    <> 'TRUE') THEN
    Insert_Element('MOVIE.COMPANY', :MOVIE.COMPANY,
:MOVIE.COMPANY);
   END IF;
ERASE('GLOBAL.original_item');
```

FIGURE 14.3   Trigger that inserts a new list item if it does not already exist.

3. Enter the following line in the PL/SQL Editor:

    :GLOBAL.original_item := :MOVIE.COMPANY;

4. Compile the trigger and close the PL/SQL Editor window.

The single line of code in this trigger declares and initializes the global variable GLOBAL.original_item.

Follow Steps 1 and 2 above to create the WHEN-VALIDATE-ITEM trigger for item COMPANY. Enter the text shown in Figure 14.3 in the body of the trigger.

In this trigger, if the current value of the list item is different from the initial value stored in GLOBAL.original_item, and if this value does not correspond to the label of an existing element in the list, then you insert the new element in the list. The function Element_Label_Exists checks for the existence in a list of at least one element with a given label. The procedure Insert_Element insert in a new element in a list with a given value and a given label. In this case, the data that users enter in MOVIE.COMPANY will serve as both the value and the label of the list's element. Therefore the call to the procedure Insert_Element is as shown in the third line of Figure 14.3. As the last action in this trigger, the global GLOBAL.original_item is erased from memory.

Note

In the present state of the form, the trigger will not compile successfully, because neither the function **Element_Label_Exists** nor the procedure **Insert_Element** are declared. However, PL/SQL Editor allows you to close the trigger even if its contents are not compiled. This feature can be used to prototype the high-level functionality of the trigger, and then move on to a lower programming level where all the implementation details are clarified.

From the PL/SQL editor window, create function **Element_Label_Exists**, as shown in Figure 14.4. The first lines of this function are familiar. You retrieve the internal ID of the list item and make sure that it exists before proceeding any further. The built-in function GET_LIST_ELEMENT_COUNT is used to retrieve the number of elements in the list. This number serves as an upper bound of the FOR loop that checks whether the input label equals any of the existing elements' labels. As you loop through the elements of the list, the function GET_LIST_ELEMENT_LABEL is used to return the label for the current element of the list.

If a match is found, the input label exists already in the list. The variable **found** is set to 'TRUE' and the FOR loop is interrupted. If the loop searches all the list elements and finds no matches, the value of variable **found** remains 'FALSE',

```
FUNCTION Element_Label_Exists (list_name VARCHAR2,
                               label     VARCHAR2)
RETURN VARCHAR2 IS
  list_id        ITEM;
  list_count     NUMBER;
  found          VARCHAR2(10) := 'FALSE';
  current_label  VARCHAR2(50);

BEGIN
  /* FIND_ITEM returns the appropriate item ID. */
  list_id := FIND_ITEM(list_name);

  IF NOT ID_NULL(list_id) THEN
    list_count := GET_LIST_ELEMENT_COUNT(list_id);

    FOR i IN 1..list_count LOOP
      current_label := GET_LIST_ELEMENT_LABEL(list_id, i);
      IF label = current_label THEN
        found := 'TRUE';
        EXIT;
      END IF;
    END LOOP;
  ELSE
    MESSAGE('List Item '||list_name||' does not exist.');
    RAISE FORM_TRIGGER_FAILURE;
  END IF;
  RETURN found;
END Element_Label_Exists;
```

FIGURE 14.4   Searching a list for a given value.

> ## Note
>
> With a minor modification, this function can be used to search for matches be-
> tween the input variable and list elements values. Instead of function
> GET_LIST_ELEMENT_LABEL, you would use function GET_LIST_
> ELEMENT_VALUE to retrieve the value of the current list element.

as it was initialized at the beginning of the function. The last statement of the
function returns the variable found to the calling environment.

Once you edit and compile the function Element_Label_Exists, create procedure Insert_Element, as shown in Figure 14.5.

The only new thing in this procedure is the use of the built-in procedure
ADD_LIST_ELEMENT. This procedure takes four input arguments. The first one
is the internal ID of the list item. The second parameter is the position in the list
where the new item will be inserted. The Procedure Insert_Element places the
new elements at the bottom of the list. If you pass the number 1 in this argument,
the elements will always be added at the top of the list. The third parameter is the
label associated with the new element, and the last parameter is its value.

```
PROCEDURE Insert_Element (list_name VARCHAR2,
                          label     VARCHAR2,
                          value     VARCHAR2) IS
  list_id    ITEM;
  list_count NUMBER;

BEGIN
  /* FIND_ITEM returns the appropriate item ID. */
  list_id := FIND_ITEM(list_name);

  IF NOT ID_NULL(list_id) THEN
    list_count := GET_LIST_ELEMENT_COUNT(list_id);
  /* Add new element at the bottom of the list. */
    ADD_LIST_ELEMENT(list_id, list_count + 1, label, value);
  ELSE
    MESSAGE('List Item '||list_name||' does not exist.');
    RAISE FORM_TRIGGER_FAILURE;
  END IF;
END Insert_Element;
```

FIGURE 14.5 Inserting a new element in a list.

> **Note**
>
> 1. If you need to delete an element from the list, you can use the built-in procedure DELETE_LIST_ELEMENT. This procedure takes as input parameters the internal ID of the list item and the position of the element in the list.
>
> 2. All the built-in program units that have been discussed in this section can take the list item internal ID or name as parameter. The use of the internal ID, after making sure that it exists, increases the robustness of your application.

14.4.5 WRITING OBJECT-INDEPENDENT CODE

The MRD application has several items that could benefit from the functionality you just added to item COMPANY. In order to avoid repeating the same actions for these items, you should create a property class based on some properties of COMPANY:

1. In the Object Navigator, create a duplicate copy of property class TEXT_ITEM and name it UPDATEABLE_COMBO.
2. Set property *Item Type* to '*List Item*'.
3. Add property *List Style* and set it to '*Combo Box*'.

Now select the triggers WHEN-NEW-ITEM-INSTANCE and WHEN-VALIDATE-ITEM attached to item COMPANY and drag them onto the property class UPDATEABLE_COMBO.

The code for these triggers explicitly uses information about item COMPANY, which would not be very helpful in a property class that you intend to use generically. Edit the contents of WHEN-NEW-ITEM-INSTANCE trigger, and replace the existing code with the following line:

```
:GLOBAL.original_item := :SYSTEM.CURSOR_VALUE;
```

SYSTEM.CURSOR_VALUE is a system variable that records the value of the item where the cursor is currently.

Edit the contents of WHEN-VALIDATE-ITEM trigger as shown in Figure 14.6.

In this trigger, SYSTEM.CURSOR_ITEM is the system variable that records the name of the item where the cursor is currently located.

```
DECLARE
  item_name VARCHAR2(80);
  item_value VARCHAR2(80);

BEGIN
  item_name := :SYSTEM.CURSOR_ITEM;
  item_value := :SYSTEM.CURSOR_VALUE;

  IF (:GLOBAL.original_item <> item_value) AND
     (Element_Label_Exists(item_name, item_value) <> 'TRUE')
       THEN
         Insert_Element(item_name, item_value, item_value);
  END IF;
  ERASE('GLOBAL.original_item');
END;
```

FIGURE 14.6 Generic trigger that inserts a new element in a list item.

Now you can delete the WHEN-NEW-ITEM-INSTANCE and WHEN-VALIDATE-ITEM triggers attached to item COMPANY. In Section 14.6.2, this and other items in the MOVIE block will inherit these triggers from the property class UPDATEABLE_COMBO.

There is a major caveat in the way this section implements the dynamic management of lists. Users will be able to enter new elements in the list and will see the new entries as long as they do not exit the application. However, because the inserted elements are maintained in temporary memory structures of Oracle Forms, as soon as the application is terminated, the modifications will be discarded. In order to make this functionality really productive and useful, you need to record these changes in permanent structures that last between sessions. Chapter 16 will explain how to use record groups to populate list items with data from the database.

14.5 GUI GUIDELINES FOR CONTROLS

As discussed in the previous chapter, when developing a GUI application you strive for a uniform and standard look of all the screens, and also for compliance with other successful applications. Remember that the goal is to be noticed as little as possible. Software applications you develop should be considered as utilities; tools in the hands of users that help them accomplish their business goals. Users should notice these applications as much as they notice the telephone set when they place or receive a call. At the same time, they should find them as reliable and easy to use as their telephone. Establishing and following standards is as important for controls as for text items in the interface of the application.

14.5.1 PUSH BUTTONS

The position and size of buttons play an important role in the ability of users to notice and use them. Depending on the orientation of the window, buttons can be placed either on the upper right-hand corner of the window or centered on the bottom of it. If the buttons are placed up and to the right of the window, they must all have the same size and be vertically aligned. If they are placed at the bottom, they must be aligned horizontally, and share the same height. It is good if they can have the same width, but this is not required.

The dimensions of the buttons must be set so that the whole text label is completely inside the margins. Buttons whose labels fall off the margins, as in this example ▣Customer▣ , give the impression of an application put together in haste.

The buttons should be grouped together by functionality. The distance between the groups should be larger than the distance between buttons of the same group. The button that is likely to be used the most by the users, usually the OK or Save button, should always be the first button from the top for vertically aligned buttons, or from the left for horizontally aligned buttons. This button should also have the *Default Button* property set to *'True'*. The Cancel or Close button should be placed immediately next to this button. If the window contains a Help button, it should be the last one, positioned at the opposite side of the default button. Limit the number of buttons in a window to no more than five.

If iconic buttons are used, they should have the same size as the icon displayed on them. Because of differences in their dimensions, text label buttons should not be mixed with iconic buttons. Use one type or the other consistently across the window. However, it is an effective GUI technique to place iconic buttons in toolbars on the sides of the window.

14.5.2 RADIO BUTTONS AND CHECK BOXES

Given the similarity in appearance between radio buttons and check boxes, you should follow the same guidelines when working with them. Radio buttons and check boxes must be aligned vertically. Each button or box must have a label to its right that briefly but clearly describes the option represented by the object. In addition, all the options that are related must be grouped visually, and a label should be placed on top of the group.

Do not place more than six to eight radio buttons or check boxes in a group. If the number of options is higher, replace radio buttons with single-selection lists, and programmatically implement multi-selection lists to replace the check boxes.

It is not recommended to use check boxes that, when checked, select all the other options in the group. The functionality can be implemented programmatically with a multi-selection list and a push button that selects all the elements of the list.

14.5.3 LISTS

Lists are controls that should replace radio buttons or check boxes in the following situations:

1. There are more than six to eight options in the group.
2. The space or the layout of the window does not allow the use of radio buttons or check boxes. In this case, drop-down list boxes and combo boxes should be considered.
3. The options in the group are likely to change. In this case, lists that can be updated and expanded dynamically should be used.

Drop-down list boxes and combo boxes created in Oracle Forms can display up to ten items at a time. You have more control in the number of elements displayed in text lists. Limit that number to no more than ten. Each list box must be labeled like any other item on the window.

If the list is very long, and users will search it frequently, consider adding auto-restriction capabilities that filter the possible matches as users type the element label in a text field. Excellent examples of lists with these features are Forms List of Values dialog box and the MS Windows Help search utility.

14.6 CONTROLS IN THE MRD APPLICATION

This section concludes the design of the principal canvases in the MRD application by adding some of the controls discussed in this section. You can continue to work with the module you used in Sections 14.4.4 and 14.4.5.

14.6.1 VISUAL ATTRIBUTES AND PROPERTY CLASSES

As in the previous chapter, you will begin the work in this section by creating a named visual attribute and a number of property classes that will facilitate the process of setting properties of GUI controls in the MRD application.

1. Create a duplicate copy of the visual attribute MS_SANS_SERIF and name it CANVAS_OBJECT. For the new visual attribute, set the property *Background Color* to *'gray'*.
2. Create a duplicate copy of the property class TEXT_ITEM and name it PUSH_BUTTON. Delete properties *Bevel*, *Rendered*, and *Query Length*. Set

Item Type to *'Button'*; add property *Width* and set it to *'60'*; set *Height* to *'15'*; set *Item Displayed* to *'1'*; set *Visual Attribute Name* to *'CANVAS_OBJECT'*; set *Mouse Navigate* to *'False'*; add property *Iconic* and set it to *'False'*; and, finally, add property *Default Button* and set it to *'False'*.

3. Create a duplicate copy of the property class TEXT_ITEM and name it CHECK_BOX. Delete properties *Bevel* and *Rendered*. Set *Item Type* to *'Check Box'*; add property *Width* and set it to *'60'*; set property *Height* to *'10'*; set *Visual Attribute Name* to *'CANVAS_OBJECT'*; set *Mouse Navigate* to *'False'*; add property *Checked Value* and set it to *'Y'*; add property *Unchecked Value* and leave it unset; add property *Check Box Other Values* and set it to *'Not Allowed'*.

4. Create a new property class and name it RADIO_BUTTON. Add property *Displayed* and set it to *'True'*; add property *Width* and set it to *'60'*; add property *Height* and set it to *'10'*; add property *Visual Attribute Name* and set it to *'CANVAS_OBJECT'*; add property *Enabled* and set it to *'True'*.

14.6.2 CONTROLS IN CANVAS CUSTOMER

Display the canvas CUSTOMER in the Layout Editor.

First, change the item STATUS into a drop-down list box. Display its properties in a Properties Window and follow these steps:

1. Set the property *Class* for STATUS to *'DROP_DOWN_LIST'*.
2. Set *Width* to *'60'*.
3. Double-click the *List Elements* property and enter the following list elements: **Active**, **Good Credit**, and **Bad Credit**. The list item values should be **A**, **G**, and **B**, respectively.
4. Set the *Default Value* property to *'A'* or *'Active'*.

Now, change the *Item Type* of GENDER from *'Text Item'* to *'Radio Group'*. You will see that it will disappear from the canvas:

1. Use the Radio Button tool in the Layout Editor tool palette to create a radio button approximately where GENDER was located. The Radio Group dialog box will appear (see Figure 14.7).
2. Click OK to add the new radio button to Gender radio group.
3. Insert the properties of this radio button from the property class RADIO_BUTTON. Set the *Name* and *Label* properties of this radio group to *'Male'*; set *Value* to *'M'*.
4. Repeat Steps 1–3 to create the radio button FEMALE. Set *Value* for this button to *'F'*.

FIGURE 14.7 Radio Group dialog box.

5. Repeat Steps 1–3 to create the radio button UNKNOWN (in the sense that data is not available). Leave the property *Value* for this button unset.

6. Group and align vertically the radio buttons. Create a rectangle box around them and place the text label Gender on top of it. For the rectangle set Fill Color to No Fill, Line Color to black, and Bevel to Inset. For the text label set Fill Color to gray, Line Color to No Line, and font to MS Sans Serif, bold, size eight.

At this point, the radio group should look like this:

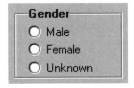

The items MYSTERY, COMEDY, DRAMA, and FOREIGN will all be implemented as check boxes. Select them all, and select Tools I Properties... from the Designer menu to display their Properties Window.

1. Inherit the properties of the selected items from the class CHECK_ITEM.

2. Delete the existing text labels to the left of the check boxes as they are no longer needed.

3. Align the check boxes vertically, create a rectangle box around them and place the text label Preferences on top of it. For the rectangle set Fill Color to No Fill, Line Color to black, and Bevel to Inset. For the text label set Fill Color to gray, Line Color to No Line, and font to MS Sans Serif, bold, size eight.

The check boxes in the Layout Editor should look like this:

Align vertically and set the widths of Customer ID, Status, Gender radio group, and Preferences check box group to minimize the vertical margins.

Now use the Push Button icon ▣ from the toolbar to create five push buttons in the upper right corner of the canvas.

1. Name the buttons COMMIT_FORM, CLOSE, MOVIE, RENTAL, and HELP.
2. Inherit their properties from the class PUSH_BUTTON.
3. Set their labels to Save, Close, Movie..., Rental..., and Help..., respectively; set the *Access Key* property to the initial letter of each button, except for COMMIT_FORM; set *Default Button* to *'True'* for button COMMIT_FORM.
4. Align the buttons vertically. Group COMMIT_FORM and CLOSE together; MOVIE and RENTAL together.

When you are finished, the buttons should look like this:

Now you are ready to wrap things up with the CUSTOMER block:

1. Create a rectangle box that separates the text items and other controls of the block from the push buttons.
2. For the rectangle, set Fill Color to No Fill, Line Color to Black, and Bevel to Raised.

3. Reduce the dimensions of the canvas to just a few pixels larger than the area occupied by the text items and controls of the CUSTOMER block.
4. Choose View | Show View from the menu to display the view and set it to the same size as the canvas.
5. In the Object Navigator resequence the tab order of items to reflect the flow of data on the screen.

Now the canvas CUSTOMER should look like Figure 14.8. Save the module before moving to the next section.

14.6.3 CONTROLS IN CANVAS MOVIE

Open the canvas MOVIE in the Layout Editor. In the block MOVIE, you will use the property class UPDATEABLE_COMBO to set the following items as combo boxes that expand dynamically during the session: DIRECTOR, PRODUCER, ACTOR, ACTRESS, and COMPANY.

1. Select these items in the Layout Editor or the Object Navigator.
2. Select Tool | Properties... from the Designer menu to pen a Properties Window for the selection.
3. Set the *Class* property to '*UPDATEABE_COMBO*'.

As said earlier, Forms will not be able to initialize the lists at runtime if no elements are defined for them in the Designer. Therefore, you must enter at least one

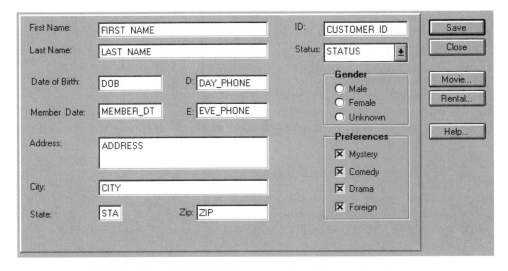

FIGURE 14.8 CUSTOMER canvas with all the controls in place.

element in the List Item Element dialog box for each of the above items. Follow the guidelines provided in Section 14.4.4 to specify a list element for these items.

Convert items RATING in the block MOVIE and STATUS in the block TAPE from text items to drop-down list boxes using the property class DROP–DOWN_LIST. Populate the lists as follows:

1. RATING should have the following list elements: NR, PG-13, R, and NC-17. The list item values will be 1, 2, 3, and 4, respectively. The properties *Default Value* and *Other Values* are '2'.
2. STATUS in the block TAPE should have the following list elements: Available, Rented, and Returned. The list item values will be A, R, and T, respectively. Its *Default Value* and *Other Values* properties are A.
3. In the Layout Editor, expand the lists, so that their elements are fully visible at runtime.

Convert STATUS item in the block MOVIE to a check box item using the property class CHECK_BOX. Set its properties as follows:

1. Set *Label* to '*Available*'.
2. Set *Checked Value* and *Default Value* to '*A*', and *Unchecked Value* to '*N*'.
3. In the Layout Editor, delete the old text label, and expand the check box until the whole label is visible.

Now create a rectangle box around the block TAPE and place the text label **Tapes for Movies** on top of it. For the rectangle set Fill Color to No Fill, Line Color to black, and Bevel to Inset. For the text label set Fill Color to gray, Line Color to No Line, and font to MS Sans Serif, bold, size eight.

In a similar fashion as in block CUSTOMER, create five push buttons in block MOVIE. These buttons should be aligned horizontally, as in Figure 14.9. Create a rectangular box to separate the items and controls from the push buttons on canvas MOVIE. Set the Bevel property of this box to raised. Adjust the size of the canvas and the view to the working area of the MOVIE canvas. As a last step, arrange the tab order of items in block MOVIE to reflect the screen layout. At this point, the canvas MOVIE should look like Figure 14.9.

14.6.4 CONTROLS IN CANVAS RENTAL

The only controls that will be added to the canvas RENTAL are horizontal push buttons, similar to the ones you added on canvas MOVIE. You can use the property class PUSH_BUTTON to create the buttons in block RENTAL or copy, paste, and modify the buttons created in the previous section following these steps:

1. In the Object Navigator, expand block MOVIE, select the five push button items, and copy them.

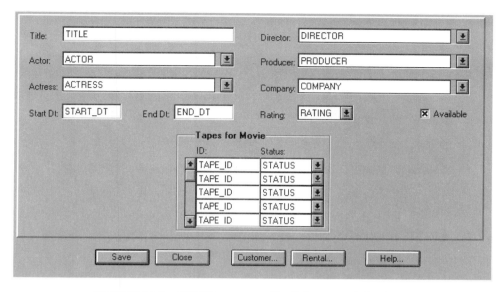

FIGURE 14.9 MOVIE canvas with all the controls in place.

2. Navigate to the Items node under RENTAL block, and paste the buttons. The new buttons, being a copy of the old ones, will be created on the canvas MOVIE.

3. With the new buttons in the RENTAL block still selected, choose Tools | Properties from the menu, and set the *Canvas* property to '*RENTAL*'.

4. Display the canvas RENTAL in the Layout Editor and move the buttons down, under the RENTAL block.

5. Select the button currently labeled Rental..., and set its *Name* to '*Movie*', and *Label* to '*Movie...*', and *Access Key* to '*M*'.

Create in this canvas a rectangle with the same properties as in the other canvases to visually divide text items from push buttons. At the end, the RENTAL canvas should look like Figure 14.10.

14.7 SUMMARY

This chapter provides information about Oracle Forms GUI controls, their properties, and functionality. Important concepts in this chapter are listed here:

❑ Push buttons
   ❑ Functional properties of push buttons
   ❑ Events of push buttons

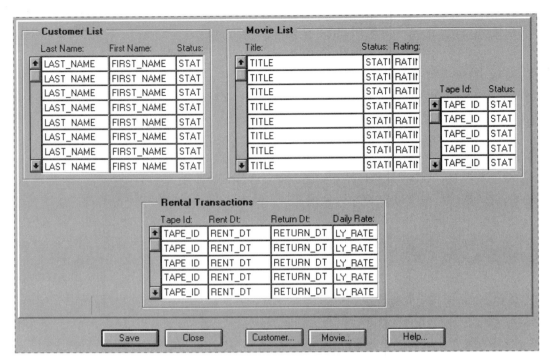

FIGURE 14.10   RENTAL canvas with all the controls in place.

- ❏ Radio groups and radio buttons
  - ❏ Properties of radio groups and radio buttons
  - ❏ Events of radio groups
- ❏ Check boxes
  - ❏ Properties of check boxes
  - ❏ Events of check boxes
- ❏ List boxes
  - ❏ Types of lists
  - ❏ Setting list properties at design time
  - ❏ Events of lists
  - ❏ Manipulating lists programmatically
  - ❏ Making the code object-independent
- ❏ GUI guidelines for controls
  - ❏ Push buttons
  - ❏ Radio buttons and check boxes
  - ❏ Lists

WINDOWS AND DIALOG BOXES

"The windows of my soul I throw
Wide open to the sun."
—John Greenleaf Whittier

All the data entry and interface items with which users interact during the lifetime of a GUI application are placed in windows. In MDI applications such as the ones you develop with Oracle Forms, multiple windows can be available, open, and visible at any time. In addition, several dialog boxes may be used to get and display data or perform specific actions.

In Oracle Forms, items and controls are placed on canvases, which then in turn are attached to windows and, through them, displayed to users at runtime. This chapter discusses the types and properties of windows, dialog boxes, canvases, and a special type of built-in dialog boxes, the alerts.

15.1 PROPERTIES OF WINDOWS

Each window has the fundamental properties that every other object enjoys in Oracle Forms such as *Name, Class, Comment,* and *Reference Information.* When a window object is created in the Object Navigator, the Designer assigns it a default name. This name should be set to a more meaningful one, that expresses the window's main functionality. You can rename a window like any other object in the Navigator, or in the Properties Window, by setting its *Name* property. The *Class* property can be set to the name of an existing property class in order to inherit the properties of the window from those of the class. Later in this chapter you will create two property classes based on the properties of windows that you can use to implement MDI sheets and dialog boxes. The *Comment* property may be used by programmers to document the window object on-line. The *Reference Information* property is available only if the window references a window in another module. It contains information about the source reference object, similar to that shown in Figure 13.2 for the case of items.

Windows have several properties that govern the way they are presented to users during the execution of the application. These properties can be set in the Designer's Properties Window for the window object. They can also be set programmatically, using the Forms built-in SET_WINDOWS_PROPERTY. Figure 15.1 represents a typical window developed in Oracle Forms.

A great number of properties for a window at runtime can be changed directly by the users through basic and standard Windows actions such as clicking the Minimize and Maximize icons, selecting from or double-clicking the windows control menu, dragging and positioning the window on the screen, or by dragging its borders and corners until the window reaches a desired size.

The properties of windows are grouped in three major categories: **Display, Functional,** and **GUI Hints.** Not all the properties that you may see in the Properties Window apply to window objects. For example, in the **Display** properties group, you can see properties related to visual attributes such as *Visual Attribute Name, Font Name,* and *Font Size.* In MS Windows and Macintosh environments,

Control Menu Icon

Title Bar

Minimize and Maximize Icons

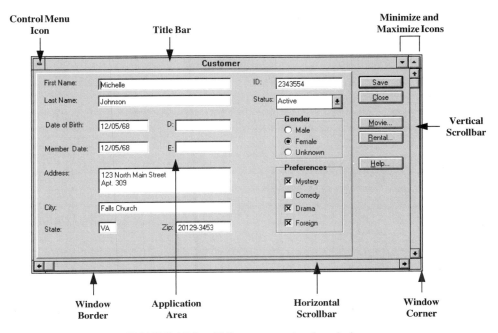

Vertical Scrollbar

Window Border

Application Area

Horizontal Scrollbar

Window Corner

FIGURE 15.1 GUI components of a window.

these properties do not have any meaning in the case of windows, and you can ignore them. The same can be said for the property *Bevel*. The following section will discuss the most important properties of windows, and how you can set them in the Designer.

15.1.1 SETTING WINDOWS PROPERTIES IN THE DESIGNER

Each window has a title bar which summarizes the functionality or the data displayed in the windows workarea. By default, when a window is created, both its name and title are set to generic strings like WINDOW0. You can set the title bar of a window by entering a string of characters in the *Title* property. If you do not provide an explicit title for the window, Forms will use its name to fill the contents of the title bar.

The position of the window is defined by the X and Y coordinates of its upper left-hand corner. In the Designer, you can set the *X Position* and *Y Position* properties to specify where on the screen the window should be displayed when users access it for the first time. After the window is displayed on the screen, users can move it around by dragging the window's title bar or by choosing the Move item from its control menu ▭. This is a standard feature of every application and should not be repressed. However, if you want to prevent users from moving the window, set the *Moveable* property in the **GUI Hints** group to *'False'*. This setting will also remove the Move item from the control menu of the window.

The initial size of the window can be set by providing values for the *Width* and *Height* properties. It is acceptable and to be expected that users will resize the window by dragging any of its borders or corners, or by selecting the Size menu item from the window's control menu ⊟. When the size of the window is reduced, it is probable that the application workarea may not be able to fit entirely inside the window. It is very important that you equip these windows with vertical and horizontal scroll bars so that users can view the hidden parts of the workarea. To do this, set the *Horizontal Scroll Bar* and *Vertical Scroll Bar* properties to *'True'*. They are both members of the **Functional** group.

If you do not want the users to be able to resize the window, set the *Fixed Size* property to *'True'*. This will hide the item Size from the control menu. The borders and the corners of the window will also disappear.

In the Designer you can also specify whether or not users will be able to change the state of the window at runtime. A window can be in one of three states: Normal, Minimized, or Maximized. The position and size of a window in Normal state are defined by the properties *X Position, Y Position, Width,* and *Height*, as described above. This is the default state in which a window is displayed. The window shown in Figure 15.1 is in Normal state.

At runtime, users can minimize a normal window by clicking the Minimize icon ⊡ or by choosing Minimize from the control menu ⊟. When the window is minimized, it is displayed in the form of an icon. For this reason, the terms "Minimize" and "Iconify" are used interchangeably when speaking about windows. Once in Minimized state, the window can be restored to its Normal state by double-clicking its icon, or by choosing Restore from the control menu. Users can also maximize the window by selecting Maximize from the control menu.

A window in Normal state can be maximized by clicking the Maximize icon ▣ or choosing Maximize from the control menu ⊟. In this state the Minimize

---

Note

By default, the *Horizontal Scroll Bar* and *Vertical Scroll Bar* properties of windows in Oracle Forms are set to *'False'*. In order to avoid the problem described above, you must change these settings to *'True'* for any window that will be resizable. You can still keep the default settings if the window will not be resizable, and its dimensions are such that all the data items and controls of the window are visible.

and Maximize icons are replaced by the Restore icon ⬧. The maximized window can be set to the Normal state by clicking the restore button, or by selecting Restore from the window's control menu. To minimize a window in Maximized state, choose Minimize from the control menu of the window.

The ability of users to minimize and maximize windows in Oracle Forms is controlled by the *Iconifiable* and *Zoomable* properties, respectively.

By default, the property *Iconifiable* is set to *'True'*, which means that users can minimize the window at runtime. When the window is iconifiable, it is always good to attach an icon to the window and a title that will be displayed under this icon. Both the title and the icon should represent the functionality of the window. They are defined by setting the *Icon Name* and *Icon Title* properties of the window. If these properties are not set explicitly, when this window is minimized, Oracle Forms will use its Runtime icon ⬛, and the title bar of the window as visual identifiers of the window in the desktop.

When setting the *Icon Name* property of a window you should keep in mind the same guidelines presented in Chapter 14 for iconic push buttons:

1. Enter only the name of the icon file, for example CUSTOMER, without the path or the extension .ICO.
2. The icon file must be in one of the directories specified in the TK21_ICONS environment variable.

By setting the *Iconifiable* property to *'False'*, you will not allow users to minimize the window. In this case, the window will not contain a Minimize icon, and its control menu will not have the Minimize item.

The default setting of the *Zoomable* property is *'True'*, which allows users to set their windows to Maximized state. If you set it to *'False'*, the maximize icon in the upper right-hand corner of the window and the Maximize item in the control menu will not appear.

The *Closeable* property is a little different from the other properties discussed in this section. Setting it to *'False'* will remove the ability to close the window with any of the standard MS Windows commands: double-clicking the window's control menu box ⬛, or pressing CTRL+F4 from the keyboard. However, setting the property to *'True'* will not enable your users to close the window with the above commands, either.

In MS Windows, a window is an object that communicates with the environment through messages. When users issue any of the two commands mentioned above, they send a message to the window that should cause it to close. If *Closeable* property is set to *'False'*, this message is not part of the messages recognized by the window. Therefore, it causes no events to occur. If the property is set to *'True'*, the message is recognized by the window, and causes the event CloseWindow. In Oracle Forms, any actions that should be taken when this event occurs must be placed in the WHEN-WINDOW-CLOSED trigger. In order to close the window, you must place PL/SQL statements that perform this or any other actions associated with closing the window. The following section shows an example of how to do this.

The **Functional** group of properties for windows contains other properties, besides the ones discussed in this section. Their meaning is related with the types of windows that can be used in Oracle Forms application. The discussion about them will be postponed until Sections 15.2.2 and 15.2.4.

15.1.2 CONTROLLING WINDOWS PROGRAMMATICALLY

As it is the case with other Oracle Forms objects, the properties of windows can be accessed and modified at runtime, using several built-in procedures and functions. The most important players in this process are the functions FIND_WINDOW, ID_NULL, GET_WINDOW_PROPERTY, and the procedure SET_WINDOW_PROPERTY.

FIND_WINDOW is used to retrieve the internal ID of a window, based on its name. The value that this function returns must be stored in a variable of type WINDOW. The function ID_NULL checks for the existence of a window based on its internal ID. The function GET_WINDOW_PROPERTY retrieves the current setting for Display properties discussed in the previous section such as title, position, and dimensions of the window. It can also be used to retrieve the current state of the window. The procedure SET_WINDOW_PROPERTY is used to set the same properties, except for the windows title.

Figure 15.2 shows a generic PL/SQL procedure that, with little modifications, can be used to retrieve or set the properties of a window object.

There is one property of windows that exists only at runtime. This is the *VISIBLE* property and it can be used to hide or display the window programmatically. If a window is not opened yet by the application, its *VISIBLE* property is set to *'False'*. If you activate the application's Window menu, the title of the window does not appear under the list of currently open windows. But if the window has already been accessed by the application, its *VISIBLE* property is set to *'True'*, and its title appears in the Window menu.

To display a window, you need to set its *VISIBLE* property to *'True'*. To close it, set the same property to *'False'*. The generic procedure displayed in Figure 15.2 can be used for this purpose. Oracle Forms provides you with two additional built-in procedures that can be used for the same purpose. They are called SHOW_WINDOW and HIDE_WINDOW.

The companion disk that comes with this book includes the module WINDYNM.FMB to demonstrate the process of dynamically showing and hiding windows in Forms. Load this application in the Designer and run it. Initially, you will see a toolbar with four push buttons in it. If you click one of the buttons, for example the one labeled First..., a window with the same name in the title bar will appear (see Figure 15.3).

```
PROCEDURE Generic_Window_Routine (window_name VARCHAR2) IS
  window_id        WINDOW;
  property_setting VARCHAR2(80);
  Window_Not_Found EXCEPTION;
BEGIN
  /* FIND_WINDOW returns the appropriate window ID.  */
  window_id := FIND_WINDOW(window_name);
  IF ID_NULL(window_id) THEN
    RAISE Window_Not_Found;
  END IF;
  /* If control comes here, window ID exists.   */
  /* PROPERTY_NAME can be POSITION, WINDOW_SIZE, etc. */
  property_setting := GET_WINDOW_PROPERTY(window_id,
                      PROPERTY_NAME);

  /* Additional processing may occur here   */

  /* PROPERTY_NAME can be POSITION, WINDOW_SIZE, etc. */
  SET_WINDOW_PROPERTY(window_id, PROPERTY_NAME,
                      property_setting);

EXCEPTION
  WHEN Window_Not_Found THEN
    MESSAGE('Window '||window_name||' does not exist.');
    RAISE FORM_TRIGGER_FAILURE;
  WHEN OTHERS THEN
    MESSAGE('Internal error occurred.');
    RAISE FORM_TRIGGER_FAILURE;
END Generic_Window_Routine;
```

FIGURE 15.2 Template program unit to access and modify properties of windows at Runtime.

Up to three windows can be opened in the application. The first two windows contain two push buttons each. The Close button closes the window in both cases. The other buttons display the window with the same title as the button's label. The third window serves to demonstrate the fact that you can display a window even if there are no data items or controls in it.

This application uses two procedures that take advantage of the built-ins SHOW_WINDOW and HIDE_WINDOW. The first procedure, called

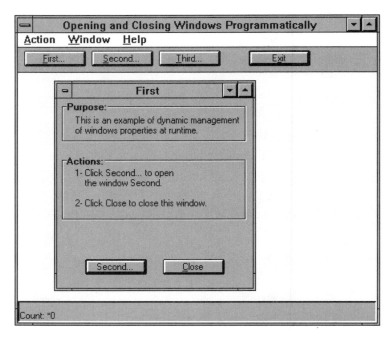

FIGURE 15.3   Hiding and displaying windows programmatically.

Open_Window, takes as parameter the window name, ensures that this window exists, and then displays it. Figure 15.4 shows the contents of this function.

The procedure Close_Window takes as input parameter the name of the window to close, and after it makes sure that the window exists and is currently visible, it closes it. The contents of this procedure are very similar to the procedure shown in Figure 15.4. The only difference is that the latter uses the built-in HIDE_WINDOW.

Open_Window and Close_Window reduce to just one line the contents of WHEN-BUTTON-PRESSED triggers for the push buttons in this application. The trigger for the button Close in the window FIRST, for example, is Close_Window('FIRST'). The statement in the trigger attached to any of the push buttons labeled Second is Open_Window('SECOND').

In Oracle Forms, displaying a window does not necessarily mean that the focus of the application will move to that window. Setting the *VISIBLE* property to *'True'* or using the procedure SHOW_WINDOW does not raise the window on top of the stack of other open windows if the focus of Oracle Forms is on an item in one of these windows. In order to better understand this, you can use the module WINDYNM1.FMB provided in the companion disk. This module is identical to WINDYNM.FMB except for an additional text item in block FIRST. (This mod-

```
PROCEDURE Open_Window (window_name VARCHAR2) IS
  window_id        WINDOW;
  Window_Not_Found EXCEPTION;

BEGIN
  window_id := FIND_WINDOW(window_name);
  IF ID_NULL(window_id) THEN
    RAISE Window_Not_Found;
  END IF;

  SHOW_WINDOW(window_id);

EXCEPTION
  WHEN Window_Not_Found THEN
    MESSAGE('Window '||window_name||' does not exist.');
    RAISE FORM_TRIGGER_FAILURE;
  WHEN OTHERS THEN
    MESSAGE('Internal error occurred in Open_Window.');
    RAISE FORM_TRIGGER_FAILURE;
END Open_Window;
```

FIGURE 15.4 Showing a window dynamically.

ule is also closer to what you will eventually develop because it contains data items and control items in several windows.)

1. Run the WINDYNM1.FMB module.
2. Open the windows FIRST and SECOND by clicking the respective buttons in the toolbar.
3. Click inside item Focus. This action places the focus of Oracle Forms in an item in block FIRST.

At this point, clicking the button Second does not activate the corresponding window anymore—the title bar of this window is not highlighted. To make this fact more noticeable, resize the window FIRST so that it completely covers the window SECOND. Now, clicking the button Second has no visual effect because the window SECOND will not appear on top of FIRST as you would expect. The only way to activate window SECOND in this situation is to select its title from this list of windows currently open maintained by the Window menu. Thus, in order to have a full functional activation of the window, you must not only set its *VISIBLE* property to *'True'*, but also navigate to a navigable item inside of it.

Another side of this discussion is to see what happens if you close the window FIRST after placing the focus of Forms on the item Focus.

Note

The discussion and the examples in this section may help you understand a little better the concept of the focus in Oracle Forms. You can think of the focus as a state in which Forms sits on an item and is ready for input.

Navigating to an item in a window will place the focus of the form on the item, activate the window, and raise it on top of the stack of other open windows. As long as the focus is in an item of the window, the window will always be the functionally active window. You can show other windows, but they will not be active unless the focus moves away from the current window either as a result of a mouse-click or programmatic statements such as GO_BLOCK or GO_ITEM.

Similarly, you cannot hide or close the window if the focus continues to be an item in that window. The only way to safely hide the window is to move the focus of Oracle Forms away first and then set its *Visible* Property to '*False*', or call the procedure HIDE_WINDOW.

---

1. Click the Close button in window FIRST. The window will be hidden from view.
2. Display either window SECOND or THIRD by clicking the appropriate button in the toolbar.

Contrary to what you expect, the window FIRST appears and the item where the focus was before closing it is selected.

15.1.3 EVENTS OF WINDOWS

There are four events that are recognized by windows in Oracle Forms. These are ActivateWindow, DeactivateWindow, ResizeWindow, and CloseWindow.

The ActivateWindow event occurs when the window becomes the application's active window. In response to this event, Forms fires the trigger WHEN-WINDOW-ACTIVATED. As explained earlier, activating a window does not necessarily mean navigating to it. In order to place the focus on the window, you must navigate to an item there.

If a window is already active and there is an attempt to activate another window, the event DeactivateWindow occurs in the first window. This event causes the trigger WHEN-WINDOW-DEACTIVATED to fire.

If a window is resized, either because users drag its borders or corners, or because its *Width* and *Height* properties are set programmatically, the event ResizeWindow occurs. As a result of this event, the trigger WHEN-WINDOW-RESIZE will fire. If the property *Fixed Size* of the window is set to '*False*', the event ResizeWindow cannot occur.

Finally, when users double-click the control menu box ▣, or press CTRL+F4 from the keyboard, the event CloseWindow occurs. For this event to happen, the window must have its *Closeable* property set to '*True*'. This event fires the trigger WHEN-WINDOW-CLOSED.

The name of the window for which the last of these events occurred is stored in the system variable SYSTEM.EVENT_WINDOW. Because windows and their events are not related functionally to blocks or items, the four triggers described above are always defined as form-level triggers.

You can find some examples of using these triggers in the module WINDYNM.FMB. Run this module and after selecting each window try to resize it. You will notice that although the borders or corners of the windows can be dragged to any size, when the mouse is released, instead of being resized, they return to the original size. The steps to implement this functionality are as follows:

1. Declare two global variables GLOBAL.Win_Width and GLOBAL.Win_Height in a form-level PRE-FORM trigger. They will hold the dimensions of a window.

2. In the trigger WHEN-WINDOW-ACTIVATED, use the procedure Get_Window_Size to store the dimensions of the current window in the global variables. The name of the current window is stored in SYSTEM.EVENT_WINDOW variable.

3. In the trigger WHEN-WINDOW-RESIZE, use the procedure Set_Window_Size to set the resized window to its original dimensions that were stored in the global variables in the previous step. Since this trigger will fire when the users complete the resizing action, they will be able to drag the window's borders and corners, but as soon as they release the mouse button, the window will snap to its original position.

If you take a look at the contents of the procedures Get_Window_Size and Set_Window_Size, you will see that they are straightforward examples of how to use the function GET_WINDOW_PROPERTY, and the procedure SET_WINDOW_PROPERTY.

There is, however, a possibility to resize the windows in this application. Here is an example of how to do this:

1. Run the module WINDYNM.FMB, and open the window FIRST.

2. Open the window THIRD. This window is now active while window FIRST is deactivated.

Note

The procedure RESIZE_WINDOW can be used as an alternative to SET_WINDOW_PROPERTY to set the dimensions of an window. Thus the statements:

```
SET_WINDOW_PROPERTY(window_id, WIDTH, win_width);
SET_WINDOW_PROPERTY(window_id, HEIGHT, win_height);
```

are equivalent to

```
RESIZE_WINDOW(window_id, win_width, win_height);
```

---

3. Move the mouse pointer over the border of the window FIRST.
4. When the mouse pointer changes shape to a resizing indicator, press the button, drag the border to a new position, and release the mouse button.

You will see that the window will not return to its original size. What is happening here?

In the scenario above, you would expect the window SECOND to be deactivated first, then the window FIRST to be activated, and, finally, the window FIRST to be resized. This is the sequence of triggers fired, but the events do not seem to follow this sequence too closely. During the actions described above, the window FIRST gets resized before anything else happens. Then, the window SECOND is deactivated, and the window FIRST is activated. At this point, the trigger WHEN-WINDOW-ACTIVATED is fired. This trigger records the new dimensions of the window assuming they are the original ones. Finally, the WHEN-WINDOW-RESIZED trigger is executed with no practical effect on the window. There is no reason for despair though, because this is the default behavior of Windows. You can try it with any MDI application and will see that, in fact, the window is resized first and then activated.

15.2 DEVELOPING MDI APPLICATIONS WITH ORACLE FORMS

Multiple Document Interface (MDI) applications are developed following the paradigm and standards established by widely successful software packages such as MS Word and Excel. The paradigm applies only to the MS Windows and Macintosh environments.

An MDI application allows users to open and maintain ready-for-use multiple windows at any one time. Each window corresponds to a specific task or functional part of the application. For example, in the MRD application, a window could be used for entering and editing data about customers, another one for movies and tapes received by the store, and yet another one to record the rental transactions that occur.

There are four basic types of windows in a MDI application: the MDI frame, MDI sheets, dialog boxes, and message boxes. The following sections explain the functionality of each type of window and how to obtain it in Oracle Forms.

15.2.1 MDI FRAME WINDOW

The MDI frame is often called the application window, because it is the initial window that is opened when the application is launched. All the other components of the application will be either attached to or placed inside the MDI frame. Figure 15.5 shows the main components of the MDI frame window.

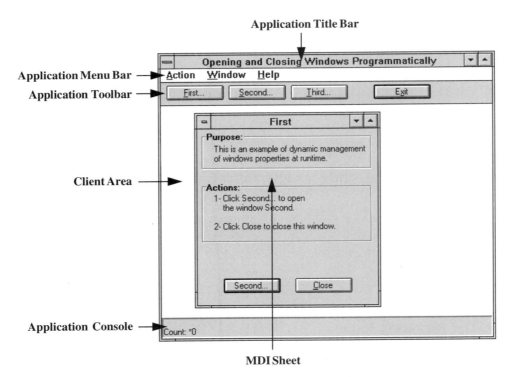

FIGURE 15.5 Components of the MDI frame.

> **Note**
>
> In environments or applications that do not follow the MDI paradigm, toolbars can be attached to any window. Oracle Forms allows you to attach toolbars to windows by setting the properties *Vertical Toolbar* or *Horizontal Toolbar* to the names of the desired toolbars.

The title bar of the MDI frame window displays the name of the application. Under the title bar, there is the application menu. Depending on the functionality of the application, several menus may be used, but all of them are attached to the MDI frame. The MDI frame serves as a placeholder for the application's toolbars as well. Horizontal toolbars go under the menu; vertical toolbars are attached along the MDI frame's left margin.

The MDI frame also contains a console, or message bar, at the bottom, which is used to display micro-help messages and other useful processing information. The area limited by the MDI frame borders, the application's console, and its toolbar or menu is called the application's client area. It is here that all the other windows of the application will be displayed. The size of the MDI frame window directly defines the size of the client workarea.

The MDI frame enjoys all the generic properties that any window has. In particular, you can specify its title, position, size, and state. Users at runtime can change the position, size, and state of the window. However, in Oracle Forms, the MDI frame windows is not an object that you can access, or one whose properties you can set in the Designer. You need to use the built-in constructs discussed in Section 15.1.2 to set these properties at runtime. In order to address the MDI frame object, you must use the internally defined constant FORMS_MDI_WINDOW. Figure 15.6 shows excerpts from the trigger WHEN-NEW-FORM-INSTANCE of module WINDYNM1.FMB.

The first line sets the title of the window to the string enclosed in the single quotes. The second line sets the size of the window to the specified arguments (in

```
SET_WINDOW_PROPERTY(FORMS_MDI_WINDOW, TITLE,
                    'Opening and Closing Windows
Programmatically');
SET_WINDOW_PROPERTY(FORMS_MDI_WINDOW, WINDOW_SIZE, 570, 220);
```

FIGURE 15.6   Setting the properties of the MDI frame window.

points). The following statements can be used to set the initial position of the MDI frame or its state, respectively:

a) SET_WINDOW_PROPERTY (FORMS_MDI_WINDOW, POSITION, 5, 5); or
b) SET_WINDOW_PROPERTY (FORMS_MDI_WINDOW, WINDOW_STATE, MAXIMIZED);

These are the only properties you can change in a MDI frame. Given its special purpose in the application, other properties that you would normally set for a window cannot be changed. Specifically, the MDI frame can always be moved, resized, minimized, maximized, restored, or closed, and it always displays scroll-bars if needed. The only actions that affect this window are double-clicking its control menu box ▣, or pressing ALT+F4. Both these actions cause the event CloseApplication to occur. This event always invokes the method EXIT_FORM, which terminates the application. Chapter 17, which discusses the process of creating menus and toolbars for an application, will explain how to attach them to the MDI frame window.

15.2.2 MDI SHEETS

MDI sheets are where most of the life of an application is spent and where most of its functionality is located. These windows can be opened as a result of users choosing options from the menu or the toolbar, or clicking controls in other windows.

There are several characteristics that a window must have in order to be considered a MDI sheet:

1. First and foremost, the MDI sheet can never appear outside the MDI frame client area. All the sizing and moving actions initiated by users or programmatically by the application's event must not cause the window to leave this area, even if it has to be hidden partially or completely from the view.
2. When the window is minimized, its icon must be placed inside the client area of the MDI frame.
3. When the window is maximized, it should be maximized to the full size of the MDI frame window. Its title should appear in parentheses appended to the application's title.
4. When the MDI sheet is initially opened, the application's focus must also navigate to one navigable item on the window, if one exists.
5. While the MDI sheet remains open, its title should always appear in the Window menu of your application. Users can activate the window by picking it from the list of currently open windows.

6. The MDI sheet should be closed if, and only if, an explicit Close message is sent to the window by the users or the application. Simply deactivating the window should not close it.

15.2.3 IMPLEMENTING MDI SHEETS

The default windows created in Oracle Forms are very close to being MDI sheet type of windows. The settings they have fulfill almost all the requirements presented above. However, their functionality must be enhanced in order to avoid the idiosyncrasies pointed out in Section 15.1.2 and to give them the full features of MDI sheets.

In particular, the following things must be added programmatically:

1. When the window is opened, Forms must navigate to a navigable item inside the window, if one exits.
2. When the window is closed, Forms must first navigate to an item that is outside the window being closed. Then, the *VISIBLE* property of this window must be set to *'False'*, thus effectively closing the window.

In order to help you in the process of creating standard MDI sheets, the companion disk includes a module called WINPROPS.FMB. There are several objects in this module that you can use to implement MDI sheets in your applications:

❑ Property class MDI_SHEET. You can use this class to inherit properties for any window that will be a MDI sheet window. The properties included in the class and their settings are shown in Figure 15.7.

For individual windows, you may override some of these properties such as *Title*, *View*, *Icon Name*, and *Icon Title*. However, in order to obtain the MDI sheet functionality in your window, you must keep the rest of the settings intact, especially those for the properties *Window Style*, *Modal*, and *Remove on Exit*. Setting the *Window Style* to *'Document'* will ensure that the windows will be displayed within the MDI frame client area. Setting the *Modal* property to *'False'* will allow users to perform other actions in the application besides the ones contained in the window. Setting the *Remove on Exit* to *'False'* will not hide the window if the users activate another window.

Among other settings that you should consider preserving for your MDI sheets are the *GUI Hints* properties. In particular, *Closeable*, *Iconifiable*, *Moveable*, and *Zoomable* should be set to *'True'*, thus allowing users to close, minimize, maximize, and move the window at Runtime. At the same time, do not forget to specify settings for the properties *Icon Title* and *Icon Name* for each individual MDI sheet.

You should also consider allowing users to resize the window by keeping the property *Fixed Size* set to *'False'*. In conjunction with this setting,

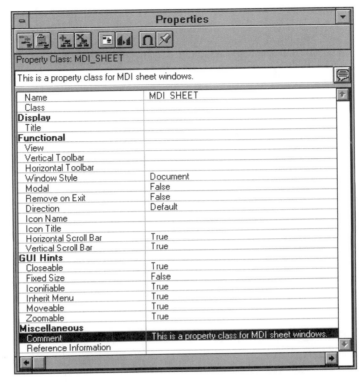

FIGURE 15.7   Properties class for MDI sheet windows.

the properties *Horizontal Scroll Bar* and *Vertical Scroll Bar* must be set to *'True'*. This way, users will be able to scroll to hidden parts of your application if they reduce the size of the window.

❏ *Form-level trigger* PRE-FORM. This trigger declares the global variable GLOBAL.Home_Item and assigns it the item name returned by the function Get_Home_Item (explained next). You can override the setting with the name

---

Note

Two other properties whose setting you should consider preserving are *Horizontal Toolbar* and *Vertical Toolbar*. In MDI applications, toolbars are always attached to the MDI frame, therefore, for MDI sheets, both these properties must be set to NULL.

of any item in the module that you choose to be the home item. Since Forms needs to navigate to this item, make sure its *Navigable* property is '*True*'.

The home item is a single unified point where Forms will place the focus each time an MDI sheet is closed. As said earlier, Forms cannot hide a window if an item on it has the focus. Therefore the home item must be in a window that will remain open throughout the application's life. This could be an MDI sheet that, based on the application's design, will not be closed by the users. An example of such a window is the Object Navigator in the Oracle Forms Designer. However, the ideal place for a home item would be the MDI frame, which is available as long as the application is running. Items cannot be placed directly on the MDI frame, but they can be arranged on a toolbar, which in turn is attached to the MDI frame. Therefore, to obtain the highest flexibility, you must create a toolbar, and use one of the items there as the home item. This should not be viewed as a restriction, since every serious GUI application today must have a toolbar with it.

❑ Function **Get_Home_Item**. This function returns the name of an item that will serve as home item for the application. Figure 15.8 shows the PL/SQL code for this function as implemented in module WINPROPS.FMB.

In this particular implementation, the home item is the first item of the first navigable block in the module. The call to the function GET_APPLICA-TION_PROPERTY retrieves the name of the form module. Then, the function GET_FORM_PROPERTY is used to get the name of the block where the current form will navigate to when it is initially started. Finally, GET_BLOCK_PROPERTY returns the name of the first item in that block. By convention and agreement among developers of your team, this item can be designed to be the application's home item.

```
FUNCTION Get_Home_Item RETURN VARCHAR2 IS
   home_item         VARCHAR2(80);
   form_module       VARCHAR2(80);
   first_block       VARCHAR2(80);
   last_item         VARCHAR2(80);
BEGIN
   form_module := GET_APPLICATION_PROPERTY(CURRENT_FORM_NAME);
   first_block := GET_FORM_PROPERTY(form_module,
                  FIRST_NAVIGATION_BLOCK);
   home_item   := GET_BLOCK_PROPERTY(first_block, FIRST_ITEM);

   RETURN home_item;
END;
```

FIGURE 15.8　Typical implementation of the home item.

❏ Procedure Open_Window(window_name   VARCHAR2,   block_name VARCHAR2). This procedure displays the window window_name, and then navigates to block block_name. No navigation occurs if block_name is NULL.

❏ Procedure Close_Window(window_name VARCHAR2). This procedure places the Forms focus on the application's home item and closes the window window_name.

❏ Trigger WHEN-WINDOW-CLOSE. This is the form-level trigger that is fired by the event CloseWindow. The body of this trigger contains only one line:

Close_Window(:SYSTEM.EVENT_WINDOW);

Here, Close_Window is the function described in the previous point.

In Section 15.7 you will use these objects to implement MDI sheets in the MRD application. You can use the steps discussed there to incorporate them into any other modules you will create in the future.

15.2.4 DIALOG BOXES

The purpose of dialog boxes is either to accept information from users in order to perform a specific task, or to provide them with the outcome and results of a certain action. Usually, when a dialog box is called, users must either complete or cancel the task that can be performed there. They cannot do anything else in the application until the dialog box is dismissed. However they can switch to another application and do something there. These dialog boxes are called modal dialog boxes. A typical modal dialog box is the Open dialog box that you can access by choosing File I Open... from the Designer menu.

There are also dialog boxes that allow users to perform other activities in the application, besides the ones related to the task that the dialog box carries out. These dialog boxes are known as nonmodal, or modeless dialog boxes. A typical example of modeless dialog boxes is the Search/Replace utility accessible by selecting Edit I Search/Replace... from the Oracle Forms Designer menu.

Dialog boxes can be displayed in response to a request from the users for a specific functionality. Several methods can be used to provide users with ways to express their request. The most popular methods in GUI environments are selecting menu items, clicking iconic tools in the toolbar, and clicking push buttons.

In MDI applications, the dialog boxes have the following properties:

1. Perform a specific task or function that complements the larger functionality of the application in general, or a MDI sheet in particular.

2. Cannot be minimized or maximized.

3. Can be moved outside the client area of the MDI frame. This is fundamentally different from the MDI sheets which are always bound by this frame.

4. Cannot be resized by the users.

5. Contain always at least two push buttons. The first one, when pressed, performs the primary task assigned to the dialog box. This is usually the default button for the dialog box, unless a destructive action will originate from pressing it. A generic name for this button is OK; a name that is better related to the task being performed such as Print, Save, etc., is preferable. The second button should allow users to close the dialog box without performing the task. This is usually labeled as the Cancel button. It is becoming a standard, if not a requirement, that the dialog boxes provide a Help button, in addition to the first two ones. By clicking this button, users can access context-sensitive help about the task supported by the dialog box.

15.2.5 IMPLEMENTING DIALOG BOXES

The module WINPROPS.FMB, mentioned in the previous section, contains a property class, called MDI_DIALOG_BOX, that you can use to develop your standard dialog boxes. The members of this class and their settings are shown in Figure 15.9.

FIGURE 15.9   Properties class for dialog boxes.

Note

The *Oracle Forms Reference Manual* states that when the Modal property of a window is set to '*False*', properties such as *Closeable*, *Iconifiable*, *Zoomable*, *Horizontal Scroll Bar*, and *Vertical Scroll Bar* are ignored. The window will display itself according to the settings for these properties independently of the setting of the *Modal* property.

As you can see from this figure, the property class MDI_DIALOG_BOX includes the same properties as the class MDI_SHEET. Some of these properties even have the same settings. However, given the different flavor that these two types of windows have, fundamental properties in dialog boxes have the opposite settings of MDI sheets.

In particular, what makes the difference between a dialog box and an MDI window is the *Window Style* property, which is set to '*Dialog*' for the former and to '*Document*' for the latter. The property *Modal* can be set to '*True*' to obtain a modal dialog box. For a modeless dialog box, the *Modal* property must be set to '*False*'. In the module WINPROPS.FMB you can find the property class MDI_MODE-LESS_DIALOG_BOX, which you may use whenever you will need to implement modeless dialog boxes. The properties of this class are all inherited from the class MDI_DIALOG_BOX, except for the *Modal* property, which is set to '*False*'.

In addition, the properties *Horizontal Scroll Bar* and *Vertical Scroll Bar* are set to '*False*' for dialog boxes. Usually you define the dimensions of these windows so that users do not need to scroll on hidden areas of the window. Because dialog boxes do not have scrollbars, the property *Fixed Size* must be set to '*True*'. You do not want the users to reduce the dialog box and then be unable to see some of the items in it. Finally, so that the dialog boxes cannot be minimized and maximized, the properties *Iconifiable* and *Zoomable* should be set to '*False*'.

```
IF ( mdi_width > win_width ) THEN
  x_coord := (mdi_width - win_width) / 2;
ELSE
  x_coord := 0;
END IF;
IF ( mdi_height > win_height ) THEN
  y coord := (mdi_height - win_height) / 2;
ELSE
  y_coord := 0;
END IF;
```

FIGURE 15.10 Computing coordinates of dialog boxes.

> **Note**
>
> MDI sheet windows do not need to have a navigable block on them in order to be displayed. In modules WINDYNM.FMB and WINDYNM1.FMB the window THIRD does not contain any navigable items, but you can still display it because the *Window Style* property is set to *'Document'*. If this property is set to *'Dialog'*, the window cannot be displayed unless there is a navigable item on it.

The module WINPROPS.FMB also contains the procedure Open_Dialog_ Box(window_name VARCHAR2, block_name VARCHAR2) which you can use to open dialog box windows. This procedure differs from Open_Window because it computes the position of the dialog box before displaying it and navigating to a block in that window. The computation of the coordinates is based on the dimensions of the MDI frame and those of the dialog box itself and aims at displaying the dialog box at the center of the MDI frame. The lines in Figure 15.10 excerpted from this procedure show how to compute the coordinates after these dimensions are stored in the variables mdi_width, mdi_height, win_width and win_height.

When implementing dialog boxes in Oracle Forms, you may want to follow this sequence of steps:

1. Create the block that contains the data items and controls that will be displayed in the dialog box in a separate canvas.
2. Create at least two push buttons. Their labels should be OK (or a more descriptive label) and Cancel. A Help button could be provided, especially for dialog boxes with complex functionality.
3. Attach the canvas where this block is created to its own window, and inherit the properties of this window from the property class MDI_DIALOG_BOX or MDI_MODELESS_DIALOG_BOX.
4. Create program units that will populate the data items of the dialog box. To improve performance, these routines should be invoked only when the dialog box is displayed.
5. Invoke the procedure Open_Dialog_Box from the appropriate locations in the application.
6. Attach WHEN-BUTTON-PRESSED triggers to the buttons in the dialog box.

15.2.6 MESSAGE BOXES

Message boxes are used to give users feedback about events and processes that occur in the application. It is important to keep users informed about what is happening in the application, to warn them about potentially destructive actions, or to indicate critical situations that have already occurred. A good reason to send a message to the users is also when queries or any other actions will last for a few seconds longer than what the users would normally expect.

Depending on the kind of information displayed, the messages can be classified as micro-help messages, informative, warning, and critical messages. The users can see the messages either in the message bar, in specially crafted dialog boxes, or in special Oracle Forms objects called alerts.

The built-in procedure MESSAGE is used to display messages in the message bar. This procedure takes as parameter a string of up to 200 characters. By default, when two messages are issued consecutively, Forms will display the first one in an alert box and will wait until users acknowledge it before displaying the second one in the messages bar. You can take advantage of this fact to display your messages in alert boxes. The following two lines provide an example of how you could do this:

```
MESSAGE ('This message will be displayed in an alert box.');
MESSAGE (' ');
```

This approach is good only if you want to display your messages in Stop alert boxes with only one OK button. If you want to display the message simply at the micro-help line, use the procedure MESSAGE with the argument NO_ ACKNOWLEDGE, as in this example:

MESSAGE ('This message will not be acknowledged', NO_ACKNOWLEDGE);

The message bar is also used to display the text string specified in the *Hint* property of the item. If you set the *Auto Hint* property of an item to '*True*', the hint message will be displayed when users navigate to it. However, this alone is not sufficient in every case. There are items such as display items, or those with the *Navigable* property set to '*False*', to which users cannot navigate. In addition, you should provide users with micro-line help without requiring them to navigate to the item itself. In GUI applications, the micro-help message for an item or control is usually displayed when the mouse moves on the item. To implement this functionality in Oracle Forms, you can place the statements shown in Figure 15.11 in a WHEN-MOUSE-ENTER trigger that will fire whenever the mouse enters the sensitive area of an item or control.

In this trigger, the system variable SYSTEM.MOUSE_ITEM is used to access the name of the item on which the mouse rests. Then, the string defined for the *Hint* property is retrieved and displayed in a message. Note that the code presented in Figure 15.11 assumes that the text in the property *Hint* is no longer than 200 bytes. In order to have this trigger fire for all the items in the form, create it as a form-level trigger.

```
DECLARE
  item_hint          VARCHAR2(200);
BEGIN
  item_hint := GET_ITEM_PROPERTY(:SYSTEM.MOUSE_ITEM, HINT_TEXT);
  MESSAGE(item_hint, NO_ACKNOWLEDGE);
END;
```

FIGURE 15.11   Displaying micro-help messages.

There are situations when you would want to display more than just a string of characters in your message. For example, you may want to add a bitmap or use some colors to convey the message better to the users. In these situations, you can build a modal dialog box in which you place text, pictures, and everything else you need. Although the line that divides dialog boxes and message boxes is not clear, you can think of the first type of objects as windows where users access some functionality of the application, and of the second types as windows where they just see some information displayed. A typical message dialog box is the About dialog box which displays the version of the application, credits, and copyright notes. You will see this in almost every application by choosing Help | About... from the menu.

15.3 ALERTS

In addition, you can use alerts to display your messages to the users. Alerts are internal objects in Oracle Forms that when invoked at runtime are displayed as modal dialog boxes. Every other operation in the application is halted until the alert is dismissed. The alert can be dismissed by pressing one of its push buttons. Every alert must have at least one button, and may have up to three buttons.

You may create alerts like any other object in the Navigator by selecting the node Alerts in the Node Display area of the Navigator and issuing any of the following commands:

a) Click the Create icon ▣ from the toolbar, or
b) Select Navigator | Create from the menu.

Designer creates the new object and names it using the default conventions. You can rename the alert after it is created.

15.3.1 SETTING PROPERTIES OF ALERTS IN THE DESIGNER

After you create an alert, you can set its properties in the Properties Window of the Designer. From the **Display** group of properties, *Title* is the only property that has an effect on the appearance of the alert. If *Title* is not set, the alert will show the string Oracle Forms in its title bar.

Although you can set all the visual attributes properties of an alert in the Properties Window, none of these settings has any real effect on the alert objects you create. The alerts will have the default visual attributes of Oracle Forms.

In the **Functional** group of properties, you can set the property *Alert Style* to '*Note*', '*Caution*', or '*Stop*'. The Note alert is used for informative messages, and it displays the icon ❶ on its left side. The Caution alert is used to warn users about actions they take that may result in considerable or irreversible loss of data. The severity icon for this alert is ⓘ. The Stop alert is used to inform users about critical errors that occurred at the Oracle Forms, Oracle Server, or operating system level, but not as a result of users actions. This alert has the icon ⊗.

The properties *Button 1*, *Button 2*, and *Button 3* are used to specify the buttons displayed in the alert and their labels. Internally, Oracle Forms assigns an access key to the labels you enter in these properties. Normally the access key is the first letter of the label, or the second one if it conflicts with an existing label, and so on. Usually, informative and critical alerts have only one button labeled OK. Warning alerts should have at least two buttons, one to proceed with the halted operation, the other to cancel it. For warning and critical alerts, a third button can be included to allow users to invoke the application's on-line help that explains why the application was halted and what to do in order to proceed safely.

Figure 15.12 shows an example of each type of alert. Module WINPROPS.FMB contains three alerts that were used to implement them. They are INFO_ALERT, WARNING_ALERT, and CRITICAL_ALERT.

The message you want to display in the alert can be specified in the *Message* property. The string you enter here can be of any length; however, Oracle Forms will display only up to the first 200 characters in the alert.

15.3.2 MODIFYING PROPERTIES OF ALERTS AT RUNTIME

There may be a considerable number of messages that your application may need to display at runtime. It will be a waste of programming resources if separate alerts were built for each message. The approach taken usually is to identify the types of alerts that will be used, and create one alert object for each of these types. Then PL/SQL code is written to dynamically retrieve the alert object that will be needed for a particular message. The built-in functions FIND_ALERT and ID_NULL are used for this purpose. The properties of this alert are set according to the situation or the message to be displayed. The procedure SET_ALERT_PROPERTY is used to override the title to the message properties of the alert. The procedure SET_BUTTON_PROPERTY is used to replace the button labels, if it is necessary. The alert then is displayed using the function SHOW_ALERT, which returns the button pressed by the users to dismiss the alert. Based on this button, you decide what action to take next.

Figure 15.13 presents the contents of the trigger that displays the warning alert shown in Figure 15.12. It is an example of how you would use the built-in procedures and functions discussed here.

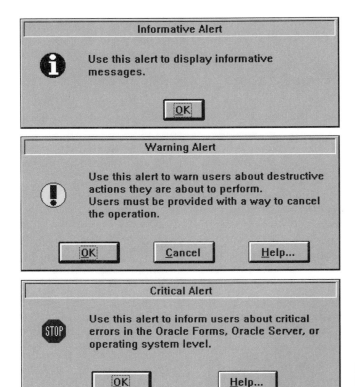

FIGURE 15.12 Example of an Informative, Warning, and Critical alert.

The first part of this procedure finds the internal ID of the alert WARN-ING_ALERT and ensures that all the subsequent invocations of alert-related, built-in procedures will act upon a valid object. Then, the title and the message of the alert are set using the procedure SET_ALERT_PROPERTY. The procedure SET_ALERT_BUTTON_PROPERTY is used to set the labels of the buttons. Finally, the alert is displayed to the users by the function SHOW_ALERT.

Despite the flexibility and the ease of use that the alerts provide, there are some problems that you need to be aware of when deciding to utilize them in your application:

1. You cannot display more than 200 characters in the message. This includes any nonprintable characters such as Tab or carriage returns. Note that *Oracle Forms Reference Manual* erroneously states that the message text cannot exceed 80 characters.

2. There does not seem to be an easy way to break the message text in several lines. In order to display the contents of the message in two lines as in Figure 15.12, white spaces were inserted between the two sentences. It took

```
DECLARE
  alert_id        ALERT;
  alert_msg       VARCHAR2(200);
  button_pressed  NUMBER;
  Alert_Not_Found EXCEPTION;

BEGIN
  alert_id := FIND_ALERT('WARNING_ALERT');
  IF ID_NULL(alert_id) THEN
    RAISE Alert_Not_Found;
  END IF;

  SET_ALERT_PROPERTY(alert_id, TITLE, 'Warning Alert');

  alert_msg := 'Use this alert to warn users about destructive
actions they are about to perform. Users must be provided with
a way to cancel the operation.';
  SET_ALERT_PROPERTY(alert_id, ALERT_MESSAGE_TEXT, alert_msg);

  SET_ALERT_BUTTON_PROPERTY(alert_id, ALERT_BUTTON1, LABEL,
                            'OK');
  SET_ALERT_BUTTON_PROPERTY(alert_id, ALERT_BUTTON2, LABEL,
                            'Cancel');
  SET_ALERT_BUTTON_PROPERTY(alert_id, ALERT_BUTTON3, LABEL,
                            'Help...');

  button_pressed := SHOW_ALERT(alert_id);
  IF button_pressed = ALERT_BUTTON1 THEN
    MESSAGE('First button was pressed.');
  ELSIF button_pressed = ALERT_BUTTON2 THEN
    MESSAGE('Second button was pressed.');
  ELSIF button_pressed = ALERT_BUTTON3 THEN
    MESSAGE('Third button was pressed.');
  END IF;

EXCEPTION
  WHEN Alert_Not_Found THEN
    MESSAGE('Alert WARNING_ALERT does not exist.');
    RAISE FORM_TRIGGER_FAILURE;
  WHEN OTHERS THEN
    MESSAGE('Internal error occurred.');
    RAISE FORM_TRIGGER_FAILURE;
END;
```

FIGURE 15.13 Setting properties of alerts dynamically.

several attempts to find the right number of white spaces that would break the lines nicely.

3. If your application uses fonts other than the Oracle Forms defaults such as MS sans-serif or Arial, the alerts will have a different look than the rest of the application.

However, the amount of work required to programmatically create message boxes with the same simplicity and flexibility that the alerts provide may not justify the benefits you will draw from them.

15.4 CANVASES AND VIEWS IN ORACLE FORMS

Canvases are a special type of objects in Oracle Forms that serve as place-holders or containers for all the data items, controls, text labels, drawings, and bitmaps that the users will see in the application. You can also think of canvases as the background for all the windows in the application. You can create canvases like any other object in the Navigator, but you can also create them together with base table blocks in the New Block Options dialog box.

15.4.1 TYPES OF CANVAS-VIEWS

There are three types of canvases in Oracle Forms: content, toolbar, and stacked canvases. Content canvases are the basic type of canvases in Oracle Forms applications. They are what you have used in the examples so far and will continue to use in the future.

Toolbar canvases are further divided in horizontal and vertical toolbar canvases. These are used to provide the applications you develop with toolbars. In an MDI application, the toolbars are attached to the MDI frame. The horizontal toolbar goes right under the menu; the vertical toolbar is attached along the left border of the MDI frame. Applications WINDYNM.FMB and WINDYNM1.FMB used earlier in the chapter to discuss the dynamic management of windows use a horizontal toolbar.

Stacked canvases are a special type of canvases that at runtime are displayed or stacked on top of another canvas. They originate from the implementation of popup pages by the character-based predecessor of Oracle Forms—SQL*Forms 3.0. In SQL*Forms, data items and boilerplate text were created on pages, which were displayed to the users at runtime. The pages would take up the entire screen, and users had to move from one page to the other in order to access their data in the entirety. Some windowing capabilities were much needed. For example, in a multiple-record tabular page, users wanted to display details about each individual record on a small area of the screen without having to switch to another page. Also, when working with a single record on a form page, there was often the need to display multiple-record listings of additional data. To provide for these needs, SQL*Forms 3.0 introduced the concept of popup pages. They were like the ordinary pages, except that they could be sized so that they would not take the entire screen. They could be shown in different locations of the screen and hidden dynamically, without affecting the underlying parent page. In the GUI versions of Oracle Forms that followed, pages were replaced with content canvases and popup pages were replaced with stacked canvases.

Views are objects closely related to canvases, often considered as unified under the name canvas-views. A view is like a rectangular box placed on top of the canvas, which governs the part of the canvas that is displayed to the users. In Figure 15.14, the large rectangle with double-lined borders represents a canvas in the Layout editor, and the single-line rectangle around the first four objects represents the view object.

The coordinates of the upper left-hand corner of the view are canvas properties (*X Position on Canvas*, and *Y Position on Canvas*). However, the *Width* and the *Height* of the view are properties of the window to which the canvas is attached. To see the relation between these properties, open any of the modules you have used in this chapter, for example WINDYNM.FMB:

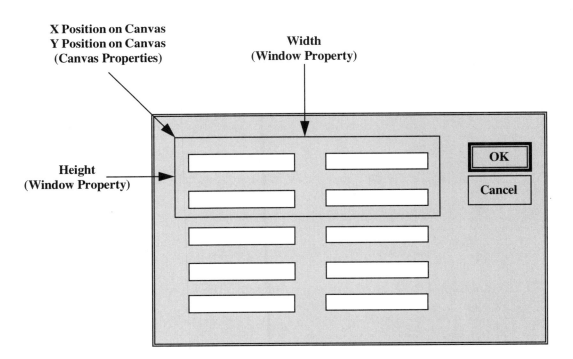

FIGURE 15.14   Views in Oracle Forms.

1. Open a Properties Window for the canvas SECOND, and pin its properties to the window.
2. Open a second Properties Window for the window SECOND, and pin its properties to the window.
3. Display the canvas SECOND in the Layout Editor, and arrange the three windows so that you can see all three of them on the screen.
4. Select View | Show View from the Layout Editor menu to display the view for the canvas SECOND.
5. Drag the upper left-hand corner of the view diagonally across the screen. With this action you have changed the coordinates and the dimensions of the view. You will see that the properties mentioned above will change simultaneously for both the canvas and the window.

In environments that support the MDI application development paradigm, such as MS Windows, Windows 95, and Macintosh, the need for stacked canvas-views is minimal. Their functionality can be implemented with standard content canvases attached to dialog box windows. The benefits of this approach—simplicity, reduced programming overhead, and an application interface with which users are familiar—are significant and should not be overlooked.

On the other hand, stacked canvas-views can be used to implement advanced application features such as balloon help and tabbed dialog box controls. If you decide to implement these features with customized code written in 3GL languages or VBX controls, you will limit the portability of the application to those environments that support such features (mainly MS Windows). Relying only on features and code inherent to the Oracle Forms, you will create applications that will inherit this functionality in any platform where Oracle Forms applications can run.

15.4.2 SETTING PROPERTIES OF CANVAS-VIEWS IN THE DESIGNER

In order to display the Properties Window for any canvas-view object in the Designer, you must select the object either in the Object Navigator or in the Layout Editor. Then proceed as follows:

a) Select Tools/Properties... from the Designer's menu, or
b) Right-click the object and select Properties... from the popup menu.

The properties of canvas views are divided in five groups: **Type, Display, Functional, Stacked View,** and **Miscellaneous**. The only property under the group **Type** is *Canvas-view Type*. Its settings yield one of the four types of canvas views discussed in the previous section.

The properties under group **Display** control the color and pattern of the canvas. By default, each canvas is created with a solid pattern and gray background color. This type of background is recommended by all GUI standards and should be satisfactory for the windows and screens of your applications. However, if you need to change these settings, you may follow any one of the following methods:

a) Set the properties *Foreground Color, Background Color,* and *Fill Pattern* in the Properties Window to the desired values, or

b) Create a named Visual Attribute object and set the property *Visual Attribute Name* for the canvas to its name.

Other properties worth mentioning in the **Display** group are *Width* and *Height*. They control the size of the canvas object. The easiest way to adjust the dimensions of a canvas is to display it in a Layout Editor window and resize it by dragging its handles. If more precision is necessary, you can set *Width* and *Height* in the Properties Window of the canvas.

The **Functional** group contains properties that govern the relationship between a canvas, its view, and the window to which it is attached. For each canvas, the property *Window* specifies the window that will manage the display of the canvas. For MDI applications, it is recommended that each canvas be attached to its own MDI frame or dialog box window. However, it is possible to attach more than one canvas to the same window. At runtime, as users navigate to items in each canvas, they will overlap each other. The property *Raise on Entry* determines when the canvas will be raised on top of all other displayed canvases. If the property is set to 'True', the canvas will move on top of the stack as soon as the Forms places its focus in any item on the canvas. If the property is set to 'False', the canvas will maintain its position in the stack of canvases as long as the focus is in an item that is visible. If the focus moves to an item that is hidden by one or more canvases, the canvas will jump on top of the stack. The properties *X Position on Canvas* and *Y Position on Canvas,* as shown in Figure 15.14, determine the upper left-hand corner of the canvas that will be displayed in the window. You may change the settings of these properties in the Properties Window, or, as explained earlier, in the Layout Editor, by moving the displayed view to the appropriate position.

The properties under the **Stacked View** group apply only to stacked canvas-views. The properties *View Width* and *View Height* determine the size of the view, whereas *Display X Position* and *Display Y Position* determine the location of the stacked view on top of the content canvas attached to the same window. In general the dimensions of the stacked canvas—governed by the properties *Width* and *Height*—are different from those of its view. To allow users to scroll to items in the stacked canvas view that are outside the boundaries of its view, and therefore invisible, you can equip the view with scrollbars by setting the properties *View Horiz. Scroll Bar* or *View Vertic. Scroll Bar* to 'True'.

15.4.3 MODIFYING PROPERTIES OF CANVAS-VIEWS AT RUNTIME

Although in the Designer, canvases and their views are represented by unified objects called canvas-views, Oracle Forms considers them as two distinct types of objects. You may already have realized this division from the discussion of the properties of canvas-views in the previous section. It becomes clear when you consider modifying these properties at Runtime.

There are four built-in program units used to retrieve and modify settings of canvases' properties. They are the functions FIND_CANVAS, ID_NULL, GET_CANVAS_PROPERTY, and the procedure SET_CANVAS_PROPERTY. The size and the visual attribute name are the only properties you can modify for a canvas. Figure 15.15 shows a procedure that changes the visual attribute property of a canvas dynamically.

The program units that retrieve and modify the properties of views are used primarily with stacked canvas views, since their properties tend to change dynamically. FIND_VIEW, ID_NULL, GET_VIEW_PROPERTY, and SET_VIEW_ PROPERTY serve the same purpose for views as the program units that correspond to canvases, windows, items, and other Oracle Forms objects. FIND_VIEW returns the internal identifier of the view object, which is of datatype Viewport. In addition, you can use the procedures SHOW_VIEW to display a view to the users, HIDE_VIEW to remove a view from the visible area of the application, and SCROLL_VIEW to scroll the viewport rectangle horizontally or vertically along the canvas.

```
PROCEDURE Set_Canvas_Visual_Attr (canvas_name VARCHAR2,
                                  va_name     VARCHAR2) IS
  canvas_id          CANVAS;
  Canvas_Not_Found   EXCEPTION;
BEGIN
  /* FIND_CANVAS returns the appropriate canvas ID.          */
  canvas_id := FIND_CANVAS (canvas_name) ;
  IF ID_NULL (canvas_id) THEN
    RAISE Canvas_Not_Found;
  END IF;
  /* If control comes here, canvas ID exists.                */
  SET_CANVAS_PROPERTY (canvas_id, VISUAL_ATTRIBUTE, va_name);

EXCEPTION
  WHEN Canvas_Not_Found THEN
    MESSAGE ('Canvas '||canvas_name||' does not exist.');
    RAISE FORM_TRIGGER_FAILURE;
  WHEN OTHERS THEN
    MESSAGE ('Internal error occurred.');
    RAISE FORM_TRIGGER_FAILURE;
END Set_Canvas_Visual_Attr;
```

FIGURE 15.15 Program unit that replaces the visual attribute of a canvas at Runtime.

Figure 15.16 shows a procedure that can be used to display balloon help for a given item. This procedure assumes that the text item with the contents of the help is located in a stacked view whose name is passed as the first argument. The procedure computes the coordinates where the stacked view will be displayed. In this case, the balloon help is aligned horizontally with the position of the mouse, but vertically is offset by the height of the item.

15.5 STEPS TO ASSOCIATE CANVASES WITH WINDOWS

As said earlier, if your goal is to create MDI applications with minimal programming efforts, you should rely mostly on content canvases attached to MDI frame or dialog box windows. In such a case, the process of associating data items and controls with canvases and windows can be summarized as follows:

1. Create a canvas where the interface object will reside. If you need to change the default background color and fill pattern of your future window, you may do this by setting the properties of the canvas that will be attached to the window.

2. Add objects on the canvas. This activity may be completed at the same time as the previous one if a new base table block and a new canvas are created in the New Block Options dialog box.

3. Create a window that will serve as the frame where the canvas will be attached. Set the properties of this window so that the window is an MDI sheet or a dialog box, depending on the needs of your application.

4. Establish a one-to-one correspondence between the window and the canvas by setting the *View* property of the window to the name of the canvas, and the *Window* property of the canvas to the name of the window.

5. Size, arrange, and align objects on the canvas as necessary.

6. Display the view in the Layout Editor and make sure its upper left hand corner matches the same corner of the canvas. You can also set the *X Position on Canvas* and *Y Position on Canvas* properties of the canvas to zero to obtain the same effect.

7. Drag the lower right-hand corner of the view so that the size of the window when it is initially displayed offers users a good picture of the data items located on the canvas. You can also set the *Width* and *Height* properties of the window at the appropriate setting, but the first method is easier because you can see the view on the screen as you are sizing it.

If the term "good picture" in the previous paragraph may sound a little vague, remember the discussion about windows and their properties. If the window is an MDI sheet, try to fit all the objects on the canvas inside the window. Make sure you don't forget those scrollbars, since users may want to change the initial di-

```
PROCEDURE Show_Balloon_Help (view_name VARCHAR2,
                            item_name VARCHAR2) IS
  view_id          VIEWPORT;
  item_id          ITEM;
  x_coord          NUMBER;
  y_coord          NUMBER;
  item_height      NUMBER;
  View_Not_Found   EXCEPTION;
  Item_Not_Found   EXCEPTION;
BEGIN
  view_id := FIND_VIEW(view_name);
  IF ID_NULL (view_id) THEN
    RAISE View_Not_Found;
  END IF;
  item_id := FIND_ITEM(item_name);
  IF ID_NULL (item_id) THEN
    RAISE Item_Not_Found;
  END IF;
  /* If control comes here, view ID and item ID exist.       */
  x_coord := :SYSTEM.MOUSE_X_POS;
  item_height := GET_ITEM_PROPERTY(item_id, HEIGHT);
  y_coord := TO_NUMBER(:SYSTEM.MOUSE_Y_POS) + item_height;

  SET_VIEW_PROPERTY(view_id, DISPLAY_X_POS, x_coord);
  SET_VIEW_PROPERTY(view_id, DISPLAY_Y_POS, y_coord);

  SHOW_VIEW(view_id);
EXCEPTION
  WHEN View_Not_Found THEN
    MESSAGE('View '||view_name||' does not exist.');
    RAISE FORM_TRIGGER_FAILURE;
  WHEN Item_Not_Found THEN
    MESSAGE('Item '||item_name||' does not exist.');
    RAISE FORM_TRIGGER_FAILURE;
  WHEN OTHERS THEN
    MESSAGE ('Internal error occurred.');
    RAISE FORM_TRIGGER_FAILURE;
END Show_Balloon_Help;
```

FIGURE 15.16   Program unit that displays a stacked canvas-view with balloon help for a given item.

mensions of the window. If the window is a dialog box—they usually are not sizable or scrollable—everything must fit inside the window. If this is not possible, consider redesigning the functionality of the dialog box. It is probably too large and may be divided in two or more dialog boxes.

15.6 OBJECT GROUPS IN ORACLE FORMS

As mentioned in the previous sections, the module WINPROPS.FMB contains a series of properties classes, triggers, and program units that you can use in the MRD application to implement the MDI sheets and dialog boxes. In order to facilitate the process of copying the objects you need from one module to another, Oracle Forms provides a special type of objects, called object groups. Object groups serve as containers in which you can store any objects in the module, except for program units. The object groups have no other purpose than to bundle in one package, objects that should go together from one module to the other. You create them like any other object in the Navigator, and populate them by simply dragging the desired object and dropping it in the group.

In order to practice the process of creating and populating object groups, follow these steps:

1. Launch the Designer and open the module WINPROPS.FMB.
2. Create a new object group and name it MDI_WINDOWS_GROUP.
3. Expand the node Property Classes. The property classes MDI_SHEET, MDI_DIALOG_BOX, and MDI_MODELESS_DIALOG_BOX are displayed.
4. Select these property classes and drag them over to the object group MDI_WINDOWS_GROUP. You will notice that they will appear under the node Object Group Children.
5. Repeat Step 3 and 4 for alerts INFO_ALERT, WARNING_ALERT, and CRITICAL_ALERT.
6. Repeat Steps 3 and 4 for triggers PRE-FORM and WHEN-WINDOW-CLOSED.

Now you are ready to copy the property classes, functions, and procedures you will need from WINPROPS.FMB to the MRD module:

1. Open the module MRD in the Designer. This is the module you have been working with all along.
2. Select the object group MDI_WINDOWS_GROUP in the WINPROPS.FMB module and drag it in the Navigator until the mouse pointer is on the Object Groups Node of the MRD module.

   You may notice that, as you drag the object group, the cursor's shape will give you a visual cue about the right position where you can drop the object in the Navigator. It will have the shape of the Stop sign as it moves over nodes of any type other than Object Groups.

3. Drop the object group in its place in the MRD applications. Oracle Forms will ask you whether you want a copy of the object or a reference to it.

If this were a commercial application development effort, and the WINPROPS.FMB were the repository of all the application's standards for your enterprise, you would reference the objects. You could still use their functionality, but you would not own their source code. This code would be stored in the central repository instead, where it could be changed in accordance with established source code version control policies and software configuration management rules. However, for the purpose of your application, you may copy the object over to your module.

4. Click the Copy button. The Copy Object Options dialog box appear.

5. Press OK to accept the default options.

Once you do that, the copy action will be completed. The beauty of object groups is that they preserve the hierarchical position of their members. You can notice that the properties classes in this group went under the Properties Classes node in the Navigator, the alerts under the Alert node, and the form-level triggers PRE-FORM and WHEN-WINDOW-CLOSED went to their appropriate location.

15.7 WINDOWS AND DIALOG BOXES IN THE MRD APPLICATION

Now you have to copy the program units Open_Window, Open_Dialog_Box, Close_Window, and Get_Home_Item, which unfortunately cannot be included in the object group. Move to the module WINPROPS.FMB again, select these program units, and drag them over to the Program Units node of the MRD application. You will notice that Designer will copy the program units without asking if you want to copy or reference them. In fact, you cannot reference program units. But, as you will see in Chapter 18, you can pack them in PL/SQL libraries and attach the libraries to the module.

At this point, you can close the WINPROPS.FMB module. You are ready to proceed with the development of the MRD application. First, set the properties of the MDI frame so that when the application is started the window is maximized and the title bar shows the string "Movie Rental Database Application."

1. Create a form-level WHEN-NEW-FORM-INSTANCE trigger.

2. Enter the contents as shown below.

```
SET_WINDOW_PROPERTY(FORMS_MDI_WINDOW, TITLE,
        'Movie Rental Database Application');
SET_WINDOW_PROPERTY(FORMS_MDI_WINDOW, WINDOW_STATE, MAXIMIZE);
```

There is only one window currently in the application:

1. Set its *Class* property to *'MDI_SHEET'*, and set each of the *Name*, *Title*, and *View* properties to *'Customer'*.
2. Select the canvas CUSTOMER and set the property *Window* to *'Customer'*.
3. In the Layout Editor for the canvas CUSTOMER, resize the canvas to comfortably include the data items, beveled rectangle, and the push buttons defined there.
4. Check View I Show View item from the menu and resize the view to match the dimensions of the canvas. Be careful not to move the view in the process. Its upper left-hand corner must still match the same corner of the canvas.
5. Uncheck the Show View menu item and save the module.

Now, create two more windows, and follow similar steps to create a one-to-one correspondence between the second window and the MOVIE canvas, and between the third window and the RENTAL canvas.

Save and generate the application, and run it if you want to take a quick look at the way the windows look. The window CUSTOMER will be initially displayed. Since the module still uses the default menu, you can choose Block I Next from this menu to navigate to block MOVIE. This action will automatically display the window MOVIE. In this window, you can select Block I Next once again to move to block RENTAL and open the window where it resides. Note that the Window menu will display the titles of the open windows, and that you can close the windows by double-clicking their control menu box. Exit the Runtime and return to the Designer when ready to proceed with the development.

The next step is to associate WHEN-BUTTON-PRESSED triggers with push buttons that will govern the navigation from window to window:

1. For the CLOSE buttons in all three windows, the statement in the trigger will be

```
Close_Window(window_name);
```

where window_name will be 'CUSTOMER', 'MOVIE', and 'RENTAL', respectively.
2. For the MOVIE buttons in the CUSTOMER and RENTAL windows, the single line in the trigger's body will be:

```
Open_Window('MOVIE', 'MOVIE');
```

3. For the RENTAL buttons in the CUSTOMER and MOVIE windows, the trigger should contain the line

```
Open_Window('RENTAL', 'RENT');
```

4. For the CUSTOMER button in the MOVIE and RENTAL windows the statement of the trigger will be

   Open_Window('CUSTOMER', 'CUSTOMER');

Create also a dialog box that will be displayed when users select About... from the Help menu.

1. Create a control block and name it CONTROL.
2. Create an item in this block and inherit its properties from the class PUSH_BUTTON. Rename it to **CLOSE_ABOUT**, set its *Canvas* property to *'ABOUT'*, and *Label* to *'Close'*.
3. Attach a WEN-BUTTON-PRESSED trigger to the new item with this line in the body:

   Close_Window('ABOUT');

4. Display the canvas ABOUT in the Layout Editor. Create a text box and put anything you would normally see in a dialog box of this kind. See Figure 15.17 for an example.
5. Resize the canvas and the view.

You should notice the fact that each of the three main windows contains two push buttons to access the other windows. Thus, in total there are six buttons, when you need only three, one for each window. These buttons must be prominently placed so that are not obfuscated by the working windows of the application. The best place would be a toolbar, like the one you used in the WINDYNM.FMB module. Only, here you will do better. You will create iconic toolbars for the principal functionality of the application. Chapter 17 will discuss the process of creating menus and toolbars for Oracle Forms applications.

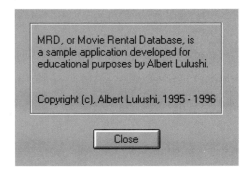

FIGURE 15.17   Sample About dialog box.

15.8 SUMMARY

This chapter discussed windows, their properties, and objects associated with them in Oracle Forms MDI windows. Important concepts in this chapter include the following:

- ❑ Properties of windows
  - ❑ Setting windows properties in the Designer
  - ❑ Controlling windows programmatically
  - ❑ Event of windows
- ❑ Developing MDI applications with Oracle Forms
  - ❑ MDI frame
  - ❑ MDI sheets
  - ❑ Implementing MDI sheets
  - ❑ Dialog boxes
  - ❑ Implementing dialog boxes
  - ❑ Message boxes
- ❑ Alerts
  - ❑ Setting properties of alerts in the Designer
  - ❑ Modifying properties of alert at runtime
- ❑ Canvases and views in Oracle Forms
  - ❑ Types of canvases
  - ❑ Setting properties of canvas-views in the Designer
  - ❑ Modifying properties of canvas-views at runtime
- ❑ Associating canvases with windows
- ❑ Object groups in Oracle Forms

Chapter 16

RECORD STRUCTURES AND OTHER OBJECTS

"Yea, from the table of my memory
I'll wipe out all trivial fond records . . ."
—William Shakespeare

- ◆ Records in Oracle Forms
- ◆ Record Groups
- ◆ Lists of Values
- ◆ Text Editors
- ◆ Parameters and Parameter Lists
- ◆ Summary

Materials presented up to this point discuss the principal structure and user interface objects in Oracle Forms. In the applications you develop you can use other objects to add to and enhance the functionality of blocks, data items, controls, windows, and dialog boxes. One of these objects, the record, is a virtual object that exists only at runtime. However, it is very important to understand its properties, and especially the events that affect its status. Others, like record groups, editors, List of Values dialog boxes, and parameter lists are objects that can be used to implement several features in the application such as tabular structures, selection and validation of data from lists, and text editing capabilities. This chapter discusses the process of creating and manipulating these objects.

16.1 RECORDS IN ORACLE FORMS

As said in Chapter 11, when analyzing the requirements of a system, you identify the object classes or entities that will take part in the system. They represent the general characteristics of a group of data items. Each individual occurrence of these data items forms an instance of the entity. For example, the entity Movie is considered as a group of data that includes a title, main actors, producers, and rating. The movie *Piano* is an instance of this entity, where all the data items have a particular value.

In the Oracle Server, entities are implemented by tables, and instances of these entities by rows in the table. In Oracle Forms applications, entities are implemented by blocks, and each individual occurrence becomes a record. Records are not objects that you can access and manipulate in the Designer. At runtime, they can be created, modified, and deleted according to the needs of the application. From an object-oriented programming perspective, since the records are instances of a block-class, the events that affect them are events that affect the class. This is the reason why, usually, methods fired by these events are implemented as block-level triggers.

16.1.1 STATES OF RECORDS, BLOCKS, AND FORMS

Before getting further into the discussion let us clarify the terminology a little bit. Sometimes we will say that an object is in a certain state, and sometimes we will say that its status is the name of the state. For example, we will say that a record is in state QUERY, or that its status is QUERY. Both expressions will mean the same thing and will be used interchangeably. The state of a record defines whether and how it will be processed by several internal events of Oracle Forms such as validation or database processing. It also affects the state of the parent block and through it the state of the form module.

A record can be in one of the following states: NEW, INSERT, QUERY, or CHANGED. The record status is NEW, if the event CreateRecord has just occurred, and the users have not entered values in any of the items in the record.

The status of all the items in a NEW record is also NEW. As soon as some data is entered in one item—either by users or as a result of programmatic assigments—the status of that item and all the other items in the record becomes CHANGED. The record switches to the state INSERT. As the users continue entering data, the status of the record will remain INSERT. When the record is committed, Oracle Forms will ensure that the record is valid, and will send an INSERT statement to the database. If the insertion is successful, the record in the Forms module becomes a twin copy of the record stored in the database. Its status now becomes QUERY. A record is in this state if it is retrieved by a query against the database as well. The state of all the items in a QUERY record is VALID. As long as users do not change any of them, the record remains in this state. However, as soon as a change is made, the status of the record and all its items becomes CHANGED. When the next CommitForm event will occur, Forms will first take the records throughout the validation check, and, if the record is valid, it will prepare and send an UPDATE statement to the database. If the transaction is completed successfully, the record status will become QUERY once again. Figure 16.1 represents the state transition diagram of a record.

The status of the records in a block defines the state of the block. The states of different blocks in the form, define the status of that module. Forms and blocks can be in one of the three states: NEW, CHANGED, or QUERY. If a block contains only one record in the NEW state, the status of the block is NEW. If at least one

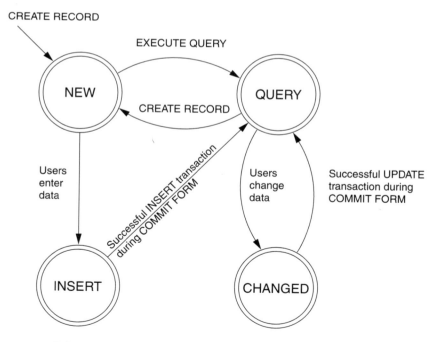

FIGURE 16.1   Transition diagram for the states of a record.

record in the block is in state QUERY, the state of the block is QUERY, even if there is a newly created record in the state NEW. If the status of at least one record in the block is INSERT or CHANGED, the block will be in the CHANGED state.

The relation between the states of blocks and the state of its parent form is similar. The form is in state NEW if and only if all its blocks are in that state. If one block switches to state QUERY, while the others are still NEW, the status of the form becomes QUERY. If the status of at least one block becomes CHANGED, the parent form will be in that state as well.

From what has been said so far, you may conclude that objects in Oracle Forms influence the state of other objects in two directions: from top down, and from bottom up. Figure 16.2 can explain this concept better. This figure shows the hierarchical organization of blocks, records, and items in a module.

When the application is first launched or when the ClearForm event occurs, the state of the module is set to NEW. This state is propagated to all the subordinate nodes one level down the tree, in other words to all the blocks in that module.

When the state of a block is set to NEW, either from a message received by its parent, or because the ClearBlock event occurred, the block will create a single NEW record. When the state of the block is set to QUERY, because the Execute-Query event occurred, the status of all the records retrieved by the query in this block is set to QUERY.

When the status of the record is NEW, either because the parent block is in this state, or because the CreateRecord event occurred in the block, the status of all the items in this record is NEW. Similarly, when the record status is QUERY, the status of all its items will become VALID.

The users do not see any of the hierarchy levels shown in Figure 16.2, except for the lowest one. On their application screens, they enter data in items or click controls to perform their job. When users modify an item, thus setting its status to CHANGED, the state is propagated all the way up to the top of the hierarchy. If, in the example of Figure 16.2, Item K is changed, it will send the message up to its parent record. This message causes the record to switch to INSERT state if it was previously in NEW, or CHANGED if it was previously in QUERY. When the state transition occurs, the record sends a signal to its parent block, which immediately sets its state to CHANGED. The block finally transmits the message to the module, thus putting it in the CHANGED state as well.

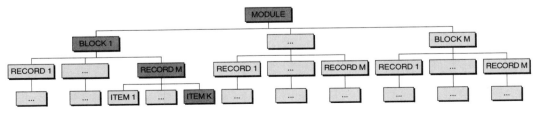

FIGURE 16.2   Hierarchy tree of objects in Oracle Forms.

Then, when the CommitForm event occurs, the process of passing status information and messages begins again, this time from the top all the way down to each item. The life of an Oracle Forms application is nothing more than a constant up-and-down of messages and state transitions, as explained here.

Oracle Forms allows you to inspect the status of the form, any of its blocks, or any of their records. The information for the objects where the cursor is currently located is stored in the systems variables SYSTEM.FORM_STATUS, SYSTEM.BLOCK_STATUS, and SYSTEM.RECORD_STATUS, respectively. You can also use the function GET_RECORD_PROPERTY to get the status of any record in any block within the application, or use the function GET_ BLOCK_PROPERTY to retrieve the status of any block in your form. There is not a way to inspect the status of an item.

The companion disk provides a form that uses the system variables to retrieve the status of the form, current block, and current record at any time during the form's life. This module, called STATUS.FMB contains two base table blocks, which you can use to query and manipulate data from the tables MOVIE and TAPE. The horizontal toolbar of the application contains three text items and a push button. When the push button is clicked, these items will display the status of the current record, block and form. Use this application to better understand the concepts discussed in this section.

16.1.2 EVENTS OF RECORDS

The previous section, while discussing the status of records, mentioned briefly some of the events related to them. This section reviews these events in more detail. The main events that affect the life of a record are EnterRecord, LeaveRecord, CreateRecord, RemoveRecord, ChangeRecordItems, and ValidateRecord.

The EnterRecord event occurs when the users navigate to an item in the record from an item that either is in a different record within the block, or is in another block altogether. Navigating from one item to the other within the same record does not constitute an EnterRecord event. If Forms can place its focus on the item within the record where users have chosen to navigate, right before entering the record, the trigger PRE-RECORD will fire. When the EnterRecord event completes successfully, the WHEN-NEW-RECORD-INSTANCE will fire.

The LeaveRecord event occurs when users navigate to an item that is in another record within the same block, or on another block. This event will cause the event ValidateRecord to occur. Depending on how the ValidateRecord event will treat items that do not pass the validation test, the LeaveRecord event may not be completed if the validation fails. However, if it is completed successfully, the trigger POST-RECORD will fire right after Forms navigates out of the record.

The CreateRecord event occurs when the built-in CREATE_RECORD is invoked, either programmatically or by pressing the [CREATE RECORD] key. During this event, Forms leaves the current record, creates a new record immediately after it, and places the focus on a new record. The trigger that fires during this event is WHEN-CREATE-RECORD. Understandably, this trigger is sandwiched between the POST-RECORD trigger that is fired when Forms leaves the original record, and the PRE-RECORD trigger that is fired when Forms is about to enter the new record. The CreateRecord event also occurs when Forms initially navigates to a new block. At the end of this event the status of the record is NEW.

The RemoveRecord event occurs either when the current block is deleted using the built-in DELETE_RECORD, or when it is cleared from the block using the built-in CLEAR_RECORD. As explained earlier in the book, these actions are different in that the first one results in the record being marked for delete by the next commit transaction, and the second one simply flushes the record from the internal structures of the block. In both cases, when the record is removed, the WHEN-REMOVE-RECORD trigger is fired.

The ChangeRecordItems event occurs whenever users change the value of a base table item in the record. As the result of this change, the record is flagged either for an INSERT or for an UPDATE during the next commit event. In response to this event, the trigger WHEN-DATABASE-RECORD will fire. At the end of the event, the status of all the items in the record is CHANGED. The status of the record is either INSERT or CHANGED, depending on the status prior to the event. This event occurs even if a control text item is changed as long as the block is a base table block and the property *Lock Record* in the **Database** group of properties of that item is set to *'True'*.

The ValidateRecord event occurs only if the record is in INSERT or CHANGED state, and either LeaveRecord or CommitForm event is initiated. If the record's status is NEW or QUERY, the record is considered as valid by Oracle Forms, therefore no validation occurs. When the ValidateRecord event occurs, the record triggers the ValidateItem event for all its dependent items. If any of these events are not successful, the ValidateRecord event itself will fail. If all the items pass the validation test, the WHEN-VALIDATE-RECORD trigger is fired. Its outcome defines the success or failure of the ValidateRecord item.

16.1.3 EVENTS OF RECORDS IN THE MRD APPLICATION

Here you will implement some of the functionality discussed in Chapter 11 in the form of block-level triggers associated with record events. Begin the process by opening the most current version of the MRD module which you saved at the end of the previous chapter. You may also use the module CH16.FMB which contains all the work done so far in the application.

There are three internal identifiers in the MRD application that will be populated with values from a sequence number generator when the records are created. These items are CUSTOMER_ID in block CUSTOMER, MOVIE_ID in block MOVIE, and TAPE_ID in block TAPE. The values for these items will come from the sequence MRD_SEQ created together with the other database objects of the application. Create first a function that returns the value from this sequence. The contents of this function are shown in Figure 16.3.

```
FUNCTION Get_Sequence_Id RETURN NUMBER IS
   seq_id    NUMBER;
BEGIN
   SELECT MRD_SEQ.NEXTVAL
   INTO seq_id
   FROM DUAL;


   RETURN seq_id;
END;
```

FIGURE 16.3   Function that Returns the Next Value from a Sequence.

Next, create WHEN-CREATE-RECORD triggers for blocks CUSTOMER, MOVIE, and TAPE. Each trigger should populate the respective ID item with a call to this function. The contents of the trigger in the block CUSTOMER, for example, are:

:CUSTOMER.CUSTOMER_ID := Get_Sequence_Id;

When records are created in block RENTAL, the values for CUSTOMER_ID and TAPE_ID come from the blocks CUST_RENT and TAPE_RENT. In a WHEN-CREATE-RECORD trigger for this block you should assign these values and set the RENT_DT to the current date as shown in the following lines:

```
:RENTAL.CUSTOMER_ID := :CUST_RENT.CUSTOMER_ID;
:RENTAL.TAPE_ID := :TAPE_RENT.TAPE_ID;
SELECT SYSDATE INTO :RENTAL.RENT_DT FROM DUAL;
```

Now use the ValidateRecord event to ensure the quality of data that will be inserted in the system. Create a WHEN-VALIDATE-RECORD trigger for the CUSTOMER block and enter its contents as shown in Figure 16.4. Similarly, create a WHEN-VALIDATE-RECORD trigger for block MOVIE and check for the uniqueness of new records based on the items TITLE and DIRECTOR. In addition, make sure in this trigger that the date items START_DT and END_DT are always specified in the right order (END_DT should always be after START_DT). This constraint should be enforceable for new and existing records, therefore you should place it outside the IF statements that checks the uniqueness of movies.

Finally, create a WHEN-VALIDATE-RECORD for block RENTAL that will ensure that the RENT_DT and RETURN_DT dates are specified in the appropriate order. Save the work done so far and generate the module.

```
DECLARE
  cust_id    VARCHAR2(20);
BEGIN
  IF :SYSTEM.RECORD_STATUS = 'INSERT' THEN
    SELECT COUNT(*)
    INTO cust_id
    FROM CUSTOMERS
    WHERE LAST_NAME = :CUSTOMER.LAST_NAME
      AND FIRST NAME_ = :CUSTOMER.FIRST_NAME
      AND MEMBER_DT = :CUSTOMER.MEMBER_DT;
    IF cust_id <> '0' THEN
      BELL;
      MESSAGE ('This customer already exists.');
      RAISE FORM_TRIGGER_FAILURE;
    END IF;
  END IF;
END;
```

FIGURE 16.4   Checking for Uniqueness of New Records.

16.2   RECORD GROUPS

Record groups are objects that provide the functionality of tabular data structures, similar to the arrays of structures in C. They allow you to combine data items of alphanumeric, numeric, and date datatypes in records that can be accessed based on the value of an index.

Note

In the WHEN-VALIDATE-RECORD trigger for blocks CUSTOMER and MOVIE, you are enforcing the uniqueness of data only for newly-inserted records. For records that already exist in the database, the IF statement will not be processed since the status of these records is no longer 'INSERT'. Thus, there is a possibility to create data that violate the uniqueness constraints. In this situation you should not allow users to update the items that are part of the check. Therefore set the property 'Update Allowed' to 'False' for FIRST_NAME, LAST_NAME, and MEMBER_DT in the CUSTOMER block and for items TITLE and DIRECTOR in the MOVIE block.

Depending on how they get populated with data, record groups are divided into query and nonquery record groups. Query record groups are created by a SQL SELECT statement. The columns in the SELECT clause of this statement become the columns of the record groups, and the records returned by the query become its rows. This type of record groups is the most flexible and usable record group. It can be created from the Designer and at Runtime and allows dynamic manipulation of the data. The nonquery record groups are created by explicitly specifying the columns they will contain. If created at runtime, they may also be populated with the data they contain, and their rows can be added or deleted programmatically. However, if created at design time, their structure and values must be specified in the Designer, and remain fixed throughout their life. For this reason, nonquery record groups created at design time are called static record groups.

In this section you will create record group structures that will be used in the MRD application. You will begin by creating a static record group. Then, you will create several query record groups that will complete the functionality of the updateable combo boxes created in Chapter 14. You will also see how record groups can be used to implement multiple-selection list boxes in Oracle Forms.

Begin the process by opening the most current version of the MRD module which you saved at the end of the previous section.

16.2.1 STATIC RECORD GROUPS

At design time, object groups can be created and renamed in the Object Navigator. When you create an object group with any of the standard commands of the Navigator, you will first see the New Record Group dialog box shown in Figure 16.5.

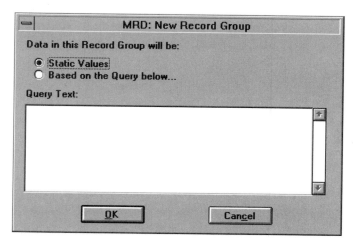

FIGURE 16.5 New Record Group dialog box.

In this dialog box you can choose the type of record group you want to create. By default, the radio box at the bottom is checked, which means that query record groups are created by default. In this case, you need to enter a SELECT statement in the Query Text field, which will create and populate the record group. If you want to create a static group, click the Static Values radio button.

From the Navigator, create a static record group and name it WINDOWS. This record group will be used to store the names of the windows in the application. It will enable you to write code that closes all the windows in the application with one single command. After selecting the type of the record group click OK in the New Record Group dialog box. The Column Specification dialog box appears (see Figure 16.6). Define here the structure of the record group WINDOWS and populate it with values.

1. Enter WINDOW_NAME in the first record of the multi-record Column Names block. Leave the datatype and length of this column at its default values.

2. Click inside Column Value detail block, and enter the names of the MDI sheet windows in the MRD module, as shown in Figure 16.6.

3. Click OK.

If you wanted to add another column to the record group, then you could insert its name under WINDOW_NAME and provide its values in the Column Values list.

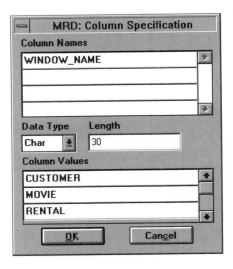

FIGURE 16.6 Column Specification dialog box for record groups.

16.2.2 QUERY RECORD GROUPS

As mentioned earlier, query record groups are created and populated by a SQL SELECT statement. If the record group is created in the Designer, only the population of the group occurs at runtime. You can also create and populate the record groups with one single step at runtime.

To create a query record group in the Designer, you must follow these steps:

1. Create the record group using any of the standard commands in the Navigator.
2. In the New Record Group dialog box, make sure the second radio button is checked. This button is followed by the label Based on the Query Below... .
3. Enter the SELECT statement in the Query Text field. This can be any valid SQL SELECT command.
4. Click OK.
5. Rename the new object group according to your needs.

In the Properties Window for the newly created object, you can see that the *Record Group Type* is now 'Query', and your statement is in the *Record Group Query* property. If you display the Column Specification dialog box, you will notice that the Column Values area of the window, which you could see and access for static record groups, is now hidden.

With the SELECT statement in hand, you can also create the record group at runtime. The built-in function CREATE_GROUP_FROM_QUERY takes as input parameter the SELECT statement, and returns the internal ID of the newly created group.

16.2.3 ACCESSING DATA OF RECORD GROUPS AT RUNTIME

In order to access the values stored in the cell of a record group, you must follow these steps:

1. Get the internal ID of the record group, based on its name, and make sure that it is a valid one. The functions FIND_GROUP and ID_NULL are used for this purpose.
2. Get the internal ID of the column where the cell is located, based on its name, and make sure that it is a valid one. The functions FIND_COLUMN and ID_NULL serve this purpose.
3. Get the number of records currently stored in the group. The function GET_ROW_COUNT returns this number.
4. Initiate a loop with the number retrieved in the previous step as the upper bound. The loop retrieves the value stored in the current cell of each record, as the iterator goes down the rows. Depending on the datatype of the value

stored in the column, one of the following functions is used to retrieve the value stored in the current cell: GET_GROUP_CHAR_CELL, GET_GROUP_ NUMBER_CELL, or GET_GROUP_DATE_CELL.

5. Use the value retrieved as required by the particular situation and the needs of your application.

In a procedure that counts all the open windows in the application, you would loop through the record group WINDOWS, get the name of each window, and check the setting of the *VISIBLE* property for that window. If it is *'TRUE'*, an internal counter is incremented by one unit. Obviously, at the end of the loop this counter will hold the number of the open windows. Figure 16.7 contains the implementation details of the function Count_Open_Windows.

16.2.4 POPULATING LIST ITEMS WITH RECORD GROUPS

In Chapter 14, you implemented several items in the block MOVIE as updateable combo lists. But a major problem with the implementation was that the lists could grow and remember the data entered by users only during one session of the application. Record groups created at runtime offer an elegant way to fix this problem with your lists.

Figure 16.8 shows the contents of the procedure Get_Movie_Lists_Values. This procedure retrieves the values stored in the database columns for an item implemented as a combo box in the block MOVIE. The name of the list item is passed to the procedure as an argument, which makes it usable for any combo list item in the MRD module.

The first part of the procedure retrieves the internal ID of the list item, and the second part build the SQL SELECT statement which will populate the list with elements. The list items in the MRD module are specified in the format BLOCK.ITEM. As base table items, ITEM corresponds to the column name in table MOVIES, from which the data will be retrieved. The value of ITEM is re-

Notes

❑ You need to select the same column twice because the first value will serve as the list element value and the second as its label.

❑ In order to avoid duplicate entries in the list, the DISTINCT keyword is included in the SELECT statement.

❑ Populating the list dynamically gives you a chance to order the list, which you cannot easily do with static lists.

```
FUNCTION Count_Open_Windows (group_name VARCHAR2,
                            group_column VARCHAR2)
RETURN NUMBER IS
  rows              NUMBER;
  rec_group_id      RecordGroup;
  column_id         GroupColumn;
  window_id         Window;
  window_name       VARCHAR2(80);
  counter           NUMBER := 0;
BEGIN
--Find ID for record group.
  rec_group_id := FIND_GROUP(group_name);
  IF ID_NULL(rec_group_id) THEN
    MESSAGE('Record Group '||group_name||' does not exist.');
    RAISE FORM_TRIGGER_FAILURE;
  END IF;
--Find ID for column of record group.
  column_id := FIND_COLUMN(group_name||'.'||group_column);
  IF ID_NULL(column_id) THEN
    MESSAGE('Column '||group_column||' does not exist in record
            group '||group_name||'.');
    RAISE FORM_TRIGGER_FAILURE;
  END IF;
--Find number of rows in record group.
  rows := GET_GROUP_ROW_COUNT(rec_group_id);
 --Loop through the records to get the window name
  FOR i IN 1..rows LOOP
    window_name := GET_GROUP_CHAR_CELL( column_id, i );
    window_id := FIND_WINDOW( window_name );
    IF ID_NULL(window_id) THEN
      MESSAGE('Window '||window_name||' does not exist.');
    RAISE FORM_TRIGGER_FAILURE;
    END IF;
    IF GET_WINDOW_PROPERTY(window_id, VISIBLE) = 'TRUE' THEN
      counter := counter+1;
    END IF;
  END LOOP;
  RETURN counter;
EXCEPTION
  WHEN OTHERS THEN
    MESSAGE('Internal error occurred in Count_Open_Windows.');
    RAISE FORM_TRIGGER_FAILURE;
END;
```

FIGURE 16.7   Counting the number of open windows in an application.

```
PROCEDURE Get_Movie_Lists_Values (list_name VARCHAR2) IS
  list_id     Item;
  col_name    VARCHAR2(80)  := SUBSTR(list_name,
                                INSTR(list_name,'.')+1);
  sql_stat    VARCHAR2(2000);

BEGIN
--Find ID for list item.
  list_id := FIND_ITEM(list_name);
  IF ID_NULL(list_id) THEN
    MESSAGE('List Item '||list_name||' does not exist.');
    RAISE FORM_TRIGGER_FAILURE;
  END IF;

--Build the SQL statement.
  sql_stat := 'SELECT DISTINCT '||list_name||', '||list_name||
             ' FROM MOVIES ORDER BY 1';

  Populate_the_List(list_id, sql_stat);

EXCEPTION
  WHEN OTHERS THEN
    MESSAGE('Internal error occurred in
Get_Movie_Lists_Values.');
    RAISE FORM_TRIGGER_FAILURE;
END Get_Movie_Lists_Values;
```

FIGURE 16.8 Procedure that populates list items dynamically.

trieved and stored in variable col_name using the SQL functions SUBSTR and INSTR. This column name is used to build the SQL statement which is then passed as an argument to the procedure Populate_the_List.

The SQL functions INSTR and SUBSTR were discussed in Chapter 9. INSTR is used to find the position in the string of the dot that separates the block name from the item name. Then the function SUBSTR returns the substring of the original string that begins from the character after the dot. This is also the name of the database column.

After the SELECT statement is prepared, it is passed together with the list ID to the procedure Populate_the_List, which will create the list elements based on the query. The contents of this procedure are shown in Figure 16.9.

This procedure is generic and can be used to populate any list item with elements returned by the SQL statement passed as a parameter. The record group

```
PROCEDURE Populate_the_List ( list_id   ITEM,
                              sql_stat VARCHAR2) IS
  group_id    RecordGroup;
  outcome     NUMBER;

BEGIN
--Create temporary record group.
  group_id := CREATE_GROUP_FROM_QUERY('List_Elements', sql_stat);
  IF ID_NULL(group_id) THEN
    MESSAGE('Record Group could not be created in
Populate_the_List.');
    RAISE FORM_TRIGGER_FAILURE;
  END IF;

--Populate record group.
  outcome := POPULATE_GROUP(group_id);
  IF outcome <> 0 THEN
    MESSAGE('Record Group could not be populated in
Populate_the_List.');
    RAISE FORM_TRIGGER_FAILURE;
  END IF;

--Populate list item
  POPULATE_LIST(list_id, group_id);

--Destroy the temporary record group to release resources
  DELETE_GROUP(group_id);

EXCEPTION
  WHEN OTHERS THEN
    MESSAGE('Internal error occurred in Populate_the_List.');
    RAISE FORM_TRIGGER_FAILURE;
END Populate_the_List;
```

FIGURE 16.9   Using record groups to populate lists dynamically.

List_Elements is created as a temporary container of the records returned by the query, using the function CREATE_GROUP_FROM_QUERY. After creating the group, the function POPULATE_GROUP adds the rows retrieved into the group. If this function completes successfully, it returns to the value zero. This is why other statements are processed only if the variable outcome is zero.

Once the rows returned by the SELECT statement are in the group, the procedure POPULATE_LIST transfers them in the list item. Finally, the temporary record group List_Elements is destroyed by invoking the procedure DELETE_GROUP. This last step is very important for two reasons:

1. It returns the memory resources to the pool of available resources when they are no longer needed.
2. It ensures that the next call to this function will be as successful as the first one. The function CREATE_GROUP_FROM_QUERY will fail if a record group with the name List_Elements already exists.

In order to add the functionality described in this section to the MRD application, create the procedures shown in Figure 16.8 and Figure 16.9. Then, append the following statements to the form-level WHEN-NEW-FORM-INSTANCE trigger:

```
Get_Movie_Lists_Values('MOVIE.ACTOR');
Get_Movie_Lists_Values('MOVIE.ACTRESS');
Get_Movie_Lists_Values('MOVIE.DIRECTOR');
Get_Movie_Lists_Values('MOVIE.COMPANY');
Get_Movie_Lists_Values('MOVIE.PRODUCER');
```

If the application will be used only by a single user at any one time, populating the list when the form is initialized is satisfactory for your needs. The fact that you get an initial snapshot of the elements of the list, coupled with the functionality added to the property class UPDATEABLE_COMBO in Chapter 14, will guarantee that your user will see all the current members of the list. However in an intensive multi-user data entry application, there may be a need to refresh the content of the list frequently. The built-in procedure CLEAR_LIST could be used to clear the contents of the current list, and the procedure Populate_the_List could be called again to take the most up-to-date snapshot of the list. It is difficult to offer a general rule about how often you should refresh the list. It is a decision that you will have to make depending on the load of your database server and on the traffic in your network. The type of functionality implemented here should be limited to lists of no more than twenty entries or so. If you expect the lists to grow larger, you may have to add some filtering capabilities that will allow your users to narrow the scope of the query before actually executing it.

Note

If the contents of the list are likely to change frequently during one session that the application will be in use, you may need to refresh it each time the list is accessed. A simple way to do this is to attach a List of Values dialog box to the text item. Section 16.3 discusses the properties of LOVs.

16.2.5 IMPLEMENTING MULTI-SELECTION LISTS WITH RECORD GROUPS

It was mentioned in Chapter 14 that multiple-selection lists are an extension of check box items. They allow your users to select several options from a long list of choices. This section will discuss the process of creating a multi-selection list.

There are several methods to implement multi-selection lists in your applications, and you can be as inventive as you would want. However, there are a few standard functions that each multi-select list should have:

1. Usually, the list of available options appears on the left, and a list of choices made up to the moment is shown to the right.
2. Double-clicking is the action with which you select an item.
3. When users select an item, they must have a visual cue that the item is selected. Normally, the selection is removed from the list of available items and transferred to the list of selected options.
4. If users select an item, they must also be able to deselect it.
5. It is desirable sometimes to select, or deselect, all the choices in an option list.

In this section, you will create a multi-selection list that will allow the users of the MRD application to pick several or all of the customers from the list of the active customers for the purpose of printing their addresses in envelopes. The list will have all the functionality described above.

Follow these steps to create the necessary data items, controls, and windows for the multi-select list in the MRD form:

1. Create a control block, a canvas, and a window, all called MAIL.
2. Inherit the properties of the window MAIL from MDI_DIALOG_BOX property class, and set its *Title* property to *'Print Envelopes'*.
3. Create a one-to-one correspondence between the canvas and the window by setting the *Window* property of the canvas to *'MAIL'* and the *View* property of the window to *'MAIL'*.
4. Create two text list items in the block MAIL. Call them AVAILABLE and SELECTED. Set their *Visual Attribute Name* property to *'MS_SANS_SERIF'*.
5. Create one element for each list with label and value NULL. You can do this by completely erasing the default entries in the List Elements and List Elements Values fields of the List Item Elements dialog box.
6. Create five push buttons and name them PRINT, SELECT_ALL, DESELECT_ALL, CLOSE_MAIL, and HELP_MAIL. Set their *Class* property to *'PUSH_BUTTON'*.
7. Set PRINT to be the default button.
8. Arrange, align, and size the items on the canvas to obtain a layout similar to the one shown in Figure 16.10.

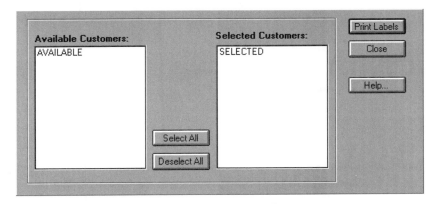

FIGURE 16.10 Multi-select lists.

Now create the program units that will implement the functionality of the multi-select list.

First, create a procedure, called Get_Customers, that will populate any of the lists with the names of all active customers in the database. This procedure is almost identical to the procedures Get_Movie_Lists_Values shown in Figure 16.8. It will ensure that the list name is a valid item's name, create a SELECT statement, and invoke the procedure Populate_the_List to add the rows returned by the query to the list.

The only difference between the procedures Get_Customers and Get_Movie_Lists_Values is the SELECT statement that will populate the lists. This statement for Get_Customers is shown in Figure 16.11.

The first and the last name of each customer are concatenated—with a space in between—and form the list elements labels. The customer ID numbers are retrieved as character values and form the list elements values. When the list will be populated from the record group created from this query, the names will be displayed on the screen, while the customer IDs will be the values of the list item behind the scene.

Figure 16.11 demonstrates two simple techniques that are often used to build dynamic SQL statements at runtime:

```
sql_stat := 'SELECT FIRST_NAME||'' ''||LAST_NAME,
            TO_CHAR(CUSTOMER_ID) '||
            'FROM CUSTOMER '||
            'WHERE STATUS = ''A'' '||
            'ORDER BY 1';
```

FIGURE 16.11 Constructing SQL statements at Runtime.

> ## Note
>
> In general, record group can be created with columns of datatypes other than CHAR. However, if these record groups will populate lists, they must have exactly two columns of CHAR datatype, of which the first will provide the list elements with labels and the second with values.

1. To store a single quote in the string, precede it with another single quote as in the WHERE clause of the statement.
2. If a character string is too long to fit in the editor window, you can split it in pieces, which are joined together by the concatenation operator ||.

The statement in Figure 16.11 is broken in several lines for the sake of clarity, but also to give you a hint. The components of this statement such as the WHERE clause or ORDER BY clause, need not be hard-coded; they can be other character strings as well. In fact, you can provide the users with a dialog box in which they can enter their query or ordering criteria at runtime. These criteria are bundled in separate strings, which then are concatenated to form the complete SELECT statement. This technique, dynamic SQL, allows you to write very generic, flexible, and situation-independent routines.

The procedure **Get_Customers** should clear both list items and populate the list item AVAILABLE when the dialog box is first accessed. In order to do this follow these steps:

1. Create a WHEN-NEW-BLOCK-INSTANCE trigger for the block MAIL.
2. In the body of the trigger add the following statement:

```
CLEAR_LIST('MAIL.AVAILABLE');
CLEAR_LIST('MAIL.SELECTED');
Get_Customers('MAIL.AVAILABLE');
```

The procedure **Get_Customers** will also be used to select or deselect all the items in the list. The code will be executed whenever the users press any of the SELECT_ALL and DESELECT_ALL push buttons. To implement the functionality for button SELECT_ALL follow these steps:

1. Create a WHEN-BUTTON-PRESSED trigger for button SELECT_ALL.
2. Enter the statements in the body of the trigger as follows:

```
CLEAR_LIST('MAIL.AVAILABLE');
Get_Customers('MAIL.SELECTED');
GO_ITEM('MAIL.SELECTED');
```

Follow these steps to implement the functionality for button SELECT_ALL:

1. Create a WHEN-BUTTON-PRESSED trigger for button DESELECT_ALL.
2. Enter the statements in the body of the trigger as follows:

```
CLEAR_LIST('MAIL.SELECTED');
Get_Customers('MAIL.AVAILABLE');
GO_ITEM('MAIL.AVAILABLE');
```

When the SELECT_ALL button is pressed, the trigger clears the list AVAIL-ABLE, populates the list SELECTED, and navigates to that list. The visual effect of this would be that all the customer names will move from the Available list box to the Selected one. Pressing the DESELECT_ALL button performs the same actions but in the reverse order of lists.

Now, create the code that will move a list element from one list to the other when users double-click it. Recall from Chapter 14 that text lists have a particular trigger (WHEN-LIST-ACTIVATED) that is fired when an element in the list is double-clicked. In this trigger you will call the procedure Move_Current_Ele-ment, which implements such a functionality.

The procedure Move_Current_Element takes as arguments the name of the list item where the element currently is and the name of the list item where this element will be inserted. The value of the element that was clicked is stored in a local variable using the built-in function NAME_IN. The procedure basically loops through the list that was clicked until it finds the element that was clicked. When this element is found, its label is retrieved using the list function GET_LIST_ELEMENT_VALUE. An element with the label and the value of the clicked element is inserted into the target list using the procedure INSERT_ELE-MENT. The element itself is deleted from the original list using the built-in DELETE_LIST_ELEMENT and the loop is terminated. Figure 16.12 contains all the details you need to create this procedure.

The fact that the procedure Move_Current_Element is generic and does not depend on the particular list items with which it is used, allows you to implement the trigger WHEN-LIST-ACTIVATED at the block level. Figure 16.13 shows the body of the trigger WHEN-LIST-ACTIVATED attached to block MAIL. Note

```
PROCEDURE Move_Current_Element (from_list_name VARCHAR2,
                                to_list_name VARCHAR2) IS
  list_id         ITEM;
  list_count      NUMBER;
  current_value   VARCHAR2(50);
  clicked_value   VARCHAR2(50) := NAME_IN(from_list_name);
  clicked_label   VARCHAR2(80);

BEGIN
  list_id := FIND_ITEM(from_list_name);
  IF ID_NULL(list_id) THEN
    MESSAGE('List Item '||from_list_name||' does not exist.');
    RAISE FORM_TRIGGER_FAILURE;
  END IF;
  list_count := GET_LIST_ELEMENT_COUNT(list_id);

  FOR i IN 1..list_count LOOP
    current_value := GET_LIST_ELEMENT_VALUE(list_id, i);
    IF clicked_value = current_value THEN
        clicked_label := GET_LIST_ELEMENT_LABEL(list_id, i);
        INSERT_ELEMENT(to_list_name, clicked_label, clicked_value);
        DELETE_LIST_ELEMENT(list_id, i);
        EXIT;
    END IF;
  END LOOP;

EXCEPTION
  WHEN OTHERS THEN
    Message('Internal error occurred in Move_Current_Element.');
    RAISE FORM_TRIGGER_FAILURE;
END Move_Current_Element;
```

FIGURE 16.12   Implementing multi-selection lists.

the system variable SYSTEM.TRIGGER_ITEM in this trigger which is used to capture the name of the button pressed that causes the trigger to fire.

You can now save and generate the module, and run it to see the functionality of the list. Select from the Oracle Forms default menu the items Block I Next or Block I Previous until the focus navigates to the block MAIL. Try selecting and deselecting several customers. Test also the Select All and Deselect All functionality.

```
DECLARE
  list_activated VARCHAR2(50) := :SYSTEM.TRIGGER_ITEM;

BEGIN
  IF list_activated = 'MAIL.SELECTED' THEN
     Move_Current_Element('MAIL.SELECTED', 'MAIL.AVAILABLE');
  ELSIF list_activated = 'MAIL.AVAILABLE' THEN
     Move_Current_Element('MAIL.AVAILABLE', 'MAIL.SELECTED');
  END IF;
END
```

FIGURE 16.13   Moving elements from one list to the other.

Note

In this case you replaced triggers of the same type (WHEN-LIST-ACTIVATED) for two objects, with a trigger of the same type, but attached to the parent of these objects. This approach allows you to reduce the number of PL/SQL objects to edit and maintain at any one time, and makes the application's logic more compact. It also makes the application leaner and more efficient at run-time. The approach can be used very successfully during the prototyping phase of the application as well. You can create the screens you need, and place the necessary data items and controls there. Then you create triggers in the upper levels of the hierarchy that contain a few calls to modularized functions and procedures. These program units need not be implemented in detail in the prototyping stage. For example, the procedure **Move_Current_Element** could simply display a message like: **Will move element from list A to list B. Development in process.** As you develop the prototype to an operational system, the messages in the program unit-bodies are replaced by the working PL/SQL statements, but the trigger will not need to be modified.

16.3 LISTS OF VALUES

Lists of Values (LOVs) are a special type of single selection lists that can be used very effectively and with little effort to display data to the users and allow them to pick the desired element. LOVs are a combination of modal dialog boxes, lists, and record groups, therefore they have characteristics from each of these type of objects:

1. LOVs are modal dialog boxes. They will prevent users from accessing any other areas of the application as long as they are displayed. Users must dismiss them by making a selection, or by canceling the operation altogether in order to be able to proceed with their work.

2. LOVs can be used to simply present data, but they are primarily used to pick a value and store it into a text item, and, from there, into a database column. Because they come packaged with a search engine and auto-reduction features, they could effectively replace list items that need to display a large number of elements. Furthermore, because the LOVs can build the list of elements they display each time they are invoked, they guarantee that the users will see the most up-to-date version of the list.

3. LOVs are built on top of record groups. In general, associating lists with record groups is a relatively easy process. However, the association of LOVs with their underlying record groups is even easier, and almost transparent for you.

16.3.1 CREATING LISTS OF VALUES

In the MRD application, you will use the LOVs to display, populate, and validate data entered in the STATE item of the address of a customer. The table STATES is created by the script that installed the database objects for the MRD application. It has only two columns and fifty rows. Each row contains the abbreviated postal code and the full name for the states in the United States in which the video rental store has customers. The functionality you will create in this section is as follows:

1. There will be a push button to the right of the STATE item that the users can click if they want to display the LOVs dialog box.

2. Users can enter the value of a state directly in the STATE item. If they enter a valid value, they will be allowed to proceed; otherwise, the LOVs dialog box will be displayed to allow users to pick the right value.

3. The LOVs will display the full names of the states, but the values stored in the item will be the abbreviated postal codes to conserve storage space.

As said earlier, under each LOVs there is a record group. The record group does not have to exist before the LOVs is created. You can create both the LOVs and the record group simultaneously in the New LOV dialog box (see Figure 16.14). To create a LOVs object, select the node List of Values in the Node Display area of the Navigator and proceed as follows:

a) Click the Create icon ▦ from the toolbar, or
b) Select Navigator | Create from the menu.

The New LOV dialog box appears.

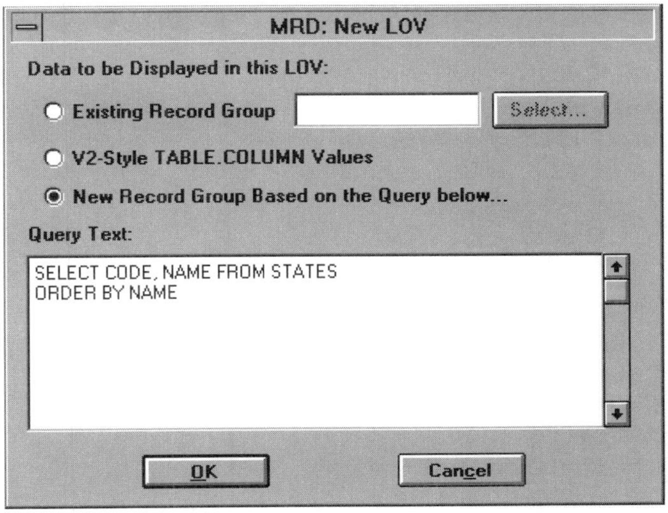

FIGURE 16.14 New LOV dialog box.

In this dialog box you can specify the type of the LOVs object. In your applications you will use LOVs based on record groups. The option V2-Style is included only for backward compatibly reasons. You will never need to create this type of LOVs in Oracle Forms.

The record groups upon which the LOVs object will be based can be created on the fly by selecting the last radio button and entering the SELECT statement in the Query Text field, as in the example of Figure 16.14. If the record group already exists, you can choose the first radio button in the list and then select it from the list of the record groups currently defined in the module.

Now create the LOVs object that will be used in this section:

1. Create a LOVs object in the Navigator. The New LOV dialog box appears.
2. Enter the SELECT statement shown in Figure 16.14.
3. Click OK. The Designer creates a LOVs object and a record group object, and assigns them default names.
4. Rename both objects to STATE.

Now, you can set the other properties of the newly created LOVs. The connection between the LOVs object and the STATE text item in the CUSTOMER block is established in the LOV Column Mapping dialog box (see Figure 16.15). This dialog box is displayed by double-clicking the property *Column Mapping* in the LOVs Properties Window.

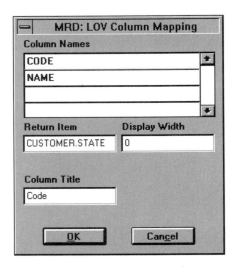

FIGURE 16.15   LOV Column Mapping dialog box.

Click the CODE column in the Column Names list, and set the Return Item field to CUSTOMER.STATE, and the Display Width to zero, as shown in Figure 16.15. With these settings, Oracle Forms will not display the column CODE in the LOVs window, and if an element is selected from the list, the value in column CODE will be stored in the STATE item. Because this column will not be displayed, the setting of the Column Title is not important in this case.

For the NAME column, the Return Item will be NULL. This means that no item in the form will receive this value. You may keep the setting for the Display Width as it is, but change the Column Title to **States**.

16.3.2 PROPERTIES OF LISTS OF VALUES

There are several properties that govern the behavior of the LOVs objects at runtime. You can set them in the Properties Window. First of all, you want the LOVs dialog box to have the same look and feel as the rest or your windows. Therefore, set its *Visual Attribute Name* property to *'CANVAS_OBJECT'*. Like any other window in your application, you want to set the coordinates, dimensions, and title of the LOVs dialog box, as well. Set both *Width* and *Height* to *'200'*, and *Title* to *'List of States'*. Remember that the dimensions settings are valid only for the initial display of the LOVs dialog box. Users then can resize the window as they want. They also depend on the coordinate units being used in the application. These settings are expressed in points.

From the other properties of the LOVs object, if *Auto Confirm* is set to *'True'*, then, when the list is reduced to one element through the auto-reduction process, that element will be picked automatically without the users having to confirm the selection. If *Auto Display* is *'True'*, each time the focus is on the item to which the

LOVs is attached, the LOVs dialog box will be displayed. The default setting for both these properties is *'False'*. The *Auto Refresh* property is set to *'True'* by default. This means that each time the LOVs dialog box will be invoked, the query through which its record group is populated will be executed. If the property is set to *'False'*, the query is executed only the first time the LOVs is invoked. If the *Long List* property is set to *'True'*, each time the LOVs dialog box is invoked, a preliminary filter is displayed were the users can display additional criteria to narrow the scope of the query. By default this property is set to *'False'*. The *Auto Skip* property is set to *'False'* by default. This causes the cursor to land on the item from which the LOVs dialog box was invoked, when a selection is made. In order to save the users the extra key stroke to navigate to the next item, you should set this property to *'True'*. In such a case, when the selection is made, the focus moves to the next item.

For the LOVs STATES preserve the default settings of all the properties except for *Auto Refresh* which should be set to *'False'* and *Auto Skip* which should be set to *'True'*. The reason for the setting of *Auto Refresh* is that the list of States will practically never change, therefore it can be populated only once when the LOVs is invoked for the first time.

16.3.3 MODIFYING PROPERTIES OF LISTS OF VALUES AT RUNTIME

Properties of LOVs can be retrieved and modified dynamically using the functions FIND_LOV, ID_NULL, GET_LOV_PROPERTY and the procedure SET_LOV_PROPERTY. There is little difference in the way you use these program units for LOVs from the way you use them for other Oracle Forms objects dicussed up to now. Figure 16.16 contains the implementation of the function Show_Centered_LOV. This function is an enhancement to the built-in SHOW_LOV because it displays the LOVs dialog box in a central position with respect to the MDI frame of the application. Add the function Show_Centered_ LOV in the module MRD since it will be used to display the LOVs STATE created earlier.

The function SHOW_LOV is used to display a LOVs dialog box. This function returns the Boolean value TRUE if the users select an item from the list, or FALSE if they cancel the dialog box. This is also the value returned by the function Show_Centered_LOV.

16.3.4 ATTACHING LISTS OF VALUES TO TEXT ITEMS

Now attach this LOVs object to the item STATE.

1. Display the Properties Window for this item.
2. Set the *LOV* property in the **Miscellaneous** group to *'STATE'*.
3. Set the property *LOV for Validation* to *'True'*.

```
FUNCTION Show_Centered_LOV (LOV_name VARCHAR2)
RETURN BOOLEN IS
  LOV_id        LOV;
  x_coord        NUMBER := 0;
  y_coord        NUMBER := 0;
  LOV_width      NUMBER;
  LOV_height     NUMBER;
  mdi_width      NUMBER;
  cell_height    NUMBER;
  current_form   VARCHAR2(80);
  LOV_Not_Found  EXCEPTION;
BEGIN
  LOV_id := FIND_LOV(LOV_name);
  IF ID_NULL(LOV_id) THEN
    RAISE LOV_Not_Found;
  END IF;

  mdi_width := GET_WINDOW_PROPERTY(FORMS_MDI_WINDOW,WIDTH) ;
  mdi_height := GET_WINDOW_PROPERTY(FORMS_MDI_WINDOW,HEIGHT) ;
  current_form := GET_APPLICATION_PROPERTY(CURRENT_FORM_NAME);
  cell_height := GET_FORM_PROPERTY(current_form,
                   CHARACTER_CELL_HEIGHT);
  mdi_height := mdi_height - 1.35*cell_height;

  LOV_width    := GET_LOV_PROPERTY(LOV_id, WIDTH);
  LOV_height   := GET_LOV_PROPERTY(LOV_id, HEIGHT);

  IF ( mdi_width > LOV_width ) THEN
    x_coord := (mdi_width - LOV_width) / 2;
  END IF;
  IF ( mdi_height > LOV_height ) THEN
    y_coord := (mdi_height - LOV_height) / 2;
  END IF;

  SET_LOV_PROPERTY(LOV_id, POSITION, x_coord, y_coord);

  RETURN (SHOW_LOV(LOV_id));
EXCEPTION
  WHEN LOV_Not_Found THEN
    MESSAGE('List of Values '||LOV_name||' does not exist.');
    RAISE FORM_TRIGGER_FAILURE;
  WHEN OTHERS THEN
    MESSAGE ('Internal error occurred in Show_Centered_LOV.');
    RAISE FORM_TRIGGER_FAILURE;
END;
```

FIGURE 16.16   Retrieving and Modifying Properties of List of Values Dynamically.

```
DECLARE
  ok_button BOOLEAN;
BEGIN
  ok_button := Show_Centered_LOV('STATE');
END;
```

FIGURE 16.17   Displaying a List of Values programmatically.

This last setting will guarantee that each value entered by the users will be checked against the LOVs list. If the entry does not match a state code, the LOVs dialog box will be displayed. The entry in the item serves as a criterion to reduce the number of elements displayed in the list.

Save, generate, and execute the form and see for yourself how the LOVs dialog box will help your users enter and validate your data. When the cursor is in the item STATE you will see the status lamp <LOV> appear in the message bar. This serves as an indicator to the users that there is a list of values associated with the item. As long as you are inside the STATE item, you will be able to display the LOVs at any time by pressing the [LIST OF VALUES] key.

When you press the [LIST OF VALUES] key, you will see the LOVs STATE displayed at the upper left-hand corner of the screen. Oracle Forms will display the dialog box according to the settings of properties *LOV X Position* and *LOV Y Position* for the STATE item or, if they are set at *'0'*, according to the settings of properties *X Position* and *Y Position* for the LOVs STATE. In order to use the function **Show_Centered_LOV**, attach the trigger KEY-LISTVAL to the item state and enter its contents as shown in Figure 16.17.

Users in a GUI platform would expect to be able to display the LOVs with a mouse click as well. For this reason you should create a push button that will serve the purpose. Exit the Runtime and return to the Designer. Follow these steps:

1. Create a push button in the block CUSTOMER and name it STATE_LOV.
2. Set its *Class* property to *'PUSH_BUTTON'*, its *Label* to *'Select...'*, and
3. Its *Access Key* to *'S'*. Align the button horizontally with the text item STATE.
4. Set the property *Navigable* to *'False'*. Users do not need to place the focus on this button. Just clicking it will be sufficient.
5. Create a WHEN-BUTTON-PRESSED trigger that will display the LOVs dialog box. Enter the contents of the trigger as shown below.

```
GO_ITEM('CUSTOMER.STATE');
DO_KEY('LIST_VALUES');
```

16.4 TEXT EDITORS

There may be occasions, when you will need to create or maintain long strings of characters in your application. If users need to access these data items often, they may find it very cumbersome having to scroll through a single-line item to read its contents.

The first thing to try in these occasions is to implement such items as multi-line text items. If it is necessary, a scrollbar can be added to them. However, depending on the size of the data, even this approach may not offer the desired results. In addition, when working with large amounts of text, users may expect to have some basic editing tools such as search and replace, or cut and paste.

The solution to these situations is to display the contents of the text item in a text editor and let the users benefit from its functionality. To implement this solution, you can use the Oracle Forms internal text editor, or a system editor such as Notepad.

The MRD application does not need any text editors of any kind, but, for the sake of discussing the topic, you can display and edit the customer's address in an editor. First, make a backup copy of the application you were working with so far and close the master copy. You will use this copy to experiment with the features of the editor.

A good way to implement the editor functionality for a text item, is the approach used by the Properties Window to give you access to properties such as *Comment*, that may contain long strings of text. You will place a push button by the side of the ADDRESS item. This button will display the editor when pressed. Continue as follows:

1. Create a push button, place it by the side of ADDRESS item, and label it Edit...
2. Create a WHEN-BUTTON-PRESSED trigger for this button, and place these statements in its body:

```
GO_ITEM('CUSTOMER.ADDRESS');
EDIT_TEXTITEM;
```

Generate and run the form and query some customer records. Click the push button you created and you will see something like Figure 16.18.

The Oracle Forms editor will adjust its size automatically, depending on the amount of text it will display. If you want to define the size, and dimensions of the window, then you replace the previous call to the EDIT_TEXTITEM in the WHEN-BUTTON-PRESSED trigger with a statement like this one:

EDIT_TEXTITEM (100, 100, 150, 150);

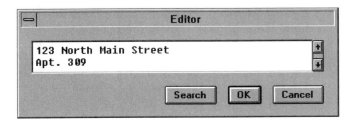

FIGURE 16.18   Oracle Forms default text editor.

The first two arguments of this statement defines the position, and the other two, the width and height of the editor dialog box.

As you can see from Figure 16.18, the visual attributes used by the default editor are the default attributes of Oracle Forms. If you want to make it look consistent with the rest of your application, or if you want to display your own title on the message box, then you can create an editor object in the Navigator and set its properties in the Properties Window:

1. Create an editor in the Object Navigator and name it ADDRESS_EDITOR.
2. Set its *Visual Attribute Name* property to *'CANVAS_OBJECT'*.
3. Set its *Title* to *'Address Editor'*, its *X Position* to *'100'*, and *Y Position* to *'100'*. Note here that you can also specify a bottom title for the dialog box or whether you want vertical and horizontal scrollbars.
4. Now, display the Properties Window for item ADDRESS, and set its *Editor* property to *'ADDRESS_EDITOR'*. Here you could override the default position of the editor, by setting the properties *Editor X Position* and *Editor Y Position*.

Generate and run the module. When you display the editor again you will see something like Figure 16.19.

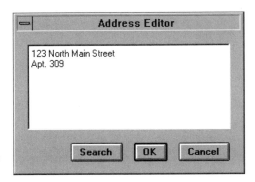

FIGURE 16.19   Oracle Forms custom text editor.

The custom editors have an additional feature that may be useful sometimes. You can use the procedures SHOW_EDITOR not only to display the editor at the location you want, but also to specify the source of text, and the destination of the contents of the dialog box, when the users dismiss it by pressing OK. In addition, this procedure sets a Boolean variable to True if the users accept the dialog or False if they cancel out of it. This procedure may come in handy on occasions when you want to keep more than one version of the text item values. However, typically the source and the destination of the text will be the same text item in the form.

Besides the internal and custom-made editors, you can also use the system editor in Oracle Forms applications. In MS Windows, this is the Notepad editor. To use the system editor in your application, set the *Editor* property of the AD-DRESS item to *'SYSTEM_EDITOR'*. Make sure that the WHEN-BUTTON-PRESSED trigger of the button Editor... still contains the following lines:

```
GO_ITEM('CUSTOMER.ADDRESS');
EDIT_TEXTITEM;
```

Now generate and run the form. When you click the Editor... button, you will see the Notepad come up. A temporary file is opened and it displays the contents of the Address item. The application in the background is disabled and will not be available until you close the Notepad window.

16.5 PARAMETERS AND PARAMETER LISTS

Within one module, variables can have a local or global scope. The scope and visibility of local variables does not extend beyond the program units in which they are defined. The global variables are visible throughout all the active modules and accessible from all their objects. Parameters implement a different flavor of

Note

In the *Oracle Forms Developer's Guide* it is stated that in order to use the Notepad editor, you must set its path in the environment variable FORMS45_EDITOR in ORACLE.INI. You do not need to do this step. In a Windows environment, Oracle Forms will recognize and use the Notepad by default.

visibility and accessibility of certain data items across the boundaries of the module. They are objects that are used to pass data between modules, for example when a form calls another, or between products, for example when an Oracle Report is executed from inside Oracle Forms.

There are two types of parameters: text and data. Text parameters are simple text strings of up to 255 bytes. They are used to pass data in and out the forms. Data parameters are also strings, but they contain the name of a record group which is already defined in the module. They are used to pass to Oracle Reports and Oracle Graphics the data that are stored in the record group.

Parameters are not passed to other modules or products individually. They are packaged in a larger object, called a parameter list. Only the internal ID of this list is passed on the other side. Based on this ID, the module or product receives the list, locates it, traverses it, and retrieves each individual parameter and its value.

In this section, you will further extend the functionality of the MAIL block, which is used to print mailing labels for customers. In Section 16.2.5, you enabled the users to select multiple customers from the list of all the active customers. Now, you will implement the functionality that is behind the mouse click on the button Print. The strategy here is as follows:

1. Go through the list of selected records and record all the CUSTOMER_ID values.
2. Build the WHERE clause of a SELECT statement that retrieves the address data only for those customers that have their CUSTOMER_ID in the set created in the previous step.
3. Hand this clause over to an Oracle Reports module that will do the actual retrieval of the data, based on the WHERE clause passed by the forms.

This strategy is implemented in the body of the trigger WHEN-BUTTON-PRESSED for the button Print (see Figure 16.20).

This trigger creates a parameter list, called Report_PL using the built-in function CREATE_PARAMETER_LIST. If the parameter list is created successfully, this function returns a non-NULL internal ID, which is stored in the variable param_list_id of datatype ParamList.

Note

Note the extra step taken at the beginning of the trigger to ensure that a parameter list called **Report_PL** does not already exist. This may seem a little over-zealous, but in an application that is developed by several programmers at the same time, how else would you guarantee that nobody else in the team is using a parameter list with this name?

```
DECLARE
  param_list_id    ParamList;
  param_list_name VARCHAR2(20) := 'Report_pl';
  sql_stat         VARCHAR2(255);

BEGIN
--Make sure that parameter list does not exist.
  param_list_id := GET_PARAMETER_LIST(param_list_name);
  IF NOT ID_NULL(param_list_id) THEN
    MESSAGE('Parameter_list '||param_list_name||' already
           exists.');
    RAISE FORM_TRIGGER_FAILURE;
  END IF;

--Create the parameter list.
  param_list_id := CREATE_PARAMETER_LIST(param_list_name);
  IF ID_NULL(param_list_id) THEN
    MESSAGE('Parameter_list '||param_list_name||' cannot be
           created.');
    RAISE FORM_TRIGGER_FAILURE;
END IF;

--Build the WHERE clause.
  sql_stat := Build_Where_Clause('MAIL.SELECTED');

--Add the WHERE clause to the parameter list.
  ADD_PARAMETER(param_list_id, 'WHERE_CLAUSE', TEXT_PARAMETER,
               sql_stat);

--Run the report that prints the label.
  RUN_PRODUCT(REPORTS, 'MRDLABEL', ASYNCHRONOUS,
             BATCH, FILESYSTEM, param_list_id, NULL);

--Destroy Parameter List
  DESTROY_PARAMETER_LIST(param_list_id);

EXCEPTION
  WHEN OTHERS THEN
    Message('Internal error occurred in WHEN-BUTTON-PRESSED.');
    RAISE FORM_TRIGGER_FAILURE;
END;
```

FIGURE 16.20 Creating and populating parameter lists.

After the parameter list is created, the function **Build_Where_Clause** will go through the list MAIL.SELECTED and build the WHERE clause that will retrieve the address of the selected customers. This is the value of the parameter that will be passed to Oracle Reports. In the report module, there will be a parameter called WHERE_CLAUSE which will receive this value. Figure 16.21 provides the implementation details of this function.

The ADD_PARAMETER procedure establishes the connection between the name of the parameter and its value. Because you are passing a simple character string, the type of this parameter is TEXT_PARAMETER. If you were to pass a record group instead, the parameter would be specified as DATA_PARA-METER.

When the WHERE clause is prepared, the report is executed using the built-in procedure RUN_PRODUCT. The meaning of the actual arguments passed to this procedure in Figure 16.18 is as follows:

REPORTS means that you will execute an Oracle Reports module. The name of this module is **MRDLABEL**. The flag ASYNCHRONOUS instructs Oracle Forms to kick off the report and not wait for it to finish. Instead, the control is returned to the users, who can continue working with other tasks in the form. The BATCH flag indicates that the Oracle Reports Runtime window will not appear to the user. The **param_list_id** is the internal ID of the parameter list you created. When Oracle Reports receives this ID, it will use it to find the memory location where the beginning of the parameter list is. Then, it will go through the individual parameters in the list to get their names and values. If the name of a parameter in the list matches the name of a predefined parameter (in your case WHERE_CLAUSE), Oracle Reports will pass the value from the parameter list to the internal parameter. The last argument in the call to RUN_PRODUCT is always NULL if a report is executed. However, if an Oracle Graphics display is being retrieved in a Forms item, the name of the chart item is stored there. You will see an example of this in Part Four of this book.

As a last step in the trigger WHEN-BUTTON-PRESSED, the parameter list is destroyed after the report is executed, in order to release the system's resources to other tasks. The purpose of the function **Build_Where_Clause** was mentioned several times. Figure 16.21 provides the implementation details of this function.

Conceptually, this function does not present anything new to you. It simply loops through the elements of a list and retrieves the value of each element. The only trick, if you can call it such, is how the WHERE clause is constructed. First you start with the string

WHERE CUSTOMER_ID IN (

```
FUNCTION Build_Where_Clause (list_name VARCHAR2)
RETURN VARCHAR2 IS
  list_id        ITEM;
  list_count     NUMBER;
  sql_stat       VARCHAR2(255) := 'WHERE CUSTOMER_ID IN (';
  current_id     VARCHAR2(50);
  sql_stat_len   NUMBER;

BEGIN
--Get a valid list ID.
  list_id := FIND_ITEM(list_name);
  IF ID_NULL(list_id) THEN
    MESSAGE('List Item '||list_name||' does not exist.');
    RAISE FORM_TRIGGER_FAILURE;
  END IF;

--Get the number of elements in the list.
  list_count := GET_LIST_ELEMENT_COUNT(list_id);

  FOR i IN 1..list_count LOOP
    sql_stat_len := LENGTH(sql_stat);
    EXIT WHEN sql_stat_len > 254;
    current_id := GET_LIST_ELEMENT_VALUE(list_id, i);
   --Add a comma after each Customer_ID.
    sql_stat := sql_stat||current_id||',';
  END LOOP;

--Remove the comma that follows the last Customer ID.
  sql_stat_len := LENGTH(sql_stat);
  sql_stat := SUBSTR(sql_stat, 1, sql_stat_len - 1);
--Finish the string with the closing parenthesis.
  sql_stat := sql_stat||')';

  return sql_stat;
EXCEPTION
  WHEN OTHERS THEN
    MESSAGE('Internal error occurred in Build_Where_Clause');
    RAISE FORM_TRIGGER_FAILURE;
END Build_Where_Clause;
```

FIGURE 16.21   Building the WHERE clause for a report.

Then, each iteration of the loop appends the value of the current element in the list, which is the CUSTOMER_ID, followed by a comma. So, for example, after the second iteration the string could look like this:

WHERE CUSTOMER_ID IN ('102934', 234849',

Before each new iteration the length of the string is tested. Since text parameters cannot contain more than 255 bytes of data, the loop is interrupted when this threshold is reached. When the loop terminates, the list will have a comma at the end. You need to remove this final comma and replace it with the matching right parentheses. If, in the previous example, the list contains only two elements, the final WHERE clause will be

WHERE CUSTOMER_ID IN ('102934', 234849')

After creating the trigger and the procedure as discussed in this section, generate and save the module. Chapter 21 will discuss in more detail the integration of Oracle Forms with Oracle Reports and Oracle Graphics. In that chapter you will also see the example of passing a record group as a parameter to Oracle Graphics.

Note

The limitation of text parameters to 255 bytes would not make this approach a feasible solution for a real life situation where hundreds of customer labels may be printed. In that case data parameters should be considered. Another alternative is to write the full SQL SELECT statement to a text file during the preparatory phase of the label printing process. Oracle Forms allows you to write data from the application program units into text files using the built-in package TEXT_IO. You would follow a similar looping approach as in Figure 16.21, but, instead of building only the WHERE clause in a local variable, you would write the whole SQL statement to the file. The Oracle Reports module, on the other hand, should be designed based on a query from an external file—the same file you write from within Oracle Forms. Thus, on the Forms side of the application you write the SQL statement to a file, whereas on the Report side you query the database based on this file, format the data, and print the labels. Chapter 21 contains an example of how the package TEXT_IO can be used to write and read text files.

16.6 SUMMARY

This chapter discussed record structures in Oracle Forms applications such as runtime records, record groups, and list of values. In addition, it explained how you can use text editors, parameters, and parameter lists. Important topics of this chapter are listed here:

- ❏ Records in Oracle Forms
  - ❏ States of records, blocks, and forms
  - ❏ Events of records
- ❏ Record groups
  - ❏ Static record groups
  - ❏ Query record groups
  - ❏ Accessing data of record groups as Runtime
  - ❏ Populating list items with record groups
  - ❏ Implementing multi-selection lists with record groups
- ❏ Lists of Values
  - ❏ Creating Lists of Values
  - ❏ Properties of Lists of Values
  - ❏ Modifying properties of Lists of Values at Runtime
  - ❏ Attaching Lists of Values to text items
- ❏ Text editors
  - ❏ Internal, custom, and system text editors
- ❏ Parameters and parameter lists
  - ❏ Types of parameters
  - ❏ Passing data to Oracle Reports using parameter lists

MENUS AND TOOLBARS

"We all know sensual pleasures taken to excess are a curse . . . it's the same with menus."

—Bob Carr

A key objective that should always be in the back of your mind when developing an application is to make it as accessible for the users as possible. You can write the best piece of software, but if it will take users several steps to get to it, nobody will be thrilled by it, and many will not even notice it. On the other hand, you do not want to open everything up as soon as the application is started. Instead users should be in charge. They should decide which parts of the application to keep available and accessible at any one moment.

The bottom line is that your application needs structure. The functionality must be organized logically and in a fashion that is natural for the business processes described by the application. Menus and toolbars are used to turn the multitude of objects and pieces of code that make up an application into an organized and well-planned tool to access and manipulate the data. This chapter discusses the process of equipping your Oracle Forms applications with menus and toolbars.

17.1 ORACLE MENUS

In Oracle Forms applications menus can be created, edited, generated, and saved in the Menu Editor. The menu modules exist independently from forms, but cannot be used unless they are attached to a form. One menu module is always attached to any form you create. This is the default menu that you have seen used in the application developed in Part One.

Chapter 8 explained how to use the Menu Editor to create the frame for a menu. This section will discuss in more detail the objects that are part of a menu module and their properties. You will also create the menu for the MRD application according to the design specifications set forth in Chapter 11.

17.1.1 CREATING THE MENU FOR THE MRD APPLICATION

The general steps you must follow when creating a menu are listed here:

1. Design the menu so that it reflects the most natural and efficient way for users to access the components of the application.
2. In the Menu Editor, lay out the structure of the menu according to the design.
3. For each menu item that users will ultimately select, define its properties according to its purpose and functionality.
4. Save and generate the menu module.
5. Attach the menu to the form module that will use it.
6. Save, generate, and run the form to test the new menu's functionality.

If necessary, these steps may be repeated more than once.

For the MRD application, you have already completed the first step. From Chapter 8, you also know how to build the structural frame of the menu in the Menu Editor. Here the focus will be on the remaining steps of the process:

1. Create a new menu module in the Designer, and name it MRD.
2. Double-click the menu type icon to its left to bring up the Menu Editor window.
3. Use the Create Right icon ▣ and Create Down icon ▣ in the Menu Editor's toolbar to quickly create the menu structure as shown in Figure 17.1. If you experience any problems, refer to the steps you followed in Chapter 8 for a similar process.
4. Save the module.

17.1.2 PROPERTIES OF MENUS

There are a few things to note here. First, as you can see from Figure 17.1, there is no need to create a Window submenu. Every form, even if no menu module is attached to it, will have the menu Window attached to its MDI frame. If a menu module is attached to the form, the Window menu will position itself in conformance with GUI standards. In the case of the MRD application, it will be inserted between the Data and Help menu items in the MAIN_MENU.

Second, the labels you enter in the Menu Editor are what the users will see when they use the menu. Therefore, proper care must be taken when they are set. In order to provide an access key for the menu item, you precede one of the letters in its label with the ampersand sign &. When the menu will be executed at runtime, this letter will be underlined. If the users are in the parent menu already, they can select the item by typing the access key from the keyboard. When specifying the access keys for a menu, you should be careful not to specify the same key for two items within the same menu. Note also that the label of those menu items that will invoke windows or dialog boxes terminates with an ellipsis.

Finally, in order not to interrupt the process of laying out the menu as shown in Figure 17.1, you do not want to stop at each and every one of them to set their properties. Instead, you proceed with the creation process keeping in mind that you will return at a later moment to fine-tune the properties of each item.

Notice for example that there are several menu items in Figure 17.1 labeled separator. These labels serve as reminders that these items will have no other purpose than separating the items of the respective menus. After you have created the menu, you can assign this functionality to all of them:

1. CTRL-CLICK each menu item labeled separator in order to select them all.
2. Choose Tools | Properties... to display the Properties Window for the selected items.
3. Set the *Menu Item Type* property to '*Separator*'. This property is the first one in the **Functional** group of properties.

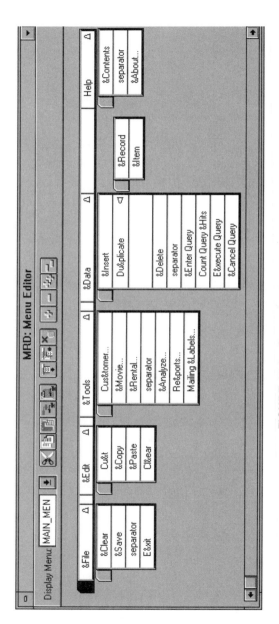

FIGURE 17.1 Structure of the MRD menu.

470

You will see that all the selected items will be changed into separating lines.

By default, the *Menu Item Type* property is set to *'Plain'* for every menu item you create. This is also the type that is encountered the most in the menus you develop. Besides *'Plain'* and *'Separator'*, the *Menu Item Type* property can be set to *'Magic'*, *'Radio'*, and *'Check'*.

When the type of a menu item is set to *'Magic'*, you can assign a built-in command or function to the item such as Cut or Copy. This is how you will implement the items of the Edit menu in your application:

1. Select all the items in the menu Edit.
2. Set the *Menu Item Type* property to *'Magic'*, and deselect the items.
3. For each individual item, set the *Magic Item* property to the setting that corresponds to its name. For example, *Magic Item* will be *'Cut'* for the menu item Cut.

The advantage of using magic items is that Oracle Forms will handle the text editing functionality and decide about its availability. Forms internally will check the context for every situation and turn on or off the appropriate menu items that can be used in that situation.

Two other special types of menu items are Radio and Check menu items. Their purpose and use is very similar to that of radio and check box items in the Forms module. Check menu items are used typically in a View submenu such as the one used in the Forms Designer, to hide and display certain objects in the application. Radio menu items are very unusual for a menu, and are used to set an application to a single state from a number of possible choices that make up the menu radio group. Functionally, these two types of menu items do not provide anything that cannot be implemented with Plain items, or that cannot be set in an Options dialog box. Keeping in mind the GUI rule that your applications must be noticed as little as possible by the users for their exotic, or unusual features, you should use primarily Plain menu items. Occasionally you may use check items, and almost never should you use radio menu items. However, should you choose to implement any of these types of menu items in your application, set the menu item type appropriately and follow the same steps that you would normally follow for Plain menu items. These steps are explained in this section.

Menu items enjoy a series of visual attribute properties related with fonts. You can also inherit these settings from named visual attributes. However, while it is justifiable to customize the visual attributes of Forms items, you should never do this for menu items. The System font, with all its default settings is used universally across all Windows applications and you should not deviate from this path.

Another property that you should never have to set is the *Icon Name*. Like iconic buttons or windows, this setting requires the name of an icon file. At runtime, the icon is displayed to the left of the menu item's label. This is once again one of those things that you can but should not do, because they are not seen in any other application. In your applications, you should represent the menu items as string labels. Iconic toolbars may be attached to the MDI frame to offer access to often-used commands.

The most important properties of a menu item, besides the *Menu Item Type* and *Label*, are the *Command Type, Command Text,* and *Accelerator*. The *Command Type* must be set to *'Null'* for menu items that will serve as separators. If the *Menu Item Type* is set to *'Magic'*, the setting of the property *Magic Item* rules the behavior of the item itself and ignores the setting of *Command Type* property. If, for example, a menu item is set to be the Magic item Cut, it will cut selected text no matter what the setting of its *Command Type* is.

For the rest of menu items (Plain, Check, and Radio), the *Command Type* can be *'Menu'*, *'PL/SQL'*, *'Plus'*, *'Forms'*, and *'Macro'*. From these settings, only the first two are the only ones used. The rest are included for backward compatibly reasons with SQL*Menus, the team mate of SQL*Forms in the Oracle's character-based application development tools.

If the *Command Type* of a menu item is set to *'Menu'*, at runtime, when users will select this menu item, a submenu will appear. The name of this submenu, is stored in the *Command Text* property. If, on the other hand, the *Command Type* is set to *'PL/SQL'*, the *Command Text* property contains the statements that are executed when the menu item is selected. You can access the *Command Text* property by double-clicking it in the Properties Window, or by double-clicking the menu object or menu item icons in the Object Navigator. When editing the *Command Text* of a Menu type item, a system editor dialog box will appear; when editing a PL/SQL menu item, the PL/SQL Editor window will be displayed.

When you create the menu in the Menu Editor, as you add new objects on the Menu Editor, the Designer defines whether their command type is Menu or Plain. In the case of the MRD menu, as you were clicking the Create Right icon to create items of the MAIN_MENU such as File, Edit, Data, Forms was setting the command of these items to PL/SQL type. When you started using the Create Down icon to create the submenus, the Designer automatically changed the command type of the previous menu items to Menu, and assigned the names of the new menu objects to the *Command Text* property.

The *Command Text* property is maintained by a plain text editor, with no PL/SQL editing capabilities when its setting is not PL/SQL. However, if the *Command Type* is set to *'PL/SQL'*, the text editor is replaced by the PL/SQL editor. This allows you to compile and check your PL/SQL statements to avoid runtime errors. In a sense, the code that you attach to each PL/SQL menu item is like a WHEN-BUTTON-PRESSED trigger attached to a push button. It will be executed when the users choose that menu item.

Another property that should not be overlooked is the *Hint* property. Similar to Oracle Forms items, the *Hint* property may contain a brief description about the function of the menu item. This description is displayed in the micro-help line of the MDI frame when the users select the item.

17.1.3 USING PL/SQL IN MENUS

Using different PL/SQL commands, you can initiate a variety of actions from your menu items. Some of these actions may correspond to Oracle Forms built-in procedures. For example, in the MRD application, all the menu items in the Data submenu correspond to built-in procedures. The *Command Text* for these items may be as simple as the name of this procedure. So, for the menu item Data | Insert the command could be

CREATE_RECORD;

The commands executed by a menu module may also be accessible from within the Oracle Forms module. They may be part of different triggers in the form. This variety of ways to perform the same action, while being very beneficial to the users, may cause configuration management nightmares for the application developers. Imagine, for example, how users will create records in your applications. They could press [CREATE RECORD], or choose Data | Insert from the menu, or click the CREATE_RECORD button that you will provide for them in the toolbar. Each of these different actions will normally invoke different PL/SQL methods. Pressing [CREATE RECORD] from the keyboard will invoke the KEY-CREREC trigger, or, in its absence, will execute the CREATE_RECORD built-in procedure. Selecting Data | Insert from the menu will fire the code placed in its *Command Text* property; and finally, clicking the iconic button in the toolbar will fire the WHEN-BUTTON-PRESSED trigger associated with it.

The problem gets even more complicated in forms with several blocks. In the MRD form, for example, the process of inserting records in the MOVIE block or in the CUSTOMER block could be different. In the form module, this problem is solved by bringing the KEY-CREREC down one level in the hierarchy. In other words, from a form level KEY-CREREC trigger, you create two block level triggers that will handle the different functionality for the two blocks. But now, in the code triggered by selecting the Insert menu item or clicking the button in the toolbar, you must first distinguish in which block the event occurred, and then act according to the situation.

It is natural to look for a way to place the code in only one place and reference it from the other two locations. An elegant solution is to place the code in the key triggers, and invoke these key triggers from the menu or the toolbar button. This solution will guarantee that the same piece of code gets executed each time. It will allow you to maintain the code in only one place. Finally, the code to be executed will be decided by the key trigger placed at the appropriate level in the objects hierarchy. To reference the code of a key trigger, or the built-in procedure that corresponds to it, you use the built-in DO_KEY. This procedure takes as input the name of the Oracle Forms built-in whose functionality is to be invoked. Following this approach, the *Command Text* for the Insert menu item will be

DO_KEY('CREATE_RECORD');

Now, whenever the menu item is selected, if there is a KEY-CREREC defined for the block or the module, that trigger will fire; otherwise, the built-in procedure CREATE-RECORD will be executed.

In the light of this discussion, set the *Command Text* for the menu items shown in the first column of Figure 17.2 to the commands specified on the second column. Note that when these commands will be implemented as iconic buttons in the toolbar, their WHEN-BUTTON-PRESSED triggers should also use these statements.

Understandably, it is desirable to take the same approach for items in the menu that do not directly map to Oracle Forms built-ins. Even for these items, you would still want to create and maintain the code in one location, and reference it from both the WHEN-BUTTON-PRESSED triggers and the *Command Text* property of the menu items. There are several ways to achieve this.

The first method follows the same strategy as the one used to take advantage of the Oracle Forms built-ins and the KEY triggers. For example, to access the CUSTOMER block data you would follow these steps:

1. Create a user-named trigger, for example CUSTOMER_SELECTED.
2. Set the *Command Text* property of Tools | Customer to

EXECUTE_TRIGGER ('CUSTOMER_SELECTED');

Menu Item Name	Command Text Property
File|Clear	DO_KEY('CLEAR_FORM');
File|Save	DO_KEY('COMMIT_FORM');
File|Exit	DO_KEY('EXIT_FORM');
Data|Insert	DO_KEY('CREATE_RECORD');
Data|Duplicate|Record	DO_KEY('DUPLICATE_RECORD');
Data|Duplicate|Item	DO_KEY('DUPLICATE_ITEM');
Data|Delete	DO_KEY('DELETE_RECORD');
Data|Enter Query	DO_KEY('ENTER_QUERY');
Data|Count Query Hits	DO_KEY('COUNT_QUERY');
Data|Execute Query	DO_KEY('EXECUTE_QUERY');

FIGURE 17.2 Command Text property settings for menu items in the MRD module.

3. The WHEN-BUTTON-PRESSED trigger for the Customer iconic button will contain the same statement:

EXECUTE_TRIGGER('CUSTOMER_SELECTED');

However, creating and maintaining user-named triggers is not recommended. This feature, useful in earlier versions of SQL*Forms, is superseded by the ability to create and use functions and procedures in later versions.

The second approach is to create a procedure that would take as parameter the name of the button pressed and, based on that name, decide which window to display, or, more generally, what action to take. However, there is a problem with this approach. Because the menu and the form are separate modules, the procedure must be present in both the modules. When the menu items will be selected, the procedure in the menu module will be executed; when the toolbar buttons will be clicked, the Forms procedure will be executed. Again, you are faced with the problem of having to maintain the same code in two different locations.

The third approach is to create a procedure as discussed above and store it in a PL/SQL library module together with every other program unit that will be shared between the menu and the form. This library is attached to the form and the menu modules, thus making its member objects available and accessible to both of them. This is the most elegant and efficient solution, because it not only allows you to maintain the code in one single point, but also to reference it from every other form or menu module that may need it. By removing the PL/SQL objects from the body of the form or menu and replacing it with a pointer to a library, you also reduce the size of these modules, thus making the application run faster. The following chapter will discuss in more detail the advantages of PL/SQL libraries in Oracle Forms applications. In that chapter you will also create the function that will be called when users select the menu item Data | Cancel Query, or any of the menu items in submenus Tools and Help. For the moment, you can place the following line in their *Command Text* property:

MESSAGE('Feature not yet implemented');

Another place where you can put PL/SQL statements in a menu is the startup code. This is a method that is fired every time a menu is loaded into memory. It is used primarily to set the initial state of the menu items. For example, in your application, you may want the users to select the last three items of the Data menu (Count Query Hits, Execute Query, and Cancel Query) only if the application is in Enter Query mode. In the startup code you could place statements that set the *ENABLED* property of these items to *'FALSE'*.

The process of retrieving and setting the properties of menu items is very similar to that of other objects you have seen so far. The example of the procedure

```
PROCEDURE Disable_Menu_Item (menu_item_name VARCHAR2) IS
  menu_item_id    MenuItem;
BEGIN
-- Find ID for menu item
  menu_item_id := FIND_MENU_ITEM(menu_item_name);
  IF ID_NULL(menu_item_id) THEN
    MESSAGE('Menu item '||menu_item_name||' does not exist.');
    RAISE FORM_TRIGGER_FAILURE;
  END IF;

  SET_MENU_ITEM_PROPERTY(menu_item_id, ENABLED, PROPERTY_FALSE);
END;
```

FIGURE 17.3 Changing menu item properties programmatically.

that would be used to disable the properties of a menu item is shown in Figure 17.3.

Using this procedure, the contents of the startup code for the menu would be as follows:

```
Disable_Menu_Item('DATA.COUNT_QUERY');
Disable_Menu_Item('DATA.EXECUTE_QUERY');
Disable_Menu_Item('DATA.CANCEL_QUERY');
```

Note however that there exist two built-in procedures that are not documented in the Oracle Forms documentation. These are ENABLE_ITEM and DISABLE_ITEM. They both take the name of the menu as a first parameter and the name of the item in that menu as a second parameter. Using these functions, the startup code of the menu will be as follows:

```
DISABLE_ITEM('DATA', 'COUNT_QUERY');
DISABLE_ITEM('DATA', 'EXECUTE_QUERY');
DISABLE_ITEM('DATA', 'CANCEL_QUERY');
```

17.1.4 ENFORCING THE SECURITY OF THE APPLICATION IN MENUS

In Oracle Forms applications you can use the definition of roles in the database to restrict the access of users to part of the system they may not be authorized to see. A role is an object defined in the Oracle Server database that is made up of a list of database users to which a set of privileges is assigned. All the privileges assigned to the role will automatically be transferred to the members of that role.

Note

Once you disable these items, there should be a point in the application where you enable them again. In that case, you can use the procedure DISABLE_ITEM. It is also good to group the statements that disable the menu items in procedures that can be called whenever the Oracle Forms mode is set to Normal. Likewise, the statements that enable the items can be grouped in a procedure that will be invoked when the application enters the Query mode. Chapter 18 discusses how to toggle the ENABLED status of menu items and toolbar buttons in your applications.

Discussing the subject of roles in the administration of Oracle databases stretches outside the topic of this book. Therefore it will be assumed that in the database that you are using to follow the examples of this book, there are two roles already created: MRD_OPERATOR and MRD_MANAGER.

  If you can connect to the database with DBA privileges, or have the privileges CREATE ROLE, GRANT ROLE, and DROP ROLE, you can create these roles yourself from the Oracle Forms Designer, following these steps:

1. Select File | Administration | Database Roles... from the menu. This menu item is enabled only if you are connected with the privileges listed above. A Role List window is displayed. It lists all the roles already defined in the database.
2. Click the button New... to create a new role. The Role Maintenance dialog box is displayed (see Figure 17.4).

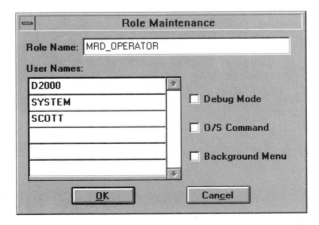

FIGURE 17.4 Role Maintenance dialog box.

> **Note**
>
> In the Role List window, you can also edit the list of users that are members of a role, or delete a role altogether.

3. Define the name for the role in the Role Name field as MRD_USER.
4. Enter all the users that will be included in the role. Note that whether you specify it or not, SYSTEM will always be a member of any role.
5. Click OK.

Follow the same steps to create a role called MRD_MANAGER. When finished, click Save in the Role List window to save the new roles to the database.

In order to use the roles to restrict access to different parts of the menu, you must first make them available to the menu module as a whole:

1. Display the Properties Window for the menu module.
2. Double-click the *Menu Module Roles* property. The Menu Module Roles dialog box will appear (see Figure 17.5).
3. Enter the names of the roles as shown in Figure 17.5.
4. Click OK.
5. Set the *Use Security* property to *'True'*.

FIGURE 17.5   Menu Module Role dialog box.

The actions have supplied the menu module with a list of available roles and instructed it to enforce the security based on these roles. Under these conditions, the menu will not allow access to any role. You must explicitly set the properties of each item so that they become available to the roles. All of the items, except for Tools | Analyze..., will be available for both roles. Therefore, the quickest way to complete the task is to do a global assignment for all of them, and then limit the access to Tools | Analyze... only for the role MRD_MANAGER:

1. Combine SHIFT+CLICK and CTRL+CLICK to select all the menu items.
2. Display the Properties Window for the selection.
3. Double-click the property *Menu Item Roles* under the **Security** group. The Menu Item Roles dialog box will be displayed (see Figure 17.6). Initially, none of the roles displayed in the list is selected.
4. Click MRD_MANAGER and SHIFT+CLICK MRD_OPERATOR to select them both.
5. Click OK.

Now, remove MRD_OPERATOR from the list of roles that have access to the menu item Tools | Analyze.

1. Select the menu item Menu | Analyze and display its Properties Window.
2. Double-click the property *Menu Item Roles* under the **Security** group. The Menu Item Roles dialog box will be displayed (see Figure 17.6). Both roles assigned to this item are selected.
3. Click MRD_OPERATOR to deselect it.
4. Click OK.

FIGURE 17.6 Menu Item Role dialog box.

Make sure that the setting for Display without Privilege property, abbreviated as *Display w/o Privilege* in the Properties Window of this menu item is *'True'*. This setting will make the menu item Analyze be always displayed, but unavailable for those users that are not part of the MRD_MANAGER role.

17.1.5 ATTACHING A MENU TO A FORM

At this point you are ready to connect the menu module developed so far with the MRD form. Save and generate the menu module and open the MRD form that you were working with at the end of the last chapter.

1. Double-click the form module icon to the left of MRD module to display its Properties Window.
2. Set the *Menu Module* to the name of the menu you just saved followed by the extension .MMX, for example MRD.MMX.

You do not need to change any of the other settings in the **Menu** group of properties. The *Menu Style* in Windows is always *'Pull-Down'*; you will access the menu from the file system, therefore *Use File* must remain set to *'True'*. If the menu had

---

Note

Oracle Forms looks for the menu module in the directories specified in the environmental variable FORMS45_PATH in the ORACLE.INI file. If your working directory is not added to FORMS45_PATH and you run the MRD module from the Designer, you will receive the error message **FRM-10221: Cannot read file mrd.**. Specifying the complete path of the menu module will solve the problem, but only temporarily. Hardcoded file names are not flexible when distributing your application to the users' environment. Another solution to this problem is to place the menu module under the same directory as the form module executable and create a program item with a working directory, the one where these executables are located.

You may also receive the following error when attempting to run the module **FRM-10256: User is not authorized to run Oracle Forms Menu.** The reason for this problem is that the account you are working with does not have privileges to query the Oracle Forms database tables for role security information. You should run the *Forms Grant* SQL script from *Developer/2000 Administration* program group as explained in Chapter 4.

multiple levels of hierarchy, you could set the *Starting Menu* property to the name of a menu other than the MAIN_MENU. This will display only those menu objects and items that are dependent on this menu in the tree. Finally, save, generate, and run the MRD module to see the menu created here.

17.2 TOOLBARS

Toolbars are rapidly becoming a standard feature in GUI applications. They group together iconic buttons and help users access functionality that is used frequently and across multiple windows. The toolbars are attached to the MDI frame either horizontally, under the menu, or vertically along the left border of the window. In this section you will create a horizontal toolbar that will be available throughout the application and will allow users to save their data, exit the application, navigate to the major parts of the application and invoke the on-line help system. You will also create a vertical toolbar that will be available only when users will be working with base table blocks. The iconic buttons here will allow them to access functions typical for these blocks such as inserting, deleting, or querying records from the database.

17.2.1 STEPS TO IMPLEMENT A TOOLBAR IN ORACLE FORMS

There is very little that you do not know about creating toolbars in Oracle Forms applications. Although you were ready to complete the task a couple of chapters earlier, it makes more sense to discuss it in this chapter. The reason is that toolbars usually go hand-in-hand with menus. Their iconic buttons represent the major functions of the system that can be selected from the menu.

The process of creating toolbars in Oracle Forms can be summarized in the following steps:

1. Create a control block that will own the iconic buttons in the toolbar.
2. Create a canvas, and define its type as Horizontal Toolbar or Vertical Toolbar, according to the type of toolbar you are creating.
3. Create each control that will be part of the toolbar. Usually, the controls are iconic buttons, but it is not uncommon to see drop-down lists boxes in toolbars as well.
4. Adjust the size of the canvas.
5. Attach the toolbar canvas to the MDI frame of the application.
6. Implement the functionality that each toolbar button will provide through PL/SQL triggers, functions, and procedures.

In the next section, you will create the toolbars for the MRD applications following these steps.

17.2.2 CREATING TOOLBARS FOR THE MRD APPLICATION

As always, you will follow the discussion here with the form you are developing. In this section you will create iconic buttons for the toolbar. The icons are provided in the directory \ICONS of the companion disk. Recall from Chapter 14 that in order for Oracle Forms to be able to attach the icon files to the buttons, the name of this directory must be specified in the TK21_ICONS environment variable in ORACLE.INI. As a preliminary step, append the directory \ICONS to the variable TK21_ICONS.

Now create the block and the canvas that will contain the iconic buttons.

1. Create a control block and name it TOOLBAR. This block will own all the iconic buttons of the toolbars.
2. Create a canvas and name it H_TOOLBAR. The buttons for the horizontal toolbar will reside on this canvas.
3. Set the *Canvas-view Type* property to *'Horizontal Toolbar'*.

All the buttons you will create will have similar properties. It is certainly a good idea to create a property class initially and use it to inherit the properties for the other objects. This property class will include the same properties as the class PUSH_BUTTON, but some of these properties will have different settings.

1. Create a duplicate copy of the property class PUSH_BUTTON and name it TOOLBAR_BUTTON.
2. Set *Width* and *Height* to *'18'*; set *Navigable* to *'False'*; and set *Iconic* to *'True'*.

Now you can create the first button of the toolbar.

1. Display the canvas H_TOOLBAR in the Layout Editor.
2. Create a push button and place it in the upper left-hand corner of the canvas. Make sure that the context for the canvas is set to the block TOOLBAR before you create the button.
3. Display the Properties Window for the buttons, and name it CLEAR_ FORM.
4. Set its *Class* property to *'TOOLBAR_ICON'*; set the *Icon Name* to *'new'*; set the *Label* to *'Clear'*; set the *Hint* property to *'Clear the application'*.

At this point, you should have a button like this ▣ on the canvas. Now create eight more push buttons. Select them all and make them inherit the properties from the TOOLBAR_BUTTON class. For each individual button, set the button-specific properties according to Figure 17.7.

Now position the buttons so that they appear grouped by functionality. The criteria you should use are listed here:

Name	Icon Name	Label	Hint
CLEAR_FORM	clearfrm	Clear	Clear the application.
COMMIT_FORM	save	Save	Save the application.
EXIT_FORM	exit	Exit	Exit the application.
CUSTOMER	customer	Customer Data	Enter and edit customer data.
MOVIE	movie	Movie Data	Enter and edit movie data.
RENTAL	rent	Rental Data	Enter and edit rental data.
ANALYZE	analyze	Analyze Trends	Analyze revenue for movies.
MAIL	mail	Print Envelopes	Print mailing labels.
HELP	help	Help	Invoke on-line help.

FIGURE 17.7   Individual settings for properties of buttons in the horizontal toolbar.

1. If the menu items that correspond to the buttons are adjacent, the buttons should be one pixel apart.
2. If there is a separator line, but the menu items are still within the same submenu, the buttons should be three pixels apart.
3. If the menu items are on different menus, the buttons should be six pixels apart.

Align the buttons horizontally, and group them by selecting Arrange I Group, so that in the future they all move together as one object. Now you can reduce the height of the canvas. Because the horizontal toolbar canvas will be attached to the MDI frame, its size will condition the height of the client area where all the MDI sheets will be displayed. Therefore it is important that these type of canvases do not take more space than they need. Finally, your horizontal toolbar should look similar to Figure 17.8.

In principle, creating the vertical toolbar is the same process:

1. Create another canvas and call it V_TOOLBAR.
2. With the context set to the block TOOLBAR, create six push buttons.
3. Inherit their common properties from the TOOLBAR_BUTTON property class.
4. Set their individual properties according to the specification in Figure 17.9.

FIGURE 17.8   Horizontal toolbar for MRD module.

Name	Icon Name	Label	Hint
CREATE_RECORD	crerec	Create	Create new record.
DELETE_RECORD	delrec	Delete	Delete current record.
ENTER_QUERY	enterqry	Enter Query	Enter query mode.
EXECUTE_QUERY	execqry	Execute Query	Execute query.
CANCEL_QUERY	canclqry	Cancel Query	Cancel query.

FIGURE 17.9 Individual settings for properties of buttons in the vertical toolbar.

After grouping and vertically aligning the buttons, and reducing the width of the canvas to an appropriate value, your vertical canvas should be similar to Figure 17.10.

Among other things, Chapter 15 discussed the process of opening and closing windows in Oracle Forms MDI applications. Recall that your application would use a home item, where the focus will land each time a window is closed. The implementation of the home item in Chapter 15 requires that it be the first item of the first block in the module. It is natural to elect one of the buttons in the horizontal toolbar as the home item for the application. The toolbar, being attached to the MDI frame, will be available as long as the application is running and will not depend on any application window. From the buttons in the horizontal toolbar, the EXIT_FORM button will always be available, to allow users to quit the application. This would be a good choice for the home item. Another one would be the button that invokes the on-line help.

The following steps designate EXIT_FORM as the home item of the MRD module:

FIGURE 17.10 Vertical toolbar for MRD module.

1. In the Object Navigator, drag the block TOOLBAR in the first position in the list of blocks.
2. Drag the button EXIT_FORM in the first position among items in the block TOOLBAR.
3. Set the *Navigable* property for this button to *'True'*. This step is necessary to allow Oracle Forms to navigate to the button.

Of course, you could have chosen the short path, by directly entering the following statement in the PRE-FORM trigger of the module:

:GLOBAL.Home_Item := 'TOOLBAR.EXIT_FORM';

Either of them is acceptable, as long as the application is well-documented, and everyone in the development team is aware of the convention.

17.2.3 ATTACHING TOOLBARS TO FORMS MODULES

Now you are ready to attach the toolbar to the MDI frame of the application:

1. Display the Properties Window for the module MRD.
2. Set the property *Horiz. MDI Toolbar* (abbreviation for Horizontal MDI Toolbar) to *'H_TOOLBAR'*.
3. Set the property *Vert. MDI Toolbar* (abbreviation for Vertical MDI Toolbar) to *'V_TOOLBAR'*.

That will do it! You can save, generate, and run the module now to take a look at the new toolbars.

17.2.4 ADDING FUNCTIONALITY TO THE MRD TOOLBAR

In this section, you will dress up the iconic buttons in the horizontal and vertical toolbars with the functionality that users will invoke by clicking each of them. This functionality will be carried out by PL/SQL statements attached to these buttons.

According to their functionality, the iconic buttons in the toolbars of the MRD module can be grouped as follows:

1. *Buttons that navigate to different windows and dialog boxes of the module.* These are the buttons CUSTOMER, MOVIE, RENTAL, ANALYZE, and MAIL.
2. *Buttons that will require special consideration.* The only button in this category would be the HELP, which will invoke the on-line help for the application.
3. *Buttons that invoke Oracle Forms built-in procedures.* These are all the remaining buttons in the horizontal or vertical toolbars.

As discussed in the previous section, the goal in this process is to modularize and concentrate the code in as few places as possible. To achieve this, create a procedure that takes the name of the button pressed, and, based on that name, executes the appropriate statements as an argument. Figure 17.11 shows contents of this procedure.

From the contents of this procedure you can appreciate the choice of names for the iconic buttons in the toolbars. Those buttons that will take the users to a particular window in the application are named after the block in the target window that will serve as landing point for the focus of Forms. This allows you to handle the navigation to all the functional areas of the application with only one line of code:

CLICK_BUTTON(button_name);

Those buttons that will correspond to Oracle Forms built-in routines, are named after the particular routine they will invoke. The one line statement **DO_KEY(button_name)** makes it possible to invoke these routines, or the corresponding key triggers, if they exist, independently of the name of the button.

It is worth discussing the particular situation when the button CANCEL_QUERY is pressed. The Oracle Forms built-in that can be used to cancel a query is

```
PROCEDURE Click_Button (button_name IN VARCHAR2) IS
BEGIN
IF button_name IN ('CUSTOMER', 'MOVIE','RENTAL') THEN
    Open_Window(button_name, button_name);
  ELSIF button_name IN ('MAIL','ABOUT')  THEN
    Open_Dialog_Box(button_name, button_name);
  ELSIF button_name IN ('ANALYZE', 'HELP') THEN
    MESSAGE('Feature not yet implemented.');
  ELSIF button_name = 'CANCEL_QUERY' AND
  :SYSTEM.MODE = 'ENTER-QUERY' THEN
    EXIT_FORM;      -- EXIT_FORM takes Oracle Forms
                    -- from Enter Query to Normal mode
  ELSE
    DO_KEY(button_name);
  END IF;
  IF NOT FORM_SUCCESS THEN
    MESSAGE('Internal error occurred in Click_Button.');
    RAISE FORM_TRIGGER_FAILURE;
  END IF;
END;
```

FIGURE 17.11   Generic procedure for toolbar icons.

EXIT_FORM. However, you need to be sure that the form is in Query mode, before issuing the call to this procedure. (If the form is in Normal mode, EXIT_FORM closes the application entirely.) The system variable SYSTEM.MODE holds the value for the state of a form when the procedure is invoked.

Note also another way used in this procedure to check the successful completion of any action by Oracle Forms. The FORM_SUCCESS is a function defined in the STANDARD package of Oracle Forms built-ins. This function returns the Boolean value TRUE if the last action of the form was successful, and FALSE if a problem occurred. There are two other similar functions, FORM_FAILURE and FORM_FATAL, which return TRUE if the last action taken by Forms failed, or resulted with a fatal error. The distinction between a failure and a fatal error is vague, therefore, if you want to check the outcome of an action, you should use the function FORM_SUCCESS, as in the example shown in Figure 17.11.

The function Click_Button enables you to invoke the functionality of any button, as long as you know the name of that button. This function can be called from several locations.

You could create a WHEN-BUTTON-PRESSED trigger, and call the function with the name of the button hard-coded in it. The trigger for the button CLEAR_FORM, for example, would contain the following line:

Click_Button('CLEAR_FORM');

You could also define the WHEN-BUTTON-PRESSED trigger at the block level, rather than for each individual button. However, thinking in object-oriented programming terms, this event is in reality related to the push buttons. Recall that the general properties of these toolbar buttons are inherited from the property class TOOLBAR_BUTTON. It is natural to create the code for the Press-Button event as a method for this property class.

As in other similar situations, in a trigger attached to a property class you want your code to be object-independent. Therefore, you should find a way to retrieve the name of the button. The system variable SYSTEM.TRIGGER_ITEM contains the name of the item that activated the trigger. This variable stores the fully-qualified name of the item, in the form BLOCK_NAME.ITEM_NAME. To strip only the item name from this string, you can use a combination of the SQL functions INSTR and SUBSTR. A similar technique was discussed in Chapter 16. INSTR is used to find the position in the string of the dot that separates the block name from the item name. Then the function SUBSTR returns the substring of the original string that begins from the character after the dot. This is also the name of the item that you pass to the procedure Click_Button.

Figure 17.12 shows the content of the trigger WHEN-BUTTON-PRESSED for the property class TOOLBAR_BUTTON.

It is not hard to notice that most of the functionality accessible from the toolbars is also accessible from several push buttons created in earlier chapters. You

```
DECLARE
  block_item       VARCHAR2(80);
  item_name        VARCHAR2(50);
  dot_pos NUMBER;
BEGIN
  block_item := :SYSTEM.TRIGGER_ITEM;
  dot_pos := INSTR(block_item, '.', 1, 1);
  item_name := SUBSTR(block_item, dot_pos + 1 );
  Click_Button(item_name);
END;
```

FIGURE 17.12   Generic trigger to activate an iconic button.

should take advantage of the work done in this section and of the carefully planned naming standards followed previously. Follow these steps to minimize the number of triggers attached to individual buttons in the MRD form:

1. Attach to the property class PUSH_BUTTON an identical trigger as the one shown in Figure 17.12.
2. Delete the item-level WHEN-BUTTON-PRESSED triggers for all the buttons in blocks CUSTOMER, MOVIE, and RENTAL, except for the buttons that close the windows.

Now, when the event ButtonPressed will occur in one of these items, for example CUSTOMER.RENTAL or MOVIE.COMMIT_FORM, Oracle Forms will execute the WHEN-BUTTON-PRESSED trigger inherited from the property class. However, if the event occurs for a button that has a proper trigger attached such as CUSTOMER.CLOSE, the item-level trigger will fire.

17.2.5 ENABLING AND DISABLING TOOLBAR BUTTONS AND MENU ITEMS DYNAMICALLY

When users launch the application, they will initially see only the MDI frame, with its menu and toolbars. Not all of the iconic buttons or menu items can be used at this time. For example, users cannot create, or delete, or save any records unless a window is open and they are on a base table block. In fact, if they try to click one of the icons in the vertical toolbar, or select any item from the Data menu, Oracle Forms will return the error message, FRM-41003: This function cannot be performed here.

It is necessary to disable some of the toolbar buttons and menu items whose functionality is not accessible upon Forms startup. However, as soon as a window with a base table block in it becomes active, the buttons and the menu items should return to their normal state. If during the process users close all the windows, these buttons and menu items should be disabled once again.

To facilitate the process of enabling and disabling objects, you need to create the following procedures:

❑ The procedure Toggle_Menu_Item, shown in Figure 17.13 toggles the *ENABLED* property of a menu item whose name is passed as an argument.
❑ The procedure Toggle_Item, shown in Figure 17.14 is very similar to the previous one and toggles the *ENABLED* property of an item whose name is passed as an argument.

With these two procedures in hand, you can create the procedure Toggle_ Enable_Property that disables the right menu items and iconic buttons at form startup or when all MDI sheets are closed and enables them when one of the MDI sheets is open. The contents of this procedure are shown in Figure 17.15.

You also need the global variable GLOBAL.Toggle_State to hold the toggle state of the application. When the form is initially loaded, the procedure Toggle_Enable_Property disables the menu items and the toolbar icons. At the same time, GLOBAL.Toggle_State must be set to *'DISABLED'*. When the first of the MDI sheet window is opened, the buttons and menu items must be set to normal state and GLOBAL.Toggle_State should be set to *'ENABLED'*. To add this functionality to the MRD module follow these steps:

```
PROCEDURE Toggle_Menu_Item (menu_item_name VARCHAR2) IS
  menu_item_id   MenuItem;
BEGIN
-- Find ID for menu item
  menu_item_id := FIND_MENU_ITEM(menu_item_name);
  IF ID_NULL(menu_item_id) THEN
    MESSAGE('Menu item '||menu_item_name||' does not exist.');
    RAISE FORM_TRIGGER_FAILURE;
  END IF;

  IF GET_MENU_ITEM_PROPERTY(menu_item_id,ENABLED) = 'TRUE' THEN
    SET_MENU_ITEM_PROPERTY(menu_item_id,ENABLED,PROPERTY_FALSE);
  ELSE
    SET_MENU_ITEM_PROPERTY(menu_item_id,ENABLED,PROPERTY_TRUE);
  END IF;
END Toggle_Menu_Item;
```

FIGURE 17.13   Procedure that toggles the ENABLED property of a menu item.

```
PROCEDURE Toggle_Item (item_name VARCHAR2) IS
  item_id  ITEM;
BEGIN
- Find ID for item
  item_id := FIND_ITEM(item_name);
  IF ID_NULL(item_id) THEN
    MESSAGE('Item '||item_name||' does not exist.');
    RAISE FORM_TRIGGER_FAILURE;
  END IF;

  IF GET_ITEM_PROPERTY(item_id,ENABLED) = 'TRUE' THEN
    SET_ITEM_PROPERTY(item_id,ENABLED,PROPERTY_FALSE);
  ELSE
    SET_ITEM_PROPERTY(item_id,ENABLED,PROPERTY_TRUE);
  END IF;
END Toggle_Item;
```

FIGURE 17.14   Procedure that toggles the ENABLED property of an item.

1. Declare the variable GLOBAL.Toggle_State in the PRE-FORM trigger.
2. Create the form-level trigger WHEN-WINDOW-ACTIVATED, and add to it the statements shown in Figure 17.16.

It is clear from these statements that when any of the MDI sheets are activated, and the status of the menu items and toolbar buttons is still disabled, the proce-

```
PROCEDURE Toggle_Enable_Property IS
BEGIN
  Toggle_Menu_Item('FILE.CLEAR_FORM');
  Toggle_Menu_Item('FILE.SAVE');
  Toggle_Menu_Item('DATA.INSERT');
  Toggle_Menu_Item('DATA.DUPLICATE');
  Toggle_Menu_Item('DATA.DELETE');
  Toggle_Menu_Item('DATA.ENTER');
  Toggle_Item('TOOLBAR.CLEAR_FORM');
  Toggle_Item('TOOLBAR.COMMIT_FORM');
  Toggle_Item('TOOLBAR.CREATE_RECORD');
  Toggle_Item('TOOLBAR.DELETE_RECORD');
  Toggle_Item('TOOLBAR.ENTER_QUERY');
END;
```

FIGURE 17.15   Procedure that enables and disables menu items and iconic buttons.

```
IF :GLOBAL.Toggle_State = 'DISABLED' AND
   :SYSTEM.EVENT_WINDOW <> 'ABOUT' THEN
    Toggle_Enable_Property;
   :GLOBAL.Toggle_State := 'ENABLED';
END IF;
```

FIGURE 17.16   Enabling menu items and iconic buttons.

dure **Toggle_Enable_Property** will be executed and will enable the objects. The flag **GLOBAL.Toggle_State** will be set to *'ENABLED'* as well. This will guarantee that when the next window is activated, this procedure will not get executed again.

The only time when the procedure **Toggle_Enable_Property** should run again is when the users close all the windows in the application. In this case, the menu items and toolbar buttons in question should no longer be accessible, and therefore, their *ENABLE* property must be set to *'FALSE'*. The global variable **GLOBAL.Toggle_State** should once again be set to *'DISABLED'*. The question is what would be the appropriate event that should make you check and see if all the windows are closed, and, if so, perform these actions.

The MRD application uses a special object as the home item where the focus should return after the window is closed. When the focus is placed on an item, the trigger WHEN-NEW-ITEM-INSTANCE fires. Thus, for all purposes, each time a window is closed, this trigger for the home item EXIT_FORM will be activated. The code that disables the objects if no windows are open should be placed in this trigger.

The best way to decide whether all the windows are closed or if there is at least one still open, is to use the function **Count_Open_Windows** that returns the number of open windows in the application. Recall that this function was implemented in Chapter 16. Now you can create the trigger WHEN-NEW-ITEM-INSTANCE for the iconic button EXIT_FORM as shown in Figure 17.17. Note that this trigger will handle the initial disabling of the objects as well.

This concludes the work you have to do with the toolbar for the MRD application. Note that although you implemented the functionality for icons CUSTOMER, MOVIE, RENTAL, ANALYZE, and MAIL, you still have to add it to the menu items. You could do it at this point, by copying the procedure **Click_Button**

```
IF Count_Open_Windows('WINDOWS', 'WINDOW_NAME') = 0 THEN
  Toggle_Enable_Property;
  :GLOBAL.Toggle_State := 'DISABLED';
END IF;
```

FIGURE 17.17   Disabling menu items and iconic toolbars.

discussed earlier over to the menu module and setting the *Command Text* for each menu item using this procedure. For example, the *Command Text* for Tools | Customer... would be

Click_Button('CUSTOMER');

The next chapter will discuss the PL/SQL libraries. There, you will create a library with code that is shared by both the form and the menu, and attach the library to each module. From that moment on, the code will be maintained in the PL/SQL library and referenced by the form or the menu.

17.2.6 ADDING BALLOON HELP TO TOOLBARS

While working with the Oracle Forms Designer you have seen how you can display popup help, also known as balloon help, for iconic buttons in toolbars of the Object Navigator, Layout Editor, Properties Window, and Menu Editor. You would like your applications to contain a similar functionality as well. While future releases of Oracle Forms will incorporate popup help with iconic toolbars, for the moment you could utilize PL/SQL libraries provided as additions to the Oracle Forms software. The library that implements the balloon help functionality is located in the directory %ORACLE_HOME%\FORMS45\PLSQLLIB and is called HINT.PLL. This library fills the contents of the balloon help with the text stored in the *Label* property of the iconic button.

The general steps to implement the balloon help functionality for the toolbars in your applications are as follows:

1. Edit the *Label* property of each iconic button to contain two or three words that describe the functionality of the button.
2. Attach the library HINT.PLL to the module that contains the toolbar. Follow instructions provided in Chapter 18 about how to attach PL/SQL libraries to an Oracle Forms module.
3. Create a form-level WHEN-MOUSE-ENTER trigger that contains the following statement as its last line:

Hint.ShowButtonHelp;

This procedure activates a timer only in the case the trigger is fired by iconic buttons. The timer will expire in 500 milliseconds, at which point, the contents of the property *Label* will be displayed in the balloon help. If you desire a different time response, you can pass its length in milliseconds to the procedure ShowButtonHelp as in the following line:

Hint.ShowButtonHelp(250);

4. Create a form-level trigger WHEN-TIMER-EXPIRED with the following statement in the first line:

Hint.ShowButtonHelpHandler;

The trigger WHEN-TIMER-EXPIRED is fired when the timer activated in the previous steps expires. The procedure ShowButtonHelpHandler itself contains the code responsible for displaying the balloon help attached to its parent iconic button.

5. In block TOOLBAR create the block-level trigger WHEN-MOUSE-LEAVE with the following statement in its body:

Hint.HideButtonHelp;

This procedure will hide the balloon help that may be currently displayed for the iconic bar as soon as the mouse leaves its sensitive area. If the timer is started by the trigger WHEN-MOUSE-ENTER, but has not yet expired, hence the balloon help is still inactive, the procedure HideButtonHelp will terminate the timer.

17.3 SUMMARY

This chapter covered the properties, functionality and usage of menus and toolbars in Oracle Forms applications. Listed here are major concepts explained in the chapter:

- ❏ Oracle menus
  - ❏ Creating menus
  - ❏ Properties of menus
  - ❏ Using PL/SQL in menus
  - ❏ Enforcing the security of the application in menus
  - ❏ Attaching a menu to a form
- ❏ Toolbars
  - ❏ Steps to implement toolbars in Oracle Forms
  - ❏ Attaching toolbars to forms modules
  - ❏ Adding functionality to toolbars
  - ❏ Enabling and disabling toolbar buttons and menu items dynamically
  - ❏ Adding balloon help to toolbars

PL/SQL OBJECTS

"One event happeneth to them all."
—*The Holy Bible,* Ecclesiastes 2:14

- ◆ Events and Triggers in Oracle Forms
- ◆ PL/SQL Libraries
- ◆ PL/SQL Packages
- ◆ Stored Program Units and Database Triggers
- ◆ Summary

So far in this book, you have used procedures and functions, and have written several triggers to implement the functionality of the MRD application. This chapter takes a closer look at these and other PL/SQL objects used in Oracle Forms. In particular, it looks at Forms as an event-driven environment and how different events activate different PL/SQL objects. It also discusses other PL/SQL objects such as stored procedures, database triggers, and packages. PL/SQL libraries, used to group together the code of PL/SQL objects, are also introduced as a way to ensure code reusability in your applications.

18.1 EVENTS AND TRIGGERS IN ORACLE FORMS

While discussing different objects used in an Oracle Forms application such as blocks, data items, controls, and records, previous chapters have also discussed the events that occur in these objects, the triggers associated with these events, and how you can place PL/SQL code in these triggers to make your application react to the events in the desired way.

18.1.1 TYPES OF EVENTS AND TRIGGERS

An Oracle Forms application is the middle ground where its users meet their data stored in the database. Users are the major players that define the events that occur in the life of a form. The events that originate from their interaction with the application are called *interface events*. Such events are clicking a mouse, pressing a push button, changing the state of a check box, selecting a radio button, or selecting from a list. When Oracle Forms was a character-based application, users could act on the application by pressing keyboard keys only. Therefore, events were mapped to a variety of keys, primarily function keys. Pressing one of these keys, for example F6, would cause a certain event to happen. Programmers would place their code in the key trigger associated with that event, and, probably add a cryptic label on the boilerplate such as **F6 -> Cust. Info**. Today, there is no need for such techniques. As examples discussed in this part have demonstrated, a push button on the window, or an iconic button on the toolbar, would be the object that users click to initiate a function or navigate to an area in the application. However, the events associated with pressing keyboard keys, and the KEY triggers are still available in Oracle Forms.

The triggers associated with user interface events are typically named after the event that fires them, in the format WHEN-*Event-Occurred*. Example of such triggers are WHEN-MOUSE-CLICK, WHEN-MOUSE-DOUBLE-CLICK, WHEN BUTTON-PRESSED, or WHEN-RADIO-CHANGED. You have used a variety of these triggers in the MRD application.

The triggers activated by pressing function keys are named KEY-*Function*. For example, in PC environments KEY-COMMIT is fired when users press F10 and KEY-CREREC is fired when they press F6. An important trigger in this category is KEY-OTHERS. This is fired whenever one of the predefined keys is pressed and no explicit trigger is associated with it. By placing the statement NULL; in this trigger, you will effectively turn off the ability of users to generate any default event of Oracle Forms by pressing one of these keys. It is a recommended action in GUI applications, where all the functionality of the system must be accessible from the menu, toolbar, or the controls of the application, and not mysteriously hidden behind a key stroke or two.

The events that are caused by the response of the database to the application's requests for information, or desire to act on the data, are called *database transaction events*. Such events are logging in and out of the database, querying data, inserting, deleting, updating, and committing. Oracle Forms divides most of these events in three phases, or subevents. The first phase is right before the transactional event occurs. The second phase is the event occurring. And the third phase comes immediately after the event.

The triggers associated with these subevents are called PRE-*Event*, ON-*Event*, and POST-*Event*. Examples of such triggers are PRE-QUERY, ON-QUERY, and POST-QUERY, fired when the DatabaseQuery event occurs; or PRE-INSERT, ON-INSERT, and POST-INSERT, fired when the DatabaseInsert event occurs. This state of affairs allows you to take certain actions in preparation for an event, when the event actually occurs, or after the event has occurred. For example, the PRE-QUERY trigger is typically used to add additional conditions in the SELECT statements of a base table block, based on the query criteria that users have entered in the query-by-example interface of the form. The POST-QUERY trigger on the other hand, is used to retrieve additional data, based on values stored in designated items for each record returned by the query. The ON-*Event* triggers are used only if you want to override the way Oracle Forms handles the event. For example, if the application is running against a non-Oracle database, triggers such as ON-INSERT, ON-DELETE, and ON-COMMIT must contain the necessary statements to perform the task in these databases. If an application will not need to access the database, you can place the statement NULL; in the ON-LOGON trigger, to bypass the logon screen that Oracle Forms displays by default, when the form is launched. The ON-*Event* triggers that are used the most, however, are the ON-ERROR and ON-MESSAGE. These are fired when Oracle Forms sends messages generated internally to the console, and can be used to trap, silence, or modify these messages.

Then, there is the gray area of events that are not caused directly by an action of the users, or a transaction with the database. These events occur internally as Forms responds to any of the events described before. The major categories of these events are navigation events and validation events. The basic navigation events are entering the object, preparing the object for input, and leaving the object. The trigger PRE-*Object* is fired when Forms enters an object. When Oracle Forms prepares an object for input, the trigger WHEN-NEW-*Object*-INSTANCE is fired. And, when Forms leaves an object, the POST-*Object* trigger is activated. In all these cases, the object can be a form, a block, a record, or a text item. The validation event occurs only for items and records, and the triggers fired during these events are WHEN-VALIDATE-ITEM and WHEN-VALIDATE-RECORD, respectively.

18.1.2 FIRING ORDER OF TRIGGERS

In order to place the code effectively in the key points of your application, it is very important to understand the sequence in which the events described above and their corresponding triggers fire. Given the large number of events and situations that can occur in a Forms application, describing the firing sequence of triggers associated with them extends far beyond the scope of this book. This section will focus only on the sequence of triggers that fire during navigational events. *Oracle Forms Reference Manual Volume 2* contains a comprehensive coverage of this topic.

To help you understand how Oracle Forms navigates from one item to the other, Figure 18.1 graphically shows the hierarchy of objects in a module. The objects in an Oracle Forms application form a connected graph. This means that if the current focus of the form is on Item 1.1.1, and the user clicks Item 2.2.1, the focus does not immediately jump to that item. Internally, Oracle Forms follows the connecting lines to navigate to the clicked item. This means that the form will first go up the tree. It will leave Item 1.1.1, Record 1.1, and Block 1. At this point, there is a line connecting the current block with the block of the target item. Forms will move to this block and navigate down the tree. It will enter Block 2, Record 2.2, and Item 2.2.1. Finally, the target block, record, and item are prepared to receive input from the user.

All the triggers associated with these events, if they exist, will fire in the sequence the events occur. Assuming that both items are text items, the sequence of triggers fired is: POST-TEXT-ITEM, POST-RECORD, POST-BLOCK when Forms is going up the tree; PRE-BLOCK, PRE-RECORD, PRE-TEXT-ITEM when Forms is going up the tree; and WHEN-NEW-BLOCK-INSTANCE, WHEN-NEW-

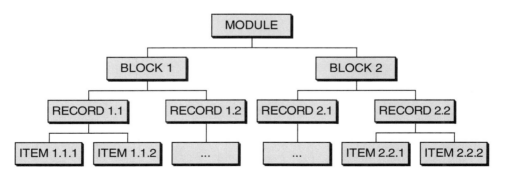

FIGURE 18.1 Hierarchy tree of objects in Oracle Forms.

RECORD-INSTANCE, WHEN-NEW-ITEM-INSTANCE when the objects are pre-pared for input.

As it can be seen from Figure 18.1, the number of nodes traversed, and therefore triggers fired, will depend on the location of the current focus and of the target item. If from Item 1.1.1 users want to go to Item 1.1.2, only the triggers POST-ITEM, PRE-ITEM, and WHEN-NEW-ITEM-INSTANCE would fire. However, if the navigation target is an item in Record 1.2, then the record-related triggers will fire as well.

The validation occurs during the process of leaving the item or the record. The validation of items will occur if their status is not VALID. A record will be validated every time its status is not QUERY. When the record is validated, all its items are validated as well.

18.1.3 TRIGGERS AS METHODS THAT ASSOCIATE OBJECTS WITH EVENTS

A form is built by drawing together resources from the pool of available objects, and the pool of available events. You start by creating objects and then program the way they behave when certain events occur. The association between an object and an event is established by a trigger attached to the object that is fired when the event occurs. Thinking of objects and events as entities, triggers are the entity introduced to resolve the many-to-many relationships that exist between these entities (see Figure 18.2).

Given the number of objects that can be part of a form and the number of events that Oracle Forms recognizes, it would be an overwhelming and impossible task to create triggers that govern the behavior of each object for each event.

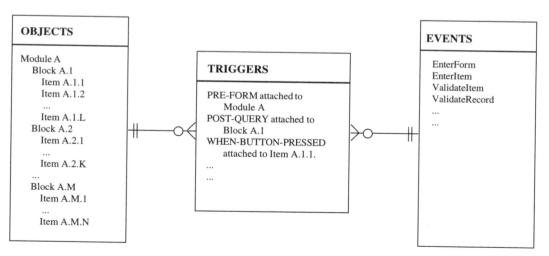

FIGURE 18.2 Relationship between objects, events, and triggers in Oracle Forms.

Fortunately, you do not have to do this. The default functionality that Oracle Forms provides takes most of the load off your shoulders. For example, very little explicit programming is required and done for database transaction events; applications mostly rely on the handling of these events by Forms. This sharing of responsibilities allows you to focus the attention where most of the programming occurs. That is the user-friendly design of the application and the handling of the user interface and validation events.

Even when you have to explicitly code triggers for an event, you can take advantage of the fact that Forms propagates events in its hierarchy of objects. If a push button is pressed, for example, Forms will look to see if there is a WHEN-BUTTON-PRESSED trigger at the button level. If there is none, it will move up to the block level in search for a trigger with that name attached to the block. If none is found, it will move up to the form level for the same purpose. By default, the first trigger encountered in this traversal from the bottom to the top of the hierarchy will be executed. This behavior allows you to modularize the code, make it more compact, and move it higher in the hierarchy of a module. The advantage here is that the number of triggers to create and maintain can be reduced significantly. If, for example, a block contains several push buttons, instead of having that many WHEN-BUTTON-PRESSED triggers, you could move the code up at the block level, and concentrate it in one single trigger that will fire each time a button in the block is pressed.

18.1.4 OVERRIDING THE DEFAULT FIRING ORDER OF TRIGGERS

There are instances when the behavior of an item in reaction to an event is slightly different from the way all its peers behave. You would still want to execute the main code that is associated with that event, and, in addition, the code that characterizes this special behavior. In such cases, you can still create and maintain the general functionality in a block-level trigger. Then, an item-level trigger is created for the same event and attached to the item that needs special attention. As said earlier, when the event occurs for this item, the default behavior of Oracle Forms is to fire the item-level trigger and stop there. By changing the property *Execution Style* for the trigger object, you can make both triggers fire.

Note

As you saw in the Chapter 17, triggers can be attached to property classes as well. Objects that inherit properties from these classes, will also inherit the triggers. Oracle Forms will execute only the class triggers even if triggers of the same type are attached to the objects or their parents.

To open the Properties Window for a trigger, you must select the trigger in the Navigator and choose Tool I Properties... from the Designer menu. The *Execution Style* property may be set to '*Override*', '*Before*', or '*After*'. '*Override*' is the default setting, and will cause Forms to execute the first trigger found going up from the item level to block and to form level. If the property is set to '*After*', the trigger in the parent object will fire first and then the trigger in the current object will be executed. This sequence is reversed when *Execution Style* is set to '*Before*'.

Of course, the property can be set recursively. For example, if there is a WHEN-BUTTON-PRESSED defined at the item, block, and form level, and you want to fire the form-level trigger first, then the block-level one, and, finally, the item-level trigger, you could set the *Execution Style* property for both the block- and item-level triggers to '*After*'. If you want the triggers to fire from bottom up, the *Execution Style* should be set to '*Before*'.

In the case when you inherit a trigger for an object from a properties class, the trigger defined in the property class will always be the only trigger to fire. Although you may set its *Execution Style* property to '*After*' or '*Before*', these settings do not affect the default firing of the trigger.

Besides *Execution Style*, the only other property that you may ever have to set for a trigger is *Fire in Enter Query Mode*. By default, this property is set to '*True*', which means that all the triggers you create will fire both in Normal and Enter Query mode. In occasions where you want to fire the trigger only in Normal mode, set this property to '*False*'.

18.1.5 RESTRICTED BUILT-IN PROGRAM UNITS

The built-in functions and procedures that come with the STANDARD package of Oracle Forms are divided in two groups: restricted and unrestricted built-ins. Restricted built-ins are those functions and procedures that affect the Oracle Forms navigation such as GO_BLOCK, GO_ITEM, CREATE_RECORD, and DELETE_RECORD. They are called restricted because their use is not allowed in triggers that fire as a result of navigational events. Such triggers are PRE-*object* and POST-*object* triggers such as PRE-BLOCK, POST-BLOCK, PRE-TEXT-ITEM, and POST-TEXT-ITEM.

This restriction is placed to avoid circular references and infinite loops in Oracle Forms applications. Indeed, imagine a situation in which you are allowed to use the restricted procedure CREATE_RECORD in a navigational trigger such as PRE-RECORD. You could easily create a block-level PRE-RECORD trigger which contains a call to CREATE_RECORD. At runtime, when users navigate to a record in the block, the following sequence of actions will occur:

1. EnterRecord event fires PRE-RECORD trigger.
2. PRE-RECORD trigger invokes CREATE_RECORD procedure.
3. CREATE_RECORD procedure creates a new record in the block and attempts to navigate to this new record.

4. The navigation attempt causes the event EnterRecord.

5. EnterRecord event fires PRE-RECORD trigger. Restart the sequence from Step 1.

It is clear that this is an infinite loop. Restricted procedures can be used in other types of triggers such as WHEN-NEW-*Object*-INSTANCE, or WHEN-*Event-Occurred*.

Unrestricted procedures, on the other hand can be used in any type of trigger. Among the most important program units in this group are all those that retrieve and set the properties of objects such as FIND_*Object*, GET_*Object*_PROPERTY, and SET_*Object*_PROPERTY. The *Oracle Forms Reference Manual* contains a complete listing of all the built-ins, together with their restricted or unrestricted type.

18.2 PL/SQL LIBRARIES

As you have been adding functionality to your application, the list of functions and procedures that implement it has been growing longer and longer. You also have faced the need to implement the same functionality in multiple modules. For example, Chapter 17 raised the problem of having to keep duplicate copies of code in the form and menu modules, in order to implement the same functionality for the iconic buttons and the menu items.

These two problems point out the need for a repository where the program units of a module should reside. This repository should not simply group functions and procedures together, but should also be accessible from all the other modules that may need any of these program units.

PL/SQL Library (PLL) modules are a special type of module in Oracle Forms that serve the purpose of a central repository for all the program units of an application. The major advantage of PLL modules is that they allow reuse of the code over and over across all the Oracle application development tools. You may store in a library PL/SQL objects that can be accessed from and used in any form or menu module, but also in reports and displays developed with Oracle Reports and Oracle Graphics.

18.2.1 CREATING AND POPULATING LIBRARIES

Chapter 4 explained how you can create, save, and compile PLL modules. This section will discuss the process of populating them with objects, and attaching PLL libraries to a form or menu module. You will follow the material introduced here as you work to create PLL libraries for the MRD application.

As a preliminary step, open the MRD module you are working with, which contains all the features you have put in the application so far.

1. In the Object Navigator, double-click the Libraries node to create a new library.
2. Save the newly created library in the same directory where the form MRD.FMB is located. Give it the name MRDMENU.PLL.
3. Create another library and name it LISTS.PLL.
4. Create a third library and name it WINDOWS.PLL.

The first library will store only those program units that must be shared between the MRD form and menu modules. The second library will contain the PL/SQL objects developed to implement the functionality of lists. The third library will be the repository for the windows-related functions and procedures. There are several reasons to split the existing program units in different libraries.

First, to say that libraries are repositories of program units, does not mean they are dumpsites, where these program units are piled up with no order or organization. There must be some organization and logical unity between the members of a library.

Second, by splitting the program units by the functional area in which they are used, you increase the chance for the reusability of the code. If in another module, you need to implement some list features, but will have only one window that will stay open all the time, all you need to reference is the library LISTS.PLL. If, on the other hand, the application has multiple windows but none of the list features included in LISTS.PLL, you would want to attach only WINDOWS.PLL to that module.

The last reason, related with the previous one, has to do with the way Oracle Forms uses libraries at runtime. When you attach a library to a module, Forms internally creates a tabular structure with the names of the program units in the library and the name and location of the library itself. At runtime, when one of these units is called, Forms will retrieve from the table the location of the PLL module where the program unit is stored and will load the entire module in the memory. It is understandable that the larger the library is, the more memory it is going to occupy when it is loaded. For this reason, you should strive to keep the size of each library as small as possible without affecting its functional completeness. If the menu module will share only one or two procedures with the form, there is no reason to include other functions or procedures that are not functionally related with the original ones.

Now, move the program units from the MRD module to the newly created libraries. You can select and cut the desired program units, and then paste them in the Program Units node of the target library. Or even easier, just drag the objects to move and drop them in the library. One way or another, move the procedures Click_Button, Toggle_Menu_Item, Toggle_Item, and Toggle_Enable_Property over to MRDMENU.PLL. Next move the function Element_Label_Exists and procedures Insert_Element, Move_Current_Element, and Populate_The_List over to module LISTS.PLL. Finally, move the function Count_Open_Windows, and Show_Centered_LOV and the procedures Close_Window, Open_Window, and Open_Dialog_Box over to module WINDOWS.PLL.

> **Note**
>
> You should not move any of the master/detail procedures created by Oracle Forms to synchronize the relations in your module. They are maintained internally by Oracle Forms, and may change if the properties of relations change. It is a golden rule of programming not to touch the code over which someone else has claimed responsibility.

You should not move the procedures Get_Customer and Get_Movie_List, or the functions Get_Home_Item, Build_Where_Clause and Get_Sequence_Id. They are too specific to the MRD module and would not justify their being in any of the three libraries, or in a library of their own.

18.2.2 COMPILING PL/SQL LIBRARIES

The next step after creating and populating a PLL library is to compile it. This is an important step, because if the library contains program units that are not compiled, Oracle Forms will not be able to load them at runtime. There are several ways to compile a PLL library.

a) Compile each individual program unit by displaying it in the PL/SQL Editor.

b) Compile only those PL/SQL objects whose status is "Compiled with Errors" or "Not Compiled" by choosing File | Compile... from the Designer menu.

c) Compile all the PL/SQL objects in the library, even those successfully compiled previously, by selecting File | Compile All... from the Designer menu.

If you try to compile the library WINDOWS.PLL, you will see a Compile dialog box similar to Figure 18.3. The compilation will stop with error.

Clicking the button Goto Error, will place the cursor at the line where the error is located. The line is in the procedure Close_Window, and contains a direct reference to the global variable GLOBAL.Home_Item. A second direct reference to that variable occurs a few lines below in the same procedure.

18.2.3 REFERENCING VARIABLES INDIRECTLY IN PL/SQL LIBRARIES

In form modules you can refer to the value stored in an item as :BLOCK_NAME.ITEM_NAME, or in a system variable as :SYSTEM.VARIABLE_NAME, or in a global variable as :GLOBAL.VARIABLE_NAME, or in a parameter as :PARAMETER.PARAMETER_NAME. Because these objects are in-

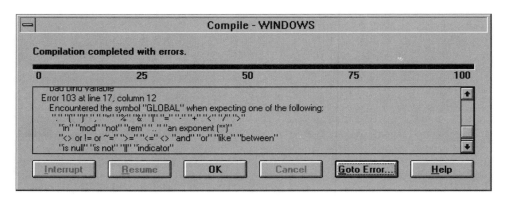

FIGURE 18.3 Compile dialog box.

ternal to the form, their values can be referenced directly. However, a PLL library is a separate module, independent of the form. It cannot and should not have any knowledge about objects that are characteristic to the form. Therefore you cannot reference directly the values of these types of variables.

Similarly, menu modules are separate modules from forms, that do not recognize their objects. The same error would have occurred if you had copied the procedure Click_Button in the menu module MRD.MMB and tried to compile it from there.

In order to reference the value of an item, system variable, global variable, or parameter outside a form module, you should use the built-in function NAME_IN. By replacing the direct reference :GLOBAL.Home_Item with the string NAME_IN('GLOBAL.Home_Item'), you still get the value of the global variable, and, at the same time create a generic program unit that can stand on its own, independently from the form module.

For the same reason, you cannot assign values directly to any of the four types of variables mentioned above. A statement like

:CUSTOMER.FIRST_NAME := 'John';

will be invalid in PLL or menu modules.

The built-in procedure COPY is used to assign values to variables without referencing them directly. The previous statement should be replaced with this statement:

COPY ('John', 'CUSTOMER.FIRST_NAME');

After you remove the direct reference to the variable :GLOBAL.Home_Item, you will be able to compile the whole WINDOWS.PLL library successfully.

When trying to compile the library WINDOWS.PLL, you will notice a similar problem with the procedure Click_Button. Here, it is the global variable SYS-

TEM.MODE that is referenced directly. Replace the direct reference with the indirect reference to its value:

NAME_IN ('SYSTEM.MODE');

The procedure Click_Button will still compile with errors because it contains references to the procedures Open_Window and Open_Dialog_Box, which now are located in module WINDOWS.PLL. You will fix this problem in the following section by attaching the library WINDOWS.PLL to MRDMENU.PLL.

The module LISTS.PLL will compile without any errors. All the code here is generic and will not cause any conflicts.

Save the changes you made in all three modules and move to the next section where you will learn how to attach these libraries to the other modules.

18.2.4 ATTACHING PL/SQL LIBRARIES

You can attach a library to a form, menu, or another library module in order to make its member program units available to other modules. The process is the same and does not depend on the type of module to which the PL/SQL library will be attached.

In order to attach the library WINDOWS.PLL to the module MRDMENU.PLL, follow these steps.

1. In the Object Navigator create a new object under the node Attached Libraries for module MRDMENU.PLL. The Attach Library dialog box will be displayed (see Figure 18.4).
2. In the Library field specify the path and name of WINDOWS.PLL. You may click Find... to open a dialog box that allows you to find the file easier.
3. Click Attach.

When you click the button Attach, an alert is displayed. It informs you that the attached library name you selected contains a nonportable directory path. It is referring to the directory where the library file is located. It also asks you to remove the path or not. If you do not remove the path, at runtime, Forms will search for the library in only one location: that specified by the path shown in the alert box.

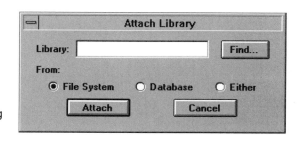

FIGURE 18.4 Attach Library dialog box.

If you remove the path, then Forms will store just the name of the library in its internal reference table. At runtime, when the library must be loaded, Forms will search the current directory and those directories specified in the environment variable FORMS45_PATH. This environment variable is defined in the [FORMS45] section of ORACLE.INI file.

Usually, attaching the libraries with the full path specified, may lead to errors during the deployment of the application. Even more so when the client machines where the application will be installed do not share the same directory structure. It is safer to remove the path when attaching the library, place all the PLL files in one designated directory, and specify the path to this directory in the FORMS45_PATH variable.

In your case, you can choose to remove the path and then add the directory to the ORACLE.INI. However, for the new FORMS45_PATH to take effect, you must restart the Designer.

When you click the button Yes in the Alert box, you will see the library added under the node Attached Libraries. If you expand its node, you will see the specifications of the members of this library. Note, however, that you cannot edit the functions or procedures here. The only point where you can edit these functions from now on is in the library module. This is the reason why unstable program units, whose structure or contents may change during the development of the system, are usually kept around in the module. Only after they are seasoned and do not need to be changed frequently, can they be moved to a library. Now you can compile successfully the module MRDMENU.PLL.

With similar actions you can attach the libraries MRDMENU.PLL and LISTS.PLL to the form module MRD.FMB. In order to complete the balloon help functionality from the last section of Chapter 17 you should also attach to this module the library HINT.PLL located in the directory %ORACLE_HOME% \FORMS45\PLSQLLIB. At the end, generate, save and close the form.

Note

Beacause the library WINDOWS.PLL is attached to MRDMENU.PLL, all its members become available to the module MRD.FMB as soon as you attach MRDMENU.PLL to it.

If you compare the size of the modules before and after the separation of program units in PL/SQL libraries you will notice that the binary file MRD.FMB shrinks by 45 percent and the executable MRD.FMX by 15 percent when PL/SQL objects are grouped in libraries attached to the form. This means that the module will be more efficient at Runtime, but also that it will be easier to work with it in the Designer.

Menu Item	Command Text Property	Menu Item	Command Text Property
File|Clear	Click_Button('CLEAR_FORM');	Data|Duplicate|Record	Click_Button('DUPLICATE_RECORD');
File|Save	Click_Button('COMMIT_FORM');	Data|Duplicate|Item	Click_Button('DUPLICATE_ITEM);
File|Exit	Click_Button('EXIT_FORM');	Data|Delete	Click_Button('DELETE_RECORD');
Tools|Customers...	Click_Button('CUSTOMER');	Data|Enter Query	Click_Button('ENTER_QUERY');
Tools|Movie...	Click_Button('MOVIE');	Data|Count Query Hits	Click_Button('COUNT_QUERY");
Tools|Rental...	Click_Button('RENTAL');	Data|Execute Query	Click_Button('EXECUTE_QUERY");
Tools|Analyze...	Click_Button('ANALYZE');	Data|Cancel Query	Click_Button('CANCEL_QUERY");
Tools|Mailing Labels...	Click_Button('MAIL');	Help|Contents	Click_Button('HELP');
Data|Insert	Click_Button('CREATE_RECORD');	Help|About...	Click_Button('ABOUT');

FIGURE 18.5 Command Text property settings for menu items in the MRD module.

Now it is time to attach the library MRDMENU.PLL to the menu module and complete the settings for the *Command Text* property of those items that were not implemented in Chapter 17.

1. Open the menu module MRD.MMB in the Designer.
2. Attach the library MRDMENU.PLL to the menu module.
3. Set the *Command Text* property for the menu items as shown in Figure 18.5.
4. Generate, save, and close the menu module.

18.3 PL/SQL PACKAGES

Functions and procedures are important PL/SQL objects that in a form module can be invoked from triggers, and in a menu module from the *Command Text* property. They allow you to group together and modularize the PL/SQL statements that are necessary to perform the functionality of the application. Packages are PL/SQL objects that take this process one step further. They bundle together data and program units in one object that access and modify the data.

Packages provide the PL/SQL implementation of several fundamental concepts of object-oriented programming such as encapsulation of data with the operations performed on the data, code reusability, dynamic binding of data types, and data hiding. They are a close equivalent in PL/SQL of the concept of classes in object-oriented programming languages such as C++.

18.3.1 COMPONENTS OF PACKAGES

Structurally, a package is divided in two parts: the specification and the body. The specification part holds the data, functions, and procedures that will be freely accessible by all the other routines that will use the package. This part also contains the specification for those program units that other programs may call, but do not need to see how they are implemented. Thus, in a sense, the specification of a package is the communication protocol of the package with the outside environment.

The body part of the package contains private information, that cannot be seen or accessed by the routines outside the package. The functions and procedures in the body are direct implementation of the program units declared in the specification part of the package. But the body part may also contain functions and procedures that are not declared in the specification part. They will not be accessible by program units other than those within the body. Figure 18.6 shows a graphical representation of the package object. It is also known as the Booch diagram of the packages, after Grady Booch, one of the founders of object-oriented programming.

In the example shown in Figure 18.6, the pseudo-package PACKAGE contains some data declaration (Data), a function specification (Function A), and a procedure specification (Procedure B). The body of the package, represented by the shaded area, contains some data declaration that are strictly local to the body, and the implementation for Function A and Procedure B. Function A, in its body calls Function C, and Procedure B calls Procedure D and Function C. The definitions for both these program units are within the package body.

The programs outside can assess and utilize only what is available in the specification part. The program unit shown in the box to the right can access the

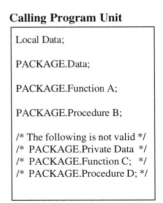

FIGURE 18.6   Graphical representation of a package.

public data and functions using the syntax PACKAGE.Data, PACKAGE.Function A, or PACKAGE.Procedure B. Implicitly, through this interface, this program unit is using the Function C, or Procedure D, only because they are used by Function A or Procedure B. However, it cannot access these objects directly. In fact, if Function A inside the package's body is modified to implement a different algorithm or data structure, the calling program would have no way of knowing about the modification.

18.3.2 BENEFITS OF PACKAGES

It is very clear to see, even from this graphical presentation, that packages encapsulate in one object the data elements and the operations or methods that manipulate them. The advantage to this approach versus the more traditional one is that it represents the world that the application describes more naturally, as an entirety of objects that interact with each other.

It is also very clear from Figure 18.6 how the hiding of code and implementation details can be achieved with a package. The benefit of hiding the code from the outside routines is that the application becomes more robust as a whole. Because the outside routines do not know how the internals of the public components of the package are implemented, there is no risk that they will become wired into the details of this package. As long as the interface, or specification, of the package remains unchanged, modifications inside the body will not force the calling routines to change their behavior or be recompiled.

Another great usage of the information hiding capability of packages is when designing and prototyping the application. In the top-down design approach, you define the high level objects and routines first, and then move in the detailed implementation. When you are still at the high-level phase, you can place all the functions and procedures declarations in the specification of a package. Then the rest of the application can continue to be developed independently. The calls to the package are made according to its specification. They will compile and execute successfully, although there is not much functionality behind them. Meanwhile, as the implementation of the package progresses, the rest of the development team does not have to modify and constantly change their code. All this work happens in the gray area of Figure 18.6, which, as said, is invisible to the rest of the world.

In order to understand the great potential that packages have to offer for code reusability, let us critique the program units developed so far for the MRD application. Several instances of them access or set properties of objects. All the utilized GET and SET built-ins can take as a parameter the name of the object. However, it was agreed from the beginning that code written that way is inefficient and prone to runtime errors that cannot be detected by the compiler at design time. Thus, it was decided that each time there was a need for one of these functions, you would use the appropriate FIND function to get the internal ID of the object, and, only if you were certain of the existence of the object, you would

```
window_id := FIND_WINDOW(window_name);
IF ID_NULL(window_id) THEN
    Message('Window '||window_name||' does not exist.');
    RAISE FORM_TRIGGER_FAILURE;
END IF;
```

FIGURE 18.7   Excerpts from Count_Open_Windows.

proceed with the other statements. This convention was followed faithfully, but, tracing back the steps now, you can find inconsistencies in the implementation of the code. Figure 18.7 shows excerpts from function Count_Open_Windows and Figure 18.8 from Close_Window. Both these functions retrieve the internal ID of a window object based on its name, and handle the case when the object does not exist.

The problem here is not just the fact that you had to code the same functionality multiple times, but that there is a great potential for discrepancies and errors. Imagine what would have been the situation in a large development team working on multiple modules in parallel. In the next section you will create a package, which will contain, among other routines, the function Get_Window_Id, which, given the name of the window, will return its internal ID if it exists, or halt the operations, if not. Then, all those lines of code in your program units will be replaced with a single call to this member of the package. Because the code in this package is generic, you could use it not just in the MRD module, but in all the other forms you will develop in the future.

Finally, the other object-oriented programming feature of packages, is the dynamic binding of data types, also known as overloading. You can create func-

```
window_id := FIND_WINDOW(window_name);
IF ID_NULL(window_id) THEN
    RAISE Window_Not_Found;
END IF;

/* Other statements are here */

EXCEPTION
/* Other statements are here */
WHEN Window_Not_Found THEN
    MESSAGE('Window '||window_name||' does not exist.');
    RAISE FORM_TRIGGER_FAILURE;
/* Other statements are here */
```

FIGURE 18.8   Excerpts from Close_Window.

tions and procedure inside a package that have the same name, but take arguments of different datatypes. For the outside routines, it becomes transparent that different program units are executed when different arguments of different datatypes are used. The package intelligently selects which routine to invoke when it receives a call, thus removing the burden of the programmers to make that selection themselves, based on the data type of the arguments.

An excellent example of overloading a routine is the function ID_NULL that has been used over and over with all the object types of Oracle Forms. This function is part of the STANDARD Extensions package of built-ins that come with the Forms. If you expand the node of this package in the Object Navigator, you can see many other examples of overloading in the Oracle Forms built-in functions and procedures.

18.3.3 CREATING A PACKAGE FOR THE MRD APPLICATION

As said earlier, a package object is made up of the specification part and the body. Although you may have all the package in the specification part, this is rarely done, since it does not offer any of the code hiding benefits of packages. The package body on the other hand cannot stand independently. It has to have a specification that goes with it.

You can create a package anywhere you can create program units: in forms, menus, and PL/SQL libraries. As an initial effort, let us create the package in a separate library:

1. Create a new library and save it to the file system with the name GEN-ERAL.PLL.
2. Create a new program unit for the library in the Object Navigator.
3. In the New Program Unit dialog box enter **Generic** in the Name field and select the Package Spec radio button to create the package specification.
4. Click OK.

Oracle Forms opens a PL/SQL editor and creates a template for the package. Enter the definitions of functions and procedures for this package as shown in Figure 18.9.

The first procedure in the package will handle an error number and string passed by a program unit. The second procedure will process any error that occurred in the program unit. Note that overloading is used here to implement the same procedure with different arguments. The function **Get_Window_Id** will return the internal ID if the window **object_name** exists, or will stop any further processing if the object does not exist. The package shown in Figure 18.9 does not use any public variables. If you had to use any of them, you would declare them between the header and the first program units specification.

Creating the package body is a very similar process:

```
PACKAGE Generic IS
  /* Handle the error raised, and passed by the program unit. */
  PROCEDURE Handle_Error(prog_unit VARCHAR2,
                         error_num NUMBER,
                         error_msg VARCHAR2);

  /* Handle the error raised by the program unit.          */
  PROCEDURE Handle_Error(prog_unit VARCHAR2);

  /* Return window ID if it exists. Halt operation otherwise. */
  FUNCTION Get_Window_Id(object_name VARCHAR2)
  RETURN Window;

END Generic;
```

FIGURE 18.9   Specification part of package Generic.

1. Create a new program unit for the library in the Object Navigator.
2. In the New Program Unit dialog box enter **Generic** in the Name field and select the Package Body radio button to create the package specification.
3. Click OK.

In the PL/SQL editor window, enter the contents of the procedures and function of the package as shown in Figure 18.10.

The first version of procedure **Handle_Error** does nothing more than display two messages, of which the last one is the error number and message passed as arguments. The second and overloaded version of procedure **Handle_Error** uses the PL/SQL functions SQLCODE and SQLERRM to retrieve the number and the text of the error that occurred. Then, these are displayed to the user together with the name of the program unit where the error occurred. The function **Get_Window_Id** retrieves the internal ID for a window based on its name. The only difference between this and previous versions of the same functionality is the way the exception OTHERS is handled. Rather than just displaying a general message, you invoke the procedure **Handle_Error** which will display the error number and message.

Compile the library and attach it to the PL/SQL library WINDOWS.PLL. Now you may replace the old code with the new statements from the package:

1. Display the procedure **Open_Window** in the PL/SQL editor.
2. Replace the lines that retrieve the internal ID for a window with the single statement:

Generic.Get_Window_Id(window_name);

```
PACKAGE BODY Generic IS
  /* Handle the error raised and passed by the program unit. */
  PROCEDURE Handle_Error(prog_unit VARCHAR2,
                         error_num NUMBER,
                         error_msg VARCHAR2)IS
BEGIN
    MESSAGE('Error in '||prog_unit||'.', NO_ACKNOWLEDGE);
    MESSAGE(TO_CHAR(error_num)||': '||error_msg||'.');
END;

/* Handle the error raised by the program unit.              */
PROCEDURE Handle_Error(prog_unit VARCHAR2)IS
  error_num     NUMBER;
  error_msg     VARCHAR2(540);
BEGIN
    error_num := SQLCODE;
    error_msg := SQLERRM;
    MESSAGE('Error in '||prog_unit||'.', NO_ACKNOWLEDGE);
    MESSAGE(TO_CHAR(error_num)||': '||error_msg||'.');
END;

/* Returns window_ID if exists. Halts operation otherwise.   */
FUNCTION Get_Window_Id(object_name VARCHAR2)
RETURN Window IS
window_id Window;
BEGIN
  window_id := FIND_WINDOW(object_name);
  IF ID_NULL(window_id) THEN
      MESSAGE('Window '||object_name||' does not exist.');
      RAISE FORM_TRIGGER_FAILURE;
  END IF;
  RETURN(window_id);
EXCEPTION
  WHEN OTHERS THEN
    Handle_Error('Get_Window_Id');
  END Get_Window_Id;
END Generic;
```

FIGURE 18.10 Body part of Generic package.

3. Replace the lines for the exception OTHERS with the statement

    Generic.Handle_Error('Open_Window');

4. Repeat Steps 1–3 for procedure **Close_Window** and function **Count_Open_ Windows**.

It is evident that the effort you did to create the package, not only reduces the size and readability of each program unit in this library, but also standardizes the behavior of these program units.

The next step is to expand the package **Generic**. You should create a function for each Oracle Forms object similar to function **Get_Window_Id**. The task is simply laborious and contains nothing worth discussing here. To save the effort, you may copy the library GENERAL.PLL from the directory where you installed the companion disk. This library, in addition to the program units shown in Figure 18.10, contains functions like **Get_Window_Id** for all the objects that you encounter in Forms.

In order not to edit the rest of the libraries the way you edited WINDOWS.PLL, you may also copy the libraries LISTS.PLL and MRDMENU.PLL. These libraries have attached to them the library GENERAL.PLL, and no path is stored, therefore you must place them all under a directory that is declared in FORMS45_PATH. Finally, the form module MRD.FMB needs some modifications of the same kind, and the library GENERAL.PLL must be attached to it as well. You may do these modifications yourself, as explained earlier.

At this point in the development process, the MRD application involves several files and modules. This is one of those situations where the configuration management of the software becomes as important as the development of new programs or the maintenance of existing ones. To help you organize and double-check that you have all the files and links you need, Figure 18.11 contains a diagram of the modules in the system and the connections among them.

18.4 STORED PROGRAM UNITS AND DATABASE TRIGGERS

In client-server database systems today, the load of computing and processing the information is divided between the database server and the clients that run the front-end application. Until a short time ago, the databases were little more than receptacles for data. The application developers had to create almost all of the system's logic and functionality in the client side. Today, all the major database packages support the ability to create application logic in the database server. In the Oracle Server, for example, you can create stored program units, including functions, procedures, and packages. You can also attach triggers with three major events that occur in a table: INSERT, DELETE, UPDATE.

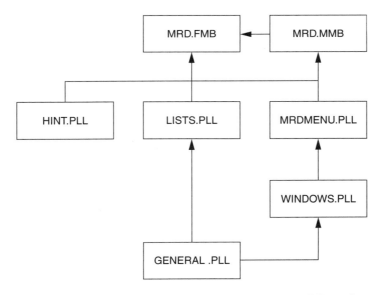

FIGURE 18.11   Software module configuration for MRD application.

The application development tools obviously have kept up with these new features. With one level of complication or another, they all support invoking remotely the stored program units in the database. However, in integrating the logic of the client and the server side of a system, and using it seamlessly, the combination of Oracle Server with Oracle Forms has two major advantages.

First, the programming language in Oracle Forms and Oracle Server is PL/SQL. This means that a developer working in the front-end application can easily switch gears and create some program units stored in the database server, when needed. If another development tool is chosen, it will be more difficult for the front-end developers to reach the level of proficiency required to develop efficient and well-performing routines in PL/SQL for the Oracle database and in the programming language used by the application development tool. Normally, in these applications, an additional person that is fluent in PL/SQL is needed to create and maintain the stored logic.

Second, it would make sense and benefit the system if the logic of the application can be shifted from one side to the other without any disruption or difficulty. Oracle Forms is the only development tool that reaches that level of integration with the Oracle Server database. As you will see later in this section, creating program units for storage in the database is similar to creating program units for the form, menu, or PLL modules. Furthermore, using Forms Designer, the program units can be moved easily between the client application and the database server. You simply drag the PL/SQL object from one side and drop it on the other. Forms Designer buffers you from all the details of creating or dropping these units in the database. This technique is also known as application logic partitioning, and tools that support it are referred to as second generation client-server tools.

18.4.1 STORED PROGRAM UNITS

As it was hinted earlier, creating stored program units in the Oracle Forms Designer is not any different from creating regular program units. In this section you will create a stored function that will be used in the ANALYZE module of the MRD application. You have seen the contents of the first function in Chapter 10. It is called Days_Between and returns the number of days between two dates passed as input arguments. Before creating this function, bring up the Designer and connect to the database. Then proceed as follows:

1. Expand the node Database Objects in the Navigator. You will initially see the list of database schemas where you can create new database objects or view existing ones. The length of this list will depend on the privileges you have on other schemas. Normally you will be able to create stored procedures only in your schema.
2. Expand the node that contains the name of your schema. Four subnodes are displayed. They represent the types of objects owned by a schema that can be viewed or accessed from the Designer.
3. Use any of the Navigator's commands to create a new stored program unit. The familiar New Program Unit dialog box will appear.
4. Enter Days_Between in the Name field and select the Function radio button.
5. Click OK. A PL/SQL Editor window comes up with a template for your function.
6. Enter the contents of the function as shown in Figure 18.12.
7. Click Save. The status lamps at the bottom of the window will be set as in Figure 18.12.

18.4.2 STORED PROGRAM UNIT PL/SQL EDITOR

The context area of the PL/SQL Editor for stored program units is a little different from that of the regular program units. It contains only the Owner and Name drop-down list boxes. The reason for this is that stored program units are objects owned by the schema, much like tables, indexes, or views. In forms, menus, or PLL modules, it is the module itself that owns the objects.

The button bar of this editor is a little different from the regular PL/SQL editor as well. Even here, the differences reflect the fact that stored program units are objects in the database. They are dropped rather than deleted, and their con-

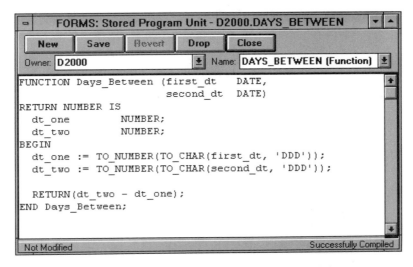

FIGURE 18.12   Stored program unit PL/SQL Editor.

tents are saved to the database, rather than to a module. When the stored program unit is saved to the database, the Oracle Server PL/SQL engine compiles it before performing the Save action. The unit is saved only if no errors are encountered.

Except for these minor differences, everything else looks as usual. However, in the background, Oracle Forms wraps together the code you enter in the editor, and sends it to the database with the request to create a stored program unit according to your specification. You do not have to do the process manually.

Despite all the likeliness between creating stored program units or regular ones, you must understand clearly that the processes are functionally different. The fact that the PL/SQL engine of the server compiles the unit, for example, is very important. This means that in stored program units you cannot use forms or menu object types such as Item or MenuItem. They are unknown data types for the server. On the other hand, data types of PL/SQL Version 2 such as Table and Record, can be used very effectively in stored program units, but cannot be moved over to the modules, which still use the version 1.1 of PL/SQL. Thus, the partitioning of the application's logic can be done easily as long as you use the fundamental data types of PL/SQL recognized by both versions.

18.4.3 DATABASE TRIGGERS

The concept of database triggers is similar to the concept of triggers in form modules. With each table in the database, you can associate methods of PL/SQL code that will be executed when the event for which the method is defined occurs. The events for which you can write database triggers are Insert, Update, and Delete.

> ## Note
>
> One good candidate for moving between the front-end application and the database server is the function Get_Sequence_Id that you created in Chapter 16 to retrieve the next value from the sequence MRD_SEQ. This function can equally reside in either side of the application. If you want to remove it from the MRD module and store it in the database, simply drag the function in the Object Navigator and drop it under the Stored Program Units node of your schema.

Using database triggers enforces a business rule about the data at the database level. It ensures that all the applications that will access the database objects will follow the rule consistently and precisely as it is defined in the object itself. Database triggers associate the flexibility of the relational model with the advantages of object-oriented programming. If the data should follow certain rules, you attach these rules to the table that will hold the data. This is the only place where the method is coded. Each application that uses the table, from that moment on, will not need to recode the rule. The method associated with the table will wait patiently until one of these applications sends the message that causes its event to occur. When this happens, the method, or trigger, will fire and execute its statements. This is the only way the method will become active.

In the MRD application, there are several rules that you could enforce globally, using database triggers. One example would be to provide the ID columns in the application with sequence-generated numbers before they are inserted in the database. In earlier chapters, you populated the ID columns during the Create Record event. However, it is more efficient to get sequence numbers when the records arrive at the database, rather than move them back and forth across the network.

18.4.4 USING DATABASE TRIGGERS TO POPULATE COLUMNS WITH SEQUENCE-GENERATED NUMBERS

This is where you will begin your work with database triggers. You want to create a trigger that will provide sequence numbers for the column CUSTOMER_ID of new records inserted in table CUSTOMER. Begin by performing these two preliminary steps:

1. Delete the block-level trigger WHEN-RECORD-CREATED in block CUSTOMER, which currently performs this task.
2. Cut the function Get_Sequence_Id from the module MRD.FMB and paste it under the Stored Program Units node.

In the Object Navigator, expand the node Tables to display all the tables you currently own. Then expand the node Customer. The nodes Triggers and Columns will be displayed underneath.

1. Create a new object for the node Triggers. The Database Triggers PL/SQL Editor appears (see Figure 18.13). Most of the objects on this window are currently disabled.
2. Click the push button New, to create a new database trigger. You will notice that the objects of the editor will be enabled now.
3. Enter the specifications for the trigger as shown in Figure 18.13. The meaning of the settings is explained in Section 18.4.5.
4. Click Save to have the Oracle Server PL/SQL engine compile and store the trigger in the database.

18.4.5 DATABASE TRIGGER PL/SQL EDITOR

There are several things to explain about the settings of the database trigger shown in Figure 18.13. Let us go through them from the top of the window down. The list boxes on the top define the context of the trigger. If you have the appropriate privileges to create triggers on tables owned by other schemas, you can use the Table Owner drop-down list box to select the schema name. You can also se-

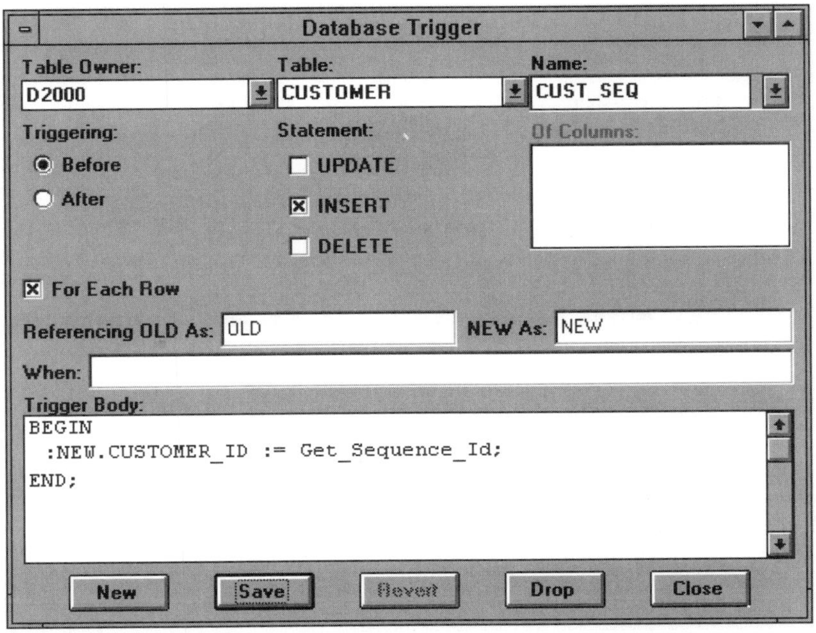

FIGURE 18.13 Database Trigger PL/SQL Editor.

lect the table where the trigger will be attached using the list Table. The combo box Name is used to specify the name of the trigger. When you create a new trigger, Oracle will provide you with a default name, but you should change it to a more descriptive and meaningful one for your application.

The check box group Statement defines the event that can activate the trigger. It can be seen here that only INSERT, UPDATE, and DELETE statements can fire a database trigger. In your case, you want the trigger to fire only when records are inserted. Therefore, the check box INSERT is checked. If the trigger should fire for more than one event, you can check more than one check box in this group. The text list Of Columns to the right is enabled only if one of the statements that will fire the trigger is UPDATE. In that case, all the columns of the table will be displayed in the list, sorted alphabetically. By default, the trigger will fire when any of these columns are updated. If you want the trigger to fire only when some specific columns are updated, you can CTRL+CLICK to select them in the list.

The radio group Triggering controls the timing of the trigger in relation to the event that causes the trigger. The database trigger can fire either before or after the statement that caused it is executed by the database. In your case, you want to put the new sequence number in the CUSTOMER_ID before the record is inserted in the table.

The check box For Each Row governs the frequency of the trigger, or how many times it will fire when the statement that causes it is executed on the table. If the check box is unchecked, the trigger will fire only once. Triggers with this setting are also called table-level triggers. If the check box is checked, the trigger will be executed for each record that the statement will affect. These triggers are also called record-level triggers. In your case, the check box is checked because you want the sequence to populate the CUSTOMER_ID for each record.

The state of the check box For Each Row influences the availability and the contents of the remaining fields in the window as well. If the box is not checked, the fields Referencing OLD As, NEW As, and When are disabled. They have a meaning only for record-level triggers. In this case, in the Trigger Body field, you must reference the components of the record by their column name, as defined in the table.

Note

Given all the possible settings of these three properties, it is easy to conclude that for any table in the database, there can be up to twelve triggers associated with it. By checking multiple check boxes in the Statement group, you can collapse up to three triggers in one, but this will not enable you to fill the free slots with other triggers. In other words, if you create a trigger of type, 'After Each Row is Inserted, Updated, or Deleted', you can no longer create a trigger of type 'After Each Row is Inserted'.

When triggers fire for each row, Oracle keeps two copies of each record affected by the statement. The state of the record in the database, before the statement is executed, is referred to as OLD. The version of that record after the statement is executed can be referenced as the NEW record. Understandably, when a record is being inserted, its OLD version contains NULL values for all the columns. The reason for this is that the record does not exist in the database until the INSERT statement is executed, and the snapshot that creates OLD is taken before this event. For a similar reason, the NEW version of a deleted record contains NULL columns. (After the DELETE is completed, the record no longer exists in the table.) If the statement is UPDATE, both NEW and OLD versions of the record will contain some values.

Both versions of the record are accessible in all the triggers. However, you cannot set the columns of the NEW record in an After trigger. Recall that this trigger will fire after the triggering statement is executed. Therefore, the NEW version of the record is created and set before the trigger enters in action. OLD and NEW are also called correlation names. Inside the Trigger Body they must be preceded by the colon, as shown in Figure 18.13.

With the settings discussed so far, the triggers can fire only in two extreme cases: either only once, or for every single row affected by the system. There can be occasions where triggers should fire only for a particular set of the records affected by the statement. Imagine, for example, that there is another application besides yours, that is using the MRD database. While you are implementing the generation of identification numbers at the database, the developers of the other application are using a fancy algorithm to come up with a unique number, based on some biographical data provided by the customer. By creating a database trigger, you are enforcing the rule globally. In other words, when a record goes for INSERT in the table CUSTOMER, the trigger will not check to see which application is sending it—yours or theirs. It will simply enforce your rule and override the value placed in the CUSTOMER_ID by the other application.

Note

In the very rare event when you will need to create a database trigger for a table named OLD or NEW, the correlation names OLD or NEW will conflict with the name of the table. Only in these cases, you will need to override the default correlation names. You can do this in the Referencing fields. If, for example, the table is named OLD, then you could replace the setting of Referencing OLD As with OLD_RECORD. Then, throughout the trigger, you could use OLD_RECORD to address the version of the record prior to the execution of the triggering statement.

In order to restrict the number of records that a record-level trigger will affect when fired, a Boolean condition can be specified in the When field. The trigger will be fired only for those records which evaluate the condition to TRUE. To avoid raising some eyebrows in the scenario presented above, you could set the When field to

NEW.CUSTOMER_ID IS NULL

With this property, the trigger will get the sequence number only for those records that are sent to the table with an unspecified CUSTOMER_ID value. Note that in this field you do not need to put the colon character in front of the correlation name. Following similar steps, you can create on your own, triggers that will populate the columns MOVIE_ID, and TAPE_ID for tables MOVIE and TAPE with numbers generated from the sequence MRD_SEQ. Make sure to delete the triggers WHEN_CREATE_RECORD for these blocks in order to avoid duplicating the functionality.

18.5 SUMMARY

The focus of this chapter are PL/SQL objects used in Oracle Forms applications. Previous chapters have provided information about triggers, functions, and procedures. This chapter summarizes concepts related to them and expands on additional objects such as PL/SQL libraries, packages, stored program units and database triggers. Major concepts discussed in this chapter are listed here:

❑ Events and triggers in Oracle Forms
  ❑ Types of events and triggers
  ❑ Firing order of triggers
  ❑ Triggers as methods that associate objects with events
  ❑ Overriding the default firing order of triggers
  ❑ Restricted built-ins
❑ PL/SQL libraries
  ❑ Creating and populating libraries
  ❑ Compiling PL/SQL libraries
  ❑ Referencing variables indirectly in PL/SQL libraries
  ❑ Attaching PL/SQL libraries to other modules
❑ PL/SQL packages
  ❑ Components of packages
  ❑ Benefits of packages
❑ Stored program units and database triggers
  ❑ Stored program units

❏ Stored program unit PL/SQL Editor
❏ Database triggers
❏ Database triggers PL/SQL Editor
❏ Using database triggers to populate columns with sequence-generated numbers

Part IV

ADVANCED PROGRAMMING WITH ORACLE FORMS

"Finit coronat opus (The end crowns the work)."
—*Latin saying*

ADVANCED TOPICS IN PL/SQL

"The chief merit of a language is clearness, and we know that nothing distracts so much from this as do unfamiliar terms."

—Galen

- ◆ Cursors in PL/SQL
- ◆ Differences Between Version 1.1 and Version 2 of PL/SQL
- ◆ Exception Handling in Oracle Forms Applications
- ◆ Summary

Previous chapters in this book have introduced and discussed fundamental concepts related to PL/SQL programming such as variables, conditional statements, and loops and how they can be used inside triggers, functions, procedures, and packages. This chapter discusses PL/SQL cursors as a type of object that allows you to create flexible and effective queries in the application. In addition, it returns once again to the problem of handling exceptions and trapping all the errors or messages that may occur during database processing.

19.1 CURSORS IN PL/SQL

Recall from Chapter 10 that when the PL/SQL engine of Oracle Forms encounters a SQL statement, it sends it to the SQL Statement Executor in the Oracle Server database for handling. When the Database Server receives the statement, it makes sure that it is a valid SQL statement and that the user issuing it has the appropriate privileges to issue that statement. If both these checks are successful, a chunk from the Database Server memory, called private SQL area, is allocated to the statement.

If this is the first time the statement has been issued against the database, Oracle will parse the statement, and will store its parsed version in another memory structure, called shared SQL area. The shared SQL area will also contain the plan Oracle will follow in order to execute the statement. Finally, the statement will be executed.

This division of the information contained within the SQL statements allows Oracle to bypass the parsing phase the next time the same statement is issued. In such a case, the private SQL area for the statement is still created, but when Oracle realizes that a parsed version of it is present in the library cache of the shared SQL area, it proceeds directly with the execution of this parsed representation. This will hold true even if the statement is issued by a different connection in the database, that may be a different user of your application.

The private SQL area contains information about the statement that can be divided in two categories. The first one is static and permanently attached to the statement. This includes, for example, the table and column names that the statement affects, and the binding information between them and the bind variables in the statement. The second category is dynamic and its size changes, depending on the actual values of the bind variables when the statement is issued. This part of the private SQL area is known as runtime area, because it expands and shrinks in size and content as the statement is executed. If, for example, the statement is a SELECT that returns 20 rows, the runtime area will be expanded to enclose those records. Figure 19.1 shows graphically how the SQL Statement Executor manages the SQL statements.

This figure assumes that statement A is sent prior to statement B. When statement A is received, Oracle binds the value, '01-SEP-94' for MEMBER_DT to the bind argument :1, and records the column names in the private SQL area of this statement—in its permanent part, to be exact. Then, the statement is parsed

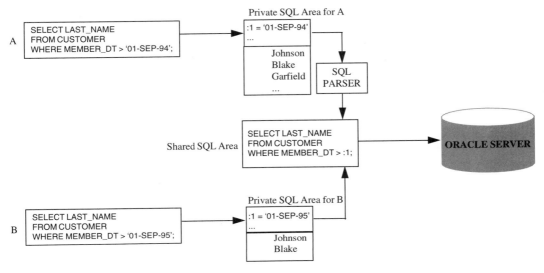

FIGURE 19.1   Execution of SQL statements by the Oracle Server.

and stored in the library cache in the shared SQL area. The execution plan that Oracle will follow is stored here as well. Finally the statement is sent to the RDBMS to retrieve the data. When statement B is received, the process is similar, except that the statement is not parsed again. After binding, statements A and B are the same. Therefore the SQL Statement Executor proceeds directly with the retrieval of data. The data returned from each query are stored in the runtime part of each statement's private SQL area.

A cursor is nothing but a name, or a handle for the memory location of the private SQL area of a statement that allows you to access the information stored there from within PL/SQL blocks.

19.1.1 DECLARING EXPLICIT CURSORS

Explicit cursors are PL/SQL objects built upon SELECT statements that allow you to better manipulate records returned by queries. They can also be used to create complex queries in a more procedural-like fashion, and in certain instances improve the performance of the application.

Cursors are declared in the DECLARE part of a PL/SQL block following the syntax

CURSOR cursor_name IS select_statement;

The SELECT statement in a cursor declaration should not contain the INTO clause that is normally used in PL/SQL. As you will see in the following section, the storage of the retrieved data into PL/SQL variables is done as a separate step with cursors. However, this statement defines the number and data type of the columns that each record returned by the query in the cursor's runtime area will have. Figure 19.2 shows two examples of cursor declaration statements.

In both of these examples, the runtime area will contain records with the same data type as the column TAPE_ID of table TAPES. If the SELECT statements would contain another column, this column would be reflected in the record set of the runtime area. The first example is not very useful because of the static nature of its SELECT statement. The cursor will contain only those records from the table TAPES that have a specific value in their MOVIE_ID column. In order for the cursor to be really effective and usable, its SELECT statement must be free of any hard-coded values, as in the second example. In this case, the cursor uses a parameter in its statement much the same way a procedure or a function would use it.

When cursors are declared in packages, you have the possibility to divide the SELECT statement of the cursor definition from its body. In the package specification, you could place statements like these:

CURSOR the_tapes(movie_id NUMBER) RETURN NUMBER;

or

CURSOR the_tapes (movie_id MOVIES.MOVIE_ID%TYPE)
RETURN TAPES.TAPE_ID%TYPE;

```
DECLARE
  CURSOR the_tapes IS
    SELECT TAPES.TAPE_ID
    FROM TAPES
    WHERE TAPES.MOVIE_ID = 101;
BEGIN
    /* Processing statements go here.    */
END;
```

```
PROCEDURE Get_Tapes (movie_id NUMBER) IS
  CURSOR the_tapes (current_id NUMBER) IS
    SELECT TAPES.TAPE_ID
    FROM TAPES
    WHERE TAPES.MOVIE_ID = current_id;
BEGIN
    /* Processing statements go here.    */
END;
```

FIGURE 19.2 Cursor declaration statements.

```
/* Definitions of other package structures may go here.    */
CURSOR the_tapes (movie_id MOVIES.MOVIE_ID%TYPE)
RETURN TAPES.TAPE_ID%TYPE
  SELECT TAPES.TAPE_ID
  FROM TAPES
  WHERE TAPES.MOVIE_ID = current_id;
/* Definitions of other package structures may go here.    */
```

FIGURE 19.3   Specifying a cursor in the body of a package.

As you can see, you must provide the data types and the number of data elements of records that the SELECT statements of the cursor will return.

Then, in the package body you specify the actual SELECT statement, as shown in Figure 19.3.

Implementing cursors this way draws all the benefits that packages bring in PL/SQL programming, as discussed in Chapter 18. In particular, it allows you to change the WHERE clause of the select statement, if need be, without affecting the programs that will use the cursor.

Note

If the SELECT statement will be a SELECT * type of statement, you can use the %ROWTYPE attribute to specify the data type of the records that the cursor will contain. For example, in the package specification mentioned above, you would use the following statement:

CURSOR the_tapes(movie_id MOVIES.MOVE_ID%TYPE) RETURN TAPES%ROWTYPE;

Then, in the specification of the package, you would have:

```
CURSOR the_tapes(movie_id MOVIES.MOVE_ID%TYPE) RETURN
TAPES%ROWTYPE
  SELECT * FROM TAPES
  WHERE TAPES.MOVIE_ID = movie_id;
```

19.1.2 METHODS AND ATTRIBUTES OF EXPLICIT CURSORS

Explicit cursors, being names of a particular memory location allocated to the SE-LECT statement, are considered as a special kind of object in PL/SQL. As such, they have their attributes and methods on which you can act.

After the cursor is declared, you can use the statement OPEN cursor_name; to execute the query contained in the cursor, and bring the records over in the runtime part of the private SQL area. If the declaration of the cursor contains parameters, the value of these parameters is specified in the OPEN statement. So, the statements that open the cursors shown in Figure 19.2 would be

OPEN the_tapes;

or

OPEN the_tapes(movie_id);

The attribute %ISOPEN keeps track of the state of the cursor. If the cursor is opened, this attribute evaluates to TRUE; otherwise, its value will be FALSE. Since an error will occur if the OPEN statement is issued against a cursor that is already open, it is always a good idea to check for the state of the cursor, before opening it.

Opening the cursor only identifies the records that the query will return. However, none of these records is returned to the calling environment, until the FETCH command is issued explicitly. When the cursor is opened, a pointer is placed on the first record retrieved by the query. When the first FETCH statement is issued, this record is returned to the calling routine and the pointer is advanced to the next record. This will continue until all the records in the runtime area are returned. The pointer to the current record can only be advanced by one record at a time. This means, for example, that the second FETCH will return only the second record, if it exists. There is no way to advance the pointer so that the fifth record is returned before its predecessors, or to set it back so that the first record is returned again.

When the FETCH statement is used, it must always be followed by an INTO clause. This clause will place the data from the fetched record into the variables of the routine that will use them. To avoid any runtime errors, these variables must have the same data type and size as the data being fetched. One way to ensure this is to declare the variable to be exactly like the table column that will correspond to it. In the examples above, for example, you would declare a variable as follows:

tape_id NUMBER;

This statement declares the variable tape_id to be a particular data type, that, in this instance, matches the data type of the column TAPE_ID in the database.

However, if the data type of this column were to change, you would have to change all the variables like the one above to match the new data type. In order to avoid these problems, the best way is to declare the variable as shown below:

tape_id TAPES.TAPE_ID%TYPE;

In this case, you are declaring the variable tape_id to be of the same data type as the corresponding database column. Whenever the type of this column changes, the attribute %TYPE will ensure that the variable tape_id will not conflict with the new type.

The number of the records fetched is stored in another attribute of the cursor, called %ROWCOUNT. Whenever the cursor is opened, this attribute is set to zero, after the first record is fetched, it is set to one, and so on. The value of this attribute can be useful if you want to retrieve only a certain number of records from the set of all the records that the cursor may contain. For example, to retrieve only the first three records, the FETCH command is issued until the %ROWCOUNT evaluates to three.

As said earlier, the FETCH statement returns the current record of the cursor to the calling environment. But what happens if the last record is fetched and another FETCH is issued? What happens when the cursor contains no records and the first FETCH is issued? To help you deal with these situations, cursors are equipped with two more attributes: %FOUND and %NOTFOUND. They are Boolean attributes that complement each other. They are both set to NULL when the cursor is opened. Then, after each FETCH, the values of these attributes are set according to the outcome of the statement. If the record was fetched successfully, %FOUND is set to TRUE, and %NOTFOUND is set to FALSE. If all the records of the cursor are fetched, the next fetch will not return a valid row, %FOUND will be set to FALSE, and %NOTFOUND to TRUE.

These attributes are used as exit conditions for loops that should retrieve all the records of a cursor, and stop safely when the last one is fetched. For these loops, the exit condition could be tested immediately after the FETCH statements and could be

EXIT WHEN cursor_name%NOTFOUND;

In this case, during the iteration after the one that fetches the last record, the FETCH statement will fail, thus setting the %NOTFOUND attribute to TRUE. This causes the iteration to stop and the control of the program to jump outside the loop.

Note however, that this exit condition relies on the cursor to contain at least one record. If the query that populates the cursor returns no records, the FETCH statement is not executed. Therefore the attribute %NOTFOUND remains set to the original value NULL. Because the exit condition of the loop does not evaluate to TRUE, its iterations will continue forever. In order to handle the case when the cursor may not have records to fetch, you can add an additional check in the exit condition of the loop for NULL values of the attributes %FOUND and %NOT-FOUND. Figure 19.4 shows two examples of using each of these attributes.

After the record is opened and used, you must close it to release the database resources it occupies. For this you issue the CLOSE statement followed by the name of the cursor to close, as in

CLOSE the_tapes;

19.1.3 USING THE FOR LOOP WITH EXPLICIT CURSORS

When you have to process some of the records from the set of all the records that are returned by a query, you must construct your code around the statements described above. In order to avoid runtime errors that may occur if the statements are not issued in the proper context, you should follow the steps below:

1. Declare the cursor in the DECLARE part of the PL/SQL block or program unit.
2. Open the cursor.
3. Create a loop with the appropriate EXIT condition that will scroll sequentially through the records of the cursor and process each record according to your needs.

```
LOOP
  FETCH the_tapes INTO tape_id;
  EXIT WHEN the_tapes%NOTFOUND OR
            the_tapes%NOTFOUND IS NULL;
  /* Processing statements go here.     */
END LOOP;
```

```
LOOP
  FETCH the_tapes INTO tape_id;
  IF the_tapes%FOUND OR
     the_tapes%FOUND IS NULL THEN
     /* Processing statements go here.    */
  ELSE
     EXIT;
  END IF;
END LOOP;
```

FIGURE 19.4 Safe exit conditions for loops that contain cursors.

4. Close the cursor.
5. Repeat Steps 2–4 where the cursor is visible if it is necessary.

Figure 19.5 shows an example of a PL/SQL block that manipulates a cursor following these steps.

Many of these steps, and the possibility of mixing them up, can be avoided by using the FOR loop with the cursor. The PL/SQL block shown in Figure 19.6 contains the same functionality as the one in Figure 19.5.

No comments are needed to point out the significant gains in simplicity that this technique represents. You do not have to explicitly open the cursor, fetch the rows in variables declared previously, and close it when done. The FOR loop will inherently open the cursor with the appropriate input variables that you specify. The index of the loop will be automatically declared as a %ROWTYPE for the records that the cursor contains. The FOR loop will fetch in this index each record until the last one, unless you exit before the last record is fetched. For each iteration, you can access the data fetched by referencing the fields of the record that is also the iterator of the loop. Finally, when the loop is exited, either because the last record was retrieved or because you chose to terminate it, the cursor is closed automatically.

```
DECLARE
  CURSOR the_tapes (current_id TAPES.MOVIE_ID%TYPE) IS
    SELECT TAPE_ID
    FROM TAPES
    WHERE MOVIE_ID = current_id;
  tape_id TAPES.TAPE_ID%TYPE;

BEGIN
  OPEN the_tapes(121);
  LOOP
    FETCH the_tapes INTO tape_id;
    EXIT WHEN the_tapes%NOTFOUND OR
              the_tapes%NOTFOUND IS NULL;
      MESSAGE('Current Tape Id is '||TO_CHAR(tape_id));
      /* Other processing statements go here. */
  END LOOP;
  CLOSE the_tapes;
END;
```

FIGURE 19.5   Example of correct usage of cursors.

```
DECLARE
  CURSOR the_tapes (current_id TAPES.TAPE_ID%TYPE) IS
        SELECT TAPE_ID
        FROM TAPES
        WHERE MOVIE_ID = current_id;

BEGIN
  FOR current_tape IN the_tapes(121) LOOP
      MESSAGE('Current Tape Id is
'||TO_CHAR(current_tape.tape_id));
        /* Other processing statements go here.  */
  END LOOP;
END;
```

FIGURE 19.6   Explicit cursor in a FOR loop.

19.1.4 IMPLICIT CURSORS

Oracle uses a cursor for every SELECT ... INTO statement that is not referenced by an explicit cursor. It also uses cursors for all INSERT, UPDATE, or DELETE statements that are processed. These are called implicit cursors to distinguish them from the ones you declare and manipulate explicitly. Although they are created and managed internally by the RDBMS, there is a way to check the attributes of

Note

Using the cursor FOR loop you can even declare the cursor on the fly. For example, you could write the following statements:

```
FOR current_movie IN (SELECT * from MOVIES) LOOP
  MESSAGE(current_movie.TITLE);
END LOOP;
```

They will inherently declare a cursor, open it, fetch each record in the index **current_movie** and close the cursor at the end of the loop.

Moreover, starting from the version 2.2 of PL/SQL, released with Oracle7 RDBMS version 7.2, cursors can be declared and manipulated like any other PL/SQL variable.

the last implicit cursor used by Oracle. This cursor can be addressed with the name SQL, and its attributes can be accessed like any other explicit cursor you create.

Of the four cursor attributes discussed in Section 19.1.2, %ISOPEN is the one you will probably never use. The simple reason is that when the control returns from the DML statement that used the cursor to the line where you may want to check the value of %ISOPEN, the cursor is already closed by the RDBMS. Therefore, this attribute for implicit cursors will always be FALSE.

The attributes %FOUND and %NOTFOUND are used to find out whether the DML statement affected any records at all. The example shown in Figure 19.7 inserts a record in the table MOVIES. Then, it inserts the tape record that corresponds to this movie in the table TAPES. It is clear that if the first INSERT fails and the second one succeeds, the table TAPES will contain an orphan record in. The attribute %FOUND is used to check the outcome of the first statement and, depending on this outcome, either proceed with the second one or not.

The attribute %ROWCOUNT returns the number of rows affected by the DML statement. Structuring your code in a similar fashion as in Figure 19.7, you can use the value stored in SQL%ROWCOUNT to take certain actions that depend on the number of the records affected by your statement.

19.1.5 EXPLICIT CURSORS IN ORACLE FORMS

Chapter 14 discussed a variety of ways in which record groups can be used to provide tabular structures in your applications. Therefore it is legitimate to question the need of explicit cursors, that, after all, provide only a subset of the functionality of record groups. Why couldn't you create record groups based on the SELECT statements shown in Figure 19.2, for example?

You certainly could, however it is more efficient to use implicit cursors, if you will not need to use any of the typical features of query record groups such as dynamic adding or deleting rows from the record set, or populating lists and Lists of Values. There are several reasons for this statement.

First, it is so much easier to manage an explicit cursor, especially if the FOR loop is used concurrently. As you saw in Section 19.1.3, this loop reduces to a minimum the number of statements needed to process the data that a cursor contains.

```
INSERT INTO MOVIES(MOVIE_ID, TITLE)
VALUES(121, 'The Piano');
IF SQL%FOUND THEN
    INSERT INTO TAPES(MOVIE_ID, TAPE_ID)
    VALUES(121, 121000);
    COMMIT;
END IF;
```

FIGURE 19.7 Checking the attributes of the SQL cursor.

> ## Note
>
> Recall that if a SELECT ... INTO statement returns no records, the predefined exception NO_DATA_FOUND is raised. If the statement returns more than one record, the exception TOO_MANY_ROWS is raised. You can use these exceptions instead of directly checking the %FOUND, %NOTFOUND, or %ROWCOUNT attributes of the implicit cursor associated with that statement.
>
> In fact, in the second case, the %ROWCOUNT attribute will not contain the number of the records returned by the query. Oracle raises the exception TOO_MANY_ROWS and sets this attributes to 1 whenever the query returns more than one record.

Second, it is more efficient to use explicit cursors, than record groups. In all cases, when the SQL statement associated with the cursor or the record group will be executed, the RDBMS will populate the private SQL area of this statement with records returned by the query. If a record group is used, these records must be moved over to the client application in order to populate its structure. With the cursor, the client does not need to allocate additional memory to hold these records. The server's memory will continue to be used to store all the records and only the record currently fetched by the cursor will reside in the client's memory structures.

In addition, cursors extend the functionality of the straightforward SELECT ... INTO statements. When used in Oracle Forms, these statements will return only one record, at most. If you will need to retrieve multiple records, you will either have to create a block object—often unacceptable for the context—or use a cursor to hold these records.

Even if you will need to return only one record, using a cursor offers improvements in the performance of the application. As explained earlier in the book, conforming with the ANSI standards of the SQL language, after fetching the first record retrieved by a SELECT ... INTO statement, Oracle will make an additional trip to the database to see if other records were returned. If there are other records in the private SQL area of the statement, none of these records will be fetched. Instead, the exception TOO_MANY_ROWS will be raised. In the PL/SQL block that contains the statement, you will have to handle this exception. If, on the other hand, there are no other records returned by the query, nothing happens.

If you know in advance that the SELECT ... INTO statement will return only one record, you can avoid the extra, and unnecessary, trip to the database by replacing that statement with a cursor. You will fetch the single record from the cursor, which is the record you need, without any further actions occurring, or exceptions raised.

A typical use of this technique can be found in POST-QUERY triggers that populate control items in a block, based on the value of a base table item in that block. For example, when a query is issued in the RENTAL block, only the values for the base table items CUSTOMER_ID and TAPE_ID are returned from the database. Based on these values, for each record, you retrieve the name of the customer that rented the tape, and the title of the movie contained in that tape. You know in advance that there is one and only one customer record with the same CUSTOMER_ID as the current rental record. Similarly, there is only one tape record with the same TAPE_ID as the fetched rental record. One, and only one, record in the MOVIES table will correspond to this tape record—the one with the same MOVIE_ID as the tape involved in the rental transaction. Given this situation, the contents of the POST-QUERY trigger for the RENTAL block in the MRD application are as shown in Figure 19.8.

The largest part of this trigger is taken by the declaration of three cursors. The first one, cust_name, will concatenate the FIRST_NAME and LAST_NAME of a customer, whose CUSTOMER_ID matches the parameter cust_id. The second cursor, movie_title, retrieves the TITLE of a movie based on its MOVIE_ID, passed as the parameter the_movie_id. The third cursor, movie_id, retrieves the MOVIE_ID of a tape record, based on the value of the parameter the_tape_id.

The first FOR loop uses the cursor cust_name to retrieve the name of the customer and store it in the control item RENTAL.CUSTOMER_NAME. In the second group of statements, the outer loop retrieves the MOVIE_ID that corresponds to the tape whose ID is in :RENTAL.TAPE_ID. Then, based on this MOVIE_ID, the inner loop retrieves the title of the movie, using the cursor movie_title.

Note

The trigger shown in Figure 19.8 utilizes the fact that the records returned by a query in block RENTAL will always contain NOT NULL values in the CUSTOMER_ID and TAPE_ID items. If this were not the case, you would invoke the cursors **cust_name** and **movie_id** only after making sure that the parameters they take are not NULL.

The example also uses the uniqueness of CUSTOMER_ID in the CUS-TOMERS table, of MOVIE_ID for a given TAPE_ID in the TAPES table, and of MOVIE_ID in the MOVIES table. If this were not true, you would place an EXIT statement after the first iteration of the loop.

```
DECLARE
  CURSOR cust_name(cust_id CUSTOMERS.CUSTOMER_ID%TYPE) IS
    SELECT FIRST_NAME||' '||LAST_NAME name
    FROM CUSTOMERS
    WHERE CUSTOMER_ID = cust_id;

  CURSOR movie_title(the_movie_id MOVIES.MOVIE_ID%TYPE) IS
    SELECT TITLE
    FROM MOVIES
    WHERE MOVIE_ID = the_movie_id;

  CURSOR movie_id (the_tape_id TAPES.TAPE_ID%TYPE) IS
    SELECT MOVIE_ID
    FROM TAPES
    WHERE TAPE_ID = the_tape_id;

BEGIN
  FOR current_customer IN cust_name(:RENTAL.CUSTOMER_ID) LOOP
    :RENTAL.CUSTOMER_NAME := current_customer.name;
  END LOOP;

  FOR current_movie IN movie_id(:RENTAL.TAPE_ID) LOOP
    FOR current_title IN movie_title(current_movie.movie_id) LOOP
      :RENTAL.MOVIE_TITLE := current_title.title;
    END LOOP;
  END LOOP;
END;
```

FIGURE 19.8   Using cursors in POST-QUERY triggers.

19.1.6 EXPLICIT CURSORS IN STORED PROGRAM UNITS

In an Oracle Forms application you can use explicit cursors in program units that reside on the client side, but also in program units stored in the database. Sometimes, the performance of the application will greatly benefit if the cursors are placed on the database side rather than on the client side. The examples that will be discussed in this section are typical situations where placing cursors in stored program units reduces significantly the network traffic between the application clients and the database server.

The first example is a stored function that takes as input arguments two dates and the ID of a customer, and returns the amount of money that the customer has spent renting movies between these two dates. The contents of this function are shown in Figure 19.9.

```
FUNCTION Compute_Customer_Revenue (from_dt      DATE,
                                   to_dt        DATE,
                                   customer_id NUMBER)
RETURN NUMBER IS
  days        NUMBER;
  revenue     NUMBER := 0;

  CURSOR customer_rentals IS
    SELECT RETURN_DT, RENT_DT, DAILY_RATE
    FROM RENTALS
    WHERE RENT_DT >= from_dt AND
      RETURN_DT <= to_dt AND
      RENTALS.CUSTOMER_ID = customer_id;
BEGIN
  FOR rental IN customer_rentals LOOP
    days := Days_Between(rental.RETURN_DT, rental.RENT_DT);
    revenue := revenue + days * rental.DAILY_RATE;
  END LOOP;

  RETURN revenue;

  EXCEPTION
    WHEN OTHERS THEN
    RAISE_APPLICATION_ERROR(-20001,
      Customer revenue cannot be computed.');
END Compute_Customer_Revenue;
```

FIGURE 19.9 Using cursors in stored program units.

As you can see from Figure 19.9, the cursor customer_rentals stores information from the RENTALS table regarding those rental transactions that were initiated between the dates passed as the first and second argument by the customer whose CUSTOMER_ID is passed as the third argument. The FOR loop parses each record in the cursor. Every such record represents a rental transaction, and the amount paid by the customer for this transaction is computed by multiplying the number of days the video is rented by the daily rate for that particular transaction. The function Days_Between, which was discussed in Chapter 18, returns the number of days between the rent and the return dates. For each iteration, the amount paid by the customer for the transaction is added to the cumulative sum paid by this customer during the given period of time. This sum is stored in the variable revenue, which is the value returned by the function when the loop terminates.

If this function is placed in the database server, each time Oracle Forms invokes it, the client application will pass three values to the server, and will receive back the amount of money generated by the customer. Only four small packets of data are exchanged across the network between the client and the server. By contrast, if this function is placed in the Oracle Forms module, the traffic is much heavier. Each iteration of the FOR loop will return the current record in the cursor to the client environment, so that the amount paid can be computed. It is obvious that the magnitude of data transported across the network depends on the number of transactions that will populate the cursor.

The function that computes the revenue in rentals generated by a movie is very similar in content. The only significant difference between Compute_Movie_

```
FUNCTION Compute_Movie_Revenue (from_dt  DATE,
                                to_dt    DATE,
                                movie_id NUMBER)
RETURN NUMBER IS
  days       NUMBER;
  revenue    NUMBER := 0;

  CURSOR movie_rentals IS
    SELECT RETURN_DT, RENT_DT, DAILY_RATE
    FROM RENTALS
    WHERE RENT_DT >= from_dt AND
      RETURN_DT <= to_dt AND
      RENTALS.TAPE_ID IN (
        SELECT TAPES.TAPE_ID
        FROM TAPES
        WHERE TAPES.MOVIE_ID = movie_id);
BEGIN
  FOR rental IN movie_rentals LOOP
    days := Days_Between(rental.RENT_DT, rental.RETURN_DT);
    revenue := revenue + days * rental.DAILY_RATE;
  END LOOP;

  RETURN revenue;

  EXCEPTION
    WHEN OTHERS THEN
    RAISE_APPLICATION_ERROR(-20002,
                'Movie revenue cannot be computed.');
END Compute_Movie_Revenue;
```

FIGURE 19.10   Using cursors in stored program units.

Revenue and Compute_Customer_Revenue is the WHERE clause of the SELECT statement that populates the cursor. The function Compute_Movie_Revenue is shown in detail in Figure 19.10. Both these functions will be used in the module ANALYZE of the MRD application. They are created in the database together with other objects used in the activities discussed in this book.

19.2 DIFFERENCES BETWEEN VERSION 1.1 AND VERSION 2 OF PL/SQL

As mentioned in several instances in this book, Oracle Forms and all other Developer/2000 tools use the version 1.1 of PL/SQL, while the Oracle7 RDBMS use version 2. It is legitimate to discuss some of the differences between the two versions.

The major differences between the two versions are the existence in PL/SQL 2 of two composite data types, tables and records, and a new scalar data type, BINARY_INTEGER, used primarily with tables, that are not found in PL/SQL 1.1. In addition, the STANDARD package of built-in functions in the last version includes the trigonometric functions SIN, COS, and TAN, the logarithmic functions LN and LOG, the exponential function EXP, and the hyperbolic trigonometric functions SINH, COSH, and TANH. Nothing new is added to the way these functions are used. Therefore, this section will discuss only the PL/SQL tables and records. Throughout this section, PL/SQL will mean PL/SQL version 2, unless otherwise noted.

19.2.1 PL/SQL TABLES

The PL/SQL table is a composite data type that allows you to implement some sort of arrays in your program units. Like arrays, they are indexed by a number, in this case a number of data type BINARY_NUMBER. In addition, each indexed position in the table allows you to store data of another scalar data type, for example, NUMBER, VARCHAR2.

In order to use a PL/SQL table, you must declare a data type of that table first. After the data type is declared, the actual table variable is declared. The statements shown in Figure 19.11 declare tables of different types.

Note

In the Oracle documentation, these components of the table are referred to as the primary key and the column, for analogy with the terminology that describes regular tables. In the future releases of Oracle, PL/SQL tables will have multiple columns of different data types, and a primary key based on multiple columns of the table.

```
TYPE CustNameType IS TABLE OF VARCHAR2(60) NOT NULL
INDEX BY BINARY_INTEGER;


TYPE MovieTitleType IS TABLE OF MOVIES.TITLE%ROWTYPE
INDEX BY BINARY_INTEGER;

customers    CustNameType;
movies       MovieTitleType;
```

FIGURE 19.11   Examples of TABLE data type objects.

The first table type **CustNameType** will not allow NULL values in its column. The second table does not place such a restriction. All the statements shown in Figure 19.11 will, obviously, be placed in the DECLARE part of a PL/SQL block. Note that it is not possible to initialize a table upon declaration.

After a table is declared, its elements can be populated or accessed through the index of the table, like usual arrays. For example, to store the name 'Michelle Johnson' in the fifth position of the table **customers** created in Figure 19.11, you would use this statement:

customers(5) := 'Michelle Johnson';

The index of the table can be any integer in the range of a BINARY_INDEX data type, including negative numbers. So, if the movie 'Piano' is stored in the fifth position of the table **movies**, the following statement assigns its value to the predeclared variable current_movie:

current_movie := movies(-5);

The structure of the table does not enforce any bounds or cohesion between its indices. This means that the table can contain elements in positions −2, 5, and 155, and these can be the only three elements of it. If the program references any other table elements, the exception NO_DATA_FOUND will be raised.

If you want to create a table that looks more like a typical array, you have to fix and record in a variable the lower bound value of the index, and keep track of the upper bound, or the size of the table, as rows are added to it. In this case, the table can provide the values of one column in an INSERT or UPDATE statement, or store the value fetched by one column of a record. Because the table supports only one scalar data type column, if the INSERT or UPDATE statement will affect multiple columns, or the cursor will return multiple columns, several table structures must be used. Furthermore, there is no easy way to delete a row from a table, once the row is added. You can set its value to NULL, but the row will still be part of the set of rows for that table.

Note

From what has been said so far, you can conclude that the PL/SQL tables require additional programming in order to become a truly useful data type. PL/SQL version 2.3, released with Oracle RDBMS version 7.3, incorporates many methods with the table data type. These methods allow you to get the index of the first and last entry in the table, the number of entries in the table, or the index of the next or previous row in the table from a given position within the table. In addition, there is a method associated with the data type that allows you to delete a single entry, or a range of entries, or all the entries in the table. These methods enhance the features and functionality of the table significantly.

In addition, this version of PL/SQL allows you to create tables of records, thus bundling together in a tabular format columns of different data types.

19.2.2 PL/SQL RECORDS

PL/SQL records are used to create record-like data types in PL/SQL program units. These data types allow you to bundle together a different number of fields of different data types. This data type extends the functionality of the attribute %ROWTYPE, which exists in PL/SQL 1.1. Records created using this attribute will contain exactly the same fields and data types as the table on which the attribute is based. Using the RECORD data type, you are not bound to one table any more. Columns from different tables can be combined with non-database fields in one unit.

Like tables, the type of record must be declared first, and then an object of that type is declared. Figure 19.12 shows two examples of record declaration. The first record groups the data for a particular tape together with the title of the movie recorded in that tape. The second record does a similar denormalizing process for the rental data. Comparing Figure 19.12 with Figure 19.11, you will notice that you can initialize components of a record, which you are not allowed to do for tables. Because of that, if a field in the record is declared as NOT NULL, it must be initialized to some value when the record is declared.

In addition, also notice that the declarations of records can be nested. The first example in Figure 19.12 declares the record type TapeType. Then, within the declaration of the record type RentalType, one of its members, tape_info, is of the record data type defined previously.

Structures of record data type, can be referenced using the usual dot notation. The following two statements are examples of how you can assign a value

```
TYPE TapeType IS RECORD
  ( movie_title MOVIES.TITLE%TYPE NOT NULL = '',
    tape_info   TAPES%ROWTYPE);

TYPE RentalType IS RECORD
  (cust_name    VARCHAR2(60) NOT NULL = '',
   tape_info    TapeType,
   rental_info RENTALS%ROWTYPE);

tapes          TapeType;
rentals        RentalType;
```

FIGURE 19.12   Examples of RECORD data type objects.

to, or retrieve a value from a field of a record. Assume that current_movie is a variable defined previously.

```
current_movie := tapes.movie_title;
rentals.tape_info.movie_title := current_movie;
```

You can also assign values to several or all the fields of a record, by making them part of the INTO clause of a SELECT ... INTO statement that retrieves data that match these fields. Cursors can be used as well.

Note

If you want to transfer data from one record to another, you can use a statement like

record_1 := record_2;

This technique can be used only if both records are of the same record type. Two records are considered of the same type only if their data types are derived from the same record type. If the data types are different record types, the records are considered different, even if their parent data types contain exactly the same fields.

You can also use TABLE data types as elements of a record, thus obtaining a more complex data structure.

19.3 EXCEPTION HANDLING IN ORACLE FORMS APPLICATIONS

Recall from Chapter 10 that when an abnormal situation occurs in a Forms application, the application responds by raising an exception. If the error is an internal error due to some invalid action or inability to perform some database transaction, the exceptions will correspond to an error number defined in the Oracle Forms or the database server software. You can also raise your own exceptions for logical errors that occur in the application.

19.3.1 PROPAGATION OF EXCEPTIONS

When an exception is raised, Oracle Forms will look for a handler clause for that exception in the PL/SQL block where the exception occurs. If one is found, the instructions contained in that handler are executed. If there is no handler, then the exception is passed to the parent block if it exists. The same check for an exception handler occurs here. The exception will continue to propagate upward until it reaches the trigger body—remember that all PL/SQL code in Oracle Forms modules is located in triggers. Figure 19.13 represents the diagram of a

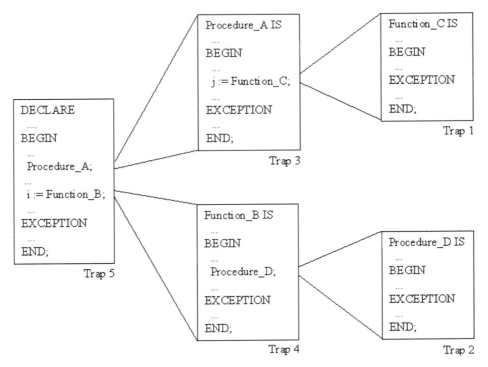

FIGURE 19.13 Trapping exceptions in Oracle Forms.

trigger that contains a call to Procedure_A and Function_B in its body. Procedure_A in turn issues a call to Function_C, and Function_B to Procedure_D. The diagram identifies the checkpoints an exception has to pass through when raised.

Any exception raised in Function_C can be handled in the EXCEPTION part of this function. If it is not trapped here, the exception will propagate to Procedure_A, where it can be handled by its EXCEPTION section, labeled as Trap 3 in the figure. If no handler is defined in Procedure_A, the exception will be propagated to the body of the calling trigger. The EXCEPTION section of this trigger, Trap 5, is the last chance to handle the raised exception. If it is not handled even here, Oracle Forms will return an error message and the trigger will fail. If in any of these steps, a handler for the exception OTHERS is used, none of the exceptions raised in the block, and all its enclosing blocks will be propagated outside the block. For example, if you place the WHEN OTHERS clause in Trap 4, all the exceptions that can be raised by Procedure_D or Function_B that are not handled by explicit handlers will be trapped and handled by the statements in this clause.

Several built-in functions can be used to check the number and the message of the error returned. ERROR_CODE returns the positive number of the error; ERROR_TYPE returns a three-character string (FRM or ORA) that indicates whether the error is an Oracle Form or Oracle Server error; ERROR_TEXT contains a description of the error that occurred. If the error is generated by the inability to execute a database transaction, two more functions can be used to get the database error number and descriptive message. These functions are DBMS_ERROR_CODE and DBMS_ERROR_TEXT. In addition, the functions SQLCODE and SQLERRM can be used, primarily in the WHEN OTHERS exception clause to retrieve the same information about errors.

Depending on the type of trigger, several things may happen upon its failure. Most of the transactional triggers such as PRE-INSERT, PRE-DELETE, POST-UPDATE, and ON-COMMIT, rollback any changes they have made prior to the failure point. The PRE-*object* and POST-*object* triggers such as PRE-TEXT-ITEM, PRE-BLOCK, and POST-RECORD, do not complete the navigation effort to the target object. A failure of the PRE-QUERY trigger will cancel the query, and, when the POST-QUERY trigger fails, the record is removed from the block. All the function KEY triggers, and most of the WHEN-*event* triggers take no action upon failure. Two triggers that behave differently are WHEN-CREATE-RECORD and WHEN-MOUSE-CLICKED. The failure of the first trigger prevents the creation of a new record; the failure of the second one prevents the navigation to the clicked item.

19.3.2 TRAPPING ERRORS IN BUILT-IN PROGRAM UNITS

Errors may also occur in built-in program units used in Forms applications. For example, if you try to navigate to an nonexistent item with the built-in procedure GO_ITEM, Oracle Forms will not be able to complete the navigation. However, differently from explicit PL/SQL statements, the failure of built-ins does not raise any exceptions. Forms has three built-in functions instead that allow you to check the outcome of the last action performed before they were called. These functions are FORM_SUCCESS, FORM_FAILURE, and FORM_FATAL. They all return a Boolean value of either TRUE or FALSE, depending on the outcome of the action.

In order to prevent Forms from performing any other actions after the failure of a built-in, the predefined exception FORM_TRIGGER_FAILURE, or any other user-defined exception must be explicitly raised. FORM_TRIGGER_FAILURE is an exception recognized only in the Oracle Forms environment. The function FORM_SUCCESS, or rather a negation of it, is randomly used to test the outcome of built-in functions or procedures. If the test shows that the built-in did not succeed, FORM_TRIGGER_FAILURE is normally raised to halt the operations. Oracle Forms will even create a procedure that uses this function and exception, if you create a default master/detail relationship between blocks. The contents of this procedure, called Check_Package_Failure, are shown in Figure 19.14.

19.3.3 EXCEPTIONS RAISED BY STORED PROGRAM UNITS

Like any other PL/SQL block, stored program units and database triggers can raise their own exceptions. If the error is an internal error of the Oracle Server, it will cause the database transaction to stop and will rollback any changes since the last savepoint. The text and number of the error are sent back to the calling form, and the functions DBMS_ERROR_CODE and DBMS_ERROR_TEXT can be used to retrieve their values. You can simulate this processing with user-defined exceptions as well. If the exception is a user-defined one, you should handle it within the stored program unit, or its enclosing blocks. If such an exception will not be handled there or in the Oracle Forms environment, an unhanded exception will be raised. In order to pass Oracle Forms an application-specific error number, and a description of the error, you can use the built-in procedure RAISE_APPLICATION_ERROR. When Forms receives an exception raised with this procedure, it will treat it like any other Oracle Server error raised internally.

The procedure RAISE_APPLICATION_ERROR is defined in the DBMS_STANDARD package that comes with the Oracle Server. This package is not known to Oracle Forms, therefore you can use the procedure only in stored

```
Procedure Check_Package_Failure IS
BEGIN
  IF NOT ( Form_Success ) THEN
    RAISE Form_Trigger_Failure;
  END IF;
END;
```

FIGURE 19.14   Procedure that tests the failure of Oracle Forms built-ins.

program units. The procedure takes two parameters. The first one is the error number, and the second one is the message text that will be associated with this number. The error number is always negative, and between −20999 and −20000. This range of numbers is reserved by the Oracle RDBMS software for user-defined errors. If you specify a number outside this range, the routine will compile successfully, but, at runtime you will get an error message.

The functions Compute_Customer_Revenue and Compute_Movie_Revenue shown in Figure 19.9 and Figure 19.10 earlier in the chapter both use RAISE_APPLICATION_ERROR to pass an error message in the case when processing errors occur.

19.3.4 TO HANDLE OR NOT TO HANDLE (AN EXCEPTION)

It is clear that by placing the clause OTHERS in the EXCEPTION part of each trigger you can trap all the errors that can be raised by the PL/SQL block contained in, or that depend on that trigger. However, it is questionable whether you want to go to that extreme, for two reasons. First, there is a great deal of functionality that comes by default in Oracle Forms. Controlling all the errors that may generate from this means rewriting this functionality on your own. Second, the Oracle Server database can be used effectively to screen data that are not compatible with the business rules that your application implements. The bottom line is that there will be errors that you will let the Oracle Forms and Oracle Server handle.

By default, Oracle Forms will send the message associated with these errors to the message line. When an error is left to be handled by the default processing of Oracle Forms, the event OnError occurs. The trigger ON-ERROR corresponds to this event. You can take advantage of this trigger in one of two ways:

1. As a last chance to trap and handle the error
2. To modify the error message that would be displayed by default.

During its processing of data and transactions, Oracle Forms issues messages of informative type for different situations. By default, these messages are sent to the console for display. In such a case, the event OnMessage occurs. The trigger that corresponds to this event is called ON-MESSAGE. You can use the ON-MESSAGE trigger to recast the message generated in a different format or to suppress a message altogether.

19.3.5 CUSTOMIZING DEFAULT ERROR PROCESSING

In this section you will add some error and message processing to the module ANALYZE.FMB. This module can be used to analyze the revenue generated by customers and by the movies of the video rental store. Open this module in the Designer, and inspect the functionality it provides so far.

Note

Errors and messages are characterized by what is called a severity level. Oracle Forms maintains this severity level in the system variable SYSTEM.MESSAGE_LEVEL. The setting of this variable controls what messages are displayed to the users. If its value is 0, all the messages will be displayed. But, if the setting of this variable is 5, messages of severity level 5 and below will not be displayed. Messages of this severity level are informative messages such as, **FRM-40401: No changes to save.**

If you want to supress messages below a certain severity level, set SYSTEM.MESSAGE_LEVEL to that level as in the following line:

:SYSTEM.MESSAGE_LEVEL := 5;

This is the only system variable whose value can not only be retrieved, but also set.

ANALYZE.FMB has only two blocks, named CUSTOMER and MOVIE. The first block displays the names of customers, their zip code and the amount they have spent renting movies from the store during a period of time. The second block contains the movie title, producer, rating, and the revenue generated by the movie in a given period of time. The module also has a control block that contains two date items and a push button labeled Calculate for each block. The users of this module can enter the dates in the From and To items and then click the Calculate button to display the amounts spent by customers, or generated by movies for that period of time.

Figure 19.15 shows the layout of the CUSTOMER block. The layout for the MOVIE block is very similar.

The AMOUNT items for both blocks are populated in POST-QUERY triggers. These triggers invoke the database-stored functions Compute_Customer_Revenue and Compute_Movie_Revenue, which were discussed in Section 19.1.6, and are shown in Figure 19.9 and Figure 19.10, respectively. The following statement represents the contents of the POST-QUERY trigger for block CUSTOMER.

```
:CUSTOMER.AMOUNT := Compute_Customer_Revenue(:CUSTOMER.CUST_FROM,
                    :CUSTOMER.CUST_TO, :CUSTOMER.CUSTOMER_ID);
```

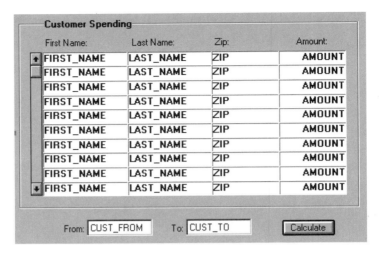

FIGURE 19.15   Layout of the CUSTOMER block in module
ANALYZE.FMB.

The contents of the POST-QUERY trigger for block MOVIE are as follows:

```
:MOVIE.AMOUNT  := Compute_Movie_Revenue(:MOVIE.MOVIE_FROM,
                        :MOVIE.MOVIE_TO, :MOVIE.MOVIE_ID);
```

If an error occurs in any of these functions, they will send an error message to the Oracle Forms environment through the procedure RAISE_APPLICATION_ ERROR. If things are left the way they are, the error goes unhandled, and you would expect the error message to be displayed in the message line. Instead, Forms will simply inform you that an unhanded exception occurred. If, for example, the error occurred in the function Compute_Cutomer_Revenue, Forms will display the following message, FRM-40735: POST-QUERY trigger raised un-handed exception ORA-20001.

   To remedy for this behavior, you will trap the error in the ON-ERROR trig-ger and redirect the error message to an alert, which will be displayed to the users. This alert is provided in the module ANALYZE.FMB. Its name is ERRORS and its title is "Processing Error". The alert has only one OK button and a STOP icon.

   Create a form level ON-ERROR trigger that contains the statements shown in Figure 19.16.

   Now, whenever the error described above occurs, Oracle Forms will not display the error message FRM-40735 quoted above, but the message associated

```
DECLARE
   alert_button  NUMBER;
   alert_message VARCHAR2(540);
BEGIN
   IF ERROR_CODE IN ( 40735) THEN
      alert_message := DBMS_ERROR_TEXT;
      SET_ALERT_PROPERTY('ERRORS', ALERT_MESSAGE_TEXT,
alert_message);
      alert_button := SHOW_ALERT('ERRORS');
   ELSE
      MESSAGE(ERROR_TYPE||'-'||TO_CHAR(ERROR_CODE)||':
'||ERROR_TEXT);
      RAISE FORM_TRIGGER_FAILURE;
   END IF;
END;
```

FIGURE 19.16   Customizing error handling in ON-ERROR triggers.

with the exceptions ORA-20001 and ORA-20002. When any other error occurs, Forms will display the message in the normal way.

There is a problem with the ON-ERROR trigger as shown above. If you encounter an error in the functions Compute_Customer_Revenue or Compute_Movie_Revenue, the error message that the alert ERRORS will display will be similar to the one shown in Figure 19.17.

It is clear that your users would not be interested in either of the other two messages that follow the first message. You should manipulate the DBMS_ERROR_TEXT string so that these messages are filtered out. As in other cases, you can use a combination of the SQL functions INSTR and SUBSTR to extract the substring you need. The following statement returns the position of the

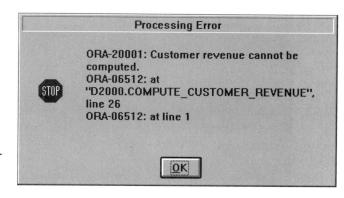

FIGURE 19.17   "Raw" Error Message Obtained from DBMS_ERROR_TEXT.

second occurrence of substring ORA- starting from the beginning of string alert_message:

pos := INSTR (alert_message, 'ORA-', 1, 2);

The first error message will be the substring of the original longer message, from the first character, to the character before the second occurrence of string ORA-. This message is retrieved by the following statement:

alert_message := SUBSTR (alert_message, 1, pos - 1);

For a general purpose application, there is another important improvement that you can make to the trigger shown in Figure 19.16. If actions that involve database transactions cannot be performed successfully, the default Oracle Forms error will be very generic. For example, if the query cannot be performed, the error message will be, FRM-40505: ORACLE error: unable to perform query. In order to find out what prevented the query from being executed, users must press the key associated with the Display Error action. In PC platforms, this will be the SHIFT+F1 key.

By specifying the error number in the IN clause of the ON-ERROR trigger, you ensure that users will not see the unhelpful FRM message, but the database message. Other good candidates for similar treatment would be the error num-

```
DECLARE
  alert_button  NUMBER;
  alert_message VARCHAR2(540);
  pos NUMBER;
BEGIN
  IF ERROR_CODE IN ( 40735, 40505, 40508, 40509, 40510 ) THEN
     alert_message := DBMS_ERROR_TEXT;
     pos := INSTR(alert_message, 'ORA-', 1, 2);
     alert_message := SUBSTR(alert_message, 1, pos - 1);
     SET_ALERT_PROPERTY('ERRORS', ALERT_MESSAGE_TEXT,
alert_message);
     alert_button := SHOW_ALERT('ERRORS');
  ELSE
     MESSAGE(ERROR_TYPE||'-'||TO_CHAR(ERROR_CODE)||':
'||ERROR_TEXT);
    RAISE FORM_TRIGGER_FAILURE;
  END IF;
END;
```

FIGURE 19.18 Improved and expanded version of ON-ERROR trigger.

bers issued when Oracle cannot insert, update, and delete, which are 40508, 40509, and 40510. The final form of the trigger ON-ERROR is shown in Figure 19.18. This trigger should serve you as a template for further enhancements of the error-reporting functionality of your application.

19.4 SUMMARY

This chapter presents advanced topics in PL/SQL programming such as cursors and their usage in Oracle Forms applications, new data types introduced in Version 2 of PL/SQL, and exception handling. Important concepts discussed are listed here:

- ❏ Cursors in PL/SQL
  - ❏ Declaring explicit cursors
  - ❏ Methods and attributes of explicit cursors
  - ❏ Using the FOR loop with explicit cursors
  - ❏ Implicit cursors
  - ❏ Explicit cursors in Oracle Forms
  - ❏ Explicit cursors in stored program units
- ❏ Differences between Version 1.1 and Version 2 of PL/SQL
  - ❏ PL/SQL tables
  - ❏ PL/SQL records
- ❏ Exception Handling in Oracle Forms Applications
  - ❏ Propagation of exceptions
  - ❏ Trapping errors in built-in program units
  - ❏ Exceptions raised by stored program units
  - ❏ To handle or not to handle (an exception)
  - ❏ Customizing default error processing

Chapter 20

DEBUGGING

"What cruel fate! What torture the bugs will this day put me to!"
—Aristophanes

No matter how good your programming abilities are, every software system you develop will be associated with a certain probability of failure. It is said that a system fails when an error occurs somewhere in one of its software modules. In general, an error is the inability of the system to exhibit the functionality that users expect from it. Testing is the process that aims at identifying the discrepancies between the systems developed and the true requirements of the customers. Identifying errors in the system and removing them is known as debugging.

There are two levels of debugging. One is a high-level debugging to ensure that the system meets the overall expectations of the customers and contains all the functionality they expect. The other is done at the application code level to ensure that functions are passed with the right parameters, the loops are repeated only as many times as necessary, and the data sent to the database is in the appropriate format.

This chapter will discuss the second level of debugging. In particular, you will learn how to run a form in the debug mode and how to use the Debugger to trace a program unit step by step.

20.1 ACCESSING THE DEBUGGER

In order to access the Debugger, you must first enable the Debug Mode in the Designer, and then run the module you want to debug. There are three ways to toggle the Debug Mode *on* and *off*:

a) In the Object Navigator, click the Debug Mode button in the vertical toolbar of the window. The Debug Mode is enabled if the icon is ▣. The Debug Mode is disabled if the icon is ▣.

b) Choose Tools | Options... to display the Options dialog box. In this dialog box, click the Runtime Options folder tab to display the options that you can set for your application at runtime. The second check box on the left is labeled Debug Mode. When it is checked, the Debug Mode is enabled.

c) Check the menu item Tools | Debug Mode to enable debugging, or uncheck it to disable debugging.

It is important that before you run a module for debugging purposes you generate it with the Debug Mode enabled. When the module is generated with Debug Mode enabled, the executable contains source code symbols that are accessible and editable from the Debugger. If the module is generated with the Debug Mode disabled, the Debugger will not be able to display any information about the source code being executed.

You can run a module in Debug Mode using the Oracle Forms Runtime engine as well. In the command line simply add the parameter debug=YES. For example, if you want to debug the module C:\MRD\MRD.FMX, the command line in the program item will be

F45RUN.EXE C:\MRD\MRD.FMX DEBUG = YES

When you run a module and the Debug Mode is enabled, the first thing that will appear is the Debugger window. This allows you to create any debugging actions that you will need, as will be discussed later in the chapter. However, in order to proceed with the execution of the module, you must close the Debugger window. Click the Close iconic button ☒ from the Debugger toolbar to dismiss this window.

Now you can run your module as usual. The Debugger will not be displayed until Oracle Forms either encounters the built-in BREAK or a predefined breakpoint in any of your program units. This is important to emphasize because if you want to use the Debugger at some point during the execution of the module, you must explicitly create a breakpoint that will interrupt the normal flow of the application and will pass the control to the Debugger.

In order to help you locate the trigger from which an error may occur, Oracle Forms Runtime has an additional parameter, called debug_messages. If you want to run the module mentioned above with this option set, you would use the following command line:

F45RUN.EXE C:\MRD\MRD.FMX DEBUG_MESSAGES=YES

Whenever you run the module with this parameter set to YES, Oracle Forms will display a message upon executing each trigger in the module. This message displays context information about the trigger such as its name and the object to which it is attached. A typical message displayed by this utility is, FRM-42400: Performing event trigger WHEN-BUTTON-PRESSED in field CUSTOMER.OK.

Thus, the steps to display the Debugger could be summarized as follows:

1. Identify the trigger, program unit, or PL/SQL block that you want to debug. You can do this from the Designer, if you have an idea where the error may be occurring. You can also run the module using Oracle Forms Runtime

---

Note

The Debugger is a utility displayed in a modal window. As long as it is active, you will not be able to access or manipulate the application running in the background other than through the Debugger actions.

with the parameter DEBUG_MESSAGES=YES, and identify the trigger that contains the violating code.

2. Create a breakpoint using the built-in procedure BREAK.
3. Generate the module with the Debug Mode option enabled.
4. Run the module until the breakpoint is reached.

20.2 COMPONENTS OF THE DEBUGGER

Figure 20.1 represents a typical Debugger window and its components. As you can see from this figure, the Debugger window may have up to three panes displayed at any one time. The Source Pane displays a read-only copy of the program unit currently being executed. The Navigator Pane contains a hierarchical listing of the objects that can be used in the Debugger. The Interpreter pane is a command line that allows you to enter statements and debug commands. Each of these panes can be sized and scrolled independently.

The Debugger window contains a toolbar with iconic buttons for the most frequently used tools. In addition, the Debugger has a menu of its own, with three items, which is inserted in the menu of your application, if one is being used.

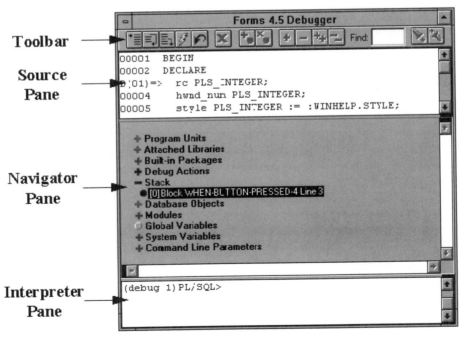

FIGURE 20.1 Components of Debugger window.

20.2.1 SOURCE PANE

The Source Pane displays a copy of the program unit that is being currently executed in the Debugger. You can use it to see the contents of the program as it is being executed. As said earlier, this is a read-only copy of the statements. You cannot edit the code in the Source Pane.

Each line in the Source Pane is preceded by a line number. If a breakpoint is defined for that line, then the line number is replaced by a symbol like B(n), where n is the internal identifier of the breakpoint. In Figure 20.1, the breakpoint defined in the third line is indicated by the symbol B(01). Similarly, if a trigger is defined for a particular line, the line number is replaced with the symbol T(n), where n is the sequence number for the trigger. The Source Pane is normally displayed. If you want to hide it, uncheck the menu item View | Source Pane.

20.2.2 NAVIGATOR PANE

The Navigator Pane allows you to list, create, and delete objects that are available in the Debugger interface. You use it in exactly the same way as you would use the Object Navigator in the Designer. You can use the Navigator Pane to create PL/SQL program units, attach PLL libraries, and even create database stored procedures and triggers. The purpose of this is to invoke their functionality from debug triggers that you may want to create.

However, the most important practical use of the Navigator Pane is to inspect and set the values of data items, variables, global variables, system variables, and parameters that are used in the application. If you want to see the values of global variables, systems variables, or Runtime parameters, simply expand the nodes Global Variables, System Variables, and Command Line Parameters.

If you want to view and edit data for objects related to modules, then expand the node Modules and its dependent nodes. For modules, you can display and change the contents of items, triggers, program units, parameter lists, and property classes.

Note

You must keep in mind that all the changes that you may make are temporarily stored in the memory structures of Oracle Forms Runtime. This means that if you edit the contents of a trigger, create a new procedure, or attach a library to the module, these changes will not be permanently recorded in the source code of your module. If you achieve your objective with these changes, you must go back in the Designer and recreate them.

You can also attach PLL libraries while the application is running in Debugger. Figure 20.2 shows the nodes of the Navigator Pane expanded to the item level. The data item File in the block WINHELP is selected and is ready to be edited. The effects of changing its contents are the same as if you entered the new data in the item when the application runs in normal mode.

In addition, you can view the contents of the stack and create debug actions, as you will see in Section 20.3. The Navigator is also displayed by default, but you can hide it by unchecking the menu item View | Navigator.

20.2.3 INTERPRETER PANE

The Interpreter Pane is a command line interface that enables you to enter Debugger commands from the PL/SQL prompt. At the same time, the Interpreter Pane echoes back the command line equivalents of actions that you may perform in the Navigator Pane.

For example, if you want to delete the breakpoint 1, you could enter the following statements at the PL/SQL> prompt:

.DELETE BREAKPOINT 1

As the other two panes, this pane is visible by default, but can be hidden by unchecking the menu item View | Interpreter Pane.

20.2.4 TOOLBAR

The toolbar of the Debugger is shown in Figure 20.3. The functionality of most of the tools here is the same as in the Object Navigator. You click the Create and Delete buttons to add or remove an object from the hierarchy tree. You can click the icons in the Expand/Collapse group to expand or collapse a node one level or

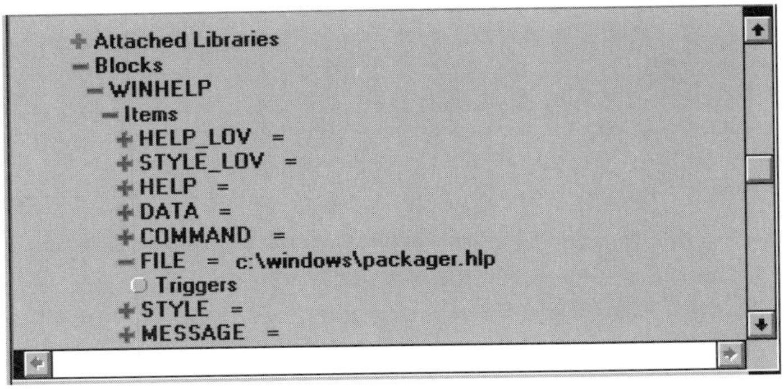

FIGURE 20.2 Changing values of items in the Debugger's Navigator pane.

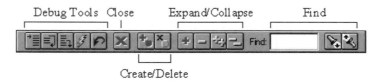

FIGURE 20.3 Oracle Forms Debugger toolbar.

all the way to the end of the hierarchy tree. The Find utility with its Search Forward and Search Backward buttons is used to quickly locate entries in the list. These commands are also available from the Navigator menu of the Debugger.

The first five buttons in the toolbar are used to carry out debugging commands:

❑ The Step Into icon is used to step inside a program unit if the current statement is a call to a function or procedure; otherwise, it just executes the command.

❑ The Step Over icon bypasses the call to a subroutine.

❑ The Step Out icon executes all the statements until the end of the current program unit.

❑ The Go icon is used to resume the execution of the program until a breakpoint is reached or there are no statements left to execute.

❑ The Reset icon abandons the execution of the current program unit and returns the control to an outer level in the Debugger.

20.3 MANAGING DEBUG ACTIONS

There are two types of objects that you can create and use during a debugging session. These are breakpoints and debug triggers. Although they are objects attached with the Debugger, breakpoints and debug triggers are usually called debug actions.

Breakpoints are the most common debug action you take. They are associated with a particular line of code that the PL/SQL engine will execute and cause the program flow to be interrupted right before this line is reached. Debug triggers are blocks of code that you may associate with the program units being debugged. They can be executed each time the Debugger is invoked, or when a particular line of code is reached. You may even create debug triggers that fire when each statement is executed.

This section explains how to create and manage these debug actions. You will use the MRD application that you have developed in previous chapters. As a preliminary step, open this module in the Designer and generate it with the Debug Mode enabled.

20.3.1 CREATING DEBUG ACTIONS

In this section you will create a breakpoint and a debug trigger in the trigger WHEN-BUTTON-PRESSED for the property class PUSH_BUTTON:

1. Run the module with the Debug Mode enabled. Before the module is initialized, the Debugger window appears.
2. In the Navigator Pane, expand the necessary nodes in order to select the trigger WHEN-BUTTON-PRESSED defined in the property class PUSH_BUTTON (These nodes are Modules, MRD, Property Classes, PUSH_BUTTON, and Triggers.) When the trigger is selected, its contents appear in the Source Pane.

Now you are ready to create the breakpoint and the debug trigger. To create a breakpoint on line 7 of the trigger, click anywhere inside the line in the Source Pane. Then follow any of these steps:

a) Double-click the line, or
b) Enter the command .BREAK in the Interpreter Pane, or
c) Select Debug | Break... from the Debugger menu. The PL/SQL Breakpoint dialog box will appear (see Figure 20.4).

The first two commands will create and enable a breakpoint attached with the particular line in the source pane. The third command is more sophisticated, because it allows you to control the Enabled/Disabled status of the breakpoint by checking or unchecking the check box Enabled. At the same time, you can associ-

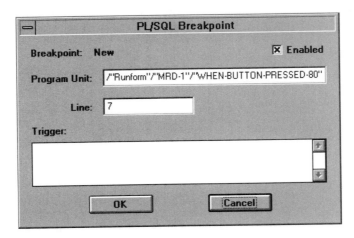

FIGURE 20.4 PL/SQL Breakpoint dialog box.

ate a trigger with the breakpoint, by entering the statements in a PL/SQL block in
the Trigger pane of the dialog box.

The process of creating a trigger is similar. To create a debug trigger on line
10 of the trigger, click anywhere inside this line in the Source Pane. Then, follow
these steps:

1. Select Debug | Break... from the Debugger menu. The PL/SQL Breakpoint
   dialog box will appear (see Figure 20.5).
2. Enter the body of the trigger in the Trigger Body pane and click OK.

Notice that the PL/SQL statements that you enter in the Trigger Body must
form a complete PL/SQL block. While in Oracle Forms triggers you could enter
just the IF statement, here you must enclose it between the keywords BEGIN and
END.

Another point that should attract your attention is the drop-down list box
Location, which allows you to define the context of the trigger just created. By de-
fault, the value of this list is Program Unit. In this case, the text fields Program
Unit and Line define the context in which this trigger will fire. If you select
Debug Entry from the list, the trigger will fire each time the Debugger is activated
due to a breakpoint, or each time one of the debug actions Step Into, Step Over,
Step Out, Go, or Reset occur.

Using the PL/SQL Trigger dialog box is obviously the easiest way to create
a debug trigger. However, you can also create them from the command line of

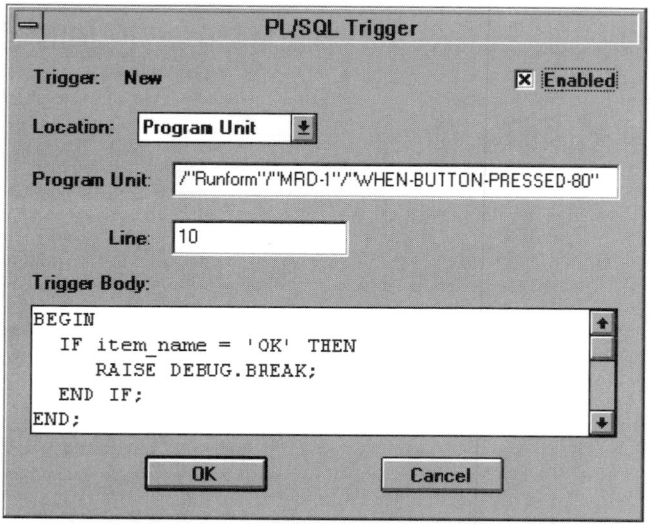

FIGURE 20.5   PL/SQL Trigger dialog box.

the Interpreter Pane. Figure 20.6 contains the commands that create the same debug trigger in the three contexts discussed above.

The first of these statements creates a trigger associated with line 8 of WHEN-BUTTON-PRESSED trigger. The second statement creates a trigger equivalent with the one you would create by choosing Debug Entry in the Location list of the dialog box PL/SQL Trigger. The third statement creates a debug trigger that will be executed for each statement.

As stated earlier, all the breakpoints or debug triggers you create in the Debugger will be available throughout the current session. However, they will not be available the next time you run the module. In order to create breakpoints that last between sessions, you should add the statement **BREAK**; before the line that will contain the breakpoint. When the form is executed in Debug Mode, this built in procedure passes the control to the Debugger.

For more complicated debug actions such as creating a complex trigger or program unit, you may save transcripts of your actions to a text file. As an example, create and use a log file that records the commands to create the debug trigger discussed previously. Exit the runtime application and run it again. When the initial debug window appears, perform the following steps:

```
PL/SQL> .TRIGGER IS
    +> BEGIN
    +> IF item_name = 'OK' THEN
    +>    RAISE DEBUG.BREAK;
    +>    END IF;
    +> END;
Trigger #1 installed at line 10 of WHEN-BUTTON-PRESSED-80
PL/SQL> .TRIGGER DEBUG IS
    +> BEGIN
    +>    IF item_name = 'OK' THEN
    +>      RAISE DEBUG.BREAK;
    +>    END IF;
    +> END;
Trigger #2 installed at interpreter entry
PL/SQL> .TRIGGER * IS
    +> BEGIN
    +>    IF item_name = 'OK' THEN
    +>       RAISE DEBUG.BREAK;
    +>    END IF;
    +> END;
Trigger #3 installed at every statement
```

FIGURE 20.6 Creating debug triggers from in the Interpreter Pane.

1. In the command line of the Interpreter Pane enter the following statement:

   .LOG FILE C:\DEBUG.LOG

   This will open a file where all the subsequent commands and Debugger responses will be logged.
2. In the Navigator Pane, select the trigger WHEN-BUTTON-PRESSED attached to the property class PUSH_BUTTON. The contents of the trigger are displayed in the Source Pane.
3. In the Source Pane, click inside line 10 of the trigger.
4. Select Debug | Break... from the Debugger menu. The PL/SQL Breakpoint dialog box will appear (see Figure 20.4).
5. Enter the body of the trigger in the Trigger Body pane and click OK.
6. In the command line of the Interpreter Pane enter the following statement:

   .LOG OFF

   This command will save and close the log file C:\DEBUG.LOG. The file can be used after you exit the application to retrieve the contents of the trigger and incorporate them with the rest of the application in the Designer. If, in subsequent runs you want to append the initial log file, you need to open it with the following statement:

   .LOG FILE C:\DEBUG.LOG

   When a log file is open, you can view its contents by selecting View | Interpreter Log... from the menu. Unfortunately, you cannot copy the contents of this window and paste them in the Command Interpreter, which would save you from re-entering long statements each time the Debugger is initialized.

20.3.2 EDITING DEBUG ACTIONS

After you create debug actions, you can go back and edit them at a later time. All the debug actions are listed in the Navigator Pane, under the Debug Actions entry. Figure 20.7 shows an example of such entries.

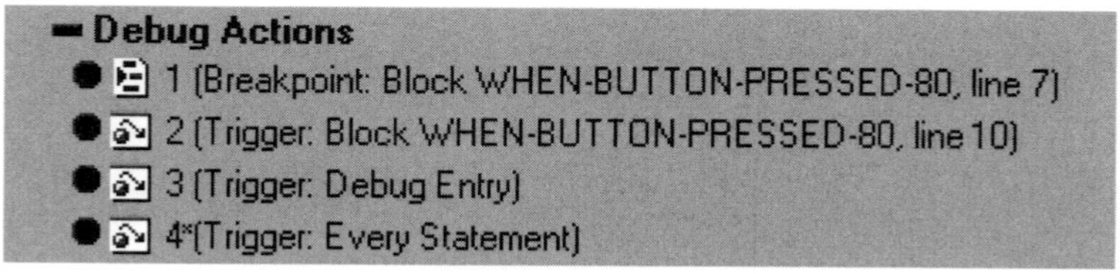

FIGURE 20.7   Debug actions.

As you can see from the figure, the information displayed contains the type of debug action, and all the relevant context information such as the program unit name, line number, and trigger type. If the debug action is disabled, as in the case of the last trigger in Figure 20.7, an asterisk sign will appear to the right of the action's identifier.

To edit any of this information, you can double-click the icons that represent the type of the debug action. Depending on the debug action, you may also choose Debug | Break... or Debug | Trigger... from the menu. Either the PL/SQL Program Unit or PL/SQL Trigger dialog box will appear (see Figure 20.4 and Figure 20.5). In these dialog boxes you can modify the debug actions according to your needs. For example, you can change the Enabled status of the debug action, its line number, and program unit name. For triggers, you can modify the body and the context as well. If you want to delete the debug action altogether, simply click the Delete icon ▧ in the toolbar, or select Navigator | Delete from the menu.

Let us conclude this section by mentioning that some of the editing of debug actions can be done from the command line of the Interpreter Pane. Figure 20.8 shows three statements issued in the Interpreter that disable the trigger first, then display its status, and finally delete it.

20.3.3 EDITING PROGRAM UNITS AND TRIGGERS

The Debug menu contains a menu item labeled Edit... . This is used to edit the program unit currently displayed in the Source Pane. When you choose this item, the PL/SQL Editor window appears (see Figure 20.9). This editor allows you to edit the contents of the program unit as you would in the Designer. However, there are two major differences in the window layout between this editor and the regular PL/SQL Editor in the Designer:

```
PL/SQL> .DISABLE TRIGGER 2
Disabling debug action 2...
PL/SQL> .DESCRIBE TRIGGER 2
Trigger: 2
   Program Unit: Block WHEN-BUTTON-PRESSED-75
   Line: 10
   Enabled: NO
PL/SQL> .DELETE TRIGGER 2
Removing debug action 2...
PL/SQL>
```

FIGURE 20.8 Editing debug actions in the Interpreter Pane.

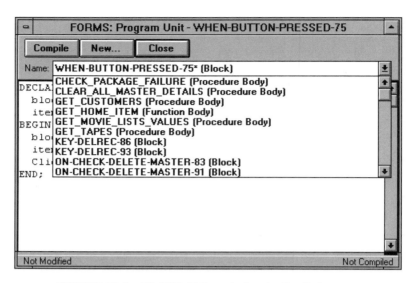

FIGURE 20.9   PL/SQL Editor window for the Debugger.

1. The absence of the Revert and Delete push buttons reflects the fact that the changes you make here will not be permanently stored in the module.
2. The drop-down list box under the push buttons contains all the program unit names of this module. Differently from the context area of the Designer's PL/SQL Editor, this list is a unified and alphabetically sorted view of all the triggers and program units in the module. To avoid naming conflicts, a sequence number is appended to the name of each trigger in the list. This is the reason why in the Debugger, trigger names are always followed by identifying numbers.

In addition to editing existing program units, you can also create program units from scratch, either by clicking the push button New... in the Debugger's PL/SQL Editor, or by creating a new object under the Program Units node in the Navigator Pane. You can also attach PLL libraries to the Debugger environment. The process is identical with attaching libraries in the Designer.

20.3.4 INSPECTING THE APPLICATION STATE

When the Runtime engine encounters a breakpoint, the flow of the program is interrupted, and control is passed to the Debugger. This gives you an opportunity to inspect the state of your application and to monitor this state at any point during the execution of the application. The Navigator Pane is where most of the actions related to this topic occur.

> # Note
>
> When creating or modifying program units in the Debugger, you may want to insert debug actions in them the same way you would insert these actions in regular program units. When the Debugger reaches such a breakpoint or debug trigger, a nesting in the levels of debugging occurs. The levels of debugging are numbered. The topmost level is assigned the number 0. When the debugging level is zero, Forms executes the code in the normal fashion and no debugging activities can occur. When a breakpoint is reached, Forms moves to debugging level one. If during the execution of statements in this level another breakpoint is encountered, Forms will move to debugging level two, and so on. The command line in the Interpreter Pane displays the current debug level. The statements in Figure 20.6 and Figure 20.8 are all issued at the debug level zero. If they were issued in the level one, the prompt in the Interpreter Pane would be (debug 1)PL/SQL>.

To inspect the values of system variables and the runtime parameters, expand the nodes with the same names in the Navigator. You cannot change the values of any of these variables, but you can view and modify the values of global variables, Forms items, and parameter lists. Follow these steps to do this:

1. Expand the appropriate node.
2. Click the label of desired object.
3. Type over the new value.

You can also inspect and modify values of variables local to the program units that are currently being executed. The names of these program units, together with the names and values of their variables are kept under the Stack node of the Navigator Pane (see Figure 20.10).

The nodes under Stack are the PL/SQL blocks that Oracle Forms is executing. Because the Execution Stack grows downward, the program unit that is at the bottom of the stack is the one being currently executed. The one immediately

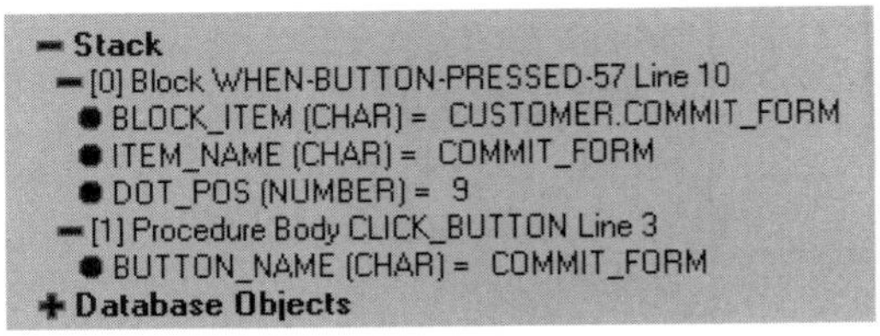

FIGURE 20.10 Viewing the Execution Stack in the Navigator Pane.

above it is the program unit that is called the current subroutine. In the case of Figure 20.10, procedure Click_Button is the current program unit, and this procedure is called from the trigger WHEN-BUTTON-PRESSED.

Each program unit in the stack is also called a frame and is identified by the number in square brackets. To select a frame, you simply click its node in the Navigator. You will notice that the Source Pane will be refreshed with the contents of the program unit that the frame represents. If there are local variables declared in this program unit, they will be listed under the frame. You can change their current values by clicking and typing over the new values.

You can also change the frame of the stack and the contents of local variables from the command line of the Interpreter Pane. The following statement sets the scope of the Debugger to frame 1 of the stack:

```
(debug 1)PL/SQL> .SET SCOPE FRAME 1
```

The following statement overwrites the value of the local variable BUTTON_NAME in the current scope with the string 'MOVIE':

```
(debug 1)PL/SQL> DEBUG.SETC ('BUTTON_NAME','MOVIE');
```

The second command uses the package DEBUG, which will be discussed in greater detail in Section 20.3.6.

20.3.5 RESUMING THE APPLICATION EXECUTION

After the program flow is interrupted and you have inspected or modified the application state, you will eventually decide to resume the execution. In general, you have three choices:

❑ **Resume the execution freely.** Oracle Forms will attempt to execute all the program units that are currently stored in the stack. If no other breakpoints are encountered, at the end of the process, the execution stack will be empty, and the Debugger window will be hidden. If Oracle Forms encounters a breakpoint in the execution path, the flow of the program is interrupted again. In order to resume free execution of the program, perform any of the following actions:
  a)   Click the Go icon 🗗 in the toolbar, or
  b)   Choose Debug | Go from the menu, or
  c)   Enter the following statement in the Interpreter Pane:

```
(debug 1)PL/SQL> .GO
```

❑ **Terminate the execution of the statements in the stack.** This action is also called resetting the debug level. In this case, Oracle Forms will not execute any further statements in the current execution thread, but will return to the next higher debug level. At the same time, the message bar will display a message similar to FRM-40748: Trigger WHEN-BUTTON-PRESSED terminated by reset command.

To reset the execution to a higher debug level, follow any of these steps:

a)   Click the Reset icon ▣ in the toolbar, or
b)   Choose Debug | Reset from the menu, or
c)   Enter the following statement in the Interpreter Pane:

```
(debug 1) PL/SQL> .RESET
```

❑   **Step through the statements in the stack.** This is probably the action that you will perform the most, because it allows you to execute only one or a few statements at a time. When these statements are executed, the control returns to the Debugger to allow you to assess their effects on the application. The most general command for stepping through the code is to choose Debug | Step... menu item from the Debugger's menu. The PL/SQL Step dialog box will appear (see Figure 20.11). The contents of this dialog box reflect the parameters that the STEP command may take.

   The radio buttons in this dialog control the mode in which the statements are executed; the value entered in the Count field controls the number of statements that will be executed in each step. By default, only one statement is executed at each step. Clicking the Apply button will issue the Step command without dismissing the dialog box, at which point you can enter a new mode or target to step to. Clicking the OK button issues the command and dismisses the dialog box. Clicking the Cancel dialog will dismiss the dialog box without any further action.

   According to the settings of the Mode radio buttons, the Debugger may Step Into, Step Over, Step Out, or Step To a target program unit. In Step Into mode, the Debugger will execute the number of statements speci-

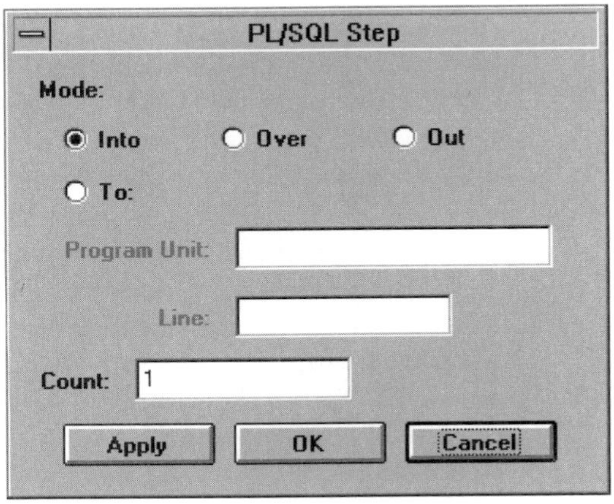

FIGURE 20.11   PL/SQL Step dialog box.

fied in Count. If any of these statements is a call to a subroutine, Debugger will descend in the subroutine. In Step Over mode, the Debugger will execute the number of statements specified, but if it encounters a subroutine call, it does not enter that routine. In Step Out mode, the Debugger will execute all the statements until the end of the current program unit and will pause when the control returns to the calling program unit. The value of Count is irrelevant for this command. When you select the Step To radio button, the data items Program Unit and Line are enabled. You can use them to enter the target program unit and line number. Debugger will execute all the statements until it reaches the specified target.

Although the PL/SQL Step dialog box offers the Step functionality in the most general level, you will rarely use it in practice. The most common Step commands, Step Into, Step Over, and Step Out, are accessible from the Debugger's toolbar. You can issue these commands by clicking the Step Into icon ▤, the Step Over icon ▤, and the Step Out icon ▤.

You may also use the command line in the Interpreter Pane for the purpose of stepping through the program units. For example, to step into the next statement, you would use this command:

```
(debug 1)PL/SQL> .STEP INTO
```

The commands Step Over or Step Out are similar, but the parameter INTO is replaced by the parameter OVER or OUT, respectively.

20.3.6 USING THE DEBUG PACKAGE

When you create debug triggers in the Debugger, you may take advantage of the functions, procedures, and exceptions defined in the package DEBUG. This is a special package because it can be accessible only at runtime, from PL/SQL code that you create in the Debugger. You have already seen two instances of using components of this package. In Figure 20.5 the exception DEBUG.BREAK is raised to instruct Forms to stop the execution of the program unit and to pass control to the Debugger. At the end of Section 20.3.4 the procedure DEBUG.SETC is used to set the value of an item.

This procedure is part of a larger group of four procedures that can be used to set values of variables, parameters, or items. The procedure DEBUG.SETC is used to set values of alphanumeric variables; DEBUG.SETN is used for integer variables; DEBUG.SETI is used to set values of PLS_INTEGER variables; and DEBUG.SETD is used with date variables.

If you want to retrieve the values of such variables, you can use four functions that correspond to the procedures above. DEBUG.GETC returns the value of an alphanumeric variable. DEBUG.GETN returns the value of a numeric variable. DEBUG.GETI returns the value of a PLS_INTEGER variable. DEBUG.GETD returns the value of a date variable. Finally, if you want to suspend the execution of the debug trigger, use the procedure DEBUG.SUSPEND.

20.4 SUMMARY

Debugger is an Oracle Forms component that allows you to debug PL/SQL code in your applications. This chapter explains its features and functionality. Major topics discussed are listed here:

- ❏ Accessing the Debugger
- ❏ Components of the Debugger
  - ❏ Source pane
  - ❏ Navigator pane
  - ❏ Interpreter pane
  - ❏ Toolbar
  - ❏ Managing Debug Actions
  - ❏ Creating debug actions
  - ❏ Editing debug actions
  - ❏ Editing program units and triggers
  - ❏ Inspecting the application state
  - ❏ Resuming the application execution
  - ❏ Using the DEBUG package

CREATING INTEGRATED DEVELOPER/2000 APPLICATIONS

"He chose to include things
That in each other are included, the whole,
The complicate, the amassing harmony."
—Wallace Stevens

- ♦ Creating Multiple-Form Applications
- ♦ Integrating Tools with RUN_PRODUCT
- ♦ Integrating Oracle Forms with Oracle Graphics
- ♦ Summary

Oracle Forms is a development tool that allows you to incorporate many useful features in your database applications. It is also a flexible tool because it can be integrated effectively with development tools from the Developer/2000 family and other environments. From Oracle Forms you can run reports using Oracle Reports or display charts using Oracle Graphics. You can also integrate Forms with the Windows environment, and other Windows applications using Dynamic Data Exchange (DDE) and Object Linking and Embedding (OLE). Through user exits and PL/SQL foreign function interface, you can use in your Forms applications functions developed in 3GL languages such as C or C++.

This chapter discusses the integration of Oracle Forms with Oracle Reports and Oracle Graphics, which are two other important Developer/2000 members. The following chapters will discuss in detail the integration of Forms in the Windows environment.

21.1 CREATING MULTIPLE-FORM APPLICATIONS

Oracle Forms is a development tool that easily supports creating applications with dozens of blocks, windows, and extended functionality. Nevertheless, there are often occasions when the functionality of a system must be split into different subsystems. Each of these subsystems may be further divided into smaller systems, which are implemented as separate Forms modules. In development efforts for large enterprise systems (developed by many programmers working in parallel), creating and maintaining separate modules which are then integrated in larger systems, is the rule more than the exception. In these systems, a module that represents the most important part of functionality is usually launched first. The other modules can be invoked by the users as and when they are needed.

There are three basic ways in which a form can invoke another form in a multi-form application:

a) Use the built-in procedure OPEN_FORM to open a form that is independent from calling form, or

b) Use the built-in procedure NEW_FORM to replace the calling form with the new form, or

c) Use the built-in procedure CALL_FORM to deactivate the calling form and invoke the new form as a modal application.

In this section you will try out each scenario by integrating two modules that have been developed in previous chapters in this book. The module MRD.FMB will continue to implement the main functionality of the MRD application. When users will want to analyze the income generated by customers and movies for the

> ## Note
>
> Recall that the ANALYZE functionality is invoked from the menu item Tool|An-
> alyze... of the MRD.MMB menu module, or by clicking the respective iconic
> button in the toolbar of MRD.FMB. In both cases, a call to the procedure
> **Push_Button('ANALYZE')** is issued. This procedure is defined in the PL/SQL
> library MRDMENU.PLL, which is attached to both the menu and the form mod-
> ule mentioned previously. Furthermore, recall that only users from the menu
> security role MRD_MANAGERS are authorized to access the analyzing func-
> tionality of the system.

movie rental store, the module ANALYZE.FMB will be activated. As a preliminary step, open the library MRDMENU.PLL, and the modules MRD.FMB and
ANALYZE.FMB in the Designer.

21.1.1 PASSING VALUES TO CALLED MODULES

When invoking a new module from an existing form, you may often need to pass
values from the current environment to the new one. One way of doing this is to
use global variables. These variables are visible across all the modules and are
used primarily for constant sharing of data between them. If you only need to initialize some values upon new form's startup, you can pass these values using parameter lists. Chapter 16 explained how you can create and populate parameter
lists. This section lists only a few features of parameter lists that are specific to the
Oracle Forms environment:

1. Each Oracle Forms module contains a parameter list called DEFAULT,
   which can be used like any other custom-created parameter lists to transfer
   values from the calling to the called form.

2. In general, parameter lists may contain text parameters or data parameters.
   This last type of parameters, formed of record groups, cannot be used to invoke a new form.

3. All the parameters passed by the calling form must have been defined at design time in the called form.

4. All the parameter values passed with parameter lists are of CHAR datatype,
   wheras the parameters in the called form may be of other datatypes such as
   DATE or NUMBER. In such case, care must be taken to populate the parameters in the calling forms with values that are convertible to the datatype
   of the parameter in the called form. In other words, if the parameter in the
   called form is of DATE datatype, the calling form must pass a value in one
   of Oracle's recognized DATE formats, for example 'DD-Mon-YY'.

21.1.2 OPENING INDEPENDENT MODULES WITH OPEN_FORM

The built-in procedure OPEN_FORM is used to open a new module independently from the calling module. The only required argument of this procedure is the name of the form. To see the effects of this procedure take the following actions:

1. Open the procedure Click_Button in the PL/SQL Editor window. This procedure is part of the PL/SQL library MRDMENU.PLL.

2. Create a new ELSIF clause for the button ANALYZE with contents as follows:

```
OPEN_FORM('ANALYZE.FMX');
```

3. Compile and save the module MRDMENU.PLL.

Now you can run the MRD module. Open one or two windows of this module, then call the ANALYZE module. You will notice that the Oracle Forms focus will be placed immediately on the new form. At the same time, the toolbar and the menu of the MRD module are replaced by those of the ANALYZE module. However, it is not difficult to notice that the windows of the MRD module are still open. They are listed under the WINDOW menu item, and can be activated at any moment either by choosing their name from this list, or by directly clicking on the target window. You will notice that each time you click the window of a different module, the MDI frame of the application will replace the menu and the toolbars with those attached to the clicked module.

As you see, when OPEN_FORM is invoked with the form name as the only argument, the new form receives focus immediately. If you want to open a form, but maintain the focus in the current form, use the following statement:

```
OPEN_FORM ('ANALYZE.FMX', NO_ACTIVATE);
```

Note

For simplicity and portability reasons this example specifies only the name of the new form module. When developing for deployment in the users' environment, you will define a working directory for your application. The example above will work if the module that will be accessed resides in this working directory.

If the module must reside in a directory other than the working directory of the application, in order to avoid hard-coding path names in the call to OPEN_FORM, you should add this directory in the specification of the environmental variable FORMS45_PATH.

This second parameter is also called the activation_mode. The other value it can take is ACTIVATE, which is also the default value of the argument.

As you use this application you may question yourself about the benefit of opening a separate module to access the ANALYZE functionality of the MRD system. The only thing that is different from the single-form environment that you have used previously is that the menus and toolbars are replaced as you move the focus from one module to the other. There are two advantages in this approach of breaking down the functionality to multiple modules.

The first advantage is generally valid for every software application you develop. The practice has shown that it is much easier to develop, maintain, and upgrade modular systems than monolithic applications. If there is a problem with the ANALYZE subsystem of the MRD application, the subsystem can be maintained without directly affecting the rest of the application.

The second advantage, which is specific to Oracle Forms applications is that invoking new modules with the procedure OPEN_FORM allows you to establish separate sessions with the database for each subsystem. This is another of those situations when the tight integration of Oracle Forms with the Oracle database server displays its benefits. The Oracle RDBMS implements all the transaction management functionality such as obtaining, holding, and releasing locks, commits, and rollbacks at the session level rather than at the schema level. The fact that Forms allows you to have multiple sessions with the database, means that you can issue transactions independently in each session. In other words, you can insert some records in the MRD module, and, without having to complete the transaction with a commit or a rollback, you can move on to the ANALYZE module and initiate a new transaction there. Committing the transaction in this second module will not commit the changes you made in the first module, because they are maintained in a separate transaction by a different session.

By default, however, OPEN_FORM opens the new module with the same database session as the calling module. To create a new independent session for the module you must complete these two steps:

1. Set the following environment variable in ORACLE.INI:

   FORMS45_SESSION=TRUE

2. Use the following statement to open the new form:

   OPEN_FORM ('ANALYZE.FMX', ACTIVATE, SESSION);

   The third parameter in this statement is called session_mode. Its default setting is NO_SESSION.

Finally, when parameters in the new form will be populated with values from the calling form, these values can be added to a parameter list. Then, the internal ID

> **Note**
>
> Obviously, in the same way you can open multiple modules independently, you can also open the same form module multiple times. Combining this with the fact that you can keep the sessions for each module separate, allows you to maintain several transactions for the same block within the application, if this is necessary.

or the name of this parameter list can be added as the last argument in the call to the procedure OPEN_FORM.

As said earlier, when multiple modules are open, you can navigate to them by directly clicking one of their windows, or by choosing its name from the list of open windows in the WINDOW menu. You can also navigate between modules programmatically. As each independent module is opened, it is assigned an internal ID. The procedure NEXT_FORM navigates to the form that has the next higher ID than the current form. When the current form is the last one to be opened, NEXT_FORM will place the focus to the first form that was opened. PREVIOUS_FORM navigates to the form with the next lower ID. When PREVIOUS_FORM is invoked from the form that was activated first, the focus is placed on the form that was opened last.

You can also use the procedure GO_FORM to navigate directly to a given form. This procedure may take as its argument the name of the form or its internal ID. Given the higher possibility of making a mistake when using the name of the form, the later version is preferred and considered safer and more efficient. Figure 21.1 shows the example of a procedure that navigates to a form if it is already opened, or opens it if it is not.

```
PROCEDURE Goto_Form (formName VARCHAR2) IS
  formID    FormModule;
BEGIN
  formID := FIND_FORM(formName);
  IF ID_NULL(formID) THEN
    OPEN_FORM(formName);
    CHECK_PACKAGE_FAILURE;
  ELSE
    GO_FORM(formID);
    CHECK_PACKAGE_FAILURE;
  END IF;
END;
```

FIGURE 21.1 Opening or navigating to modules programmatically.

At the conclusion of this section, let us discuss some things that you must be aware of when invoking independent forms with OPEN_FORM.

1. Because each opened module will take a share of the system resources, you should be careful with the number of modules that are open at any one time. Educate the users to maintaining open only those modules that are indispensable, and close the ones that are not needed.

2. OPEN_FORM is a restricted procedure which cannot be called when the application is in Query Mode.

3. When the focus moves from one module to another either because the module is opened with the ACTIVATE activation mode, or because a user-initiated or programmatic navigation occurs, none of the usual POST-*object*, PRE-*object*, and WHEN-NEW-*object*-INSTANCE triggers will fire. The only triggers fired are WHEN-WINDOW-DEACTIVATED in the module that opens or initiates the navigation to the new module, and WHEN-WINDOW-ACTIVATED in the target module.

4. The menu item WINDOW will list the titles of the windows as they are defined in each individual module. This could lead to more than one window with the same title being open and displayed in the list. For example, the windows that hold CUSTOMER block data for each of the modules MRD and ANALYZE could inadvertently be titled Customer. In order to help your users associate windows with the module that owns them, you should include some sort of indication about the purpose of the module in the window title. For this reason, the windows in module ANALYZE.FMB are called 'Customer Revenue' and 'Movie Revenue'.

5. The MDI frame is a common object shared by all the modules being opened. Changes that a module makes to the MDI frame such as setting its title, remain visible until overwritten, even after the module is closed.

21.1.3 POST, COMMIT, AND ROLLBACK

Before discussing the other two ways used to call modules from existing Oracle Forms modules, let us shed some more light on the concepts of posting, committing, and rolling back transactions. Recall from previous discussions that in order to mark certain points in a transaction you use savepoints. The main purpose of the savepoint is to undo or rollback only a part of the transaction, without losing all the work performed from the moment the transaction began. When interacting with the database, Oracle Forms uses savepoints and rollbacks on your behalf.

By default, a savepoint is issued when the Oracle Forms Runtime is initially launched, each time a new form is loaded in memory using NEW_FORM or CALL_FORM, and each time the procedures POST and COMMIT_FORM procedures are invoked.

The procedures POST and COMMIT_FORM are similar in the sense that they both write the data to the database. In the process, all the default validation and commit processing of Forms occurs in the same manner. However, they are fundamentally different, because the data written by POST are not committed and can be rolled back. By contrast when COMMIT_FORM is issued, all the data since the beginning of the transaction, including those temporarily stored by POST are written permanently to the database.

Rollbacks can be issued when either of the procedures CLEAR_FORM, EXIT_FORM, or NEW_FORM are invoked. Each of these procedures takes an argument called rollback_mode. By default, the value of this argument is TO_SAVEPOINT. With this value, all the uncommitted changes in the current module, including those that are posted, will be discarded when any of the above procedures are complete. The other two values that this argument can take are NO_ROLLBACK and FULL_ROLLBACK. When you use NO_ROLLBACK, Oracle Forms does not perform any rollback. Only the changes in the current module that are not posted or committed will be lost at the end of the procedures mentioned above. In the case of EXIT_FORM and NEW_FORM, the data posted in the current module and all the locks obtained by this module will be preserved even after the module is removed from memory. When the argument rollback_mode takes the value FULL_ROLLBACK, Oracle Forms wipes out all the pending changes, even those posted. The rollback occurs at the session level, rather than at the module level, which occurs when TO_SAVEPOINT is used. This means that changes made but not yet committed in the current form, and in all the other forms that called or were called by this form, will be lost.

21.1.4 REPLACING MODULES WITH NEW_FORM

One of the major drawbacks of opening multiple modules using OPEN_FORM is the toll each of these modules takes on the memory available to the system. Before deciding to open a module independently, you must consider whether you can release the resources occupied by the current form. If it is the case that the users will not need to have both forms available at the same time, you can replace the old form with the new form using the procedure NEW_FORM. The general syntax of this procedure is

NEW_FORM (module_name, rollback_mode, query_mode, parameter_list);

The meaning and usage of the first and last of the arguments above is the same as for the procedure OPEN_FORM, explained in Section 21.1.2. When Oracle Forms encounters the procedure NEW_FORM, it exits the current form and launches the form module_name. If parametric values will be passed from the current form to the new form, these values are placed in a parameter list.

The meaning of the argument rollback_mode is as explained in the previous section. Its default value is TO_SAVEPOINT, but it can take the additional values

NO_ROLLBACK and FULL_ROLLBACK. By default, users will be able to query and manipulate data in this form like in any other form. If you want to restrict them to use the form only for query purposes, you can set the query_mode argument to QUERY_ONLY. The default value of this argument is NO_QUERY_ONLY.

When the requirements of your application allow you to replace the modules, NEW_FORM offers a good and efficient solution to the problem of building multiple-form applications. However, like OPEN_FORM, this procedure is a restricted procedure that can be used only in Normal Mode.

21.1.5 CALLING MODAL MODULES WITH CALL_FORM

This is an option that you should consider only in very rare occasions, if at all. There are three basic reasons for this argument:

1. When you use CALL_FORM to invoke another module, Oracle Forms keeps the current form running in the background, disabled and unavailable to the users, while running the new module. Thus, the memory resources will be used without users seeing any benefits of it.
2. A certain amount of the memory allocated to a module opened with CALL_FORM is locked until that module is exited.
3. In a GUI application, the only application modal windows should be dialog boxes. It is certainly not necessary, and not efficient, to have a whole module running as a modal form.

The general syntax of this procedure is

CALL_FORM (module_name, display, switch_menu, query_mode,
parameter_list);

The meaning of parameters such as module_name, query_mode, and parameter_list, is explained in Sections 21.1.2 and 21.1.4. The argument display can take one of the two values: HIDE and NO_HIDE. The value HIDE, which is also the default value, means that Oracle Forms will hide the current form from the view before displaying the new called form. When the called form is exited, the background form becomes active again. If NO_HIDE is specified, the calling form remains visible, and its windows can be activated, resized, minimized, and maximized. However, any items, controls, or toolbars associated with it are disabled and not available.

The argument switch_menu controls whether the called form uses the menu of the calling module or its own menu. The default value of this argument is NO_REPLACE, which means that both modules will share the same menu module associated with the calling module. If this argument is set to DO_REPLACE, the menu module attached to the called form takes over and replaces the menu of the original module.

Despite the inherent disadvantages, the procedure CALL_FORM has a feature that the other two procedures discussed previously do not enjoy. CALL_FORM is not a restricted procedure, which means that it can be used equally well in Query Mode and in Normal Mode.

21.2 INTEGRATING TOOLS WITH RUN_PRODUCT

RUN_PRODUCT is a built-in procedure that allows you to invoke from Oracle Forms other components of the Developer/2000 family of tools. You can use this procedure to call Oracle Forms, Oracle Reports, Oracle Graphics, and Oracle Book modules; however, it is used mostly to invoke Reports and Graphics, less often Book modules, and almost never other Forms modules.

The previous section discussed the different alternatives you have to invoke other forms from within a form module. OPEN_FORM, NEW_FORM, and CALL_FORM limit considerably the need and the use of RUN_PRODUCT to call other forms. As you will see in the following section, Graphics is integrated with Oracle Forms as well, through chart items and the PLL library OG. Often, you will prefer to use these last resources to display data graphically in your application. This leaves Oracle Reports as the primary tool invoked with RUN_PRODUCT, and Oracle Book as a distant candidate.

RUN_PRODUCT takes several arguments as input. Its general syntax is

RUN_PRODUCT (product, document, commmode, execmode,
location, list, display);

The meaning of each argument is explained as follows:

❑ **Product** represents the type of application that will be invoked. Its values can be FORMS, REPORTS, GRAPHICS, or BOOK.

❑ **Document** specifies the name of the document to be loaded. This is the file name if the document is maintained as a file in the directory structure, or the module name if it is stored in the database. When the document argument specifies a file, you can specify its full path, or provide only the file name. In this last case, the product will look for the file in the working directory and in the default directory defined for the tool, which in general is %ORACLE_HOME%\BIN.

❑ **Commmode** is an abbreviation for communication mode and defines when the control will return to calling form after the call to the product is issued.

If the value of this argument is SYNCHRONOUS, the new application is modal with respect to the calling module. Users cannot perform any actions in the form while the called application is active. Only when this application is exited, does the control return to the calling forms. If the value of the argument commmode is ASYNCHRONOUS, RUN_PRODUCT issues the call to the new product and returns immediately the control to the parent form, even if the invoked application may not have been displayed completely.

❑ Execmode is an argument whose value controls the execution mode of the invoked tool. All the tools that are invoked with RUN_PRODUCT are executed either in BATCH, or RUNTIME mode; all, with the exception of Oracle Forms modules. In the rare event you will invoke Forms with this procedure, you must always use the value RUNTIME. When the value of the argument execmode is set to BATCH, the invoked product is executed without the intervention of the users. A meaningful situation when you would use this argument is when you want to run a report in the background and possibly send it directly to the printer. However, when calling Graphics or Oracle Book modules, which are of a more interactive character than Reports, the value of this argument should be set to RUNTIME. In such a case, the new application is fully available to the users.

❑ Location is an argument that is related with the value of the argument document. It can take only two values: FILESYSTEM and DB. The first value indicates that the module is stored in the file system, and the name of the file is defined in the argument document. The second value means that the module is stored in the database. In this case, document contains the name of the database module.

❑ List is the name or the internal ID of a parameter list with values that the calling form will pass to the invoked application. As mentioned earlier, the parameter list can either contain text string values or record groups. Oracle Forms can be called only with TEXT_PARAMETER parameter lists. Another restriction that applies across the board is that when a record group is passed as a parameter list, the new product must be invoked synchronously.

❑ Display requires a value only if you are invoking an Oracle Graphic display. In this case, the value of this argument is the name of the chart item that will serve as container for the chart. When other tools are invoked, the setting of this argument does not bear a meaning.

In Chapter 16, you created a trigger associated with the push button PRINT in the block MAIL of the MRD module. This trigger builds a parameter list and calls the report MRDLABEL, which ultimately prints the labels. Figure 21.2 shows the contents of this trigger.

As you can see from this figure, the execution mode is set to RUNTIME because the users must set the orientation of the report to landscape before sending

```
DECLARE
  param_list_id    ParamList;
  param_list_name VARCHAR2(20) := 'Report_pl';
  sql_stat         VARCHAR2(255);

BEGIN
--Make sure that parameter list does not exist.
  param_list_id := GET_PARAMETER_LIST(param_list_name);
  IF NOT ID_NULL(param_list_id) THEN
    MESSAGE('Parameter_list '||param_list_name||' already exists.');
    RAISE FORM_TRIGGER_FAILURE;
  END IF;

--Create the parameter list.
  param_list_id := CREATE_PARAMETER_LIST(param_list_name);
  IF ID_NULL(param_list_id) THEN
    MESSAGE('Parameter_list '||param_list_name||' cannot be created.');
    RAISE FORM_TRIGGER_FAILURE;
  END IF;

--Build the WHERE clause.
  sql_stat := Build_Where_Clause('MAIL.SELECTED');

--Add the WHERE clause to the parameter list.
  ADD_PARAMETER(param_list_id, 'WHERE_CLAUSE', TEXT_PARAMETER,
                sql_stat);

--Run the report that prints the label.
  RUN_PRODUCT(REPORTS, 'MRDLABEL', ASYNCHRONOUS,
  RUNTIME, FILESYSTEM, param_list_id, NULL);

--Destroy Parameter List
  DESTROY_PARAMETER_LIST(param_list_id);

EXCEPTION
  WHEN OTHERS THEN
    Message('Internal error occurred in WHEN-BUTTON-PRESSED.');
    RAISE FORM_TRIGGER_FAILURE;
END;
```

FIGURE 21.2   Invoking reports with RUN_PRODUCT.

the data to the printer. You also want the control to return to the users immediately after they invoke the report. Therefore, the communication mode argument is set to ASYNCHRONOUS.

21.3 INTEGRATING ORACLE FORMS WITH ORACLE GRAPHICS

Oracle Graphics is a member of the Developer/2000 family of tools that has excellent integration capabilities with Oracle Forms. Functionally, it complements the features provided by the Forms, because it allows you to graphically display and summarize data. Therefore, it is quite natural that Oracle puts a great amount of effort in the seamless integration of these three products.

There are three approaches you can take to include Oracle Graphics displays in your applications:

a) Invoke the tool using the built-in procedure RUN_PRODUCT, or
b) Use the functionality provided by the PL/SQL library OG, or
c) Use the OLE Compound Documents and OLE Automation technology.

The first two options require that you create a chart item that will serve as a container where the Graphics display will reside. The integration achieved by these options is based on the features provided by Developer/2000. One of the major advantages provided by this approach is that the integrated application you develop can be ported with no additional efforts in all the platforms where Developer/2000 tools will run. With the third approach, you still need a container to hold the Oracle Graphics display, but this container is an OLE Container item, rather than a chart item.

The first approach was discussed in detail in the previous section, therefore it will not be revisited again here. Simply recall that whenever you invoke a Graphics display with RUN_PRODUCT, a chart item must have been created in the Designer, and the name of this item provided as the last argument to the pro-

---

Note

It is usually easier and more efficient to integrate Oracle Graphics and Oracle Forms with one of the first two techniques listed above. The OLE server capabilities of Oracle Graphics are normally used to display graphs from within other Windows products.

cedure. The chapters to come will discuss in detail the OLE technology and the integration of object classes generated by OLE application servers in Oracle Forms. The remaining approach will be discussed in the rest of this chapter.

You will work with the module ANALYZE.FMB in which you will insert two Oracle Graphics charts. The first one will display the cumulative amount of revenue collected by the video rental store for a given period of time. The revenues will be grouped by zip codes of the customers that rent the movies. The second chart will look at the revenues from a different angle. The income from video rentals will be grouped based on the ratings of the movies. Before moving to the next section, open the module ANALYZE.FMB in the Designer.

21.3.1 CREATING CHART ITEMS

As said earlier, in order to integrate Oracle Graphics with Oracle Forms, you must first provide a container in the Forms which will contain the display. These containers are a distinct type of items, called chart items. As with other types of items, there are three basic ways to create chart items in your Forms module:

a) Directly draw the item on the canvas in the Layout Editor, or
b) Specify the type of item in the New Block Options dialog box, upon creation of a new base table block, or
c) Modify the *Item Type* property of an existing item to 'Chart Item'.

In order to create a new chart item in the CUSTOMER canvas, take these steps:

1. Display the canvas in the Layout Editor, and set the context to the block CONTROL.
2. Click the Chart Item icon ▣ from the tool palette, and draw a square-shaped chart item to the right of the Amount column in the CUSTOMER block.
3. Double-click the newly created item to display its Properties Window, and rename it to REVENUE_BY_ZIP.
4. Arrange the layout of the canvas, so that it looks similar to Figure 21.3.
5. Perform similar steps to create the chart item REVENUE_BY_RATING in the MOVIE canvas.

While you are in the Properties Window, take a look at the properties that a chart item has. You can notice that, besides the properties in the **Display** group, these items enjoy very few other properties. Even in the **Display** group, only the first few properties that control the position and dimensions of the chart item on the canvas have a visual effect on the item itself. Visual attribute properties are over-

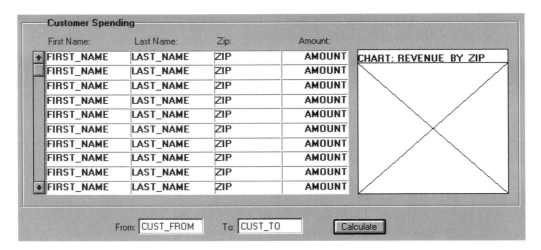

FIGURE 21.3   Layout of canvas CUSTOMER in module ANALYZE.FMB.

written by the attributes of the graphics chart when it populated the container. Notice also that chart items are always control items. For these items, properties that govern the interaction with the database are meaningless. Thus, these items are simply and merely containers that will host the application objects developed in Oracle Graphics. All their functionality is provided by the interface with Oracle Graphics.

21.3.2 THE OG PACKAGE

In order to activate Oracle Graphics displays and exchange data between them and form modules in your application, you can use the PL/SQL package OG. This package is provided in the form of a PLL library together with the other software modules. By default, it is installed in the directory %ORACLE_HOME% \FORMS45\PLSQLLIB, together with other useful libraries such as HINT.PLL used in Chapter 17.

The core functionality of this package is a series of program units that allow you to open and close Oracle Graphics displays, exchange data with them, invoke program units defined in them, and trigger mouse events in these displays. Here is a brief description of each program unit defined in the OG package:

❑   OG.OPEN. This procedure allows you to activate an Oracle Graphics display and associate it with a chart item in your form module. The general syntax of this procedure is

OG.OPEN (display, item, clip, refresh, parameter_list);

The first two arguments are the only two required and specify the file name of the chart to display and the chart item that will serve as a container for this display, respectively. The arguments clip and refresh are of Boolean datatype. The first one controls the way the bitmap representation of the display will populate the chart item. If it is TRUE, which is also the default value, the chart item will preserve the dimensions defined in the Designer, and the display will be clipped if it cannot entirely fit in this item. When clip is FALSE, the size of the display will change at Runtime to match the dimensions of the chart item. The default setting of the argument refresh is TRUE, and this setting updates the Graphics display upon its opening. If you set this argument to FALSE, the display presented initially is a static bitmap that may not represent the true relationship of data in the databases. Eventually, you will have to bring the display up to date using the procedure OG.REFRESH. If any values are to be passed from the Forms environment to the Graphics display, these values can be bundled in the form of a parameter list, whose name is passed on by the argument parameter_list.

❑ OG.CLOSE. The specification of this procedure is

OG.CLOSE(display, item);

It simply closes the Oracle Graphics display associated with the chart item.

❑ OG.REFRESH. The general syntax of this procedure is

OG.REFRESH(display, item, parameter_list);

This procedure updates the pictorial representation of the Graphics display in the chart item container. If, for example, the data upon which the chart is built are based upon a query, the query is re-executed, and the display updated accordingly.

❑ OG.INTERPRET. This is an important procedure because it allows you to send to Oracle Graphics PL/SQL statements for execution. These statements

Note

All the remaining program units in the OG package will take at least two arguments: display and item. They have the same meaning as in the procedure OG.OPEN. In order for these procedures to complete successfully, the Oracle Graphics display and the Oracle Forms chart item passed in these arguments must have been previously bound together by the procedure OG.OPEN.

can range in length and complexity from simple one-line program unit calls to full-blown PL/SQL blocks. The general syntax of this procedure is

OG.INTERPRET(display, item, plsql_string, refresh, parameter_list);

The first three arguments are required, and the last two are only optionally defined. Figure 21.4 later in this section shows an example of how the plsql_string argument is prepared and passed to this procedure.

❑ OG.GETCHARPARAM. This is a function that returns the value of an alphanumeric parameter defined in the Graphics display. The general syntax of this function is

char_parameter_value := OG.GETCHARPARAM(display, item,
display_parameter);

❑ OG.GETNUMPARAM. This function is similar in purpose with the previous function, except that it returns the value of a numeric parameter in the display. The syntax of this function is:

num_parameter_value := OG.GETNUMPARAM(display, item,
display_paramter);

It is interesting to open a parenthesis here and discuss the implementation of these last two functions. They are very similar even in the details defined in their bodies, and perform the following steps:

1. Open a temporary file for Write.
2. Write to this file the value of the parameter passed as argument.
3. Close the temporary file.
4. Open the temporary file for Read.
5. Read the value stored in that file to a local variable.
6. Close the temporary file.
7. Return this value to the calling environment.

Note

In both these functions, the argument **display_parameter** is the name of the parameter in the Oracle Graphics display whose value you want to retrieve. This parameter must have been defined in the Oracle Graphics Designer at design time.

```
FUNCTION getnumparam (
  display       IN VARCHAR2,
  item          IN VARCHAR2,
  param         IN VARCHAR2
) RETURN NUMBER IS

strval VARCHAR2(255);
tfp TEXT_IO.FILE_TYPE;
strint VARCHAR2(255);

BEGIN
strint :=
'DECLARE '                                               ||
'tfp TEXT_IO.FILE_TYPE;'                                  ||
'BEGIN '                                                  ||
'tfp:=TEXT_IO.FOPEN(''ogtmp.dat'',''w'');'               ||
'TEXT_IO.PUT_LINE (tfp, TO_CHAR(:' || param || '));'     ||
'TEXT_IO.FCLOSE(tfp);'                                    ||
'END;';

  og.interpret (display, item, strint, FALSE);

-- *Temporary* means of getting data back
-- from Oracle Graphics. In future releases
-- we will pass data directly. For now,
-- we use a temporary file...
  tfp := TEXT_IO.FOPEN ('ogtmp.dat', 'r');
  TEXT_IO.GET_LINE (tfp, strval);
  TEXT_IO.FCLOSE (tfp);

  return TO_NUMBER(strval);

END;
```

FIGURE 21.4   Example of OG.INTERPRET.

The implementation of these steps is split between the Oracle Graphics and the function in the OG package. The first three steps are bundled together in the form of an anonymous PL/SQL block, which is passed to Oracle Graphics for execution using the procedure OG.INTERPRET discussed above. Figure 21.4 shows the implementation details of the function OG.GETNUMPARAM. This is also a good example of how to use the procedure OG.INTERPRET.

> **Note**
>
> While parameter lists allow you to pass values and data from Forms to graphics, the functions OG.GETNUMPARAM and OG.GETCHARPARAM are used to transfer data in the opposite direction. You can use them to return to Forms values of parameters defined in an Oracle Graphics display.

This function makes use of TEXT_IO, which is another package that comes with Developer/2000 and allows you to manipulate text files.

❏ OG.MOUSEDOWN. This procedure allows you to simulate the event MouseDown on the Oracle Graphics display. The primary reason for its use is to seamlessly transmit the event of clicking a chart item in Oracle Forms onto the Graphics environment. The ultimate effect is the same as if the MouseDown event had occurred in the Graphics display. The display object on which the mouse goes down becomes event-active, and receives all the mouse events until the next MouseDown event, upon which a new event-active object is defined.

The general syntax of this procedure is

OG.MOUSEDOWN(display, item, x, y, refresh, clickcount, button,
constrained, parameter_list);

The first two arguments of this procedure are required; the remaining arguments are all optional. The arguments display, item, refresh, and parameter_list have the same meaning as in the other program units discussed previously. The arguments x and y represent the coordinates of the mouse when it was clicked. You need to specify these coordinates only when you want to make the Graphics display believe that the MouseDown event occurred in a location other than the actual location of the mouse. If you do not specify any of these coordinates, the current mouse coordinates stored in the system variables SYSTEM.MOUSE_X_POS and SYSTEM.MOUSE_Y_POS are used. The argument clickcount contains the number of times the MouseDown event occurred. In a regular click, this value is 1; in a double-click it is 2. The argument button is the button pressed. Its default value is 1, which denotes the left button. If it is 2, a right click occurred. Finally, the Boolean argument constrained is set to TRUE only if the SHIFT key was pressed simultaneously with the MouseDown event. Its value is FALSE in all other cases.

Note

The procedures OG.MOUSEDOWN and OG.MOUSEUP provide for arguments like **clickcount, button,** and **constrained,** and their meaning is documented in the *Oracle Forms Advanced Techniques* manual. However, at least in the current stage of functionality that Oracle Graphics enjoys, they do not have any impact on the way mouse events are passed from Forms to Graphics displays. Oracle Graphics recognizes only the following mouse events: MouseDown, MouseUp, MouseMoveDown, MouseMoveUp. Any values you provide for the arguments mentioned are ignored in the procedure MouseUp-Down defined in package OG. Both OG.MOUSEDOWN and OG.MOUSEUP ultimately invoke this procedure to implement their functionality.

❑ OG.MOUSEUP. This procedure triggers the MouseUp event in an Oracle Graphics display. It is very similar to the procedure OG.MOUSEDOWN. The general syntax of this procedure is

OG.MOUSEUP(display, item, x, y, refresh, button, constrained,
parameter_list);

Notice that in the case of this procedure, the argument clickcount is not required as it does not make sense in general to count the number of times the mouse button is released.

In this section you already saw the implementation of one procedure from the package OG. If you examine the contents of the other functions and procedures included in this package, you will notice that the program units described above are nothing more than a convenient API layer on top of the generic RUN_PRODUCT routine. A skillful combination of parameters in these program units prior to calling RUN_PRODUCT provides for all the added flexibility and ease of programming that OG has to offer. These parameters are passed in the form of a parameter list.

21.3.3 USING OG PACKAGE IN ANALYZE MODULE

In Section 21.3.1 you created two chart items that will display in graphical form summary data about the revenue of the video rental store. These graphs are implemented in the form of two Oracle Graphics displays, provided in the companion disk as modules BYZIP.OGD and BYRATING.OGD. Now you will integrate

```
SELECT
  SUM((RETURN_DT - RENT_DT) * DAILY_RATE) amount,
  ZIP
FROM RENTALS R, CUSTOMERS C
WHERE RENT_DT <= TO_DATE(:from_dt)
  AND RETURN_DT >= TO_DATE(:to_dt)
  AND R.CUSTOMER_ID = C.CUSTOMER_ID
GROUP BY ZIP
```

FIGURE 21.5   SQL statement that populates the display BYZIP.OGD.

these displays with the chart items created previously, using program units from package OG.

The module BYZIP.OGD displays the sum generated by rental transactions between two given dates in the form of a pie chart organized by the zip code of the customers that initiated and paid for these transactions. The module BYRAT-ING.OGD displays a similar sum in the form of a bar chart, organized by the rating categories of the movies offered for rent. Figure 21.5 shows the SQL query that is used to populate the chart BYZIP.OGD. Figure 21.6 shows the SQL query that is used to populate the chart BYRATING.OGD.

Both displays store the range dates in the parameters from_dt and to_dt. You will pass values for these parameters when you invoke the displays from the Forms module ANALYZE.FMB. In each display a drill-down relationship is defined. In BYZIP.OGD the drill-down relationship is defined in such a way that when users click on a slice of the pie, the zip code represented by that slice is stored in the parameter zip. In BYRATING.OGD when users click a bar, the rating that the bar represents will be stored in the parameter rating.

With this information in hand, you are ready to integrate these two displays with the chart item containers REVENUE_BY_ZIP and REVENUE_BY_RATING defined in block CONTROL of module ANALYZE.FMB:

```
SELECT
  SUM((RETURN_DT - RENT_DT) * DAILY_RATE) amount,
  DECODE(RATING, 1, 'G', 2, 'PG-13', 3, 'R', 4, 'NC-17') rating
FROM RENTALS R, TAPES T, MOVIES M
WHERE RENT_DT >= TO_DATE(:start_dt)
  AND RETURN_DT <= TO_DATE(:end_dt)
  AND R.TAPE_ID = T.TAPE_ID
  AND T.MOVIE_ID = M.MOVIE_ID
GROUP BY RATING
```

FIGURE 21.6   SQL statement that populates the display BYRATING.OGD.

1. Attach the library OG.PLL. This is located in the directory %ORACLE_ HOME%\FORMS45\PLSQLLIB. (This directory is normally in the FORMS45_PATH of ORACLE.INI.)

2. Define two global variables in a PRE-FORM trigger that will store the names of the Graphics displays; for example,

```
:GLOBAL.byzip := 'ZIP.OGD';
:GLOBAL.byrating := 'BYRATING.OGD';
```

3. Create a WHEN-NEW-BLOCK-INSTANCE trigger for block CUSTOMER. It should contain the following line:

```
OG.OPEN (:GLOBAL.byzip, 'CONTROL.REVENUE_BY_ZIP',
            FALSE, FALSE);
```

Recall from the previous section that these options will open the display file whose name is in **GLOBAL.byzip** and attach it to the chart item CON-TROL.REVENUE_BY_ZIP. The display will be resized and will not be up-dated right away.

4. Create a WHEN-NEW-BLOCK-INSTANCE trigger for block MOVIE. It should contain the following line:

```
OG.OPEN (:GLOBAL.byrating, 'CONTROL.REVENUE_BY_RATING',
            FALSE, FALSE);
```

At this point, save, generate, and run the module. You will notice that none of the displays contains their graph. This is because the queries that populate them are not executed if the **refresh** argument is FALSE. You do not want to set the **refresh** argument to TRUE in the call to OG.OPEN because you want to give the users the opportunity to enter the range dates for the analysis. The code that will populate

---

Note

As explained in other cases, you should avoid hardcoding path names in your applications. Unfortunately, the only way to specify only the file names for Graphics displays is to place them in the directory defined by FORMS45 envi-ronment variable in ORACLE.INI. The value of this variable is typically C:\ORAWIN\FORMS45.

the displays should be invoked when users enter the range dates and click the button labeled Calculate in each window.

1. Return in the Designer and create a WHEN-BUTTON-PRESSED trigger for push button CUST_CALC.
2. Enter the contents of this trigger as shown in Figure 21.7.
3. Create a WHEN-BUTTON-PRESSED trigger for push button MOVIE_CALC.
4. Enter the contents of this trigger similar to what is shown in Figure 21.7. Make the appropriate modifications in the calls to procedures ADD_PARA-METER and OG.REFRESH.

It is clear from Figure 21.7 how you pass the range dates to the appropriate graphics display in the form of text parameters. When the procedure OG.RE-FRESH will be activated, these values will be passed on to the actual parameters defined in each display. Based on these values, the charts will be updated with revenues for the specified period.

```
DECLARE
  plist ParamList;
BEGIN
  plist := CREATE_PARAMETER_LIST('revenues');
  IF ID_NULL (plist) THEN
    MESSAGE('Cannot create parameter list.');
    RAISE FORM_TRIGGER_FAILURE;
  END IF;

  ADD_PARAMETER(plist, 'from_dt', TEXT_PARAMETER,
              TO_CHAR(:CONTROL.CUST_FROM));
  ADD_PARAMETER(plist, 'to_dt', TEXT_PARAMETER,
              TO_CHAR(:CONTROL.CUST_TO));
  OG.REFRESH(:GLOBAL.byzip, 'CONTROL.REVENUE_BY_ZIP', plist);

  DESTROY_PARAMETER_LIST(plist);

EXCEPTION
  WHEN OTHERS THEN
    MESSAGE('Error occurred in block CUSTOMER.');
    RAISE FORM_TRIGGER_FAILURE;
END;
```

FIGURE 21.7 Refreshing the contents of a chart in Oracle Forms.

You want the users to restrict the records displayed in each block by clicking areas in the display. If, for example, they click the slice of the pie chart that corresponds to zip code 22043, the block CUSTOMER should display only those customers who live in that zip code area. If users click the bar corresponding to rating category PG-13, only movies from this category should be displayed in the block MOVIE.

Recall that there is a drill-down relationship defined in each display which stores the value of the clicked slice or chart in a parameter. You want to retrieve these values in the Oracle Forms environment and then use them as query criteria for the respective blocks.

1. Add the following global variables declarations to the trigger PRE-FORM:

```
:GLOBAL.zip := NULL;
:GLOBAL.rating := NULL;
```

2. Display the Properties Window for block CUSTOMER and set the *WHERE* property in the **Database** group as follows:

ZIP = :GLOBAL.zip

3. Display the Properties Window for block MOVIE and set the *WHERE* property in the **Database** group as follows:

RATING = :GLOBAL.rating

These two properties ensure that whenever queries are executed in these blocks, the statements you specified as their settings will become part of the WHERE clause in the SELECT statement that Oracle Forms will build. To achieve the goal, you need to store in GLOBAL.zip and GLOBAL.rating the values clicked by the users.

1. Create a trigger WHEN-MOUSE-CLICK for chart item CONTROL.REVENUE_BY_ZIP.
2. Enter the contents of this trigger as shown in Figure 21.8.
3. Create a trigger WHEN-MOUSE-CLICK for chart item CONTROL.REVENUE_BY_RATING.
4. Enter similar contents for this trigger that apply to the context of block MOVIE.

Finally, save, generate, and run the module to test its functionality.

```
OG.MOUSEDOWN(:GLOBAL.byzip, 'CONTROL.REVENUE_BY_ZIP');
:GLOBAL.zip := OG.GETCHARPARAM(:GLOBAL.byzip,
'CONTROL.REVENUE_BY_ZIP', 'ZIP');
GO_BLOCK('CUSTOMER');
EXECUTE_QUERY;
```

FIGURE 21.8   Retrieving values from Oracle Graphics into Oracle Forms.

21.4 SUMMARY

This chapter discussed the process of creating integrated Developer/2000 applications composed of several Oracle Forms, Reports, and Graphics modules. Important concepts of this chapter are listed here:

- ❑ Creating multiple-form applications
    - ❑ Passing values to called modules
    - ❑ Opening independent modules with OPEN_FORM
    - ❑ POST, COMMIT, and ROLLBACK
    - ❑ Replacing modules with NEW_FORM
    - ❑ Calling modal modules with CALL_FORM
- ❑ Integrating tools with RUN_PRODUCT
- ❑ Integrating Oracle Forms with Oracle Graphics
    - ❑ Creating chart items
    - ❑ The OG package
    - ❑ Using the OG package in Forms modules

DYNAMIC DATA EXCHANGE

"Only connect! That was the whole of her sermon."
—Edward Morgan Forster

With the move of Oracle Forms in the Windows environment, a whole variety of features used in this platform became available to Forms applications. The most evident ones were the ability to create MDI applications, to put some cut and paste functionality in these applications, to respond to mouse events, and to exchange data with other applications through DDE. It was not until the release of Oracle Forms 4.5 though, that applications developed in MS Windows became real members of the class of advanced Windows applications. Two major features were incorporated in Forms with this release. The first one is the ability to directly exchange information between applications with no intermediate steps such as converting, downloading, or uploading of data. The second one is the ability to control other applications from within the Forms applications; to send instructions and commands they understand from within the PL/SQL triggers and program units.

Oracle Forms implements the integration with other Windows applications through the support for Dynamic Data Exchange (DDE) and Object Linking and Embedding (OLE). This chapter explains the meaning of DDE and its role in the integration of MS Windows applications in general, and Oracle Forms with these applications in particular. The following chapters discuss OLE and how it is supported by Forms. Chapter 25 discusses how to access members of DLL libraries of functions and take advantage of these functions in our Forms applications.

22.1 WHAT IS DDE?

DDE is a set of functions defined in Windows that allows programs to communicate. The communication between processes is established using shared memory resources to exchange the data between applications. Because the DDE functions are implemented at the operating system level, they are standard and will allow any two applications that follow their conventions to communicate and exchange data with each other. Because these functions can be incorporated in the programming scripts of each application, they allow programmers to automate the process of establishing connections and exchanging data among applications.

22.1.1 DDE COMPONENTS

The process that occurs when two applications are engaged in a DDE transaction is called *conversation*. For a conversation to take place, the following conditions must be met:

1. Both applications support the DDE communication protocol.
2. Both applications are running simultaneously.

Like any other conversation, the DDE conversation must be initiated by one party. The application that issues a request for communication is called the *DDE client*. The other application that responds to such a request is called *DDE server*. Once the DDE client initiates a conversation, it is also responsible for the agenda of the conversation. In other words, it can send data to the server, receive data from the server, ask the server to execute certain actions, or decide to terminate the conversation. The DDE server, on the other hand, is passive, and responds to incoming requests from the clients. It receives data from them, services their requests for information, or executes the commands according to their instructions.

DDE clients need a name to address the servers. This name is also called the application name, and is usually the name of the .EXE file of the program. For example, for MS Excel, the file name is EXCEL.EXE and the application name is *Excel*; for MS Word, the names are WINWORD.EXE and *Winword*; for WordPerfect, the names are WPWIN.EXE and *Wpwin*; but for Lotus 1-2-3, the names are LOTUSW.EXE and *Lotus*.

The metaphor of conversation for applications that communicate using DDE extends a little further than what is said above. Like any other conversation, the DDE conversation focuses on one *topic*. When the DDE client issues a request for conversation, it must inform the DDE server about the topic that will be the subject of the conversation. The DDE mechanism in Windows divides DDE servers in several topics. Some topics are specific to the application and, therefore, are called special topics. The special topics may vary from one server application to another. However, most servers support the special topic called *system*, which, in turn, can be used to get the names of other special topics supported by the application. For DDE servers that support the MDI paradigm, each document is a topic for DDE conversation. The name of the topic in this case is the fully qualified path of the file in which the document is saved. Suppose, for example, that C:\EXCEL\EXPENSE.XLS is the name of the Excel spreadsheet that contains your monthly expenses. If you want to access it from another application using DDE, the topic of conversation will also be C:\EXCEL\EXPENSE.XLS. However, if you want to access a new spreadsheet from the client application, you would use BOOK1 as the topic of the conversation with Excel. When working with other servers, you would use the appropriate extensions and names for new documents.

It is obvious that the same client and server applications may simultaneously engage in conversations about different topics. For example, from an Oracle Forms application (the DDE client), you may send some data to an Excel spreadsheet (DDE server), and receive other data from a second spreadsheet. Windows considers each combination of the DDE server and topic as a unique *channel* of communication. When the client initiates a conversation with a server about a given topic, Windows opens a DDE channel, assigns it an internal ID, and informs the DDE client about it. As long as the conversation is active, the client uses this ID, or channel, to exchange data with or transmit commands about the topic to the server. In the example above, the first DDE channel would be established between the Forms module and the spreadsheet that will be the destination of data. The second channel would be established between the Forms module and the spreadsheet that is the source of data.

After a DDE communication channel is established, the DDE client may exchange data with the server. In the DDE context, the named objects in the server where these data elements reside are called *items*. Items can be used to receive data from clients or to store information that can be uploaded by them during a DDE conversation. The items that can be used in DDE transactions depend on the DDE server and on the topic of conversation. For special topics such as *System*, the items will depend on the specific applications. When the topic is set on a document, the variety and number of items is larger. If the application is a spreadsheet application such as Excel, Lotus 1-2-3, or QuatroPro, each cell can be an item. Ranges of cells and named blocks can also be items.

The fact that each cell in a spreadsheet can be accessed directly as an object, places them among the DDE servers that are the easiest to use. Word processing applications are a little harder to work with, because their structure is not as fragmented in objects. However, all the major word processing packages such as MS Word, WordPerfect, or AmiPro, support bookmarks, which allows you to name certain areas within a document. These bookmarks are used for navigation and cross-referencing from within the document, or as items in DDE communications. Figure 22.1 shows graphically the components of a typical DDE conversation.

22.1.2 DDE ACTIONS

Actions in a DDE conversation can originate only from the client application. As explained, the server will respond only to the incoming requests from the clients. This division of responsibilities is reflected in the type of support that different applications offer to DDE communications. There are applications such as MS Word, Excel, or WordPerfect, that can be DDE clients, as well as DDE servers. These applications are able not only to issue DDE commands, but also understand DDE commands that other clients send to them. There are other applications, such as Oracle Forms, that can behave only as DDE clients. They cannot respond to the DDE instructions sent by other applications.

The fundamental layer of functions used in DDE communications is defined in the Dynamic Data Exchange Management Library (DDEML) included with the MS Windows software. Each client application builds an Application Programming Interface (API) layer on top of it, which brings inevitable differences in implementation from one application to the other. The way DDE is implemented in Oracle Forms, for example, is different from that of MS Excel. However, each client application supports at least five basic operations in its implementation of a DDE. These are *Initiate*, *Request*, *Poke*, *Execute*, and *Terminate*.

Assuming that both the client and server applications are running, a DDE communication channel must be established between them before any exchange of data can occur. The process that establishes this channel is called Initiate. During the initiation process, the client application *agrees* with the server application on a particular topic about which they will converse during the session.

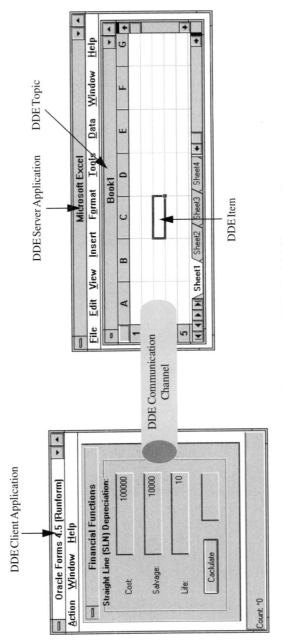

FIGURE 22.1 Components of a typical DDE conversation.

After the communication channel is established, the client and server may exchange data. The action through which the client application receives data from the server is called Request. The operation through which data is sent from the client to the server is called Poke. The DDE client may also instruct the server to perform certain actions. The commands for these actions are transmitted during the Execute operation. Finally, when the DDE conversation is completed, the Terminate action is used to close the communication channel.

Many DDE client applications provide for the operations of *Advise* and *Unadvise*, to detect any changes in the data stored by the server application. The Advise operation is a message sent to the client application whenever a change occurs in the server application. This message may trigger the necessary actions to be taken when changes occur such as sending the new data from the server to the client. The Unadvise command is used to end the Advise operation.

22.2 DDE IN DEVELOPER/2000 TOOLS

As mentioned earlier, Oracle Forms can play only the client part in a DDE communication transaction. This is true with all the other Developer/2000 applications, including Oracle Reports and Oracle Graphics. The DDE functionality in all these tools is implemented using a common interface provided by the package DDE. This package allows you to access DDE servers from within PL/SQL triggers and program units. Although this section and the rest of this chapter will focus on the usage of the DDE package with Oracle Forms, the concepts discussed here apply to the other members of Developer/2000 family.

22.2.1 PROGRAM UNITS IN DDE PACKAGE

The DDE package contains five program units that provide for the five fundamental processes in every DDE communication:

❑ DDE.INITIATE. This is a function that establishes a communication channel between Oracle Forms and a DDE topic on the server application. The function returns to the calling environment the internal identifier that Windows assigns to the channel. This identifier can be used to funnel data through the channel from the Forms module to the server, and vice-versa.

❑ DDE.REQUEST. This is a procedure that places data from an item in the server into a buffer declared in the PL/SQL program unit. The data can then be accessed from this buffer and used in the Forms application.

❑ DDE.POKE. This is a procedure that sends data from the Forms module to an item in the DDE server application.

❑ DDE.EXECUTE. This is a procedure used to send a command over to the server. The command must be a valid command recognizable by the server.

> **Note**
>
> When using the procedures DDE.REQUEST, DDE.POKE, and DDE.EXE-CUTE, Oracle Forms expects a confirmation message back from the server that acknowledges the receipt of the command. All these procedures take a parameter which allows you to tell Oracle Forms how long to wait for the acknowledgment, before deciding that the procedure failed. The value of this time-out parameter is specified in milliseconds, and it defaults to 1000 milliseconds. If the default value is used, Forms will issue the data exchange request or command to the server. If the server has not responded within one second, Forms will raise the appropriate exception, informing the calling program that the instruction failed.

Most of the DDE servers support their own programming languages that allow creation of macros or subprograms. For example, all the MS Office tools have some dialect of Basic as their programming language. DDE.EXE-CUTE allows you to invoke these macros or subroutines from within Oracle Forms.

❏ DDE.TERMINATE. This procedure closes the DDE communication channel that was opened with DDE.INITIATE.

As mentioned above, DDE communication between two applications may occur only if both applications are running. The DDE package enables you to launch an application that is not currently running in order to exchange data with it through the DDE bridge. The function DDE.APP_BEGIN may be used in this case. This function returns an internal identifier for the application. If an application started with DDE.APP_BEGIN is running and you want to place the focus of Windows on it, the procedure DDE.APP_FOCUS can be used. This procedure takes as a parameter the internal ID assigned to the application by DDE.APP_BEGIN. Finally, if you want to close an application started with DDE.APP_BEGIN, you can invoke the procedure DDE.APP_END, which takes as parameter the internal ID of the application.

22.2.2 DATA FORMATS

For the data exchange operations (Request and Poke), the procedures DDE.RE-QUEST and DDE.POKE will also need to know the format of the data to transfer. As explained earlier, Oracle Forms uses the underlying operating system DDE functions and procedures to carry out the processes. Therefore, these data formats must either be the predefined MS Windows datatypes, or user-defined formats registered with MS Windows.

The MS Windows predefined data formats are part of a number of global constants, described in the Windows API documentation. They are also defined as constants in the DDE package, which allows you to use them in the DDE operations from within Oracle Forms. The numeric value of these constants can be accessed through the function DDE.GETFORMATNUM. Furthermore, this function can be used to register a new user-defined format. If you know the value of the format, and want to retrieve its name in the form of a character string, you may use the function DDE.GETFORMATSTR.

The companion disk includes a small application, called FORMATS.FMB, that allows you to inspect the names and values of the predefined MS Windows data formats, and to create new ones. This application consists of a text list that you can use to scroll the data formats currently available. For the current list element, the numeric value and the name of the format are displayed on the side. Figure 22.2 shows the dialog box where this list is displayed.

If you want to create a new data format follow these steps:

1. Click the button New Format. You will see that the fields Value and String Name will be cleared.
2. Click inside the item String Name and enter the name of the new format.
3. Press ENTER when done. You will see the numeric value that MS Windows will assign to the new format displayed in the Values item. The new format is added to the end of the list.

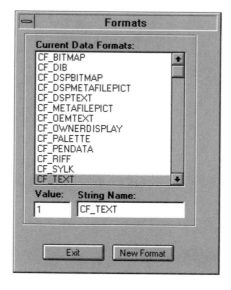

FIGURE 22.2   Data formats defined in the Oracle Forms DDE package.

If you inspect the contents of the trigger WHEN-LIST-CHANGED attached to the text list, you will see the following lines:

```
:FORMATS.VALUE := DDE.GETFORMATNUM(:FORMATS.FORMAT);
:FORMATS.TEXT :=
DDE.GETFORMATSTR(DDE.GETFORMATNUM(:FORMATS.FORMAT));
```

The first statement retrieves the value of the format for the current element of the list. The second statement retrieves the string name of this format based on its numeric value.

The contents of the trigger WHEN-VALIDATE-ITEM attached to the item FORMATS.TEXT are as follows:

```
:FORMATS.VALUE := DDE.GETFORMATNUM(:FORMATS.TEXT);
Insert_Element('FORMATS.FORMAT', :FORMATS.TEXT,
               TO_CHAR(:FORMATS.VALUE));
```

It is clear here that the value generated by MS Windows for the new item is generated first and then inserted at the end of the list.

22.2.3 EXCEPTIONS IN THE DDE PACKAGE

Besides the functions and data formats discussed in the previous two functions, the DDE package contains a series of predefined exceptions that allow you to handle several situations and errors in the DDE transactions you will program. Some of these exceptions can be raised by specific program units; others are raised as a result of failures in memory or in the MS Windows DDE layer.

The application support function DDE.APP_BEGIN, can raise the exception DDE.DDE_APP_FAILURE if the application specified as the parameter of the function cannot be launched. The other two functions of the same group,

Note

Although the data type conversion functions are available in the DDE package, it is very unlikely that you will ever need to use them in your application. The reason for this statement is that with DDE, applications can exchange data only in the text format. Therefore, in all the POKE and REQUEST statements you will write, the data format will be DDE.CF_TEXT.

DDE.APP_FOCUS and DDE.APP_END, raise the exception DDE.DDE_APP_ NOT_FOUND if the application ID passed as a parameter does not correspond to a currently running application.

If the function DDE.INITIATE fails to establish a communication channel between Oracle Forms and the server, the exceptions DDE.DDE_INIT_FAILED or DDE.DMLERR_NO_CONV_ESTABLISHED may be raised.

If Oracle Forms issues a data exchange instruction or command against the server using DDE.REQUEST, DDE.EXECUTE, or DDE.POKE, and the time-out interval specified in these procedures expires without the server acknowledging the request, the following exceptions may be raised: DDE.DMLERR_DATAACK-TIMEOUT, DDE.DMLERR_EXECACKTIMEOUT, or DDE.DMLERR_POKEACK-TIMEOUT.

If any of the parameters passed to the previous routines is not specified correctly, the following exceptions may be raised: DDE.DDE_PARAM_ERR, DDE.DMLERR_INVALIDPARAMETER, or DDE.DMLERR_NOTPROCESSED.

If the server was busy when the DDE operation request was sent, the exception DDE.DMLERR_BUSY is raised; if the server application terminates before servicing the operations, the exception DDE.DMLERR_SERVER_DIED is raised.

The data type translation function DDE.GETFORMATSTR can raise the exception DDE.FMT_NOT_FOUND if the format number supplied as parameter does not exist. The other function of this category, DDE.GETFORMATNUM, can raise the exception DDE.FMT_NOT_REG if the string name of the format passed as parameter is not a predefined MS Windows format, or cannot be registered as a user-defined format. Finally, all the program units may raise the generic errors DDE.DMLERR_MEMORY_ERROR and DDE.DMLERR_SYS_ERROR.

You must handle these exceptions in the program units you create, in order to ensure that the DDE commands will either complete successfully or terminate gracefully, in case an error occurs.

22.3 EXAMPLES OF DDE WITH ORACLE FORMS

This section presents and discusses several examples of communication between Oracle Forms and other Windows applications. It will start with an example that uses Excel as DDE server. Then, you will see how MS Word can be used as a server. In the last part, you will make Oracle Forms interact with the Windows Program Manager through DDE.

For each instance you will use a separate Forms application. The templates for these applications are provided on the companion disk. They contain the block and data items for each application and their layout in the canvas. The names of the modules are DDEEXCL.FMB, DDEWORD.FMB and DDEPROG.FMB. In the rest of the chapter you will add the DDE communication functionality to these templates. The final versions of these applications are also provided for you to consult. These files are DDEEXCLF.FMB, DDEWORDF.FMB, and DDEPROGF.FMB, respectively.

Despite the different functionality of each module, some general steps will be followed in each of them. These steps are listed:

1. Start the DDE server.
2. Establish a communication channel between the Oracle Forms and a topic in the application server.
3. Perform the necessary DDE operations.
4. Terminate the DDE communication.
5. Shut down the DDE server launched in Step 1.

These steps, especially Steps 2–4, may be repeated several times during the life of the Forms module.

22.3.1 INTEGRATING ORACLE FORMS WITH SPREADSHEETS

The integration of Oracle Forms applications with spreadsheet packages such as Excel, Lotus 1-2-3, or QuatroPro, is probably the most fruitful way of using the DDE technology with Oracle Forms. Each spreadsheet created with any of the above packages is divided in a hierarchy of sheets, rows, and columns. Their cells are fully qualified by specifying the names of the objects above. These cells, on the other hand, are items with which you exchange data during a DDE conversation. Thus, spreadsheets have a large number of items so that you can reference or exchange data in your applications. Another advantage of exchanging data with spreadsheets is their excellent support for a variety of functions such as financial, mathematical, trigonometric, and statistical functions. By establishing a communication channel between Oracle Forms and one of these spreadsheets, you increase by orders of magnitude the ability to compute and analyze the data stored in the database.

In the DDEEXCL.FMB module, you will implement two financial functions from MS Excel. The first one can be used to compute the straight-line depreciation of an asset for a given period of time. The second one can be used to return the periodic payment for an annuity based on constant payments and a constant interest rate over a given period of time. Start the Oracle Forms Designer and open the module DDEEXCL.FMB. This module has only one canvas, which looks like Figure 22.3.

A quick inspection of the contents of this module will reveal that all three blocks of this module are control blocks. The left half of the screen contains the items of block SLN, which will be used to compute the straight-line depreciation of an asset. COST will be used to enter the initial value of the asset. SALVAGE will contain the value of the asset at the end of the depreciation period. The number of periods over which the asset will be depreciated will be entered in the item

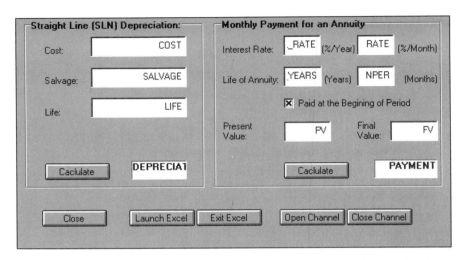

FIGURE 22.3 Layout of a Forms application that interacts with Excel using DDE.

LIFE. As an example, if you pay $3,000 to purchase a computer for your home business, and, for tax purposes, intend to depreciate ninety percent of its value over four years, you could set COST to 3000, SALVAGE to 300, and LIFE to 4. Then, click the push button Calculate. This button will invoke the Excel function that will calculate the depreciation and will store it in the display item DEPRECIATION.

The right half of the screen contains the items of block PMT, where you will compute the periodic payment for an annuity. The first two items store the interest rate in percentage points. The ANNUAL_RATE item is provided for convenience, since rates usually are defined in these terms. However, the formula for the payment will use the monthly percentage rate which is computed and stored in the item RATE. NUM_YEARS is the life of the annuity in years. Based on the value entered here, the number of periods, or months, in the life of the annuity is computed and stored in the item NPER. The check item TYPE is used to specify the type of payment for the annuity. If the box is checked, the payment is made at the beginning of the month; if the box is not checked, the annuity is paid at the end of the month. The items PV and FV are used to provide the present value of the annuity and its final value at the end of the payment period. The push button CALCULATE invokes the Excel function PMT, which calculates and stores in item PAYMENT the periodic payment for the annuity based on the data entered. As an example, to calculate how much you will have to pay for a mortgage of $150,000, at a fixed rate of 8% APR, payable in 30 years, you should set ANNUAL_RATE to 8, NUM_YEARS to 30, PV to 150000, FV to 0, and click the push button Calculate.

Finally, this module contains five push buttons, horizontally aligned at the bottom, which belong to the block CONTROL. The first one to the left closes the Forms application. The next two buttons to the right start and terminate Excel.

```
DECLARE
  appl_name VARCHAR2(255);
BEGIN
  IF :GLOBAL.application_id IS NOT NULL THEN
     MESSAGE('Application is already running.');
  ELSE
     appl_name := 'C:\EXCEL\EXCEL.EXE';
     :GLOBAL.application_id := DDE.APP_BEGIN(appl_name,
                               DDE.APP_MODE_NORMAL);
  END IF;
EXCEPTION
  WHEN DDE.DDE_APP_FAILURE THEN
     MESSAGE('Could not launch application for DDE operations.');
     RAISE FORM_TRIGGER_FAILURE;
  WHEN OTHERS THEN
     MESSAGE('Error: '||TO_CHAR(SQLCODE)||' '||SQLERRM);
     RAISE FORM_TRIGGER_FAILURE;
END;
```

FIGURE 22.4   Launching a DDE server application.

The fourth button establishes a communication channel with Excel, and the last one closes it (see Figure 22.3).

In this module, you will need to access the application ID that Windows assigns to Excel when started from several program units. Likewise, the internal ID assigned to the communication channel when established will be used in several triggers and program units. These internal IDs will be stored in two global variables, called GLOBAL.application_id and GLOBAL.channel_id. Declare these variables in a PRE-FORM trigger and assign the NULL value to both of them.

Now create the necessary triggers to the push buttons in the module's button palette:

❑ Create a WHEN-BUTTON-PRESSED trigger for the item LAUNCH and enter the statements shown in Figure 22.4 in the body of the trigger.

Note

The statements shown in this figure assume that Excel is installed in the directory C:\EXCEL. If your environment differs, provide the appropriate location of EXCEL.EXE.

As you can see from this figure, when the application is launched for the first time, its ID is stored in the global variable GLOBAL.application_id. This avoids repeated startups of the server application when an instance has been started previously and is available for use. Notice that the application is started in Normal mode. To start it minimized or maximized, the parameter DDE.APP_MODE_NORMAL in DDE.APP_BEGIN should be replaced with DDE.APP_MODE_MINIMIZED or DDE.APP_MODE_MAXIMIZED.

❑ Now create the WHEN-BUTTON-PRESSED trigger for button CLOSE, and enter the statements shown in Figure 22.5 in its body.

    The only statement that may require some clarification in this figure is the use of the procedure DDE.APP_FOCUS to make Excel the current application before terminating it. When you send data over to Excel items, they will be stored temporarily in a new document. When DDE.APP_END instructs the application to terminate, Excel will prompt you to save the modified document. The prompt will not be visible normally, unless Excel is given the Windows focus.

❑ The contents of the trigger WHEN-BUTTON-PRESSED for the button EXIT_FORM are very similar to the previous trigger. In fact, the DECLARE

```
DECLARE
  application_id PLS_INTEGER;
BEGIN
  IF :GLOBAL.application_id IS NULL THEN
     MESSAGE('Cannot terminate an instance that is not
initiated by this application.');
  ELSE
     application_id := TO_NUMBER(:GLOBAL.application_id);
     DDE.APP_FOCUS(application_id);
     DDE.APP_END(application_id);
     :GLOBAL.application_id := NULL;
     :GLOBAL.channel_id := NULL;
  END IF;
EXCEPTION
  WHEN DDE.DDE_APP_NOT_FOUND THEN
     MESSAGE('Could not find application for DDE operations.');
     RAISE FORM_TRIGGER_FAILURE;
  WHEN OTHERS THEN
     MESSAGE('Error: '||TO_CHAR(SQLCODE)||' '||SQLERRM);
     RAISE FORM_TRIGGER_FAILURE;
END;
```

FIGURE 22.5   Terminating a DDE server application.

> **Note**
>
> Note that when the server application is terminated, Windows will no longer recognize its internal ID, or the ID of any DDE channel that was established with the application. Therefore you must set to NULL the global variables that store these ID values in the application.

and EXCEPTION parts of these triggers are identical. In the execution part, you should end the instance of Excel that may have been started previously, and then invoke the built-in procedure EXIT_FORM.

❑ The trigger WHEN-BUTTON-PRESSED for button OPEN_CHANNEL invokes DDE.INITIATE to establish a communication channel with Excel. The topic of conversation will be BOOK1, which is the document that Excel opens by default when it is started. Figure 22.6 provides the necessary details to implement this trigger.

This trigger checks first for a communications channel that may already exist. It assumes that Excel is not available if it is not started from

```
BEGIN
  IF :GLOBAL.channel_id IS NOT NULL THEN
    MESSAGE('Communication channel already established.');
  ELSIF :GLOBAL.application_id IS NULL THEN
    MESSAGE('Application must be launched first.');
  ELSE
    :GLOBAL.channel_id := DDE.INITIATE('EXCEL', 'BOOK1');
  END IF;
EXCEPTION
  WHEN DDE.DDE_INIT_FAILED THEN
    MESSAGE('Could not initialize DDE communication channel.');
    RAISE FORM_TRIGGER_FAILURE;
  WHEN DDE.DMLERR_NO_CONV_ESTABLISHED THEN
    MESSAGE('Could not establish DDE communication channel.');
    RAISE FORM_TRIGGER_FAILURE;
  WHEN OTHERS THEN
    MESSAGE('Error: '||TO_CHAR(SQLCODE)||' '||SQLERRM);
    RAISE FORM_TRIGGER_FAILURE;
END;
```

FIGURE 22.6 Establishing a DDE communication channel.

within our application. This means that although the users may be working with Excel on their own, the trigger will not take advantage of the instance that they are already running. To complete the functionality it is designed to perform, this application should launch its own duplicate instance of Excel instead. This is certainly a drawback inherent in the way DDE is designed to work. The computer resources will not be used efficiently. However, from a data security perspective, it may be considered an advantage as well, because it protects the documents that the users may be editing in the other instance from accidental modifications.

❑   The approach and layout of the trigger WHEN-BUTTON-PRESSED for button CLOSE_CHANNEL are similar to those described above. This trigger simply checks that a DDE communications channel is open, and, if so, invokes DDE.TERMINATE procedure to close it. Figure 22.7 shows the details of this trigger.

So far, you have implemented the functionality that starts Excel, establishes the communication channel between Excel and Forms, terminates this channel, and closes Excel. In order to complete the task, you must create the PL/SQL program units that transfer the data from Forms items to Excel cells, invoke the functions SLN and PMT in Excel, and return the results of these functions to Oracle Forms.

Create a function called Calc_SLN, and enter its specifications as shown in Figure 22.8.

This function takes as parameter the communication channel ID established previously and the numeric arguments required to compute the straight-line de-

```
DECLARE
  channel_id       PLS_INTEGER;
BEGIN
  IF :GLOBAL.channel_id IS NULL THEN
     MESSAGE('No communication channels are open at this time.');
  ELSE
     channel_id := TO_NUMBER(:GLOBAL.channel_id);
     DDE.TERMINATE(channel_id);
     :GLOBAL.channel_id := NULL;
  END IF;
EXCEPTION
  WHEN OTHERS THEN
     MESSAGE('Error: '||TO_CHAR(SQLCODE)||' '||SQLERRM);
     RAISE FORM_TRIGGER_FAILURE;
END;
```

FIGURE 22.7   Terminating a DDE communication channel.

```
FUNCTION Calc_SLN (channel_id PLS_INTEGER,
                   cost        NUMBER,
                   salvage     NUMBER,
                   life        NUMBER)
RETURN NUMBER IS
  return_value VARCHAR2(100) := '';
BEGIN
  DDE.POKE(channel_id, 'R1C1', TO_CHAR(cost), DDE.CF_TEXT, 1000);
  DDE.POKE(channel_id, 'R1C2', TO_CHAR(salvage), DDE.CF_TEXT, 1000);
  DDE.POKE(channel_id, 'R1C3', TO_CHAR(life), DDE.CF_TEXT, 1000);
  DDE.POKE(channel_id, 'R1C4', '=TEXT(SLN(A1, B1, C1), 0.00)',
           DDE.CF_TEXT, 1000);

  DDE.REQUEST(channel_id, 'R1C4', return_value, DDE.CF_TEXT, 1000);

  RETURN(TO_NUMBER(return_value));
EXCEPTION
  WHEN OTHERS THEN
     MESSAGE('Error: '||TO_CHAR(SQLCODE)||' '||SQLERRM);
     RAISE FORM_TRIGGER_FAILURE;
END;
```

FIGURE 22.8 Calculating the straight-line depreciation of an asset.

preciation. The first three statements in the execution part of the function transfer the data from the input arguments of the function to Excel cells. Note the fact that these data are all converted to text strings before being handed over to the DDE.POKE function for transmission.

The last POKE statement is similar in structure to the previous three. It does little more than send a stream of characters from the form to the spreadsheet. This string, however is different from the previous three. It is not just raw data, but contains a command that will direct Excel to compute the SLN function and format the outcome. The SLN function will take as arguments the data stored earlier in cells A1, B1, and C1.

Note

When you send data over, these items are referred to as R1C1, R1C2, and R1C3, but in order to refer to the contents of these cells in Excel, you must use the notations A1, B1, and C1.

The value computed by the function SLN must be returned to Forms through the DDE communication channel. Therefore, it must be in text format. This is the reason why the Excel data conversion function TEXT is called after the SLN function, and before the DDE.REQUEST function transfers the result back to the form module.

Now create the trigger WHEN-BUTTON-PRESSED for button CALCU-LATE in the block SLN. The contents of this trigger should be as shown in Figure 22.9.

This trigger first checks that a DDE communication channel is established, and then invokes the function **Calc_SLN** with values entered in the items of block SLN as arguments. The properties of these items are set to ensure that the arguments passed to the function will be valid ones. For example, the property *Required* is set to *'True'*, and the property *Low Range Value* is set to *'0'*. This means that before the trigger shown in Figure 22.9 is activated, non-negative numbers must be entered in the text items of block SLN. In a general case, you should check for the validity of the arguments before sending the data over to Excel for computation.

There is no conceptual difference in the way you calculate the monthly payments for an annuity. Without repeating the detailed discussion above, Figure 22.10 presents the contents of function **Calc_PMT**.

Figure 22.11 contains the contents of trigger WHEN-BUTTON-PRESSED for the button PMT.CALCULATE.

After you enter these last two program units, save and generate the form. Make sure to use it in order to answer the questions posed at the beginning of the section. You will find, for example, that over the next four years, you can depreciate your $3,000 computer by $675 every year. The monthly payments for your 30-year, fixed 8% APR, $150,000 mortgage will be $1,093 per month if you pay at the beginning of the month, but $1,101 per month if you pay at the end of it. Notice

```
DECLARE
  channel_id PLS_INTEGER;
BEGIN
  IF :GLOBAL.channel_id IS NOT NULL THEN
      channel_id := TO_NUMBER(:GLOBAL.channel_id);
      :SLN.DEPRECIATION := Calc_SLN(channel_id, :SLN.COST,
                             :SLN.SALVAGE, :SLN.LIFE);
  ELSE
      MESSAGE('A communication channel must be established first.');
  END IF;
END;
```

FIGURE 22.9   Calling the function Calc_SLN.

```
FUNCTION Calc_PMT (channel_id PLS_INTEGER,
                   rate        NUMBER,
                   nper        NUMBER,
                   pv          NUMBER,
                   fv          NUMBER,
                   type        NUMBER)
RETURN NUMBER IS
  return_value VARCHAR2(1024) := '';
BEGIN
  DDE.POKE(channel_id, 'R1C1', TO_CHAR(rate), DDE.CF_TEXT, 1000);
  DDE.POKE(channel_id, 'R1C2', TO_CHAR(nper), DDE.CF_TEXT, 1000);
  DDE.POKE(channel_id, 'R1C3', TO_CHAR(pv),   DDE.CF_TEXT, 1000);
  DDE.POKE(channel_id, 'R1C4', TO_CHAR(fv),   DDE.CF_TEXT, 1000);
  DDE.POKE(channel_id, 'R1C5', TO_CHAR(type), DDE.CF_TEXT, 1000);
  DDE.POKE(channel_id, 'R1C6', '=TEXT(PMT(A1, B1, C1, D1, E1),
           0.00)', DDE.CF_TEXT, 1000);

  DDE.REQUEST(channel_id, 'R1C6', return_value, DDE.CF_TEXT,
              1000);

  RETURN(TO_NUMBER(return_value));
EXCEPTION
  WHEN OTHERS THEN
     MESSAGE('Error: '||TO_CHAR(SQLCODE)||' '||SQLERRM);
     RAISE FORM_TRIGGER_FAILURE;
END;
```

FIGURE 22.10 Calculating the periodic payment for an annuity.

```
DECLARE
  channel_id PLS_INTEGER;
BEGIN
  IF :GLOBAL.channel_id IS NOT NULL THEN
     channel_id := TO_NUMBER(:GLOBAL.channel_id);
     :PMT.PAYMENT := Calc_PMT(channel_id, :PMT.RATE/100, :PMT.NPER,
                              :PMT.PV, :PMT.FV, :PMT.TYPE);
  ELSE
     MESSAGE('A communication channel must be established first.');
  END IF;
END;
```

FIGURE 22.11 Invoking function Calc_PMT.

> ## Note
>
> Using this formula, you can see yet another convincing proof of the power of the compound interest (interest earned on interest) that often goes unnoticed. Had you started saving ten years ago, when your baby was born, the monthly sum you had to contribute to your savings would have been only $215. To reach the $100,000 objective with the same amount of monthly investment, but starting today, ten years late, you have to guaranty a steady rate of return of 23% for the next ten years.

that the value calculated will be a negative number, to indicate that this is cash that will flow away from you for the annuity term.

You can use the PMT block for a variety of other purposes. Suppose, for example, that your heir will go to college in ten years, and you want to have $100,000 saved for her Law degree by then. Your local municipal bonds offer a 6% return on the investment and you want to see how much you need to save every month to reach your goal. In the block PMT, set ANNUAL_RATE to 6, NUM_YEARS to 10, PV to 0, FV to 100000, and click the push button Calculate. You will see that you will need to send $607 at the beginning of each month to your investor.

Finally, at the conclusion of this section let us emphasize the fact that although the example here was tailored around MS Excel, minimal modifications are required to adapt it to other spreadsheet packages such as Lotus 1-2-3 or QuatroPro. They all support the same functionality, more or less, and in a very similar fashion.

22.3.2 INTEGRATING ORACLE FORMS WITH WORD PROCESSORS

Spreadsheets provide a high number of items that can be used as data containers in DDE transactions. This feature originates from the highly structured organization of these applications. Word processing packages such as MS Word, WordPerfect, or AmiPro, given their nature, have a smaller number of objects loosely organized inside their documents. Therefore, when word processors are used as server applications in DDE transactions, the number of choices you have for items is limited.

Nevertheless, as you will see in this section, these applications can be used successfully to expand the functionality of Oracle Forms applications. The most popular combination of word processors and database packages is the creation of form letters. Form letters are documents based on a template, which differ from each other in a limited number of points. For example, the video store discussed in this book may need to send reminders to customers who fail to return their videos on time. The content and format of each letter will be similar to the one shown in Figure 22.12.

Certain data in this letter will reflect information that is already stored in the database such as the customer name and address or the title of the movie. It would certainly be nice if you could spare the account representatives the effort of typing all these data elements for each letter they send out.

In order to implement the transfer of data from the form module to the letter template, some items must exist or be defined in the document. Word processing applications use bookmarks as DDE items. Bookmarks are markers of certain areas of text in the document. Every word processor provides for ways to create bookmarks. For example, in MS Word you would take the following steps:

1. Select the text that will be marked.
2. Choose Edit | Bookmark from the menu. The Bookmark dialog box will appear (see Figure 22.13).

VIDEO RENTAL STORE

8123 Lincoln Avenue
Falls Church, VA 33334-2121

November 17, 1995

Michelle Johnson
123 North Main Street Apt. 309
Falls Church, VA 20129

Dear Michelle:

This is a reminder about the movie *The Piano,* which is now 30 days past due. If there is a problem with the video tape, please call me at once so we can correct it.

Thank you for your business and for your prompt attention to this matter.

Sincerely,

Robert S. Walker
Account Representative

P.S. If you have already returned the movie, please accept our thanks and disregard this notice.

FIGURE 22.12   Typical form letter that can be produced by integrating Oracle Forms with word processors.

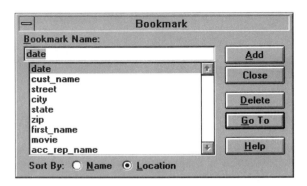

FIGURE 22.13   MS Word Bookmark dialog box.

3. Type the new name in the Bookmark Name field.
4. Press the Add button to create the new bookmark.

Figure 22.13 also shows the bookmarks that are created in the template document LETTER.DOC. This document is provided in the companion disk and will be used in this section in combination with the Oracle Forms module DDE-WORD.FMB. The bookmarks are ordered by their location in the document. If the contents of Figure 22.13 are compared with the template document shown in Figure 22.12, it is not difficult to identify the location of each bookmark. You can also open the document LETTER.DOC and press F5 to go to any bookmark you want. Furthermore, you can have Word display the bookmarks inside square brackets by following these steps:

1. Chose Tools | Options... from the MS Word menu. The Options dialog box appears.
2. Select View tab.
3. In the Show group, check the check box item Bookmarks and then click the OK button.

As it was the case with the module in the previous section, DDEWORD.FMB contains a template of the form to which you will add the DDE functionality. The layout of the items in this module is shown in Figure 22.14.

All the base table items in this block are query-only, and can be used to retrieve the name and address of the customer and the title of the movie that the customer has failed to return. The text item field TEMPLATE, at the bottom of the window, is where the location of the letter template document is stored. The information entered here will be used to open the template when MS Word is initially launched, and will also serve as a topic of conversation when the DDE communication channel will be established. The text item ACC_REP_NAME will be used to send the name of the account representative to the Word document.

The functionality attached to the first five push buttons is almost identical to the functionality attached to these buttons in the module DDEEXL.FMB. The only

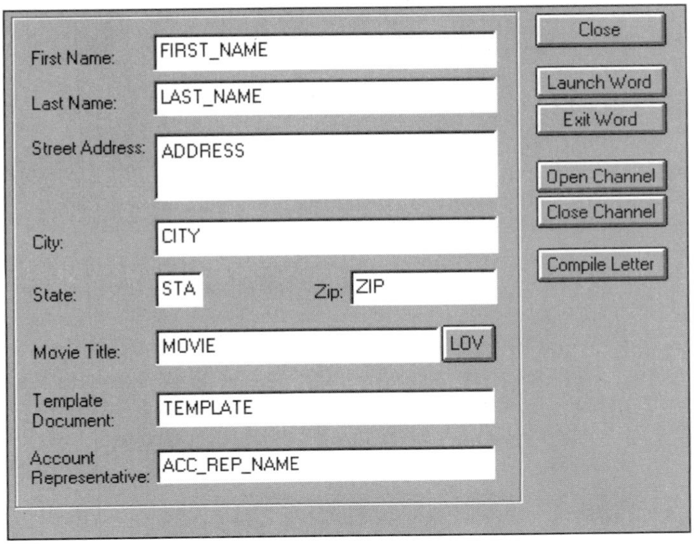

FIGURE 22.14 Layout of a Forms application that interacts with MS Word using DDE.

changes that should be made in order to reflect the new type of DDE server are as follows:

1. In the WHEN-BUTTON-PRESSED for button LAUNCH, the name of the application is defined by the command below:

   appl_name := 'C:\WINWORD\WINWORD.EXE 'll:CUSTOMER.TEMPLATE;

2. In the WHEN-BUTTON-PRESSED for button OPEN_CHANNEL the DDE communication channel is initialized with this statement:

   :GLOBAL.channel_id := DDE.INITIATE
   ('WINWORD', :CUSTOMER.TEMPLATE);

Note

In the module DDEWORD.FMB, as in DDEEXCL.FMB, the location of WIN-WORD.EXE is hardcoded. You must ensure that you use the right path for your environment.

These triggers are already included in the module DDEWORD.FMB, and you may inspect them on your own if you have any questions regarding their functionality. Here the focus will be on the trigger associated with the button COMPILE. When this trigger is executed, it initially performs some minor arrangements and formatting of the data queried in the CUSTOMER block. Then it passes these data elements to the procedure Compile_Letter, which will ultimately send them to the MS Word document, and display the letter to the user. The contents of this procedure are shown in Figure 22.15.

You can see from this figure how the function DDE.POKE is used to transfer the data from the Oracle Forms environment to the MS Word document items. These items are addressed using the bookmark names defined in the template document.

The only thing that is left now to complete the task is to create the WHEN-BUTTON-PRESSED trigger for button COMPILE. In this trigger, before issuing the call to the procedure Compile_Letter, you need to prepare some of its arguments, so that they match the format of the data elements in the template letter. For example, you will retrieve the SYSTEM date and convert it in the format

```
PROCEDURE Compile_Letter (channel_id   PLS_INTEGER,
                          date          VARCHAR2,
                          cust_name     VARCHAR2,
                          street        VARCHAR2,
                          city          VARCHAR2,
                          state         VARCHAR2,
                          zip           VARCHAR2,
                          first_name    VARCHAR2,
                          movie         VARCHAR2,
                          acc_rep_name VARCHAR2) IS
BEGIN
  DDE.POKE(channel_id, 'date',         date,         DDE.CF_TEXT, 1000);
  DDE.POKE(channel_id, 'cust_name',    cust_name,    DDE.CF_TEXT, 1000);
  DDE.POKE(channel_id, 'street',       street,       DDE.CF_TEXT, 1000);
  DDE.POKE(channel_id, 'city',         city,         DDE.CF_TEXT, 1000);
  DDE.POKE(channel_id, 'state',        state,        DDE.CF_TEXT, 1000);
  DDE.POKE(channel_id, 'zip',          zip,          DDE.CF_TEXT, 1000);
  DDE.POKE(channel_id, 'first_name',   first_name,   DDE.CF_TEXT, 1000);
  DDE.POKE(channel_id, 'movie',        movie,        DDE.CF_TEXT, 1000);
  DDE.POKE(channel_id, 'acc_rep_name', acc_rep_name, DDE.CF_TEXT, 1000);
EXCEPTION
  WHEN OTHERS THEN
    MESSAGE('Error: '||TO_CHAR(SQLCODE)||' '||SQLERRM);
    RAISE FORM_TRIGGER_FAILURE;
END;
```

FIGURE 22.15   Transferring data to MS Word through a DDE communication channel.

Note

Each Word document has three bookmarks built in its structure. Their names are \doc, \startofdoc, and \endofdoc. The first bookmark represents the entire document. If, for example, you want to transfer the contents of a document in an Oracle Forms item, you would use the following statement:

 DDE.REQUEST (channel_id, '\doc', buffer_name, DDE.CF_TEXT, 1000);

The other two bookmarks represent the beginning and the end of the document, respectively, but do not actually contain any data. Consider, for example, the following statement:

 DDE.POKE (channel_id, '\startofdoc', 'At the beginning of document.', DDE.CF_TEXT, 1000);

This statement will add the string in quotes at the beginning of the document, but will not overwrite any existing data. The bookmark \startofdoc itself will remain to the left of the new string, at the beginning of the document.

Besides these bookmarks, Word sets and updates a number of other predefined bookmarks, which are documented in the on-line help under topic *Predefined Bookmarks*. Note the important fact that these built-in bookmarks must be preceded by the '\' character in order to be recognized by MS Word.

Month DD, YYYY which is more appropriate in a business letter than the default DD-MON-YY format. You will also concatenate the first and last names of the customer.

After the procedure Compile_Letter sends the data to the MS Word document, the users should have the ability to do any last minute editing and send the letter to the printer. Therefore the last statement of the trigger sets the focus of Windows on the MS Word document. Figure 22.16 shows the contents of this trigger.

22.3.3 CONTROLLING OTHER PROGRAMS FROM WITHIN ORACLE FORMS

The examples presented in the previous two sections show how Oracle Forms modules can exchange data with other applications. In this section you will see how to send commands from form modules to another application using a DDE communication channel.

```
DECLARE
  appl_id     PLS_INTEGER;
  channel_id PLS_INTEGER;
  date        VARCHAR2(50);
  cust_name   VARCHAR2(60);
BEGIN
  IF :GLOBAL.channel_id IS NOT NULL THEN
     channel_id := TO_NUMBER(:GLOBAL.channel_id);
     SELECT TO_CHAR(SYSDATE, 'Month DD, YYYY') INTO date FROM DUAL;
     cust_name := :CUSTOMER.FIRST_NAME||' '||:CUSTOMER.LAST_NAME;

     Compile_Letter(channel_id, date, cust_name, :CUSTOMER.ADDRESS,
                   :CUSTOMER.CITY, :CUSTOMER.STATE, :CUSTOMER.ZIP,
                   :CUSTOMER.FIRST_NAME, :CUSTOMER.MOVIE,
                   :CUSTOMER.ACC_REP_NAME);

     appl_id := TO_NUMBER(:GLOBAL.application_id);
     DDE.APP_FOCUS(appl_id);
  ELSE
     MESSAGE('A communication channel must be established first.');
  END IF;
END;
```

FIGURE 22.16   Trigger that transfers data from Oracle Forms to MS Word.

For the DDE to work, both the client and the server applications must be up and running at the same time. However, there is one server application that is always running as long as Windows is running. This is the Windows shell program, also known as the Program Manager. By establishing a DDE communication channel between Oracle Forms and the Program Manager, you will be able to send commands and directives to the Windows shell from within Forms.

In this section you will use the module DDEPROG.FMB, which contains only five push buttons aligned horizontally. The first three of these buttons, labeled Close, Open Channel, and Close Channel, have a similar functionality as their counterparts in the modules discussed in the previous sections. Note that in this case, you do not need push buttons to launch or terminate the DDE server, since this server, the Program Manager, will be available during the life of your application.

For the Windows Program Manager, both the Service and the Topic of conversation are called PROGMAN. Recall that they are required to initiate a communication link through DDE. Therefore, the statement that establishes this link in the WHEN-BUTTON-PRESSED trigger of the Open Channel button is:

:GLOBAL.channel_id := DDE.INITIATE ('PROGMAN', 'PROGMAN');

In the triggers associated with the other two buttons, Create and Delete, you will send some commands to the Program Manager. Among the most frequently used commands with the Program Manager are **CreateGroup**, **AddItem**, **DeleteItem**, **ShowGroup**, and **DeleteGroup**. These commands are issued primarily by installation utilities, in order to create the necessary program groups and items to access the applications. Here you will access them from within Oracle Forms using the DDE functionality. The discussion has practical importance, because you can follow the same approach to create your own installation utility, as a tool in the cumbersome process of deploying an application to environments that are not configured consistently.

As mentioned earlier, the function DDE.EXECUTE allows us to send a command string to the server application through the DDE communication channel. This command string is enclosed in single quotes and may contain one or more commands recognizable by the server. Each command must be enclosed in square brackets. For example, to create a program group called *Chapter 22*, you could use the following statement:

DDE.EXECUTE (channel_id, '[CreateGroup(Chapter 22)]', 1000);

If, on the other hand, you want to send the instruction to create the group together with that to show the group, you would use the following statement:

DDE.EXECUTE (channel_id, '[CreateGroup(Chapter 22)]
[ShowGroup(Chapter 22, 1)]', 1000);

As you can see from these statements, the function **CreateGroup** takes the name of the group to be created as the only argument. This name will become the label that will be displayed in the title bar of the group's window or with its icon in the Program Manager. The function **DeleteGroup** takes only the group name as a parameter as well. This function deletes a group from the Program Manager.

The function **ShowGroup** takes two parameters. The first one is the name of the group to be displayed. The second parameter is the mode in which the window of the group is set when the function is executed. The values of this parameter range from 1 to 8. When values 1, 2, and 3 are used, the window will be displayed in Normal, Minimized, and Maximized mode, respectively.

In the module DDEPROG.FMB you will enable users to create a program group called *Chapter 22* and add program items to it. These program items will open the MS Word document that served as a letter template in the previous section. They will also run the modules DDEEXCL.FMB and DDEWORD.FMB. Other program items could be added to this group as well. The function **AddItem** is used to add a program item to the current program group. Let us briefly discuss this function, before moving to the actual implementation of its functionality in the trigger.

The function **AddItem** may take up to eight parameters. The description and sequence of these parameters is as follows: Command Line, Description, Icon Source File, Icon Index, X Position, Y Position, Working Directory, and Shortcut Key. You may realize that this is the same information that you provide in the Program Item Properties dialog box when you create a new program item from the Program Manager.

The Command Line is the statement that will be executed when the icon of the item will be double-clicked. Description will be the label that will go underneath the icon of the program item in its parent program group. Icon Source File is the file that contains the icon for the item. Since this file may contain several icons, the Icon Index allows you to pick the one you want. X Position and Y Position are the initial coordinates of the program item icon in the window of the parent program group. The Working Directory is the directory where the files of the program item are located and where new files will be created. The Shortcut Key is a combination of the CTRL, SHIFT, or ALT keys, usually CTRL+ALT, with a character from the keyboard that allows you to switch to the application when it is running or to launch it from the Program Manager.

Now you are ready to create the WHEN-BUTTON-PRESSED triggers for buttons CREATE and DELETE. Figure 22.17 shows the contents of the first trigger.

The first call to DDE.EXECUTE creates the program group called *Chapter 22*. The second call creates a program item that will open the MS Word document C:\MRD\LETTER.DOC. The description for this program item will be *Letter Template*. Its icon will be drawn from the MS Word executable file. The horizontal position for the icon will be 30, and the working directory of the program will be C:\WINWORD. The next two EXECUTE statements create two additional program items for modules DDEEXCL.FMX and DDEWORD.FMX. Finally, after the program groups are added, the ShowGroup command is issued to display the new program group in Normal Mode. Depending on your environment, the actual directory names that you will use in the trigger may be different, but the approach is the same.

Note

You may choose not to specify some parameters in the **AddItem** program. However, if other parameters that follow them are specified, you must maintain their position with an empty space. In the statements in Figure 22.17, although the icon index, or vertical position parameters, are not specified, an empty space followed by a comma is used to represent them. The empty space is not needed for the shortcut key parameters because there are no other parameters specified after it.

```
DECLARE
  channel_id PLS_INTEGER;
BEGIN
  IF :GLOBAL.channel_id IS NOT NULL THEN
     channel_id := TO_NUMBER(:GLOBAL.channel_id);
     DDE.EXECUTE(channel_id, '[CreateGroup(Chapter 22)]', 1000);
     DDE.EXECUTE(channel_id, '[AddItem(winword c:\mrd\letter.doc,
               Letter Template, c:\winword\winword.exe, , 30, ,
               c:\winword)]', 1000);
     DDE.EXECUTE(channel_id, '[AddItem(f45run.exe c:\forms\ddeexcl.fmx,
               Forms & Excel, f45run.exe, , 110, ,
               c:\orawin\bin)]', 1000);
     DDE.EXECUTE(channel_id, '[AddItem(f45run.exe c:\forms\ddeword.fmx,
               Forms & Word, f45run.exe, , 190, ,
               c:\orawin\bin)]', 1000);
     DDE.EXECUTE(channel_id, '[ShowGroup(Chapter 22, 1)]', 1000);
  ELSE
     MESSAGE('A communication channel must be established first.');
  END IF;
END;
```

FIGURE 22.17 Executing Program Manager commands from Oracle Forms.

The trigger attached to button DELETE will be very similar to the trigger discussed above. The only difference is that all the DDE.EXECUTE statements there are replaced by the following line:

DDE.EXECUTE (channel_id, '[DeleteGroup(Chapter 22)]', 1000);

When you are finished with the editing of both triggers, save, generate, and run the module DDEPROG.FMB. Click the Open Channel button to initiate a conversation with the Program Manager. Click the button Create to create the program group with the program items discussed above. The picture you should see will be similar to Figure 22.18. If you do not want to keep this program group in your desktop, return to the module DDEPROG.FMB and click the button Delete to remove it from the Program Manager.

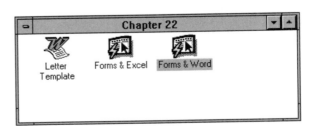

FIGURE 22.18 Program group and program items created from Oracle Forms.

22.4 SUMMARY

This chapter discussed one of the earliest Windows technologies for data sharing and exchange between applications: Dynamic Data Exchange, or DDE. Major concepts explained in the chapter are presented here:

- ❑ Definition of DDE
    - ❑ DDE components
    - ❑ DDE actions
- ❑ DDE in Developer/2000 Tools
    - ❑ Components of DDE package
    - ❑ Data formats
    - ❑ Exceptions in the DDE package
- ❑ DDE in Oracle Forms
    - ❑ Integrating Oracle Forms with spreadsheets
    - ❑ Integrating Oracle Forms with word processors
    - ❑ Controlling other programs from within Oracle Forms

OLE

"If there's one thing a computer is good at, it's helping you combine diverse elements."

—Michael Hawley

OLE is a technology that is based on the integration and reusability of different software components in one application. This chapter discusses certain aspects of it, and how they relate to applications that you develop with Oracle Forms. In particular, it explains the OLE Documents technology, which allows the creation of compound documents through the linking or embedding of objects.

23.1   WHAT IS OLE?

Although initially OLE was an abbreviation for Object Linking and Embedding, today the acronym represents much more meaning and functionality. In 1991, software engineers at Microsoft came up with a solution to create compound documents, which was called Object Linking and Embedding 1, or OLE 1. This allowed applications such as MS Word to represent text, side by side with spreadsheets from Excel, charts from MS Graph, bitmaps from drawing packages, and so on. The concept revolutionized the way these packages were used and led to the concept of office suites of applications such as Microsoft Office, or Lotus SmartSuite, which tend and provide for the needs of modern offices for document creation and editing. However, the initial design of OLE 1 needed fine-tuning, optimization, and other improvements. The result of these efforts was OLE 2 conceived, designed, and released in 1992 to 1993. At this point, people in Redmond, Washington stepped back and looked at what their architects had done. They realized that the framework of the new OLE extends far and beyond the creation of compound documents. Compound documents are still a major part of it, but the design is so generic that it supports a whole new way of looking at the software development process. For this reason, Microsoft promoted OLE as its principal technology for the integration of software components. Furthermore, the architecture is so flexible that new pieces can be added to the picture without requiring any revisions of it. Therefore, the numbering of OLE was dropped, to signify that there will be no OLE 3, 4, or 5.

This section will summarize as best as possible the concepts of OLE that you will use in your Oracle Forms applications. For a full discussion of the technology, you should refer to books purposely written on the subject. An excellent reference is *Inside OLE* (Second Edition, Microsoft Press, 1995) by Kraig Brockschmidt, a Program Manager in the Microsoft's OLE development team.

23.1.1   THE NEED FOR OLE

In several software engineering books, the metaphor of building a house is used to describe the process of developing software applications. In both cases, clients get together with the construction team to explain what they want and how it should look like. Design plans are created, which clients eventually sign off, and the construction process begins. During this process users may inspect the progress of work, may require some new features or drop some previous requirements. At the end of it, users get the keys to the house, the constructors pocket the money, and everybody lives happily thereafter.

For all its didactic advantages, the metaphor is not exactly correct, especially if you consider it in the reverse direction. Think for a minute of constructing a house in the same fashion in which many software systems are built today. First of all you make sure to fence a territory large enough to contain several houses like the one you will build. You will be wasting some resources, but users must pay for them if they want an efficient house. Then, you place "No Trespassing" signs all over the fence, so that nobody else wanders in your territory. If somebody is able to obtain a pass to visit your compound, you will constantly keep an eye, probably a leash, on them, just in case. Then off to the real job of building the house!

You break the job in several tasks, subtasks, steps, and substeps, and divide your resources so that the project is completed on time. Some of your people are responsible for producing nails of all sizes. After they are done with this, they will switch to the production of light bulbs. Another team will be responsible for the production of bricks and door knobs. Yet another one will take care of the tiles, faucets, and glass. You have meticulously covered everything, and count on your teams to finish on time so that the real construction can begin. When this day arrives, your people become carpenters, brick layers, painters, and electricians. Some of them move on to build the furniture, and others to decorate the house. A few others are responsible for putting together instructions on how to go from one room to another, on how to turn the oven on, and how to adjust the air temperature.

Then the day when your project is completed arrives and you hand the keys over to your clients, together with a list of disclaimers and known problems with the house. If they ever want to rearrange the furniture in the living room, they should be aware that this will affect the heat pump in the basement. They cannot invite more that five guests per night, and you are not to be held responsible for that. The paintings in the kids room are nailed to the wall and should not be removed, otherwise the roof may leak. And the list may go on like this.

If houses were really built this way, we would all be living in monolithic, Flintstone-type houses, too cold in winter, too hot in summer, far and isolated from each other. But we have constructed houses for centuries and we have learned to do better than that. Today we divide the work and specialize in certain aspects of the process. Hardware equipment and tools are produced by hardware companies. Construction materials are made by some other type of companies. Building contractors purchase these materials and equipment according to the customer demand, and provide skilled workers, brick layers, plumbers, and electricians to actually build the house. Furniture, decorations, and appliances for the house can be purchased from yet another group of companies. What is more important, we can customize and add to our houses the features we want. We can all go to the store, buy furniture packaged so that it fits in the trunk of the car, and bring it back home. A list of a few instructions and drawings is sufficient to put the piece of furniture together in a matter of minutes.

Unfortunately, many software systems encountered today are built and continue to be built like monolithic applications, that limit the functionality and the ability of users to integrate them with other applications. The challenge facing the information technology world is to transform the application development from a process in which everything is done from scratch, into a process where software engineers, and even end-users, put together pieces of premade software objects into fully fledged and fully functional applications. These components can be purchased independently from manufacturers that specialize in their production and testing, much like we buy nails or paint in our local hardware store.

OLE is the framework that allows the integration of these software objects into one application. OLE provides the protocol that enables products made by different vendors to communicate and exchange information with each other. This protocol is defined at the binary, or machine language level, and is not dependent on any programming language. This means that the OLE framework will accommodate objects created with procedural and object-oriented languages alike, as long as these objects contain the necessary binary information.

23.1.2 COMPONENT SOFTWARE TECHNOLOGY

OLE is not an application development environment. It is an architecture that integrates object-based software services. A number of these services are provided by the OLE framework; additional customized services may be created and added to the framework. Every application that follows the OLE protocol may use any of these services, no matter who developed them or when, where, and how they were developed. In other words, the fact that Oracle Forms conforms to the OLE standards allows you to use any of the services provided by other OLE service providers such as word processing, spreadsheets, graphics, sound, and video. Thinking in terms of the metaphorical house, OLE tells you the standard jacks to install. These very same standards are followed by electrical appliance manufacturers. This ensures that you will be able to plug and use anywhere around the house a VCR, a TV set, a stereo, or an iron. OLE brings to software engineering common sense standards established long ago in other industries.

On the other hand, OLE is an extendible architecture of services. As new services become available, they can replace or be added to existing ones without affecting the rest of the application that uses them. When a new version of the word processor embedded in the Forms application becomes available, all you will need to do is install the new version, without having to modify the form module itself. Just like when replacing the ten-year-old TV set with a home entertainment center, you simply plug in the new equipment in an existing jack, without having to rewire the electrical circuits of the house.

Each OLE service is provided by a particular application called the OLE server. For example, word processing is a service that may be provided by applications such as MS Word or WordPerfect. The service contains one or more software components. For example, MS Word has a text editing component, a drawing component, and a chart editing component. These components are made up of one or more objects. Word.Basic, for example, is an object that is part of the text editing component of MS Word. Each object has several attributes, properties, and methods associated with it. Semantically related methods and features are bound together in groups called interfaces. OLE ensures communication between services through their interfaces. OLE cannot and does not allow access to internal or private variables of an object. The only way to access the service is by going through its interface.

Remember that all this is done at binary level and is language independent. Thus, OLE extends the object-oriented paradigm from the source code language-dependent level to the machine language level. Objects normally developed with object-oriented tools remain isolated until OLE features are added to them. Their interaction with other objects is limited within the boundaries of the application of which they are a part. When these objects become part of an OLE software component, some or all of their functionality is exposed to the other components through the interfaces. These interfaces allow components to be plugged into other applications that may have been developed in an entirely different programming environment, from a different vendor.

23.1.3 OLE CLIENTS AND OLE SERVERS

The OLE technology uses the concepts of client and server like other technologies in the computer world. The client is an application that requests and uses the services of another application. The server is the one who provides these services. The Component Object Model (COM) is the fundamental layer of OLE technology that ensures the integration between clients and servers. Based on this model, when an OLE client requests a service, it is really asking to interface with the component of a server. All the available components with which the client can interface are registered during the installation process of their respective software packages in the registry database of the machine. The client will pick from this database the component to interface with, or rather an internal class identifier (CLSID) of this component. This unique identifier is used to start the server application, instantiate a new copy of the object in memory, and return to the client an interface pointer for the object. Recall that in the OLE terminology, the interface is a set of methods used to access, modify, or act upon an object. This means that this interface pointer will display to the client all the functionality of the server.

Suppose, for example, that you want to add text editing services to your Oracle Forms application. You have to query the registry database for word processors installed in your machine. When you pick one, say MS Word, you are sending its unique internal class identifier to the OLE mechanism of Windows. This mechanism uses this CLSID to retrieve, from the registry, information about the directory in which Word is installed and how to start it up. Windows uses this information to start the server, and instantiate a Word object. The pointer to this new instance of Word is returned to Forms, which uses it to access all the functionality that this application provides.

23.1.4 THE REGISTRY DATABASE

This database is a file called REG.DAT, stored in the Windows directory, for example, C:\WINDOWS. Its contents are updated and maintained by the Windows shell and change as programs are installed on the machine. You can also view or edit its contents using the Registration Information Editor, also known as *regedit*. You can run this program by selecting File I Run from the Program Manager of File Manager menu, and entering regedit in the command line field. The first window you will see is similar to Figure 23.1. It lists all the programs installed in your machine.

The registry database is not used only for OLE services, therefore you will see programs in this window that do not support OLE, such as Card File. If you double-click an entry in the list you will see the Modify File Type dialog box. This dialog box allows you to view and edit the data that control the behavior of Windows when a file associated with a particular program is opened from the File Manager or Program Manager.

You are interested however in the contents of this database used to identify programs as OLE servers. In order to see this information you need to run the advanced interface of the Registration Information Editor:

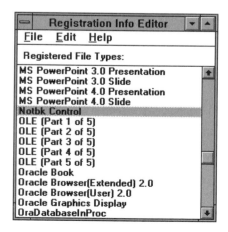

FIGURE 23.1   Registration Information Editor.

1. Choose File | Run from the menu of File Manager or Program Manager.
2. Enter regedit /v in the command line field. The Registration Info Editor dialog box will be displayed (see Figure 23.2).

Figure 23.2 shows the contents of the registry for MS Word 6.0 application. The long string of digits enclosed in the curly brackets is the class identifier CLSID. This is also displayed in the Full Path field. Note the LocalServer item which points to the path where Word is currently installed: C:\WINWORD \WINWORD.EXE. This is where Windows will search for the server to activate during OLE processes. Figure 23.2 contains other data items such as DefaultIcon or Verb; the meaning of which will be discussed in the coming sections. Note also the last three lines, which identify the server Word Basic. This server generates Word objects that will be used in OLE Automation processes discussed in Chapter 24.

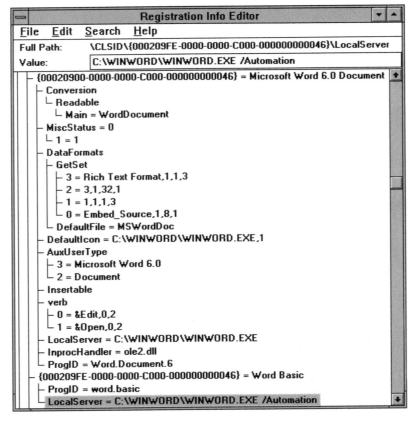

FIGURE 23.2   Detailed view of Registration Information Editor.

23.2 OLE DOCUMENTS TECHNOLOGY

OLE Documents is a part of OLE technologies—a significant one, as a matter of fact—that handles the process of creating and managing compound documents. Specifically, it deals with the embedding or linking of objects from OLE servers in the body of OLE client applications. Compound documents initially were text processing files where users needed to insert drawings, pictures, spreadsheets, or, in general, data from other applications. The existing capabilities of Windows, such as Clipboard operations, were not sufficient to meet these needs. Often, during the Cut and Paste actions, data were lost. In the cases when the operation was successful, meaningful data, such as rows and columns from a spreadsheet, were replaced by pictures in metafile or bitmap format, where most of the original content of data was lost. Object Linking and Embedding, OLE 1, was born to satisfy such needs. OLE 2 was the effort to fix the flaws of the original design and extend the original architecture of OLE. The extension was such that it now supports a whole range of other OLE technologies such as Property Pages and OLE controls. Therefore, the original functionality of OLE (creation and maintenance of compound documents), is now called OLE Documents.

The meaning of documents has changed as well. Today a compound document does not have to be a file produced with a text editor. Any application that implements the client side of the OLE Documents technology enables itself to store and manipulate objects created by any OLE server. The support of Oracle Forms for this technology makes it possible to create front-end applications that provide not only strong database features, but also the functionality and features of an array of other applications. The OLE concept of code reusability at the binary level allows you to use the inventive work of other programmers as if it was yours, without violating any of their intellectual property rights. Furthermore, the support of the Oracle7 database for LONG RAW datatype columns provides you with a way to permanently and dynamically bind up to two gigabytes of text, pictures, multi-media, and other types of files, with the record structures in which you organize the data. The following sections discuss how to implement linking and embedding of OLE components in Oracle Forms applications.

23.2.1 THE COMPOSERS APPLICATION

In this part, you will work with the application COMPOSER.FMB while different components of object linking and embedding are explained. This is a simple two-block form, whose layout is shown in Figure 23.3.

The block COMPOSER contains biographical information about composers such as name, date of birth, death, and nationality. The block WORK contains a listing of works from these composers. Both of these blocks correspond to database tables with the same names. As you see in the picture, the original template of the application contains ample free space to the right of both blocks. You will

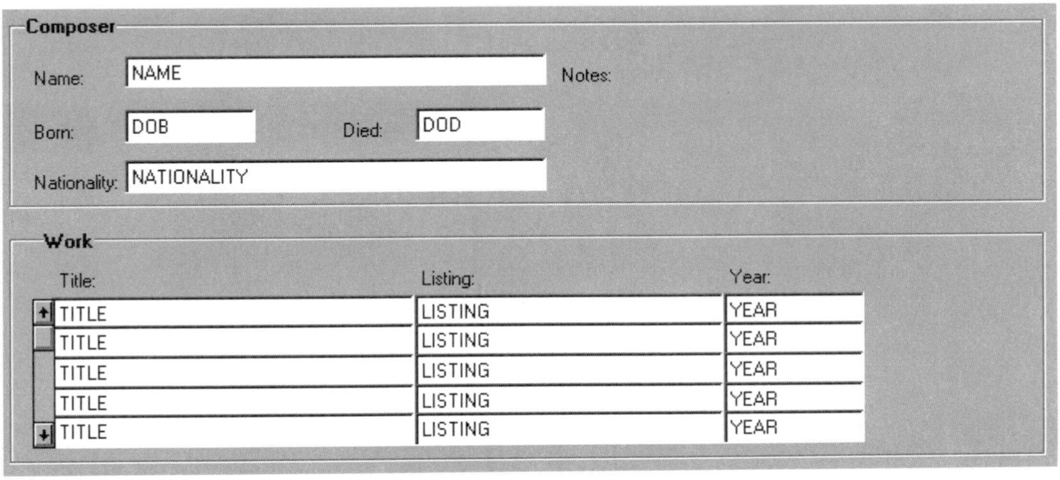

FIGURE 23.3   Layout of module COMPOSER.FMB.

fill this space in the following sections with two OLE containers. These items will allow you at runtime to store biographical information about composers and samples of their music in the database. The information can be queried, viewed, played, and edited like any other data element in the form module.

As a preliminary step, open the module COMPOSER.FMB in the Oracle Forms Designer, generate, and run it to become familiar with the kind of data that the tables contain.

23.2.2   OLE CONTAINERS IN ORACLE FORMS

In this section you will create a container in the COMPOSER block that will help users store samples of works from different composers in the database:

1. Open the canvas COMPOSER in the Layout Editor and set the context to the block COMPOSER.
2. Click the OLE2 Object icon ▣ in the tool palette, and create the OLE container in the space to the right of the text label **Notes** in this block.
3. Double-click the newly created item to display its Properties Window. You will see that the *Item Type* property for the item is set to *'OLE Container'*.
4. Set the name of the item to BIOGRAPHY and the property *Items Displayed* to *'1'*.

While you still are in the Properties Window, let us discuss the **Functional** properties of the OLE container items.

FIGURE 23.4   OLE Menu dialog box.

The *OLE In-Place Activation* property is set to *'False'* by default. This means that the object will be activated in a window of its own, different from the window in which your application is running. If you want to activate the object within the borders of the OLE container in the form, set this property to *'True'*. Section 23.3 will discuss this property in more detail. Closely related with this setting is also the property *OLE Do In Out*, which will be discussed in that section as well.

The *OLE Activation Style* controls how you in the Designer, or the users at runtime will activate the object in the OLE container. The default setting is *'Double-click'*. If you want the object to become active as soon as the focus moves on it, set the property to *'Focus-in'*. If the setting of this property is *'Manual'*, you can activate the object only by selecting an item from the popup menu displayed when you right-click the object.

The ability of the OLE object to respond to the right-click event is controlled by the property *Show OLE Popup Menu*, which by default is set to *'True'*. You can see the items in the popup menu by double-clicking the property *OLE Popup Menu Items*. The OLE Menu dialog box will appear (see Figure 23.4).

By default, all the items in the list are displayed in the popup menu. Their availability is determined by the object and clipboard contents. For example, if there is nothing copied in the clipboard, the item Paste will be disabled. You will never see the label Object of the last item in this list. This label will be replaced by the name of the actual object you will store in the container.

Note

From all the properties of the Functional group for OLE Container items, the *OLE Popup Menu Items* is the only one that can be manipulated programmatically, as well as in the Designer. You can use the built-ins GET_ITEM_PROPERTY and SET_ITEM_PROPERTY to retrieve and set its settings as you would do for any other property.

The property *OLE Resize Style* controls how the object is displayed inside the container. *'Crop'* is the default setting and means that the object will be cropped to fit the size of the container defined in the Designer. If the setting is *'Scale'*, the object is reduced or enlarged as necessary to fit the container. This is used mostly for pictures and bitmap objects. If the setting is *'Initial'*, it is the container that will be resized to fit the size of the OLE object. However, this is done only when the object is initially created. Subsequent retrievals of the object do not change the dimensions of the container. If you want the container to adjust its size so that it fits the object in any situation, set the property to *'Dynamic'*.

The *OLE Tenant Types* property defines the type of objects that reside within the OLE container. These objects can either be embedded or linked, but there can also be objects that were linked previously and the link is broken presently. The next sections will discuss these type of objects. If you want the OLE container in your form to host any of these types of objects, set its *OLE Tenant Types* property to *'Any'*. This is also the default setting. If you do not want any objects to reside in the container, set the property to *'None'*. This is not a particularly useful setting. If the container should host only embedded or linked objects, set the property to *'Embedded'* or *'Linked'*. In the case when the object was previously linked and the link is broken, set the property *OLE Tenant Types* to *'Static'*. This will display only an image of the object previously linked.

The property *Show OLE Tenant Type*, when set to *'True'* as it is by default, is supposed to indicate the type of object that resides in the container. However, this setting does not have any visual effects on the borders of the OLE container item.

The way the OLE object is displayed within the container is also controlled by the property *OLE Tenant Aspect*. By default, this property is set to *'Content'*, which means that the content of the object will be displayed inside the container according to the setting of property *OLE Resize Style*. If the *OLE Tenant Aspect* is set to *'Icon'*, the container will represent the OLE object as an icon. This setting should be coordinated with the way the object is created, in the Insert dialog box, which we will discuss in the following sections. The property can also be set to *'Thumbnail Preview'*, which offers a reduced version of the object.

Last, but not least, is the property *OLE Class*. By default, this property is not set, which means that you in the Designer or your users at runtime can insert OLE objects from any class that is available in the machine. If you want to restrict the contents of the container to only one particular class, double-click this property in the Properties Window for the item. A List of Values dialog box will appear with all the OLE classes currently installed in your machine (see Figure 23.5).

If, for example, you select ExcelChart from the list, the only objects that can be inserted in the container will be MS Excel charts, produced by this class. As you can see, you can either restrict the contents of the item to be OLE objects from one class only, or you cannot restrict them at all.

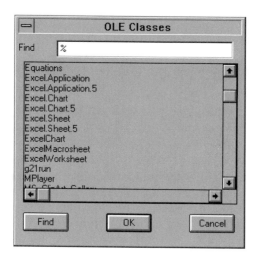

FIGURE 23.5   OLE Classes List Of Values dialog box.

23.2.3   EMBEDDING OBJECTS IN ORACLE FORMS

In the COMPOSER.FMB module, you will implement the item BIOGRAPHY as an OLE container that will store embedded objects. First size its dimensions in the Layout Editor to a rectangle that fills the empty space left to the right of the other data items in the block COMPOSER. Then follow these steps:

1. Double-click the object to display its Properties Window.
2. Set the *OLE Tenant Types* property to '*Embedding*'.
3. Save and generate the module.

Now, take off your designer hat and run the module to see how you would work with the new OLE container in the form from a users perspective. Query the COMPOSER block for composer Franz Liszt.

1. Move the mouse pointer over the OLE container created previously and right-click. The popup menu for OLE items is displayed. If you had nothing copied in the clipboard, you will notice that only the Insert Object... item in this menu is enabled. Otherwise, Paste and Paste Special... will also be enabled.
2. Select Insert Object... from the popup menu. The Insert Object dialog box will appear (see Figure 23.6).

   In this dialog box, you can select the type of object to insert in the container from the text list. The contents of this list are determined by the setting of *OLE Class* property in the Designer, and by the OLE classes currently stored in the Windows registry. Because you did not set the *OLE Class* property for this item, Windows is showing all the OLE objects that are currently installed in the machine.

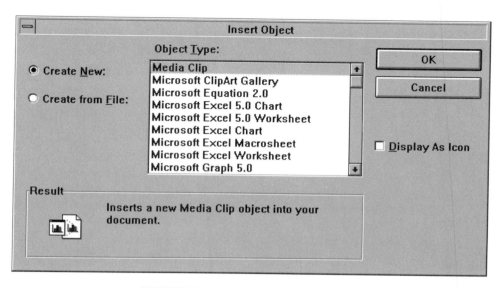

FIGURE 23.6   Insert Object dialog box.

3. Scroll down the list and select the object type Microsoft Word 6.0 Document. You will notice that the message in the Result text box will change according to the object currently selected.
4. Click OK.

At this point two things may happen. If MS Word is not running, Windows will launch it and create a new document window with the title Document in Unnamed. If you were working with Word previously, the application will be activated and the same new document window will be created. The MS Word File menu is also slightly different from what you see normally:

❏ The menu item Close now appears as Close and Return to Unnamed. By selecting this item, you will close the window and return to Oracle Forms. Word will prompt you to save any changes you may have made.

❏ The menu item Save is now replaced by Update. The normal Save operation in Word now updates the Oracle Forms container item with the contents of the document.

❏ The menu item Save All is replaced by Save and Update All. When you select this item, Word will save any open file documents, and will update any OLE container with the data from their corresponding documents.

The Forms application has changed slightly as well. If you switch to it, you will notice that the OLE container item that you are editing in Word is displayed with diagonal lines across it. This is an indicator that the object is being edited. The rest of the application is in its normal state and you can continue to enter and edit data in the other items. However, you should keep in mind how Oracle Forms processes its transactions. For example, if in the middle of editing the Biography in a Word document, you return to Forms and navigate to another record in the COMPOSER block, Forms will simply disconnect its link with MS Word, which in turn will close the window without saving any of the new changes.

In the MS Word document that represents the notes for Liszt enter the text shown in Figure 23.7. Select File | Close and Return to Unnamed from the Word menu.

Figure 23.7 purposely shows the horizontal ruler for the document. As you can see, the width of the document is reduced so that the entire line fits inside the OLE container in the Forms module. The left margin is also shifted right, so that the bullets do not appear attached to the left border of the container. These are cosmetic changes intended to make the document readable without requiring the users to access Word in edit mode to see its contents.

In the case described above, you created the embedded Word document from scratch. It is also possible to create it based on an existing file. Query the record for Chopin in the block and follow the first two steps described previously to insert a MS Word object in the Notes container. In the Insert Object dialog box (see Figure 23.6), click the radio button Create from File. The dialog box will be transformed as shown in Figure 23.8.

The OLE object classes in Figure 23.5 are now replaced by a text item where you can specify the name of the file that you want to embed:

1. Click the Browse... button to display a standard dialog box that allows you to select the file you want to embed.
2. Select the file CHOPIN.DOC located in the same directory where the module COMPOSER.FMB is installed. Notice that when you select this file, the words Microsoft Word 6.0 will appear above the text field. Based on the selection you made, Windows queries the registration database for the name

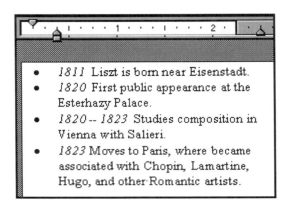

FIGURE 23.7   Editing and embedded OLE document.

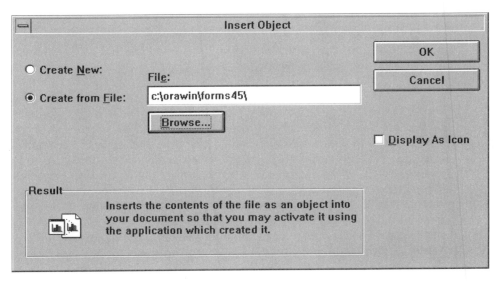

FIGURE 23.8   Insert Object dialog box with the Create from File option checked.

of the OLE class that created the file. This name is passed to Oracle Forms, which will prepare its container to store the new object.

3. Click OK to complete the task.

23.2.4   CONVERTING EMBEDDED OBJECTS

The problem you tried to solve when creating the document for the first record applies to the second one as well. The document contained in the file CHOPIN.DOC is a normal size document, and only the upper left part of it appears inside the container. In fact, unless the documents you will embed have only a few lines, you will always be faced with the problem of the actual size of the document being larger than the actual size of the container. You can alter the setting of *OLE Resize Style* property, however, none of the other alternatives offers a problem-free solution. *'Scale'*, as said earlier, should be used with pictures and graphics. If the object contains text, the letters will be scrambled and will overlap each other in the scaling process. The other two settings, *'Dynamic'* and *'Initial'*, which size the container according to the dimensions of the document, are not desirable if you expect the document to be large. A full-page or multi-page document will cover other items in the form.

One solution, which should always be considered for large-size objects, is to display them as icons. As a user, you can do this by following these steps:

1. Right-click the OLE object to display its popup menu. Note that the last item of this menu, by default called Object, now is called Document Object to reflect the type of object embedded.

2. Select Document Object from the popup menu. Another smaller menu appears.

3. Select Convert..., which is the last item in the menu. The Convert dialog box appears (see Figure 23.9).

The current type of object is displayed in the upper part of this window. The Object Type list box in the center of the dialog displays the types to which the current object could be possibly converted. If, for example, WordPerfect is installed, it will appear in the list and both radio buttons to the left would be enabled. If you select the first radio button, the object will be converted from Word to WordPerfect document. If you select the second button, the object will be activated as a WordPerfect document. This is a very important advantage provided by the OLE mechanism. It allows you to create and embed data with one class, and view the data with every other compatible OLE class. The fact that MS Word was used to create notes for these two composers does not prevent users who have WordPerfect or AmiPro installed in their desktops from viewing and manipulating these data. The OLE functionality will ensure that the appropriate conversions occur, just as when file documents are converted from one tool to another.

To display the embedded object as an icon, check the check box Display as Icon to the right of the dialog. As soon as you do this, one of the MS Word icons will be displayed, with the label Document displayed underneath. Notice also that the message in the text box in the lower part of the window will change to reflect the fact that the object will now be displayed as an icon. Click the push button Change Icon... to display the Change Icon dialog box (see Figure 23.10).

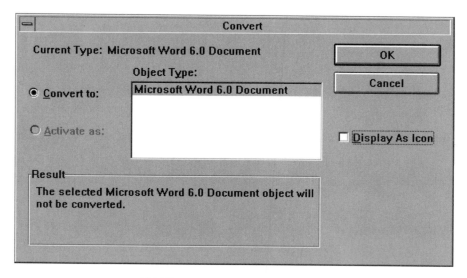

FIGURE 23.9   Convert dialog box.

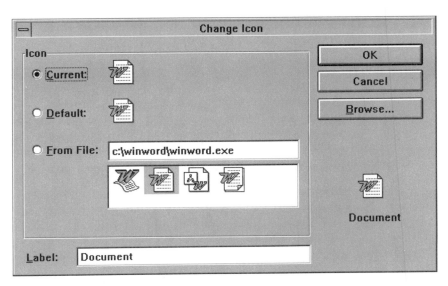

FIGURE 23.10   Change Icon dialog box.

In this dialog box, the radio button Current displays the icon currently selected in the previous dialog. The default icon, the file that contains the icon, and its
position inside the file are also displayed. Where is this information stored? If you
look back at Figure 23.2 which contains the registration information for MS Word in
the Windows Registry, you will see that there is an entry there, called DefaultIcon,
which points to the file name and position for the icon. If you want to change the
default setting, pick one of the available icons in the WINDWORD.EXE file, or click
the push button Browse... to search for another icon file in the directory tree. After
you select the icon and click OK in both dialog boxes, you will return back to the
form. Now the embedded object is represented only by the icon you have chosen.

If you expect all the objects that will be embedded in a container to be too
large to fit inside the container, you may want to set their display status to an
icon from the Designer. You can do this by setting their *OLE Tenant Aspect* property to *'Icon'*. This will not guarantee that the objects will be displayed as such
though. Users must still choose to display the object as an icon when creating the
object. They do this by checking the check box Display as Icon in the Insert Object
dialog box (see Figure 23.6 and Figure 23.8).

23.2.5   VERBS OF EMBEDDED OBJECTS

In the previous section you were asked to display the popup menu and then the
submenu associated with the last item, Document Object. Besides the option Convert Object, this submenu contains two other items, which are known as the verbs
of the OLE object. These verbs represent the interface that the OLE object exposes

Note

There is a pitfall here in the way Oracle Forms updates the display of its data items. After you convert the item to display its data as an icon, you would think that the record should be flagged for an update. However, if you commit the data, Forms will display the message, **FRM-40401: No changes to save.** If you re-query the block, the record that comes from the database will still be displayed as before. Your new instruction to display as an icon is lost.

So, did the item change or not? This is an evasive question, which can be answered with either a Yes or a No. By converting the item to an icon you did not change the contents of the Word document, which leads Forms to believe that no change occurred. Therefore, the record is not marked for an update. However, for embedded objects, Forms stores to the database not simply the contents of the object, but also side information such as the fact that the object should be displayed as an icon. When you change these settings, the OLE container should be considered as changed.

To overcome this inconsistency, after you convert the OLE object to an icon, force an update on the container item by opening its contents in the server application window and closing the window right away. You do not need to do any changes, because simply invoking the OLE server will make Forms believe that the item changed.

The fact that an OLE container is flagged for update as soon as its contents are displayed in a server window, is of course another inconsistency in the implementation of OLE objects by Oracle Forms.

It is interesting to mention that going in the opposite direction does not create any of these problems. In other words, if you change the display mode of an object from Icon to Normal, the change will be stored in the database.

to client applications, or, in other words, actions that can be performed on the object.

Usually every embedded object has a verb called Edit, which allows you to modify the contents of the object in the server application. Then, most of the document-based OLE servers offer on Open verb which opens the documents. These two verbs are synonymous for embedded objects. Multimedia servers such as MS Video for Windows or Soundo'LE have a verb called Play which allows you to play the contents of the object. When the OLE server is installed, together

```
├─ PlayerFrameClass = Quick Time Movie
  ├─ CLSID = {00044EBB-0000-0000-C000-000000000046}
  └─ protocol
     └─ StdFileEditing
        ├─ server = c:\windows\player.exe
        ├─ verb
        │  ├─ 0 = &Playback
        │  ├─ 1 = &Activate Movie Player
        │  └─ 2 = Play &Options...
        └─ Handler = c:\windows\system\qthndlr.dll
```

FIGURE 23.11   Verbs for an OLE class.

with other information, it also registers its verbs with the Windows registry. It is here that you can look up the verbs supported by any application. Looking back at Figure 23.1, you can see that the verbs for MS Word are Edit and Open. Figure 23.11 shows the contents recorded in the Registration Database for the application Quick Time Movie Player™ by Apple Computer, Inc.

The verb that is listed first is the action that will be executed when the OLE object is double-clicked in the container.

23.3   IN-PLACE ACTIVATION OF EMBEDDED OBJECTS

In all the examples you have worked with so far, the OLE server applications are displayed in their own windows, separate from the Forms application that invoked them. In a sense, the focus in this approach is placed on the application. When users work with the form module, they are in an Oracle Forms window; when they need to edit the biographical notes for some composer, they switch to MS Word. Although this is the way the software tools work internally, there is no reason why this should be transparent to the users. They would be more interested to work with an application that is centered around one document, and does not require switching back and forth between different windows.

One of the great improvements that were implemented by OLE 2 is the ability to bring all the necessary functionality for editing an embedded object inside the OLE container of the document. The approach is very elegant, because instead of asking users to go to the OLE server to edit the application, the internal negotiation between the client and the server, all based on the OLE protocol, brings the application to the user. This extended functionality of embedded objects is called in-place activation.

In order to enable an OLE container item for in-place activation, you must set its *In-Place Activation* property to *'True'*. Do so for the item BIOGRAPHY in the

> ## Note
>
> In his book *Inside OLE*, Kraig Brockschmidt tells the story of how people at Microsoft, with the contribution of their marketing folks, managed to rename the functionality several times. The original name, *in-situ editing*, was found to be too academic. For fear that not too many programmers would grasp the meaning of the Latin word, it was changed to *in-place editing*. However, since the new OLE was much wider than just editing compound documents, the term *editing* was replaced with *activation*. Then, in the euphoric move to place a visual in front of everything, the term was changed to *Visual Editing*(™). The trademark was obtained for the new name as well. Therefore, depending on who you talk to, and what kind of literature you read, you may encounter all of these terms.

block COMPOSER. In addition, rearrange the items in this block, so that they look like Figure 23.12.

The reason for this rearrangement is to enlarge the dimensions of the OLE container. Now that the editing will be in-place, Word will enlarge or reduce the view of the document proportionally with the width of the container. As shown in Figure 23.12, the document will be displayed approximately at normal size. But if you reduce the width of the item to half, the view of the document will be only 50%. This will make it very hard to see the characters being typed. Remember that this will not affect the way characters look after the editing is completed, only while Word is active.

After these arrangements, save, generate and execute the form. For any record, double-click the OLE container. You will notice that the OLE container will yield to a MS Word document in which you can enter your notes. Pay attention to the fact that the Oracle Forms menu is now replaced by the MS Word

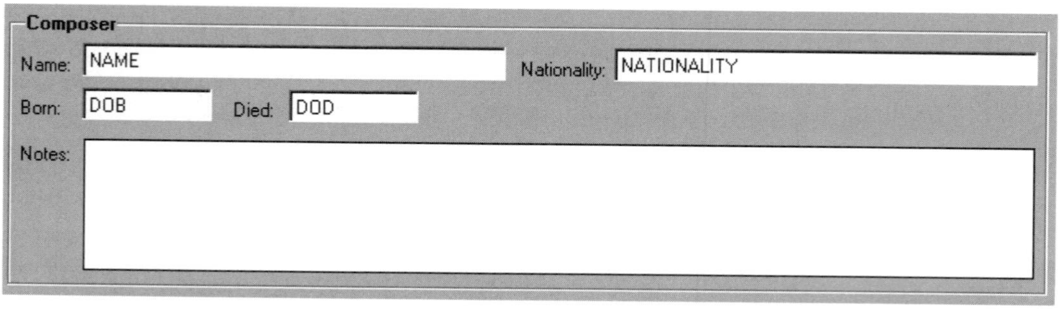

FIGURE 23.12 Block COMPOSER rearranged.

menu and toolbars (see Figure 23.13). For all purposes, you are in Word, just as before, except that now you do not have to do the editing in another window.

The container is now surrounded by a hatched border line. As you move the mouse over the border you will see it change shape to indicate that you can move the container around the window, or you can resize it to your needs. The position and dimensions will be valid only while you are editing. As soon as you click outside the hatched border, the container will return to its original size and the text you entered will be displayed inside of it.

Notice that the Word menu for this type of embedded object is a little different from what you are used to seeing. The main difference is that the File submenu disappears altogether. It is assumed that the client application will perform all the actions that normally go under this menu. While for other applications this may not be a draw-back, in Forms, this fact will not allow you, for example, to print the contents of the document directly to the printer, which you could do in other cases.

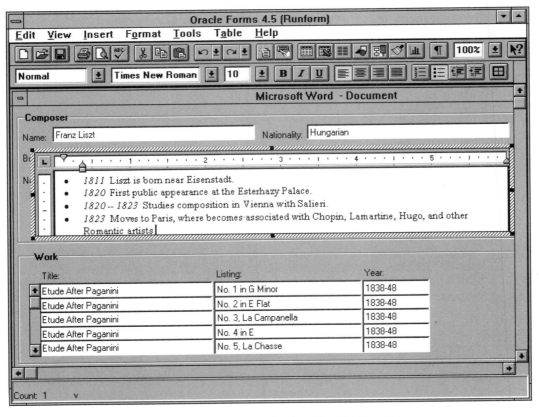

FIGURE 23.13 In-Place activation of an OLE container.

> ## Note
>
> If you have more than one embedded object with the *OLE In-Place Activation* property set to '*True*', by default, the editing window can be active for each of them at the same time. This is because the property *OLE Do In Out* is set to '*True*'. If you want the window of an object to be deactivated even if users activate the editing window of another object, set this property to '*False*'.

Another difference is that all the items in the View menu that allow you to control the view size of the document are disabled. This is also true for the Zoom Control drop-down list box in the toolbar. This is the reason why you had to size the item in the Designer, so that the view offered is one with which users can work comfortably.

23.4   LINKING OBJECTS IN ORACLE FORMS

As you were working through the examples discussed in the previous sections, you probably experienced some performance problems during the update and retrieval of records, especially if you are accessing the database across a busy network. The reason is the amount of data that was associated with each embedded object that you inserted in the database. Although you entered only a few lines in the biographical notes of the composers, Oracle Forms had to store all the native data required to instruct the embedded objects to start themselves up the next time you need to edit them. This is how the embedding is designed to work.

In a compound document, embedding objects from other application servers will increase the size of the file to which the document is saved. This eventually could lead to problems, because the larger the size of the file, the longer it will take the application to open and load it into memory. It is easier to reach the critical point where deterioration of the performance becomes noticeable if the file is loaded in a file server. It is even easier to reach this point when a third processing party—the database server—is added to the picture.

In order to alleviate the burden of the application, linking of objects should be considered as a serious alternative. Functionality-wise there is no difference between linking and embedding. The container treats the objects equally, by executing the same code, no matter whether they are linked or embedded. The only difference is that an embedded object, as said earlier, encapsulates within itself all the data, whereas the data for a linked object reside elsewhere, in a file. The object stored in the client container is just a pictorial representation of the data, with a pointer to the location of the file where the rest of the data resides.

In this section, you will link some of the records of works of composers with 60-second samples of these works. The sound files were recorded using the standard Windows Sound Recorder and can be played using the Microsoft's Media Player or any other application that support the feature.

Start by creating a container in the WORK block where these samples will be stored:

1. Set the content in the Layout Editor to the block WORK.
2. Click the OLE2 Object icon 🔳 in the tool palette, and create the OLE container to the right of the YEAR column. You will see that Designer will create five objects, one for each displayed record in the block.
3. Double-click the newly created item to display its Properties Window.
4. Set the name of the item to WORK and the property *Items Displayed* in the **Records** group to '1'.

Now, set some of the **Functional** properties of the item to fit your situation.

1. Set the property *OLE Tenant Type* to '*Linked*'. Users can link the files even if this property is set to '*Any*', but this setting would not prevent them from embedding these files. You must avoid embedding especially for multimedia files which are quite large.
2. Set the property *OLE Class* to '*Mplayer*', or any other sound playing application that you have installed in your machine. This is another difference with the way you used the OLE objects in the previous sections. There you could enter any type of data for the composer, a document with biographical data,

---

Note

These pointers, called *monikers*, are not what is normally understood when the term is used in programming languages such as C or C++. They are not as simple as the name of the file where the data is stored either. The normal file name is just a string of characters. An application does not know what to do with it, unless some additional instructions accompany it. The monikers are OLE constructs that encapsulate names with instructions on what to do with these names. These instructions primarily direct the moniker to find the object with that name and to return a pointer to the interface or the set of methods, that the object offers to the outside world. *Moniker* is a British slang for nickname.

a portrait in picture format, or a video clip. Here, you are narrowing the scope of objects to only sound objects.

3. Set the property *OLE Tenant Aspect* to *'Icon'*. This is how you would normally display objects such as sound or video clips.

4. Return in the Layout Editor and set the dimensions of the container to a size appropriate to display an icon.

Save, generate, and run the module to use the new functionality from a user's perspective.

1. Query the record for Franz Liszt, and click on the record that represents its third etude after Paganini, also known as **La Campanella**.

2. Right-click the OLE container and choose Insert Object... from the popup menu. The Insert Object dialog box appears. This looks very similar to the one shown in Figure 23.8. However, if you read carefully the contents of the text box at the bottom of the window and compare them with Figure 23.8, you can realize the different context in which you are operating now. While in the previous sections you were embedding the object to the OLE container, here only a picture of the file will be inserted, and a link will be established between this picture and the file itself.

3. Click Browse... and locate the file LISZT03.WAV stored in the same directory as the module COMPOSER.FMB.

4. Check the Display As Icon check box.

5. Click OK to return to the Forms application.

At this point, you can double-click the icon to listen to the music. You can also select the verb Play from the popup menu. If you select the verb Edit, the application server will run, and the sound file will be loaded, so that you can edit it.

Pay attention to an item in the popup menu which was disabled when you were working with embedded objects, but is enabled now. This is Links.... Select it and you will see the Links dialog box similar to Figure 23.14.

The central area of this dialog repeats the information displayed at the bottom. The Source is the name and location of the file linked to the OLE object. The Type corresponds to the OLE class that produced the object. The update mode by default is Automatic. This means that whenever the contents of the file change, the modifications will be seen immediately and automatically by the OLE container. If the radio item Manual is checked instead, the only way to update the OLE container is to click the button Update Now in the Links dialog box.

In this dialog box, you can also change the file linked with the OLE container by clicking the Change Source... button. A standard dialog box will be dis-

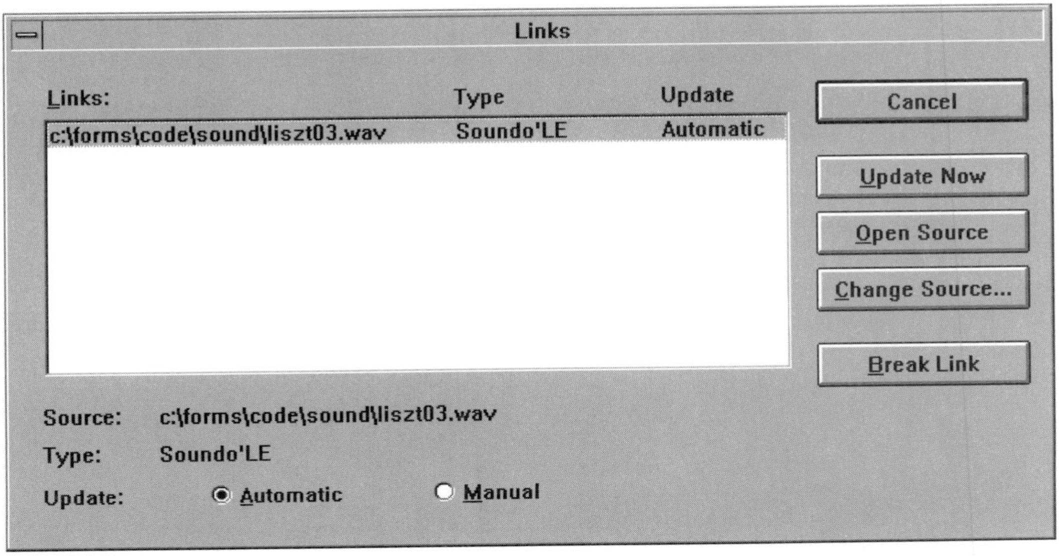

FIGURE 23.14   Links dialog box.

played which you can use to search for the new file. If you want to launch the server application, click the button Open Source. This will also close the Links dialog box. Note that this action is equivalent to selecting Edit from the popup menu of the OLE object.

Finally, if you click the button Break Link, the link between the OLE container and the file will be disrupted. You will be left with just a static picture of the object, and any editing functionality will be lost. In this case only the icon would remain after you break the link. If the object is an Excel graph, what remains after the link with the source file is broken is just a pictorial representation of the chart, with no data or editing capabilities behind it.

Note

The theme of the music in the file you were working with in this section comes from the third movement of Paganini's second violin concerto, which is also called "La Campanella." In that movement, you can hear the sound of a little bell that accompanies the music in the background. In Italian, the word for a small bell is *campanella*.

23.5 LINKING AND EMBEDDING IN ORACLE FORMS DESIGNER

When you define an Oracle Forms item as an OLE container, you can use all of the features discussed so far from the Designer, as well as at runtime. You should be cautious about how you use the functionality, though. Linking or embedding an object in the Designer is similar to setting the *Default Value* property for a normal item. Whenever a new record is created, its OLE container will be populated with the object that you stored there at design time. This may result in objects being saved unnecessarily in the database.

However, you can use the Designer to see the effects of different settings for the properties of the OLE items. You can also size the containers to the right dimensions. For example, in Section 23.3, several objects were embedded in the BIOGRAPHY item until the right size of the object was found.

23.6 MANIPULATING COMPOUND DOCUMENTS PROGRAMMATICALLY

There are occasions when you want to modify the default interface provided by the OLE functionality, in order to make the application more robust, or to protect the data from unwarranted modifications. In the example discussed in the previous section, users are free to edit and modify the contents of the records files at their will. In a corporate-wide application, only authorized users may have the privilege to edit such data. The rest of the users who create links to these files, should be able to view the data, or play the recording in this case, but not modify them.

Oracle Forms provides a PL/SQL package, called FORMS_OLE, which allows you to simulate programmatically the functionality between the OLE client and OLE server applications. In this section, you will use components of this package to create an interface such that users can link sound files to the OLE containers, play these files, or break the links at their will. However, they will be forbidden from editing these files.

You will continue work with the module COMPOSER.FMB and with the block WORK in particular.

1. Display the Properties Window for the OLE container item WORK.
2. Make sure that the property *OLE Tenant Type* is still set to 'Linked', *OLE Class* to 'Mplayer', and *OLE Tenant Aspect* to 'Icon'.
3. Set the *OLE Activation Style* property to 'Manual'. This will prevent users from activating the object by double-clicking or placing the focus in the item.

4. Double-click the property *OLE Popup Menu Items* to display the OLE Menu dialog box as shown in Figure 23.4.

5. Select the last item in the list, called Object, and uncheck the check box Enable.

With these settings, you have left the users only the possibility to insert objects from one specific class—Mplayer. By disabling the Object menu item, you are not allowing them to access the verbs of these objects. This way you are globally blocking their interface with the object, so that you can take control and grant them access only to the functionality you want.

Give the users back the ability to play the sound files:

1. Create a push button in the block WORK.

2. Set its *Name* and *Label* to 'Play', and set its *Items Displayed* property to '1'.

3. Size the button and place it below the OLE container on the canvas.

4. Create a WHEN-BUTTON-PRESSED trigger for the button, and enter in the body of the trigger the statements shown in Figure 23.15.

In the first group of statements in the trigger, the internal ID of the item is retrieved. Then, the function FORMS_OLE.SERVER_ACTIVE is used to check whether the server application is currently running or not. This function returns a Boolean value of TRUE if the server is running and FALSE if not. This value is stored in a variable.

Immediately after the call to function FORMS_OLE.SERVER_ACTIVE, you check if an error occurred or not. The reason for this check is that the users may be trying to play an item that is not inserted yet. In this case, the call to the previous function will generate the error message, **FRM-41344: OLE object not defined for WORK in the current record.** In the trigger, this error message is followed with an instruction on what to do to insert an object.

If the server is not running, the function FORMS_OLE.ACTIVATE_SERVER will start it up. This function establishes a bridge between the OLE container and the server application. The function FORMS_OLE.CLOSE_SERVER has the reverse effect of breaking this connection.

The function FORMS_OLE.GET_VERB_COUNT returns the number of verbs defined for the object. Since this number is returned in a character format, you convert it to numeric format in order to use it as the upper bound for a loop that will search for the verb Play in the list of available verbs. Inside the loop, the function FORMS_OLE.GET_VERB_NAME is used to retrieve the name of the verb based on the index value. When the verb Play is found, the procedure FORMS_OLE.EXEC_VERB is used to actually invoke the action that this verb represents. This is equivalent to selecting the verb from the popup menu of the OLE object.

```
DECLARE
  container_id    Item;
  container_name  VARCHAR2(60):='WORK.WORK';
  running         BOOLEAN;
  verb_count      VARCHAR2(10);
  verb            VARCHAR2(50);
BEGIN
  container_id := FIND_ITEM(container_name);
  IF ID_NULL(container_id) THEN
     MESSAGE('Item '||container_name||' does not exist.');
     RAISE FORM_TRIGGER_FAILURE;
  END IF;

  running := FORMS_OLE.SERVER_ACTIVE(container_id);
  IF NOT FORM_SUCCESS THEN
     MESSAGE('Right-click the icon above button Play and
              select Insert Object... from the menu.');
     RAISE FORM_TRIGGER_FAILURE;
  END IF;
  IF NOT running THEN
     FORMS_OLE.ACTIVATE_SERVER(container_id);
  END IF;

  verb_count := FORMS_OLE.GET_VERB_COUNT(container_id);
  FOR i IN 1..TO_NUMBER(verb_count) LOOP
     verb := FORMS_OLE.GET_VERB_NAME(container_id, i);
     IF UPPER(verb) = 'PLAY' THEN
        FORMS_OLE.EXEC_VERB(container_id, i);
        EXIT;
     END IF;
  END LOOP;
EXCEPTION
  WHEN OTHERS THEN
    MESSAGE('Error: '||TO_CHAR(SQLCODE)||'-'||SQLERRM);
    RAISE FORM_TRIGGER_FAILURE;
END;
```

FIGURE 23.15 Manipulating OLE objects programmatically.

> ## Note
>
> Another function that is part of this package is FORMS_OLE.GET_INTER-FACE_POINTER, which takes as input parameter the name or internal ID of an OLE container and returns a pointer or handle to the OLE object that resides in that item. You will use this function in the next chapter, in the discussion about OLE Automation.

The final version of this application is provided in the companion disk under the name COMP_F.FMB.

23.7 SUMMARY

This chapter discusses the OLE technology and how it applies to the development of Oracle Forms applications. The first part of it is an overview of OLE, and the second part explains the use of OLE Documents in Oracle Forms. Important topics in this chapter are listed here:

- ❏ What is OLE?
  - ❏ The need for OLE
  - ❏ Component software technology
  - ❏ OLE clients and OLE servers
  - ❏ The registry database
- ❏ OLE documents technology
  - ❏ The composers application
  - ❏ OLE containers in Oracle Forms
  - ❏ Embedding objects in Oracle Forms
  - ❏ Converting embedded objects
  - ❏ Verbs of embedded objects
- ❏ In-Place Activation of embedded objects
- ❏ Linking objects in Oracle Forms
- ❏ Linking and embedding in Oracle Forms Designer
- ❏ Manipulating compound documents programmatically

OLE AUTOMATION
AND VBX CONTROLS

"Give me where to stand, and I will move the earth."
—Archimedes (said with reference to the lever—
the world's first automation tool)

♦ OLE Automation

♦ OLE Automation in Oracle Forms

♦ OLE Controls

♦ VBX Controls

♦ Summary

Chapter 23 offered an overview of OLE technology as a whole and focused on OLE Documents, which is an important component of it. You learned how to use Oracle Forms as OLE containers and integrate them with OLE server applications. As it was emphasized in that chapter, today, OLE provides much more functionality than mere creation of compound documents through linking and embedding.

An area that is being explored intensively and offers a great perspective is the OLE Automation technology, which is a set of protocols and constructs that allows creation of universal applications that access and use features from an array of other applications with the goal to facilitate and automate processes that otherwise would require human intervention. The first part of this chapter will discuss how OLE Automation can be implemented from an Oracle Forms environment.

Another area where OLE promises to offer a lot is the creation and use of OLE controls. Their advent in the computing world is quite recent, and is another proof of the extendible architecture of OLE. OLE controls did not exist when OLE was designed; however, they fit perfectly well in the framework of objects and interfaces defined by OLE. The second half of this chapter discusses OLE controls. In practical terms, it focuses on the support that Oracle Forms offers for the predecessors of OLE controls: Visual Basic Custom Controls, also known as VBX controls.

24.1 OLE AUTOMATION

The modern workplace relies heavily on the utilization of software products for the purpose of facilitating and substituting several tedious and labor-intensive tasks such as document editing, financial calculations, plotting of charts and graphs, and storage and retrieval of data. In each area, several applications have distinguished themselves as being full of features, which are easy to learn, access, and use. However, despite the strong capabilities that each individual package offers, much to be desired is left on their integration and cooperation.

Imagine for a second the activities of a payroll office in a typical enterprise today. Periodically, its staff must download data from a database where all the employees log their time onto a spreadsheet package, where several complicated computations are made, charts are drawn, and financial analysis of the company's welfare is done. Then, some of these data may go to a printer where paychecks for the employees are printed. Someone working on the monthly report for the company's executives needs to cut and paste some charts. Yet another person sends notification messages by e-mail to certain employees whose records may need some verification and supplemental information. This web of activity is a busy hive of working bees, running around to keep the company healthy and prosperous.

Unfortunately, too much of this energy may be wasted on tasks of a secondary nature such as figuring out how to transfer the data across applications, ensuring that the right data elements are available when people need them, or restricting access to data to unauthorized persons. Today there exists the technology to automate a considerable amount of these tasks at the software level. This technology is OLE Automation, an important component of the OLE functionality as a whole, which was introduced as a significant improvement of the initial OLE 1.

OLE Automation is a set of standard interfaces and data types designed to enable applications to exchange data with each other and to drive their respective components programmatically. OLE Automation makes possible the use of the native language of an application to control and manipulate other applications. In the scenario presented above, if all the individual applications support OLE Automation, it is possible to write a script in any of them, that would download the data from the database, format and calculate the spreadsheet, create the necessary charts, paste them in the monthly report, send the paychecks to the printer, and send the e-mail messages to the employees that must be notified. All the human interface can be encapsulated in this program unit. Thus the computers will do what they are good at, and the humans will be relieved to do more creative and productive work.

OLE Automation is based on the concepts of *automation objects* and *automation controllers*. The automation objects are OLE objects which have a special type of interface which displays all their methods, properties, and arguments to the outside environment. This interface, called *dispatch interface* or *dispinterface*, assigns a unique identifier, known as dispID, to each member function or property of the object. An outside application which can access the automation object through its class identifier CLSID, can also use the dispinterface to query the dispIDs provided by the object. Each method or property can then be invoked based on this identifier. On the other side of the equation stand the automation controllers. They provide programmers with language structures that can be used to access the properties and execute the methods of the OLE automation objects. The automation controllers use the dispID to access the properties of an object or to invoke its methods. OLE Automation is a very important technological standard, because it allows applications to use their own native language scripts to drive any other application that implements the dispinterface according to this standard.

24.2 OLE AUTOMATION IN ORACLE FORMS

Oracle Forms, and all the other Developer/2000 tools, are OLE automation controller applications. You can create program units in PL/SQL that drive any OLE automation object such as a word processor, a spreadsheet, or a drawing package. This functionality is provided by the package OLE2, which comes with these tools. The following section discusses the contents of this package, and in Sections 24.2.2 and 24.2.3 you will use it to implement OLE Automation features in some sample Oracle Forms applications.

24.2.1 OLE2 PACKAGE

The OLE2 package provides a small number of data types and program units, which are generic enough to allow you to control any OLE automation object. Each OLE automation object in Oracle Forms is represented and accessed by a variable of data type OLE2.OBJ_TYPE. You can create an object from scratch by using the function OLE2.CREATE_OBJ. This function takes as argument the name of an OLE class installed in your machine. The Windows registry is queried with this name, the class identifier CLSID is retrieved, and this information is used to start the server application and create a new object instance of the specified class. The function returns a pointer to that object. After you have finished work with the automation object, you can use the procedure OLE2.RELEASE_OBJ to release all the system resources that the object is using.

As said in the previous section, once the automation controller, in the case of Oracle Forms, obtains a handle to the automation object, the dispinterface of the object will reveal all its properties and methods. You can use three functions of the OLE2 package to get different properties of the object. If the property is numeric use the function OLE2.GET_NUM_PROPERTY; if the property setting is alphanumeric use the function OLE2.GET_CHAR_PROPERTY; if the property setting is another OLE automation object, the function OLE2.GET_OBJ_PROPERTY returns a pointer to this object. If you want to set the property of an object, use the procedure OLE2.SET_PROPERTY.

Four members of the OLE2 package are used to invoke the object's methods. If the method is a procedure, the procedure OLE2.INVOKE is used. When the method is a function that returns a number, alphanumeric string, or another automation object, the functions OLE2.INVOKE_NUM, OLE2.INVOKE_CHAR, and OLE2.INVOKE_OBJ are used respectively.

Each of the program units for accessing the properties and methods of a function take as parameters the pointer to the object and the name of the property or method. Any parameters that may be required are passed in the form of an argument list. Argument lists are special objects of data type OLE2.LIST_TYPE. They can be created with the function OLE2.CREATE_ARGLIST, which returns an internal identifier for the list. Arguments are added with the procedure OLE2.ADD_ARG. The order of the arguments must be exactly as required by the

Note

In Oracle Forms, you can achieve the same functionality by using the function FORMS_OLE.GET_INTERFACE_POINTER as well.

method. Finally, when the list is no longer needed, its resources can be returned to the available pool by invoking the procedure OLE2.DESTROY_ARGLIST.

24.2.2 OLE AUTOMATION WITH SPREADSHEETS

In this section you will use the OLE Automation features of Oracle Forms to implement the functionality created in Chapter 22 using DDE communication channels. The template modules that you will work with in this section are called OLEEXCL.FMB and OLEWORD.FMB. The finished versions of these modules, which contain the features you will implement in this section, are provided with the names OLEEXCLF.FMB and OLEWORDF.FMB.

Start the Designer and open the module OLEEXCL.FMB. The canvas layout of this module is shown in Figure 24.1. The layout is similar to that of module DDEEXCL.FMB. The main difference is that in OLE Automation, you do not need any communication channel like in DDE. This is the reason why in this module there is only one button to launch Excel, and another one to close it, but no buttons to open or close a channel. For the same reason, the PRE-FORM trigger declares only one global variable **GLOBAL.application_id**.

The trigger WHEN-BUTTON-PRESSED for the buttons Launch Excel will create an OLE Automation object from the class EXCEL.APPLICATION.5, and will store a pointer to it in the global variable **GLOBAL.application_id**. Obviously, if the object already exists, a new one will not be instantiated. Create the trigger and enter its contents as shown in Figure 24.2.

Now, create a WHEN-BUTTON-PRESSED trigger for the button Exit Excel. This trigger will invoke the OLE2.RELEASE_OBJ procedure to free up the resources taken by the object. The variable **GLOBAL.application_id** will also be set to NULL. The contents of this trigger are shown in Figure 24.3.

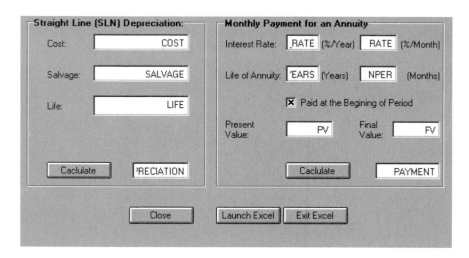

FIGURE 24.1   Layout of module OLEEXCL.FMB.

```
DECLARE
  appl_name VARCHAR2(255) := 'EXCEL.APPLICATION.5';
BEGIN
  IF :GLOBAL.application_id IS NOT NULL THEN
     MESSAGE('Application is already running.');
  ELSE
     :GLOBAL.application_id := OLE2.CREATE_OBJ(appl_name);
  END IF;
EXCEPTION
  WHEN OTHERS THEN
     MESSAGE('Error: '||TO_CHAR(SQLCODE)||' '||SQLERRM);
     RAISE FORM_TRIGGER_FAILURE;
END;
```

FIGURE 24.2   Initializing an Excel OLE Automation object.

The contents of the trigger for the button Close will be very similar to Figure 24.3. Here you would still check to see if the automation object is created by the application. If this is the case, you discard it using OLE2.RELEASE_OBJ. Then you invoke EXIT_FORM to terminate the application.

In the triggers WHEN-BUTTON-PRESSED for the buttons Calculate in both blocks, you should ensure first that the automation object is already initialized. Then you call the functions **Calc_SLN** and **Calc_PMT**, whose return values populate the items SLN.DEPRECIATION and PMT.PAYMENT, respectively. The ar-

```
DECLARE
  application_id PLS_INTEGER;
BEGIN
  IF :GLOBAL.application_id IS NULL THEN
     MESSAGE('Cannot terminate an instance that is not
initiated by this application.');
  ELSE
     application_id := TO_NUMBER(:GLOBAL.application_id);
     OLE2.RELEASE_OBJ(application_id);
     :GLOBAL.application_id := NULL;
  END IF;
EXCEPTION
  WHEN OTHERS THEN
     MESSAGE('Error: '||TO_CHAR(SQLCODE)||' '||SQLERRM);
     RAISE FORM_TRIGGER_FAILURE;
END;
```

FIGURE 24.3   Deleting an OLE Automation object.

```
DECLARE
  application_id PLS_INTEGER;
BEGIN
  IF :GLOBAL.application_id IS NOT NULL THEN
      application_id := TO_NUMBER(:GLOBAL.application_id);
      :SLN.DEPRECIATION := Calc_SLN( application_id, :SLN.COST,
                                     :SLN.SALVAGE, :SLN.LIFE);
  ELSE
      MESSAGE('The application must be started first.');
  END IF;
END;
```

FIGURE 24.4   Invoking function Calc_SLN.

guments passed with these functions are the interface pointer to the Excel spread-sheet object and the values entered in the text item of the respective blocks. The property *Required* is set to '*True*' for all these items, therefore you will not have to check whether they are NULL before calling the functions.

Figure 24.4 shows the contents of trigger WHEN-BUTTON-PRESSED for button Calculate in block SLN. Figure 24.5 shows the contents of trigger WHEN-BUTTON-PRESSED for button Calculate in the block PMT.

Now, create the functions **Calc_SLN** and **Calc_PMT**. Because of the similarities between these functions, it is sufficient to show only one of them in detail, and leave the implementation of the second function to you. Figure 24.6 shows the contents of function **Calc_SNL**.

The first part of this function creates an argument list, and adds to it the three input arguments that will be passed to the Excel function SNL. Then the function OLE2.GET_NUM_PROPERTY is used to return the value that function SLN computes based on the arguments in the list. This is also the value returned from the function **Calc_SLN**. At the end of this function, the argument list is destroyed, in order to free the resources it occupies. The function **Calc_PMT** will differ only in the number of arguments added to the argument list, and in the fact that the Excel function PMT is used instead of SLN. Save, generate, and run the module in order to see its new functionality.

24.2.3   OLE AUTOMATION WITH WORD PROCESSORS

Open the module OLEWORD.FMB, which you will use to transfer data from the Oracle database to a MS Word form letter. A similar functionality was supported by the module DDEWORD.FMB discussed in Chapter 22. However, as you will see here, the functionality you can add using the OLE Automation technology is much more powerful and transparent for the user than in the DDE approach.

Chapter 22 discusses in detail the template letter that will be used in this application. In a nutshell, several bookmarks are defined in the document. Each of

```
DECLARE
  application_id PLS_INTEGER;
BEGIN
  IF :GLOBAL.application_id IS NOT NULL THEN
      application_id := TO_NUMBER(:GLOBAL.application_id);
      :PMT.PAYMENT := Calc_PMT(application_id, :PMT.RATE/100, :PMT.NPER,
                              :PMT.PV, :PMT.FV, :PMT.TYPE);
  ELSE
      MESSAGE('The application must be started first.');
  END IF;
END;
```

FIGURE 24.5 Invoking function Calc_PMT.

these bookmarks will be populated with data from the record of the current customer, when the letter will be compiled. This is how much functionality you implemented in Chapter 22. If users of that application want to perform any action with the document such as printing, saving it to a file for record-keeping purposes, or running the spell checker, they have to switch to the MS Word window

```
FUNCTION Calc_SLN (application_id PLS_INTEGER,
                   cost          NUMBER,
                   salvage       NUMBER,
                   life          NUMBER)
RETURN NUMBER IS
  arg_list         OLE2.LIST_TYPE;
  return_value     NUMBER;
BEGIN
  arg_list := OLE2.CREATE_ARGLIST;
  OLE2.ADD_ARG(arg_list, cost);
  OLE2.ADD_ARG(arg_list, salvage);
  OLE2.ADD_ARG(arg_list, life);

  return_value := OLE2.GET_NUM_PROPERTY(application_id, 'SLN', arg_list);
  OLE2.DESTROY_ARGLIST(arg_list);

  RETURN(return_value);
EXCEPTION
  WHEN OTHERS THEN
      MESSAGE('Error: '||TO_CHAR(SQLCODE)||' '||SQLERRM);
      RAISE FORM_TRIGGER_FAILURE;
END;
```

FIGURE 24.6 Using OLE Automation to calculate the straight-line depreciation of an asset.

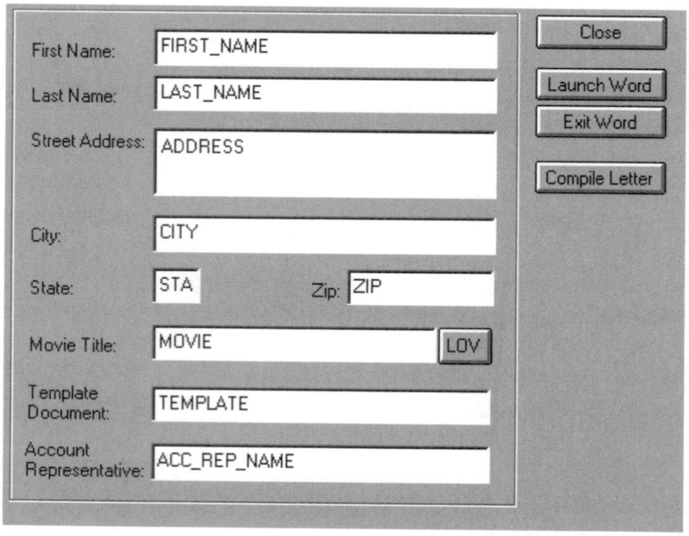

FIGURE 24.7   Layout of module OLEWORD.FMB.

and do it there. You will see here how easy it is to incorporate this functionality inside the Forms application, using the OLE2 package. Figure 24.7 shows the layout of the module OLEWORD.FMB.

The contents of the WHEN-BUTTON-PRESSED trigger for button Launch Word are almost the same as what Figure 24.2 shows. The only difference is that here the application name is WORD.BASIC instead of EXCEL.APPLICATION.5. The triggers for buttons Exit Word and Close are exactly the same as in the module OLEEXCL.FMB. All three triggers are provided in the template module OLEWORD.FMB.

The only thing left to discuss is the trigger that actually compiles the letter. In this trigger you will implement more functionality than you did in the DDE application, simply because the OLE Automation mechanism allows you to access all the functions of MS Word and every other server application with great ease and simplicity.

Specifically, these are the actions that will be taken when the users press the Compile Letter button:

1. The trigger will check if the application is already started, and will proceed only if this is the case.

2. The trigger will retrieve the current system date, and will concatenate the first and last names of the customer. These two steps are the same as in the DDE application.

3. The trigger will calculate the name of a file where this letter will be saved. The directory will be the same where the template is saved; the extension of the file will be .DOC; the name of the file will be the first eight characters of the string formed by concatenating the last name with the first name. For example, if the template is retrieved from C:\FORMAPPS\LETTER.DOC, and the customer name is Michelle Johnson, the form letter for her will be saved as C:\FORMAPPS\JOHNSONM.DOC.

4. The trigger will open the template file from the location provided by the user.

5. The bookmarks defined in this file will be replaced with data provided in the items of block CUSTOMER.

6. The file will be saved under the new name.

7. The file will be sent to the printer.

8. The file will be closed.

As you can see from these steps, despite some tricks done initially to render user-entered data in an appropriate form, the core functionality of this trigger is issuing MS Word commands from PL/SQL. For the sake of simplicity, uniformity, and reusability of the code, you should concentrate these functions in a PL/SQL library which can be attached to the OLEWORD.FMB module, and any other module where you will need to add this functionality in the future.

1. In the Object Navigator create a new library module and name it OLE-WORD.PLL.

2. Create a package specification program unit called Word, with contents as shown in Figure 24.8.

3. Create the package body of WORD and declare a variable of data type OLE2.OBJ_TYPE, called appl_id. Use the following statement to initialize the variable to the value of GLOBAL.application_id:

```
appl_id OLE2.OBJ_TYPE:= TO_NUMBER(NAME_IN('GLOBAL.
application_id'));
```

```
PACKAGE WORD IS
  PROCEDURE File_Open (file VARCHAR2);
  PROCEDURE File_Save_As (file VARCHAR2);
  PROCEDURE File_Print;
  PROCEDURE File_Close;
  PROCEDURE Replace_Bookmark (bookmark VARCHAR2, content VARCHAR2);
END;
```

FIGURE 24.8 PL/SQL package for OLE Automation with MS Word.

```
PROCEDURE File_Open (file VARCHAR2) IS
  arg_list OLE2.LIST_TYPE;
BEGIN
    arg_list := OLE2.CREATE_ARGLIST;
    OLE2.ADD_ARG(arg_list, file);
    OLE2.INVOKE(appl_id, 'FileOpen', arg_list);
    OLE2.DESTROY_ARGLIST(arg_list);
END;
```

FIGURE 24.9   Opening a MS Word file using OLE Automation.

Recall that in nonform modules you must reference global variables indirectly.

4. Create the body for procedure **File_Open**. The contents of this procedure are shown in Figure 24.9.

5. Create the body for procedure **File_Save_As**. The only difference between this and the previous procedure is that instead of MS Word method FileOpen you will use FileSaveAs with the procedure OLE2.INVOKE.

6. Create the body for procedures **File_Print** and **File_Close**. Each of them contains a single line. These are the statements that should be placed in each procedure:

    For **File_Print**   OLE2.INVOKE(appl_id, 'FilePrint');
    For **File_Close**   OLE2.INVOKE(appl_id, 'FileClose');

7. Finally, implement the body of procedure **Replace_Bookmark**. The contents of this function are shown in Figure 24.10.

At this point, compile and save the OLEWORD.FMB module, and attach it to your form. Now, you are ready to create the body of the trigger WHEN-BUTTON-PRESSED for button Compile Letter. Recall that in this trigger you want to save each new document to a file named after the customer to whom the letter is sent. The name of this file is relatively easy to create. You can concatenate the last name with the first name, and then use the function SUBSTR to get the first eight characters of this string. Getting the directory path from the definition of the letter template entered by the users is a little trickier. First you should get the position of the last back-slash character '\' in the template name. For this, you can use the function INSTR with the following parameters:

last_slash_pos := INST(:CUSTOMER.TEMPLATE, '\', -1, 1);

Recall from Chapter 10 that these parameters make INSTR return the position of the first occurrence of character '\' in the string stored in CUSTOMER.TEM-

```
PROCEDURE Replace_Bookmark (bookmark VARCHAR2,
                           content VARCHAR2) IS
  arg_list OLE2.LIST_TYPE;
BEGIN
  arg_list := OLE2.CREATE_ARGLIST;
  OLE2.ADD_ARG(arg_list, bookmark);
  OLE2.INVOKE(appl_id, 'EditGoTo', arg_list);
  OLE2.DESTROY_ARGLIST(arg_list);

  arg_list := OLE2.CREATE_ARGLIST;
  OLE2.ADD_ARG(arg_list, content);
  OLE2.INVOKE(appl_id, 'Insert', arg_list);
  OLE2.DESTROY_ARGLIST(arg_list);
END;
```

FIGURE 24.10   Replacing bookmarks in MS Word using OLE Automation.

PLATE, starting from the end of the string (the reason for setting the third argument to -1). Then, you can use SUBSTR to return the part of :CUSTOMER.TEMPLATE from the first character to the character in the position defined in the previous step. This string will be the directory where the new file will be stored. You can also provide users with a text item in the form, similar to TEMPLATE, where they themselves can specify the directory where the new file will be located. Figure 24.11 shows the detailed implementation of this trigger.

As you can see from the examples discussed in this and the previous section, OLE Automation offers you great possibilities to make the most out of the investment made in different software packages. Integrating these products with

Note

There is a caveat that you should be aware of in this procedure. Given the way bookmarks are implemented in Word, overwriting their previous contents with new data will erase them as named objects in the document. This means that any of the customer-specific files generated by OLEWORD.FMB will not contain the bookmarks. To get around to this problem, and for many other great tips on integrating Windows applications using DDE and OLE, you may reference *Making Windows Applications Work Together*, by Rob Krumm (M&T Books, 1994).

```
DECLARE
  date             VARCHAR2(50);
  cust_name        VARCHAR2(60);
  work_dir         VARCHAR2(144);
  new_file         VARCHAR2(60);
  last_slash_pos   NUMBER;
BEGIN
  IF :GLOBAL.application_id IS NULL THEN
     MESSAGE('The application must be started first.');
     RAISE FORM_TRIGGER_FAILURE;
  END IF;
  SELECT TO_CHAR(SYSDATE, 'Month DD, YYYY') INTO date FROM DUAL;
  cust_name := :CUSTOMER.FIRST_NAME||' '||:CUSTOMER.LAST_NAME;

  new_file := :CUSTOMER.LAST_NAME||:CUSTOMER.FIRST_NAME;
  new_file := SUBSTR(new_file, 1, 8)||'.doc';
  last_slash_pos := INSTR(:CUSTOMER.TEMPLATE, '\', -1, 1);
  work_dir := SUBSTR(:CUSTOMER.TEMPLATE, 1, last_slash_pos);
  new_file := work_dir||new_file;

  Word.File_Open(:CUSTOMER.TEMPLATE);
  Word.Replace_Bookmark('date',           date);
  Word.Replace_Bookmark('cust_name',       cust_name);
  Word.Replace_Bookmark('street',          :CUSTOMER.ADDRESS);
  Word.Replace_Bookmark('city',            :CUSTOMER.CITY);
  Word.Replace_Bookmark('state',           :CUSTOMER.STATE);
  Word.Replace_Bookmark('zip',             :CUSTOMER.ZIP);
  Word.Replace_Bookmark('first_name',      :CUSTOMER.FIRST_NAME);
  Word.Replace_Bookmark('movie',           :CUSTOMER.MOVIE);
  Word.Replace_Bookmark('acc_rep_name',    :CUSTOMER.ACC_REP_NAME);
  Word.File_Save_As(new_file);
  MESSAGE('File saved in: '''||UPPER(new_file)||'''.');
  Word.File_Print;
  Word.File_Close;
END;
```

FIGURE 24.11   Transferring data from Oracle Forms to MS Word using OLE
Automation.

the Oracle Forms applications is also a very straightforward and easy process. In fact, the main difficulty you may encounter is not as much in the actual PL/SQL code you write, as in finding the names of the native functions you should use, and the parameters they take. This obviously requires programming skills not just in Oracle Forms, but also in the third-party products you will decide to integrate. There are several ways to overcome this difficulty. One would be to expand the development team with people that have solid experience with these tools. The users community—people that use the word processing, spreadsheet, and graphic applications every day—would provide you with some surprisingly good experts on the subject. Ask them to share with you the toolbox of macros and utilities they may have created over the years.

Another way is to take advantage of the large variety of books written on Windows applications that cover their programming macro languages. The book by Rob Krumm mentioned earlier is representative of such books.

Then, if you are one of those do-it-yourself personalities, you may want to take a plunge in the on-line documentation that each of these tools provides. The contents page for each application that supports programming usually contains a section that provides references and examples for each function and procedure supported by the tool. For example, in MS Word this section is called *Programming with Microsoft Word*; in Excel it is called *Programming with Visual Basic*.

Finally, you can use the functions you want to reference from Oracle Forms in the native environment and record the session in the form of a macro. This macro then can be inspected to identify which functions were called and how their parameters were passed. Figure 24.12, for example, shows the macro that was used to identify the functions needed in the OLEWORD.FMB module. The names of the functions in this figure are highlighted for the sake of clarity.

As you can see from this figure, the number of arguments for some of these functions such as FileOpen, FileSaveAs, or FilePrint, may be overwhelming at times. However, only a few of them are required. The remaining arguments can maintain their default values.

24.3 OLE CONTROLS

In everyday life we constantly use devices, big and small, to perform certain actions or to control the performance and execution of others. Although today we are surrounded by a myriad of electronic devices and buttons, we have used controls for a long time. In fact, the history of humanity can be seen as a constant evolution of our abilities to refine these devices, and make them take us to new heights and achievements. Nobody knows the genius who first invented the wheel, or the lever, but without that person, wonders such as the Great Pyramids would not exist. The industrial revolution was generated and nourished by the eagerness of people to replace manual labor with mechanical devices. The infor-

```
Sub MAIN

FileOpen .Name = "LETTER.DOC", .ConfirmConversions = 0,
.ReadOnly = 0, .AddToMru = 0, .PasswordDoc = "", .PasswordDot
= "", .Revert = 0, .WritePasswordDoc = "", .WritePasswordDot
= ""

EditGoTo .Destination = "date"
Insert "November 12, 1995"

FileSaveAs .Name = "JOHNSONM.DOC", .Format = 0, .LockAnnot = 0,
.Password = "", .AddToMru = 1, .WritePassword = "",
.RecommendReadOnly = 0, .EmbedFonts = 0, .NativePictureFormat
= 0, .FormsData = 0

FilePrint .AppendPrFile = 0, .Range = "0", .PrToFileName = "",
.From = "", .To = "", .Type = 0, .NumCopies = "1", .Pages = "",
.Order = 0, .PrintToFile = 0, .Collate = 1, .FileName = ""

FileClose

End Sub
```

FIGURE 24.12   MS Word macro used to locate WORD.BASIC methods used in OLEWORD.FMB.

mation revolution, of which we are experiencing just the beginning, is replacing mechanical devices with automated tools that can be controlled by a panel full of buttons, switches, and keys. We are so accustomed to these controls and devices in our life that we don't notice most of them until they break: the door knob does not turn, the elevator button will not work, or the remote control is broken.

The revolution that graphical user interface environments brought in the computing industry was to build graphical screens based on the metaphor of the controls that we use every day. The GUI designers rightly assumed that people, used to pushing buttons to request service in hotel rooms or to switching light buttons on and off, would also feel comfortable working with applications that offer similar controls to perform their functions.

Originally, the types of controls used in the software industry were limited to push buttons, radio buttons, check boxes, list boxes, scroll bars, spin boxes, and a few others. Visual Basic introduced the powerful technique of integrating custom-made controls with applications. These controls are referred to as Visual Basic Extension, or VBXs, for short. They allow you to use in your applications, the functionality and methods of objects developed by third-party vendors. VBXs allow you to purchase well-designed standard interface objects, thus providing more time for the understanding of your users' needs, and the creation of software systems that meet them. In the following sections you will learn to integrate VBX with applications developed in Oracle Forms.

Despite the popularity among application developers, the design of VBXs was not free of errors and hasty decisions. However, it was not until Microsoft embarked on the long journey to create a 32-bit operating system that they realized that this design contained major flaws. In fact, VBXs would not migrate well, if at all, in the new systems. Therefore, new designs were put together. By this time, though, the OLE technology was well-established. The newest components added to the technology were the OLE controls. They are at the top of the other technologies in the sense that they build on them, especially on OLE Documents, In-Place Activation, and OLE Automation. To maintain the analogy with their distant relatives, the OLE controls are referred to as OCX controls.

OLE controls are still in their infancy stage; however, their perspective seems very promising. They will bring to the software industry the remarkable advances that we are experiencing in other areas of technology. Take the cars that we drive today, for example. We sit in comfortable seats, turn on the ignition key, switch gears, and drive. We turn the wheel, press the gas or brake pedals, or press a button to turn the lights on. A great deal of things must happen in order for each of these things to occur; however, we are shielded from all these details. All we have and need is a panel where each of these functions is represented by a switch, a button, or a control, which we use to get the car going. OLE controls promise to bring exactly that in software systems. They are objects that encapsulate a large number of services, properties, and methods, which are exposed to the other software programs to use and benefit from.

24.4 VBX CONTROLS

VBX controls, as mentioned earlier, were introduced as extensions to the standard programming interface provided by Visual Basic. They are packages of objects that encapsulate properties and methods in a way that is easier for the users to access. Each VBX control is characterized by its properties, events, and methods. Properties are named attributes of the control, which govern its appearance such as background or foreground color, its size, position on the canvas, and so on. When VBXs are used in Oracle Forms, many of these properties are converted automatically to the native Oracle Forms properties. There are also properties that control the behavior of the object. These properties usually are appended to the list of properties for the item. Events are actions that the control is programmed to recognize. Such events can be sparked externally, by user actions such as clicking an area of the control, or internally, by programmatically changing the state of a control or some of its properties. Methods are program units such as functions and procedures that act upon an item. This section will discuss how to manipulate such objects as Oracle Forms items. You will work with examples to integrate VBX controls with Forms applications.

24.4.1 PROPERTIES OF VBX CONTROL ITEMS

In Oracle Forms, VBX controls are a special type of item that share many common characteristics with other items. They can be used to enter, retrieve, and manipulate data from the database. In addition, they can also be used to provide a better and friendlier interface to the applications.

There are several ways to create a VBX control item in a form:

a) Click the VBX Control iconic button 🔲 in the Layout Editor's tool palette and draw the control on the canvas, or

b) Set the type of item to VBX Control in the Items tab of the New Block Options dialog box, upon creation of a new base table block., or

c) Set the *Item Type* property of an existing item to '*VBX Item*'.

When a new VBX control is created, it is like an empty container on the canvas. It will not come to life until a control is attached to it from the file system. The three properties that are used to populate an Oracle Forms VBX control container with a control are all under the **Functional** group in the Properties Window for the item. The names of these properties are *VBX Control File*, *VBX Control Name*, and *VBX Control Value Property*.

The setting of the first property is the name of the DLL file in which the control object is located. Traditionally, these files have the extension .VBX, and are installed in the Windows' SYSTEM directory by the installation utility of the control's vendor. One such file may contain several VBX controls inside of it. To choose one of them, you pick its name from the list of objects in the property *VBX Control Name*.

At the beginning of this section it was said that VBX controls can be used to manipulate data. You must select one of the properties of the control as the

---

Note

These properties are set in the same order in which they are described above. You must set first the *VBX Control File* property to a valid file name, before being able to set the *VBX Control Name* to one of the objects this file contains. Only after you have set the object can you elect one of its properties to determine the value of the VBX item, if such will be the case.

one whose value will determine the value of the item itself. For this purpose, you set the property *VBX Control Value Property* to one of the properties of the control.

After the VBX item is assigned a VBX control, all the properties of this control are added at the bottom of the item's list of properties in the **Miscellaneous** group. In the Properties Windows you can change the settings of these properties according to your needs.

24.4.2 MANIPULATING VBX CONTROLS PROGRAMMATICALLY

Oracle Forms provides a simple add-on package that allows you to access and modify VBX control items from within PL/SQL program units. This package is called VBX. Two important members of this package are the function VBX.GET_PROPERTY and the procedure VBX.SET_PROPERTY. The first one returns the setting of a property for a given VBX item; the second one sets the property for a given item to the specified value. As it is the case with other similar constructs, these program units take either the name or the internal identifier of the item as their first parameter. Moreover, the function VBX.GET_VALUE_PROPERTY retrieves the setting of the property *VBX Control Value*, and the procedure VBX.SET_VALUE_PROPERTY sets this property to a new value. This is the only one from the three Functional properties of a VBX control item that can be set at runtime.

You can also invoke the methods that the VBX control displays to the outside world. The interface that the package VBX provides for this purpose is the procedure VBX.INVOKE_METHOD. This procedure takes as parameters the name or ID of the items and the name of the method that should be invoked. If the method takes any parameters, up to four of them can be passed with this procedure in the form of alphanumeric characters.

Finally, you can trap and respond to events of a VBX control, or catalyze new ones programmatically. When an event defined for a control occurs, its name is stored in the Oracle Forms system variable SYSTEM.CUSTOM_EVENT. This also causes the trigger WHEN-CUSTOM-ITEM-EVENT to execute. This behavior allows you to create an item-level trigger with this name, and attach it to the VBX control item whose events you want to capture. Then, in the body of the trigger, you would place a series of IF statements that compare the value stores in the SYSTEM.CUSTOM_EVENT variable with the name of the event to which you want to react. Inside the IF clause you place the code that will be executed as a response to such an event.

In order to trigger an event programmatically, the procedure VBX.FIRE_EVENT is used. This procedure takes three arguments. The first one is the name or ID of the VBX control item. The second argument is the name of the event that you want to trigger. The third argument is the name or the internal identifier of a parameter list which contains all the parameters necessary for the trigger to be activated.

Note

As is the case with OLE Automation discussed in the first part of this chapter, when you manipulate a VBX Control programmatically, the problem is not how to do this with the PL/SQL constructs available. As seen in this section, the program units of the package VBX make this task almost trivial. The most laborious part is to figure out which properties to set, which methods to invoke, or which events to respond to. For this, you must carefully review all the documentation available to you from the VBX control vendor. This documentation, in general, is organized in separate sections that describe the properties, events, and methods of each control.

24.4.3   VBX CONTROLS IN ORACLE FORMS—KNOB.VBX

In this and the following section you will use a scaled-down version of the form that you used in the OLE Automation part of the chapter to discuss the integration of Oracle Forms and Excel through this technology. The name of the module is VBXEXCL.FMB. Open this form in the Designer, and display its canvas in the Layout Editor. You will see that in comparison with OLEEXCL.FMB, this module contains only the SLN block. The functionality of this block is exactly as in the module OLEEXCL.FMB. It implements the Excel function SLN to compute the straight-line depreciation of an asset. In this section you will create two VBX controls that will facilitate the data entry for the items SALVAGE and LIFE.

The first control is called KNOB.VBX, and is provided by the Oracle Corporation together with its Developer/2000 software. You will use it to facilitate the entry of the amount that will be salvaged at the end of the asset's life. The lower bound of this amount will be zero; the upper bound will be the cost of the asset at the beginning of the period. The second control is called SPIN.VBX, and is one of the custom controls that comes with Visual Basic. In the following section, you will implement a spin button with this control that will facilitate the entry of years in the LIFE item of the asset.

Now add the first VBX control to your form:

1. Create a VBX control item to the right of the item SALVAGE and display its Properties Window.

2. Name the item KNOB, and set its property *Mirror Item* to 'SALVAGE'. This way, the changes in the value of the knob will be reflected in the value of SALVAGE and vice-versa. At the same time, you should set its *Data Type* to 'NUMBER', the same as SALVAGE.

> ## Note
>
> This section assumes that both these controls are located in your Windows SYSTEM directory, although this is not necessary for using them.
>
> In order to use these VBXs at runtime, you need the library VBRUN300.DLL, or VBRUN400.DLL. They are part of the Visual Basic version 3.0 or 4.0 software, but can be retrieved free of charge from several on-line services and bulletin boards.
>
> You can use the VBX KNOB.VBX both in the Designer and at runtime. However, in order to use the control SPIN.VBX in the Designer, you need to have a license of the Visual Basic software. You do not need a license to use the control at runtime. This arrangement is standard in the VBX control industry.

3. Double-click the property *VBX Control File*. A standard Open dialog box will be displayed. Use it to find the file KNOB.VBX in the Windows system directory. When you select the file name, you will notice that Oracle Forms automatically sets the property *VBX Control Name* to 'KNOB1' and *VBX Control Value Property* to 'Value Current'. These settings are the ones you want to use in this case.

At the same time, several properties are added to the Miscellaneous group for this item. These properties and their original settings are presented in Figure 24.13.

Among these properties you will probably never change the color-related ones. They are specified in the form of hexadecimal numbers, and unfortunately no color palette is attached. If you want to add a text label on top of the control, set the property *Caption* to the desired string. The property *Caption Position* provides several possibilities as to where to place this label. If you want to change the position or size of the marker along the radius of the knob, you can set the properties *Marker Edge Offset* and *Marker Size*. Higher values for the first property correspond to a marker closer to the center. If you want to change the mouse pointer when it enters the sensitive area of the control, set the property *MousePointer* to one of the several options. Set this property to '2—Cross'.

The properties that you will likely change the most are the last four Value properties. The *Minimum Value* and *Maximum Value* define the range within which the values will oscillate. You can leave both these properties to their default settings. Dynamically, you will set the *Maximum Value* to the value entered in the COST item.

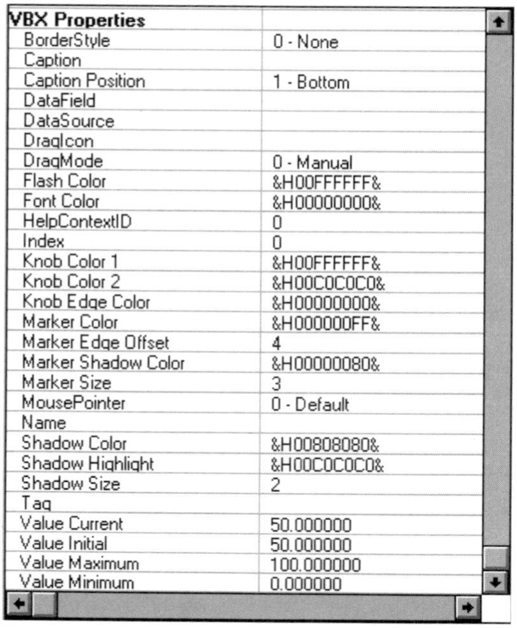

VBX Properties	
BorderStyle	0 - None
Caption	
Caption Position	1 - Bottom
DataField	
DataSource	
DragIcon	
DragMode	0 - Manual
Flash Color	&H00FFFFFF&
Font Color	&H00000000&
HelpContextID	0
Index	0
Knob Color 1	&H00FFFFFF&
Knob Color 2	&H00C0C0C0&
Knob Edge Color	&H00000000&
Marker Color	&H000000FF&
Marker Edge Offset	4
Marker Shadow Color	&H00000080&
Marker Size	3
MousePointer	0 - Default
Name	
Shadow Color	&H00808080&
Shadow Highlight	&H00C0C0C0&
Shadow Size	2
Tag	
Value Current	50.000000
Value Initial	50.000000
Value Maximum	100.000000
Value Minimum	0.000000

FIGURE 24.13   Default settings for KNOB.VBX control.

Value Initial is the value that the knob will have when initialized. This value defines the initial position of the marker on the circle, as well. Set this property to zero. *Value Current* is the value that the control will assign to the Forms item by default. Recall that the property *VBX Control Value Property* is set to '*Value Current*', which means that the current value of the knob will also be the value of the item. Set this property to '*0*' as well.

Now, create a WHEN-VALIDATE-ITEM trigger for item COST with the following statement in its body:

VBX.SET_PROPERTY ('KNOB', 'Value Maximum', TO_CHAR(:SLN.COST));

This will ensure that whenever the value of COST will change, the upper bound of the knob's values will reflect that change.

In order to initialize the upper bound and the position of the marker to the default values for the items COST and SALVAGE, create a WHEN-NEW-RECORD-INSTANCE with the following two lines in its body:

```
VBX.SET_PROPERTY ('KNOB', 'Value Maximum', TO_CHAR(:SLN.COST));
VBX.SET_PROPERTY ('KNOB', 'Value Current', TO_CHAR(:SLN.SALVAGE));
```

Now you can save, generate, and run the form. Drag the knob's marker to change the value of SALVAGE and vice-versa. See also how changing the value of COST will modify the upper range of the knob.

24.4.4   VBX CONTROLS IN ORACLE FORMS—SPIN.VBX

Now create a spin control that will allow users to easily change the values entered in item LIFE:

1. Create a VBX control item on the right of the item LIFE, and display its Properties Window.
2. Name the item SPIN, and set its property *Mirror Item* to '*LIFE*'. Make sure to set its *Data Type* to '*NUMBER*', the same as LIFE.
3. Set the property *VBX Control File* to the name of the file '*SPIN.VBX*'. When you select the file name, you will notice that Oracle Forms automatically sets the property *VBX Control Name* to '*SpinButton*' and *VBX Control Value Property* to '*Name*'. Accept these settings.

Take a look now at the properties displayed for this VBX Control. As you can see here, there are not too many properties that you can set for this control. The reason is that the SpinButton control is used primarily for the two events SpinUp and SpinDown associated with it. SpinUp occurs when the users click the up arrow; SpinDown occurs when the down arrow is used. If the mouse is kept pressed on one of the arrows, the corresponding event will be repeated at a frequency that is determined by the setting of the property *Delay*. This specifies the delay, in milliseconds, between two consecutive events.

By default, the orientation of the spin arrows is vertical. If you want to create a horizontal spin control, set the property *SpinOrientation* to '*1—Horizontal*'. In such case, the events SpinUp and SpinDown will correspond to pressing the right and left arrows.

Keeping these things in consideration, create the code that will increase or decrease the value of item LIFE by one unit each time when the events SpinUp and SpinDown occur. The strategy to follow in this case is as follows:

1. Create an item-level trigger WHEN-CUSTOM-ITEM-EVENT for the item SPIN.
2. Retrieve the name of the event from the variable SYSTEM.CUSTOM_ITEM_EVENT.
3. Execute the PL/SQL statement according to the event.

Figure 24.14 shows in detail the contents of this trigger. Initially, the trigger retrieves the settings for properties RANGE_HIGH and RANGE_LOW for item SLN.LIFE. Then, the event name is retrieved from SYSTEM.CUSTOM_ITEM_EVENT. If the event is MouseUp, the value of :SLN.LIFE is increased by one unit. However, if there is an upper bound specified for the item, and this bound is reached, no increment occurs. The processing of the event MouseDown is symmetric. Obviously, in case there are other conditions that the data stored on the item must fulfill, the contents of the trigger will be more complex. Save, generate,

```
DECLARE
  event      VARCHAR2(50);
  upper      NUMBER;
  lower      NUMBER;
BEGIN
  upper := TO_NUMBER(GET_ITEM_PROPERTY('SLN.LIFE', RANGE_HIGH));
  lower := TO_NUMBER(GET_ITEM_PROPERTY('SLN.LIFE', RANGE_LOW));
  event := :SYSTEM.CUSTOM_ITEM_EVENT;

  IF event = 'SpinUp' THEN
     IF :SLN.LIFE < upper OR upper IS NULL THEN
        :SLN.LIFE := :SLN.LIFE + 1;
     END IF;
  ELSIF event = 'SpinDown' THEN
     IF lower < :SLN.LIFE OR lower IS NULL THEN
        :SLN.LIFE := :SLN.LIFE - 1;
     END IF;
  END IF;
END;
```

FIGURE 24.14   Responding to VBX control events.

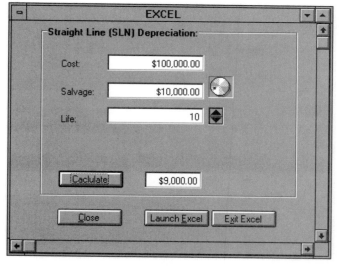

FIGURE 24.15   Implementation of VBX controls in Oracle Forms.

and run the application to see the new functionality. Figure 24.15 shows the appearance of the window at runtime.

24.5 SUMMARY

This chapter is a continuation of the previous chapter and focuses on OLE Automation, OLE Controls, and VBX Controls. Important concepts discussed are listed here:

- ❑ OLE Automation
- ❑ OLE Automation in Oracle Forms
    - ❑ OLE2 package
    - ❑ OLE Automation with spreadsheets
    - ❑ OLE Automation with word processors
- ❑ OLE controls
- ❑ VBX controls
    - ❑ Properties of VBX control items
    - ❑ Manipulating VBX controls programmatically
    - ❑ VBX controls in Oracle Forms—KNOB.VBX
    - ❑ VBX controls in Oracle Forms—SPIN.VBX

FOREIGN FUNCTIONS INTERFACE

"Skilled in the works of both languages."
—Horace

- Types of Foreign Functions
- Sample Foreign Functions
- User Exit Interface
- PL/SQL Foreign Function Interface
- Summary

Another important add-on functionality provided by Oracle Forms, besides DDE and OLE integration, is the utilization of modules created with Third Generation Languages (3GL) tools such as C, FORTRAN, and COBOL. The functions and procedures in these modules can be accessed in the form of user exits and foreign functions interface directly from PL/SQL. This chapter will discuss the process of creating and accessing C functions, and most importantly, Windows Software Development Kit (SDK) functions both from user exits and the PL/SQL foreign functions interface.

25.1 TYPES OF FOREIGN FUNCTIONS

In MS Windows, foreign functions can be accessible only if they are bundled in a Dynamic Link Library (DLL) file. Therefore, any programming language or compiler that can create DLL can also be used to write a library of foreign functions that will be used from Oracle Forms. If the foreign function contains only language constructs that belong to the native language, for example C, the function is called a non-Oracle foreign function. The reason for this name is that from within these functions, you cannot access any of the Oracle Forms variables and items, or the Oracle database. You write these functions using the compiler of the host language.

If you want your functions to access the Oracle database independently, you create the so-called Oracle Call Interface (OCI) functions. However, these functions do not allow you to access variable values from Oracle Forms or other development tools. Therefore, they are rarely used in Oracle Forms applications.

When it is desirable that the foreign functions have access to the Oracle Forms variables or the Oracle database, you can use Oracle Precompilers to create these functions. In Oracle Precompilers functions you can combine valid syntactic constructs of the host language with SQL statements, PL/SQL blocks, and Oracle Forms variables. The precompiler interprets these files and produces source files that contain only host-language statements. All SQL or PL/SQL statements are converted to their equivalents in the host language. You can compile and link this file as you would normally do with any other file. For example, you use the Pro*C precompiler to create an Oracle Precompiler function for the C language. This function is saved in a file with the extension .PC. When Pro*C processes this file, it checks for the accuracy of SQL and PL/SQL statements contained therein. If no errors are encountered, a file with the extension .C is produced at the end of the process. This file then can be passed to the C compiler for normal compilation and linking processing.

The Oracle Precompiler functions can use any of the host-language statements. In addition, they can execute any SQL statement by preceding it with the keywords EXEC SQL. To execute Oracle Precompiler options that are not standard SQL commands, you prefix them with the keywords EXEC ORACLE.

Another important set of statements used in precompiler functions are those that transfer data, context information, and messages between Oracle Forms items or variables and host-language variables. These statements are EXEC TOOLS GET, EXEC TOOLS SET, EXEC TOOLS MESSAGE, EXEC TOOLS GET CONTEXT, and EXEC TOOLS SET CONTEXT.

The statement EXEC TOOLS GET is used to pass values from Oracle Forms variables such as items, parameters, and global and system variables to variables in the 3GL program. The statement EXEC TOOLS SET sets an Oracle Forms variable to a value currently stored in the host-language variable. EXEC TOOLS MESSAGE allows you to send a message from the foreign function to the Oracle Forms environment. Finally, the statements EXEC TOOLS SET CONTEXT and EXEC TOOLS GET CONTEXT are used to maintain certain values globally, across calls of foreign functions, much in the same way global variables in Oracle Forms preserve values across program units. EXEC TOOLS SET CONTEXT is used to associate the desired value with a context name, and EXEC TOOLS GET CONTEXT is used to retrieve the value previously stored in a context variable.

25.2 SAMPLE FOREIGN FUNCTIONS

In this chapter, you will use several C functions to discuss their implementation in user exit interfaces and PL/SQL foreign functions interface. This section describes the contents of these functions, and in Section 25.3.2 you will create a DLL library that contains these functions. This library will be used to access these functions from within Oracle Forms. The samples of this chapter were compiled using Microsoft Visual C++ 1.52. If you are using a different compiler, you should use the appropriate instructions for creating DLL projects, however, you will not have to modify any of the source code files.

25.2.1 MODULES UEERROR.H AND UEERROR.C

The module UEERROR.H is a header file that contains the definition of Failure, Fatal, and Success codes that other functions will return. It also contains the declaration for a function that will display an error message to the Oracle Forms users, if this is necessary.

The module UEERROR.C contains the function that displays an error message that is raised by one of the other functions. The contents of this function are shown in Figure 25.1.

There are three functions from the Windows SDK toolkit that are used in function **UEError**:

❑ The function **wsprintf** formats the characters in the third argument according to the specifications in the format-control string, specified by the second argument. The formatted character is stored in the buffer provided by the first argument. In your case, you are formatting the title and the text of the error message as character strings.

```
#include <windows.h>

#include "ueerror.h"


void UEError ( LPSTR messageTitle, LPSTR messageText )
{
    char text[200],
         title[80];

    wsprintf (title,"%s",messageTitle);
    wsprintf (text,"%s",messageText);

    MessageBox ( GetActiveWindow(),text,title,MB_ICONSTOP);
}
```

FIGURE 25.1   C function that displays a message box.

❑ The function MessageBox creates and displays a message box window. The first argument in this function is the handle of the window that will be the parent of the dialog box. The following two arguments contain respectively the text and the title of the message box. The last argument defines the style of the dialog box. In this case, the message box will contain a stop-sign icon and one OK button to dismiss it. The function returns the numeric value of the button that was pressed to dismiss the dialog box.

❑ The function GetActiveWindow is used to return the handle of the window that is the active windows when the message box is created. This also serves as the parent window for the new message box. You may also set this parameter to NULL.

Note

The example shown in Figure 25.1 can also serve as a template for implementing your own customized message boxes. Recall from Chapter 15 that Oracle Forms uses alerts to display messages to the users. However, in order to use some standard Windows dialog boxes, you may call directly the Windows SDK function **MessageBox.** If, for example, you set the last parameter to MB_ICONQUESTION | MB_YESNOCANCEL, the message box will display a questions mark icon (which cannot be obtained by alerts) and three buttons: Yes, No, and Cancel.

25.2.2   MODULE HELP.C

This file contains the definitions for the functions WinHelpIndex, WinHelpContents, WinHelpQuit, WinHelpSearchOn, and WinHelpContext. Figure 25.2 shows the contents of the function WinHelpIndex. Given the similarity between the contents of this function with the remaining four functions, they will not be discussed in this section.

The input argument of this function will be a string like WinHelpIndex file=c:\example\helpfile.hlp. The function strtok is used to parse the string in different tokens. In the first call, this function scans the argument inputArgs until it reaches the first blank space. The pointer to this string is returned to the variable parameter. The successive call reads the next token from the string inputArg, until the character '=' is found. This token must be the keyword FILE for the processing to continue. Another call to strtok returns the string up to the first empty space that is found, which is also the name of the help file passed as the input argument. Note that to retrieve any other tokens after the first one, the first argument to strtok must be NULL.

After the name of the file is parsed, the function OpenFile is used to check for the existence of the file. When the parameter OF_EXIST is used, Windows opens and closes the file without affecting any of its attributes. If the file does not exist, the function returns the value -1, in which case, you inform the user about the invalid file name.

Finally, when you are sure about the existence of the file, the Windows function WinHelp is invoked. This function starts the Windows Help engine in different configurations, depending on the arguments passed. The first argument is a handle to the window that is requesting help. The second is a pointer to the name of the file to be opened. The last two arguments are used in combination to specify the type of help to be displayed and other additional data required to display it. In the case shown in Figure 25.2, the parameter HELP_INDEX will open the topic "Index" defined within the help file.

Note

Fundamentally, all these functions invoke the Windows SDK function **WinHelp.** Their differences come from different values of the arguments passed to this function. The meaning of these values and arguments is documented in any book that covers the Windows SDK and in the on-line help that comes with programming tools such as Visual Basic, or compilers such as Microsoft Visual C++ and Borland C++.

```
#include <windows.h>
#include <string.h>
#include <stdio.h>
#include <stdlib.h>

#include "ueerror.h"


/*
** user_exit('WinHelpIndex file=c:\example\helpfile.hlp');
**          Opens the help file at the "Index"
*/
int WinHelpIndex(inputArgs)
    char        *inputArgs;
{
    HWND          hParentWin;
    OFSTRUCT      of;
    HANDLE        hFile;
    char          *fileName, *Parameter;

    char          errorTitle[80] = "Error in User Exit WinHelpIndex";
    char          invalidFile[80] = "Invalid WinHelp File Name.";
    char          invalidFileParameter[100] = "Invalid FILE Parameter.";

    Parameter = strtok(inputArgs," ");
    Parameter = strtok(NULL,"=");

    if ( strcmp(strupr(Parameter),"FILE")==0 )
        fileName = strtok(NULL," ");
    else
    {
        UEError(errorTitle, invalidFileParameter);
        return FATAL_ERR;
    }

    hFile = OpenFile((LPSTR)fileName,&of,OF_EXIST);

    if ( hFile != -1 ) // OpenFile returns -1 if unsuccessful
    {
        hParentWin = GetActiveWindow();
        WinHelp(hParentWin,(LPSTR) fileName,HELP_INDEX,NULL);
    }
    else
    {
        UEError(errorTitle, invalidFile);
        return FATAL_ERR;
    }

    return SUCCESS;
} /* WinHelpIndex */
```

FIGURE 25.2   C function that invokes Windows Help utility.

The WinHelpContents function invokes WinHelp with the parameter HELP_CONTENTS, which displays the Help contents topic as defined in the [OPTIONS] section of the Help project file. The function WinHelpQuit invokes WinHelp with the parameter HELP_QUIT. This instructs the Help engine that Help is no longer needed for the application that opened it. Windows closes the Help file and, if no other applications are using Help, it dismisses the Help engine.

For all these functions, the fourth parameter is not needed, therefore it is set to NULL. For the remaining two functions however, this parameter is used. In the function WinHelpSearchOn, the statement that calls WinHelp is as in the following line:

```
WinHelp(hParentWin,(LPSTR) fileName,HELP_KEY, (DWORD)
        (LPSTR) Parameter);
```

The argument HELP_KEY instructs WinHelp that help is requested on the string contained in the Parameter. If there is exactly one topic that matches this string, this topic is displayed. Otherwise the Search dialog box is displayed to allow users to select the appropriate topic.

In the function WinHelpContext, the function WinHelp is invoked as follows:

```
WinHelp(hParentWin,(LPSTR) fileName,HELP_CONTEXT,
        (DWORD) numericContext);
```

In this case, the parameter HELP_CONTEXT informs WINHELP to display Help for the topic identified by the context number contained in the fourth parameter. This number must have been defined in the [MAP] section of the Help project file.

Obviously, in these functions, an additional step is required to parse the fourth parameter. For a detailed description of these functions, refer to module HELP.C provided in the companion disk.

25.2.3 MODULE FILENAME.PC

This file contains the definition of the function GetFileName, which makes use of another Windows SDK function, GetOpenFileName, to display a dialog box similar to Open or Save, which will allow users to browse the directory structure, search for a file, and return its name to an Oracle Forms item. The steps of this function are described below:

1. Initialize and set data items such as the title of the dialog box, or the error message.
2. Use the function GetSystemDirectory to retrieve the current system directory. This will be the initial directory displayed by the dialog box.
3. Replace the wildcard—by convention this is the last character of szFilter—with the NULL character '\0'. For example, if the variable szFilter was ini-

tialized to "All Files (*.*) | *.* | ", at the end of the FOR loop, its value will be "All Files (*.*)\0*.*\0".

4. Get the handle of the current window that will serve as the parent for the Get File Name dialog box.

5. Clear and initialize the structure ofn, based on the data prepared in the previous steps.

6. Invoke the function GetOpenFileName which takes the structure ofn and uses it to populate the components of the dialog box. If the user selects a file from the dialog box, this function returns a non-zero value and stores the name of the file in the lpstrFile member of the structure. This string is placed in the buffer that will store the name of the selected file.

Figure 25.3 shows the details of this function.

As you can see from Figure 25.3, the function GetFileName stores the name of the file selected by users in the buffer szBuffer which is passed as an argument to this function by the calling environment. In order to make this value available to Oracle Forms, you must transfer it from this buffer to a variable in Forms. The function ReturnFileName serves this purpose. Because this function will access Forms items, the Oracle Pro*C Compiler must be used. This function is contained in the file FILENAME.PC, as well, and is shown in detail in Figure 25.4.

As you can notice, this function parses the input argument string in a similar fashion as the WinHelp functions discussed previously. Note, however, that the variables that will be used in the SQL statement are declared in a separate DECLARE section, bounded by the EXEC SQL BEGIN DECLARE and EXEC SQL END DECLARE statements. Furthermore, you should also notice that PL/SQL variables of VARCHAR data type are structures of two components. After you precompile the file FILENAME.PC, you can open the module FILENAME.C generated by the Pro*C precompiler. You will see that the precompiler has replaced the declaration

VARCHAR FormsItemName[256];

with the following statements:

```
struct {
unsigned short len;
unsigned char arr[256];
} FormsItemName;
```

In the rest of the function, you can reference both components of this structure. As you can see from Figure 25.4, the component FormsItemName.arr is where the contents of the variable reside; the component FormsItemName.len holds the number of characters currently stored in the first component.

```c
#include <windows.h>
#include <string.h>
#include <commdlg.h>
#include <memory.h>

#include "ueerror.h"

int    GetFileName ( LPSTR szBuffer )
{
     HWND          hParentWin;
     OPENFILENAME  ofn;
     char          szDirName[256], szFile[256], szFileTitle[256];
     UINT          i, cbString;
     char          chReplace, /* string separator for szFilter */
                   szFilter[256] = "All Files (*.*)|*.*|",
                   dialogTitle[80] = "Get File Name\0";

     /* Get the system directory name, and store in szDirName */
     GetSystemDirectory(szDirName, sizeof(szDirName));
     szFile[0] = '\0';

     cbString = lstrlen(szFilter);
     chReplace = szFilter[cbString - 1]; /* retrieve wildcard */
     for (i = 0; szFilter[i] != '\0'; i++) { /* Replace wildcard with '\0' */
         if (szFilter[i] == chReplace)
            szFilter[i] = '\0';
     }

     hParentWin = GetActiveWindow();

     /* Set all structure members to zero. */
     memset(&ofn, 0, sizeof(OPENFILENAME));

     /* Initialize structure members. */
     ofn.lStructSize = sizeof(OPENFILENAME);
     ofn.hwndOwner = hParentWin;
     ofn.lpstrFilter = szFilter;
     ofn.nFilterIndex = 1;
     ofn.lpstrFile= szFile;
     ofn.nMaxFile = sizeof(szFile);
     ofn.lpstrFileTitle = szFileTitle;
     ofn.nMaxFileTitle = sizeof(szFileTitle);
     ofn.lpstrInitialDir = szDirName;
     ofn.Flags = OFN_SHOWHELP | OFN_PATHMUSTEXIST | OFN_FILEMUSTEXIST;
     ofn.lpstrTitle = dialogTitle;

     if (GetOpenFileName(&ofn))
         lstrcpy (szBuffer,ofn.lpstrFile);
     else     {
         *szBuffer=0;
     return FATAL_ERR;
     }
    return SUCCESS;
}
```

FIGURE 25.3   C function that displays a standard Open dialog box.

```
int ReturnFileName(inputArgs)
  char *inputArgs;
{
  char *Parameter, szBuffer[256], *itemName,
  errorTitle[80] = "Error in User Exit RetrieveFileName\0",
  invalidItemParameter[80] = "Invalid Parameter.  ITEM was expected.\0",
  errorMsg[80] = "Cannot invoke the Get File Name dialog box.\0";

  EXEC SQL INCLUDE SQLCA;

  EXEC SQL BEGIN DECLARE SECTION;
       VARCHAR fileName[256];
       VARCHAR FormsItemName[256];
  EXEC SQL END DECLARE SECTION;

  Parameter = strtok(inputArgs," ");
  Parameter = strtok(NULL,"=");

  if ( strcmp(strupr(Parameter),"ITEM")==0 )
       itemName =  strtok(NULL," ");
  else  {
       UEError(errorTitle, invalidItemParameter);
       return FATAL_ERR;
  }

  if ( GetFileName ( szBuffer ) == SUCCESS )  {
       strcpy(FormsItemName.arr, itemName);
       FormsItemName.len = strlen( itemName );
       strcpy(fileName.arr, szBuffer);
       fileName.len = strlen( szBuffer );

       EXEC TOOLS SET :FormsItemName VALUES (:fileName);
  }
  else  {
       UEError(errorTitle, errorMsg);
       return FATAL_ERR;
  }

  return SUCCESS;
} /* ReturnFileName */
```

FIGURE 25.4   Pro*C Function that passes values to Oracle Forms variables.

25.3   USER EXIT INTERFACE

In order to access the above functions from a user exit in Oracle Forms, a Dynamic Link Library must be built to contain these and a few other functions. In this section you will create this library and the user exits calls step by step. If you have Pro*C installed in your machine, precompile the module FILENAME.PC. The output of this process will be the module FILENAME.C, which contains only C statements. This module is provided in the case where you do not have access to the Pro*C software. As a preliminary step, create a separate directory, where all the C functions will be placed and the DLLs will be created. Name this directory UE_CH25.

25.3.1   IAPXTB CONTROL STRUCTURE

IAPXTB is a tabular structure of pointers to the functions of a given DLL library that can be accessed from user exits. When Oracle Forms is installed, two templates of this structure are provided in the directory %ORACLE_HOME%\ FORMS45\USEREXIT. The first one, UE_XTB.C, contains a sample IAPXTB structure with only one function. The second template, UE_XTBN.C, contains only an empty structure, with no functions declared. Each line in the structure should follow the format shown below:

"Function_Name", CFunctionName, XITCC,

The string included in the double quotes contains the name of the function that will be used to refer to the function from a user exit. The second variable is the name of the function as defined in the host language module. The third variable is a reference to the programming language in which this function is created. XITCC denotes the C language, XITCOB denotes COBOL, and XITFOR denotes FORTRAN.

In your case, the IAPXTB structure is defined in the module UE_CH25.C, which you should copy from the companion disk into the directory UE_CH25. The contents of this function are shown in Figure 25.5.

The first part of this module declares functions that are contained in other modules. The central part of it is taken by the IAPXTB structure. Note that the IAPXTAB structure does not contain every function of the library, but only those functions that you will need to access from user exits.

The first line of this module is an **#include** statement for the header file UE.H. This file is found in the %ORACLE_HOME%\FORMS45\USEREXIT directory and must be copied in the directory UE_CH25 as well.

```
#include "ue.h"

extern ReturnFileName();
extern WinHelpIndex();
extern WinHelpContents();
extern WinHelpQuit();
extern WinHelpSearchOn();
extern WinHelpContext();

/* Define the user exit table */
extern   exitr iapxtb[] = {   /* Holds exit routine pointers */
        "ReturnFileName",   ReturnFileName, XITCC,
        "WinHelpIndex",     WinHelpIndex, XITCC,
        "WinHelpContents",  WinHelpContents, XITCC,
        "WinHelpQuit",      WinHelpQuit, XITCC,
        "WinHelpSearchOn",  WinHelpSearchOn, XITCC,
        "WinHelpContext",   WinHelpContext, XITCC,
       (char *) 0, 0, 0           /* zero entry marks the end */
}; /* end iapxtb  */
```

FIGURE 25.5   Contents of IAPXTB user exit structure.

25.3.2 CREATING THE DLL FILE

Now you are ready to create the new Dynamic Link Library file:

1. Launch the Microsoft Visual C++ compiler.
2. Choose Project | New... from the menu. The New Project dialog box is displayed (see Figure 25.6).
3. Set the Project Name to UE_CH25.
4. Select Windows Dynamic Link Library (.DLL) from the Project Type drop-down list box.

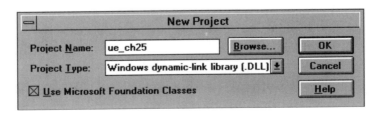

FIGURE 25.6   Microsoft Visual C++ New Project dialog box.

5. Click OK. The Edit - UE_CH25.MAK dialog box appears (see Figure 25.7). In this dialog box, you can add and delete members in the project file UE_CH25.MAK.

6. Click the button Add All to add all the C files listed in Figure 25.7.

7. Recall that the file FILENAME.C is created by the Oracle Pro*C Precompiler. In order to be able to link these files successfully, you should add to the project the libraries SQL16WIN.LIB and SQX16WIN.LIB. These libraries are provided in the companion disk and are both installed in the directory %ORACLE_HOME%\FORMS45\USEREXIT. If you have the Pro*C compiler installed in your machine, you may find these files in the directory %ORACLE_HOME%\PRO20\USEREXIT as well.

8. The directory %ORACLE_HOME%\FORMS45\USEREXIT contains some other files that you must include every time you create a user exit DLL. These files are F45XTB.DEF, UEZ.OBJ, OSSEWP.OBJ, and F45R.LIB. Oracle Forms records in the F45XTB.DEF file the export statements for functions that it uses to assess other user exit functions that you create. These statements must not be changed.

9. When all the files described above are added to the project, click button Close in the Edit UE_CH25.MAK dialog box.

10. Choose Project | Build UE_CH25.DLL, or Project | Rebuild UE_CH25.DLL from the menu to compile, link, and build the Dynamic Link Library.

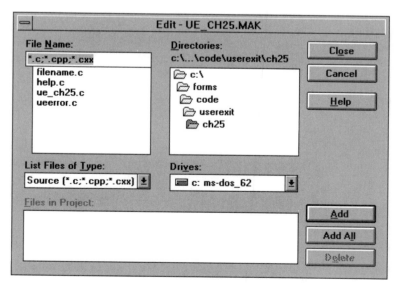

FIGURE 25.7   Microsoft Visual C++ Edit Makefile dialog box.

25.3.3 DEPLOYING THE USER EXIT DLL

By default, Oracle Forms will recognize user exits defined in the library F45XTB.DLL located in the directory %ORACLE_HOME%\BIN. One way to deploy the library built in the previous section is to rename it to F45XTB.DLL, and move it to that directory. This will obviously overwrite any functions that you may have previously linked in the F45XTB.DLL. For large applications, with a significant number of user exits, it is not recommended that all the foreign function be packed in the default DLL. Besides resource contention problems that may arise when a sizable DLL is loaded in the memory, you may also experience problems if multiple users access the library at the same time.

The other, more elegant approach is to bundle together related functions in separate DLLs, and to add the locations of these files in the definition of the environment variable FORMS45_USEREXIT. This variable is defined in the ORACLE.INI file. Spreading the foreign functions across multiple DLLs provides for a more flexible application that will better utilize the systems resources, and will be easier to maintain and upgrade in the future. In order to be able to follow the examples in the following section, you must make the new DLL available to the Oracle Forms user exits, in any of the two ways described above.

25.3.4 CALLING USER EXITS IN ORACLE FORMS

Now, you are ready to invoke the user exits created in the previous sections in the Oracle Forms applications you have worked with in this book. You can use the functions that invoke the Windows Help engine to add MS Windows help to these applications. As an example, you could integrate the file MRD.HLP with the application Movie Rental Database. This file is provided together with the other MRD application modules in the companion disk. It is assumed that you have copied it in the directory C:\MRD.

First, start by adding the call to the user exit from the Help menu item and the Help iconic button in the toolbar. The PL/SQL code executed from both these places is Click_Button('HELP'). Therefore you should edit this function in the PLL module MRDMENU.PLL.

1. Start the Oracle Forms Designer and open the PLL module MRDMENU.PLL.
2. Open the procedure Click_Button in the PL/SQL editor.
3. Enter the following statement in the PL/SQL editor for menu item Contents:

USER_EXIT('WinHelpContents FILE=MRD.HLP');

4. Compile and save the library module.

Now, open the form module MRD.FMB and add user exit calls to the Windows Help utility. Recall that there is a Help button defined in the windows

CUSTOMER, MOVIE, RENTAL, and MAIL. In order to add context-sensitive help to your application you should create a WHEN-BUTTON-PRESSED trigger for each of them. The triggers should contain the following statement:

```
USER_EXIT('WinHelpContext FILE= C:\MRD\MRD.HLP CONTEXT= i');
```

In this statement, i is the context number that has been associated with each particular Help topic in the [MAP] section of the Help project file MRD.HPJ. The following is a list of the context numbers for the principal windows of the application.

Customer	1
Movie	2
Rental	3
Mail	4

Save and generate the form module and run it to see the newly added Help functionality.

Now, integrate the functionality to browse the directory tree in search of a file. There are several forms that would benefit from such functionality. The module OLEWORD.FMB that you used in Chapter 24, for example, requires the use of a template form for the customer letter. You could improve the functionality of this module, by allowing users to search for the file that contains this template.

Note

The built-in procedure USER_EXIT, may take as a second argument an error message that is returned to Oracle Forms in case the call to the foreign function fails. Oracle Forms considers the call to a user exit like a call to any of its built-in program units, in the sense that no errors raised within the foreign function are passed to the calling environment. You can use the functions FORM_SUCCESS, FORM_FATAL, and FORM_FAILURE to check the outcome of a user exit routine. For example, the following lines represent a template for calling foreign functions from user exits in Oracle Forms:

```
USER_EXIT('ForeignFunctionName Arguments', 'Error
message');
IF NOT FORM_SUSSESS THEN
    /* Call to foreign function failed. */
END IF;
```

1. Open the module OLEWORD.FMB in the Designer.
2. In the Layout Editor create a push button labeled Browse..., and place it to the right of the data item TEMPLATE.
3. Create a WHEN-BUTTON-PRESSED trigger for this button. Enter the following statement in the body of the trigger:

   USER_EXIT('ReturnFileName ITEM=CUSTOMER.TEMPLATE');

4. Save, generate, and run the module to test the newly added functionality.

25.4 PL/SQL FOREIGN FUNCTION INTERFACE

Traditionally, Oracle Forms applications have been able to invoke and use foreign functions through user exits. Oracle Forms 4.5 enables you to access these functions directly from PL/SQL, by using the components of the ORA_FFI package. In order to be able to use this package, the foreign functions must be C functions bundled in a Dynamic Link Library, static library, or any executable application, created by you or by a third-party vendor.

25.4.1 COMPARING USER EXITS WITH THE PL/SQL FOREIGN FUNCTION INTERFACE

In order to access a foreign function from the PL/SQL, you must imitate the interface of this function with a PL/SQL function. This feature, under certain circumstances makes the PL/SQL interface more advantageous and flexible than the user exits.

A drawback of the user exits is that you must create and link at least the IAPXTB structure together with the other functions that you want to access. If these functions are located in third-party API modules, you will generally have to create a functional layer in the 3GL target language, in order to be able to compile and link these functions together in one DLL that can be addressed by the user exits. This means that you must switch repeatedly between PL/SQL programming and 3GL programming. The configuration of the application will also become more difficult to maintain in track, because of the number of additional files that need to be maintained. (Recall how many files you had to edit, compile, and link in the user exit examples in the previous sections.)

Another drawback of the user exit interface to foreign functions is that user exits written in straight C cannot directly return values to the Oracle Forms variables. In the example of function ReturnFileName in Section 25.2.3, you were able to return the file name chosen by the user only by using Oracle Precompiler statements. Although Pro*C is easy to learn and similar to C, the fact remains that you add to the system complexity by choosing to implement the function through a user exit.

Recall also that in order to invoke foreign functions from user exits, these foreign functions must be in a Dynamic Link Library. Furthermore, you must build the front-end IAPXTB matrix and often a layer of C functions on top of the existing DLL function. None of these is required when you access the functions through the PL/SQL interface. The member functions of the package ORA_FFI are all you will need to integrate foreign functions from any source in your Oracle Forms applications. Section 25.4.2 provides details about the components of this package and Section 25.4.3 shows you how to use these components to create the foreign functions interface manually.

Finally, Oracle Corporation provides a tool—Foreign Function Interface Generator—that facilitates the task of building a PL/SQL interface to any DLL library. This tool is the form module FFIGEN.FMB and is installed in the %ORACLE_HOME%\FORMS45\DEMOS\FOREIGN directory. Section 25.4.4 describes the tool and shows you how to use it to automate the process of creating this interface.

25.4.2   ORA_FFI PACKAGE

The ORA_FFI package contains data types, functions, procedures, and exceptions that are used in order to access foreign functions from PL/SQL program units.

There are three types of special objects used in the PL/SQL interface to foreign functions: libraries, functions, and pointers. Libraries represent the Dynamic Link Library, the static library, or the executable file that contains the foreign functions that will be accessed. In PL/SQL program units the libraries are addressed through handles, which are objects of ORA_FFI.LIBHANDLETYPE data type. Similarly, member functions of these libraries are accessed through handles of type ORA_FFI.FUNCHANDLETYPE. In rare occasions, you may need to implement unspecified pointers in your programs, similar to the void pointer in C. To obtain such variables, you must declare them of ORA_FFI.POINTERTYPE data type.

The following statement declares the variable lh_User as a library handle:

lh_User ORA_FFI.LIBHANDLETYPE;

The following statement declares the variable fh_WinHelp as a function handle:

fh_WinHelp ORA_FFI.FUNCHANDLETYPE;

The following statement declares the variable dwData as a pointer:

dwData ORA_FFI.POINTERTYPE;

The package ORA_FFI provides three functions that allow you to check if a library is currently loaded in memory, to load it if this is not the case, or to unload

> ## Note
>
> The data type ORA_FFI.POINTERTYPE is in reality a record structure with only one element in it called *handle*. This element is of NUMBER data type, which limits the use of these pointers. The following statement assigns the value 5 to the variable dwData:
>
> **dwData.handle := 5;**

it when no longer needed. The function ORA_FFI.FIND_LIBRARY takes as an argument the name of a library and returns a handle to it, if the library is previously loaded. Otherwise, this function raises the exception ORA_FFI.FFI_ERROR. The function ORA_FFI.LOAD_LIBRARY takes as parameter the directory and the name of the library. If the library file is located in the current system directory, or in a directory that is included in the PATH environment variable, you may set the directory argument to NULL, and provide simply the library name. The function loads the library and returns a handle to it. If the loading process is not successful the function returns NULL. When you are finished using the functions in a library, you may want to unload it, in order to release the system resources it occupies. Use the procedure ORA_FFI.UNLOAD_LIBRARY for this purpose. This procedure takes as argument the handle of the library to be unloaded.

Figure 25.8 shows sample code that registers the Windows library USER.EXE, and the user exit library that you developed in the previous sections. Once the library is loaded, all its member functions become available for you to use. As a preliminary step though, you must initialize them. Initializing a function is a process that involves the following three steps:

```
BEGIN
  lh_USER := ORA_FFI.FIND_LIBRARY('USER.EXE');
EXCEPTION WHEN ORA_FFI.FFI_ERROR THEN
  lh_USER := ORA_FFI.LOAD_LIBRARY(NULL,'USER.EXE');
END;
```

```
BEGIN
  lh_UE_CH25 := ORA_FFI.FIND_LIBRARY('UE_CH25.DLL');
EXCEPTION WHEN ORA_FFI.FFI_ERROR THEN
  lh_USER :=
ORA_FFI.LOAD_LIBRARY('C:\FORMS\USEREXIT\','UE_CH25.DLL');
END;
```

FIGURE 25.8   Loading DLL libraries with ORA_FFI procedures.

> **Note**
>
> The library USER.EXE is located in the directory \WINDOWS\SYSTEM, which is always accessible to Windows. This is the reason why you do not need to specify the directory in the function that loads this library. On the other hand, the directory must be specified in the second case, assuming that the directory C:\FORMAPPS\USEREXIT is not in the path. Note how the directory name must be terminated with the back slash character '\'.

1. Register the function using ORA_FFI.REGISTER_FUNCTION. This function takes as arguments the library handle where the foreign function is located, the name of the function, and the calling standard used by the function. The value of the last argument can be either ORA_FFI.PASCAL_STD for functions that follow the Pascal/FORTRAN naming and calling standards, or ORA_FFI.C_STD for those functions that follow the C naming and calling standards.

> **Note**
>
> When C or C++ declarators (functions, arrays, and pointers) are preceded by the keyword __pascal, the compiler uses the Pascal/FORTRAN naming and calling convention. The Pascal/FORTRAN naming convention requires that all names be converted to uppercase. The Pascal/FORTRAN calling convention requires that the arguments of a function be pushed from left to right.
>
> When the names of variables or functions are preceded by the keyword __cdecl, the compiler is instructed to follow the C naming and calling conventions. The C naming conventions require that the names of variables and functions be preceded by an underscore character, and the case sensitivity be maintained. The C calling convention requires that the arguments of a function be pushed from right to left.
>
> The C naming and calling conventions are the default. Therefore, unless you use the keyword __pascal, all the variables and functions you use in your programs will follow these conventions.
>
> However, almost all the Windows SDK functions and variables follow the Pascal/FORTRAN naming and calling conventions.

Specified Value	Corresponding C Datatype
ORA_FFI.C_CHAR	char
ORA_FFI.C_CHAR_PTR	char·*
ORA_FFI.C_SHORT	short
ORA_FFI.C_SHORT_PTR	short·*
ORA_FFI.C_INT	int
ORA_FFI.C_INT_PTR	int·*
ORA_FFI.C_DOUBLE	double
ORA_FFI.C_DOUBLE_PTR	double·*
ORA_FFI.C_LONG	long
ORA_FFI.C_LONG_PTR	long·*
ORA_FFI.C_FLOAT	float
ORA_FFI.C_FLOAT_PTR	float·*
ORA_FFI.C_DVOID_PTR	void·*

FIGURE 25.9 Mapping of argument types to C data types.

2. Use the procedure ORA_FFI.REGISTER_PARAMETER to register the type of each argument of the function. This procedure takes as arguments the handle to the function and the C data type of the function argument being registered. The values that the second argument may take are presented in Figure 25.9.

3. Use the procedure ORA_FFI.REGISTER_RETURN to register the return type of the foreign function. This procedure is very similar to the procedure ORA_FFI.REGISTER_PARAMETER. It takes as first argument the handle of the function, and as second argument the C data type that will be returned by the function.

In the general case, all the above steps must be performed in order to properly initialize a foreign function. However, depending on the type of function being initialized, Step 2 or Step 3 may not be necessary. If, for example, the C function does not take any arguments, you may skip Step 2. If the function return type is void, thus the function is a procedure, you do need to register a return type, therefore, the Step 3 may be skipped.

Figure 25.10 shows examples of initialization of three functions from the Windows SDK USER library.

The first group of statements registers the functions WinHelp, the types of arguments, and its return type. The second group of statements registers the procedure SetWindowText, and the data types of its two arguments. This procedure sets the title of the window whose handle is passed in the first argument to the character string contained in the second argument. Finally, the last two statements register the function GetActiveWindow and its return type. This function does not take any arguments and returns a handle to the window that is currently active.

```
fh_WinHelp := ORA_FFI.REGISTER_FUNCTION(lh_USER,'WinHelp',ORA_FFI.PASCAL_STD);
ORA_FFI.REGISTER_PARAMETER(fh_WinHelp,ORA_FFI.C_INT);
ORA_FFI.REGISTER_PARAMETER(fh_WinHelp,ORA_FFI.C_CHAR_PTR);
ORA_FFI.REGISTER_PARAMETER(fh_WinHelp,ORA_FFI.C_INT);
ORA_FFI.REGISTER_PARAMETER(fh_WinHelp,ORA_FFI.C_DVOID_PTR);
ORA_FFI.REGISTER_RETURN(fh_WinHelp,ORA_FFI.C_INT);

fh_SetWindowText := ORA_FFI.REGISTER_FUNCTION(lh_USER,'SetWindowText',ORA_FFI.
                   PASCAL_STD);
ORA_FFI.REGISTER_PARAMETER(fh_SetWindowText,ORA_FFI.C_INT);
ORA_FFI.REGISTER_PARAMETER(fh_SetWindowText,ORA_FFI.C_CHAR_PTR);

fh_GetActiveWindow := ORA_FFI.REGISTER_FUNCTION(lh_USER,'GetActiveWindow',
                   ORA_FFI.PASCAL_STD);
ORA_FFI.REGISTER_RETURN(fh_GetActiveWindow,ORA_FFI.C_INT);
```

FIGURE 25.10 Different cases of C functions initialization.

Let us conclude this section by mentioning the function ORA_FFI.IS_NULL _PTR. You can use this function to check if any library handle, function handle, or pointer is NULL. In such case, the function returns the Boolean value TRUE; otherwise it returns the value FALSE.

25.4.3 IMPLEMENTING THE PL/SQL FOREIGN FUNCTION INTERFACE

In this section, you will create a PL/SQL interface to several functions from the Windows USER.EXE library. Some of these functions such as WinHelp, GetActiveWindow, and SetWindowText, were introduced in the previous section, where you learned how to register them, their parameter types, and return data type. In addition to these, you will also use the function MessageBox, to display message boxes quickly and easily without going through Oracle Forms alerts. For a detailed description of the use of these functions and their parameters, you should consult the Windows SDK documentation that comes with compilers such as Microsoft Visual C++, or Borland C++, or Visual Basic.

The module you will work with in this section is called PLSQLFF1.FMB. This is a one-block form that can display message boxes and Windows Help using the Windows SDK functions mentioned above. The layout of this form is presented in Figure 25.11.

In the first half of the window you will be able to enter the title, text, and style of the message box that will be displayed. In the second half you can enter the name of the help file, the command, and additional data, if required by the command. For the items STYLE and COMMAND, list of values will help you choose the appropriate value of the parameter. In the rest of this section you will create the triggers and program units that will display the message box and the help file according to the specified parameters.

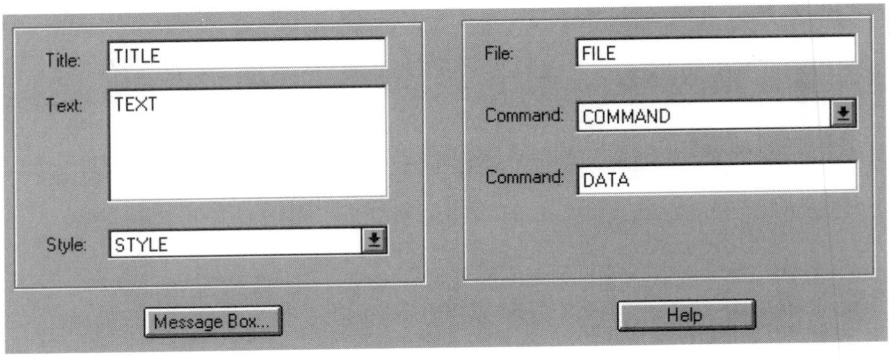

FIGURE 25.11　Layout of module CH25.FMB.

The program units that will carry out this functionality will be encapsulated in a package. Because this package will implement the foreign function interface with the library USER.EXE, its name will be FFI_USER. Start the development activity by creating the specification for this package:

1. Launch the Oracle Forms Designer, and open the module PLSQLFF1.FMB.
2. Create a package specification called FFI_USER.
3. Enter the contents of the package specification as shown in Figure 25.12.

```
PACKAGE FFI_USER IS
  FUNCTION WinHelp (hwnd IN PLS_INTEGER,
    lpszHelpFile IN OUT VARCHAR2,
    fuCommand IN PLS_INTEGER,
    dwData IN OUT ORA_FFI.POINTERTYPE)
  RETURN PLS_INTEGER;

  FUNCTION GetActiveWindow
  RETURN PLS_INTEGER;

  FUNCTION MessageBox ( hwndParent IN PLS_INTEGER,
    lpszText IN OUT VARCHAR2,
    lpszTitle IN OUT VARCHAR2,
    fuStyle IN PLS_INTEGER)
  RETURN PLS_INTEGER;
END;
```

FIGURE 25.12　Specification for package FFI_USER.

```
BOOL WinHelp(hwnd, lpszHelpFile, fuCommand, dwData)
   HWND hwnd;              /* handle of window requesting help   */
   LPCSTR lpszHelpFile; /* address of directory-path string  */
   UINT fuCommand;        /* type of help                      */
   DWORD dwData;          /* additional data                   */

HWND GetActiveWindow(void)

int MessageBox(hwndParent, lpszText, lpszTitle, fuStyle)
   HWND hwndParent;       /* handle of parent window          */
   LPCSTR lpszText;       /* address of text in message box   */
   LPCSTR lpszTitle;      /* address of title of message box  */
   UINT fuStyle;          /* style of message box             */
```

FIGURE 25.13   Definitions of the Windows functions in the USER.EXE Library.

Defining these functions, their return types, number of arguments, and the data type for each argument is as easy as looking up the definition of the corresponding functions in the Windows SDK documentation. Figure 25.13 shows the definitions of these functions in the Windows library.

An important difference is that the data types of arguments and the return type of the functions in the package FFI_USER are PL/SQL data types. Given that the other program units in the Oracle Forms application will access these functions only through the package specification interface, you guaranty that they will not have to rely on any implementation details of these functions.

When creating the program units for the body of this package you should follow these steps:

1. Declare variables that will store the handle to the foreign functions library and the foreign functions that will be used from that library.
2. Load the C library, and register the functions, their return type, and the data types of all their parameters. This should be done in the execution part of the package body.
3. For each function in the package specification, create a subordinate function, whose only purpose is to associate the C foreign function, or rather its handle, with the PL/SQL data types and return type of the function.
4. Create the body of each function declared in the package specification. The ultimate purpose of this function is to issue a call to the subordinate function created in the previous step. This function then, will bind the data passed as arguments with the C function through the function handle. The foreign function will be executed, and will return a value to the PL/SQL environment.

The previous section explained how you can implement the first two steps. You simply declare the desired variables using the data types defined in the package

```
PACKAGE BODY FFI_USER IS
   lh_User ORA_FFI.LIBHANDLETYPE;
   fh_WinHelp ORA_FFI.FUNCHANDLETYPE;
   fh_GetActiveWindow ORA_FFI.FUNCHANDLETYPE;
   fh_MessageBox ORA_FFI.FUNCHANDLETYPE;

/* Function declarations will go here. */

BEGIN
  BEGIN
    lh_USER := ORA_FFI.find_library('USER.EXE');
  EXCEPTION WHEN ORA_FFI.FFI_ERROR THEN
    lh_USER := ORA_FFI.load_library(NULL,'USER.EXE');
  END;

  fh_WinHelp :=
  ORA_FFI.REGISTER_FUNCTION(lh_USER,'WinHelp',ORA_FFI.PASCAL_STD);
  ORA_FFI.REGISTER_PARAMETER(fh_WinHelp,ORA_FFI.C_INT);
  ORA_FFI.REGISTER_PARAMETER(fh_WinHelp,ORA_FFI.C_CHAR_PTR);
  ORA_FFI.REGISTER_PARAMETER(fh_WinHelp,ORA_FFI.C_INT);
  ORA_FFI.REGISTER_PARAMETER(fh_WinHelp,ORA_FFI.C_DVOID_PTR);
  ORA_FFI.REGISTER_RETURN(fh_WinHelp,ORA_FFI.C_INT);

  fh_GetActiveWindow :=

  ORA_FFI.REGISTER_FUNCTION(lh_USER,'GetActiveWindow',ORA_FFI.PASCAL_STD);
  ORA_FFI.REGISTER_RETURN(fh_GetActiveWindow,ORA_FFI.C_INT);

  fh_MessageBox :=

  ORA_FFI.REGISTER_FUNCTION(lh_USER,'MessageBox',ORA_FFI.PASCAL_STD);
  ORA_FFI.REGISTER_PARAMETER(fh_MessageBox,ORA_FFI.C_INT);
  ORA_FFI.REGISTER_PARAMETER(fh_MessageBox,ORA_FFI.C_CHAR_PTR);
  ORA_FFI.REGISTER_PARAMETER(fh_MessageBox,ORA_FFI.C_CHAR_PTR);
  ORA_FFI.REGISTER_PARAMETER(fh_MessageBox,ORA_FFI.C_INT);
  ORA_FFI.REGISTER_RETURN(fh_MessageBox,ORA_FFI.C_INT);
END;
```

FIGURE 25.14 Declaring and initializing the functions in package FFI_USER.

ORA_FFI. Then, you use the necessary functions from this package to load the library and register the foreign functions, their arguments, and their return values. In order to do this in your case, create a package body, name it FFI_USER, and enter its contents as shown in Figure 25.14. Be aware that the package shown in this figure is not complete yet and will not compile successfully.

Now you are ready to create the functions that will implement the interface of the package. These functions should be created in the declaration part of the

```
FUNCTION icd_WinHelp (funcHandle IN ORA_FFI.FUNCHANDLETYPE,
  hwnd IN PLS_INTEGER,
  lpszHelpFile IN OUT VARCHAR2,
  fuCommand IN PLS_INTEGER,
  dwData IN OUT ORA_FFI.POINTERTYPE)
RETURN PLS_INTEGER;
PRAGMA INTERFACE(C,icd_WinHelp,11265);

FUNCTION WinHelp (hwnd IN PLS_INTEGER,
  lpszHelpFile IN OUT VARCHAR2,
  fuCommand IN PLS_INTEGER,
  dwData IN OUT ORA_FFI.POINTERTYPE)
RETURN PLS_INTEGER IS
  rc PLS_INTEGER;
BEGIN
  rc := icd_WinHelp(fh_WinHelp, hwnd, lpszHelpFile, fuCommand, dwData);
  RETURN (rc);
END ;
```

FIGURE 25.15   Using the PRAGMA directive to bind PL/SQL variables with foreign functions.

package body, immediately after the statements that declare the handle variables to the library and the foreign functions. Figure 25.15 contains the details of the functions that are needed to implement the interface with the WinHelp function.

First, the subordinate function icd_WinHelp is declared. This is very similar to the WinHelp function declared in the package specification. It returns the same type of data and takes the same arguments as this function. One important difference to point out is that the function icd_WinHelp takes as its first argument the handle to the foreign function registered previously. Another significant difference with PL/SQL program units you have seen so far is that this function is passed for execution to the component of Oracle Forms that interfaces with C libraries. The PRAGMA directive instructs the compiler to execute this branching.

The statements in the body of function WinHelp are self-explanatory. The main purpose of this function is to bind the arguments with the foreign function handle by issuing a call to the function icd_WinHelp, which, in turn, will call the

Note

The only argument that you may change in the PRAGMA INTERFACE statement is the middle one that specifies the function name. The first and the third arguments must be exactly as shown in Figure 25.15 for all the cases.

foreign function. For the sake of simplicity, the statements shown in Figure 25.15 assume that all the arguments are valid. You may place other statements in the body of these functions to ensure that the appropriate data is passed along, or that any errors that may occur are trapped and handled.

The process of creating the functions GetActiveWindow and MessageBox is entirely similar. The contents of these functions are shown in Figure 25.16.

At this point you are ready to create the WHEN-BUTTON-PRESSED triggers for push buttons MESSAGE and HELP. Both these triggers will ultimately call the functions MessageBox and WinHelp from the package FFI_USER. Since both these functions require a window handle as their first parameter, the function GetActiveWindow is invoked prior to each of the other two functions. Figure

```
FUNCTION icd_GetActiveWindow (funcHandle IN ORA_FFI.FUNCHANDLETYPE)
RETURN PLS_INTEGER;
PRAGMA INTERFACE(C,icd_GetActiveWindow,11265);

FUNCTION GetActiveWindow
RETURN PLS_INTEGER IS
  rc PLS_INTEGER;
BEGIN
  rc := icd_GetActiveWindow(fh_GetActiveWindow);
  RETURN (rc);
END ;

FUNCTION icd_MessageBox(funcHandle IN ORA_FFI.FUNCHANDLETYPE,
  hwndParent IN PLS_INTEGER,
  lpszText IN OUT VARCHAR2,
  lpszTitle IN OUT VARCHAR2,
  fuStyle IN PLS_INTEGER)
RETURN PLS_INTEGER;
PRAGMA INTERFACE(C,icd_MessageBox,11265);

FUNCTION MessageBox (hwndParent IN PLS_INTEGER,
  lpszText IN OUT VARCHAR2,
  lpszTitle IN OUT VARCHAR2,
  fuStyle IN PLS_INTEGER)
RETURN PLS_INTEGER IS
  rc PLS_INTEGER;
BEGIN
  rc :=
icd_MessageBox(fh_MessageBox,hwndParent,lpszText,lpszTitle,fuStyle);
  RETURN (rc);
END ;
```

FIGURE 25.16   Accessing Windows SDK functions with ORA_FFI.

```
DECLARE
  rc PLS_INTEGER;
  hwnd PLS_INTEGER;
  command PLS_INTEGER := :WINHELP.COMMAND;
BEGIN
  hwnd := FFI_USER.GetActiveWindow;
  rc := FFI_USER.WinHelp (hwnd, :WINHELP.FILE, command, :WINHELP.DATA);
END;
```

```
DECLARE
  rc PLS_INTEGER;
  hwnd PLS_INTEGER;
  style PLS_INTEGER := :WINHELP.STYLE;
BEGIN
  hwnd := FFI_USER.GetActiveWindow;
  rc := FFI_USER.MessageBox (hwnd, :WINHELP.TEXT, :WINHELP.TITLE,
style);
END;
```

FIGURE 25.17   Calling foreign functions from PL/SQL triggers.

25.17 shows the contents of the triggers attached to the Help button and to the Message Box button, respectively.

By carefully examining the functions shown in this chapter, you will notice that all the variables that will correspond to C pointer types are declared as IN OUT variables. This allows Forms to treat these parameters as initialized variables, for which the appropriate memory is already allocated. If the default mode of the parameters (IN) is used, these parameters act like constants inside the body of the functions. In order for the subsequent call to the foreign function to work, you must declare a local variable, assign it the value of the parameter, and pass this local variable to the foreign function. Figure 25.18 shows an example of the function **WinHelp** implemented with IN parameters.

25.4.4   THE FOREIGN FUNCTION INTERFACE GENERATOR

Together with the Oracle Forms software, Oracle Corporation ships a variety of demonstration applications that are installed in %ORACLE_HOME%\ FORMS45\DEMOS directory. They all contain useful techniques and examples you should become familiar with. In the context of creating a PL/SQL interface to foreign functions, the module ORAFFI.FMB reduces the programming effort significantly, and minimizes the possibility of errors. The Foreign Function Interface Generator (FFIGen) application allows you to specify in one unified screen the name of the PL/SQL package to be created, the DLL library that contains the for-

```
FUNCTION WinHelp (hwnd IN PLS_INTEGER,
  lpszHelpFile IN VARCHAR2,
  fuCommand IN PLS_INTEGER,
  dwData IN ORA_FFI.POINTERTYPE)
RETURN PLS_INTEGER IS
  hwnd_1 PLS_INTEGER := hwnd;
  lpszHelpFile_1 VARCHAR2(144) := lpszHelpFile;
  fuCommand_1 PLS_INTEGER := fuCommand;
  dwData_1 ORA_FFI.POINTERTYPE := dwData;
  rc PLS_INTEGER;
BEGIN
  rc := i_WinHelp(fh_WinHelp, hwnd_1, lpszHelpFile_1,
fuCommand_1, dwData_1);
  RETURN (rc);
END;
```

FIGURE 25.18 Interfacing with foreign functions with IN arguments.

eign functions, and each function to be included in the package with information about its arguments and return datatype. The information you provide is stored in database tables and is used to generate a .PLL file which contains the PL/SQL package that interfaces with the foreign functions in the specified DLL.

FFIGen application has three components:

1. FFIGEN.SQL contains the SQL statements that create the application tables and insert the necessary data to generate the package WINSAMPLE used in another Oracle Forms demo.
2. FFIGEN.FMB contains the binary code for the form of FFIGen.
3. FFIGEN.MMB contains the binary code for the menu of FFIGen.

The installation utility installs the executables FFIGEN.FMX and FFIGEN.MMX as well. In case they are missing in your environment, you should generate them prior to using the application.

You can run the FFIGen application from the Forms Demo application in the Developer/2000 Demos program group or using the Oracle Forms Runtime tool. However, if you intend to use it frequently, it is better to create a separate program item in any program group you desire. The following steps assume that Oracle Forms executables are installed in C:\ORAWIN\BIN and the modules for the FFI-Gen application are in C:\ORAWIN\FORMS45\DEMOS\FOREIGN directory.

1. Create a program and specify the Description as

Foreign Function Interface Generator

2. Specify the Command Line as

   C:\ORAWIN\BIN\F45RUN.EXE
   C:\ORAWIN\FORMS45\DEMOS\FOREIGN\FFIGEN.FMX

3. Specify the Working Directory as

   C:\ORAWIN\FORMS45\DEMOS\FOREIGN

4. Choose an icon for this program item or simply accept the default Oracle
   Forms Runtime icon.

In the remaining part of this section, you will use the FFIGen application to generate the package FFI_USER which you created manually in Section 25.4.3. First,
launch the application and create the necessary database objects:

1. Double-click the program item created above. The Oracle Forms Logon dialog box appears.
2. Specify the username, password, and database connection string in the
   Logon dialog box. If the logon is successful and the FFIGen database objects
   do not exist in the schema you specify, the dialog box Foreign Function
   Demo Setup will appear (see Figure 25.19).
3. Click Create Tables button to create the FFIGen application tables. In this
   case, the script FFIGEN.SQL is executed. Alternatively, you may elect to run
   this script from SQL*Plus prior to invoking FFIGen for the first time.

After the logon and the installation of database objects is successful, you will see
the Foreign Function Interface Generator Demo window. This window contains
information about the package WINSAMPLE. In the following steps you will insert the information required to generate the package FFI_USER:

1. Click in the Package Name item, under WinSample and enter **FFI_USER**.
2. Click inside Dynamic Link Library Name item and enter **USER.EXE**.
3. Click inside Description item and enter comments for this package.

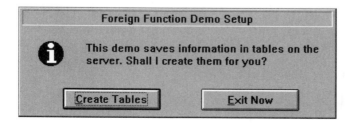

FIGURE 25.19   Foreign Function
Demo Setup dialog box.

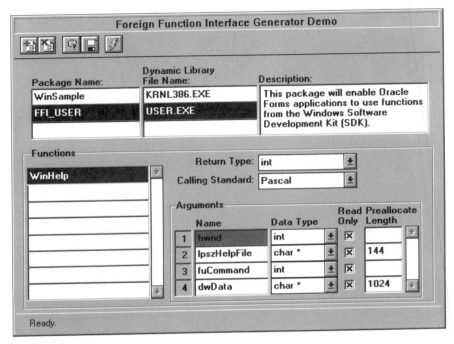

FIGURE 25.20   Foreign Function Interface Generator window.

4. Click in the Functions block and enter the information for function Win-Help, its return type, and arguments as shown in Figure 25.20.

5. Click under the function WinHelp, save the changes when prompted, and enter the information for function GetActiveWindow. As discussed earlier in the chapter, this function does not take any arguments, its return type is *int*, and the calling standard is *Pascal*.

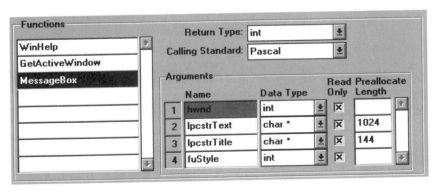

FIGURE 25.21   Specifications for GetActiveWindow function.

> **Note**
>
> You should always check the checkbox Read Only for IN arguments. For IN OUT or OUT variables this checkbox should not be checked. Furthermore, if the function will return some value to an argument, you must allocate enough space to that argument to hold the value. You do this by entering a value in the Preallocate Length field.

6. Click under the function GetActiveWindow, and enter the information for function MessageBox as shown in Figure 25.21.
7. Click the Save icon ⬛ to save the changes.
8. Click the Generate icon 🗐 to create the library FFI_USER.PLD in the working directory.

These steps are equivalent to the tedious manual coding effort described in Section 25.4.3. They result in a library that can be used in the module PLSQLFFI.FMB. Since FFI_USER.PLD is the text version of this library, you must convert it to .PLL format before attaching it to the form PLSQLFFI.FMB:

1. Launch the Oracle Forms Designer if it is not already running.
2. Select File | Administration | Convert... from the menu. The Convert dialog box appears (see Figure 25.22).
3. Specify the settings in the Convert dialog box as shown in Figure 25.22. Use the Browse utility to search for FFI_USER.PLD in the working directory of FFIGen application.
4. Click Convert. The text file FFI_USER.PLD is converted into the PLL file FFI_USER.PLL.

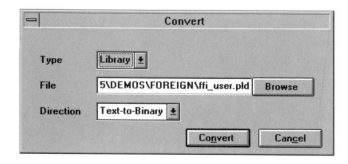

FIGURE 25.22 Convert dialog box.

> ## Note
>
> This is a quick and very effective way to create a package that provides you with a large amount of functionality. It is recommended that you use the FFIGen application whenever you need to create a PL/SQL interface to foreign functions. If you need to customize the contents of some of the functions or document your functions, you can edit the components of the generated package, but you will not have to do the heavy-duty programming prone to inconsistencies and errors required to manually develop this package.

5. Open FFI_USER.PLL in the Designer and select File | Compile... from the menu. The library should compile without errors.

6. Save FFI_USER.PLL in the same directory as PLSQLFFI.FMB.

7. Attach the library FFI_USER.PLL to PLSQLFFI.FMB and use the components of package FFI_USER as explained at the end of Section 25.4.3.

25.4.5 GENERATING FOREIGN FUNCTION INTERFACE PACKAGES FROM PROCEDURE BUILDER

The ORA_FFI packages contain a procedure that has not been mentioned so far in this discussion. Its name is ORA_FFI.GENERATE_FOREIGN, and can be used only in the Oracle Procedure Builder environment. After you load the C library and register all the functions and arguments that you want to use, you can invoke this procedure to create a PL/SQL package that will govern the PL/SQL interface with these functions. In this section you will perform the steps to accomplish this:

1. Launch the Oracle Procedure Builder.

2. Choose File | Load... from the menu. The Load Program Unit dialog box will appear.

3. Click the Browse... button if necessary to select the file FFI_USER.TXT, located under the same directory as the module CH25.FMB.

4. Click Load.

You will see that a procedure called FFI_USER is created when the file is loaded. If you display the contents of this procedure in the PL/SQL editor, you will notice that its body contains the type declarations and statements shown in Figure 25.14. To complete the process of creating the package, follow these steps:

> ## Note
>
> This method is certainly better than manual coding of the foreign function interface, but should be considered only if you cannot use the FFIGen application. Besides the fact that it still requires programming of the initialization part of the package, the package that it generates still requires editing for readability and documentation purposes. For example, an inspection of the package generated with this method will show that the arguments to the functions are named arg0, arg1, and so on, which are not very meaningful and should be clarified.

1. Enter the following lines at the end of the procedure, and compile it when done:

```
ORA_FFI.GENERATE_FOREIGN (lh_USER);
ORA_FFI.UNLOAD_LIBRARY (lh_USER);
```

2. Choose Tools|PL/SQL Interpreter... from the menu. The PL/SQL Interpreter window becomes the active window.
3, At the PL/SQL> prompt enter the following command:

.EXECUTE PROC FFI_USER

If you switch back to the Navigator, you will see that two new objects are created: the package specification FFI_USER and package body FFI_USER. This is a fully functional package that you can put in a library, attach to any module, and use in your applications.

25.5 SUMMARY

This chapter discussed the integration of Oracle Forms with Dynamic Loadable Libraries. It explained the traditional way to access these functions, through user exits. It also explained the new functionality of Oracle Forms 4.5, PL/SQL foreign function interface. Important concepts in this chapter are listed here:

❏ Types of Foreign Functions
❏ Sample Foreign Functions
   ❏ Access Windows SDK functions

- ❏ Accessing Windows Help utility
- ❏ Pro*C modules
- ❏ User Exit Interface
  - ❏ IAPXTB control structure
  - ❏ Creating the user exit DLL file
  - ❏ Deploying the user exit DLL
  - ❏ Calling user exits in Oracle Forms
- ❏ PL/SQL Foreign Function Interface
  - ❏ Comparing user exits with the PL/SQL Foreign Function Interface
  - ❏ ORA_FFI package
  - ❏ Implementing the PL/SQL Foreign Function Interface
  - ❏ The Foreign Function Interface Generator
  - ❏ Generating Foreign Function Interface packages from Procedure Builder

UNDERSTANDING THE ORACLE SERVER

by Marina Krakovsky

- This book provides a comprehensive overview of Oracle 7 architecture and administration, without getting buried in the technical jargon.

- Loaded with illustrations and examples written in a clear and simple language.

BUILDING INTELLIGENT DATABASES with ORACLE PL/SQL, Triggers, and Stored Procedures

by Kevin Owens

- This book shows how to develop business applications, such as payroll or accounting software, using Oracle PL/SQL, triggers, and stored procedures.

- Illustrates through examples how to create and optimize applications using Oracle Triggers and stored procedure language.

- Supports Oracle 7.X database system.

- Includes a diskette featuring the source code samples found in the book.

P T R
P H

Professional Technical Reference

PRENTICE HALL

• *The Professional's Choice* •

http://www.prenhall.com

LICENSE AGREEMENT AND LIMITED WARRANTY

READ THE FOLLOWING TERMS AND CONDITIONS CAREFULLY BEFORE OPENING THIS DISK PACKAGE. THIS LEGAL DOCUMENT IS AN AGREEMENT BETWEEN YOU AND PRENTICE-HALL, INC. (THE "COMPANY"). BY OPENING THIS SEALED DISK PACKAGE, YOU ARE AGREEING TO BE BOUND BY THESE TERMS AND CONDITIONS. IF YOU DO NOT AGREE WITH THESE TERMS AND CONDITIONS, DO NOT OPEN THE DISK PACKAGE. PROMPTLY RETURN THE UNOPENED DISK PACKAGE AND ALL ACCOMPANYING ITEMS TO THE PLACE YOU OBTAINED THEM FOR A FULL REFUND OF ANY SUMS YOU HAVE PAID.

1. **GRANT OF LICENSE:** In consideration of your payment of the license fee, which is part of the price you paid for this product, and your agreement to abide by the terms and conditions of this Agreement, the Company grants to you a nonexclusive right to use and display the copy of the enclosed software program (hereinafter the "SOFTWARE") on a single computer (i.e., with a single CPU) at a single location so long as you comply with the terms of this Agreement. The Company reserves all rights not expressly granted to you under this Agreement.

2. **OWNERSHIP OF SOFTWARE:** You own only the magnetic or physical media (the enclosed disks) on which the SOFTWARE is recorded or fixed, but the Company retains all the rights, title, and ownership to the SOFTWARE recorded on the original disk copy(ies) and all subsequent copies of the SOFTWARE, regardless of the form or media on which the original or other copies may exist. This license is not a sale of the original SOFTWARE or any copy to you.

3. **COPY RESTRICTIONS:** This SOFTWARE and the accompanying printed materials and user manual (the "Documentation") are the subject of copyright. You may not copy the Documentation or the SOFTWARE, except that you may make a single copy of the SOFTWARE for backup or archival purposes only. You may be held legally responsible for any copying or copyright infringement which is caused or encouraged by your failure to abide by the terms of this restriction.

4. **USE RESTRICTIONS:** You may not network the SOFTWARE or otherwise use it on more than one computer or computer terminal at the same time. You may physically transfer the SOFTWARE from one computer to another provided that the SOFTWARE is used on only one computer at a time. You may not distribute copies of the SOFTWARE or Documentation to others. You may not reverse engineer, disassemble, decompile, modify, adapt, translate, or create derivative works based on the SOFTWARE or the Documentation without the prior written consent of the Company.

5. **TRANSFER RESTRICTIONS:** The enclosed SOFTWARE is licensed only to you and may not be transferred to any one else without the prior written consent of the Company. Any unauthorized transfer of the SOFTWARE shall result in the immediate termination of this Agreement.

6. **TERMINATION:** This license is effective until terminated. This license will terminate automatically without notice from the Company and become null and void if you fail to comply with any provisions or limitations of this license. Upon termination, you shall destroy the Documentation and all copies of the SOFTWARE. All provisions of this Agreement as to warranties, limitation of liability, remedies or damages, and our ownership rights shall survive termination.

7. **MISCELLANEOUS:** This Agreement shall be construed in accordance with the laws of the United States of America and the State of New York and shall benefit the Company, its affiliates, and assignees.

8. **LIMITED WARRANTY AND DISCLAIMER OF WARRANTY:** The Company warrants that the SOFTWARE, when properly used in accordance with the Documentation, will operate in substantial conformity with the description of the SOFTWARE set forth in the Documentation. The Company does not warrant that the SOFTWARE will meet your requirements or that the operation of the SOFTWARE will be uninterrupted or error-free. The Company warrants that the media on which the

SOFTWARE is delivered shall be free from defects in materials and workmanship under normal use for a period of thirty (30) days from the date of your purchase. Your only remedy and the Company's only obligation under these limited warranties is, at the Company's option, return of the warranted item for a refund of any amounts paid by you or replacement of the item. Any replacement of SOFTWARE or media under the warranties shall not extend the original warranty period. The limited warranty set forth above shall not apply to any SOFTWARE which the Company determines in good faith has been subject to misuse, neglect, improper installation, repair, alteration, or damage by you. EXCEPT FOR THE EXPRESSED WARRANTIES SET FORTH ABOVE, THE COMPANY DISCLAIMS ALL WARRANTIES, EXPRESS OR IMPLIED, INCLUDING WITHOUT LIMITATION, THE IMPLIED WARRANTIES OF MERCHANTABILITY AND FITNESS FOR A PARTICULAR PURPOSE. EXCEPT FOR THE EXPRESS WARRANTY SET FORTH ABOVE, THE COMPANY DOES NOT WARRANT, GUARANTEE, OR MAKE ANY REPRESENTATION REGARDING THE USE OR THE RESULTS OF THE USE OF THE SOFTWARE IN TERMS OF ITS CORRECTNESS, ACCURACY, RELIABILITY, CURRENTNESS, OR OTHERWISE.

IN NO EVENT, SHALL THE COMPANY OR ITS EMPLOYEES, AGENTS, SUPPLIERS, OR CONTRACTORS BE LIABLE FOR ANY INCIDENTAL, INDIRECT, SPECIAL, OR CONSEQUENTIAL DAMAGES ARISING OUT OF OR IN CONNECTION WITH THE LICENSE GRANTED UNDER THIS AGREEMENT, OR FOR LOSS OF USE, LOSS OF DATA, LOSS OF INCOME OR PROFIT, OR OTHER LOSSES, SUSTAINED AS A RESULT OF INJURY TO ANY PERSON, OR LOSS OF OR DAMAGE TO PROPERTY, OR CLAIMS OF THIRD PARTIES, EVEN IF THE COMPANY OR AN AUTHORIZED REPRESENTATIVE OF THE COMPANY HAS BEEN ADVISED OF THE POSSIBILITY OF SUCH DAMAGES. IN NO EVENT SHALL LIABILITY OF THE COMPANY FOR DAMAGES WITH RESPECT TO THE SOFTWARE EXCEED THE AMOUNTS ACTUALLY PAID BY YOU, IF ANY, FOR THE SOFTWARE.

SOME JURISDICTIONS DO NOT ALLOW THE LIMITATION OF IMPLIED WARRANTIES OR LIABILITY FOR INCIDENTAL, INDIRECT, SPECIAL, OR CONSEQUENTIAL DAMAGES, SO THE ABOVE LIMITATIONS MAY NOT ALWAYS APPLY. THE WARRANTIES IN THIS AGREEMENT GIVE YOU SPECIFIC LEGAL RIGHTS AND YOU MAY ALSO HAVE OTHER RIGHTS WHICH VARY IN ACCORDANCE WITH LOCAL LAW.

ACKNOWLEDGMENT

YOU ACKNOWLEDGE THAT YOU HAVE READ THIS AGREEMENT, UNDERSTAND IT ,AND AGREE TO BE BOUND BY ITS TERMS AND CONDITIONS. YOU ALSO AGREE THAT THIS AGREEMENT IS THE COMPLETE AND EXCLUSIVE STATEMENT OF THE AGREEMENT BETWEEN YOU AND THE COMPANY AND SUPERSEDES ALL PROPOSALS OR PRIOR AGREEMENTS, ORAL, OR WRITTEN, AND ANY OTHER COMMUNICATIONS BETWEEN YOU AND THE COMPANY OR ANY REPRESENTATIVE OF THE COMPANY RELATING TO THE SUBJECT MATTER OF THIS AGREEMENT.

Should you have any questions concerning this Agreement or if you wish to contact the Company for any reason, please contact in writing at the address below or call the at the telephone number provided.

PTR Customer Service
Prentice Hall PTR
One Lake Street
Upper Saddle River, New Jersey 07458

Telephone: 201-236-7105